The Challenge of Democracy

D1370238

Lesson 14 Paper Proposal

31 due

F
5 - 7
Pages
final

E
2 - 3
Pages
for
proposal

find the happy spot
declare whose going to win
What happened to spark debate

how did it get into gov't system
(courts, mayor, congress)

how will the decision be made
what each side thinks of issue

MW L2: Read Ch. 1

858

858) 361-8940

'NAVY' in subject line

EDITION
3

Cengage Advantage Books:

The Challenge of Democracy American Government in Global Politics

Essentials Edition

KENNETH JANDA
Northwestern University

JEFFREY M. BERRY
Tufts University

JERRY GOLDMAN
Northwestern University

Updated and Abridged by
KEVIN W. HULA
Loyola University Maryland

WADSWORTH
CENGAGE Learning™

Australia • Brazil • Japan • Korea • Mexico • Singapore • Spain • United Kingdom • United States

WADSWORTH
CENGAGE Learning

Cengage Advantage Books: The Challenge of Democracy: American Government in Global Politics, Essentials Edition, Third Edition

Kenneth Janda, Jeffrey M. Berry, Jerry Goldman, Kevin W. Hula

Publisher: Suzanne Jeans

Executive Editor: Carolyn Merrill

Acquisitions Editor: Anita Devine

Development Editor: Betty Slack

Development Editor, Advantage Edition: Laura Ross

Media Editor: Laura Hildebrand

Marketing Manager: Lydia LeStar

Senior Marketing Communications Manager: Heather Baxley

Content Project Manager: Alison Eigel Zade

Art Director: Linda Helcher

Production Technology Analyst: Jeff Joubert

Print Buyer: Fola Orekoya

Rights Acquisition Specialist, Image: Jennifer Meyer Dare

Senior Rights Acquisition Specialist, Text: Jennifer Meyer Dare

Production Service: Cenveo Publisher Services

Interior and Cover Designer: Rokusek Design

Compositor: Cenveo Publisher Services

Books in this series:

- **The Challenge of Democracy: American Government in Global Politics, Eleventh Edition**
  Kenneth Janda, Jeffrey M. Berry, Jerry Goldman

- **The Challenge of Democracy: American Government in Global Politics, Essentials Edition, Eighth Edition**
  Kenneth Janda, Jeffrey M. Berry, Jerry Goldman, Kevin W. Hula

- **Cengage Advantage Books: The Challenge of Democracy: American Government in Global Politics, Essentials Edition, Third Edition**
  Kenneth Janda, Jeffrey M. Berry, Jerry Goldman, Kevin W. Hula

For product information and technology assistance, contact us at **Cengage Learning Customer & Sales Support, 1-800-354-9706.**

For permission to use material from this text or product, submit all requests online at **www.cengage.com/permissions**.
Further permissions questions can be emailed to **permissionrequest@cengage.com**.

Library of Congress Control Number: 2010935870

ISBN-13: 978-1-111-83258-2
ISBN-10: 1-111-83258-7

Wadsworth
20 Channel Center Street
Boston MA 02210
USA

Cengage Learning products are represented in Canada by Nelson Education, Ltd.

Cengage Learning is a leading provider of customized learning solutions with office locations around the globe, including Singapore, the United Kingdom, Australia, Mexico, Brazil and Japan. Locate your local office at **international.cengage.com/region**.

For your course and learning solutions, visit **www.cengage.com**.

Purchase any of our products at your local college store or at our preferred online store **www.cengagebrain.com**.

Printed in The United States of America
1 2 3 4 5 6 7 15 14 13 12 11

Brief Contents

Contents

Boxed Features

Compared with What?

Politics of Global Change

Preface

The Third Edition of *Cengage Advantage Books: The Challenge of Democracy, The Essentials*, is a fully-updated, two-color, value-priced version of the Eighth Edition of *The Challenge of Democracy, The Essentials*. Our goal was to offer an up-to-date, lower-cost alternative to the *Essentials* text without diminishing any of the qualities that have made it so successful. The new *Advantage Essentials* format mirrors that of the *Essentials* as it draws upon and synthesizes the best approaches found in the Brief edition and Student Choice edition. In addition, we sought to make the text as current as possible by incorporating events occurring throughout 2011.

Key Content Updates

The text includes coverage of the latest political events that have emerged since the publication of the last edition. Key updates include discussion of the following:

- The challenges of leadership for chief executives, ranging from the earthquake, tsunami, and nuclear disaster facing Japanese Prime Minister Naoto Kan to President Obama's authorization of drone warfare in Pakistan and the mission that killed Osama bin Laden.
- The 2010 elections, including 2009–2010 campaign spending, state ballot propositions, and the 112th Congress.
- Updated statistics such as the 2010 decennial census, including Hispanic population growth in the United States and the redistribution of votes in the Electoral College.
- President Obama's fiscal year (FY) 2012 budget proposal, with its implications for the deficit, debt, and entitlement programs.
- The media, noting the continued decline of newspaper revenues, generational differences in news access, and the rise of news consumption through wireless mobile devices.
- Updated and completely new opening vignettes covering the war on terror, and the demonstrations and resulting regime changes in Tunisia and Egypt.

Thematic Framework

Because we wanted to write a book that students would actually read, we sought to discuss politics—a complex subject—in a captivating and understandable way. American politics is not dull, and its textbooks need not be either. But equally important, we wanted to produce a book that students would credit for stimulating their thinking about politics. While offering all the essential information about American government and politics, we believed that it was most important to give students a framework for analyzing politics that they could use long after their studies ended. To accomplish these goals, we built *The Challenge of Democracy* around three dynamic themes that are relevant to today's world: the clash among the values of *freedom, order, and equality;* the tensions between *pluralist and majoritarian visions of democracy;* and the fundamental ways that *globalization* is changing American politics.

Freedom, Order, and Equality

The first theme is introduced in Chapter 1 ("Dilemmas of Democracy"), where we suggest that American politics often reflects conflicts between the values of freedom and order and between the values of freedom and equality. These value conflicts are prominent in contemporary American society, and they help to explain political controversy and consensus in earlier eras.

For instance, in Chapter 2 ("The Constitution") we argue that the Constitution was designed to promote order and it virtually ignored issues of political and social equality. Equality was later served, however, by several amendments to the Constitution. In Chapter 12 ("Order and Civil Liberties") and Chapter 13 ("Equality and Civil Rights") we demonstrate that many of this nation's most controversial issues represent conflicts among individuals or groups who hold differing views on the values of freedom, order, and equality. Views on issues such as abortion are not just isolated opinions; they also reflect choices about the philosophy citizens want government to follow. Yet choosing among these values is difficult, sometimes excruciatingly so.

Pluralist and Majoritarian Visions of Democracy

The second theme, also introduced in Chapter 1, asks students to consider two competing models of democratic government. One way that government can make decisions is by means of *majoritarian* principles—that is, by taking the actions desired by a majority of citizens. A contrasting model of government, *pluralism,* is built around the interaction of decision makers in government with groups concerned about issues that affect them.

These models are not mere abstractions; we use them to illustrate the dynamics of the American political system. In Chapter 9 ("The Presidency") we discuss the problem of divided government. More often than not over the past forty years, the party that controlled the White House did not control both houses of Congress. When these two branches of government are divided between the two parties, majoritarian government is difficult. Even when the same party controls both branches, the majoritarian model is not always realized. In Chapter 7 ("Interest Groups") we see the forces of pluralism at work. Interest groups of all types populate Washington, and these organizations represent the diverse array of interests that define our society. At the same time, the chapter explores ways in which pluralism favors wealthier, better-organized interests.

Globalization's Impact on American Politics

The third theme, the impact of globalization on American politics, is introduced in Chapter 1 and then discussed throughout the text. The traditional notion of national sovereignty holds that each government is free to govern in the manner it feels best. As the world becomes a smaller place, however, national sovereignty is tested in many ways. When a country is committing human rights violations—putting people in jail for merely disagreeing with the government in power—should other countries try to pressure it to comply with common norms of justice? Do the democracies of the world have a responsibility to use their influences to try to limit the abuses of the powerless in societies where they are abused? These are just a few of the questions we explore.

Throughout the book we stress that students must make their own choices among the competing values and models of government. Although the four of us hold diverse and strong opinions about which choices are best, we do not believe it is our role to tell students our own answers to the broad questions we pose. Instead, we want our readers to learn firsthand that a democracy requires thoughtful choices. That is why we titled our book *The Challenge of Democracy.*

Features of This Edition

The Third Edition of *Cengage Advantage Books: The Challenge of Democracy, The Essentials,* includes a number of useful pedagogical features for students.

Chapter-Opening Vignettes

As in previous editions, each chapter begins with a vignette designed to draw students into the substance of that chapter while simultaneously examining one or more of the themes of the book and relating chapter content to current world events. For example, Chapter 1 ("Dilemmas of Democracy") looks at the massive demonstrations that toppled long-time authoritarian heads of state in North Africa and the Middle East in 2011. We introduce the concept of globalization and the tension that exists between freedom and order in democratic and authoritarian regimes alike. In Chapter 9 ("The Presidency") we examine the clandestine war in Pakistan against al Qaeda and the Taliban as we introduce the challenges and decisions facing the president in his role as commander in chief. Other topics include the national controversy over Arizona's crackdown on illegal aliens (Chapter 3, "Federalism"), the challenges party affiliation poses for lobbying firms when control of Congress changes (Chapter 7, "Interest Groups"), the difficulty of implementing President Obama's campaign promise to close the detention facility at Guantánamo (Chapter 8, "Congress"), and the emergence of the tea party movement (Chapter 5, "Participation and Voting"). More than three-quarters of the vignettes in this edition are either entirely new or significantly revised.

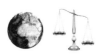

"Politics of Global Change" and "Compared with What?"

Two boxed features appear in *Cengage Advantage Books: The Challenge of Democracy, The Essentials.* The first, "Politics of Global Change" (found in even-numbered chapters), examines various elements of political change, some troubling, some hopeful, particularly in light of the spread of globalization. Topics include democratization around the globe (Chapter 2, "The Constitution"), attempts to develop a global regulatory framework to address global warming (Chapter 10, "The Bureaucracy"), and the link between global financial interdependence and deficit spending (Chapter 14, "Policymaking and the Budget").

We firmly believe that students can better evaluate how our political system works when they compare it with politics in other countries, so a second boxed feature, "Compared with What?"

(found in odd-numbered chapters), introduces a comparative perspective to the book, challenging students to compare the American political system with that of other countries around the world. In Chapter 1 ("Dilemmas of Democracy"), for example, we present international polling data showing significant differences in the importance people place on the competing values or order and freedom. In Chapter 5 ("Participation and Voting"), we compare voter turnout in the United States with turnout in sixteen other democracies. In Chapter 11 ("The Courts"), we compare five systems for judicial selection used around the world.

In-Text Reference Materials

The text contains an array of pedagogical tools designed for student self-assessment and reinforcement, including *chapter-opening outlines* and learning objective *focus questions* that correspond to each major section of the book; *Test Prepper* questions at the end of each chapter to check for understanding; *key terms* that appear in the margins of the text pages where the words are defined; *marginal icons* linking students to website material, which includes online quizzing and multimedia assets; and *Tying It Together* chapter summaries that provide brief responses to each focus question, helping students synthesize chapter themes and directing them to areas that may require further study. Finally, at the end of the book, we have included a copy of the Declaration of Independence and the Constitution for student reference.

For the Instructor: Innovative Teaching Tools

Our job as authors did not end with writing this text. From the beginning, we have been centrally involved with producing a tightly integrated set of instructional materials to accompany the text. With help from other political scientists and educational specialists at Cengage Learning, these ancillary materials have grown and improved over time.

Multimedia and Online Teaching Resources

Cengage Learning now offers these exciting resources for instructors:

PowerLecture DVD with JoinIn™ Student Response System, and ExamView®
ISBN-13: 9781111945879 | ISBN-10: 111194587X

An all-in-one multimedia resource for class preparation, presentation and testing, this DVD includes Microsoft® PowerPoint® slides, a Test Bank in both Microsoft® Word and ExamView® formats, an Instructor's Manual, and a Resource Integration Guide. The book-specific slides of lecture outlines, as well as photos, figures, and tables from the text, make it easy for you to assemble lectures for your course, while the media-enhanced slides for each chapter can be used on their own or easily integrated with the book-specific PowerPoint outlines. These media-enhanced slides include audio and video clips, new animated learning modules illustrating key concepts, tables, statistical charts, and more. The Test Bank includes multiple-choice and essay questions, along with their answers and page references. An Instructor's Manual includes learning objectives, chapter outlines, discussion questions, class activities and projects suggestions, tips on integrating media into your class, suggested readings and Web resources, and a section especially designed to help teaching assistants and adjunct instructors. JoinIn™ offers book-specific "clicker" questions that test and track student comprehension of key concepts—political polling questions simulate voting and the results can be compared to national data, leading to lively discussions; Visual Literacy questions tied to images from the book add high-interest feedback during your lecture. Finally, the Resource Integration Guide outlines the resources available to instructors and students within the chapter-by-chapter framework of the book, suggesting how and when each supplement can be used to optimize learning. Contact your Cengage representative to receive a copy upon adoption.

CourseMate

Political Science CourseMate with eBook
1133232698 | 9781133232698 PAC
113323271X | 9781133232711 IAC
1133232701 | 9781133232704 SSO

Cengage Learning's Political Science CourseMate brings course concepts to life with interactive learning, study tools, and exam preparation tools that support the printed textbook. Use Engagement Tracker to assess student preparation and engagement in the course, and watch student comprehension soar as your class works with the textbook-specific website. An interactive eBook allows students to take notes, highlight, search, and interact with embedded media (such as quizzes, flashcards, and videos). Other resources include critical thinking activities, simulations, animated learning modules, and interactive timelines.

CourseReader: American Government
111147995X | 9781111479954 CourseReader 0-30: American Government Printed Access Card
1111479976 | 9781111479978 CourseReader 0-30: American Government Instant Access Code
1111479968 | 9781111479961 CourseReader 0-30: American Government SSO
1111680566 | 9781111680565 CourseReader 0-60: American Government Printed Access Card
1111680558 | 9781111680558 CourseReader 0-60: American Government Instant Access Code
111168054X | 9781111680541 CourseReader 0-60: American Government SSO
1111680590 | 9781111680596 CourseReader Unlimited: American Government Printed Access Card
1111680582 | 9781111680589 CourseReader Unlimited: American Government Instant Access Code
1111680574 | 9781111680572 CourseReader Unlimited: American Government SSO

CourseReader for American Government is a fully customizable online reader which provides access to hundreds of readings, audio, and video selections from multiple disciplines. This easy to use solution allows you to select exactly the content you need for your courses, and is loaded with convenient pedagogical features like highlighting, printing, note taking, and audio downloads. YOU have the freedom to assign individualized content at an affordable price. CourseReader: American Government is the perfect complement to any class.

Companion Site
ISBN-13: 9781133043720 | ISBN-10: 1133043720

This password-protected website for instructors features all of the free student assets, plus an instructor's manual (learning objectives, chapter outlines, discussion questions, class activities and projects suggestions, tips on integrating media into your class, suggested readings and Web resources, and a section especially designed to help teaching assistants and adjunct instructors), and book-specific PowerPoint® presentations (lecture outlines, photos and figures). Also included is the Instructor's Guide to YouTube. Organized by fifteen topics, the guide follows the sequence of an American government course and includes a preface with tips on how to use Internet videos in class, links to video clips, clip

descriptions, and discussion questions. Access from www.cengage
.com/login.

WebTUTOR™

WebTutor with eBook on WebCT
1133233104 | 9781133233107 PAC
1133233090 | 9781133233091 IAC

Rich with content for your American government course, this
Web-based teaching and learning tool integrates with your
school's learning management system and includes course management, study/mastery, and communication tools. A wealth of
student learning activities includes simulations, animated learning
modules, videos and primary sources with accompanying quizzing, timelines, audio summaries and flashcards. Chapter-based
practice quizzes offer immediate feedback and link to the interactive eBook so students can focus their efforts where they need to.
A fully-customizable test bank, PowerPoint lectures, suggested
Discussion Board topics and Writing Assignments, along with a
Course Materials Guide that describes all of the content in the
course and how to use it, shortcut your course preparation time.
Use WebTutor™ to provide virtual office hours, post your syllabus,
and track student progress—all directly from your learning management system.

WebTUTOR™

WebTutor with eBook on Blackboard
1133233082 | 9781133233084 PAC
1133233074 | 9781133233077 IAC

Rich with content for your American government course, this
Web-based teaching and learning tool integrates with your
school's learning management system and includes course management, study/mastery, and communication tools. A wealth of
student learning activities includes simulations, animated learning
modules, videos and primary sources with accompanying quizzing, timelines, audio summaries and flashcards. Chapter-based
practice quizzes offer immediate feedback and link to the interactive eBook so students can focus their efforts where they need to.
A fully-customizable test bank, PowerPoint lectures, suggested
Discussion Board topics and Writing Assignments, along with a
Course Materials Guide that describes all of the content in the
course and how to use it, shortcut your course preparation time.
Use WebTutor™ to provide virtual office hours, post your syllabus,
and track student progress—all directly from your learning management system.

Political Science News Resource Center
1439040753 | 9781439040751 PAC
1439040745 | 9781439040744 IAC

Cengage Learning's Political Science News Resource Center provides you with up-to-the-minute in-depth analysis and robust content from worldwide news outlets to help you incorporate the political science headlines of today into your students' learning experience. The Resource Center includes the American Government NewsWatch website which is updated at least four times a day with news and information for the American Government course via video, podcasts, and hundreds of articles from leading journals, magazines, and newspapers from the United States and around the world. Sources include the *Political Science Quarterly*, *The New Republic*, *The National Review*, *The Christian Science Monitor*, and *The New York Times*. Also included is the KnowNow! American Government Blog – the go-to current events blog for students and teachers of American Government.

Political Theatre DVD 2.0
ISBN-13: 9780495793601 | ISBN-10: 0495793604

Bring politics home to students with Political Theatre 2.0, up-to-date through the 2008 election season. This is the second edition of this 3-DVD series and includes real video clips that show American political thought throughout the public sector. Clips include both classic and contemporary political advertisements, speeches, interviews and more. Available to adopters of Cengage textbooks, version 2.0 provides added functionality with this updated edition.

JoinIn™ Student Response System – Political Theatre 2.0, 2nd Edition
ISBN-13: 9780495798293 | ISBN-10: 0495798290

For even more interaction, combine Political Theatre with the innovative teaching tool of a classroom response system through JoinIn™. Poll your students with questions created for you or create your own questions. Built within the Microsoft® PowerPoint® software, it's easy to integrate into your current lectures in conjunction with the "clicker" hardware of your choice.

The Wadsworth News DVD for American Government 2013, 1st Edition
ISBN-13: 9781133313724 | ISBN-10: 1133313728

This collection of two- to five-minute video clips on relevant political issues serves as a great lecture or discussion launcher. An introduction for context, as well as discussion questions, accompanies each clip.

Table of Contents:

15. THE PRESIDENCY.
    Video 1: President Obama Uses Executive Orders to Reverse Bush Policies.
    Video 2: President Obama Energy Policy Focuses on Long-Term Change.
16. PUBLIC OPINION.
    Video 1: Exit Polls Project Winners and Demographic Trends.
    Video 2: The Difficulty of Predicting Iowa Caucus Outcomes.
17. VOTING AND PARTICIPATION.
    Video 1: Inconsistencies in Voting Procedures from State to State.
    Video 2: Voting Machine Accountability in Question.

ABC News DVD: Speeches by Barack Obama, 1st Edition
ISBN-13: 9781439082478 | ISBN-10: 1439082472

DVD of nine famous speeches by President Barack Obama, from 2004 through his inauguration, including his speech at the 2004 Democratic National Convention; his 2008 speech on race, "A More Perfect Union"; and his 2009 inaugural address. Speeches are divided into short video segments for easy, time-efficient viewing. This instructor supplement also features critical-thinking questions and answers for each speech, designed to spark classroom discussion.

Latino-American Politics Supplement, 2nd Edition
Schmidt/Shelley/Bardes/Ford/Maxwell/Crain/Santos
ISBN-13: 9781111344818 | ISBN-10: 1111344817

This updated thirty-two-page supplement uses real examples to detail politics related to Latino Americans.

Instructor's Guide to YouTube for Political Science

Instructors have access to the Instructor's Guide to YouTube, which shows American government instructors where on the Internet to find videos that can be used as learning tools in class. Organized by fifteen topics, the guide follows the sequence of an American government course and includes a preface with tips on how to use Internet videos in class.

USPolitics.org

The Third Edition continues to be supported by **uspolitics.org**, Kenneth Janda's personal website for *The Challenge of Democracy*. His site offers a variety of teaching aids to instructors who adopt any version of *The Challenge of Democracy* for courses in American politics. It is divided into two sides: the student side is open to all users, but the instructor side is limited to teachers who register online at **uspolitics.org** as *Challenge* adopters. The site offers some material not contained on Cengage Learning's own website, yet it also provides convenient links to the publisher's site.

For more information on the teaching tools that accompany *The Challenge of Democracy,* please contact your Cengage Learning sales representative.

For the Student: Effective Learning Aids

CourseMate

- **CourseMate.** CourseMate, accessible at www.cengagebrain .com/shop/ISBN/1111832587, offers students a variety of rich online learning resources designed to enhance the student experience. These resources include video activities, audio summaries, critical-thinking activities, simulations, animated learning modules, interactive timelines, primary source quizzes, flashcards, learning objectives, glossaries, and crossword puzzles. All resources are correlated with key chapter learning concepts, and students can browse or search for content in a variety of ways.
- **IDEAlog.** IDEAlog, which won the 2005 Instructional Software Award from the American Political Science Association, is closely tied to the text's "value conflicts" theme. It is directly accessible at http://IDEAlog.org and is also available on the student website. IDEAlog first asks students to rate themselves on the two-dimensional trade-off of freedom versus order and freedom versus equality. It then presents them with twenty questions, ten dealing with the conflict of freedom versus order and ten pertaining to freedom versus equality. Students' responses to these questions are classified according to libertarian, conservative, liberal, or communitarian ideological tendencies.

We invite your questions, suggestions, and criticisms of the teaching/learning package and *The Challenge of Democracy.* You may contact us at our respective institutions or through our collective e-mail address cod@northwestern.edu.

Acknowledgments

All authors are indebted to others for inspiration and assistance in various forms; textbook authors are notoriously so. For the eleventh edition of the comprehensive version, from which this version was created, we were fortunate enough to have Professor Deborah Schildkraut of Tufts University revise the chapters covering "The Media," "Congress," and "Domestic Policy." She contributed greatly to the quality of this new version of *The Challenge of Democracy.* We want to again thank Patricia Conley, a Visiting Professor at the University of Chicago, for her work on earlier editions of the book.

We again want to single out Professor Paul Manna of the College of William and Mary, who has assisted us in many different ways. Lukasz Hankus of nonstopworkshop.com provided invaluable support for the new and improved version of IDEAlog; Kimball Brace, President of Election Data Services, supplied us with updated election data; Robert Coen, Northwestern University Professor Emeritus of Economics, gave us a careful review of the chapter coverage of "Economic Policy"; Axel Dreher, at KOF, the Swiss Economic Institute, contributed data on globalization; and Simon Winchester helped us understand the history of the 1883 Krakatoa volcanic eruption. Timely information technology suggestions and assistance came from Jeff Parsons of the Oyez Project, Professor James Ferolo of Bradley University, and Dr. Francesco Stagno d'Alcontres of Centro Linguistico d'Ateneo Messinese. We also wish to express our gratitude to Julieta Suarez-Cao of Northwestern University, Hope Lozano-Bielat of Boston University, and Andrew Gruen of Cambridge University for their helpful research assistance.

We have been fortunate to obtain the help of many outstanding political scientists across the country who provided us with critical reviews of our work as it has progressed through ten separate editions. We found their comments enormously helpful, and we thank them for taking valuable time away from their own teaching and research to write their detailed reports. More specifically, our thanks go to the following:

David Ahern, *University of Dayton*

Philip C. Aka, *Chicago State University*

James Anderson, *Texas A&M University*

Greg Andranovich, *California State University, Los Angeles*

Theodore Arrington, *University of North Carolina, Charlotte*

Denise Baer, *Northeastern University*

Richard Barke, *Georgia Institute of Technology*

Brian Bearry, *University of Texas at Dallas*

Linda L. M. Bennett, *Wittenberg University*

Stephen Earl Bennett, *University of Cincinnati*

Elizabeth Bergman, *California State Polytechnic University, Pomona*

Thad Beyle, *University of North Carolina, Chapel Hill*

Bruce Bimber, *University of California–Santa Barbara*

Michael Binford, *Georgia State University*

Bonnie Browne, *Texas A&M University*

Jeffrey L. Brudney, *Cleveland State University*

Jane Bryant, *John A. Logan College*

J. Vincent Buck, *California State University, Fullerton*

Gregory A. Caldeira, *Ohio State University*

David E. Camacho, *Northern Arizona University*

Robert Casier, *Santa Barbara City College*

James Chalmers, *Wayne State University*

John Chubb, *Stanford University*

Allan Cigler, *University of Kansas*

Stanley Clark, *California State University, Bakersfield*

Ronald Claunch, *Stephen F. Austin State University*

Guy C. Clifford, *Bridgewater State College*

Gary Copeland, *University of Oklahoma*

Ruth A. Corbett, *Chabot College*

W. Douglas Costain, *University of Colorado at Boulder*

Cornelius P. Cotter, *University of Wisconsin–Milwaukee*

James L. Danielson, *Minnesota State University, Moorhead*

Christine L. Day, *University of New Orleans*

David A. Deese, *Boston College*

Victor D'Lugin, *University of Florida*

Douglas C. Dow, *University of Texas at Dallas*

Art English, *University of Arkansas*

Matthew Eshbaugh-Soha, *University of North Texas*

Tim Fackler, *University of Texas, Austin*

Dennis Falcon, *Cerritos Community College*

Henry Fearnley, *College of Marin*

Elizabeth Flores, *Del Mar College*

Patricia S. Florestano, *University of Maryland*

Richard Foglesong, *Rollins College*

Steve Frank, *St. Cloud State University*

Mitchel Gerber, *Hofstra University*

Dana K. Glencross, *Oklahoma City Community College*

Dorith Grant-Wisdom, *Howard University*

Paul Gronke, *Duke University*

Sara A. Grove, *Shippensburg University*

David J. Hadley, *Wabash College*

Willie Hamilton, *Mt. San Jacinto College*

Kenneth Hayes, *University of Maine*

Ronald Hedlund, *University of Wisconsin-Milwaukee*

Richard Heil, *Fort Hays State University*

Beth Henschen, *The Institute for Community and Regional Development, Eastern Michigan University*

Marjorie Randon Hershey, *Indiana University*

Roberta Herzberg, *Indiana University*

Jack E. Holmes, *Hope College*

Peter Howse, *American River College*

Ronald J. Hrebenar, *University of Utah*

James B. Johnson, *University of Nebraska at Omaha*

William R. Keech, *Carnegie Mellon University*

Scott Keeter, *Pew Center*

Sarah W. Keidan, *Oakland Community College (Michigan)*

Linda Camp Keith, *Collin County Community College*

Beat Kernen, *Southwest Missouri State University*

Haroon Khan, *Henderson State University*

Dwight Kiel, *Central Florida University*

Nancy Pearson Kinney, *Washtenaw Community College*

Vance Krites, *Indiana University of Pennsylvania*

Clyde Kuhn, *California State University, Sacramento*

Jack Lampe, *Southwest Texas Junior College*

William Lester, *Jacksonville State University*

Brad Lockerbie, *University of Georgia*

Joseph Losco, *Ball State University*

Philip Loy, *Taylor University*

Stan Luger, *University of Northern Colorado*

David Madlock, *University of Memphis*

Michael Maggiotto, *University of South Carolina*

Edward S. Malecki, *California State University, Los Angeles*

Michael Margolis, *University of Cincinnati-McMicken College of Arts and Sciences*

Thomas R. Marshall, *University of Texas at Arlington*

Janet Martin, *Bowdoin College*

Steve J. Mazurana, *University of Northern Colorado*

Michael McConachie, *Collin College*

Wayne McIntosh, *University of Maryland*

David McLaughlin, *Northwest Missouri State University*

Don Melton, *Arapahoe Community College*

Melissa Michelson, *California State University, East Bay*

Dana Morales, *Montgomery College*

Jim Morrow, *Tulsa Junior College*

David Moskowitz, *The University of North Carolina, Charlotte*

William Mugleston, *Mountain View College*

William Murin, *University of Wisconsin-Parkside*

David Nice, *Washington State University*

David A. Nordquest, *Pennsylvania State University, Erie*

Bruce Odom, *Trinity Valley Community College*

Laura Katz Olson, *Lehigh University*

Bruce Oppenheimer, *Vanderbilt University*

Richard Pacelle, *Indiana University*

William J. Parente, *University of Scranton*

Tony Payan, *University of Texas, El Paso*

Robert Pecorella, *St. John's University*

James Perkins, *San Antonio College*

Denny E. Pilant, *Southwest Missouri State University*

Marc Pufong, *Valdosta State University*

Curtis Reithel, *University of Wisconsin-La Crosse*

Russell Renka, *Southeast Missouri State University*

Chester D. Rhoan, *Chabot College*

Michael J. Rich, *Emory University*

Richard S. Rich, *Virginia Tech*

Ronald I. Rubin, *Borough of Manhattan Community College, CUNY*

Gilbert K. St. Clair, *University of New Mexico*

Barbara Salmore, *Drew University*

Todd M. Schaefer, *Central Washington University*

Denise Scheberle, *University of Wisconsin-Green Bay*

Paul R. Schulman, *Mills College*

William A. Schultze, *San Diego State University*

Thomas Sevener, *Santa Rosa Junior College*

Kenneth S. Sherrill, *Hunter College*

Sanford R. Silverburg, *Catawba College*

Mark Silverstein, *Boston University*

Charles Sohner, *El Camino College*

Robert J. Spitzer, *SUNY Cortland*

Terry Spurlock, *Trinity Valley Community College*
Candy Stevens Smith, *Texarkana College*
Dale Story, *University of Texas at Arlington*
Nicholas Strinkowski, *Clark College*
Neal Tate, *University of North Texas*
James A. Thurber, *The American University*
Ronnie Tucker, *Shippensburg University*
John Tuman, *University of Nevada, Las Vegas*
Bedford Umez, *Lee College*
David Uranga, *Pasadena City College*
Eric M. Uslaner, *University of Maryland*
Lawson Veasey, *Jacksonville State University*
Charles E. Walcott, *Virginia Tech*

Richard J. Waldman, *University of Maryland*
Thomas G. Walker, *Emory University*
Benjamin Walter, *Vanderbilt University*
Shirley Ann Warshaw, *Gettysburg College*
Gary D. Wekkin, *University of Central Arkansas*
Jonathan West, *University of Miami*
Zaphon Wilson, *Armstrong Atlantic State University*
John Winkle, *University of Mississippi*
Clifford Wirth, *University of New Hampshire*
Wayne Wolf, *South Suburban College*
Mikel Wyckoff, *Northern Illinois University*
Ann Wynia, *North Hennepin Community College*
Jerry L. Yeric, *University of North Texas*

Finally, we want to thank the many people at Wadsworth/Cengage Learning who helped make this *Advantage Essentials* version a reality. There's not enough room here to list all the individuals who helped us with the previous editions and versions, so we say a collective thank you for the superb work you did on *The Challenge of Democracy*. Political Science Editor Anita Devine jumped head-first into the project and could not have been more supportive and helpful throughout the process. Laura Ross developed the *Advantage Edition*, was a delight to work with, and kept us on schedule. Our direct production contacts were extraordinarily efficient and helpful. A million thanks to Alison Eigel Zade and Rajachitra Suresh, who seemed to create order out of the chaos we created. Finally, thanks, too, to the sales representatives who do such a terrific job of bringing each new edition of *The Challenge of Democracy* to the attention of those who might use it.

K. J.   J. B.   J. G.   K. H.

DEDICATED TO THESE PEOPLE WHO TAUGHT US:

Henry Teune, collaborating with K. J. in studying the Indiana legislature

Robert Peabody, inspiring J. B. during graduate study at Johns Hopkins

Richard B. Meltzer, for 50+ years of friendship with J. G.

Allan J. Cigler, introducing K. H. to the thrill of politics

Dilemmas of Democracy

REUTERS/Jose Luis Magana/Landov

Visit www.cengagebrain.com/shop/ISBN/1111832587 for flashcards, web quizzes, videos and more!

CourseMate

FOCUS QUESTIONS

1. How is the American government affected by increasing globalization?
2. How does government serve its citizens?
3. What are the critical values, conflicts, and political ideologies that affect the decisions and policies made by the American government?
4. What criteria can we use to determine if our government is democratic?
5. What are the challenges of establishing and sustaining true democratic governments around the world?

After nearly thirty years of authoritarian rule, Egyptian President Hosni Mubarak fled Cairo on February 11, 2011. He was ousted after eighteen tumultuous days of street protests. President Obama said, "The people of Egypt have spoken, their voices have been heard, and Egypt will never be the same."[1]

Why begin a book on American government with a revolution in an Arab nation over 5,000 miles away? Because what happened in Egypt dramatically illustrates the key concepts—freedom, order, equality, and forms of democracy—underlying our book's title, *The Challenge of Democracy*. Mubarak enforced order and stability in Egypt at the cost of freedom and equality for its 80 million people, many of whom were unemployed and living in poverty.[2] He also held rigged elections, denying any semblance of democracy.[3]

During the uprising, the United States faced a dilemma: whether to support Mubarak—our ally against Islamic terrorism and for peace with Israel[4]—or to back his people's call for freedom and democracy.[5] This dilemma reflects our book's subtitle, *American Government in Global Politics*, and its supporting theme, globalization. What happens abroad today can have profound effects on the United States tomorrow.

The revolt in Egypt was inspired by weeks of popular protests in Tunisia that ousted its longtime president Zine El Abidine Ben Ali.[6] Protests began when a 26-year-old street vendor, humiliated by police and despairing over his inability to earn a living, burned himself in public.[7] Spurred by Facebook and Twitter postings, thousands of young Tunisians braved bullets and mobbed the streets to protest his plight and their lack of political freedom and economic equality. On February 14, Ben Ali fled on a plane to Saudi Arabia. The Arab television network, Al Jazeera, broadcast the events across the Middle East.[8]

3

Egyptians closely followed everything on Al Jazeera. The youth traded text messages such as, "Mubarak, your plane is waiting for you!"[9] As in Tunisia, a Facebook page personified the Egyptian protest. In June 2010, plainclothes police seized 28-year-old businessman Kalid Said, presumably because he knew of police corruption. Soon, a Facebook page posted cell phone photos from the morgue showing Said's battered face along with YouTube videos of him in life, happy and smiling.[10] "We Are All Kalid Said" became Egypt's most visited dissident site, spreading news about planned protests.

Activists planned a mass demonstration on January 25, 2011. Thousands of protesters gathered in Tahrir (Liberation) Square to demand Mubarak's ouster and stayed there for days. On January 27, authorities shut down the Internet and cell phone services.[11] On February 2, pro-Mubarak forces on camels and horses attacked the protesters, leading to pitched battles shown on Al Jazeera.[12] Mubarak called in the army, but it refused to fire on its own people. On February 3, the Cairo office of Al Jazeera was attacked and burned, and its satellite carriers silenced.[13] On February 10, Mubarak tried to defuse the protest by granting extra powers to a new vice president while remaining president. Tahrir Square erupted in outrage. The next day Mubarak stepped down, flying by helicopter to his palace in a distant city. President Obama quickly proclaimed, "The people of Egypt have spoken."

Egyptian generals took over and called for elections under a new democratic constitution. Whether Egypt becomes a democracy remains to be seen. Nevertheless, the fall of an authoritarian ruler to popular pressure in the largest Arab country has fundamentally changed politics in the Middle East, where we relied on authoritarian allies to supply oil, fight against terrorism, and negotiate with Israel. How much should we value freedom and equality abroad over orderly government by friendly strong men? Indeed, how much should we value freedom, order, and equality at home?

Our main interest in this text is the purpose, value, and operation of government as practiced in the United States. We probe the relationship between individual freedoms and personal security, and how government ensures security by establishing order through making and enforcing its laws. We also examine the relationship between individual freedom and social equality as reflected in government policies, which often confront underlying dilemmas such as these. As the spread of protests in the Middle East indicates, however, we live in an era of globalization—a term for the increasing interdependence of citizens and nations across the world. So we must consider how politics at home and abroad interrelate—which is increasingly important to understanding our government.[14]

We hope to improve your understanding of the world by analyzing the norms, or values, that people use to judge political events. Our purpose is not to preach what people ought to favor in making policy decisions; it is to teach what values are at stake.

Teaching without preaching is not easy; no one can completely exclude personal values from political analysis. But our

globalization
The increasing interdependence of citizens and nations across the world.

approach minimizes the problem by concentrating on the dilemmas that confront governments when they are forced to choose between important policies that threaten equally cherished values, such as freedom of speech and personal security.

A prominent scholar defined *politics* as "the authoritative allocation of values for a society."[15] Every government policy reflects a choice between conflicting values. All government policies reinforce certain values (norms) at the expense of others. We want you to interpret policy issues (for example, should assisted suicide go unpunished?) with an understanding of the fundamental values in question (freedom of action versus order and protection of life) and the broader political context (liberal or conservative politics).

By looking beyond the specifics to the underlying normative principles, you should be able to make more sense out of politics. Our framework for analysis does not encompass all the complexities of American government, but it should help your knowledge grow by improving your comprehension of political information. We begin by considering the basic purposes of government. In short, why do we need it?

balance of values

The Globalization of American Government

Most people do not like being told what to do. Fewer still like being coerced into acting a certain way. Yet billions of people in countries across the world willingly submit to the coercive power of government. They accept laws that state on which side of the road to drive, what constitutes a contract, how to dispose of human waste—and how much they must pay to support the government that makes these coercive laws.

In the first half of the twentieth century, people thought of government mainly in territorial terms. Indeed, a standard definition of government was the legitimate use of force—including firearms, imprisonment, and execution—within specified geographical boundaries to control human behavior. The term is also used to refer to the body authorized to exercise that power. Since the Peace of Westphalia in 1648 ended the Thirty Years' War in Europe, international relations and diplomacy have been based on the principle of national sovereignty, defined as "a political entity's externally recognized right to exercise final authority over its affairs."[16] Simply put, national sovereignty means that each national government has

government
The legitimate use of force to control human behavior; also, the organization or agency authorized to exercise that force.

national sovereignty
A political entity's externally recognized right to exercise final authority over its affairs.

the right to govern its people as it wishes, without interference from other nations.

Although the League of Nations and later the United Nations were supposed to introduce supranational order into the world, even these international organizations explicitly respected national sovereignty as the guiding principle of international relations. The U.N. Charter, Article 2.1, states, "The Organization is based on the principle of the sovereign equality of all its Members."

National sovereignty, however, is threatened under globalization. Consider the international community's concern with starving refugees in the Darfur region of Sudan. The U.N. Security Council resolved to send troops to end the ethnic conflict that cost some 400,000 lives. The Sudanese government, suspected of causing the conflict, opposed the U.N. action as violating its sovereignty.[17] Nevertheless, the humanitarian crisis in Sudan became closely monitored by the U.N., which took action against a member state.

Global forces also generate pressures for international law. Consider the 1982 Law of the Sea Treaty, which governs maritime law from mineral rights to shipping lanes under an International Seabed Authority. Although President Reagan did not sign it, the treaty came into force in 1994 when it was ratified by sixty nations. President Clinton then signed the treaty, but conservative senators kept it from being ratified, fearing loss of U.S. sovereignty. After global warming began to melt the Arctic ice, the U.S. Navy backed the treaty for guaranteeing free passage through international straits, and oil and mining companies favored its 350-mile grant of mineral rights around Alaska. It was reported out of committee for Senate consideration in 2007 with President Bush's support.[18] The treaty still remained unratified during Obama's first year.

Our government, you might be surprised to learn, is worried about this trend of holding nations accountable to international law. In fact, in 2002, the United States "annulled" its signature to the 1998 treaty to create an International Criminal Court that would define and try crimes against humanity.[19] Why would the United States oppose such an international court? One reason is its concern that U.S. soldiers stationed abroad might be arrested and tried in that court.[20] Another reason is the death penalty, practiced in most of the United States but abolished by more than half the countries in the world and all countries in the European Union. Indeed, in 1996, the International Commission of Jurists condemned our death penalty as "arbitrarily and racially discriminatory," and there is a

Sealand: Rebuilding a (Micro-)Nation

The Principality of Sealand is perched on a World War II military platform approximately six miles off the southeast coast of England. Located in international waters, the platform was acquired in 1967 by Paddy Roy Bates, a retired British officer who declared it a sovereign nation and lived there with his family for decades. In 2006, Sealand experienced a devastating fire that crippled its infrastructure. The tiny island country underwent extensive renovation, after which Prince Roy announced that the micro-nation was seeking "inward investment" in the form of purchase or long-term lease.

(© Kim Gilmour/Alamy)

concerted campaign across Europe to force the sovereign United States of America to terminate capital punishment.[21]

As the world's sole superpower, should the United States be above international law if its sovereignty is threatened by nations that don't share *our* values? What action should we follow if this situation occurs?

Although this text is about American national government, it recognizes the growing impact of international politics and world opinion on U.S. politics. We are closely tied through trade to former enemies (we now import more goods from China—still communist—than from France and Britain combined), and we are thoroughly embedded in a worldwide economic, social, and political network. More than ever before, we must discuss American politics while

IDEALOG.ORG

Our IDEAlog.org self-test poses twenty questions about political values seen in Figure 1.2 (see p. 23). One of the questions in the IDEAlog self-test is about immigration. Take the quiz and see how you respond.

casting an eye to other countries to see how foreign affairs affect our government and how American politics affects government in other nations.

The Purposes of Government

All governments require their citizens to surrender some freedom as part of being governed. Why do people surrender their freedom to this control? To obtain the benefits of government. Throughout history, government seems to have served two major purposes: maintaining order (preserving life and protecting property) and providing public goods. More recently, some governments have pursued a third and more controversial purpose: promoting equality.

Maintaining Order

Maintaining order is the oldest objective of government. **Order** in this context is rich with meaning. Let's start with "law and order." Maintaining order in this sense means establishing the rule of law to preserve life and to protect property. To the seventeenth-century English philosopher Thomas Hobbes (1588–1679), preserving life was the most important function of government. In his classic philosophical treatise, *Leviathan* (1651), Hobbes described life without government as life in a "state of nature." Without rules, people would live as predators do, stealing and killing for their personal benefit. In Hobbes's classic phrase, life in a state of nature would be "solitary, poor, nasty, brutish, and short." He believed that a single ruler, or sovereign, must possess unquestioned authority to guarantee the safety of the weak to protect them from the attacks of the strong. He believed that complete obedience to the sovereign's strict laws was a small price to pay for the security of living in a civil society.

Most of us can only imagine what a state of nature would be like. But in some parts of the world, people live in a state of lawlessness. That has been the situation in Somalia since 1991, when the government was toppled and warlords feuded over territory. Today, the government controls only a portion of the capital, Mogadishu, and Somali pirates seize ships off its shore with impunity.[22] Throughout history, authoritarian rulers have used people's fears of civil disorder to justify taking power and becoming the new established order.

Hobbes's conception of life in the cruel state of nature led him to view government primarily as a means of guaranteeing people's

order
Established ways of social behavior. Maintaining order is the oldest purpose of government.

survival. Other theorists, taking survival for granted, believed that government protected order by preserving private property (goods and land owned by individuals). Foremost among them was John Locke (1632–1704), another English philosopher. In *Two Treatises on Government* (1690), he wrote that the protection of life, liberty, and property was the basic objective of government. His thinking strongly influenced the Declaration of Independence, which identifies "Life, Liberty, and the pursuit of Happiness" as "unalienable Rights" of citizens under government.

Not everyone believes that the protection of private property is a valid objective of government. The German philosopher Karl Marx (1818–1883) rejected the private ownership of property used in the production of goods or services. Marx's ideas form the basis of communism, a complex theory that gives ownership of all land and productive facilities to the people—in effect, to the government. In line with communist theory, the 1977 constitution of the former Soviet Union declared that the nation's land, minerals, waters, and forests "are the exclusive property of the state." In addition, "The state owns the basic means of production in industry, construction, and agriculture; means of transport and communication; the banks, the property of state-run trade organizations and public utilities, and other state-run undertakings."[23] Even today's market-oriented China still clings to the principle that all land belongs to the state, and not until 2007 did it pass a law that protected private homes and businesses.[24]

Providing Public Goods

After governments have established basic order, they can pursue other ends. Using their coercive powers, they can tax citizens to raise funds to spend on **public goods**, which are benefits and services that are available to everyone, such as education, sanitation, and parks. Public goods benefit all citizens but are not likely to be produced by the voluntary acts of individuals. The government of ancient Rome, for example, built aqueducts to carry fresh water from the mountains to the city. Road building is another public good provided by the government since ancient times.

Some government enterprises that have been common in other countries—running railroads, operating coal mines, generating electric power—are politically controversial or even unacceptable in the United States. Hence, many people objected when the Bush administration took over General Motors and Chrysler in 2008 to

communism
A political system in which, in theory, ownership of all land and productive facilities is in the hands of the people and all goods are equally shared. The production and distribution of goods are controlled by an authoritarian government.

public goods
Benefits and services, such as parks and sanitation, that benefit all citizens but are not likely to be produced voluntarily by individuals.

facilitate an orderly bankruptcy. Many Americans believe public goods and services should be provided by private business operating for profit.

Promoting Equality

The promotion of equality has not always been a major objective of government. It gained prominence in the twentieth century, in the aftermath of industrialization and urbanization. Confronted by the contrast of poverty amid plenty, some political leaders in European nations pioneered extensive government programs to improve life for the poor. Under the emerging concept of the welfare state, government's role expanded to provide individuals with medical care, education, and a guaranteed income "from cradle to grave." Sweden, Britain, and other nations adopted welfare programs aimed at reducing social inequalities. This relatively new purpose of government has been by far the most controversial. People often oppose taxation for public goods (such as building roads and schools) because of its cost alone. They oppose more strongly taxation for government programs to promote economic and social equality on principle.

The key issue here is the government's role in redistributing income, that is, taking from the wealthy to give to the poor. Charity (voluntary giving to the poor) has a strong basis in Western religious traditions; using the power of the state to support the poor does not. Using the state to redistribute income was originally a radical idea, set forth by Marx as the ultimate principle of developed communism: "from each according to his ability, to each according to his needs."[25] This extreme has never been realized in any government, not even in communist states. But over time, taking from the rich to help the needy has become a legitimate function of most governments.

That function is not without controversy, however. Especially since the Great Depression of the 1930s, the government's role in redistributing income to promote economic equality has been a major source of policy debate in the United States. In 2006, for example, Democrats in the Senate blocked a bill passed in the House that would have raised the minimum wage from $5.15 to $7.25. They objected to the bill because it would have also cut the estate tax for the wealthy. The minimum wage increase was ultimately passed in 2007, but only by attaching it to a bill funding the war effort in Iraq.

IDEALOG.ORG

How do you feel about government programs that reduce income differences between rich and poor? Take IDEALog's self-test.

Government can also promote social equality through policies that do not redistribute income. For example, in 2000 Vermont passed a law allowing persons of the same sex to enter a "civil union" granting access to similar benefits enjoyed by persons of different sexes through marriage. By 2011 Vermont had replaced the term *civil unions* with marriage, and the legislatures or courts in Massachusetts, New Hampshire, Connecticut, Iowa, the District of Columbia, and New York put same-sex marriage laws into effect. In this instance, laws advancing social equality may clash with different social values held by other citizens. Indeed, thirty-one states blocked same-sex marriages through public referenda, and public ballot measures in Maine and California repealed same-sex marriage laws passed in those states.[26]

A Conceptual Framework for Analyzing Government

Citizens have very different views on how vigorously they want government to maintain order, provide public goods, and promote equality. Of the three objectives, providing public goods usually is less controversial than maintaining order or promoting equality. After all, government spending for highways, schools, and parks carries benefits for nearly every citizen. Moreover, these services merely cost money. The cost of maintaining order and promoting equality is greater than money; it usually means a trade-off of basic values.

To understand government and the political process, you must be able to recognize these trade-offs and identify the basic values they entail. You need to take a much broader view than that offered by examining specific political events. You need to use political concepts. A *concept* is a generalized idea of a class of items or thoughts. It groups various events, objects, or qualities under a common classification or label.

The framework that supports this text consists of five concepts that figure prominently in political analysis. We regard these five concepts as especially important to a broad understanding of American politics, and we use them repeatedly. This framework will help you evaluate political events long after you have read this book.

The five concepts that we emphasize relate to (1) what government tries to do and (2) how it decides to do it. The concepts that relate to what government tries to do are *order, freedom,* and *equality.* All governments by definition value order; maintaining order is part of the meaning of government. Most governments at least claim to preserve individual freedom while they maintain order, although they vary widely in the extent to which they succeed. Few governments even profess to guarantee equality, and governments differ greatly in policies that pit equality against freedom. Our conceptual framework should help you evaluate the extent to which the United States pursues all three values through its government.

How government chooses the proper mix of order, freedom, and equality in its policymaking has to do with the process of choice. We evaluate the American governmental process using two models of democratic government: *majoritarian* and *pluralist*. Many governments profess to be democracies. Whether they are or not depends on their (and our) meaning of the term. Even countries that Americans agree are democracies, such as the United States and Britain, differ substantially in the type of democracy they practice. We can use our conceptual models of democratic government both to classify the type of democracy practiced in the United States and to evaluate the government's success in fulfilling that model.

The five concepts can be organized into two groups:

1. Concepts that identify the values pursued by government:
   - Freedom
   - Order
   - Equality
2. Concepts that describe models of democratic government:
   - Majoritarian democracy
   - Pluralist democracy

First we examine freedom, order, and equality as conflicting values pursued by government. Later in this chapter, we discuss majoritarian democracy and pluralist democracy as alternative institutional models for implementing democratic government.

The Concepts of Freedom, Order, and Equality

These three terms—*freedom, order,* and *equality*—have a range of connotations in American politics. Both *freedom* and *equality* are positive terms that politicians have learned to use to their own advantage. Consequently, *freedom* and *equality* mean different things to different people at different times, depending on the political context in which they are used. *Order,* however, has negative connotations for many people because it brings to mind government intrusion in private lives. Except during periods of social strife or external threat (e.g., after September 11, 2001), few politicians in Western democracies call openly for more order. Because all governments infringe on freedom, we examine that concept first.

Freedom. *Freedom* can be used in two major senses: freedom *of* and freedom *from.* Franklin Delano Roosevelt used the word in each sense in a speech he made shortly before the United States entered World War II. He described four freedoms: freedom *of* religion, freedom *of* speech, freedom *from* fear, and freedom *from* want. **Freedom of** is the absence of constraints on behavior. It is freedom to do something. In this sense, *freedom* is synonymous with *liberty.*[27] **Freedom from** suggests immunity from something undesirable or negative, such as fear and want. In the modern political context, *freedom from* often connotes the fight against exploitation and oppression. The cry of the civil rights movement in the 1960s, "Freedom Now!" conveyed this meaning. If you recognize that *freedom* in the latter sense means immunity from discrimination, you can see that it comes close to the concept of equality.[28] In this book, we avoid using *freedom* to mean "freedom from"; for this sense of the word, we simply use *equality.* When we use *freedom,* we mean "freedom of."

Order. When *order* is viewed in the narrow sense of preserving life and protecting property, most citizens would concede the importance of maintaining order and thereby grant the need for government. But when *order* is viewed in the broader sense of preserving the social order, people are more likely to argue that maintaining order is not a legitimate function of government. *Social order* refers to established patterns of authority in society and to traditional modes of behavior. However, it is important to remember that social order can change. Today, perfectly respectable men and women wear bathing suits that would have caused a scandal a hundred years ago.

A government can protect the established order by using its **police power**—its authority to safeguard residents' safety, health, welfare, and morals. The extent to which government should use this authority is a topic of ongoing debate in the United States and is constantly being redefined by the courts. After September 11, 2001, new laws were passed increasing government's power to investigate suspicious activities by foreign nationals in order to

freedom of
An absence of constraints on behavior, as in *freedom of speech* or *freedom of religion.*

freedom from
Immunity, as in *freedom from want.*

police power
The authority of government to maintain order and safeguard citizens' safety, health, welfare, and morals.

deter terrorism. After the underwear bomber was thwarted from blowing up an airliner on Christmas Day 2009, the Transportation Security Administration began deploying 450 advanced full-body scanners to probe through clothing.[29] Despite their desire to be safe from further attacks, some citizens feared the erosion of their civil liberties.

Most governments are inherently conservative; they tend to resist social change. But some governments aim to radically restructure the social order. Social change is most dramatic when a government is overthrown through force and replaced. This can occur through an internal revolution or a "regime change" effected externally. Societies can also work to change social patterns more gradually through the legal process. Our use of the term *order* in this book encompasses all three aspects: preserving life, protecting property, and maintaining traditional patterns of social relationships.

Equality. Like *freedom* and *order, equality* is used in different senses to support different causes. Political equality in elections is easy to define: each citizen has one and only one vote. This basic concept is central to democratic theory, a subject we explore at length later in this chapter. But when some people advocate political equality, they mean more than "one person, one vote." These people contend that an urban ghetto dweller and the chairman of the board of Microsoft are not politically equal despite the fact that each has one vote. Through occupation or wealth, some citizens are more able than others to influence political decisions. For example, wealthy citizens can exert influence by advertising in the mass media or contacting friends in high places. Lacking great wealth and political connections, most citizens do not have such influence. Thus, some analysts argue that equality in wealth, education, and status—that is, social equality—is necessary for true political equality.

There are two routes to promoting social equality: providing equal opportunities and ensuring equal outcomes. **Equality of opportunity** means that each person has the same chance to succeed in life. This idea is deeply ingrained in American culture. The U.S. Constitution prohibits titles of nobility, and owning property is not a requirement for holding public office. Public schools and libraries are free to all. For many people, the concept of social equality is satisfied by offering equal opportunities for advancement—it is not essential that people actually end up being equal. For others, true social equality means nothing less than **equality of outcome**.[30] They believe that society must see to it that people are

political equality
Equality in political decision making: one vote per person, with all votes counted equally.

social equality
Equality in wealth, education, and status.

equality of opportunity
The idea that each person is guaranteed the same chance to succeed in life.

equality of outcome
The concept that society must ensure that people are equal, and governments must design policies to redistribute wealth and status to achieve economic and social equality.

equal. According to this view, it is not enough that governments provide people with equal opportunities; they must also design policies to redistribute wealth and status so that economic and social equality are achieved.

Some link equality of outcome with the concept of government-supported rights—the idea that every citizen is entitled to certain benefits of government, that government should guarantee its citizens adequate (if not equal) housing, employment, medical care, and income. If citizens are entitled to government benefits as a matter of right, government efforts to promote equality of outcome become legitimized.

Clearly, the concept of equality of outcome is very different from that of equality of opportunity, and it requires a much greater degree of government activity. It also clashes more directly with the concept of freedom. By taking from one person to give to another, which is necessary for the redistribution of income and status, the government creates winners and losers. The winners may believe that justice has been served by the redistribution. The losers often feel strongly that their freedom to enjoy their income and status has suffered.

Two Dilemmas of Government

The two major dilemmas facing American government in the early years of the twenty-first century stem from the oldest and the newest objectives of government: maintaining order and promoting equality. Both order and equality are important social values, but government cannot pursue either without sacrificing a third important value: individual freedom. The clash between freedom and order forms the *original* dilemma of government; the clash between freedom and equality forms the *modern* dilemma of government. Although the dilemmas are very different, each involves trading off some amount of freedom for another value.

The Original Dilemma: Freedom Versus Order. The conflict between freedom and order originates in the very meaning of *government* as the legitimate use of force to control human behavior. How much freedom a citizen must surrender to government is a dilemma that has occupied philosophers for hundreds of years. The original purpose of government was to protect life and property, to make citizens safe from violence. How well is the American government doing today in providing law and order to its citizens? More than

rights
The benefits of government to which every citizen is entitled.

66 percent of the respondents in a 2009 national survey said that there were areas within a mile of their home where they were "afraid to walk alone at night."[31]

Contrast the fear of crime in urban America with the sense of personal safety while walking in Moscow, Warsaw, or Prague when the old communist governments still ruled in Eastern Europe. It was common to see old and young strolling late at night along the streets and in the parks of those cities. The communist regimes gave their police great powers to control guns, monitor citizens' movements, and arrest and imprison suspicious people, which enabled them to do a better job of maintaining order. Communist governments deliberately chose order over freedom.

In the abstract, people value both freedom and order; in real life, the two values inherently conflict. By definition, any policy that strengthens one value takes away from the other. In a democracy, policy choices hinge on how much citizens value freedom and how much they value order.

The Modern Dilemma: Freedom Versus Equality. Popular opinion has it that freedom and equality go hand in hand. In reality, these two values usually clash when governments enact policies to promote social equality. Because social equality is a relatively recent government objective, deciding between policies that promote equality at the expense of freedom, and vice versa, is the modern dilemma of politics. Consider these examples:

- During the 1970s, the courts ordered the busing of schoolchildren to achieve equal proportions of blacks and whites in public schools. This action was motivated by concern for educational equality, but it also impaired freedom of choice.
- During the 1980s, some states passed legislation that went beyond giving men and women equal pay for equal work to the more radical notion of pay equity—equal pay for comparable work. Women were to be paid at a rate equal to men's even if they had different jobs, providing the women's jobs were of "comparable worth" (meaning the skills and responsibilities were comparable).
- During the 1990s, Congress prohibited discrimination in employment, public services, and public accommodations on the basis of physical or mental disabilities. Under the 1990 Americans with Disabilities Act, businesses with twenty-five or more employees could not pass over an otherwise qualified disabled person in employment or promotion, and new buses and trains had to be made accessible to them.

The Importance of Order and Freedom in Other Nations

Compared with citizens in twenty-nine other nations, Americans do not value order very much. The World Values Survey asked respondents to select which of four national goals was "very important":

- Maintaining order in the nation
- Giving people more say in important government decisions
- Fighting rising prices
- Protecting freedom of speech

The United States ranked twenty-eighth in the list of those selecting "maintaining order" as very important. Although American citizens do not value government control of social behavior as much as others, Americans do value freedom of speech more highly. Citizens in only three countries favor protecting freedom of speech more than citizens in the United States.

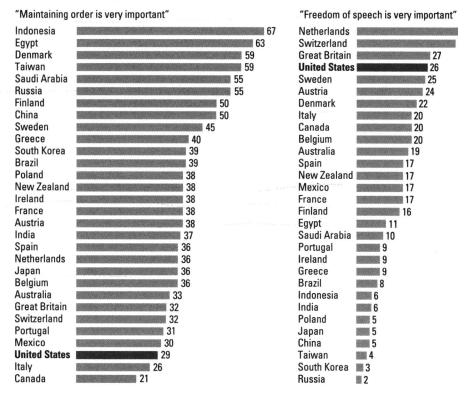

"Maintaining order is very important"

Country	Percentage
Indonesia	67
Egypt	63
Denmark	59
Taiwan	59
Saudi Arabia	55
Russia	55
Finland	50
China	50
Sweden	45
Greece	40
South Korea	39
Brazil	39
Poland	38
New Zealand	38
Ireland	38
France	38
Austria	38
India	37
Spain	36
Netherlands	36
Japan	36
Belgium	36
Australia	33
Great Britain	32
Switzerland	32
Portugal	31
Mexico	30
United States	29
Italy	26
Canada	21

Percentage of respondents who value "order"

"Freedom of speech is very important"

Country	Percentage
Netherlands	39
Switzerland	36
Great Britain	27
United States	26
Sweden	25
Austria	24
Denmark	22
Italy	20
Canada	20
Belgium	20
Australia	19
Spain	17
New Zealand	17
Mexico	17
France	17
Finland	16
Egypt	11
Saudi Arabia	10
Portugal	9
Ireland	9
Greece	9
Brazil	8
Indonesia	6
India	6
Poland	5
Japan	5
China	5
Taiwan	4
South Korea	3
Russia	2

Percentage of respondents who value "freedom"

Source: These are combined data from the 1999–2001 and 2005–2007 waves of the World Values Survey. See Ronald Inglehart, "Materialist/Postmaterialist Priorities among Publics around the World" (discussion paper presented at ISR, University of Michigan, 14 February 2008).

- During the first decade of the 2000s, Congress passed the Genetic Information Nondiscrimination Act (GINA). Signed by President Bush in 2008, it prohibited companies from discriminating in hiring based on an individual's genetic tests, genetic tests of a family member, and family medical history.

The clash between freedom and order is obvious, but the clash between freedom and equality is more subtle. Americans, who think of freedom and equality as complementary rather than conflicting values, often do not notice the clash between those two values. When forced to choose between them, however, Americans are far more likely than people in other countries to choose freedom over equality.

The conflicts among freedom, order, and equality explain a great deal of the political conflict in the United States. The conflicts also underlie the ideologies that people use to structure their understanding of politics.

Ideology and the Scope of Government

Some people hold an assortment of values and beliefs that produce contradictory opinions on government policies. Others organize their opinions into a **political ideology**: a consistent set of values and beliefs about the proper purpose and scope of government.

How far should government go to maintain order, provide public goods, and promote equality? We can analyze answers to this question by referring to philosophies about the proper scope of government—the range of permissible activities. Imagine a continuum. At one end is the belief that government should do everything; at the other is the belief that government should not exist. These extreme ideologies—from "least government" to "most government"—and those that fall in between are shown in Figure 1.1.

Totalitarianism. **Totalitarianism** is the belief that government should have unlimited power. A totalitarian government controls all sectors of society: business, labor, education, religion, sports, the arts, and others. A true totalitarian favors a network of laws, rules, and regulations that guides every aspect of individual behavior.

Socialism. Whereas totalitarianism refers to government in general, socialism pertains to government's role in the economy. Like communism, socialism is an economic system based on Marxist theory.

political ideology
A consistent set of values and beliefs about the proper purpose and scope of government.

totalitarianism
A political philosophy that advocates unlimited power for the government to enable it to control all sectors of society.

socialism
A form of rule in which the central government plays a strong role in regulating existing private industry and directing the economy, although it does allow some private ownership of productive capacity.

FIGURE 1.1 Ideology and the Scope of Government

LEAST GOVERNMENT				MOST GOVERNMENT

POLITICAL THEORIES			
Anarchism	Libertarianism	Liberalism	Totalitarianism

ECONOMIC THEORIES		
Laissez Faire	Capitalism	Socialism

POPULAR POLITICAL LABELS IN AMERICA	
Conservative	Liberal

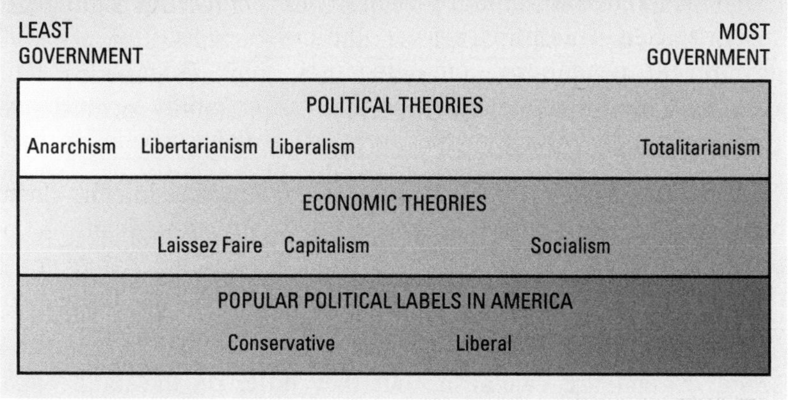

We can classify political ideologies according to the scope of action that people are willing to allow government in dealing with social and economic problems. In this chart, the three rows map out various philosophical positions along an underlying continuum ranging from "least" to "most" government. Notice that conventional politics in the United States spans only a narrow portion of the theoretical possibilities for government action. In popular usage, liberals favor a greater scope of government, and conservatives want a narrower scope. But over time, the traditional distinction has eroded and now oversimplifies the differences between liberals and conservatives. Figure 1.2 (p. 23) offers a more discriminating classification of liberals and conservatives.

(© Cengage Learning 2013)

Under socialism (and communism), the scope of government extends to ownership or control of the basic industries that produce goods and services (communications, heavy industry, transportation). Although socialism favors a strong role for government in regulating private industry and directing the economy, it allows more room than communism does for private ownership of productive capacity.

Communism in theory was supposed to result in a withering away of the state, but communist governments in practice tended toward totalitarianism, controlling economic, political, and social life through a dominant party organization. Some socialist governments, however, practice **democratic socialism**. They guarantee civil liberties (such as freedom of speech and freedom of religion) and allow their citizens to determine the extent of the government's activity through free elections and competitive political parties. The governments of Britain, Sweden, Germany, and France, among other democracies, have at times been avowedly socialist.

> **democratic socialism**
> A socialist form of government that guarantees civil liberties such as freedom of speech and religion. Citizens determine the extent of government activity through free elections and competitive political parties.

Capitalism. Capitalism also relates to the government's role in the economy. In contrast to both socialism and communism, **capitalism** supports free enterprise—private businesses operating without government regulations. Some theorists, most notably the late economist Milton Friedman, argue that free enterprise is necessary for free politics.[32] Whether this argument is valid depends in part on our understanding of democracy, a subject we discuss later in this chapter.

The United States is decidedly a capitalist country, more so than most other Western nations. But our government does extend its authority into the economic sphere, regulating private businesses and directing the overall economy. Both American liberals and conservatives embrace capitalism, but they differ on the nature and amount of government intervention in the economy that is necessary or desirable.

Libertarianism. **Libertarianism** opposes all government action except that which is necessary to protect life and property. For example, libertarians believe that social programs that provide food, clothing, and shelter are outside the proper scope of government. They also oppose any government intervention in the economy. This kind of economic policy is called laissez faire, a French phrase that means "let (people) do (as they please)." Such an extreme policy extends beyond the free enterprise advocated by most capitalists.

Anarchism. Anarchism stands opposite totalitarianism on the political continuum. Anarchists oppose all government in any form. As a political philosophy, **anarchism** values absolute freedom above all else. Like totalitarianism, it is not a popular philosophy, but it does have adherents on the political fringes. Discussing old and new forms of anarchy, Joseph Kahn said, "Nothing has revived anarchism like globalization."[33]

Liberals and Conservatives. As shown in Figure 1.1, practical politics in the United States ranges over only the central portion of the continuum. The extreme positions, totalitarianism and anarchism, are rarely argued in public debate. And in this era of distrust of "big government," few American politicians would openly advocate socialism. Most debate is limited to a narrow range of political thought. On one side are people commonly called *liberals;* on the other are *conservatives*. In popular usage, liberals favor more government,

capitalism
The system of government that favors free enterprise (privately owned businesses operating without government regulation).

libertarianism
A political ideology that is opposed to all government action except as necessary to protect life and property.

laissez faire
An economic doctrine that opposes any form of government intervention in business.

anarchism
A political philosophy that opposes government in any form.

Anarchists in Action

Anarchism as a philosophy views government as an unnecessary evil used by the wealthy to exploit the poor. In June 2010, a small group of young anarchists broke away from an otherwise peaceful protest against the G20 summit meeting in Toronto, Canada. While the main body of protestors marched to raise awareness of the negative impacts of globalization on the poor, the young anarchists vandalized businesses and ultimately burned police cars.

(AP Photo/The Canadian Press, Chris Young)

conservatives less. This distinction is clear when the issue is government spending to provide public goods. **Liberals** are willing to use government to promote equality but not order. Thus, they generally favor generous government support for education, wildlife protection, public transportation, and a whole range of social programs. **Conservatives** want smaller government budgets and fewer government programs. They support free enterprise and argue against government job programs, regulation of business, and legislation of working conditions and wage rates. In short, they prefer to use government to promote order rather than equality.

In other areas, liberal and conservative ideologies are less consistent. The differences no longer hinge on the narrow question of the government's role in providing public goods. Liberals still favor more government and conservatives less, but this is no longer the critical difference between them. Today, that difference stems from their attitudes toward the purpose of government. Conservatives support the original purpose of government: to maintain

liberals
Those who are willing to use government to promote equality but not order.

conservatives
Those who are willing to use government to promote order but not equality.

social order. They are willing to use the coercive power of the state
to force citizens to be orderly. But they would not stop with defining, preventing, and punishing crime. They tend to want to preserve traditional patterns of social relations—the domestic role of
women and the importance of religion in school and family life,
for example.

Liberals are less likely than conservatives to want to use government power to maintain order. Liberals do not shy away from
using government coercion, but they use it for a different purpose:
to promote equality. They support laws that ensure equal treatment
of homosexuals in employment, housing, and education; laws that
force private businesses to hire and promote women and members
of minority groups; and laws that require public transportation to
provide equal access to people with disabilities. Conservatives do
not oppose equality, but they do not value it to the extent of using
the government's power to enforce it. For liberals, the use of that
power to promote equality is both valid and necessary.

A Two-Dimensional Classification of Ideologies

To classify liberal and conservative ideologies more accurately, we
have to incorporate the values of freedom, order, and equality into
the classification.[34] We can do this using the model in Figure 1.2.
It depicts the conflicting values along two separate dimensions,
each anchored in maximum freedom at the lower left. One dimension extends horizontally from maximum freedom on the left to
maximum order on the right. The other extends vertically from
maximum freedom at the bottom to maximum equality at the top.
Each box represents a different ideological type: libertarians, liberals, conservatives, and communitarians.[35]

Libertarians value freedom more than they value order or
equality (we will use *libertarian* for people who have libertarian
tendencies but may not accept the whole philosophy). In practical
terms, libertarians want minimal government intervention in both
the economic and the social spheres. For example, they oppose
affirmative action laws and laws that restrict transmission of sexually explicit material. Liberals value freedom more than order but
not more than equality. They oppose laws that ban sexually
explicit publications but support affirmative action. Conservatives
value freedom more than equality but would restrict freedom to
preserve social order. Conservatives oppose affirmative action but
favor laws that restrict pornography.

libertarians
Those who are opposed to
using government to pro-
mote either order or equality.

FIGURE 1.2   Ideologies: A Two-Dimensional Framework

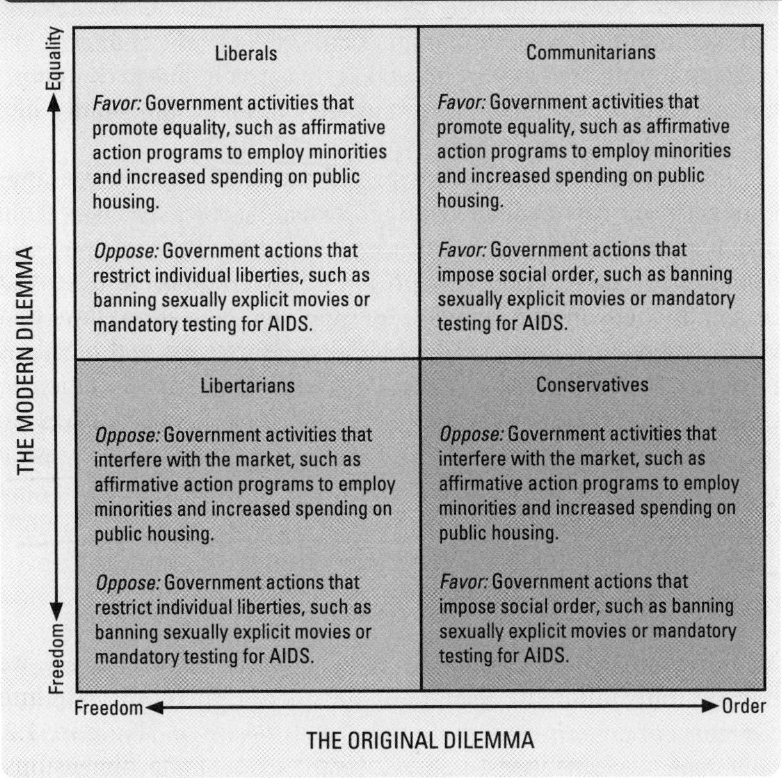

THE MODERN DILEMMA

Equality ↑

Liberals

Favor: Government activities that promote equality, such as affirmative action programs to employ minorities and increased spending on public housing.

Oppose: Government actions that restrict individual liberties, such as banning sexually explicit movies or mandatory testing for AIDS.

Communitarians

Favor: Government activities that promote equality, such as affirmative action programs to employ minorities and increased spending on public housing.

Favor: Government actions that impose social order, such as banning sexually explicit movies or mandatory testing for AIDS.

Libertarians

Oppose: Government activities that interfere with the market, such as affirmative action programs to employ minorities and increased spending on public housing.

Oppose: Government actions that restrict individual liberties, such as banning sexually explicit movies or mandatory testing for AIDS.

Conservatives

Oppose: Government activities that interfere with the market, such as affirmative action programs to employ minorities and increased spending on public housing.

Favor: Government actions that impose social order, such as banning sexually explicit movies or mandatory testing for AIDS.

Freedom ↓

Freedom ◄————————————► Order

THE ORIGINAL DILEMMA

The four ideological types are defined by the values they favor in resolving the two major dilemmas of government: how much freedom should be sacrificed in pursuit of order and equality, respectively. Test yourself by thinking about the values that are most important to you. Which box in the figure best represents your combination of values?

(© Cengage Learning 2013)

Finally, at the upper right in Figure 1.2, we have a group that values both equality and order more than freedom. Its members support both affirmative action laws and laws that restrict pornography. We will call this new group communitarians.[36] The term is used narrowly in contemporary politics to reflect the philosophy of the Communitarian Network, a political movement founded by sociologist Amitai Etzioni.[37] This movement rejects both the liberal–conservative classification and the libertarian argument that "individuals should be left on their own to pursue their choices, rights, and self-interests."[38] Like liberals, Etzioni's communitarians believe that there is a role for government in helping the disadvantaged. Like conservatives, they believe that government should be used to promote moral values—preserving the family through more stringent divorce laws and limiting the dissemination of pornography, for example.[39] However, the Communitarian Network is not dedicated to big government. According to

communitarians
Those who are willing to use government to promote both order and equality.

its platform, "The government should step in only to the extent that other social subsystems fail, rather than seek to replace them."[40] Our definition of communitarian (small "c") clearly embraces the Communitarian Network's philosophy, but it is broader: communitarians favor government programs that promote both order and equality, somewhat in keeping with socialist theory.

By analyzing political ideologies on two dimensions rather than one, we can explain why people can seem to be liberal on one issue (favoring a broader scope of government action) and conservative on another (favoring less government action). The reason hinges on the purpose of a given government action: Which value does it promote: order or equality? According to our typology, only libertarians and communitarians are consistent in their attitudes toward the scope of government activity, whatever its purpose. Libertarians value freedom so highly that they oppose most government efforts to enforce either order or equality. Communitarians (in our use) are inclined to trade off freedom for both order and equality. Liberals and conservatives, in contrast, favor or oppose government activity depending on its purpose. As you will learn in Chapter 4, large groups of Americans fall into each of the four ideological categories. Because Americans increasingly choose four different resolutions to the original and modern dilemmas of government, the simple labels *liberal* and *conservative* no longer describe contemporary political ideologies as well as they did in the 1930s, 1940s, and 1950s.

The American Governmental Process: Majoritarian or Pluralist?

After his inauguration as president, Barack Obama's discussions about the economy with congressional Democrats and Republicans revealed that the parties were united on only one thing: something should be done to stimulate the economy and to prevent it from declining further. The collapse of the real estate bubble and the broad economic downturn in 2008 led not only to Obama's decisive victory over Republican John McCain a few months earlier but also to strong gains for Democrats in Congress, putting them in firm control of both the House and Senate.

The Republican leaders stood fast for their party's philosophy of small government and low taxes, recommending that the stimulus package emphasize tax cuts and tax incentives. The Democrats supported direct government spending on public works like roads and bridges, thus putting some of the unemployed immediately to work. Along with infrastructure support, the plan included large payments to the states to help them avoid laying off employees since state tax revenues plummeted in the wake of the recession. A small tax cut for low- and middle-income workers was also part of the Democratic package.

While there was no conclusive answer among economists about which philosophy was better, that underlying question was academic: as Obama pointed out, he and the congressional Democrats won the election.[41] Their philosophy would carry the day, and Democratic majorities in the House and Senate backed the plan.[42]

On the surface it seemed like democracy had worked its will as the majority had spoken. Yet beneath the surface of the Democratic plan, another dynamic was at work. The overall package appropriated $787 billion to be spent to try to reverse the downward spiral of the recession. But as the specifics of the spending plan were being formulated by Congress, there was a vast array of choices as to exactly what the money would be spent on. Interest groups lobbied Congress furiously for their own priorities. Business was especially active as different industries pushed legislators to support spending or create tax breaks that would help that particular industry. Some got what they wanted; others were disappointed. Representatives and senators listened to the many voices of the different parts of the American economy and then made their choices. The 2008 election faded into the background as legislators negotiated among themselves with an eye on which types of businesses and nonprofits in their districts or states would gain under alternative proposals.

These are very different models of government. Should Congress follow the president, who won a majority of the vote, in interpreting his stimulus package as what the people want? Or is majority opinion a blunt and imprecise instrument, and should closer consideration be given to the rich and diverse constituencies that form our body politic?

To this point, our discussion of political ideologies has centered on conflicting views about the values government should pursue. We now examine how government should decide what to do. In particular, we set forth two criteria for judging whether a government's decision-making process is democratic, one emphasizing majority rule and the other emphasizing the role of interest groups.

The Theory of Democratic Government

Americans have a simple answer to the question, "Who should govern?" It is, "The people." Unfortunately, this answer is too simple. It fails to say who *the people* are. Should we include young children? Recent immigrants? Illegal aliens? This answer also fails to indicate how "the people" should do the governing. Should they be assembled in a stadium? Vote by mail? Choose representatives to govern for them? We need to take a close look at what "government by the people" really means.

The word *democracy* originated in Greek writings around the fifth century B.C. *Demos* referred to the common people, the masses; *kratos* meant "power." The ancient Greeks were afraid of **democracy**, which they viewed as rule by rank-and-file citizens. That fear is evident in the term *demagogue*. We use that term today to refer to a politician who appeals to and often deceives the masses by manipulating their emotions and prejudices.

Many centuries after the Greeks defined *democracy,* the idea still carried the connotation of mob rule. When George Washington was president, opponents of a new political party disparagingly called it a *democratic* party. No one would do that in politics today. In fact, the names of more than 20 percent of the world's political parties contain some variation of the word *democracy.*[43]

There are two major schools of thought about what constitutes democracy. The first believes democracy is a form of government, and it emphasizes the procedures that enable the people to govern: meeting to discuss issues, voting in elections, and running for public office, for example. The second sees democracy in the substance of government policies, in freedom of religion and providing for human needs. The *procedural* approach focuses on how decisions are made; the *substantive* approach is concerned with what government does.

The Procedural View of Democracy. **Procedural democratic theory** sets forth principles that describe how government should make decisions. These principles address three distinct questions:

1. *Who should participate* in decision making?
2. *How much should* each participant's vote count?
3. *How many* votes are needed to reach a decision?

According to procedural democratic theory, all adults within the boundaries of the political community should participate in government decision making. We refer to this principle as **universal participation**. How much should each participant's vote count?

★ **democracy**
A system of government in which, in theory, the people rule, either directly or indirectly.

★ **procedural democratic theory**
A view of democracy as being embodied in a decision-making process that involves universal participation, political equality, majority rule, and responsiveness.

★ **universal participation**
The concept that everyone in a democracy should participate in governmental decision making.

According to procedural theory, all votes should count equally. This is the principle of political equality. Note that universal participation and political equality are two distinct principles. It is not enough for everyone to participate in a decision; all votes must carry equal weight.

Finally, procedural theory prescribes that a group should decide to do what the majority of its participants wants to do. This principle is called majority rule. (If participants divide over more than two alternatives and none receives a majority, the principle usually defaults to *plurality* rule, in which the group should do what the largest group of participants wants, even if fewer than half of those involved hold that view.)

A Complication: Direct Versus Indirect Democracy. Universal participation, political equality, and majority rule are widely recognized as necessary for democratic decision making. Small, simple societies can achieve all three with direct or **participatory democracy**, in which all members of the group meet to make decisions, observing political equality and majority rule. However, in the United States and nearly all other democracies, participatory democracy is rare. Clearly, all Americans cannot gather at the Capitol in Washington, D.C., to decide defense policy.

The framers of the U.S. Constitution had their own conception of democracy. They instituted **representative democracy**, a system in which citizens participate in government by electing public officials to make government decisions on their behalf. Within the context of representative democracy, we adhere to the principles of universal participation, political equality, and majority rule to guarantee that elections are democratic. But what happens after the election?

Suppose the elected representatives do not make the decisions the people would have made if they had gathered for the same purpose. To account for this possibility in representative government, procedural theory provides a fourth decision-making principle: **responsiveness**. Elected representatives should follow the general contours of public opinion as they formulate complex pieces of legislation.[44]

By adding responsiveness to deal with the case of indirect democracy, we now have four principles of procedural democracy:

- Universal participation
- Political equality

majority rule
The principle—basic to procedural democratic theory—that the decision of a group must reflect the preference of more than half of those participating; a simple majority.

participatory democracy
A system of government where rank-and-file citizens rule themselves rather than electing representatives to govern on their behalf.

representative democracy
A system of government where citizens elect public officials to govern on their behalf.

responsiveness
A decision-making principle, necessitated by representative government, that implies that elected representatives should do what the majority of people wants.

- Majority rule
- Government responsiveness to public opinion

The Substantive View of Democracy. According to procedural theory, the principle of responsiveness is absolute: the government should do what the majority wants, regardless of what that is. At first this seems a reasonable way to protect the rights of citizens in a representative democracy. But what about the rights of minorities? To limit the government's responsiveness to public opinion, we must look outside procedural democratic theory to substantive democratic theory. Substantive democratic theory focuses on the substance of government policies, not on the procedures followed in making those policies. It argues that in a democratic government, certain principles must be embodied in government policies. Substantive theorists would reject a law that requires Bible reading in schools because it would violate a substantive principle, the freedom of religion. The core of the substantive principles of American democracy is embedded in the Bill of Rights and other amendments to the U.S. Constitution.

In defining the principles that underlie democratic government—and the policies of that government—most substantive theorists agree on a basic criterion: government policies should guarantee *civil liberties* (freedom of behavior such as freedom of religion and freedom of expression) and *civil rights* (powers or privileges that government may not arbitrarily deny to individuals, such as protection against discrimination in employment and housing). But agreement among substantive theorists breaks down when discussion moves from civil rights to *social rights* (adequate health care, quality education, decent housing) and *economic rights* (private property, steady employment). For example, some insist that policies that promote social equality are essential to democratic government. Others restrict the requirements of substantive democracy to policies that safeguard civil liberties and civil rights.[45]

A theorist's political ideology tends to explain his or her position on what democracy really requires in substantive policies. Conservative theorists have a narrow view of the scope of democratic government and a narrow view of the social and economic rights guaranteed by that government. Liberal theorists believe that a democratic government should guarantee its citizens a much broader spectrum of social and economic rights.

Procedural Democracy Versus Substantive Democracy. The problem with the substantive view of democracy is that it does not provide

IDEALOG.ORG

Should the government try to improve the standard of living for all poor Americans? Take IDEAlog's self-test.

VS.

substantive democratic theory
The view that democracy is embodied in the substance of government policies rather than in the policymaking procedure.

clear, precise criteria that allow us to determine whether a government is democratic. Substantive theorists are free to promote their pet values—separation of church and state, guaranteed employment, equal rights for women, or whatever else—under the guise of substantive democracy.

The procedural viewpoint also has a problem. Although it presents specific criteria for democratic government, those criteria can produce undesirable social policies that prey on minorities. This clashes with **minority rights**—the idea that all citizens are entitled to certain rights that cannot be denied by the majority. One way to protect minority rights is to limit the principle of majority rule by requiring a two-thirds majority or some other extraordinary majority when decisions must be made on certain subjects. Another way is to put the issue in the Constitution, beyond the reach of majority rule.

Clearly, procedural democracy and substantive democracy are not always compatible. In choosing one over the other, we are also choosing to focus on either procedures or policies. As authors of this text, we favor a compromise between the two. On the whole, we favor the procedural conception of democracy because it more closely approaches the classical definition of *democracy:* "government by the people." And procedural democracy is founded on clear, well-established rules for decision making. But the theory has a serious drawback: it allows a democratic government to enact policies that can violate the substantive principles of democracy. Thus, pure procedural democracy should be diluted so that minority rights and civil liberties are guaranteed as part of the structure of government.

Institutional Models of Democracy

Some democratic theorists favor institutions that tie government decisions closely to the desires of the majority of citizens. If most citizens want laws against the sale of pornography, then the government should outlaw pornography. If citizens want more money spent on defense and less on social welfare (or vice versa), the government should act accordingly. For these theorists, the essence of democratic government is majority rule and responsiveness. Other theorists place less importance on these principles. They do not believe in relying heavily on mass opinion; instead, they favor institutions that allow groups of citizens to defend their interests in the public policymaking process.

minority rights
The benefits of government that cannot be denied to any citizens by majority decisions.

Both schools hold a procedural view of democracy but differ in how they interpret "government by the people." We can summarize these theoretical positions using two alternative models of democracy. As a model, each is a hypothetical plan, a blueprint, for achieving democratic government through institutional mechanisms. The *majoritarian* model values participation by the people in general; the *pluralist* model values participation by the people in groups.

The Majoritarian Model of Democracy. The **majoritarian model of democracy** relies on our intuitive notion of what is fair. It interprets "government by the people" as government by the *majority* of the people. To force the government to respond to public opinion, the majoritarian model depends on several mechanisms that allow the people to participate directly.

The popular election of government officials is the primary mechanism for democratic government in the majoritarian model. Citizens are expected to control their representatives' behavior by choosing wisely in the first place and by reelecting or voting out public officials according to their performance.

Majoritarian theorists also see elections as a means for deciding government policies. An election on a policy issue is called a *referendum.* When a policy question is put on the ballot by the action of citizens circulating petitions and gathering a required minimum number of signatures, it is called an *initiative*. Twenty-one states allow their legislatures to put referenda before the voters and give their citizens the right to place initiatives on the ballot. Five other states make provision for one mechanism or the other.[46] Eighteen states also allow for the *recall* of state officials, a means of forcing a special election for an up or down vote on a sitting governor or state judge.

In the United States, no provisions exist for referenda at the federal level. Some other countries do allow policy questions to be put before the public. In a national referendum in 2009, a clear majority of voters in Switzerland voted to ban construction of minarets on any of the country's mosques. (Minarets are the thin spires atop a mosque.) This vote was clearly hostile to the country's small (5 percent) Muslim population. One of the dangers of referenda is the power of a majority to treat a minority in a harsh or intimidating way.[47]

The majoritarian model contends that citizens can control their government if they have adequate mechanisms for popular

majoritarian model of democracy
The classical theory of democracy in which government by the people is interpreted as government by the majority of the people.

Now *That's* a Town Meeting

For over 600 years, citizens of Appenzell Inner-Rhodes, the smallest canton (like a township) in Switzerland, have gathered in the town square on the last Sunday in April to make political decisions by raised hands. At a recent meeting, Appenzellers adopted a leash law for dogs, approved updating property files on a computer, chose a new building commissioner, and acted on other public business before adjourning until the next year. Even with a long tradition like this one, things can change. Because of Easter's position on the calendar in 2011, the gathering for that year was postponed until May 1.

(REUTERS/Arnd Wiegmann)

participation. It also assumes that citizens are knowledgeable about government and politics, want to participate in the political process, and make rational decisions in voting for their elected representatives.

Critics contend that Americans are not knowledgeable enough for majoritarian democracy to work. They point to research that shows that only 36 percent of a national sample of voters said that they follow news about politics "very closely."[48] Two scholars who have studied citizens' interest in politics conclude that most Americans favor "stealth" democracy, "in which ordinary people do not have to get involved."[49] If most citizens feel that way, then majoritarian democracy is not viable, even with the wonders of modern information technology. Defenders of majoritarian democracy respond that although individual Americans may have only limited knowledge of or interest in government, the American public as a whole still has coherent and stable opinions on the major policy questions.

An Alternative Model: Pluralist Democracy. For years, political scientists struggled valiantly to reconcile the majoritarian model of democracy with polls that showed a widespread ignorance of politics among the American people. When only a little more than half of the adult population bothers to vote in presidential elections, our form of democracy seems to be government by *some of* the people.

The 1950s saw the evolution of an alternative interpretation of democracy, one tailored to the limited knowledge and participation of the real electorate, not the ideal one. It was based on the concept of *pluralism:* that modern society consists of innumerable groups that share economic, religious, ethnic, or cultural interests. Often people with similar interests organize formal groups. When an organized group seeks to influence government policy, it is called an **interest group.** Many interest groups regularly spend a great deal of time and money trying to influence government policy (see Chapter 7). Among them are the American Hospital Association, the National Association of Manufacturers, the National Education Association, the Associated Milk Producers, and the National Organization for Women.

The **pluralist model of democracy** interprets "government by the people" to mean government by people operating through competing interest groups. According to this model, democracy exists when many (plural) organizations operate separately from the government, press their interests on the government, and even challenge the government.[50] Compared with majoritarian thinking, pluralist theory shifts the focus of democratic government from the mass electorate to organized groups. It changes the criterion for democratic government from responsiveness to mass public opinion to responsiveness to organized groups of citizens.

A decentralized, complex government structure offers the access and openness necessary for pluralist democracy. For pluralists, the ideal system is one that divides government authority among numerous institutions with overlapping authority. Under such a system, competing interest groups have alternative points of access to present and argue their claims. When the National Association for the Advancement of Colored People could not get Congress to outlaw segregated schools in the South, it turned to the federal court system, which did what Congress would not do. According to the ideal of pluralist democracy, if all opposing interests are allowed to organize and if the system can be kept open so that all substantial claims have an opportunity to be heard, the decision will serve the diverse needs of a pluralist society. Countries going through the

interest group
An organized group of individuals that seeks to influence public policy. Also called a *lobby.*

pluralist model of democracy
An interpretation of democracy in which government by the people is taken to mean government by people operating through competing interest groups.

process of democratization can find the emergence of pluralism a challenge as new groups mean new demands upon government.

On one level, pluralism is alive and well. Interest groups in Washington are thriving, and the rise of many citizen groups has broadened representation beyond traditional business, labor, and professional groups.[51] But on another level, political scientist Robert Putnam has documented declining participation in a wide variety of organizations. Americans are less inclined to be active members of civic groups like parent–teacher associations, the League of Woman Voters, and the Lions Club. Civic participation is a fundamental part of American democracy because it generates the social glue that helps to generate trust and cooperation in the political system.[52]

The Majoritarian Model Versus the Pluralist Model. In majoritarian democracy, the mass public, not interest groups, controls government actions. The citizenry must be knowledgeable about government and willing to participate in the electoral process. Majoritarian democracy relies on electoral mechanisms that harness the power of the majority to make decisions. Conclusive elections and a centralized structure of government are mechanisms that aid majority rule. Cohesive political parties with well-defined programs also contribute to majoritarian democracy, because they offer voters a clear way to distinguish alternative sets of policies.

Pluralism does not demand much knowledge from citizens in general. It requires specialized knowledge only from groups of citizens, in particular their leaders. In contrast to majoritarian democracy, pluralist democracy seeks to limit majority action so that interest groups can be heard. It relies on strong interest groups and a decentralized government structure—mechanisms that interfere with majority rule, thereby protecting minority interests. We could even say that pluralism allows minorities to rule.

An Undemocratic Model: Elite Theory. If pluralist democracy allows minorities to rule, how does it differ from elite theory—the view that a small group of people (a minority) makes most important government decisions? According to elite theory, important government decisions are made by an identifiable and stable minority that shares certain characteristics, usually vast wealth and business connections.[53] Elite theory appeals to many people, especially those who believe that wealth dominates politics.

According to elite theory, the United States is not a democracy but an oligarchy.[54] Although the voters appear to control the government

elite theory
The view that a small group of people actually makes most of the important government decisions.

oligarchy
A system of government in which power is concentrated in the hands of a few people.

through elections, elite theorists argue that the powerful few in society manage to define the issues and constrain the outcomes of government decisions to suit their own interests. Clearly, elite theory describes a government that operates in an undemocratic fashion.

Political scientists have conducted numerous studies designed to test the validity of elite theory. Not all of those studies have come to the same conclusion, but the preponderance of evidence documenting government decisions on many different issues does not generally support elite theory—at least in the sense that an identifiable ruling elite usually gets its way. Not surprisingly, elite theorists reject this view. They argue that studies of decisions made on individual issues do not adequately test the influence of the power elite. Rather, they contend that much of the elite's power comes from its ability to keep things off the political agenda—that is, its power derives from its ability to keep people from questioning fundamental assumptions about American capitalism.[55]

Elite theory remains part of the debate about the nature of American government and is forcefully argued by some severe critics of the American political system. Although we do not believe that the scholarly evidence supports elite theory, we do recognize that contemporary American pluralism favors some segments of society over others. The poor are chronically unorganized and are not well represented by interest groups. In contrast, business is better represented than any other sector of the public. Thus, one can endorse pluralist democracy as a more accurate description than elitism in American politics without believing that all groups are equally well represented.

Elite Theory Versus Pluralist Theory. The key difference between elite theory and pluralist theory lies in the durability of the ruling minority. In contrast to elite theory, pluralist theory does not define government conflict in terms of a minority versus the majority; instead, it sees many minorities vying with one another in each policy area. Pluralist democracy makes a virtue of the struggle between competing interests. It argues for government that accommodates this struggle and channels the result into government action. According to pluralist democracy, the public is best served if the government structure provides access for different groups to press their claims in competition with one another.

Note that pluralist democracy does not insist that all groups have equal influence on government decisions. In the political struggle, wealthy, well-organized groups have an inherent advantage over poorer, inadequately organized groups. In fact, unorganized segments of the population may not even get their concerns placed on the agenda for government consideration. Indeed, studies of the congressional agenda demonstrate that it is characterized by little in the way of legislation concerned with poor or low-income Americans, while business-related bills are plentiful.[56] This is a critical weakness of pluralism. However, pluralists contend that so long as all groups are able to participate vigorously in the decision-making process, the process is democratic.

Democracy and Globalization

While no government perfectly achieves the goals of the majoritarian or pluralist models of democracy, some nations approach these ideals closely enough to be considered practicing democracies. Governments can meet some criteria for a procedural democracy (universal participation, political equality, majority rule, and government responsiveness to public opinion) and fail to meet others. They can also differ in the extent to which they support freedom of speech and freedom of association, which create the necessary conditions for the practice of democracy. Various scholars and organizations have developed complicated databases that rate countries on a long list of indicators, providing a means of comparing countries along all criteria.[57] One research institution has found a global trend toward freedom every decade since 1975, though in the past few years there has been a slight drop in the number of democracies.[58] **Democratization** is a difficult process, and many countries fail completely or succeed only in the short run and lapse into a form of authoritarianism.

One reason that democratization can be so difficult is that ethnic and religious conflict is epidemic. Such conflict complicates efforts to democratize because antagonisms can run so deep that opposing groups do not want to grant political legitimacy to each other. As a result, ethnic and religious rivals are often more interested in achieving a form of government that oppresses their opponents (or, in their minds, maintains order) than in establishing a real democracy. These internal challenges can raise significant challenges for the global community. After toppling the Taliban government in Afghanistan and Saddam Hussein's regime in Iraq, the U.S. government faced the much more daunting task of creating enduring democratic institutions in two countries rife with ethnic, tribal, and religious conflicts.

democratization
A process of transition as a country attempts to move from an authoritarian form of government to a democratic one.

The political and economic instability that typically accompanies transitions to democracy also makes new democratic governments vulnerable to attack by their opponents. The military will often revolt and take over the government on the grounds that progress cannot occur until order is restored. The open political conflict that emerges in a new democracy may not be easily harnessed into a well-functioning government that tolerates opposition.[59] Despite such difficulties, strong forces are pushing authoritarian governments toward democratization. Nations find it difficult to succeed economically in today's world without establishing a market economy, and market economies (that is, capitalism) give people substantial freedoms. Thus, authoritarian rulers may see economic reforms as a threat to their regime.

American Democracy: More Pluralist Than Majoritarian

It is not idle speculation to ask what kind of democracy is practiced in the United States. The answer to this question can help us understand why our government can be called democratic despite a low level of citizen participation in politics and despite government actions that run contrary to public opinion.

Throughout this book, we probe to determine how well the United States fits the two alternative models of democracy: majoritarian and pluralist. If our answer is not already apparent, it soon will be. We argue that the political system in the United States rates relatively low according to the majoritarian model of democracy but fulfills the pluralist model very well. Yet the pluralist model is far from a perfect representation of democracy. Its principal drawback is that it favors the well organized, and the poor are the least likely to be members of interest groups. As one advocate of majoritarian democracy once wrote, "The flaw in the pluralist heaven is that the heavenly chorus sings with a strong upper-class accent."[60]

This evaluation of the pluralist nature of American democracy may not mean much to you now. But you will learn that the pluralist model makes the United States look far more democratic than the majoritarian model would. Eventually, you will have to decide the answers to three questions: Is the pluralist model truly an adequate expression of democracy, or is it a perversion of classical ideals designed to portray America as democratic when it is not? Does the majoritarian model result in a "better" type of democracy? If so, could new mechanisms of government be devised to produce a desirable mix of majority rule and minority rights? These questions should play in the back of your mind as you read about the workings of American government in meeting the challenge of democracy.

Tying It Together

1. How is the American government affected by increasing globalization?
   - National sovereignty: each national government has the right to govern its people as it wishes, without interference from other nations.
   - As globalization increases, human rights weigh more heavily in international politics.
     - Some believe that nations should be held accountable to international law.
     - The U.S. government worries that international law would require us to abide by laws based on other nations' values rather than our own.
   - The American government must recognize it is part of a worldwide economic, social, and political network. Foreign affairs must be evaluated by how they affect the U.S. government and, conversely, how American politics affects governments in other nations.

2. How does government serve its citizens?
   - Maintaining order: the rule of law is established to preserve life and to protect property.
     - Communism is the theory that gives ownership of all land and productive facilities to the government.
   - Providing public goods: benefits and services are available to everyone, such as education, sanitation, and parks.
   - Promoting equality: the government's role in redistributing income is a relatively new purpose of government and is highly controversial.

3. What are the critical values, conflicts, and political ideologies that affect the decisions and policies made by the American government?
   - Concepts that identify the values pursued by government:
     - Freedom: *freedom of* is the freedom to do something such as practice the religion you choose and freedom of speech.

Freedom from is the freedom from something negative and often means the fight against exploitation and oppression.
- Order: order includes preserving life, protecting property, and maintaining traditional patterns of social relationships.
- Equality: *social inequality* is the equality in wealth, education, and status and this can be promoted by *equality of opportunity* and *equality of outcome.*

- Dilemmas facing government:
  - The original dilemma: freedom versus order.
  - The modern dilemma: freedom versus equality.
- Political ideologies of the scope of government:
  - Totalitarianism: government should have unlimited power.
  - Socialism: the scope of government extends to ownership or control of basic industries that produce goods and services.
  - Capitalism: free enterprise such as private business should operate without government regulations.
  - Libertarianism: all government action is opposed except that which is necessary to protect life and property.
  - Anarchism: anarchists oppose all government, in any form.
- Liberals and conservatives:
  - Liberals are willing to use the government to promote equality but not order.
  - Conservatives value order over freedom and freedom over equality.
  - Today, the differences between liberals and conservatives are not clear cut.
  - Communitarians value both equality and order more than freedom.
  - Libertarians value individual freedom highly and frown upon government action to pursue equality and order.

4. What criteria can we use to determine if our government is democratic?
- Procedural democratic theory: includes universal participation, political equality, majority rule, and government responsiveness to public opinion.
- Substantive democratic theory: focuses on the substance but not the procedures of democracy. Government policies should guarantee civil liberties and civil rights, but there is no agreement on social and economic rights.
- Models of democracy:
  - The majoritarian model interprets government by the people as a majority of the people.
  - The pluralistic model interprets government by the people to mean people operating through competing interest groups.

- An undemocratic model:
  - Elite theory is the idea that a small group of people make the most important government decisions.

5. What are the challenges of establishing and sustaining true democratic governments around the world?
   - Ethnic and religious rivalries interfere with a government's ability to recognize all citizens' interests.
   - Governmental instability caused by the transition to democracy can lead to vulnerability for a new democracy.
   - Inevitable economic reforms often bring greater freedom, which authoritarian rulers often see as a threat to their leadership.

Test Prepper 1.1

The Globalization of American Government

True or False?
1. The principle of national sovereignty has been used to define a government's right to self-determination since the seventeenth century.
2. Government is the legitimate use of force within specified geographic boundaries to control human behavior.
3. National sovereignty is challenged by globalization.

Comprehension
4. Why does the United States oppose an international court?
5. Why do international politics and world opinion have an impact on U.S. politics?

Test Prepper 1.2

The Purposes of Government

True or False?
1. Governments generally use their coercive powers to promote the sale of public goods.
2. The view that property is owned by the people rather than by individuals was an idea set forth by Karl Marx and served as the ultimate principle of developed communism.
3. Since the Great Depression, the U.S. government's role in redistributing income to promote economic equality has been a major source of policy debate in the United States.

Comprehension

4. According to the communist ideology, who is the rightful owner of all land and productive facilities such as manufacturing plants?
5. What are some ways that government can promote social equality?

Test Prepper 1.3

A Conceptual Framework

True or False?

1. New laws passed after September 11, 2001, dramatically increased government police power.
2. Political ideologies are simplistic explanations of people's political views.
3. For liberals, the use of government power to promote equality is unnecessary and a misuse of power.

Comprehension

4. What are the two major dilemmas that have historically faced governments?
5. Why do the labels *liberal* and *conservative* not describe political ideologies as well as they did in the 1930s, 1940s, and 1950s?

Test Prepper 1.4

Majoritarian or Pluralist?

True or False?

1. Participatory democracy is necessary to have representative democracy.
2. According to procedural theory, the government should do what the public wants it to do.
3. According to elite theory, the United States is an oligarchy, and government power is in the hands of an elite.

Comprehension

4. How does the pluralistic model of democracy interpret "government by the people"?
5. When and how was democracy first defined? Was democracy originally thought of as a positive concept?

Test Prepper 1.5

Democracy and Globalization

True or False?

1. Since the nineteenth century, most countries have fully met all the criteria necessary to be judged a true democracy.
2. Authoritarian rulers see economic reforms as a threat to their regime.

3. Internal challenges, such as ethnic and religious conflict, can raise significant challenges for not only a country but also the global community.

Comprehension

4. Does the U.S. government more closely fit the pluralistic model or the majoritarian model?
5. Can all countries establish and sustain democratic governments if they wish to?

CourseMate CL Resources:

Visit www.cengagebrain.com/shop/ISBN/1111832587 for flashcards, web quizzes, videos and more!

Hisham Ibrahim/Getty Images

CourseMate

Visit www.cengagebrain.com/shop/
ISBN/1111832587 for flashcards,
web quizzes, videos
and more!

FOCUS QUESTIONS

1. How did circumstances in the American colonies in the mid-eighteenth century lead to the movement for a new government?

2. How did the revolutionaries structure the government of their new republic, and was it successful?

3. How did the confederation come to agreement on a national constitution?

4. What were the basic ideas and articles that created the final version of the Constitution?

5. How did the founders achieve ratification of the Constitution?

6. What methods are used to alter the Constitution?

7. What are the unique features of the U.S. Constitution?

"You are the 'Conventionists' of Europe. You therefore have the power vested in any political body: to succeed or to fail," claimed Chairman Valéry Giscard d'Estaing in his introductory speech on February 26, 2002, to the members of the Convention on the Future of Europe. The purpose of the convention, according to Chairman Giscard d'Estaing, was for the members to "agree to propose a concept of the European Union which matches our continental dimension and the requirements of the 21st century, a concept which can bring unity to our continent and respect for its diversity." If the members succeeded, he reassured them, no doubt they would in essence write "a new chapter in the history of Europe."[1] Integrating and governing twenty-five nation-states—many of them at one time or another bitter enemies—with a population of 500 million is, to say the least, a daunting task.

Over two centuries earlier, from his home at Mount Vernon, George Washington penned a letter to James Madison on March 31, 1787. "I am glad to find," Washington wrote, "that Congress have recommended to the States to appear in the Convention proposed to be holden in Philadelphia in May. I think the reasons in favor, have the preponderancy of those against the measure."[2] Roughly two months later, in May, Washington would be selected by a unanimous vote to preside over the Constitutional Convention, known then as the Federal Convention, which was charged with revising the Articles of Confederation. Acting beyond its mandate, the body produced instead a new document altogether, which remains the oldest operating national constitution in the world.

The heads of state or government from twenty-eight countries signed the treaty establishing a constitution for Europe on October 29, 2004, and submitted the text to their respective governments for ratification. Unlike the U.S. Constitution, which required ratification by only nine of the thirteen states, the European constitution required ratification by *all* the signatories. As Americans discovered under the Articles of Confederation, unanimity is difficult to achieve. After ratification by nine European countries, voters in France and the Netherlands rejected the constitution in May and June 2005, dooming the document.

Although the processes on both sides of the Atlantic may have differed in 1787 and today, the political passions that these efforts spawned have been equally intense and highlight the fragility inherent in designing a constitution. And no wonder. The questions that challenged America's founders and confronted the women and men charged with setting a future course for Europe do not have easy or obvious answers. A thoughtful European observer asked the same kinds of questions that confronted the delegates at Philadelphia: "How can a balance be achieved in the representation of large and small states? How much power should be conferred upon the federal level, and what should be the jurisdiction of the EU [European Union] today? What fundamental set of values underpins political unity? Is there a European equivalent to 'life, liberty and the pursuit of happiness'?"[3]

The next attempt at a solution took the form of a new treaty, called the Treaty of Lisbon or the Reform Treaty, which was signed on December 13, 2007, during a European summit. Except for Ireland, all member nations submitted the treaty to their respective legislatures. The treaty's approval required unanimity. The Reform Treaty presented a still-longer version of the previous constitutional text, but dropped nearly all the state-like symbols and terminology (the European flag and anthem, among others). It planned for a European Union president, created a diplomatic service under a single foreign-affairs head, and smoothed the ability to make decisions by reducing the number of areas that called for unanimity among member nations. Ireland rejected the treaty in a 2008 referendum, halting once more the effort toward European integration. But the sobering effects of economic toil soon gave Ireland a chance to reconsider. In October 2009, Irish voters agreed to the treaty by a substantial margin, hoping that the new EU would stave off economic catastrophe caused by the worldwide collapse in the financial sector.[4] Finally, on December 1, 2009, the treaty went into effect, bringing the European Union one step closer to unity.

The American experience is sure to shed light on the issues emerging in Europe's quest for unity. This chapter poses some questions about the U.S. Constitution. How did it evolve? What form did it take? What values does it reflect? How can it be altered? And which model of democracy, majoritarian or pluralist, does it better fit? In these answers may lie hints of the formidable tasks facing the European Union.

The Revolutionary Roots of the Constitution

The Constitution of the United States is startlingly short—just 4,300 words. But those 4,300 words define the basic structure of our national government. (In contrast, the failed European constitution was more than 60,000 words long. The Reform Treaty was over 68,500 words.) A comprehensive document, the Constitution divides the government into three branches and describes the powers of those branches, their relationship to each other, the interaction between the government and the governed, and the relationship between the national government and the states. The Constitution makes itself the supreme law of the land and binds every government official to support it.

Most Americans revere the Constitution as political scripture. To charge that a political action is unconstitutional is akin to claiming that it is unholy. So the Constitution has taken on symbolic value that has strengthened its authority as the basis of American government. Strong belief in the Constitution has led many politicians to abandon party for principle when constitutional issues are at stake.

The U.S. Constitution, written in 1787 for an agricultural society huddled along the coast of a wild new land, now guides the political life of a massive urban society in the nuclear age. To fully understand the reasons for the stability of the Constitution—and of the political system it created—we must first look at its historical roots, which lie in colonial America.

Harmony.eu?

In November 2009, leaders of the twenty-seven countries of the European Union chose Herman Von Rompuy as the EU's first president and Catherine Ashton as the High Representative for foreign policy. The choice of these respected but little-known figures may foretell a less united and forceful political union. Mr. Rompuy, an economist by training, enjoys writing haiku. One recent effort may shed light on his new role: "A fly zooms, buzzes; Spins and is lost in the room; He does no one harm."

(© European Union, 2010)

Freedom in Colonial America

Although they were British subjects, the American colonists in the eighteenth century enjoyed a degree of freedom denied most other people in the world at that time. In Europe, ancient custom and the relics of feudalism restricted private property, compelled support for established religion, and restricted access to trades and professions; Americans were relatively free of such controls. Also, in America, colonists enjoyed almost complete freedom of speech, press, and assembly.[5]

By 1763, Britain and the colonies had reached a compromise between imperial control and colonial self-government. America's foreign affairs and overseas trade were to be controlled by the king and Parliament (the British legislature); the rest was left to home rule. But the cost of administering the colonies was substantial. Because Americans benefited the most, their English countrymen contended that Americans should bear that cost.

Uniquely American Protest

Americans protested the Tea Act (1773) by holding the Boston Tea Party *(background, left)* and by using a unique form of painful punishment, tarring and feathering, on the tax collector (see "Stamp Act" upside-down on the Liberty Tree). An early treatise on the subject offered the following instructions: "First, strip a person naked, then heat the tar until it is thin, and pour upon the naked flesh, or rub it over with a tar brush. After which, sprinkle decently upon the tar, whilst it is yet warm, as many feathers as will stick to it."

(Courtesy of the John Carter Brown Library at Brown University)

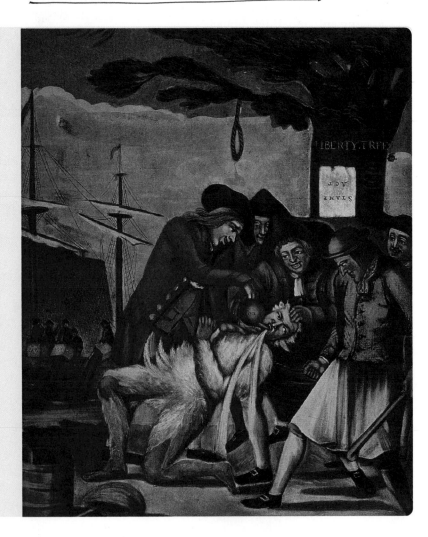

The Road to Revolution

The British believed that taxing the colonies was the obvious way to meet the costs of administering the colonies. The colonists did not agree. They especially did not want to be taxed by a distant government in which they had no representation. During the decade preceding the outbreak of hostilities in 1775, this issue was to convert increasing numbers of colonists from loyal British subjects seeking the rights of Englishmen to revolutionaries seeking the end of British rule over the American colonies.

On the night of December 16, 1773, a group of colonists reacted to a British duty on tea by organizing the Boston Tea Party. A mob boarded three ships and emptied 342 chests of that valuable substance into Boston Harbor. In an attempt to reassert British control over its recalcitrant colonists, Parliament passed the Coercive (or "Intolerable") Acts (1774). One act imposed a blockade on Boston until the tea was paid for; another gave royal governors the power to quarter British soldiers in private homes. Now the taxation issue was secondary; more important was the conflict between British demands for order and American demands for liberty. The Virginia and Massachusetts assemblies summoned a continental congress, an assembly that would speak and act for the people of all the colonies.

The First Continental Congress met in Philadelphia in September 1774. The objective of the assembly was to restore harmony between Great Britain and the American colonies. A leader of the Continental Congress, called the president, was elected. (The terms *president* and *congress* in American government trace their origins to the First Continental Congress.) In October 1774, the delegates adopted a statement of rights and principles; many of these later found their way into the Declaration of Independence and the Constitution. For example, the congress claimed a right "to life, liberty, and property" and a right "peaceably to assemble, consider of their grievances, and petition the king." Then the congress adjourned, planning to reconvene in May 1775.

Revolutionary Action

By early 1775, however, a movement that the colonists themselves were calling a revolution had already begun. Colonists in Massachusetts were fighting the British at Concord and Lexington. Delegates to the Second Continental Congress, meeting in May, faced a dilemma: Should they prepare for war, or should they try to reconcile with Britain? As conditions deteriorated, the Second Continental Congress remained in session to serve as the government of the colony-states.

On June 7, 1776, the Virginia delegation called on the Continental Congress to resolve "that these United Colonies are, and of right ought to be, free and Independent States, that they are absolved from all allegiance to the British Crown, and that all political connection between them and the State of Great Britain is, and ought to be, totally dissolved." A committee of five men was appointed to prepare a proclamation expressing the colonies' reasons for declaring independence.

The Declaration of Independence

Thomas Jefferson, a young farmer and lawyer from Virginia, drafted the proclamation. Jefferson's document, the **Declaration of Independence**, expressed simply, clearly, and rationally the arguments in support of separation from Great Britain.

The principles underlying the declaration were rooted in the writings of the English philosopher John Locke and had been expressed many times before by speakers in congress and in the colonial assemblies. Locke argued that people have God-given, or natural, rights that are inalienable—that is, they cannot be taken away by any government. According to Locke, all legitimate political authority exists to preserve these natural rights and is based on the consent of those who are governed. The idea of consent is derived from social contract theory, which states that the people agree to establish rulers for certain purposes and have the right to resist or remove rulers who violate those purposes.[6]

Jefferson used similar arguments in the Declaration of Independence:

> We hold these truths to be self-evident, that all men are created equal, that they are endowed by their Creator with certain unalienable rights, that among these are life, liberty, and the pursuit of happiness. That to secure these rights, governments are instituted among men, deriving their just powers from the consent of the governed. That whenever any form of government becomes destructive of these ends, it is the right of the people to alter or to abolish it, and to institute new government, laying its foundation on such principles, and organizing its power in such form, as to them shall seem most likely to effect their safety and happiness.

Declaration of Independence
Drafted by Thomas Jefferson, the document that proclaimed the right of the colonies to separate from Great Britain.

social contract theory
The belief that the people agree to set up rulers for certain purposes and thus have the right to resist or remove rulers who act against those purposes.

Historian Jack Rakove maintains that Jefferson was not proposing equality for individuals. Rather, he was asserting the equality of peoples to enjoy the same rights of self-government that other peoples enjoyed: "It was the collective right of revolution and self-government that the Declaration was written to justify—not a visionary or even utopian notion of equality within American society itself."[7]

Jefferson's simple yet impassioned statement of faith in democracy reverberates to this day. He went on to list the many deliberate acts of the king that had exceeded the legitimate role of government. Finally, Jefferson declared that the colonies were "Free and Independent States," with no political connection to Great Britain.

The major premise of the Declaration of Independence is that the people have a right to revolt if they determine that their government is denying them their legitimate rights. The long list of the king's actions was evidence of such denial, so the people had the right to rebel and form a new government. On July 2, 1776, the Second Continental Congress finally voted for independence. The vote was by state, and the motion carried 11 to 0. (Rhode Island was not present, and the New York delegation, lacking instructions, did not cast its yea vote until July 15.) Two days later, on July 4, the Declaration of Independence was approved with few changes.

The War of Independence lasted far longer than anyone had expected. It began in a moment of confusion, when a shot rang out as British soldiers approached the town of Lexington on the way to Concord, Massachusetts, on April 19, 1775. The end came six and a half years later, on October 19, 1781, with Lord Cornwallis's surrender of his six-thousand-man army at Yorktown, Virginia. It was a costly war: more died and were wounded in relation to the population than in any other conflict except the Civil War.[8]

From Revolution to Confederation

By declaring their independence from England, the colonies left themselves without any real central government, so the revolutionaries proclaimed the creation of a republic. Strictly speaking, a **republic** is government without a monarch, but the term had come to mean a government based on the consent of the governed, whose power is exercised by representatives who are responsible to them. A republic need not be a democracy, and this was fine with the founders; at that time, democracy was associated with mob rule and instability (see Chapter 1). The revolutionaries were

republic
A government without a monarch; a government rooted in the consent of the governed, whose power is exercised by elected representatives responsible to the governed.

less concerned with determining who would control their new government than with limiting the powers of that government. They had revolted in the name of liberty, and now they wanted a government with sharply defined powers. To make sure they got one, they meant to define its structure and powers in writing.

The Articles of Confederation

Barely a week after the Declaration of Independence was signed, the Second Continental Congress received a committee report entitled "Articles of Confederation and Perpetual Union." A **confederation** is a loose association of independent states that agree to cooperate on specified matters. In a confederation, the states retain their sovereignty, which means that each has supreme power within its borders. The central government is weak; it can only coordinate, not control, the actions of its sovereign states.

The **Articles of Confederation**, the compact among the thirteen original colonies that established the United States, was finally adopted on November 15, 1777. The Articles jealously guarded state sovereignty; their provisions clearly reflected the delegates' fears of a strong central government. Under the Articles, each state, regardless of its size, had one vote in the congress. Votes on financing the war and other important issues required the consent of at least nine of the thirteen states.

The common danger—Britain—forced the young republic to function under the Articles, but this first try at a government was inadequate to the task. The delegates had succeeded in crafting a national government that was largely powerless. The Articles failed for at least four reasons. First, they did not give the national government the power to tax. As a result, the congress had to plead for money from the states to pay for the war and carry on the affairs of the new nation. Second, the Articles made no provision for an independent leadership position to direct the government (the president was merely the presiding officer of the congress). The omission was deliberate—the colonists feared the reestablishment of a monarchy—but it left the nation without a leader. Third, the Articles did not allow the national government to regulate interstate and foreign commerce. (When John Adams proposed that the confederation enter into a commercial treaty with Britain after the war, he was asked, "Would you like one treaty or thirteen, Mr. Adams?").[9] Finally, the Articles could not be amended without the unanimous agreement of the congress and

confederation
A loose association of independent states that agree to cooperate on specified matters.

Articles of Confederation
The compact among the thirteen original states that established the first government of the United States.

the assent of all the state legislatures; thus, each state had the power to veto any changes to the confederation.

The goal of the delegates who drew up the Articles of Confederation was to retain power in the states. This was consistent with republicanism, which viewed the remote power of a national government as a danger to liberty. In this sense alone, the Articles were a grand success: they completely hobbled the infant government.

Disorder Under the Confederation

Once the Revolution ended and independence was a reality, it became clear that the national government had neither the economic nor the military power to function. Freed from wartime austerity, Americans rushed to purchase goods from abroad. Debt mounted, and bankruptcy followed for many.

The problem was particularly severe in Massachusetts, where high interest rates and high state taxes were forcing farmers into bankruptcy. In 1786 and 1787, farmers under the leadership of Daniel Shays, a Revolutionary War veteran, carried out a series of insurrections to protest against high taxes levied by the state to retire its wartime debt.[10] With the congress unable to secure funds from the states to help out, the governor of Massachusetts eventually called out the militia and restored order.[11] Shays's Rebellion demonstrated the impotence of the confederation and the urgent need to suppress insurrection and maintain domestic order.

From Confederation to Constitution

Order, the original purpose of government, was breaking down under the Articles of Confederation. The "league of friendship" envisioned in the Articles was not enough to hold the nation together in peacetime. So in 1786, Virginia invited the states to attend a convention at Annapolis to explore revisions to the Articles of Confederation. Although only five states sent delegates, they seized the opportunity to call for another meeting in Philadelphia the next year. The congress agreed to the convention but limited its mission to "the sole and express purpose of revising the Articles of Confederation."

Shays's Rebellion lent a sense of urgency to the task before the Philadelphia convention. The congress's inability to confront the rebellion was evidence that a stronger national government was necessary to preserve order and property—to protect the states from internal as well as external dangers. "While the Declaration was directed against an excess of authority," remarked Supreme Court Justice Robert H. Jackson some 150 years later, "the Constitution [that followed the Articles of Confederation] was directed against anarchy."[12]

The Constitutional Convention officially opened on May 25, 1787. Although its delegates were authorized only to revise the Articles of Confederation, within the first week of debate, Edmund Randolph of Virginia presented a long list of changes, suggested by fellow Virginian James Madison, that would replace the weak confederation of states with a powerful national government. The delegates unanimously agreed to debate Randolph's proposal, which was called the **Virginia Plan**. Almost immediately, then, they rejected the idea of amending the Articles of Confederation, working instead to create an entirely new constitution.

The Virginia Plan

The Virginia Plan dominated the convention's deliberations for the rest of the summer, making several important proposals for a strong central government:

- That the powers of the government be divided among three separate branches: a **legislative branch** for making laws, an **executive branch** for enforcing laws, and a **judicial branch** for interpreting laws.
- That the legislature consist of two houses. The first would be chosen by the people and the second by the members of the first house from among persons nominated by the state legislatures.
- That each state's representation in the legislature be in proportion to taxes paid to the national government or in proportion to its free population.
- That an executive of unspecified size be selected by the legislature and serve for a single term.
- That the national judiciary include one or more supreme courts and other lower courts, with judges appointed for life by the legislature.
- That the executive and a number of national judges serve as a council of revision, to approve or veto (disapprove) legislative acts. Their veto could be overridden, however, by a vote of both houses of the legislature.

Virginia Plan
A set of proposals for a new government, submitted to the Constitutional Convention of 1787; included separation of the government into three branches, division of the legislature into two houses, and proportional representation in the legislature.

legislative branch
The lawmaking branch of government.

executive branch
The law-enforcing branch of government.

judicial branch
The law-interpreting branch of government.

- That the scope of powers of all three branches be far greater than that assigned the national government by the Articles of Confederation and include the power of the legislature to override state laws.

By proposing a powerful national legislature that could override state laws, the Virginia Plan clearly advocated a new form of government. It was a mixed structure, with more authority over the states and new authority over the people.

Madison was a monumental force in the ensuing debate on the proposals. However, the constitution that emerged from the convention bore only partial resemblance to the document Madison wanted to create. He endorsed seventy-one specific proposals, but he ended up on the losing side on forty of them.[13] And the parts of the Virginia Plan that were ultimately adopted in the U.S. Constitution were not adopted without challenge. Conflict revolved primarily around the basis of representation in the legislature, the method of choosing legislators, and the structure of the executive branch.

The New Jersey Plan

When in 1787 it appeared that much of the Virginia Plan would be approved by the big states, the small states united in opposition. William Paterson of New Jersey introduced an alternative set of resolutions, written to preserve the spirit of the Articles of Confederation by amending rather than replacing them. The **New Jersey Plan** included the following proposals:

- That a single-chamber legislature have the power to raise revenue and regulate commerce.
- That the states have equal representation in the legislature and choose the members of that body.
- That a multiperson executive be elected by the legislature, with powers similar to those listed in the Virginia Plan but without the right to veto legislation.
- That a supreme judiciary tribunal be created with a very limited jurisdiction. (There was no provision for a system of national courts.)
- That the acts of the legislature be binding on the states—that is, be regarded as the "supreme law of the respective states," with force used to compel obedience.

The New Jersey Plan was defeated in the first major convention vote, 7 to 3. However, the small states had enough support to force a compromise on the issue of representation in the legislature.

New Jersey Plan Submitted by the head of the New Jersey delegation to the Constitutional Convention of 1787, a set of nine resolutions that would have, in effect, preserved the Articles of Confederation by amending rather than replacing them.

The Great Compromise

The Virginia Plan's provision for a two-chamber legislature was never seriously challenged, but the idea of representation according to population generated heated debate. The small states demanded equal representation for all states. A committee was created to resolve the deadlock. It consisted of one delegate from each state, chosen by secret ballot. After working through the Independence Day recess, the committee reported reaching the **Great Compromise** (sometimes called the *Connecticut Compromise* because it was proposed by Roger Sherman of the Connecticut delegation). Representation in the House of Representatives would be apportioned according to the population of each state. Initially, there would be fifty-six members. Revenue-raising acts would originate in the House. Most important, the states would be represented equally in the Senate, by two senators each. Senators would be selected by their state legislatures, not directly by the people.

The delegates accepted the Great Compromise. The smaller states got their equal representation and the larger states their proportional representation. The small states might dominate the Senate and the big states might control the House, but because all legislation had to be approved by both chambers, neither group would be able to dominate the other. To assure perpetual state equality, no amendment to the Constitution could violate the equal state representation principle.[14]

Compromise on the Presidency

Conflict replaced compromise when the delegates turned to the executive branch. They agreed on a one-person executive—a president—but they disagreed on how the executive would be selected and the term of office. The delegates distrusted the people's judgment; some feared that popular election would arouse public passions. Consequently, the delegates rejected the idea. At the same time, representatives of the small states feared that election by the legislature would allow the larger states to control the executive.

Once again they compromised, creating the *electoral college,* a cumbersome system consisting of a group of electors chosen for the sole purpose of selecting the president and vice president. Each state legislature would choose a number of electors equal to the number of its representatives in Congress. Each elector would then vote for two people. The candidate with the most votes would become president, provided that the number of votes constituted a

Great Compromise
Submitted by the Connecticut delegation to the Constitutional Convention of 1787, and thus also known as the *Connecticut Compromise,* a plan calling for a bicameral legislature in which the House of Representatives would be apportioned according to population and the states would be represented equally in the Senate.

majority; the person with the next greatest number of votes would become vice president. (This procedure was changed in 1804 by the Twelfth Amendment, which mandates separate votes for each office.) If no candidate won a majority, the House of Representatives would choose a president, with each state casting one vote.

The electoral college compromise eliminated the fear of a popular vote for president. At the same time, it satisfied the small states. If the electoral college failed to produce a president—which the delegates expected would happen—an election by the House would give every state the same voice in the selection process.

The delegates agreed that the president's term of office should be four years and that the president should be eligible for reelection with no limit on the number of terms.

The delegates realized that removing a president from office would be a very serious political matter. For that reason, they involved the other two branches of government in the process. The House alone was empowered to charge a president with "Treason, Bribery, or other high Crimes and Misdemeanors" by a majority vote. The Senate was given sole power to try such impeachments. It could convict and thus remove a president only by a two-thirds vote. The chief justice of the United States was required to preside over the Senate trial.

The Final Product

Once the delegates resolved their major disagreements, they dispatched the remaining issues relatively quickly. A committee was appointed to draft a constitution. The Preamble, which was the last section to be drafted, begins with a phrase that would have been impossible to write when the convention opened. This single sentence sets forth the four elements that form the foundation of the American political tradition:[15]

- *It creates a people:* "We the People of the United States" was a dramatic departure from a loose confederation of states.
- *It explains the reason for the Constitution:* "in Order to form a more perfect Union" was an indirect way of saying that the first effort, under the Articles of Confederation, had been inadequate.
- *It articulates goals:* "[to] establish Justice, insure domestic Tranquility, provide for the common defense, promote the general Welfare, and secure the Blessings of Liberty to ourselves and our posterity"—in other words, the government exists to promote order and freedom.

- *It fashions a government:* "do ordain and establish this Constitution for the United States of America."

The Basic Principles

In creating the Constitution, the founders relied on four political principles that together established a revolutionary new political order: republicanism, federalism, separation of powers, and checks and balances.

Republicanism is a form of government in which power resides in the people and is exercised by their elected representatives. The framers were determined to avoid aristocracy (rule by a hereditary class), monarchy (rule by one), and direct democracy (rule by the people). A republic was both new and daring; no people had ever been governed by a republic on so vast a scale. Indeed, the framers themselves were far from sure that their government could be sustained. After the convention ended, Benjamin Franklin was asked what sort of government the new nation would have. "A republic," he replied, "if you can keep it."

Federalism is the division of power between a central government and regional units. It makes citizens subject to two different bodies of law. A federal system stands between two competing government structures. On one side is unitary government, in which all power is vested in a central government. On the other side stands confederation, a loose union with powerful states. The Constitution embodied a division of power, but it conferred substantial powers on the national government at the expense of the states.

According to the Constitution, the powers vested in the national and state governments are derived from the people, who remain the ultimate sovereign. National and state governments can exercise their powers over persons and property within their own spheres of authority. But by participating in the electoral process or amending their governing charters, the people can restrain both the national and the state governments if necessary to preserve liberty.

The Constitution lists the powers of the national government and the powers denied to the states. All other powers remain with the states. However, the Constitution does not clearly describe the spheres of authority within which these powers can be exercised. As we will discuss in Chapter 3, limits on the exercise of power by the national government and the states have evolved as a result of political and military conflict; moreover, the limits have proved changeable.

republicanism
A form of government in which power resides in the people and is exercised by their elected representatives.

federalism
The division of power between a central government and regional governments.

FIGURE 2.1   The Constitution and the Electoral Process

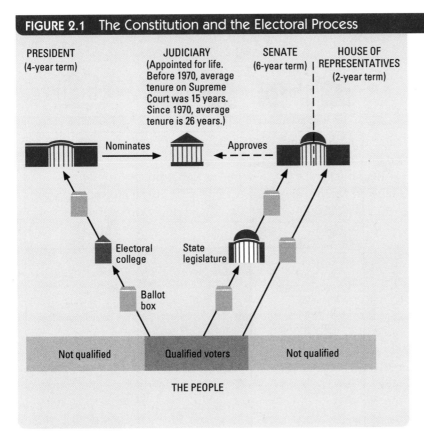

PRESIDENT
(4-year term)

JUDICIARY
(Appointed for life.
Before 1970, average
tenure on Supreme
Court was 15 years.
Since 1970, average
tenure is 26 years.)

SENATE
(6-year term)

HOUSE OF
REPRESENTATIVES
(2-year term)

Nominates → ← Approves

Electoral
college

State
legislature

Ballot
box

Not qualified   Qualified voters   Not qualified

THE PEOPLE

The framers were afraid of majority rule, and that fear is reflected in the electoral process for national office described in the Constitution. The people, speaking through the voters, participated directly only in the choice of their representatives in the House. The president and senators were elected indirectly, through the electoral college and state legislatures. (Direct election of senators did not become law until 1913, when the Seventeenth Amendment was ratified.) Judicial appointments are, and always have been, far removed from representative links to the people. Judges are nominated by the president and approved by the Senate.

(© Cengage Learning 2013)

Separation of powers and checks and balances are two distinct principles, but both are necessary to ensure that one branch does not dominate the government. **Separation of powers** is the assignment of the lawmaking, law-enforcing, and law-interpreting functions of government to independent legislative, executive, and judicial branches, respectively. Separation of powers safeguards liberty by ensuring that all government power does not fall into the hands of a single person or group of people. However, the Constitution constrained majority rule by limiting the people's direct influence on the electoral process (see Figure 2.1). In theory, separation of powers means that one branch cannot exercise the powers of the other branches. In practice, however, the separation is far from complete. One scholar has suggested that what we have instead is "separate institutions sharing powers."[16]

Checks and balances is a means of giving each branch of government some scrutiny of and control over the other branches. The aim is to prevent the exclusive exercise of certain powers by any

separation of powers
The assignment of lawmaking, law-enforcing, and law-interpreting functions to separate branches of government.

checks and balances
A government structure that gives each branch some scrutiny of and control over the other branches.

FIGURE 2.2 — Separation of Powers and Checks and Balances

Separation of powers is the assignment of lawmaking, law-enforcing, and law-interpreting functions to the legislative, executive, and judicial branches, respectively. The phenomenon is illustrated by the diagonal from upper left to lower right in the figure.

Checks and balances give each branch some power over the other branches. For example, the executive branch possesses some legislative power, and the legislative branch possesses some executive power. These checks and balances are listed outside the diagonal.

(© Cengage Learning 2013)

BRANCHES OF GOVERNMENT

POWERS OF GOVERNMENT

	The legislature can:	The executive can:	The judiciary can:
Legislative	• Make laws	• Veto legislation • Recommend legislation	• Review legislative acts
Executive	• Confirm executive appointments (Senate) • Override executive veto • Reject foreign treaties	• Enforce laws	• Review executive acts • Issue injunctions
Judicial	• Impeach • Create or eliminate courts	• Grant pardons • Nominate judges	• Interpret laws

one of the three branches. For example, only Congress can enact laws. But the president (through the veto power) can cancel them, and the courts (by finding that a law violates the Constitution) can strike them down. The process goes on as Congress and the president sometimes begin the legislative process anew, attempting to reformulate laws to address the flaws identified by the Supreme Court in its decisions. In a "check on a check," Congress can override a president's veto by an **extraordinary majority,** two-thirds of each chamber. Congress is also empowered to propose amendments to the Constitution, counteracting the courts' power to invalidate. Figure 2.2 depicts the relationship between separation of powers and checks and balances.

extraordinary majority
Majority greater than that required by majority rule, that is, greater than 50 percent plus one.

The Articles of the Constitution

In addition to the Preamble, the Constitution contains seven articles. The first three establish the separate branches of government and specify their internal operations and powers. The remaining four define the relationships among the states, explain the process of amendment, declare the supremacy of national law, and explain the procedure for ratifying the Constitution.

Article I: The Legislative Article. In structuring their new government, the framers began with the legislative branch because they thought lawmaking was the most important function of a republican government. Article I is the most detailed and therefore the longest of all the articles. It defines the bicameral (two-chamber) character of the Congress and describes the internal operating procedures of the House of Representatives and the Senate. Section 8 of Article I expresses the principle of **enumerated powers,** which means that Congress can exercise only the powers that the Constitution assigns to it. Eighteen powers are enumerated; the first seventeen are specific powers (for example, the power to regulate interstate commerce).

The last clause in Section 8, known as the **necessary and proper clause** (or the *elastic clause*), gives Congress the means to execute the enumerated powers (see the Appendix). This clause is the basis of Congress's **implied powers**—those powers that Congress must have in order to execute its enumerated powers. For example, the power to levy and collect taxes (clause 1) and the power to coin money and regulate its value (clause 5), when joined with the necessary and proper clause (clause 18), imply that Congress has the power to charter a bank. Otherwise, the national government would have no means of managing the money it collects through its power to tax. Implied powers clearly expand the enumerated powers conferred on Congress by the Constitution.

Article II: The Executive Article. Article II sets the president's term of office, the procedure for electing a president through the electoral college, the qualifications for becoming president, and the president's duties and powers. The last include acting as commander in chief of the military; making treaties (which must be ratified by a two-thirds vote in the Senate); and appointing government officers, diplomats, and judges (again, with the advice and consent of the Senate).

The president also has legislative powers—part of the constitutional system of checks and balances. For example, the Constitution requires that the president periodically inform the Congress of the

enumerated powers
The powers explicitly granted to Congress by the Constitution.

necessary and proper clause
The last clause in Section 8 of Article I of the Constitution, which gives Congress the means to execute its enumerated powers. This clause is the basis for Congress's implied powers. Also called the *elastic clause*.

implied powers
Those powers that Congress requires in order to execute its enumerated powers.

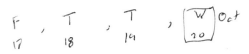

"State of the Union" and of the policies and programs that the executive branch intends to advocate in the coming year. Today this is done annually, in the president's State of the Union address. Under special circumstances, the president can also convene or adjourn Congress. Additionally, the duty to "take Care that the Laws be faithfully executed" in Section 3 has provided presidents with a reservoir of power.

Article III: The Judicial Article. The third article was left purposely vague. The Constitution established the Supreme Court as the highest court in the land. But beyond that, the framers were unable to agree on the need for a national judiciary, or its size, its composition, or the procedures it should follow. They left these issues to the Congress, which resolved them by creating a system of federal—that is, national—courts separate from the state courts.

Unless they are impeached, federal judges serve for life. They are appointed to indefinite terms "during good Behavior," and their salaries cannot be lowered while they hold office. These stipulations reinforce the separation of powers; they see to it that judges are independent of the other branches and that they do not have to fear retribution for their exercise of judicial power.

Congress exercises a potential check on the judicial branch through its power to create (and eliminate) lower federal courts. Congress can also restrict the power of the federal courts to decide cases. And, as we have noted, the president appoints—with the advice and consent of the Senate—the justices of the Supreme Court and the judges of the lower federal courts. In recent decades this has become highly politicized.

Article III does not explicitly give the courts the power of **judicial review**, the authority to invalidate congressional or presidential actions. That power has been inferred from the logic, structure, and theory of the Constitution and from important decisions by the Supreme Court itself.

The Remaining Articles. The remaining four articles of the Constitution cover a lot of ground. Article IV requires that the judicial acts and criminal warrants of each state be honored in all other states, and it forbids discrimination against citizens of one state by another state. This provision promotes equality; it keeps the states from treating outsiders differently from their own citizens. The origin of this clause can be traced to the Articles of Confederation. Article IV also allows the addition of new states and stipulates that

judicial review
The power to declare government acts invalid because they violate the Constitution.

the national government will protect the states against foreign invasion and domestic violence.

Article V specifies the methods for amending (changing) the Constitution and guarantees equal state representation in the Senate. We will have more to say about this shortly.

An important component of Article VI is the **supremacy clause**, which asserts that when they conflict with state or local laws, the Constitution, national laws, and treaties take precedence. The stipulation is vital to the operation of federalism. In keeping with the supremacy clause, Article VI requires that all national and state officials, elected or appointed, take an oath to support the Constitution. The article also mandates that religion cannot be a prerequisite for holding government office.

Article VII describes the ratification process, stipulating that approval by conventions in nine states would be necessary for the Constitution to take effect.

The Framers' Motives

What forces motivated the framers? Surely economic issues were important, but they were not the major issues. The single most important factor leading to the Constitutional Convention was the inability of the national or state governments to maintain order under the loose structure of the Articles of Confederation. Certainly, order required the protection of property, but the framers had a view of property that extended beyond their portfolios of government securities. They wanted to protect their homes, their families, and their means of livelihood from impending anarchy.

Although they disagreed bitterly on the structure and mechanics of the national government, the framers agreed on the most vital issues. For example, three crucial features of the Constitution—the power to tax, the necessary and proper clause, and the supremacy clause—were approved unanimously and without debate. Indeed, the motivation to create order was so strong that the framers were willing to draft clauses that protected the most undemocratic of all institutions: slavery.

The Slavery Issue

The institution of slavery was well ingrained in American life at the time of the Constitutional Convention, and slavery helped shape the Constitution, although it is mentioned nowhere by name. It is

supremacy clause
The clause of Article VI of the Constitution that asserts that national laws take precedence over state and local laws when they conflict.

doubtful, in fact, that there would have been a Constitution if the delegates had had to resolve the slavery issue.

The question of representation in the House of Representatives brought the issue close to the surface of the debate at the Constitutional Convention and led to the Great Compromise. Representation in the House was to be based on population. But who would be counted in the "population"? Eventually the delegates agreed unanimously that in apportioning representation in the House and in assessing direct taxes, the population of each state was to be determined by adding "the whole Number of free Persons" and "three fifths of all other Persons" (Article I, Section 2). The phrase "all other Persons" is, of course, a substitute for "slaves."

The three-fifths clause gave states with large slave populations (in the South) greater representation in Congress than states with small slave populations (in the North). The compromise left the South with 47 percent of the House seats, a sizable minority, but in all likelihood a losing one on slavery issues.[17] The overrepresentation resulting from the South's large slave populations translated into greater southern influence in selecting the president as well, because the electoral college was based on the size of the states' congressional delegations. The three-fifths clause also undertaxed states with large slave populations.

Another issue centered on the slave trade. Several southern delegates were uncompromising in their defense of it, while other delegates favored prohibition. The delegates compromised, agreeing that the slave trade could not be ended until twenty years had elapsed (Article I, Section 9). Also, the delegates agreed, without serious challenge, that fugitive slaves be returned to their masters (Article IV, Section 2).

In addressing these points, the framers in essence condoned slavery. Clearly, slavery existed in stark opposition to the idea that "all men are created equal," and though many slaveholders, including Jefferson and Madison, agonized over it, few made serious efforts to free their own slaves. Most Americans seemed indifferent to slavery. Nonetheless, the eradication of slavery proceeded gradually in certain states. By 1787, Connecticut, Massachusetts, New Jersey, New York, Pennsylvania, Rhode Island, and Vermont had abolished slavery or provided for gradual emancipation. This slow but perceptible shift on the slavery issue in many states masked a volcanic force capable of destroying the Constitutional Convention and the Union.

Selling the Constitution

On September 17, 1787, nearly four months after the Constitutional Convention opened, the delegates convened for the last time to sign the final version of their handiwork. Because several delegates were unwilling to sign the document, the last paragraph was craftily worded to give the impression of unanimity: "Done in Convention by the Unanimous Consent of the States present." However, before it could take effect, the Constitution had to be ratified by a minimum of nine state conventions. In each, support was far from unanimous.

The proponents of the new charter, who wanted a strong national government, called themselves *Federalists*. The opponents of the Constitution were quickly dubbed *Antifederalists*. They claimed, however, that they were true Federalists because they wanted to protect the states from the tyranny of a strong national government. The viewpoints of the two groups formed the bases of the first American political parties.

The *Federalist* Papers

Beginning in October 1787, an exceptional series of eighty-five newspaper articles defending the Constitution appeared under the title *The Federalist: A Commentary on the Constitution of the United States*. The essays bore the pen name "Publius" and were written primarily by James Madison and Alexander Hamilton, with some assistance from John Jay. Logically and calmly, Publius argued in favor of ratification. Reprinted extensively during the ratification battle, the *Federalist* papers remain the best single commentary we have on the meaning of the Constitution and the political theory it embodies.

Not to be outdone, the Antifederalists offered their own intellectual basis for rejecting the Constitution. In several essays, the most influential authored under the pseudonyms "Brutus" and "Federal Farmer," they attacked the centralization of power in a strong national government, claiming it would obliterate the states, violate the social contract of the Declaration of Independence, and destroy liberty in the process. They defended the status quo, maintaining that the Articles of Confederation established true federal principles.[18]

Of all the *Federalist* papers, the most magnificent and most frequently cited is *Federalist* No. 10, written by James Madison. He argued that the proposed constitution was designed "to break and control the violence of faction." "By a faction," Madison wrote, "I understand a number of citizens, whether amounting to a majority or minority of the whole, who are united and actuated by some common impulse of passion, or of interest, adverse to the rights of other citizens, or to the permanent and aggregate interests of the community."

Madison was discussing what we described in Chapter 1 as *pluralism*. What Madison called factions are today called interest groups or even political parties. According to Madison, "The most common and durable source of factions has been the various and unequal distribution of property." Madison was concerned not with reducing inequalities of wealth (which he took for granted) but with controlling the seemingly inevitable conflict that stems from them. The Constitution, he argued, was well constructed for this purpose.

Through the mechanism of representation, wrote Madison, the Constitution would prevent a "tyranny of the majority" (mob rule). The government would not be controlled directly by the people; rather, it would be controlled indirectly by their elected representatives. And those representatives would have the intelligence and understanding to serve the larger interests of the nation. Moreover, the federal system would require that majorities form first within each state, then organize for effective action at the national level. This and the vastness of the country would make it unlikely that a majority would form that would "invade the rights of other citizens."

The purpose of *Federalist* No. 10 was to demonstrate that the proposed government was not likely to be ruled by any faction. Contrary to conventional wisdom, Madison argued, the key to controlling the evils of faction is to have a large republic—the larger, the better. The more diverse the society is, the less likely it is that an unjust majority can form. Madison certainly had no intention of creating a majoritarian democracy; his view of popular government was much more consistent with the model of pluralist democracy discussed in Chapter 1.

Madison pressed his argument from a different angle in *Federalist* No. 51. Asserting that "ambition must be made to counteract ambition," he argued that the separation of powers and checks and balances would control tyranny from any source. If power is distributed equally across the three branches, then each branch has the capacity to counteract the other. In Madison's words, "usurpations are guarded against by a division of the government into distinct and separate departments." Because legislative power tends to predominate in republican governments, legislative authority is divided between the Senate and the House of Representatives, which have different methods of selection and terms of office. Additional protection comes through federalism, which divides power "between two distinct governments"—national and state—and subdivides "the portion allotted to each . . . among distinct and separate departments."

The Antifederalists wanted additional separation of powers and additional checks and balances, which, they maintained, would eliminate the threat of tyranny entirely. The Federalists believed that this would make decisive national action virtually impossible. But to ensure ratification, they agreed to a compromise.

A Concession: The Bill of Rights

Despite the eloquence of the *Federalist* papers, many prominent citizens, including Thomas Jefferson, were unhappy that the Constitution did not list basic civil liberties—the individual freedoms guaranteed to citizens. The omission of a bill of rights was the chief obstacle to the adoption of the Constitution by the states. The colonists had just rebelled against the British government to preserve their basic freedoms. Why didn't the proposed Constitution spell out those freedoms?

The answer was rooted in logic, not politics. Because the national government was limited to those powers that were granted to it and because no power was granted to abridge the people's liberties, a list of guaranteed freedoms was not necessary. In *Federalist* No. 84, Hamilton went even further, arguing that the addition of a bill of rights would be dangerous. Because it is not possible to list all prohibited powers, wrote Hamilton, any attempt to provide a partial list would make the remaining areas vulnerable to government abuse.

But logic was no match for fear. Many states agreed to ratify the Constitution only after George Washington suggested that a list of guarantees be added through the amendment process. More than one hundred amendments were proposed by the states. These were eventually narrowed down to twelve, which Congress approved and sent to the states. Ten of them became part of the Constitution in 1791, after securing the approval of the required three-fourths of the states. Collectively, these ten amendments are known as the **Bill of Rights**. They restrain the national government from tampering with fundamental rights and civil liberties and emphasize the limited character of the national government's power (see Table 2.1).

IDEALOG.ORG

Do you think the government should or should not restrict violence and sex on cable television? Take IDEAlog's self-test.

Bill of Rights
The first ten amendments to the Constitution. They prevent the national government from tampering with fundamental rights and civil liberties and emphasize the limited character of national power.

TABLE 2.1   The Bill of Rights

The first ten amendments to the Constitution are known as the Bill of Rights. The following is a list of those amendments, grouped conceptually. For the actual order and wording of the Bill of Rights, see the Appendix.

Guarantees	Amendment
Guarantees for Participation in the Political Process	
No government abridgment of speech or press; no government abridgment of peaceable assembly; no government abridgment of petitioning government for redress.	1
Guarantees Respecting Personal Beliefs	
No government establishment of religion; no government prohibition of free religious exercise.	1
Guarantees of Personal Privacy	
Owners' consent necessary to quarter troops in private homes in peacetime; quartering during war must be lawful.	3
Government cannot engage in unreasonable searches and seizures; warrants to search and seize require probable cause.	4
No compulsion to testify against oneself in criminal cases.	5
Guarantees Against Government's Overreaching	
Serious crimes require a grand jury indictment; no repeated prosecution for the same offense; no loss of life, liberty, or property without due process; no taking of property for public use without just compensation.	5
Criminal defendants will have a speedy public trial by impartial local jury; defendants are informed of accusation; defendants may confront witnesses against them; defendants may use judicial process to obtain favorable witnesses; defendants may have legal assistance for their defense.	6
Civil lawsuits can be tried by juries if controversy exceeds $20; in jury trials, fact-finding is a jury function.	7
No excessive bail; no excessive fines; no cruel and unusual punishment.	8
Other Guarantees	
The people have the right to bear arms.	2
No government trespass on unspecified fundamental rights.	9
The states or the people retain all powers not delegated to the national government or denied to the states.	10

Ratification

The Constitution officially took effect on its ratification by the ninth state, New Hampshire, on June 21, 1788. However, the success of the new government was not ensured until July 1788, by which time the Constitution was ratified by the key states of Virginia and New York after lengthy debate.

The reflection and deliberation that attended the creation and ratification of the Constitution signaled to the world that a new government could be launched peacefully. The French observer Alexis de Tocqueville (1805–1859) later wrote:

> That which is new in the history of societies is to see a great people, warned by its lawgivers that the wheels of government are stopping, turn its attention on itself without haste or fear, sound the depth of the ill, and then wait for two years to find the remedy at leisure, and then finally, when the remedy has been indicated, submit to it voluntarily without its costing humanity a single tear or drop of blood.[19]

Constitutional Change

The founders realized that the Constitution would have to be changed from time to time. To this end, they specified a formal amendment process—a process that was used almost immediately to add the Bill of Rights. With the passage of time, the Constitution also has been altered through judicial interpretation and changes in political practice.

The Formal Amendment Process

The amendment process has two stages: proposal and ratification. Both are necessary for an amendment to become part of the Constitution. The Constitution provides two alternative methods for completing each stage (see Figure 2.3). Amendments can be proposed by a two-thirds vote in both the House of Representatives and the Senate or by a national convention, summoned by Congress at the request of two-thirds of the state legislatures. All constitutional amendments to date have been proposed by the first method.

A proposed amendment can be ratified by a vote of the legislatures of three-fourths of the states or by a vote of constitutional conventions held in three-fourths of the states. Congress chooses the method of ratification. It has used the state convention method only once, for the Twenty-first Amendment, which repealed the

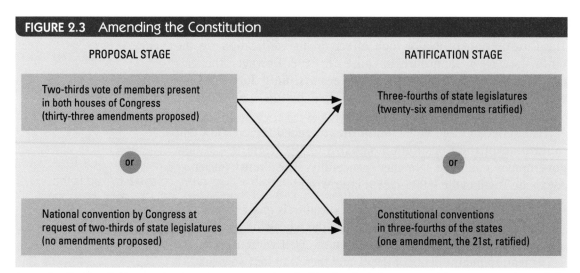

FIGURE 2.3 Amending the Constitution

Amending the Constitution requires two stages: proposal and ratification. Both Congress and the states can play a role in the proposal stage, but ratification is a process that must be fought in the states themselves. Once a state has ratified an amendment, it cannot retract its action. However, a state may reject an amendment and then reconsider its decision.

(© Cengage Learning 2013)

Eighteenth Amendment (on Prohibition). Note that the amendment process requires the exercise of extraordinary majorities (two-thirds and three-fourths). The framers purposely made it difficult to propose and ratify amendments. They wanted only the most significant issues to lead to constitutional change. Calling a national convention to propose an amendment has never been tried. Certainly the method raises several thorny questions, the most significant of which concerns what limits, if any, there are on the business of the convention. Would a national convention called to consider a particular amendment be within its bounds to rewrite the Constitution? No one really knows.

Most of the Constitution's twenty-seven amendments were adopted to help keep it abreast of changes in political thinking. The first ten amendments (the Bill of Rights) were the price of ratification, but they have been fundamental to our system of government. The last seventeen amendments fall into three main categories: they make public policy, correct deficiencies in the government's structure, or promote equality (see Table 2.2).

Since 1787, about ten thousand constitutional amendments have been introduced, but only a fraction have passed the proposal stage. However, once an amendment has been voted by the Congress, chances of ratification are high. Only six amendments submitted to the states have failed to be ratified.

TABLE 2.2		Constitutional Amendments: 11 Through 27		
No.	**Proposed**	**Ratified**	**Intent***	**Subject**
11	1794	1795	G	Prohibits an individual from suing a state in federal court without the state's consent.
12	1803	1804	G	Requires the electoral college to vote separately for president and vice president.
13	1865	1865	E	Prohibits slavery.
14	1866	1868	E	Gives citizenship to all persons born or naturalized in the United States (including former slaves); prevents states from depriving any person of "life, liberty, or property, without due process of law"; and declares that no state shall deprive any person of "the equal protection of the laws."
15	1869	1870	E	Guarantees that citizens' right to vote cannot be denied "on account of race, color, or previous condition of servitude."
16	1909	1913	E	Gives Congress the power to collect an income tax.
17	1912	1913	E	Provides for popular election of senators, who were formerly elected by state legislatures.
18	1917	1919	P	Prohibits the making and selling of intoxicating liquors.
19	1919	1920	E	Guarantees that citizens' right to vote cannot be denied "on account of sex."
20	1932	1933	G	Changes the presidential inauguration from March 4 to January 20 and sets January 3 for the opening date of Congress.
21	1933	1933	P	Repeals the Eighteenth Amendment.
22	1947	1951	G	Limits a president to two terms.
23	1960	1961	E	Gives citizens of Washington, D.C., the right to vote for president.
24	1962	1964	E	Prohibits charging citizens a poll tax to vote in presidential or congressional elections.
25	1965	1967	G	Provides for succession in event of death, removal from office, incapacity, or resignation of the president or vice president.
26	1971	1971	E	Lowers the voting age to eighteen.
27	1789	1992	G	Bars immediate pay increases to members of Congress.

*P: amendments legislating public policy; G: amendments correcting perceived deficiencies in government structure; E: amendments advancing equality.

Interpretation by the Courts

In *Marbury* v. *Madison* (1803), the Supreme Court declared that the courts have the power to nullify government acts when they conflict with the Constitution. (We will elaborate on this power, known as judicial review, in Chapter 11.) The exercise of judicial review forces the courts to interpret the Constitution. In a way, this makes a lot of sense. The judiciary is the law-interpreting branch of the government; as the supreme law of the land, the Constitution is fair game for judicial interpretation. Judicial review is the courts' main check on the other branches of government. But in interpreting the Constitution, the courts cannot help but give new meaning to its provisions. This is why judicial interpretation is a principal form of constitutional change.

Political Practice

The Constitution is silent on many issues. It says nothing about political parties or the president's cabinet, for example, yet both have exercised considerable influence in American politics. Some constitutional provisions have fallen out of use. The electors in the electoral college, for example, were supposed to exercise their own judgment in voting for president and vice president. Today the electors function simply as a rubber stamp, validating the outcome of election contests in their states.

Meanwhile, political practice has altered the distribution of power without changes in the Constitution. The framers intended Congress to be the strongest branch of government. But the president has come to overshadow Congress. Presidents such as Abraham Lincoln and Franklin Roosevelt used their powers imaginatively to respond to national crises, and their actions paved the way for future presidents to enlarge the powers of the office.

An Evaluation of the Constitution

The U.S. Constitution is one of the world's most praised political documents. It is the oldest written national constitution and one of the most widely copied, sometimes word for word. It is also one of the shortest. The brevity of the Constitution may be one of its greatest strengths. The framers simply laid out a structural framework for government; they did not describe relationships and powers in detail. For example, the Constitution gives Congress the power to regulate "Commerce . . . among the several States," but it does not define *interstate commerce*. Such general wording allows interpretation in keeping with contemporary political, social, and technological developments.

The generality of the U.S. Constitution stands in stark contrast to the specificity of most state constitutions. The California Constitution, for example, provides that "fruit and nut-bearing trees under the age of four years from the time of planting in orchard form and grapevines under the age of three years from the time of planting in vineyard form . . . shall be exempt from taxation" (Article XIII, Section 12). Because they are so specific, most state constitutions are much longer than the U.S. Constitution.

Freedom, Order, and Equality in the Constitution

The revolutionaries constructed a new form of government—a *federal* government—that was strong enough to maintain order but not so strong that it could dominate the states or infringe on individual freedoms. In short, the Constitution provided a judicious balance between order and freedom. It paid virtually no attention to equality. (Recall that the equality premise in the Declaration of Independence was meant for the colonists as a people, not as individuals.)

Consider social equality. The Constitution never mentioned *slavery*, a controversial issue even when it was written. As we have seen, the Constitution implicitly condones slavery in several articles. Not until ratification of the Thirteenth Amendment in 1865 was slavery prohibited. The Constitution was designed long before social equality was ever conceived as an objective of government. In fact, in *Federalist* No. 10, Madison held that protection of the "diversities in the faculties of men from which the rights of property originate" is "the first object of government."

More than a century later, the Constitution was changed to incorporate a key device for the promotion of social equality: the income tax. The Sixteenth Amendment (1913) gave Congress the power to collect an income tax; it was proposed and ratified to replace a law that had been declared unconstitutional in an 1895 court case. The income tax had long been seen as a means of putting into effect the concept of *progressive taxation,* in which the tax rate increases with income. The Sixteenth Amendment gave progressive taxation a constitutional basis.[20] Progressive taxation promotes social equality through the redistribution of income—that is, high-income people are taxed at higher rates to help fund social programs that benefit lower-income people taxed at lower rates.

Politics of Global Change

A New Birth of Freedom: Exporting American Constitutionalism

When the founders drafted the U.S. Constitution in 1787, they hardly started from scratch. Leaders such as James Madison and John Adams drew on the failed experiences of the Articles of Confederation to chart a new course for our national government. They also leaned heavily on the ideas of great democratic thinkers of the past. Today, given the two-hundred-twenty-year track record of the United States, it is no wonder that many other nations have looked to the American experience as they embark on their own democratic experiments.

In the past fifteen years especially, democratizing countries on nearly every continent have developed new governing institutions by drawing at least in part on important principles from the U.S. Constitution and Bill of Rights. This is certainly the case in the former communist countries of Eastern Europe, which are in their third decade of newly established democratic rule. Enshrining democratic ideals in a written constitution corresponds to the ascendancy of freedom worldwide (see the accompanying figure). Free and partially free countries are in ascendance; not-free countries are in decline.

Echoing the U.S. Declaration of Independence and the Constitution's preamble, for example, Article 1 of the Estonian constitution declares unequivocally, ". . . the supreme power of the state is vested in the people." Specific guarantees protecting individual rights and liberties are also written in great detail in the constitutions of these new democracies. The Latvian constitution, for example, takes a strong stand on the defense of privacy, stating that "everyone has the right to inviolability of his or her private life, home and correspondence."

Some of these newly democratic nations, however, have opted for a constitutional design with a separation of powers less rigid than one established by the American model. A parliamentary system poses fewer constraints on executive authority as long as it is sustained by a legislative majority. As long as prime ministers are backed by the popular vote expressed via a parliamentary majority, they can remain in office indefinitely. However, they can be

Social equality itself has never been, and is not now, a prime *constitutional* value. The Constitution has been much more effective in securing order and freedom. Nor did the Constitution take a stand on political equality. It left voting qualifications to the states, specifying only that people who could vote for "the most numerous Branch of the State Legislature" could also vote for representatives to Congress (Article I, Section 2). Most states at that time allowed only taxpaying or property-owning white males to vote. Such inequalities have been rectified by several amendments. The United States is not unique in revisiting the balance among freedom, order, removed from office as soon as they lose their popular support by means of a parliamentary non-confidence vote. For instance, if an election changes the composition of the parliament, the new majority can select a new prime minister. Under the same scenario, the U.S. president—who can be removed from office only by impeachment—is forced to govern facing a hostile majority and possible gridlock.

Because there is no ready-made formula for building a successful democracy, only time will tell whether these young constitutions will perform well in practice.

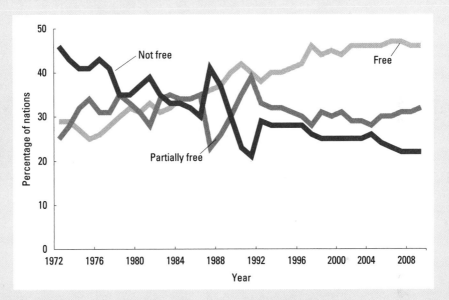

Sources: International Institute for Democracy, *The Rebirth of Democracy: 12 Constitutions of Central and Eastern Europe,* 2nd ed. (Amsterdam: Council of Europe, 1996); A. E. Dick Howard, "Liberty's Text: 10 Amendments That Changed the World," *Washington Post,* 15 December 1991, p. C3; Freedom House, "Freedom in the World 2009," available at http://www.freedom house.org/uploads/fiw09/tablesandcharts/Table of Independent Countries FIW 2009.pdf and http://www.freedomhouse.org/uploads/Chart116File163.pdf (accessed on 22 December 2009).

and equality within its constitution. Many other nations have pursued equally dramatic changes to their constitutions over the last decade. (See "Politics of Global Change: A New Birth of Freedom.")

The Constitution and Models of Democracy

Think back to our discussion of the models of democracy in Chapter 1. Which model does the Constitution fit: the pluralist or majoritarian? Actually, it is hard to imagine a government framework better suited to the pluralist model of democracy than the Constitution of the United States. It is also hard to imagine a document more at odds with the

We Want Beer

"We want beer" may be a popular refrain at tailgating parties and on certain college campuses today, but it was the basis of political protest in October 1932 when more than 20,000 protesters, many of them women, demanded repeal of the Eighteenth Amendment. The amendment, which was ratified in 1919, banned the manufacture, sale, and transportation of alcoholic beverages. The amendment was spurred by moral and social reform groups, such as the Women's Christian Temperance Union, founded by Evanston, Illinois, resident Frances Willard in 1874. The amendment proved to be an utter failure. People continued to drink, but their alcohol came from illegal sources.

(AP Photo)

majoritarian model. Consider Madison's claim, in *Federalist* No. 10, that government inevitably involves conflicting factions. This concept coincides perfectly with pluralist theory (see Chapter 1). Then recall his description in *Federalist* No. 51 of the Constitution's ability to guard against the concentration of power in the majority through separation of powers and checks and balances. This concept—avoiding a single center of government power that might fall under majority control—also fits perfectly with pluralist democracy.

The delegates to the Constitutional Convention intended to create a republic, a government based on majority consent; they did not intend to create a democracy, which rests on majority rule. They succeeded admirably in creating that republic. In doing so, they also produced a government that developed into a democracy—but a particular type of democracy. The framers neither wanted nor got a democracy that fit the majoritarian model. They may have wanted and they certainly did create a government that conforms to the pluralist model.

Tying It Together

1. How did circumstances in the American colonies in the mid-eighteenth century lead to the movement for a new government?
   - American colonists
     - were free of the restrictions of feudalism.
     - enjoyed almost complete freedom of speech, press, and assembly.
     - were unwilling to pay taxes to a distant government in which they had no representation.
   - Colonial desire for liberty conflicted with British attempts to maintain order.
   - Two continental congresses were convened to determine how to ensure colonists' rights.
   - Congressional delegates accepted the Declaration of Independence in 1776, which asserted the right of individuals to revolt if their government denied their rights.

2. How did the revolutionaries structure the government of their new republic, and was it successful?
   - The Articles of Confederation established an alliance between the independent states while severely limiting the power of a central government.
   - Under the terms of the confederation, the newly formed government
     - was unable to tax.
     - lacked an independent leader.
     - could not regulate commerce or international trade.
     - was unable to amend the Articles of Confederation without unanimous agreement of Congress and state legislative approval.
   - The inability of the confederation to deal with insurrections demonstrated the need for an empowered central government that could maintain order.

3. How did the confederation come to agreement on a national constitution?
   - A constitutional convention, initially authorized to revise the Articles of Confederation, determined instead to debate the Virginia Plan.
   - The Virginia Plan introduced several important ideas that would create a powerful national government:
     - three separate branches of government.
     - division of the legislature into two houses.
     - proportional representation.
   - Fearing control by the larger states, the small states recommended the New Jersey Plan to amend the Articles of Confederation.
   - While the New Jersey Plan was rejected by the Convention, smaller states did force a compromise on representation.
   - The delegates accepted the Great Compromise, which determined the responsibilities and means of electing state representatives and the president.
   - The delegates agreed to a presidential term of four years with unlimited terms.
   - A procedure was agreed upon for the impeachment of the president that included both houses as well as the judiciary.

4. What were the basic ideas and articles that created the final version of the Constitution?
   - The Preamble forms the foundation for the Constitution because it
     - defines a people.
     - explains the reason for the Constitution.
     - articulates goals.
     - fashions a government.
   - The basic principles the founders relied upon were
     - republicanism.
     - separation of powers.
     - checks and balances.
   - The Articles of the Constitution:
     - Article I specifies the enumerated and implied powers of Congress.
     - Article II describes the president's term, election process, qualifications, duties, and powers.
     - Article III establishes the Supreme Court and gives Congress the authority to establish a federal court system.
     - Article IV specifies the rights and responsibilities of the states.
     - Article V specifies the constitutional amendment process.
     - Article VI asserts the supremacy clause, requires that elected officials take an oath of loyalty to the Constitution, and mandates that religion cannot be a prerequisite to office.
     - Article VII describes the ratification process.

5. How did the founders achieve ratification of the Constitution?
   - Nine states were needed to ratify the Constitution.
   - Federalists were the proponents of the Constitution while Antifederalists, fearful of an overly powerful national government, were opponents.
   - The *Federalist* papers supported the Constitution and were widely read throughout the states.
   - In *Federalist* No. 10 and No. 51, James Madison developed arguments for the Constitution that foreshadowed a pluralist theory of democracy.
   - Both sides agreed to the Bill of Rights: ten amendments that restrained the national government from tampering with rights and civil liberties as well as clarified the limit of its power.
   - The Constitution was ratified on June 21, 1788.

6. What methods are used to alter the Constitution?
   - Amendments can be proposed by a two-thirds vote in both houses of Congress or by national convention. Amendments can be ratified by a vote of the legislatures of three-fourths of the states or by a vote of conventions in three-fourths of the states.
   - Change can occur by judicial review and interpretation.
   - Change can occur by political practice.

7. What are the unique features of the U.S. Constitution?
   - The Constitution is one of the shortest constitutions.
   - It lays out a structural framework for government without describing relationships and powers in detail.
   - Its general wording allows for contemporary interpretation.
   - It originally focused on protecting freedom and maintaining order but has been amended to support social equality.
   - It fits perfectly with the pluralistic model of government.

Test Prepper 2.1

The Revolutionary Roots of the Constitution

True or False?

1. In 1763, the colonists and the British were in agreement regarding how much control the British would have in making decisions regarding the colonists.
2. John Locke's writings, including his belief that people have inalienable, God-given, natural rights, were very influential in the writing of the Declaration of Independence.
3. The War of Independence lasted from April 19, 1780, to October 19, 1781.

Comprehension

4. What impact did the Coercive Acts of 1774 have on the colonies?
5. What was the major dilemma the delegates of the Second Continental Congress faced?

Test Prepper 2.2

From Revolution to Confederation

True or False?

1. A republic must be a democracy to be a true republic.
2. In a confederation, states abandon their sovereignty, meaning they surrender supreme power within their borders.
3. One goal of the delegates who drew up the Articles of Confederation was to retain power in the states.

Comprehension

4. What is the significance of Shays's Rebellion on the development of the Constitution?
5. Why did the Articles of Confederation ultimately fail?

Test Prepper 2.3

From Confederation to Constitution

True or False?

1. The New Jersey Plan was an effort by small states to preserve the spirit of the Articles of Confederation.
2. The Great Compromise was also known as the Connecticut Compromise, as it was proposed by Roger Sherman of the Connecticut delegation.
3. The electoral college allowed for a presidential candidate to win by popular vote.

Comprehension

4. Why did delegates from the smaller states accept the Great Compromise?
5. On what grounds could a president be impeached?

Test Prepper 2.4

The Final Product

True or False?

1. The power of Congress to override a veto is one way to establish a "check on a check."
2. In addition to the Preamble, the Constitution includes three articles.
3. Judicial review is the power of the courts to declare government acts invalid because they violate the Constitution.

Comprehension

4. What is the meaning and importance of the supremacy clause found in Article VI?
5. What were the motives of those who framed the Constitution?

Selling the Constitution

True or False?

1. The Bill of Rights provided assurances that the state governments would be constrained from limiting basic civil liberties.
2. James Madison argued that the Constitution would prevent a "tyranny of the majority" by creating a small and limited republic.
3. The success of the new Constitution was ensured when the ninth state ratified it.

Comprehension

4. How did the *Federalist* papers help win ratification for the Constitution?
5. Why were prominent citizens such as Thomas Jefferson unhappy that the Constitution did not list basic civil liberties?

Constitutional Change

True or False?

1. All constitutional amendments to date have been approved by national convention.
2. Congress chooses between two methods of ratification for amendments it proposes.
3. Chances of ratification of an amendment are high once Congress has voted it through the proposal stage.

Comprehension

4. How does political practice often alter the American political system without any formal amendment to the Constitution?
5. Describe the two stages of amending the Constitution.

An Evaluation of the Constitution

True or False?

1. The U.S. Constitution is much more complex than state constitutions because it has a much greater area of responsibility.
2. The specificity of the U.S. Constitution is its greatest strength.
3. Social equality is never mentioned in the U.S. Constitution.

Comprehension

4. To what degree has social equality played a central role in the Constitution?
5. Does the Constitution fit the pluralist or majoritarian model of democracy? Support your opinion with arguments and examples.

CourseMate CL Resources:

Visit www.cengagebrain.com/shop/ISBN/1111832587 for flashcards, web quizzes, videos and more!

CHAPTER

3

Federalism

AP Photo/Ross D. Franklin

FOCUS QUESTIONS

1. What is federalism, and what theories and metaphors help to explain it?
2. What forces prompt change in the relationships between national and state governments?
3. How do views about American federalism influence politics and policy?
4. How is federalism related to the outcome of state and local elections?
5. How do citizens interact with the intergovernmental system?
6. How does federalism promote pluralism?

"The problem is all these illegals," said Luis, a legal Mexican immigrant who has lived and worked in Arizona for 16 years. "They come here expecting to find paradise, and it isn't. You have to work hard for everything. But at least there is work."[1] These are difficult times, especially in Arizona. The Great Recession (2007–2009), the ensuing trail of high unemployment, and the housing market collapse wreaked devastation on the state. Illegal immigration surged along with increased drug smuggling, human trafficking, and associated gang violence across Arizona's 362-mile border with Mexico.

For years, Arizonans—including Luis and his fellow legal immigrants—have borne the burden of illegals who have sought work and opportunity in the United States. President George W. Bush was determined to reform immigration laws, staunching the illegal tide, but he failed. Immigration reform was political kryptonite, weakening even the most powerful politicians who tried to address the issue. The public seethed at the prospect of illegals taking jobs from American citizens; of illegals using the social safety net to secure heath care, education, and housing; and of pregnant illegals crossing the border and delivering their babies on American soil, thus qualifying their children immediately for American citizenship.[2] All of this and more proved too much for conservative Arizonans and their politicians.

In 2010, under Governor Jan Brewer, the state legislature adopted a law—SB1070—taking immigration matters into its own hands. The law is both broad and strict; it goes far beyond efforts in other states to address the problem of illegal immigration. More significantly, it goes further than the United States government has chosen to go.

U.S. law requires foreigners who are not citizens living in the United States—called *aliens*—to register with the government and carry their registration papers. Arizona's SB1070 took this requirement a step further by criminalizing the failure to carry the necessary papers. The new law obligates the police to determine a person's immigration status, when practicable during a "lawful stop, detention or arrest," if there is reasonable suspicion that the person is an illegal alien. The law also cracked down on those who hire, transport, or shelter illegal aliens.[3] Critics argued that citizens or legal aliens with brown skin would be caught up in such sweeps. Defenders of the law maintained that racial profiling was prohibited.

David Salgado, a Phoenix police officer, challenged SB1070 in federal court on the ground that the provisions forced him into an untenable dilemma. On the one hand, if he enforced the law, he would be engaged in racial profiling by stopping only members of a given racial class to check for proper immigration status. On the other hand, if he failed to enforce the law, he would be subject to sanctions from his superiors, including the prospect of losing his job.[4]

The national government intervened in the lawsuit, sending one of its highest-ranking officials from the Justice Department to argue its position. The argument did not focus on racial profiling, the issue that animated the press and the public. Rather, the United States rested its case on federalism grounds: the Constitution and laws of the United States place the matter of immigration solely in the hands of the national government, and the states remain duty-bound under the Constitution's supremacy clause (Article VI) to bow to national authority.

On July 28, 2010, just one day before the law was to go into effect, federal judge Susan Bolton blocked the main provisions of the law, including the requirement that police check the immigration status of those arrested or stopped. Her reasoning adopted the position of the United States: principles of federalism give exclusive power over immigration matters to the national government, trumping state efforts at regulating or enforcing national immigration laws as in Arizona.[5]

Two elements of federalism are at work here. The first element is the respective **sovereignty**, or quality of being supreme in power or authority, of national and state governments. In the case of Arizona's efforts to confront illegal immigration, this distinction between different sovereignties was clear to Judge Bolton: authority rests principally with the national government. She did not invalidate the entire law, but only those portions that intrude on the national government's delegated or implied powers. The states cannot simply act on their own when the Constitution (Article I, Section 8, Clause 4) and laws of the United States assign responsibility for immigration and naturalization to the national government. A second element of federalism is the power of national (i.e., federal) courts to assure the supremacy of the U.S. Constitution and national laws. Such power was necessary, though not sufficient, to yoke separate states into one nation, or as the motto goes, "E pluribus unum."

sovereignty
The quality of being supreme in power or authority.

In this chapter, we examine American federalism in theory and in practice. Is the division of power between the nation and states a matter of constitutional principle or practical politics? How does the balance of power between the nation and states relate to the conflicts between freedom and order and between freedom and equality? Does the growth of federalism abroad affect us here at home? Does federalism reflect the pluralist or the majoritarian model of democracy?

Theories and Metaphors

The delegates who met in Philadelphia in 1787 tackled the problem of making one nation out of thirteen independent states by inventing a new political form—federal government—that combined features of a confederacy with features of unitary government (see Chapter 2). Under the principle of **federalism**, two or more governments exercise power and authority over the same people and the same territory. For example, the governments of the United States and Pennsylvania share certain powers (the power to tax, for instance), but other powers belong exclusively to one or the other. As James Madison wrote in *Federalist* No. 10, "The federal Constitution forms a happy combination . . . [of] the great and aggregate interests being referred to the national, and the local and particular to state governments." So the power to coin money belongs to the national government, but the power to grant divorces remains a state prerogative. By contrast, authority over state militias may sometimes belong to the national government and sometimes to the states. The history of American federalism reveals that it has not always been easy to draw a line between what is "great and aggregate" and what is "local and particular."*

Nevertheless, federalism offered a solution to citizens' fears that they would be ruled by majorities from different regions and different interests and values. Federalism also provided a new political model. The history of American federalism is full of attempts to capture its true meaning in an adjective or metaphor. By one reckoning, scholars have generated nearly five hundred ways to describe federalism.[6] We will concentrate on two such representations: dual federalism and cooperative federalism.

Dual Federalism

The term **dual federalism** sums up a theory about the proper relationship between the national government and the states. This theory has four essential parts. First, the national government rules by enumerated powers only. Second, the national government has a limited set of constitutional purposes. Third, each government

federalism
The division of power between a central government and regional governments.

dual federalism
A view that holds the Constitution is a compact among sovereign states, so that the powers of the national government are fixed and limited.

---

*The phrase Americans commonly use to refer to their central government—*federal government*—muddies the waters even more. Technically, we have a federal system of government, which encompasses both the national and state governments. To avoid confusion from here on, we use the term *national government* rather than *federal government* when we are talking about the central government.

Made in the U.S.A.

Young boys working in a Macon, Georgia, cotton mill (1909). The U.S. Supreme Court decided in 1918 that Congress had no power to limit the excesses of child labor. According to the Court, that power belonged to the states, which resisted imposing limits for fear such legislation would drive businesses to other (less restrictive) states.

(Library of Congress)

unit—nation and state—is sovereign within its sphere. And fourth, the relationship between nation and states is best characterized by tension rather than cooperation.[7]

Dual federalism portrays the states as powerful components of the federal system—in some ways, the equals of the national government. Under dual federalism, the functions and responsibilities of the national and state governments are theoretically different and practically separate from each other. Dual federalism sees the Constitution as a compact among sovereign states. Of primary importance in dual federalism are **states' rights,** a concept that reserves to the states all rights not specifically conferred on the national government by the Constitution. Claims of states' rights often come from opponents of a national government policy. Their argument is that the people have not delegated the power to make such policy, and thus the power remains in the states or the people. Proponents of states' rights believe that the powers of the national government should be interpreted narrowly. They insist that the activities of Congress should be confined to the enumerated powers. They support their view by quoting the Tenth Amendment: "The powers not delegated to the United States by the Constitution, nor prohibited by it to the States, are reserved to the states respectively, or to the people." Conversely, those people favoring national action frequently point to the Constitution's elastic clause, which gives Congress the **implied powers** needed to execute its enumerated powers (see Chapter 2).

states' rights
The idea that all rights not specifically conferred on the national government by the Constitution are reserved to the states.

implied powers
Those powers that Congress requires in order to execute its enumerated powers.

FIGURE 3.1   Metaphors for Federalism

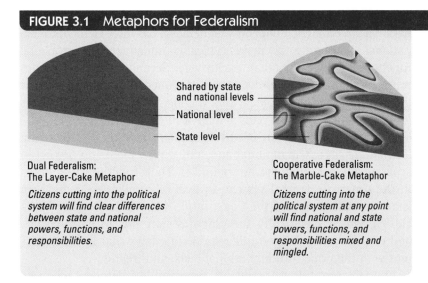

Shared by state
and national levels

National level

State level

The two views of federalism
can be represented
graphically.

(© Cengage Learning 2013)

**Dual Federalism:
The Layer-Cake Metaphor**

*Citizens cutting into the political
system will find clear differences
between state and national
powers, functions, and
responsibilities.*

**Cooperative Federalism:
The Marble-Cake Metaphor**

*Citizens cutting into the
political system at any point
will find national and state
powers, functions, and
responsibilities mixed and
mingled.*

Political scientists use a metaphor to describe dual federalism. They call it *layer-cake federalism*; the powers and functions of national and state governments are as separate as the layers of a cake (see Figure 3.1). Each government is supreme in its own "layer," its own sphere of action; the two layers are distinct; and the dimensions of each layer are fixed by the Constitution.

Dual federalism has been challenged on historical and other grounds. Some critics argue that if the national government is really a creation of the states, it is a creation of only thirteen states—those that ratified the Constitution. The other thirty-seven states were admitted after the national government came into being and were created by that government out of land it had acquired. Another challenge has to do with the ratification process. Remember that special conventions in the original thirteen states, not the states' legislatures, ratified the Constitution. Ratification, then, was an act of the people, not the states. Moreover, the Preamble to the Constitution begins, "We the people of the United States," not, "We the States." The question of where the people fit into the federal system is not handled well by dual federalism.

Cooperative Federalism

Cooperative federalism, a phrase coined in the 1930s, is a different theory of the relationship between national and state governments. It acknowledges the increasing overlap in state and national functions

cooperative federalism
A view that holds that the Constitution is an agreement among people who are citizens of both state and nation, so there is little distinction between state powers and national powers.

and rejects the idea of separate spheres, or layers, for the states and the national government. Cooperative federalism has three elements. First, national and state agencies typically undertake governmental functions jointly rather than exclusively. Second, nation and states routinely share power. Third, power is not concentrated at any government level or in any agency; this fragmentation of responsibilities gives people and groups access to many centers of influence.

The bakery metaphor used to describe this kind of federalism is a *marble cake*. The national and state governments do not act in separate spheres; they are intermingled. Their functions are mixed in the American federal system. Critical to cooperative federalism is an expansive view of the Constitution's supremacy clause (Article VI), which specifically subordinates state law to national law and charges every judge to disregard state laws that are inconsistent with the Constitution, national laws, and treaties.

In contrast to dual federalism, cooperative federalism blurs the distinction between national and state powers. Some scholars argue that the layer-cake metaphor has never accurately described the American political structure.[8] The national and state governments have many common objectives and have often cooperated to achieve them. In the nineteenth century, for example, cooperation, not separation, made it possible to develop transportation systems such as canals and to establish state land-grant colleges.

A critical difference between the theories of dual and cooperative federalism is the way they interpret two sections of the Constitution that set out the terms of the relationship between the national and state governments. Article I, Section 8, lists the enumerated powers of Congress and then concludes with the **elastic clause**, which gives Congress the power to "make all Laws which shall be necessary and proper for carrying into Execution the foregoing Powers." The Tenth Amendment reserves for the states or the people "powers" not given to the national government or denied to the states by the Constitution. Dual federalism postulates an inflexible elastic clause and a capacious Tenth Amendment. Cooperative federalism postulates suppleness in the elastic clause and confines the Tenth Amendment to a self-evident, obvious truth.

elastic clause
The last clause in Section 8 of Article I of the Constitution, which gives Congress the means to execute its enumerated powers. This clause is the basis for Congress's implied powers. Also called the *necessary and proper clause.*

The Dynamics of Federalism

Although the Constitution defines a kind of federalism, the actual balance of power between nation and states has always been more a matter of politics than of formal theory. Three broad principles help to underscore why. First, rather than operating in a mechanical fashion, American federalism is a flexible and dynamic system. The Constitution's inherent ambiguities about federalism generate not only constraints but also opportunities for politicians, citizens, and interest groups to push ideas that they care about. Second, due to this flexibility, public officials across levels of government often make policy decisions based on pragmatic considerations without regard to theories of what American federalism should look like. Politics and policy goals rather than pure theoretical or ideological commitments about federalism tend to dominate decision making. Third, there is a growing recognition among public officials and citizens that public problems (those involving trade-offs between freedom, order, and equality) cut across governmental boundaries. This section develops the first claim; we explore the other two later in this chapter.

The overall point these three claims illustrate is that understanding American federalism requires knowing more than simply the powers that the Constitution assigns the different levels of government. Real understanding requires recognizing the forces that can prompt changes in relationships between the national government and the states. In this section, we focus on four specific forces: national crises and demands, judicial interpretation, the expansion of grants-in-aid, and the professionalization of state governments.

National Crises and Demands

The elastic clause of the Constitution gives Congress the power to make all laws that are "necessary and proper" to carry out its responsibilities. By using this power in combination with its enumerated powers, Congress has been able to increase the scope of the national government tremendously. The greatest change has come in times of crisis and national emergency, such as the Civil War, the world wars, the Great Depression, the aftermath of 9/11, or the 2007–2009 Great Recession. Consider the Great Depression.

The problems of the Great Depression proved too extensive for either state governments or private businesses to handle, so the national government assumed a heavy share of responsibility for providing relief and pursuing economic recovery. Under the New Deal, President Franklin D. Roosevelt's response to the depression, Congress enacted various emergency relief programs to stimulate economic activity and help the unemployed. Many measures required the cooperation of national and state governments. Through the

IDEALOG.ORG

Do you prefer a bigger government with more services or a smaller government with fewer services? Take IDEAlog's self-test.

regulations it attached to funds, the national government extended its power and control over the states.[9]

Some call the New Deal era revolutionary. There is no doubt that the period was critical in reshaping federalism in the United States, and the interaction between the national and state governments clearly resembled the marble-cake metaphor more than the alternative. But perhaps the most significant change was in the way Americans thought about their problems and the role of the national government in solving them. Difficulties that at one time had been seen as personal or local problems were now national problems, requiring national solutions. The general welfare, broadly defined, became a legitimate concern of the national government.

In other respects, however, the New Deal was not very revolutionary. For example, Congress did not claim any new powers to address the nation's economic problems. It simply used its constitutional powers to suit the circumstances.

Concerns over terrorist attacks on U.S. soil have expanded national power. The month after the events of September 11, 2001, the Congress swiftly passed and the president signed into law the USA-PATRIOT Act (P.L. 107-56). Among other provisions, the law expanded significantly the surveillance and investigative powers of the Department of Justice. After some disagreement about its structure and organization, federal policymakers also created the Department of Homeland Security in 2002, a new department that united over twenty separate federal agencies under a common administrative structure.[10] These efforts sparked much debate regarding the appropriate limits of the national government's power over the lives of American citizens and the prerogatives of other levels of government.

The role of the national government has also grown as it has responded to needs and demands that state and local governments were unwilling or unable to meet. To address the severe economic downturn saddling the nation, President Obama proposed and Congress quickly passed a $787 billion economic stimulus package in February 2009. No Republicans in the House of Representatives and only three Republicans in the Senate voted for the legislation, a clear signal of the charged partisan atmosphere in Washington. The American Recovery and Reinvestment Act (ARRA) offered substantial direct aid to states beleaguered by the recession in the form of Medicaid payments, extended unemployment benefits, school and infrastructure spending, and other grants. Several Republican governors rejected the money, arguing that the strings attached would mandate the states to more spending in the future. But the bluster receded as furious state legislators in both parties demanded the much-needed funds. When the deadline arrived, all governors signed on.[11]

Judicial Interpretation

How federal courts have interpreted the Constitution and federal law is another factor that has influenced the relationship between the national government and the states. The U.S. Supreme Court, the umpire of the federal system, settles disputes over the powers of the national and state governments by deciding whether the actions of either are unconstitutional (see Chapter 11). In the nineteenth and early twentieth centuries, the Supreme Court often decided in favor of the states. Then for nearly sixty years, from 1937 to 1995, the Court almost always supported the national government in contests involving the balance of power between nation and states. Since 1995, the Supreme Court has tended to favor states' rights, but not without some important exceptions.

Ends and Means. Early in the nineteenth century, the nationalist interpretation of federalism triumphed over states' rights. In 1819, under Chief Justice John Marshall, the Supreme Court expanded the role of the national government in *McCulloch* v. *Maryland*. The Court was asked to rule whether Congress had the power to establish a national bank and, if so, whether states had the power to tax that bank. In a unanimous opinion that Marshall wrote, the Court conceded that Congress had only the powers conferred on it by the Constitution, which nowhere mentioned banks. However, Article I granted to Congress the authority to enact all laws "necessary and proper" to the execution of Congress's enumerated powers. Marshall gave a broad interpretation to this elastic clause: "Let the end be legitimate, let it be within the scope of the constitution, and all means which are appropriate, which are plainly adapted to that end, which are not prohibited, but consistent with the letter and spirit of the constitution, are constitutional."

The Court clearly agreed that Congress had the power to charter a bank. But did the states (in this case, Maryland) have the power to tax the bank? Arguing that "the power to tax involves the power to destroy," Marshall insisted that states could not tax the national government because the bank represents the interests of the whole nation; a state may not tax those it does not represent. Therefore, a state tax that interferes with the power of Congress to make law is void.[12]

Commerce for a New Nation. Especially from the late 1930s to the mid-1990s, the Supreme Court's interpretation of the Constitution's **commerce clause** was a major factor that increased the national government's power. The third clause of Article I, Section 8, states that "Congress shall have Power . . . To regulate Commerce . . . among the several States." In early Court decisions, beginning with *Gibbons* v. *Ogden* in 1824, Chief Justice Marshall interpreted the word *commerce* broadly to include virtually every form of commercial activity. But later courts would take a narrower view of that power.[13]

States' Rights and Dual Federalism. Roger B. Taney became chief justice in 1836, and during his tenure (1836–1864), the Court's federalism decisions began to favor the states. The Taney Court took a more restrictive view of commerce and imposed firm limits on the powers of the national government. As Taney saw it, the Constitution spoke "not only in the same words, but with the same meaning and intent with which it spoke when it came from the hands of its framers and was voted on and adopted by the people of the United States." In the infamous *Dred Scott* decision (1857), for example, the Court decided that Congress had no power to prohibit slavery in the territories.[14]

Federalism and the New Deal. The judicial winds shifted again during the Great Depression. After originally disagreeing with FDR's and the Congress's position that the economic crisis was a national problem demanding national action, in 1937, with no change in personnel, the Court began to alter its course and upheld several major New Deal measures. Perhaps the Court was responding to the 1936 election returns (Roosevelt had been reelected in a landslide, and the Democrats commanded a substantial majority in Congress). Or perhaps the Court sought to defuse the president's threat to enlarge the Court with justices sympathetic to his views. In any event, the Court abandoned its effort to maintain a rigid boundary between national and state power.[15]

The Umpire Strikes Back. In the 1990s, a series of important U.S. Supreme Court rulings involving the commerce clause suggested that the states' rights position was gaining ground. The Court's 5 to 4 ruling in *United States* v. *Lopez* held that Congress exceeded its authority under the commerce clause when it enacted a law in 1990 banning the possession of a gun in or near a school.[16] A conservative majority, headed by Chief Justice William H. Rehnquist, concluded that having a gun in a school zone "has nothing to do with 'commerce' or any sort of economic enterprise, however broadly one might define those terms." Justices Sandra Day O'Connor, Antonin Scalia, Anthony Kennedy, and

commerce clause
The third clause of Article I, Section 8, of the Constitution, which gives Congress the power to regulate commerce among the states.

Clarence Thomas, all appointed by Republicans, joined in Rehnquist's opinion, putting the brakes on congressional power.

Another piece of gun-control legislation, known as the Brady Bill, produced similar results. The 1993 bill mandated the creation by November 1998 of a national system to check the background of prospective gun buyers in order to weed out, among others, convicted felons and the mentally ill. In the meantime, it created a temporary system that called for local law enforcement officials to perform background checks and report their findings to gun dealers in their community. Several sheriffs challenged the law.

The Supreme Court agreed with the sheriffs, delivering a double-barreled blow to the local-enforcement provision in June 1997. In *Printz* v. *United States,* the Court concluded that Congress could not require local officials to implement a regulatory scheme imposed by the national government. In language that seemingly invoked layer-cake federalism, Justice Antonin Scalia, writing for the five-member conservative majority, argued that locally enforced background checks violated the principle of dual sovereignty by allowing the national government "to impress into its service—and at no cost to itself—the police officers of the 50 States." In addition, the scheme violated the principle of separation of powers, by congressional transfer of the president's responsibility to faithfully execute national laws to local law enforcement officials.[17]

IDEALOG.ORG

One of the questions in the IDEAlog self-test deals with stricter gun-control laws. How did you answer that question?

Federalism's Shifting Scales. In 2000, the Court struck down congressional legislation that had allowed federal court lawsuits pursuing money damages for victims of crimes "motivated by gender." The Violence Against Women Act violated both the commerce clause and Section 5 of the Fourteenth Amendment. The majority declared that "the Constitution requires a distinction between what is truly national and what is truly local."[18]

The recent pattern promoting states' rights in federalism cases is not without significant exceptions. Perhaps the best-known decision bucking the trend is *Bush* v. *Gore.* In that decision the Court overruled the Florida Supreme Court's interpretation of Florida election law and ordered a halt to Florida ballot recounts, effectively ending the 2000 presidential election contest. In *Lawrence and Garner* v. *Texas,* an unrelated case from 2003, the Court also ruled against the states when it declared unconstitutional, by a 6 to 3 vote, a Texas law that had outlawed homosexual conduct between consenting adults. In the process, the decision also overturned a prior Court decision from the 1980s that had upheld Georgia's authority to maintain a similar law.[19]

How far, then, might the "necessary and proper" lawmaking power discussed in *McCulloch* v. *Maryland* extend in practice today? In *U.S.* v. *Comstock* (2010), the U.S. Supreme Court ruled (7–2) that the national government could keep dangerous sex offenders in prison after their sentences were completed if they posed an ongoing threat to the public. Justice Breyer wrote that "in determining whether the Necessary and Proper Clause grants Congress the legislative authority to enact a particular federal statute, we look to see whether the statute constitutes a means that is rationally related to the implementation of a constitutionally enumerated power."[20] Though Congress's authority to criminalize behavior, build prisons, and imprison violators of federal law is also not explicitly discussed in the Constitution, the Court has long recognized these powers as means of executing the enumerated powers.

Grants-in-Aid

Since the 1960s, the national government's use of financial incentives has rivaled its use of legislation and judicial interpretation as a means of shaping relationships between national and state governments. The principal method the national government uses to make money available to the states is grants-in-aid.

A **grant-in-aid** is money paid by one level of government to another level of government, to be spent for a specific purpose. Most grants-in-aid come with standards or requirements prescribed by Congress. Many are awarded on a matching basis: a recipient must make some contribution of its own, which is then matched by the national government. Grants-in-aid take two general forms: categorical grants and block grants.

Categorical grants target specific purposes, and restrictions on their use typically leave the recipient relatively little discretion. Recipients today include state governments, local governments, and public and private nonprofit organizations. There are two kinds of categorical grants: formula grants and project grants. As their name implies, **formula grants** are distributed according to a particular formula, which specifies who is eligible for the grant and how much each eligible applicant will receive. The formulas may weigh such factors as state per capita income, number of school-age children, urban population, and number of families below the poverty line. Most grants, however, are **project grants**, awarded on the basis of competitive applications. Recent grants have focused on health (substance abuse and HIV-AIDS programs); natural resources and the environment (asbestos and toxic pollution); and education, training, and employment (for disabled, homeless, and elderly persons).

grant-in-aid
Money provided by one level of government to another, to be spent for a given purpose.

categorical grant
A grant-in-aid targeted for a specific purpose by formula or by project.

formula grant
A categorical grant distributed according to a particular formula that specifies who is eligible for the grant and how much each eligible applicant will receive.

project grant
A categorical grant awarded on the basis of competitive applications submitted by prospective recipients.

In contrast to categorical grants, Congress awards **block grants** for broad, general purposes. They allow recipient governments considerable freedom in deciding how to allocate money to individual programs. Whereas a categorical grant might be given to promote a very specific activity—say, developing an ethnic heritage curriculum—a block grant might be earmarked for elementary, secondary, and vocational education. The state or local government receiving the block grant would then choose the specific educational programs to fund with it.

Grants-in-aid are a method of redistributing income. Money is collected by the national government from citizens of all fifty states and then funneled back to state and local governments. Many grants have worked to remove gross inequalities among states and their residents. But the formulas used to redistribute this income are not impartial; they are highly political, established through a process of congressional horse trading. Whatever its form or purpose, grant money comes with strings attached. Some strings are there to ensure that the money is used for the purpose for which it was given. Other regulations are designed to evaluate how well the grant is working. Still others are designed to achieve some broad national goal, a goal that is not always closely related to the specific purpose of the grant. For example, in October 2000, President Bill Clinton signed legislation establishing a tough national standard of .08 percent blood-alcohol level for drunk driving. States that refused to impose this lower standard by 2004 stood to lose millions in government highway construction money.[21] Not surprisingly, every state with a higher blood alcohol standard responded to the legislation by passing its own law lowering the standard to .08 percent.

Professionalization of State Governments

A final important factor that has produced dynamic changes in the American federal system has been the emergence of state governments as more capable policy actors. Not long ago, states were described as the weak links in the American policy system. In an oft-quoted book, former North Carolina governor Terry Sanford leveled heavy criticisms at the states, calling them ineffective, indecisive, and inattentive organizations that may have lost their relevance in an increasingly complicated nation and world.[22] Writing nearly twenty years earlier, journalist Robert Allen was even less kind; he called the states "the tawdriest, most incompetent, most stultifying unit in the nation's political structure."[23]

How times have changed. Since the 1960s especially, states have become much more capable and forceful policy actors. These changes have contributed to dynamic changes in the American

block grant
A grant-in-aid awarded for general purposes, allowing the recipient great discretion in spending the grant money.

Compared with What?

Working for the Public

The national government in the United States employs about 2 million people. But if we factor in individuals employed through federal grants and contracts, the number of federal government employees balloons to around 15 million. When we factor in all public employees at the national, state, and local levels, we get a greater sense of the presence of government in our lives.

Figure A compares the number of public sector workers at all levels controlling for population across several countries. In this comparison, public sector employment is about 71 workers for every 1,000 Americans. This is about average across all the countries compared. Public sector employment in the United States is about half of that in Norway and Sweden, much smaller countries with substantial public welfare programs.

Figure A   Public Sector Employment as a Percentage of Total Population (2005)

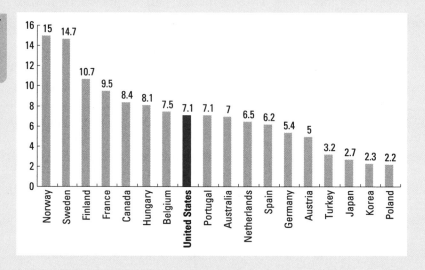

federal system. If the situation was so bleak less than five decades ago, what has happened since then?[24]

First, the states have made many internal changes that have fostered their capabilities. Both governors and state legislators now employ more capably trained and experienced policy staff rather than part-time assistants. Second, legislatures now meet more days during the year, and elected officials in states receive higher salaries than in the past. Third, the appeal of higher salaries has helped to attract more highly qualified people to run for state office. Fourth, the increasing ability

Public sector employment in the United States is greater than that in the economically powerful countries of Germany and Japan.

The distribution of public sector employment between the national level on one hand and the state and local levels on the other produces a different picture. (See Figure B.) By far, most public sector workers in the United States are found at the state and local levels. Higher state and local employment is also characteristic of other federal systems, such as those of Australia, Germany, and Canada.

So if you ponder the question "Where is my government?" a postal worker could satisfy the federal part of the answer. Local government employees are far more numerous, working at the firehouse, the police station, the county health office, or your local public school.

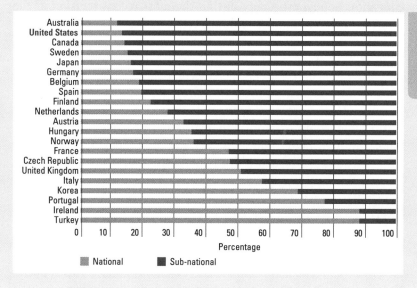

Figure B   Distribution of Employment between the National and Subnational Levels of Government (2005)

Sources: Adam Sheingate, "Why Can't Americans See the State?" *The Forum* 7, no. 4 (2010): 1–14; Paul C. Light, "The New True Size of Government," *Organizational Performance Initiative: Research Brief, Number 2* (Robert F. Wagner Graduate School of Public Service, New York University, August 2006), p. 11.

of states to raise revenue, through state tax and budgetary reforms that have transpired since the 1960s, has given states greater leverage in designing and directing policy. And, fifth, the unelected officials who administer state programs in areas such as transportation, social services, and law enforcement have become better educated. For instance, professional and service occupations account for more than the half of all jobs at the state and local levels. In 2006, professional workers represented one-fifth of all state and local government employees. Most of these professional jobs require a college degree.[25]

Changes in national policy have also helped the states to develop. Many federal grants-in-aid include components designed explicitly to foster capacity-building measures in state governments. One example is the Elementary and Secondary Education Act (ESEA), which became law in 1965. This act, passed as part of President Lyndon Johnson's Great Society effort, was designed to provide federal assistance to the nation's disadvantaged students. Although it is often overlooked, Title V of the law contained several provisions designed to strengthen state departments of education, the agencies that would be responsible for administering the bulk of other programs contained in the ESEA. Those new capabilities, which subsequent federal laws and internal state efforts have fostered, continue to influence the shape of both federal and state education policy, especially during the most recent revision of the ESEA as the No Child Left Behind Act of 2001.[26]

All of this is not to say that the states are without problems of their own. In some ways, they have been victims of their own success. Now that state capitals have become more viable venues where citizens and interest groups can agitate for their causes, the states have begun to face ever-increasing demands. Those requests can strain state administrators and legislative or gubernatorial staffs who, although better educated and equipped than their predecessors, still struggle to set priorities and please their constituents.

Ideology, Policymaking, and American Federalism

American federalism appears to be in constant motion. This is due in large part to what some political scientists call policy entrepreneurs—citizens, interest groups, and officials inside government—who attempt to persuade others to accept a particular view of the proper balance of freedom, order, and equality. The American federal system provides myriad opportunities for interested parties to push for their ideas.

In essence, the existence of national and state governments—specifically, their executive, legislative, and judicial branches and their bureaucratic agencies—offers these entrepreneurs several different venues where they can attempt to influence policy and politics. The most creative of these entrepreneurs can work at multiple levels of government simultaneously.

In this section, we explore how views about American federalism can influence the shape of the nation's politics and policy. We also relate these issues to our ongoing discussion of political ideology, which we introduced in Chapter 1 (see Figure 1.2).

Ideology, Policymaking, and Federalism in Theory

To begin our discussion in this section, it will be helpful to return to the cake metaphors that describe dual and cooperative federalism. Looking at those models of the nation's federal system helps capture some of what could be considered conventional wisdom about political ideology and federalism—in particular, the views of conservatives and liberals. In their efforts to limit the scope of the national government, conservatives are often associated with the layer-cake metaphor. In contrast, liberals, believing that one of the functions of the national government is to bring about equality, are more likely to find the marble-cake metaphor more desirable.

Conservatives are often portrayed as believing that different states have different problems and resources and that returning control to state governments would promote diversity. States would be free to experiment with alternative ways to confront their problems. Another view often attributed to conservatives is that the national government is too remote, too tied to special interests, and not responsive to the public at large. The national government over-regulates and tries to promote too much uniformity. States, on the other hand, are closer to the people and better able to respond to specific local needs.

In contrast, pundits and scholars often argue that what conservatives hope for, liberals fear. Liberals remember, so the argument goes, that the states' rights model allowed political and social inequalities and supported racism. Blacks and city dwellers were often left virtually unrepresented by white state legislators, who disproportionately served rural interests. Liberals believe the states remain unwilling to protect the rights or provide for the needs of their citizens, whether those citizens are consumers seeking protection from business interests, defendants requiring guarantees of due process of law, or poor people seeking a minimum standard of living.

Recent presidencies provide evidence in support of these generalities about liberals and conservatives, but they also indicate that politics and policy are more nuanced than ideology alone could predict. Consider the cases of three Republican presidents.

In 1969, Richard Nixon advocated giving more power to state and local governments. Nixon wanted to decentralize national policies through an effort called *New Federalism.* Nixon's New Federalism called for combining and reformulating categorical grants into block grants. The shift had dramatic implications for federalism. Block grants were seen as a way to redress the imbalance of power between Washington and the states and localities. New Federalism was nothing more than dual federalism in modern dress.

Ronald Reagan took office in 1981. Reagan promised a "new New Federalism" to restore a proper constitutional relationship between the national, state, and local governments. The national government, he said, treated "elected state and local officials as if they were nothing more than administrative agents for federal authority."[27]

Reagan's commitment to reducing federal taxes and spending meant that the states would have to foot an increasing share of the bill for government services (see Figure 3.2). In the late 1970s, the national government funded up to 23 percent of all state and local government spending. By the late 1980s, its contribution had declined

FIGURE 3.2   The National Government's Contribution to State and Local Governments

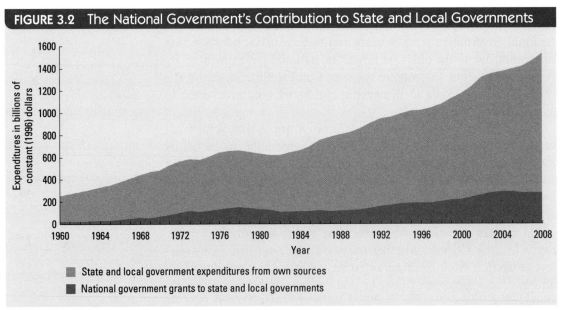

The national government contributes money to the states through grants. While state spending has increased steadily over the last fifty years, the percentage of total state spending contributed by the national government since 1960 has ranged between 8 percent in 1960 and 23 percent in 1978. Though the federal share of state spending dropped to 15 percent during the late 1980s, it crept back up to approximately 20 percent by 2001, where it hovers today.

Source: Calculations from Historical Tables, *Budget of the United States Government,* FY2011, Table 15.2 (adjusted to 2005 dollars).

to less than 15 percent. That figure inched up steadily throughout the Clinton presidency and has hovered around 20 percent since 2001.

When George W. Bush won the White House in 2000, there appeared to develop yet another bend in the nation's federalism road. Generally, Bush, who described himself as a "compassionate conservative," was "notably inattentive to federalism considerations in office," expanding federal authority in areas where Republicans were loathe to tread such as education, prescription drug coverage, and driver's licenses.[28]

Ideology, Policymaking, and Federalism in Practice

Despite the apparent consistencies between presidential preferences regarding federalism and refrains such as "liberals love the national government" and "conservatives favor states' rights," these simplifications are often misleading. To grasp the differences between conservatives and liberals, one has to understand not only these general labels but also the purposes of government under discussion. Consider an example from the debates over the federal preemption of state power.

National Intervention in State Functions. The power of Congress to enact laws that have the national government assume total or partial responsibility for a state government function is called **preemption**.[29] When the national government shoulders a new government function, it restricts the discretionary power of the states. Congressional prohibition of state or local taxation of the Internet is an example of complete preemption.[30] It represents a loss of billions of dollars to state and local governments. Partial preemption occurs with the enactment of minimum national standards that states must meet if they wish to regulate the field. The Do Not Call Implementation Act of 2003 is an example of partial preemption. States retained authority to regulate telemarketing provided they met the minimum standards spelled out by the act.[31]

Congressional preemption statutes infringe on state powers in two ways: through mandates and restraints. A **mandate** is a requirement that a state undertake an activity or provide a service in keeping with minimum national standards. A mandate might require that states remove specified pollutants from public drinking water supplies. In contrast, a **restraint** forbids state government from exercising a certain power. A restraint might prohibit states from dumping sewage into the ocean.

preemption
The power of Congress to enact laws by which the national government assumes total or partial responsibility for a state government function.

mandate
A requirement that a state undertake an activity or provide a service in keeping with minimum national standards.

restraint
A requirement laid down by act of Congress prohibiting a state or local government from exercising a certain power.

Label Me

Food labeling follows a single national standard today as a result of the Nutrition Labeling and Education Act of 1990. The act preempted states from imposing different labeling requirements.

(© Sarah-Maria Vischer/The Image Works)

Nutrition Facts
Serving Size ¾ cup (31g)
Servings Per Container about 11

Amount Per Serving	Cinnamon Toast Crunch	with ½ cup skim milk
Calories	130	170
Calories from Fat	30	30
	% Daily Value**	
Total Fat 3g*	**5%**	**5%**
Saturated Fat 0.5g	**2%**	**2%**
Trans Fat 0g		
Polyunsaturated Fat 0.5g		
Monounsaturated Fat 2g		
Cholesterol 0mg	**0%**	**1%**
Sodium 220mg	**9%**	**12%**
Potassium 45mg	**1%**	**7%**
Total Carbohydrate 25g	**8%**	**10%**
Dietary Fiber 1g	**4%**	**4%**
Sugars 10g		
Other Carbohydrate 14g		
Protein 1g		
Vitamin A	10%	15%
Vitamin C	10%	10%
Calcium	10%	25%
Iron	25%	25%
Vitamin D	10%	25%
Thiamin	25%	30%
Riboflavin	25%	35%
Niacin	25%	25%
Vitamin B$_6$	25%	25%
Folic Acid	25%	25%
Vitamin B$_{12}$	25%	35%
Phosphorus	4%	15%
Magnesium	2%	6%
Zinc	25%	30%
Copper	2%	2%

* Amount in cereal. A serving of cereal plus skim milk provides 3g total fat, less than 5mg cholesterol, 280mg sodium, 250mg potassium, 30g total carbohydrate (16g sugars) and 5g protein.
** Percent Daily Values are based on a 2,000 calorie diet. Your daily values may be higher or lower depending on your calorie needs:

	Calories	2,000	2,500
Total Fat	Less than	65g	80g
Sat Fat	Less than	20g	25g
Cholesterol	Less than	300mg	300mg
Sodium	Less than	2,400mg	2,400mg
Potassium		3,500mg	3,500mg
Total Carbohydrate		300g	375g
Dietary Fiber		25g	30g

coercive federalism
A view that the national government may impose its policy preferences on the states through regulations in the form of mandates and restraints.

Preemption is a modern power. Congress passed only twenty-nine preemptive acts before 1900. In the ensuing sixty years, Congress had preempted the power of states to legislate in certain areas an additional 153 times. The pace of preemption has accelerated. By 2000, or in just forty years, Congress enacted an additional 329 preemption statutes.[32] From 2001 to 2005, 64 new laws preempted state authority.[33] The vast majority of these recent preemption efforts were partial preemptions dealing with terrorism or environmental protection.

The increased use of preemption has given birth to a new theory of federalism. The pressure to expand national power inherent in cooperative federalism has reduced the national government's reliance on fiscal tools such as grants-in-aid. Instead, the national government has come to rely on regulatory tools such as mandates and restraints to assure the supremacy of federal policy. According to this view, cooperative federalism has morphed into **coercive federalism**.[34]

Constraining Unfunded Mandates. State and local government officials have long voiced strong objections to the national government's practice of imposing requirements on the states without providing the financial support needed to satisfy them. By 1992, more than 170 congressional acts had established partially or wholly unfunded mandates.[35] One of the early results of the Republican-led 104th Congress (1995–1997) was the Unfunded Mandates Relief Act of 1995. The legislation requires the Congressional Budget Office to prepare cost estimates of any proposed national legislation that would impose more than $50 million a year in costs on state and local governments or more than $100 million a year in costs on private business. It also requires a cost analysis of the impact of agency regulations.

Many mandates have fallen outside the precise contours of the Relief Act. Although it is likely that the cost estimates have served to temper or withdraw some mandates, the Relief Act has acted merely as a "speed bump," slowing down others rather than deterring new efforts at regulation.[36] (It is important to note that the law does not apply to legislation protecting constitutional rights and civil rights or to antidiscrimination laws.)

The act's critics argue that large proportions of state appropriation budgets still must cover the costs of programs imposed by the national government. The National Conference of State Legislatures estimated, for example, that Real ID—a federally mandated program that imposes security, authentication, and issuance standards upon states when issuing driver's licenses and identification cards—will cost $11 billion through 2012.[37] Since 2004, the national government has passed along more than $130 billion worth of unfunded mandates to the states.[38]

If Republicans were expecting a return of powers to the states during the presidency of George W. Bush, then they were likely disappointed. On his watch, the national government increased its power over the states. Through coercive federalism, the national government now calls the tune for still more activities that were once the sole province of individual states.

Federalism and Electoral Politics

While federalism affects the shape of American public policy, it also plays a significant role in electoral politics. We will have much more to say about elections in Chapter 6. For now, we focus on the ways that federalism is related to the outcome of state and national elections.

National Capital–State Capital Links

State capitals often serve as proving grounds for politicians who aspire to national office. After gaining experience in a state legislature or serving in a statewide elected position (governor or attorney general, for example), elected officials frequently draw on that experience in making a pitch for service in the U.S. House, Senate, or even the White House. The role that state political experience can play in making a run for the presidency seems to have become increasingly important in recent decades. Consider that four of the last six candidates who were elected to the highest office in the land, a period dating back to 1976, had formerly served as governors: Jimmy Carter (Georgia), Ronald Reagan (California), Bill Clinton (Arkansas), and George W. Bush (Texas). George H. W. Bush and Barack Obama are the exceptions to this otherwise long streak.

It is hard to underestimate the value of previous political experience in attempting to mount a campaign for national office. In addition to simply learning the craft of being a politician, experience in state politics can be critically important for helping a candidate to build up a network of contacts, staunch constituents, and potential fundraisers. Past governors also have the benefit of being plugged into organizations such as the National Governors Association and the Republican and Democratic governors' groups, which can help to cultivate national-level name recognition, friendships, and a reputation in Washington. Finally, considering that presidential elections are really a series of fifty different state-level contests, given the structure of the electoral college, a candidate for the White House can benefit tremendously from a friendly governor who can call into action his or her own political network on the candidate's behalf.

Congressional Redistricting

Perhaps even more important than activities on the campaign trail is the decennial process of congressional redistricting, which reveals crucial connections between federalism and the nation's electoral politics. Most generally, **redistricting** refers to the process of redrawing boundaries for electoral jurisdictions. This process occurs at all levels of government, and becomes an extremely high-stakes game in the two years after each decennial national census in the United States. During that window of time, the U.S. Census Bureau produces and releases updated population counts for the nation. Those figures are used to determine the number of seats that each state will have in the U.S. House, which are apportioned based on population.

redistricting
The process of redrawing boundaries for electoral jurisdictions.

While it is relatively straightforward to determine how many seats each state will have, where the new district lines will be drawn is a complicated and highly political affair. Even in states that may not have lost or gained seats due to population shifts within a state–some areas grow at a rapid rate, while others lose population, for example–the task of redistricting carries huge stakes. In large part, this is because state legislatures typically have the task of drawing the lines that define the congressional districts in their states. Given that this process happens only once every ten years and because the careers of U.S. House members and their party's relatively long-term fortunes in Congress can turn on decisions made in these state-level political debates, it is no wonder that the redistricting process commands significant national attention.

Another way that federalism can influence redistricting is through a process called *preclearance*. Under Section 5 of the Voting Rights Act, several states are required to submit their redistricting plans to the U.S. Department of Justice for approval. The process is quite complicated, but in essence it requires that states show how their proposed plans will not be "retrogressive in purpose or effect," meaning they will not dilute minority voting strength. Passing the test of preclearance, however, does not mean that a state's redistricting plans cannot be challenged for civil rights purposes or other grounds as defined in federal law and court decisions, such as rulings affirming the one person–one vote principle.

In short, both the politics of drawing congressional boundaries and the interactions between Justice Department officials and state legislators responsible for preclearance reveal the intimate connections between federalism and the redistricting process.[39]

Federalism and the American Intergovernmental System

We have concentrated in this chapter on the roles the national and state governments play in shaping the federal system. Although the Constitution explicitly recognizes only national and state governments, the American federal system has spawned a multitude of local governments as well. A 2007 census counted over eighty-nine thousand.[40] It is worth considering these units because they help to illustrate the third main principle we outlined near the beginning of this chapter: a growing recognition among public figures and citizens that public problems cut across governmental boundaries.

Americans are citizens of both nation and state, but they also come under the jurisdiction of various local government units. These units include **municipal governments**, the governments of

municipal governments
The government unit that administers a city or town.

Whose Rules?

Grand Staircase–Escalante National Monument in southern Utah was established by presidential decree in 1996. It sits on 1.7 million acres of austere and rugged land. The decree irked local residents, who had hoped for greater industrial development, which is now barred. They have fought back by claiming ownership of hundreds of miles of dirt roads, dry washes, and riverbeds in the monument. The conflicting signs illustrate the controversy. On the left, the local government, Kane County, approves use of all-terrain vehicles. On the right, the national government signals just the opposite.

(Kevin Moloney/The New York Times/Redux)

county government
The government unit that administers a county.

school district
An area for which a local government unit administers elementary and secondary school programs.

special district
A government unit created to perform particular functions, especially when those functions are best performed across jurisdictional boundaries.

cities and towns. Municipalities, in turn, are located in (or may contain or share boundaries with) counties, which are administered by **county governments**. (Sixteen states further divide counties into townships.) Most Americans also live in a **school district**, which is responsible for administering local elementary and secondary educational programs. They also may be served by one or more **special districts**, government units created to perform particular functions, typically when those functions—such as fire protection and water purification and distribution—are best performed across jurisdictional boundaries. All of these local governments are created by state governments, either in their constitutions or through legislation.

In theory, at least, one benefit of localizing government is that it brings government close to the people; it gives them an opportunity to participate in the political process, to have a direct impact on policy. From this perspective, overlapping governments appear compatible with a majoritarian view of democracy.

The reality is somewhat different, however. In fact, voter turnout in local contests tends to be very low, even though the impact of individual votes is much greater. Furthermore, the fragmentation of powers, functions, and responsibilities among national, state, and local governments makes government as a whole seem complicated and hence incomprehensible and inaccessible to ordinary people. In addition, most people have little time to devote to public affairs. These factors tend to discourage individual citizens from pursuing politics and, in turn, enhance the influence of organized groups, which have the resources—time, money, and know-how—to sway policymaking (see Chapter 7). Instead of bringing government closer to the people and reinforcing majoritarian democracy, then, the system's complexity tends to encourage pluralism.

The large number of governments also makes it possible for government at some level to respond to the diversity of conditions that prevail in different parts of the country. States and cities differ enormously in population, size, economic resources, climate, and other characteristics. Smaller political units are better able to respond to particular local conditions and can generally do so more quickly than larger units. Smaller units, however, may not be able to muster the economic resources to meet some challenges. Consequently, in a growing number of areas, citizens have come to see the advantages of coordinating efforts and sharing burdens across levels of government.

Supreme Court Justice Anthony Kennedy once observed that "federalism was our Nation's own discovery. The Framers split the atom of sovereignty. It was the genius of their idea that our citizens would have two political capacities, one state and one federal, each protected from incursion by the other."[41]

Federalism and Pluralism

Our federal system of government was designed to allay citizens' fears that they might be ruled by a majority in a distant region with whom they did not necessarily agree or share interests. By recognizing the legitimacy of the states as political divisions, the federal system also recognized the importance of diversity. The existence and cultivation of diverse interests are hallmarks of pluralism.

Both of the main competing theories of federalism support pluralism, but in somewhat different ways. The layer-cake approach of dual federalism aims to decentralize government, shifting power to the states. It recognizes the importance of local rather than national standards and applauds the diversity of those standards. The variety allows the people at least a choice of policies under which to live, if not a direct voice in policymaking.

In contrast, the marble cake of cooperative federalism is perfectly willing to override local standards for national ones depending on the issue at stake. Yet this view of federalism, while more amenable to national prerogatives, is highly responsive to all manner of pressures from groups and policy entrepreneurs, including pressure at one level of government from those unsuccessful at other levels. By blurring the lines of national and state responsibility, this kind of federalism encourages petitioners to try their luck at whichever level of government offers them the best chance of success.

Tying It Together

1. What is federalism, and what theories and metaphors help to explain it?
   - Federalism is a political model for government in which power is divided between a central government and regional governments.
   - Dual federalism defines the relationship between the national government and the states.
     - This concept is illustrated by the layer-cake metaphor.
     - Each governmental unit is sovereign within its sphere.
     - The relationship between nation and state is characterized by tension rather than cooperation.
   - Cooperative federalism presumes that national and state agencies work together and share power and that this power is fragmented.
     - This concept is illustrated by the marble-cake metaphor.
     - Cooperative federalism blurs the distinction between national and state governments.

2. What forces prompt change in the relationships between national and state governments?
   - Congress has increased national power during times of crisis and national emergency.

- The Supreme Court settles disputes regarding the balance of power between the states and national government.
- The national government often uses financial incentives (e.g., grants-in-aid) to persuade states to act in desired ways.
- State governments have increased their abilities by making internal changes, holding more legislative sessions, attracting more qualified people, and hiring better-educated administrators.

3. How do views about American federalism influence politics and policy?
   - Conservatives are often associated with the layer-cake metaphor, believing in clear divisions of power between state and national government.
   - Liberals usually prefer the marble-cake view, believing in overlapping powers between state and national government.
   - Conflicting views on federalism persist.
   - In practice, the national government
     - takes over responsibility for state functions by preemption.
     - issues a mandate to require states to act in a particular way.
     - limits the use of state power by issuing a restraint.
     - uses funding as a means to control the states.

4. How is federalism related to the outcome of state and local elections?
   - State governments act as proving grounds for politicians who want to achieve national recognition and office.
   - Redistricting can change political careers through changes in district size and location of voting districts.

5. How do citizens interact with the intergovernmental system?
   - Americans are citizens of both the nation and their state.
   - Americans are also under the jurisdiction of local governments. These governments include municipal, county, school, and special districts.
   - Fragmentation can make government seem complex, leading to a lack of participation that reinforces pluralism.
   - The large number of governments allows for responsiveness at some level, which benefits citizens.

6. How does federalism promote pluralism?
   - By recognizing the legitimacy of the state, the federal system recognizes diversity, which promotes pluralism.
   - The layer-cake model of federalism shifts power to the states, which gives people choice according to local needs.
   - The marble-cake model is highly responsive to special interests.

Theories and Metaphors

True or False?
1. Federalism divides and balances the power between the fifty state governments so one does not become more powerful than another.
2. Dual federalism emphasizes the elastic clause and the implied powers of Congress.
3. In marble-cake federalism, the powers of states are strictly separate from those of the national government.

Comprehension
4. Why is an expansive view of the supremacy clause so important to cooperative federalism?
5. What two sections of the Constitution differentiate *dual federalism* and *cooperative federalism,* and how do they do so?

The Dynamics of Federalism

True or False?
1. The two general forms of grants-in-aid are block grants and categorical grants.
2. Since the New Deal, the Supreme Court has consistently sided with the states in questions of federalism and the balance of power.
3. State governments are more capable policy actors now than they were before 1960.

Comprehension
4. How has the Supreme Court's interpretation of the commerce clause increased national power?
5. Give an example of the use of the elastic clause during a national crisis.

Ideology, Policymaking, and American Federalism

True or False?
1. The national government sends a substantially smaller percentage of the national budget to the state today than it did in the 1960s.
2. President Jimmy Carter wanted to decentralize national policies with *New Federalism.*
3. The national government can issue a mandate to the states only if it provides necessary funding for that mandate.

Comprehension
4. What arguments do conservatives use to keep power in the hands of the states?
5. Explain how political ideology is related to federalism in theory and in practice.

Federalism and Electoral Politics

True or False?

1. Candidates for national office don't really benefit from experience gained in state office because state and national governments have completely different functions.
2. Redistricting refers to redrawing electoral jurisdictions.
3. Redistricting occurs prior to each congressional election.

Comprehension

4. What are three advantages of previous political experience when running for office?
5. How does the process of preclearance illustrate the tensions inherent in federalism?

Federalism and the American Intergovernmental System

True or False?

1. Municipal government is a synonym for state government.
2. Special districts are set up by state governments to oversee particular activities that often occur across jurisdictional boundaries.
3. Voter turnout tends to be higher in local elections because the impact of local elections is greater on the everyday lives of voters.

Comprehension

4. How does the large number of different governments help politicians to be more responsive?
5. Describe a weakness of smaller government units mentioned in this section of your textbook.

Federalism and Pluralism

True or False?

1. The layer-cake analogy of dual federalism aims to decentralize government and shift power to the states.
2. Marble cake federalism allows individuals and interest groups to petition officials at whichever level of government offers them the best chance of success.

Comprehension

3. How do both of the cake models of federalism support pluralism?
4. Who do you feel is responsible for responding to disasters such as the H1N1 flu: the local, state, or national government?

CourseMate CL Resources:

Visit www.cengagebrain.com/shop/ISBN/1111832587 for flashcards, web quizzes, videos and more!

Public Opinion, Political Socialization, and the Media

Justyna Furmanczyk/Shutterstock.com

FOCUS QUESTIONS

1. What is public opinion, how is it collected, and what is its place in the two models of democracy?
2. How are political values formed?
3. How do the social backgrounds of individuals influence their opinions?
4. To what degree do people's opinions on specific issues reflect their political ideologies?
5. Apart from ideology, what other factors influence public opinion?
6. How do the media promote two-way communication between government and its citizens?
7. Where do citizens acquire political knowledge, and what role do the media play in this process?
8. What influence do the media have over democratic government and its objectives?

On December 8, 2009, the state of Ohio executed Kenneth Biros in a novel way. Condemned to death for his 1991 crime—brutally raping and murdering a woman—Biros was injected with a massive dose of barbiturate. The single drug replaced the typical three-drug execution cocktail: sodium pentothal to produce unconsciousness, pancuronium bromide to cause paralysis, and potassium chloride to stop the heart.[1] The cocktail or some variant has been used in over one thousand lethal injections in thirty-six states since the late 1970s.[2]

Lethal injection was adopted as a more humane method of execution than alternatives (e.g., electrocution, hanging), but the three drugs can be difficult to administer. Three months earlier, in fact, Ohio failed to execute Romell Broom (convicted of abduction, rape, and murder of a 14-year-old girl) after sticking him with a needle for nearly two hours, unable to find a usable vein.[3] Two Kentucky inmates had contended that the method constituted cruel and unusual punishment, outlawed by the Constitution, but the Supreme Court ruled 7 to 2 against them in April 2008.[4]

Two months later, however, an Ohio judge ruled that stricter Ohio law required "avoidance of any unnecessary risk of pain" in executions and struck down the cocktail method.[5] After the December one-drug injection produced no complications, Ohio used it again on January 7, 2010, executing Vernon Smith for killing a shopkeeper in a 1993 robbery. Experts expected that other states would soon adopt the Ohio model.[6]

The death penalty is very popular in the United States, regularly backed over several decades two to one in national surveys.[7] Nevertheless, it is outlawed in two-thirds of the world's countries, including *every* other major Western democracy.[8] In 2008, 93 percent of all executions were carried out in only five nations—China, Iran, Saudi Arabia, Pakistan, and the United States[9]— putting us in uncomfortable company. Since the 1990s, however, death sentences have declined in the United States, and in 2011 Illinois became the sixteenth state to repeal the death penalty—in part due to high costs of litigation.[10]

We can learn much about the role of public opinion in America by reviewing how our government has punished violent criminals. During most of American history, government execution of people who threatened the social order was legal. In colonial times, capital punishment was imposed not just for murder but also for antisocial behavior— denying the "true" God, cursing one's parents, committing adultery, practicing witchcraft, even being a rebellious child.[11] Over the years, writers, editors, and clergy argued for abolishing the death sentence, and a few states responded by eliminating capital punishment. But the outbreak of World War I fed the public's fear of foreigners and radicals, leading to renewed support for the death penalty. The security needs of World War II and the postwar fears of Soviet communism fueled continued support for capital punishment.

After anticommunist hysteria subsided in the late 1950s, public opposition to the death penalty increased. But public opinion was neither strong enough nor stable enough to force state legislatures to outlaw it. In keeping with the pluralist model of democracy, efforts to abolish the death penalty shifted from the legislative arena to the courts. The opponents argued that the death penalty is cruel and unusual punishment and is therefore unconstitutional. Their argument apparently had some effect on public opinion: in 1966, a plurality of respondents opposed the death penalty for the first (and only) time since the Gallup Organization began polling the public on the question of capital punishment.

The states responded to this shift in public opinion by reducing the number of executions, until they stopped completely in 1968 in anticipation of a Supreme Court decision. By then, however, public opinion had again reversed in favor of capital punishment. Nevertheless, in 1972, the Court ruled in a 5–4 decision that the death penalty as imposed by existing state laws was unconstitutional.[12] The decision was not well received in many states, and thirty-five state legislatures passed new laws to get around the ruling. Meanwhile, as the nation's homicide rate increased, public approval of the death penalty jumped almost ten points and continued climbing.

In 1976, the Supreme Court changed its position and upheld three new state laws that let judges consider the defendant's record and the nature of the crime in deciding whether to impose a sentence of death.[13] The Court also rejected the argument that punishment by death violates the Constitution and noted that public opinion favors the death penalty. Through the end of the 1970s, however, only three criminals were executed. Eventually, the states began to heed public concern about the crime rate. Over one thousand executions have taken place since the 1976 Supreme Court ruling.[14]

Although public support for the death penalty remains high, Americans are divided on the issue. A majority of white Americans favor the death penalty for a person convicted of murder, while a majority of African Americans oppose the death penalty.[15] Conservatives are more likely to support the death penalty than liberals. Eighty-one percent of all Republicans favor the death penalty, whereas only 48 percent of all Democrats do. Many Americans are concerned that innocent persons have been executed.[16] Indeed, since 1973, over 135 death row inmates have been exonerated of their crimes by new evidence such as DNA testing.[17]

The history of public thinking on the death penalty reveals several characteristics of public opinion:

- *The public's attitudes toward a given government policy can vary over time, often dramatically.* Opinions about capital punishment tend to fluctuate with threats to the social order. The public is more likely to favor capital punishment in times of war and when fears of foreign subversion and crime rates are high.
- *Public opinion places boundaries on allowable types of public policy.* Stoning or beheading criminals is not acceptable to the American public (and surely not to courts interpreting the Constitution). Until recently, administering a lethal injection to a murderer was not controversial.[18]
- *If asked by pollsters, citizens are willing to register opinions on matters outside their expertise.* People clearly believe execution by lethal injection is more humane than electrocution, asphyxiation in the gas chamber, or hanging. But how can the public know enough about execution to make these judgments?
- *Governments tend to respond to public opinion.* State laws for and against capital punishment have reflected swings in the public mood. The Supreme Court's 1972 decision against capital punishment came when public opinion on the death penalty was sharply divided; the Court's approval of capital punishment in 1976 coincided with a rise in public approval of the death penalty.
- *The government sometimes does not do what the people want.* Although public opinion overwhelmingly favors the death penalty for murder, there were only forty-six executions in 2010 (but there were fourteen thousand murders that year).[19]

The last two conclusions bear on our discussion of the majoritarian and pluralist models of democracy discussed in Chapter 1. Here we probe more deeply into the nature, shape, depth, and formation of public opinion in a democratic government. What is the place of public opinion in a democracy? How do people acquire their opinions? What are the major lines of division in public opinion? How do individuals' ideology and knowledge affect their opinions?

Public Opinion and the Models of Democracy

Public opinion is simply the collective attitudes of the citizens on a given issue or question. Opinion polling, which involves interviewing a random sample of citizens to estimate public opinion as a whole, is such a common feature of contemporary life that we often forget it is a modern invention, dating only from the 1930s (see Figure 4.1). In fact, survey methodology did not develop into a powerful research tool until the advent of computers in the 1950s.

Before polling became an accepted part of the American scene, politicians, journalists, and everyone else could argue about what the people wanted, but no one really knew. Today, sampling methods and opinion polling have altered the debate about the majoritarian and pluralist models of democracy. Now that we know how often government policy runs against majority opinion, it becomes harder to defend the U.S. government as democratic under the majoritarian model. Even at a time when Americans overwhelmingly favored the death penalty for murderers, the Supreme Court decided that existing state laws applying capital punishment were unconstitutional. Even after the Court approved new state laws as constitutional, relatively few murderers were actually executed.

The two models of democracy make different assumptions about public opinion. The majoritarian model assumes that a majority of the people hold clear, consistent opinions on government policy. The pluralist model assumes that the public is often uninformed and ambivalent about specific issues, and opinion polls frequently support that claim. What are the bases of public opinion? What principles, if any, do people use to organize their beliefs and attitudes about politics? Exactly how do individuals form their political opinions? We look for answers to these questions in this chapter. In later chapters, we assess the effect of public opinion on government policies. The results should help you make up your own mind about the viability of the majoritarian and pluralist models in a functioning democracy.

public opinion
The collected attitudes of citizens concerning a given issue or question.

political socialization
The complex process by which people acquire their political values.

Political Socialization

Public opinion is grounded in political values. People acquire their values through **political socialization**, a complex process through which individuals become aware of politics, learn political facts,

FIGURE 4.1 Gallup Poll Accuracy

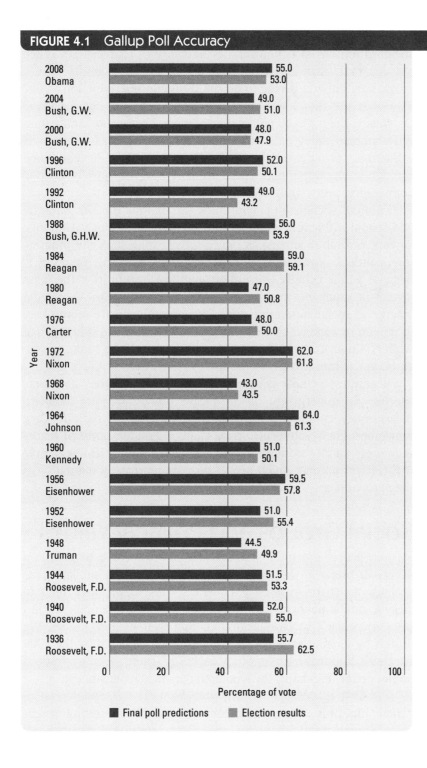

Year	Final poll predictions	Election results
2008 Obama	55.0	53.0
2004 Bush, G.W.	49.0	51.0
2000 Bush, G.W.	48.0	47.9
1996 Clinton	52.0	50.1
1992 Clinton	49.0	43.2
1988 Bush, G.H.W.	56.0	53.9
1984 Reagan	59.0	59.1
1980 Reagan	47.0	50.8
1976 Carter	48.0	50.0
1972 Nixon	62.0	61.8
1968 Nixon	43.0	43.5
1964 Johnson	64.0	61.3
1960 Kennedy	51.0	50.1
1956 Eisenhower	59.5	57.8
1952 Eisenhower	51.0	55.4
1948 Truman	44.5	49.9
1944 Roosevelt, F.D.	51.5	53.3
1940 Roosevelt, F.D.	52.0	55.0
1936 Roosevelt, F.D.	55.7	62.5

Percentage of vote

■ Final poll predictions ■ Election results

One of the nation's oldest polls was started by George Gallup in the 1930s. The accuracy of the Gallup Poll in predicting presidential elections over seventy years is charted here. Although it is not always on the mark, its predictions have been fairly close to election results. The poll was most notably wrong in 1948, when it predicted that Thomas Dewey, the Republican candidate, would defeat the Democratic incumbent, Harry Truman, underestimating Truman's vote by 5.4 percentage points. In 1992, the Gallup Poll was off by an even larger margin, but this time it did identify the winner, Bill Clinton. Gallup's final prediction for the 2000 election declared the race "too close to call." Indeed, the race in the electoral college remained too close to call for weeks after the election.

and form political values. Think for a moment about your political socialization. What is your earliest memory of a president? When did you first learn about political parties? If you identify with a party, how did you decide to do so? If you do not, why don't you? Who was the first liberal you ever met? The first conservative? Obviously, the paths to political awareness, knowledge, and values differ among individuals, but most people are exposed to the same influences, or agents of socialization, especially in childhood through young adulthood. These influences include family, school, community, peers, and, of course, television.

Political socialization continues throughout life. As parental and school influences wane in adulthood, peer groups (neighbors, coworkers, club members) assume a greater importance in promoting political awareness and developing political opinions.[20] Because adults usually learn about political events from the mass media—newspapers, magazines, television, and radio—the media emerge as socialization agents.[21] Older Americans are more likely to rely on newspaper and television news for political information, while younger Americans are more likely to turn to radio, magazines, or the Internet.[22]

Regardless of how people learn about politics, they gain perspective on government as they grow older. They are likely to measure new candidates (and new ideas) against the old ones they remember. Their values also may change. Finally, political learning comes simply through exposure and familiarity. One example is the act of voting, which people do with increasing regularity as they grow older.

Social Groups and Political Values

No two people are influenced by precisely the same socialization agents in precisely the same way. Still, people with similar backgrounds do share learning experiences; this means they tend to develop similar political opinions. In this section, we examine the ties between people's social backgrounds and their political values. We do this by looking at responses to two questions posed by the 2008 American National Election Study (ANES).[23] These specific questions do not define or exhaust the typology; they merely illustrate it.

The first question deals with abortion. The interviewer said, "There has been some discussion about abortion during recent years. Which opinion on this page best agrees with your view? You can just tell me the number of the opinion you choose":

1. "By law, abortion should never be permitted" [15 percent agreed].
2. "The law should permit abortion only in case of rape, incest, or when the woman's life is in danger" [27 percent].
3. "The law should permit abortion for reasons other than rape, incest, or danger to the woman's life, but only after the need for the abortion has been clearly established" [18 percent].
4. "By law, a woman should be able to obtain an abortion as a matter of personal choice" [40 percent].[24]

Those who chose the last category most clearly valued individual freedom over order imposed by government. Moreover, evidence shows that the pro-choice respondents also have concerns about broader issues of social order, such as the role of women and the legitimacy of alternative lifestyles.[25]

The second question pertained to the role of government in guaranteeing employment:

> Some people feel the government in Washington should see to it that every person has a job and a good standard of living. Suppose that these people are at one end of the scale. . . . Others think the government should just let each person get ahead on his own. Suppose these people are at the other end. . . . Where would you put yourself on this scale, or haven't you thought much about this?

Excluding those people who "haven't thought much" about this question, 31 percent of the respondents wanted government to provide every person with a living, and 20 percent were undecided. That left 49 percent who wanted the government to let people "get ahead" on their own. These respondents, who opposed government efforts to promote equality, apparently valued freedom over equality.

Overall, the responses to each of these questions were divided approximately equally. Somewhat more than half of the respondents (58 percent) felt that government should not broadly prohibit abortion, and just short of a majority (49 percent) thought the government should not guarantee everyone a job and a good standard of living. However, sharp differences in attitudes emerged for both issues when the respondents were grouped by socioeconomic factors: education, income, region, race, religion, and sex. The differences are shown in Figure 4.2 as positive and negative deviations from the national averages for each question.

Bars that extend to the right identify groups that are more likely than most Americans to sacrifice freedom for a given value of government, either equality or order. Next, we examine the opinion patterns more closely for each socioeconomic group.

Education

Education increases people's awareness and understanding of political issues. Higher education also promotes tolerance of unpopular opinions and behavior and invites citizens to see issues in terms of civil rights and liberties.[26] This result is clear in the left-hand column of Figure 4.2, which shows that people with less education are more likely to support restrictions on abortion while people with more education are more likely to view abortion as a matter of a woman's choice.[27] When confronted with a choice between personal freedom and social order, college-educated individuals tend to choose freedom.

With regard to the role of government in reducing income inequality, the right-hand column in Figure 4.2 shows that people with less education favor government action to guarantee jobs. Those with more education tend to oppose government action, favoring freedom over equality.

Income

In many countries, differences in social class, based on social background and occupation, divide people in their politics.[28] In the United States, the vast majority of citizens regard themselves as "middle class." Yet as Figure 4.2 shows, wealth is consistently linked to opinions favoring a limited government role in equality and less consistently to opinions about order. Those with lower incomes are more likely to favor government guarantees of employment and living conditions. Those with incomes under $60,000 also favor outlawing abortion more than those earning over $60,000. Wealth and education tend to have a similar impact on opinion: the groups with more education and higher income prefer freedom to order or equality.

Region

Early in our country's history, regional differences were politically important—important enough to spark a civil war between North and South. For nearly 100 years after the Civil War, regional differences continued to affect American politics. The moneyed Northeast was

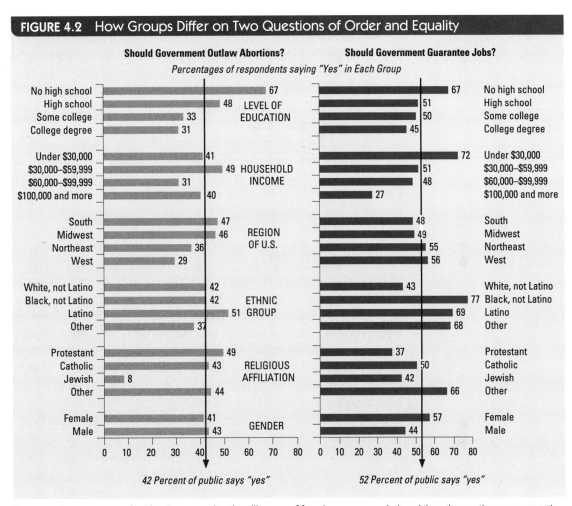

FIGURE 4.2 How Groups Differ on Two Questions of Order and Equality

Two questions—one on abortion (representing the dilemma of freedom versus order) and the other on the government's role in guaranteeing employment (freedom versus equality)—were asked of a national sample in 2008. Public opinion for the nation as a whole was sharply divided on each question. These two graphs show how respondents in several social groups responded to each question. The vertical lines indicate overall public opinion for the two questions.

Source: Data from *2008 American National Election Study,* undertaken in collaboration by Stanford University and the University of Michigan.

thought to control the purse strings of capitalism. The Midwest was long regarded as the stronghold of isolationism in foreign affairs. The South was practically a one-party region, almost completely Democratic. And the individualistic West pioneered its own mixture of progressive politics.

In the past, differences in wealth fed cultural differences between regions. In recent decades, however, the movement of people and wealth away from the Northeast and Midwest to the Sunbelt states in the South and Southwest has equalized the per capita income of the regions. One product of this equalization is that the "solid South" is no longer solidly Democratic.[29] In fact, the South has tended to vote for Republican candidates for president since 1968, and the majority of southern members of Congress are now Republicans.

Figure 4.2 shows differences among the four major regions of the United States on social and economic issues. Respondents in the South and Midwest were more likely to support restrictions on abortion. However, people in the Northeast and West were more supportive of government efforts to equalize income.

Race and Ethnicity

In the early twentieth century, the major ethnic minority groups in America were immigrants from Ireland, Italy, Germany, Poland, and other European countries. They came to the United States in waves during the late 1800s and early 1900s and found themselves in a strange land, usually without money and unable to speak English. Moreover, their religious backgrounds, mainly Catholic and Jewish, differed from that of the predominantly Protestant earlier settlers. These urban ethnics and their descendants became part of the great coalition of Democratic voters that President Franklin Roosevelt forged in the 1930s. And for years after, the European ethnics supported liberal candidates and causes more strongly than the original Anglo-Saxon immigrants did.[30]

From the Civil War through the civil rights movement of the 1950s and 1960s, African Americans fought to secure basic political rights such as the right to vote. Initially mobilized by the Republican Party, the party of Lincoln, following the Civil War, African Americans later forged strong ties with the Democratic Party during the New Deal era. Today, African Americans are still more likely to support liberal candidates and identify with the Democratic Party. African Americans make up almost 13 percent of the population, with sizable voting blocs in southern states and northern cities.

Latinos (people of Latin American origin) are commonly but inaccurately referred to as a racial group. The vast majority of Latinos in the United States are white, but there is a notable black Latino population as well. Latinos made up 16 percent of the population in 2010, but the U.S. Census Bureau estimates that they will comprise 23 percent of the population by 2030.[31] Latinos who speak Spanish are also known as Hispanics. At the national level, Latinos have lagged behind African Americans in mobilizing and gaining political office. However, they make up over 45 percent of the population in New Mexico and 37 percent in California and Texas.[32]

Asians account for approximately 5 percent of the population, and Native Americans constitute just over 1 percent. Like other minority groups, their political impact is greatest in the cities or regions where they are concentrated and greater in number. For instance, Asian Americans constitute 39 percent of the population in Hawaii and over 12 percent in California; Native Americans make up 15 percent of the population of Alaska and almost 10 percent of New Mexico.[33]

Members of minority groups display somewhat similar political attitudes on questions pertaining to equality.[34] The reasons are twofold.[35] First, racial minorities (excepting second-generation Asians) tend to have low **socioeconomic status**, a combination of education, occupation, status, and income. Second, all racial minorities have been targets of racial prejudice and discrimination and have benefited from government actions in support of equality. The right-hand column in Figure 4.2 clearly shows the effects of race on the freedom–equality issue. All minority groups, particularly African Americans, are more likely than whites to favor government action to improve economic opportunity. The abortion issue produces less difference, although Latinos favor government restrictions on abortion slightly more than other groups do.

Religion

Since the last major wave of European immigration in the 1930s and 1940s, the religious makeup of the United States has remained fairly stable. Today, 56 percent of the population is Protestant or non-Catholic Christian, about 22 percent is Catholic, less than 2 percent is Jewish, 7 percent reports some other faith, and about 13 percent professes no religion.[36] For many years, analysts found strong and consistent differences in the opinions of Protestants, Catholics, and Jews. Protestants were more conservative than Catholics, and Catholics tended to be more conservative than Jews.

As Figure 4.2 indicates, broad religious groupings have little effect on attitudes about economic equality but more influence on attitudes about social order. Protestants favor government action to limit abortion even more than Catholics. Jews overwhelmingly favor abortion rights. Differences among religious groups have

socioeconomic status
Position in society, based on a combination of education, occupational status, and income.

emerged across many contemporary social and political issues. Differences among religious subgroups are significant. Evangelical Protestants are much more likely than members of other Protestant religious groups to oppose gay marriage and support the death penalty while favoring right-to-life over abortion. Evangelicals and Jews are more likely to express support for Israel in Middle Eastern politics. Religious beliefs have been at the center of national and local debates over issues such as stem cell research, human cloning, and the teaching of evolution or intelligent design as the appropriate explanation for the development of life on Earth.[37]

Word of God?

A person's religiosity may be as important as his or her denominational identification in predicting political opinions. One measure of people's religiosity in a Christian-Judaic society is their opinion about the Bible. When asked about the nature of the Bible in 2008, about 38 percent of respondents said it was the actual word of God. About 44 percent regarded it as inspired by God but believed it should not be taken literally. The remaining 18 percent viewed it as an ancient book of history, legends, fables, and moral precepts recorded by humans. Those who believed that the Bible is the literal word of God strongly favored government action to limit abortion. They were also much more likely to think that "creationism," a theory of the origin and development of life on Earth based on a strict reading of the Bible, should be taught in public schools alongside the theory of evolution.

(Data from the 2008 American National Election Survey. Photo: Stephen Morton/Stringer/Getty Images)

Gender

Men and women differ with respect to their political opinions on a broad array of social and political issues. As shown in the right-hand column of Figure 4.2, women are more likely to favor government actions to promote equality. Women are also consistently more supportive than men of both affirmative action and government spending for social programs. They are consistently less supportive of the death penalty and going to war.[38] Men and women differ less on the abortion issue (see the left-hand column of Figure 4.2). Contemporary party politics is marked by a gender gap: women tend to identify with the Democratic Party more than men do (see Figure 6.2 on page 200). In the 2004 presidential election, 48 percent of the female voters supported Bush's reelection compared to 55 percent of the male voters.[39] A similar gender gap occurred in the 2008 presidential race. While 56 percent of all female voters cast ballots for Barack Obama, only 49 percent of the male voters did so. John McCain received support from 43 percent of the female voters and 48 percent of the male voters.

From Values to Ideology

We have just seen that differences in groups' responses on two survey questions reflect those groups' value choices between freedom and order and between freedom and equality. But to what degree do people's opinions on specific issues reflect explicit political ideology (the set of values and beliefs that they hold about the purpose and scope of government)? Political scientists generally agree that ideology influences public opinion on specific issues; they have much less consensus on the extent to which people explicitly think in ideological terms.[40] They also agree that the public's ideological thinking cannot be categorized adequately in conventional liberal–conservative terms.[41]

The Degree of Ideological Thinking in Public Opinion

Although today's media frequently use the terms *liberal* and *conservative,* some people think these terms are no longer relevant to American politics. Indeed, voters don't tend to use ideological concepts when discussing politics.[42]

In one poll, voters were asked what they thought when someone was described as "liberal" or "conservative."[43] Few responded in explicitly political terms. Rather, most people gave dictionary definitions: "'liberals' are generous (a *liberal* portion). And 'conservatives' are moderate or cautious (a *conservative* estimate)."[44] The two most frequent responses for *conservative* were "fiscally responsible or tight" (17 percent) and "closed-minded" (10 percent). For *liberal,* the top two were "open-minded" (14 percent) and "free-spending" (8 percent). Only about 6 percent of the sample mentioned "degree of government involvement" in describing liberals and conservatives. The tendency to respond to questions by using ideological terms grows with increasing education, which helps people understand political issues and relate them to one another. People's personal political socialization can also lead them to think ideologically.

The Quality of Ideological Thinking in Public Opinion

What people's ideological self-placement means in the twenty-first century is not clear. At one time, the liberal–conservative continuum represented a single dimension: attitudes toward the scope of government activity. Liberals were in favor of more government action to provide public goods, and conservatives were in favor of less. The simple distinction is not as useful today. Many people who call themselves liberals no longer favor government activism in general, and many self-styled conservatives no longer oppose it in principle. Attitudes toward government also depend on which party controls the government.[45] As a result, many people have difficulty deciding whether they are liberal or conservative.

Studies of the public's ideological thinking find that two themes run through people's minds when they are asked to describe liberals and conservatives. First, people associate liberals with change and conservatives with tradition. This theme corresponds to the distinction between liberals and conservatives on the exercise of freedom and the maintenance of order.[46]

The other theme has to do with equality. The conflict between freedom and equality was at the heart of President Roosevelt's New Deal economic policies (social security, minimum wage legislation, farm price supports) in the 1930s. The policies expanded the interventionist role of the national government in order to promote greater economic equality, and attitudes toward government intervention in the economy served to distinguish liberals from conservatives for decades afterward.[47] Attitudes toward government interventionism still underlie opinions about domestic economic policies.[48] Liberals support intervention to promote their ideas of economic equality; conservatives favor less government intervention and more individual freedom in economic activities.

In Chapter 1, we proposed an alternative ideological classification based on people's relative evaluations of freedom, order, and equality. We described liberals as people who believe that government should promote equality, even if some freedom is lost in the process, but who oppose surrendering freedom to government-imposed order. Conservatives do not oppose equality in and of itself but put a higher value on freedom than on equality when the two conflict. Yet conservatives are not above restricting freedom when threatened with the loss of order. So both groups value freedom, but one is more willing to trade freedom for equality, and the other is more inclined to trade freedom for order. If you have trouble thinking about these trade-offs on a single dimension, you are in good company. The liberal–conservative continuum presented to survey respondents takes a two-dimensional concept and squeezes it into a one-dimensional format.[49]

> **IDEALOG.ORG**
>
> How did you answer the questions about abortion and government-guaranteed employment on the self-test?

Ideological Types in the United States

Our ideological typology in Chapter 1 (see Figure 1.2 on page 23) classifies people as Liberals if they favor freedom over order and equality over freedom. (We will use capital letters in this section to signify our ideological classification; lowercase signifies ideological self-placement.) Conversely, Conservatives favor freedom over equality and order over freedom. Libertarians favor freedom over both equality and order—the opposite of Communitarians.[50] By cross-tabulating people's answers to the two questions from the 2008 American National Election Study about freedom versus order (abortion) and freedom versus equality (government job guarantees), we can classify respondents according to their ideological tendencies. As shown in Figure 4.3, a substantial portion of respondents falls within each of the quadrants.* This indicates that people do not decide about government activity according to a one-dimensional ideological continuum. Were that the case, responses to the two questions would cluster diagonally in the Liberal and Conservative boxes.

---

*Remember, however, that these categories—like the letter grades A, B, C, and D for courses—are rigid. The respondents' answers to both questions varied in intensity but were reduced to a simple yes or no to simplify this analysis. Many respondents would cluster toward the center of Figure 4.3 if their attitudes were represented more sensitively.

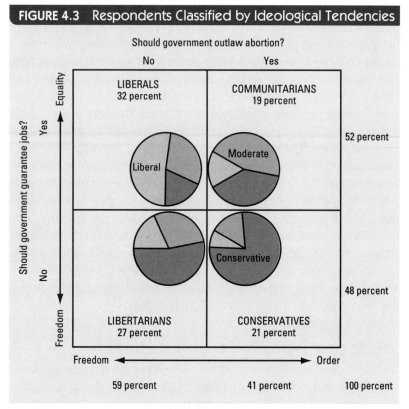

FIGURE 4.3   Respondents Classified by Ideological Tendencies

In the 2008 election survey, respondents were asked whether abortion should be outlawed by government or a matter of personal choice, and whether government should guarantee people a job and a good standard of living or people should get ahead on their own. (The questions are given verbatim at the beginning of the "Social Groups and Political Values" section of this chapter.) These two questions presented choices between freedom and order and between freedom and equality. People's responses to the two questions showed no correlation, demonstrating that these value choices cannot be explained by a simple liberal–conservative continuum. The pie charts in the center show the proportion of each group self-describing themselves as liberal, moderate, or conservative on the traditional one-dimensional scale.

Source: *2008 American National Election Study,* undertaken in collaboration by Stanford University and the University of Michigan.

The Liberal pattern occurred most frequently (32 percent), with the Libertarians next (27 percent) and Conservatives (21 percent) barely outscoring Communitarians (19 percent). Of more interest is the relationship between the pie charts in the figure and the quadrants in which they appear. The pie charts represent the proportion of respondents in the same survey *who described themselves* as liberal, moderate, or conservative.

In Figure 4.3, three-quarters of those we can label Conservatives because of their answers to the questions on order and equality also described *themselves* as conservatives, while more than half of our Liberals were also self-described liberals. In contrast, those we classified as Communitarian or Libertarian according to the order and equality questions showed less consistency in classifying themselves as liberal, moderate, or conservative.

Respondents who easily place themselves on a single dimension running from liberal to conservative often contradict their self-placement when answering questions that trade freedom for either order or equality.[51] A two-dimensional typology such as that in Figure 4.3 allows us to analyze responses more meaningfully.[52] One reason so many Americans classify themselves as conservative on a one-dimensional scale is that they have no option to classify themselves as libertarian.

The ideological typology reflects important differences between social groups. Communitarians are prominent among African Americans and Latinos (33 percent) and among people with no high school degree (42 percent), groups that tend to look favorably on the benefits of government. Regional differences are small among the types, except that 44 percent of respondents in the West score as Liberal. Women tend to be Liberal (38 percent) and men Libertarian (33 percent). Indeed, Libertarians account for 51 percent of men making more than $100,000, who may believe that they have little need for government.

This more refined analysis of political ideology explains why even Americans who pay close attention to politics find it difficult to locate themselves on the liberal–conservative continuum. Their problem is that they are liberal on some issues and conservative on others. Forced to choose along just one dimension, they opt for the middle category: moderate. However, our analysis also indicates that many people who classify themselves as liberals or conservatives do fit these two categories in our typology. There is value, then, in the liberal–conservative distinction, as long as we understand its limitations.

Forming Political Opinions

We have seen that people acquire political values through socialization and that different social groups develop different sets of political values. We also have learned that some people, but only a minority, think about politics ideologically, holding a consistent set of political attitudes and beliefs. But how do those who are not ideologues—in other words, most citizens—form political opinions? How informed are people about politics? What can we say about the quality of public opinion?

Political Knowledge

In the United States today, the level of education is high and media coverage of national and international events is extensive, yet the average American displays an astonishing lack of political knowledge.[53]

In a study of political knowledge, political scientists Delli Carpini and Keeter analyzed approximately 3,700 individual survey items that measured some type of factual knowledge about public affairs.[54] They found that "many of the basic institutions and procedures of government are known to half or more of the public, as are the relative positions of the parties on many major issues."[55] Yet, political knowledge is not randomly distributed within our society. "In particular, women, African Americans, the poor, and the young tend to be substantially less knowledgeable about politics than are men, whites, the affluent, and older citizens."[56] Changing news formats in the past twenty years—the emergence of around the clock cable news and the Internet—do not seem to have increased the level of political knowledge for most Americans.[57] Education is the strongest single predictor of political knowledge.

Researchers have not found any meaningful relationship between political sophistication and self-placement on the liberal-conservative scale—that is, people with equal knowledge about public affairs and levels of conceptualization are as likely to call themselves liberals as conservatives.[58] Nor is there any systematic relationship between Republican and Democratic partisanship and test scores on general political knowledge.[59] However, individuals who strongly believe in certain causes may be impervious to information that questions their beliefs; they may even create false memories that support their beliefs.[60]

Costs, Benefits, and Cues

self-interest principle
The implication that people choose what benefits them personally.

Perhaps people do not think in ideological terms or know a wide variety of political facts, but they can tell whether a policy is likely to directly help or hurt them. The **self-interest principle** states that people choose what benefits them personally.[61] The principle plays an obvious role in how people form opinions on policies with clear costs and benefits. Taxpayers tend to prefer low taxes to high taxes. Smokers tend to oppose bans on smoking in public places. Some people evaluate incumbent presidents according to whether they are better or worse off than they were four years ago. Group leaders often cue group members, telling them what they should support or oppose.[62]

In some cases, individuals are unable to determine personal costs or benefits. This tends to be true of foreign policy. Here, many people have no opinion, or their opinions are not firmly held and are likely to change quite easily given almost any new information. For example, public approval of the war in Iraq and of former president George W. Bush's handling of the war varied with positive news such as Iraqi elections and negative news such as the number of military casualties.

Public opinion that is not based on a complicated ideology may also emerge from the skillful use of cues. Individuals may use heuristics—mental shortcuts that require hardly any information—to make fairly reliable political judgments.[63] For instance, citizens can use political party labels to compensate for low levels of information about the policy positions of candidates.[64] Similarly, citizens take cues from trusted government officials and interest groups regarding the wisdom of bills pending in Congress or the ideology of Supreme Court nominees.

Political Leadership

Public opinion on specific issues is molded by political leaders, journalists, and policy experts. Politicians serve as cue givers to members of the public. Citizens with favorable views of a politician may be more likely to support his or her values and policy agenda. In one study, 49 percent of respondents were uncomfortable with the statement, "I have never believed the Constitution required our schools to be religion free zones," when it was presented anonymously; only 34 percent claimed to be uncomfortable when the statement was attributed to former president Bill Clinton.[65] In a different study, African Americans were presented with a statement about the need for blacks to rely more on themselves to get ahead in society; respondents agreed with the statement when it was attributed to black political figures (Jesse Jackson and Clarence Thomas) and disagreed when the statement was attributed to white political figures (George H. W. Bush and Ted Kennedy).[66]

Politicians routinely make appeals to the public on the basis of shared political ideology and self-interest. Competition and controversy among political elites provide the public with a great deal of information. But politicians are well aware that citizen understanding of and support for an issue depend on how issues are framed. They compete to provide a story line or idea that suggests the essence of political events and policy issues.[67]

The ability of political leaders to affect public opinion has been enhanced enormously by the growth of the broadcast media, especially television.[68] The majoritarian model of democracy assumes that government officials respond to public opinion. But the evidence is substantial that this causal sequence is reversed—that public opinion responds instead to the actions of government officials.[69] If this is true, how much potential is there for public opinion to be manipulated by political leaders through the mass media?

The Media in America

"We never talk anymore" is a common lament of couples who are not getting along very well. In politics, too, citizens and their government need to communicate in order to get along well. *Communication* is the process of transmitting information from one individual or group to another. *Mass* communication is the process by which information is transmitted to large, heterogeneous, widely dispersed audiences. The term **mass media** refers to the means for communicating to these audiences. The mass media are commonly divided into two types. *Print media* (newspapers, magazines) communicate information through the publication of written words and pictures. *Broadcast media* (radio, television) communicate information electronically through sounds and images. The worldwide network of personal computers, commonly called the Internet, can also be classified as broadcast technology, and the Internet has grown in size so that it also qualifies as a mass media.

Our focus here is on the role of the media in promoting communication from government to its citizens and from citizens to their government. In totalitarian governments, information flows more freely in one direction (from government to people) than in the other. In democratic governments, information must flow freely in both directions; a democratic government can respond to public opinion only if its citizens can make their opinions known. Moreover, the electorate can hold government officials accountable for

mass media
The means employed in mass communication, often divided into print media and broadcast media.

their actions only if voters know what their government has done, is doing, and plans to do. Because the mass media provide the major channels for this two-way flow of information, they have the dual capability of reflecting and shaping our political views.

The media are not the only means of communication between citizens and government. Agents of socialization (especially schools) function as "linkage mechanisms" that promote such communication. In the next three chapters, we discuss other major mechanisms for communication: voting, political parties and election campaigns, and interest groups.

The Internet

Alongside the four most traditional forms of mass media—newspapers, magazines, radio, and television—the Internet has rapidly grown into an important conduit for political information. What we today call the Internet began in 1969 when, with support from the U.S. Defense Department's Advanced Research Projects Agency, computers at four universities were linked to form ARPANET. In its early years, the Internet was used mainly to transmit e-mail among researchers. In 1991, a group of European physicists devised a standardized system for encoding and transmitting a wide range of materials, including graphics and photographs, over the Internet, and the World Wide Web (WWW) was born. In January 1993 there were only fifty websites.[70] Today there are over 100 million sites and over a billion Web users.[71] The Internet was soon incorporated into politics, and today virtually every government agency and political organization has a website.

The Internet has also created a new venue for traditional print media outlets to offer their wares. On the Web, local publications such as the *Topeka Capital Journal* are no more difficult to access than national newspapers such as the *New York Times*. What television networks such as ABC and CNN offer in national and international news exists alongside the local coverage of individual stations such as Baltimore's WJZ, and Americans are logging in for news from all these outlets. But with these opportunities for expanded access, significant challenges have arisen, particularly for newspapers. Online news access is generally free, while newspapers charge a subscription fee. Online competition has been an insurmountable challenge for many newspapers, which are already in financial difficulties. Between 2006 and 2010, newspaper advertising revenues dropped 48 percent and newsrooms shed 25 percent of their staff.

Some, like Denver's 150-year-old *Rocky Mountain News,* have gone out of business. Others, like the *Los Angeles Times* and the *Chicago Tribune,* filed for bankruptcy. Still others, like Seattle's 146-year-old *Post-Intelligencer,* became web-only operations in 2009.[72]

Almost 79 percent of Americans use the Internet, and most of them are under the age of sixty-five.[73] Internet users tend to be well educated and concentrated in large cities and suburbs. Those individuals who rely on the Internet as their main source of news tend to be very critical of traditional news media; they are much more likely to say that news organizations are politically biased.[74]

Private citizens operate their own websites on politics and public affairs, daily posting their political thoughts and critical comments. These blogs (short for weblogs) have had dramatic effects on news reporting. Congressional investigations into whether the Bush administration's firings of nine U.S. attorneys in 2007 were unlawfully motivated by political concerns originated as a story on a political blog. It was eventually picked up by traditional news outlets, led to congressional hearings and court proceedings, and ultimately ushered in the resignation of Attorney General Alberto Gonzales. During the 2008 primaries, an unpaid writer for the Huffington Post political blog broke the news that Barack Obama told a group of supporters that rural voters are "bitter" and that they "cling to guns or religion."[75] This quote went on to become a major news story and was an issue throughout the rest of the campaign. As these incidents illustrate, the influence of political blogs in American politics has been largely indirect, by influencing the types of stories that get picked up by the "mainstream media."

Private Ownership of the Media

In the United States, people take private ownership of the media for granted. In other Western democratic countries, the print media (both newspapers and magazines) are privately owned, but the broadcast media often are not. Private ownership of both print and broadcast media gives the news industry in America more political freedom than in any other country in the world, but it also makes the media more dependent on advertising revenues. To make a profit, the news operations of the mass media in America must appeal to the audiences they serve. The primary criterion of a story's **newsworthiness** is usually its audience appeal, which is judged according to its potential impact on readers or listeners, its degree of sensationalism (exemplified by violence, conflict, disaster, or

newsworthiness
The degree to which a news story is important enough to be covered in the mass media.

Politics of Global Change

The Growth of Cable in a Wireless Age

You might think that the World Wide Web relies on satellite technology. In fact, most Internet messages to distant lands run along the ocean floor. Undersea fiber-optic cables now carry most of the world's Internet, wireless, and fixed-line traffic. Over time, advances in technology have significantly reduced the costs of laying the cable and of transmission. Global bandwidth usage keeps growing and is predicted to double every 1.4 years.

As demand increases, telecommunications companies are racing to lay more cable and connect more parts of the world. New cables have been proposed for Africa, the Middle East, and even Greenland. And most countries like having more than one cable route as a backup in case one route fails. In the age of globalization, Internet-dependent businesses and nations want a reliable connection.

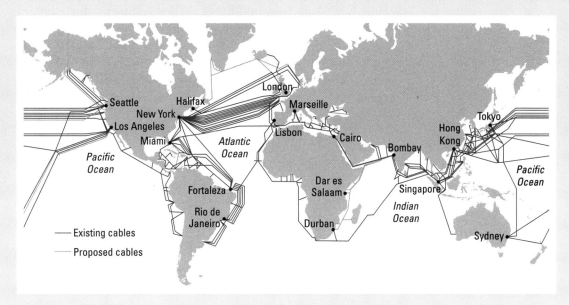

Source: Christopher Rhoads, "Internet Logjams Spur Cable Boom," *Wall Street Journal,* 8 February 2008, p. A1. Copyright 2008 by Dow Jones & Company, Inc. Reproduced with permission of Dow Jones & Company, Inc., in the format textbook via Copyright Clearance Center.

scandal), its treatment of familiar people or life situations, its close-to-home character, and its timeliness.[76]

Media owners can make more money by either increasing their audiences or acquiring additional publications or stations. A decided trend toward concentrated ownership of the media increases the risk that a few major owners could control the news flow to promote their own political interests. In fact, the number of *independent newspapers* has declined as newspaper chains (owners of two or more newspapers in different cities) have acquired more newspapers. The Gannett chain, which owns *USA Today,* now also publishes eighty-one other daily newspapers in the United States and seventeen in the United Kingdom.[77]

As with newspapers, chains sometimes own television stations in different cities, and ownership sometimes extends across different media. None of the three original television networks remains an independent corporation: the Walt Disney Company owns ABC. NBC has been owned by General Electric for years. In late 2009, cable company Comcast announced that it is planning to acquire NBC from General Electric. When complete, this merger is set to create a conglomerate that would "hold the most significant collection of cable television assets in the world."[78] The Fox Network is owned by Rupert Murdoch's News Corporation, which also controls 20th Century Fox movie studios, Fox News, the FX cable channel, MySpace, publisher HarperCollins, and the well-known *Wall Street Journal* newspaper.[79]

Government Regulation of the Media

Although most of the mass media in the United States are privately owned, they do not operate free of government regulation. The broadcast media, however, are subject to more regulations than the print media.

The Federal Communications Act of 1934 created the **Federal Communications Commission (FCC)** to regulate the broadcast and telephone industries. The FCC has five members (no more than three from the same political party) nominated by the president for terms of five years. The commissioners can be removed from office only through impeachment and conviction. Consequently, the FCC is considered an independent regulatory commission: it is insulated from political control by the president or Congress. (We discuss independent regulatory commissions in Chapter 10.) Today, the FCC's charge includes regulating interstate and international

Federal Communications Commission (FCC)
An independent federal agency that regulates interstate and international communication by radio, television, telephone, telegraph, cable, and satellite.

communications by radio, television, telephone, telegraph, cable, and satellite.

For six decades—as technological change made television commonplace and brought the invention of computers, fax machines, and satellite transmissions—the communications industry was regulated under the basic framework of the 1934 law that created the FCC. Then, pressured by businesses that wanted to exploit new electronic technologies, Congress, in a bipartisan effort, swept away most existing regulations in the Telecommunications Act of 1996.

The 1996 law relaxed or scrapped limitations on media ownership. For example, broadcasters were previously limited to owning only twelve TV stations and forty radio stations. Now there are no limits on the number of TV stations one company may own, as long as its coverage does not extend beyond 35 percent of the market nationwide. The 1996 law set no national limits for radio ownership and relaxed local limits. In addition, it lifted rate regulations for cable systems, allowed cross-ownership of cable and telephone companies, and allowed local and long-distance telephone companies to compete with one another and to sell television services. Although even those who wrote the law could not predict its long-range effect, the law quickly spurred a series of media group megamergers and expanded ownership of local stations by the networks.

The First Amendment to the Constitution prohibits Congress from abridging the freedom of the press. Over time, *the press* has come to mean all the mass media, and the courts have decided many cases that define how far freedom of the press extends under the law. The most important of these cases are often quite complex. Usually the courts strike down government attempts to restrain the press from publishing or broadcasting the information, reports, or opinions it finds newsworthy. One notable exception concerns strategic information during wartime; the courts have supported censorship of information such as the sailing schedules of troop ships or the planned movements of troops in battle. Otherwise, they have recognized a strong constitutional case against press censorship.

Because the broadcast media are licensed to use the public airwaves, they are subject to additional regulation, beyond that applied to the print media, of the content of their news coverage. The basis for the FCC's regulation of content lies in its charge to ensure that radio and television stations "serve the public interest, convenience, and necessity." With its **equal opportunities rule**, the FCC requires any broadcast station that gives or sells time to a

equal opportunities rule
Under the Federal Communications Act of 1934, the requirement that if a broadcast station gives or sells time to a candidate for any public office, it must make available an equal amount of time under the same conditions to all other candidates for that office.

candidate for public office to make an equal amount of time available under the same conditions to all other candidates for that office. The **reasonable access rule** requires that commercial stations make their facilities available for the expression of conflicting views or issues from all responsible elements in the community. Two related rules were struck down by a U.S. court of appeals in 2000. The *political editorial rule* required stations that endorsed a candidate to provide free reply time to political opponents. The *personal attack rule* required stations to provide free response time to candidates and others whose integrity was attacked on the air. Opponents of these rules had long charged that they stifled debate by discouraging broadcasters from adopting editorial positions.[80]

Reporting and Following the News

In this section we discuss how the media cover political affairs, and we examine where citizens acquire their political knowledge. We also look at what people learn from the media, and we probe the media's effects on public opinion, the political agenda, and political socialization.

Covering National Politics

Washington, D.C., has by far the biggest press corps of any city in the world—nearly 7,000 congressionally accredited reporters: 2,000 from newspapers, 1,800 from periodicals, 2,500 from radio and television, and over 350 photographers.[81] Only a small portion of these reporters is admitted to fill the fifty seats in the White House press briefing room. As recently as the Truman administration, reporters enjoyed informal personal relationships with the president. Today, the media's relationship with the president is mediated primarily through the Office of the Press Secretary.

White House correspondents rely heavily on information they receive from the president's staff, each piece carefully crafted in an attempt to control the news report. The most frequent form is the news release, a prepared text distributed to reporters in the hope that they will use it verbatim. A daily news briefing enables reporters to question the press secretary about news releases. A news conference provides an opportunity to question high-level officials in the executive branch—including the president on occasion. News conferences appear to be freewheeling, but officials tend to rehearse precise answers to anticipated questions.

reasonable access rule
An FCC rule that requires broadcast stations to make their facilities available for the expression of conflicting views or issues by all responsible elements in the community.

Occasionally, information is given "on background," which means that reporters can use the information but cannot identify the source except in a vague reference such as "a senior official says." Information disclosed "off the record" cannot be printed. Journalists who violate these well-known conditions risk losing their welcome at the White House.

Reporters occasionally benefit from leaks of information released by officials who are guaranteed anonymity. The best-known example was a source known as "Deep Throat" during the Watergate scandal. Deep Throat provided *Washington Post* reporter Bob Woodward critical information linking the Nixon White House to crimes committed during the 1972 campaign and the subsequent cover-up. Facing impeachment, President Nixon ultimately chose to resign. Despite rampant speculation, Deep Throat's identity was kept secret for over thirty years, until he and his family revealed that he was W. Mark Felt, the number two man at the FBI during Watergate. Officials may leak news to interfere with others' political plans or to float ideas ("trial balloons") past the public and other political leaders to gauge their reactions. Sometimes a carefully placed leak turns into a gusher of media coverage through the practice of "pack journalism"—the tendency of journalists to adopt similar viewpoints toward the news simply because they hang around together, exchanging information and defining the day's news with one another.

Presenting the News

Media executives, news editors, and prominent reporters function as **gatekeepers** in directing the news flow: they decide which events to report and how to handle the elements in those stories. They not only select what topics go through the gate but also are expected to uphold standards of careful reporting and principled journalism. The rise of the Internet, however, has made more information and points of view available to the public and journalists alike. A 2007 survey of journalists found that 59 percent said that they look to political blogs sometimes or regularly as part of their news-gathering process.[82] However, the Internet has no gatekeepers and thus no constraints on its content. While it is a powerful research tool with the ability to deliver information quickly, it can spread factual errors and rumors as well.

The established media cannot communicate everything about public affairs. There is neither space in newspapers or magazines nor time on television or radio to do so. Time limitations impose

gatekeepers
Media executives, news editors, and prominent reporters who decide which events to report and which elements in those stories to emphasize.

especially severe constraints on television news broadcasting. Each half-hour network news program devotes only about twenty minutes to the news (the rest of the time is taken up by commercials), and there is even less news on local television.

During elections, personification encourages **horse race journalism,** in which media coverage becomes a matter of which candidate is leading in the polls and who raised the most money. Over three-quarters of Americans say that they want more coverage of candidates' positions on the issues; almost half would also like less coverage of who is leading in the polls.[83] Yet studies of network news coverage of presidential campaigns find that horse race coverage dominates. Journalists cover the horse race because it offers new material daily, whereas the candidates' programs remain the same.[84]

Where the Public Gets Its News

Until the early 1960s, most people reported getting more political news from newspapers than from any other source. Television nudged out newspapers as the public's major source of news in the early 1960s. Since 2010, 18–29 year olds have reported getting most of their news from the Internet, though older Americans still name television as their primary source for news.[85] Over half of the public consults multiple sources of news during the day—perhaps reading the paper at breakfast, checking the Internet at work, and ending the day watching television news.[86] Older Americans spend more time watching, reading, or listening to news; people under the age of thirty spend less.[87]

A 2009 survey found a majority of Americans identifying the Internet as their preferred way to get news if they could choose only one source.[88] What kind of websites are they using? The online version of national newspapers or national television stations were much more popular for news than Internet-only sources such as blogs. The growth in online news consumption has been accompanied by a dramatic rise in news access through mobile devices. Almost half of all adults in a 2011 survey reported getting local news and information through a cell phone or tablet.[89]

What People Remember and Know

horse race journalism
Election coverage by the mass media that focuses on which candidate is ahead rather than on national issues.

If, as surveys indicate, 80 percent of the public reads or hears the news each day, how much political information do these people absorb? By all accounts, not much. A national survey in the late fall of 2010 asked respondents about current events and important

political figures. Only 41 percent of the public knew that relations between nuclear rivals India and Pakistan were unfriendly, slightly fewer (38 percent) could identify the incoming Speaker of the House, John Boehner, and only 16 percent were aware that more than half of the $700 billion Troubled Asset Relief Program (TARP) financial bailout had been repaid. Only 15 percent could name the prime minister of close ally Great Britain (David Cameron).[90]

Numerous studies have found that those who rely on television for their news score lower on tests of knowledge about public affairs than those who rely on print media.[91] Among media researchers, this finding has led to the **television hypothesis**—the belief that television is to blame for the low level of citizens' knowledge about public affairs.[92] We know that television tends to squeeze public policy issues into one-minute or, at most, two-minute fragments, which makes it difficult to explain candidates' positions.

Television also tends to cast abstract issues in personal terms to generate the visual content that the medium needs.[93] However, other research has questioned the hypothesis and found that "television was more successful in communicating information about topics that were of low salience [significance] to the audience, while print media were superior in conveying information about

television hypothesis
The belief that television is to blame for the low level of citizens' knowledge about public affairs.

topics that had high salience."[94] Regardless of how well newspapers convey information, readership is declining.

Influencing Public Opinion

Americans overwhelmingly believe that the media exert a strong influence on their political institutions, and almost nine out of ten Americans believe that the media strongly influence public opinion.[95] However, measuring the extent of media influence on public opinion is difficult.[96] Because few of us learn about political events except through the media, it could be argued that the media create public opinion simply by reporting events. Consider the major oil well leak off the coast of Louisiana in 2010. Surely months of video footage of oil being pumped into the Gulf affected American public opinion toward the safety of offshore drilling.

Documenting general effects of media on opinions about general issues in the news is difficult. Doris Graber, a leading scholar on the media, reported several studies that carefully documented media influence. For example, more pretrial publicity for serious criminal cases leads to full trials rather than settlement through plea-bargaining; media attention to more obscure foreign policy issues tends to force them onto the policy agenda.[97] Television network coverage of the returns on the night of the 2000 presidential election may have profoundly affected public opinion toward both major candidates. In a report commissioned by cable news network CNN, three journalism experts concluded that the networks' unanimous declarations of George W. Bush's victory that night "created a premature impression" that he had defeated Al Gore before the Florida outcome had been decided. The impression carried through the postelection challenge: "Gore was perceived as the challenger and labeled a 'sore loser' for trying to steal the election."[98]

Setting the Political Agenda

Despite the media's potential for influencing public opinion, most scholars believe that the media's greatest impact on politics is found in their power to set the **political agenda**—a list of issues that people identify as needing government attention. Those who set the political agenda define which issues government decision makers should discuss and debate.

The mass media in the United States have traditionally played an important role in defining the political agenda. Television, which brings pictures and sound into almost every home, has enormous

political agenda
A list of issues that need government attention.

potential for setting the political agenda. A careful study designed to isolate and examine television's effects on public opinion concluded, "By attending to some problems and ignoring others, television news shapes the American public's political priorities."[99] Indeed, the further removed a viewer is from public affairs, "the stronger the agenda-setting power of television news."[100]

One study found varying correlations between media coverage and what the public sees as "the most important problem facing this country today," depending on the type of event. Public opinion was especially responsive to media coverage of recurring problems such as inflation and unemployment.[101] The media's ability to influence public opinion by defining "the news" makes politicians eager to influence media coverage. Politicians attempt to affect not only public opinion but also the opinions of other political leaders.[102]

In a curious sense, the mass media have become a network for communicating among attentive elites, all trying to influence one another or to assess others' weaknesses and strengths. If the White House is under pressure on some policy matter, it might supply a representative to appear on one of the Sunday morning talk shows, such as *Meet the Press* or *Face the Nation.* The White House's goal would be to influence the thinking of other insiders (who faithfully watch these programs) as much as to influence the opinions of the relatively few ordinary citizens who watch these particular programs.

Socializing the Citizenry

The mass media act as important agents of political socialization.[103] Young people who rarely follow the news by choice nevertheless acquire political values through the entertainment function of the broadcast media. Years ago, children learned from radio programs; now they learn from television. What children learned from radio was quite different from what they are learning now, however. In the golden days of radio, youngsters listening to popular radio dramas heard repeatedly that "crime does not pay." The message never varied: criminals are bad; the police are good; criminals get caught and are severely punished for their crimes.

Television today does not portray the criminal justice system in the same way, even in police dramas. Consider programs such as *24* and *In Justice,* which have portrayed police and FBI agents as lawbreakers. Other series, such as *Law and Order, Prison Break,* and *The Shield,* sometimes portray a tainted criminal justice system and institutionalized corruption.[104] Certainly one cannot easily argue that television's entertainment programs help prepare law-abiding citizens.

So the media play contradictory roles in the process of political socialization. On the one hand, they promote popular support for government by joining in the celebration of national holidays, heroes' birthdays, political anniversaries, and civic accomplishments. On the other hand, the media erode public confidence by publicizing citizens' grievances, airing investigative reports of agency malfeasance, and even showing dramas about crooked cops.[105]

Evaluating the Media in Government

Are the media fair or biased in reporting the news? What contributions do they make to democratic government? What effects do they have on freedom, order, and equality?

Is Reporting Biased?

News reports are presented as objective reality, yet critics of modern journalism contend that news is filtered through the ideological biases of the owners and editors (the gatekeepers) and of the reporters themselves. Even citizens tend to be skeptical of the news. Democrats and Republicans show distinct differences in which media organizations they find most credible (see Figure 4.4). The argument that news is politically biased has two sides. On the one hand, news reporters are criticized in best-selling books for tilting their stories in a liberal direction, promoting social equality, and undercutting social order.[106] On the other hand, wealthy and conservative media owners are suspected—in other best-selling books—of preserving inequalities and reinforcing the existing order by serving a relentless round of entertainment that numbs the public's capacity for critical analysis.[107]

Although the picture is far from clear, available evidence seems to confirm the charge of liberal leanings among reporters in the major news media. In a 2007 survey of journalists, 32 percent of the national press considered themselves "liberal," compared with only 8 percent who said they were "conservative."[108] Content analysis of the tone of ABC, CBS, and NBC network coverage of presidential campaigns from 1988 to 2004 concluded that Democratic candidates received much more "good press" than Republicans in every election but 1988, when

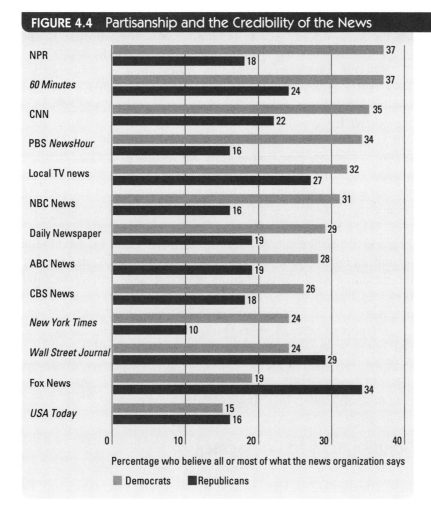

FIGURE 4.4 Partisanship and the Credibility of the News

NPR — Democrats 37, Republicans 18
60 Minutes — Democrats 37, Republicans 24
CNN — Democrats 35, Republicans 22
PBS *NewsHour* — Democrats 34, Republicans 16
Local TV news — Democrats 32, Republicans 27
NBC News — Democrats 31, Republicans 16
Daily Newspaper — Democrats 29, Republicans 19
ABC News — Democrats 28, Republicans 19
CBS News — Democrats 26, Republicans 18
New York Times — Democrats 24, Republicans 10
Wall Street Journal — Democrats 24, Republicans 29
Fox News — Democrats 19, Republicans 34
USA Today — Democrats 15, Republicans 16

Percentage who believe all or most of what the news organization says

■ Democrats ■ Republicans

Respondents were asked to rate broadcast and print media according to whether the respondent believes "all or most" or "nothing" of what the organization says. The table lists the results broken down by partisan identification. In general, Republicans are more skeptical of the media than Democrats. Republicans rate the Fox News channel and the *Wall Street Journal* most highly, while Democrats favor the PBS *News Hour,* CNN, and National Public Radio (NPR).

Source: "Section 7: Media Credibility," in 2008 Pew Research Center for the People and the Press, News Consumption and Believability Study, 17 August 2008, found at http://people-press.org/reports/pdf/444.pdf, p. 59. Copyright © PEW Research Center. Reproduced by permission.

the Republican candidate benefited from better press.[109] However, one medium—talk radio—is dominated by conservative views.

To some extent, working journalists in the national and local media are at odds with their own editors, who tend to be more conservative.[110] The editors, in their function as gatekeepers, tend to tone down reporters' liberal leanings by editing their stories or not placing them well in the medium. Newspaper publishers are also free to endorse candidates, and almost all daily newspapers once openly endorsed one of the two major party candidates for president. In sixteen of eighteen elections from 1932 to 2000, newspaper editorials favored the Republican candidate. In 2004, however, more editorials backed challenger John Kerry (208) than Bush (189). In 2008, the number of endorsements for Barack Obama far surpassed the number for John McCain: 287 vs. 159. That year, the *Chicago Tribune* endorsed a Democrat for the first time in its 162-year history.[111]

Without question, incumbents—as opposed to challengers—enjoy much more news coverage simply from holding office and issuing official statements. The less prominent that the office is, the greater is the advantage from such free news coverage. Non-campaign news coverage leads to greater incumbent name recognition at election time, particularly for members of Congress (see Chapter 8). This coverage effect is independent of any bias in reporting on campaigns. For more prominent offices such as the presidency, however, a different news dynamic may come into play. When a powerful incumbent runs for reelection, journalists may feel a special responsibility to counteract his or her advantage by putting the opposite partisan spin on the news.[112] Thus, whether the media coverage of campaigns is seen as pro-Democratic (and therefore liberal) or pro-Republican (and therefore conservative) depends on which party is in office at the time.

A report of network news stories broadcast during the general election in 2008, when there was no incumbent, found that Obama received overwhelmingly positive coverage: 68 percent of stories about Obama were deemed positive. In stark contrast, only 33 percent of stories about McCain were considered positive.[113]

Contributions to Democracy

In a democracy, communication must move in two directions: from government to citizens and from citizens to government. In fact, political communication in the United States seldom goes directly from government to citizens without passing through the media. The point is important because news reporters tend to be highly critical of politicians; they consider it their job to search for inaccuracies in fact and weaknesses in argument—practicing **watchdog journalism**.[114] Some observers have characterized the news media and the government as adversaries—each mistrusting the other, locked in competition for popular favor while trying to get the record straight. To the extent that this is true, the media serve both the majoritarian and the pluralist models of democracy well by improving the quality of information transmitted to the people about their government.[115]

The mass media transmit information in the opposite direction by reporting citizens' reactions to political events and government

watchdog journalism
Journalism that scrutinizes public and business institutions and publicizes perceived misconduct.

actions. The press has traditionally reflected public opinion (and often created it) while defining the news and suggesting courses of government action. But the media's role in reflecting public opinion has become much more refined in the information age. After commercial polls (such as the Gallup and Roper polls) were established in the 1930s, newspapers began to report reliable readings of public opinion. By the 1970s, some news organizations acquired their own survey research divisions. Occasionally print and electronic media have joined forces to conduct major national surveys. For example, the well-respected *New York Times*/CBS News Poll conducts surveys that are first aired on the *CBS Evening News* and then analyzed at length in the *Times*.

Although polls sometimes create opinions just by asking questions, their net effect has been to generate more accurate knowledge of public opinion and to report that knowledge back to the public. Widespread knowledge of public opinion does not guarantee government responsiveness to popular demands, but such knowledge is necessary if government is to function according to the majoritarian model of democracy.

Effects on Freedom, Order, and Equality

The media in the United States have played an important role in advancing equality, especially racial equality. Throughout the civil rights movement of the 1950s and 1960s, the media gave national coverage to conflict in the South, as black children tried to attend white schools and civil rights workers were beaten and even killed in the effort to register black voters. Partly because of this media coverage, civil rights moved up on the political agenda, and coalitions were formed in Congress to pass new laws promoting racial equality. Women's rights have also been advanced by the media, which have reported instances of blatant sexual discrimination exposed by groups working for sexual equality. In general, the mass media offer spokespersons for any disadvantaged group an opportunity to state their case before a national audience and to work for a place on the political agenda.

Although the media are willing to encourage government action to promote equality at the cost of some personal freedom, they resist government attempts to infringe on freedom of the press to promote order.[116] While the public tends to support a free press in theory, public support is not universal and wavers in practice. Asked whether it is more important "that the government be able to censor news stories it feels threaten national security OR that the news media be able to report stories they feel are in the national interest," about one-third of the respondents in a 2006 national survey favored government censorship.[117]

The media's ability to report whatever they wish, whenever they wish, certainly erodes efforts to maintain order. For example, sensational media coverage of terrorist acts gives terrorists the publicity they seek; portrayal of brutal killings and rapes on television encourages copycat crimes, committed "as seen on TV." Freedom of the press is a noble value and has been important to democratic government. But we should not ignore the fact that democracies sometimes pay a price for pursuing it without qualification.

Tying It Together

1. What is public opinion, how is it collected, and what is its place in the two models of democracy?
   - Public opinion is the collective attitude of the citizens on a given issue or question.
   - Opinions are gathered through sampling methods such as polling.
   - The majoritarian model assumes that most people hold clear opinions on political issues; however, public opinion is often different from government policy.
   - The pluralistic model believes voters are often uninformed about political issues; this is generally consistent with the public opinion.

2. How are political values formed?
   - Public opinion is grounded in political values.
   - Values are acquired through the political socialization process.
   - Political socialization is the path to political awareness, knowledge, and values.
   - Everyone's political socialization is different and continuously formed by
     - family.
     - school.
     - peer group.

- community.
- the media.

3. How do the social backgrounds of individuals influence their opinions?
   - Individuals are influenced by similar socialization agents in different ways.
   - People's political values and voting choices are tied to their backgrounds, which include
     - education.
     - income.
     - religion.
     - race and ethnicity.
     - region.
     - gender.

4. To what degree do people's opinions on specific issues reflect their political ideology?
   - Ideology influences public opinion on specific issues.
   - The public's ideological thinking cannot be categorized in conventional liberal–conservative terms.
   - Significant portions of the public are also communitarians or libertarians.
   - When it comes to freedom and order, people associate liberals with change and conservatives with tradition.
   - When it comes to economic equality, people view liberals as supporting intervention and conservatives as favoring less government intervention.

5. Apart from ideology, what other factors influence public opinion?
   - Americans have political opinions even on topics on which they have little knowledge.
   - Strongly held opinions may not change, even when voters are presented with new information questioning those beliefs.
   - Education is the strongest predictor of political knowledge.
   - Equal levels of political understanding may produce different political views due to self-interest.
   - The influence of political leaders is enhanced through the mass media.

6. How do the media promote two-way communication between government and its citizens?
   - The mass media are a means for communicating to voters.

- The Internet is a source for communication through websites, both for media outlets to provide information and individuals to express opinions.
- In the United States, the media are owned by private individuals, which promotes political freedom.
- The First Amendment to the Constitution prohibits Congress from abridging the freedom of the press, which has come to mean mass media.
- The equal opportunities rule requires broadcasters to give equal time to all candidates in a political race.
- The reasonable access rule requires stations to give time to conflicting views.

7. Where do citizens acquire political knowledge, and what role do the media play in this process?
   - The mass media are an important part of the political socialization process.
   - Newspapers gave way to television as the source for people's news about politics, and today the Internet is surpassing newspapers as a news source.
   - More than half the public consults multiple sources of news during the day.
   - Those who rely on television tend to remember less information about public affairs; this is also called the television hypothesis.
   - The media's greatest potential for influencing public opinion is setting the political agenda.

8. What influence do the media have over democratic government and its objectives?
   - Reporting is filtered through ideological biases of the media's owners, editors, and reporters.
   - A large proportion of the public distrusts the media because of perceived biases. In practice, national journalists tend to be liberal and editors tend to be conservative.
   - The media contribute to the two-way communication between government and voters.
   - Journalists practice watchdog journalism to provide an external check on government.
   - The media encourage government action to promote equality but not action to limit freedom of the press.

Public Opinion and Models of Democracy

True or False?

1. Government action is always consistent with public opinion on major issues such as the death penalty.
2. Gallup polls always accurately predict election results.
3. Survey methodology did not develop into a powerful research tool until the 1950s.

Comprehension

4. How is public opinion gathered today?
5. How accurate are the Gallup Poll's electoral predictions?

Political Socialization

True or False?

1. Political opinions rarely change over time.
2. Many external factors influence a person's political opinions.
3. Political socialization is a simple process by which people acquire their political values.

Comprehension

4. How do people acquire their political values?
5. What forms of media are older Americans likely to rely on? Younger Americans?

Social Groups and Political Values

True or False?

1. The impact of regional effects on public opinion is increasing.
2. People with higher degrees of education tend to favor equality over freedom.
3. Contemporary politics is marked by a gender gap.

Comprehension

4. Does religion play a role in political values?
5. Why are the terms *pro-life* and *pro-choice* inadequate to characterize many people's opinions about abortion?

From Values to Ideology

True or False?

1. Most voters identify liberals and conservatives primarily in political terms based upon the degree of government involvement in society.

2. People form their opinions of government activity based on an unwavering, one-dimensional ideological standard.
3. Both liberals and conservatives value freedom, but neither is willing to trade freedom for any other value.

Comprehension
4. Why do Americans often find it hard to label themselves as liberals or conservatives?
5. What effect did President Roosevelt's New Deal economic policies have on the role of the national government?

Test Prepper 4.5

Forming Political Opinions

True or False?
1. Education is the factor that best predicts political knowledge.
2. People with equal knowledge about public affairs and levels of conceptualization are more likely to call themselves liberals than conservatives.

Comprehension
3. What is the self-interest principle?
4. How do political leaders mold public opinion on specific issues?

Test Prepper 4.6

The Media in America

True or False?
1. Freedom of the press has never been limited by the Supreme Court.
2. The Internet as we know it today began in 1969 when computers at four universities were linked to form ARPANET.
3. Newsworthiness is the degree to which a news story is important enough to be covered in the mass media.

Comprehension
4. Why is the equal opportunities rule important?
5. What is the FCC, and what purpose does it serve?

Test Prepper 4.7

Reporting and Following the News

True or False?
1. Americans believe the media exert a strong influence on public opinion.
2. Surveys say that 80 percent of Americans read or hear the news each day.

3. Gatekeepers decide which events to report and which elements in those events and stories to emphasize.

Comprehension

4. Explain the term *horse race journalism*.
5. What do scholars believe is the media's greatest impact on politics?

Test Prepper 4.8
Evaluating the Media in Government

True or False?

1. The mass media's only role as an intermediary between government and the public is to tell the public what the government is doing.
2. The net effect of polls has been to generate more accurate knowledge of public opinion and to report that knowledge back to the public.

Comprehension

3. How have the mass media contributed to democracy?
4. How have the media advanced equality in the United States?

CourseMate CL Resources:

Visit www.cengagebrain.com/shop/ISBN/1111832587 for flashcards, web quizzes, videos and more!

AP Photo/Lauren Victoria Burke

FOCUS QUESTIONS

1. What are the ways citizens can participate in government?
2. What is unconventional participation, and why is it practiced?
3. How can citizens participate in government in more conventional ways?
4. How does society promote participation?
5. How do Americans participate through voting?
6. What is the relationship of political participation to the values of freedom, equality, and order?
7. What are the purposes of elections, and how do these serve the models of democracy?

Angry citizens packed town halls across the country in the summer of 2009. They gathered to confront Democratic members of Congress over President Obama's health-care plan. The experience of Representative Tim Bishop (D-N.Y.) was typical. Videos of his June town hall meeting showed participants screaming questions and shouting him down. According to the *Wall Street Journal*, "Mr. Bishop would begin to respond to a question and a participant would yell, 'Answer the question!' At one point, Mr. Bishop yelled back, 'I'm trying to!'"[1] The scene was repeated at countless meetings with Democratic members of Congress in different places.[2]

People's anger erupted in other ways. Members of Congress were hanged in effigy, protesters carried signs linking the health plan with Nazism (and communism), demonstrations provoked fistfights, and fights led to hospitalizations.[3] On September 12, thousands of protesters traveled to Washington, filling the west lawn of the Capitol and spilling onto the National Mall.[4] It was mostly a grassroots response to Obama's policies, but with a Republican complexion. Of fifty-four demonstrators on a bus from Tallahassee, Florida, forty-four identified themselves as Republican, eight as independent, and two as Libertarian.[5] Most speakers were little-known activists, but they also included several members of Congress.

A featured speaker was former Republican majority leader Dick Armey of Texas, now president of FreedomWorks, a Washington-based political group advocating smaller government and lower taxes.[6] In March, FreedomWorks had launched a twenty-five-city "Tea Party Tour" to oppose Obama, the Democrats, and their alleged socialist agenda.[7] (The *tea party* term derived from the colonists' 1773 act of dumping British tea into Boston harbor in protest of Britain's new tax on tea.)[8] For the 2009 protestors, TEA reportedly stood for "Taxed Enough Already."

Republican leaders were in a quandary over how to relate to these antigovernment protesters, who persisted after the summer. While party leaders welcomed the populist opposition to Democratic plans, they worried about containing the new activists' anger, often directed at Republicans too. Catherina Wojtowicz, coordinator of the Chicago tea party group, said, "Personally, I'm just as fed up with the Republican Party as the Democratic Party."[9]

Like the colonists in 1773, tea party activists in 2009 employed unconventional forms of political protest that today are constitutionally protected. Do Americans protest more or less than citizens in other countries? What other options do people have to participate in politics? How well does political protest fit with either the pluralist or majoritarian models of democracy?

In this chapter, we seek to answer these and other important questions about popular participation in government. We begin by studying participation in democratic government, distinguishing between conventional and unconventional participation. Then we evaluate the nature and extent of both types of participation in American politics. Next, we study the expansion of voting rights and voting as the major mechanism for mass participation in politics. Finally, we examine the extent to which the various forms of political participation serve the values of freedom, equality, and order and the majoritarian and pluralist models of democracy.

Democracy and Political Participation

Government ought to be run by the people. That is the democratic ideal in a nutshell. But how much and what kind of citizen participation are necessary for democratic government? Champions of direct democracy believe that if citizens do not participate directly in government affairs, making government decisions among themselves, they should give up all pretense of living in a democracy. More practical observers contend that people can govern indirectly through their elected representatives. And they maintain that choosing leaders through elections—formal procedures for voting—is the only workable approach to democracy in a large, complex nation.

Elections are a necessary condition of democracy, but they do not guarantee democratic government. Before the collapse of communism, the former Soviet Union regularly held elections in which more than 90 percent of the electorate turned out to vote, but it certainly did not function as a democracy, because there was only one party. Both the majoritarian and the pluralist models of democracy rely on voting to varying degrees, but both models expect citizens to participate in politics in other ways. For example, they expect citizens to discuss politics, form interest groups, contact public officials, campaign for political parties, run for office, and even protest government decisions.

We define **political participation** as "those actions of citizens that attempt to influence the structure of government, the selection of government officials, or the policies of government or to support government and politics."[10] This definition embraces both conventional and unconventional forms of political participation. **Conventional participation** is relatively routine behavior that uses the established institutions of representative government, especially campaigning for candidates and voting in elections. **Unconventional participation** is relatively uncommon behavior that challenges or defies established institutions or the dominant culture (and thus is personally stressful to participants and their opponents).

Voting, displaying a campaign poster in the front yard, and writing letters to public officials are examples of conventional political participation; staging sit-down strikes in public buildings, spray-painting political slogans on walls, and chanting slogans outside officials' windows are examples of unconventional participation. Political demonstrations can be conventional (carrying signs outside an abortion clinic) or unconventional (linking arms to prevent entrance to the clinic). Terrorism is an extreme case of unconventional political behavior. Indeed, the U.S. legal code defines **terrorism** as "premeditated, politically motivated violence perpetrated against noncombatant targets by subnational groups or clandestine agents, usually intended to influence an audience."[11] Timothy McVeigh, a decorated veteran of the 1991 Gulf War, chose to bomb the federal building in Oklahoma City in 1995 because it would provide good camera coverage. Executed in 2001 for taking 168 lives, McVeigh said he bombed the building because the national government had become a police state hostile to gun owners, religious sects, and patriotic militia groups.[12] Although terrorist acts are political acts by definition, they go far beyond what we consider political *participation* in this chapter. Such extreme acts

political participation
Actions of private citizens by which they seek to influence or support government and politics.

conventional participation
Relatively routine political behavior that uses institutional channels and is acceptable to the dominant culture.

unconventional participation
Relatively uncommon political behavior that challenges or defies established institutions and dominant norms.

terrorism
Premeditated, politically motivated violence perpetrated against noncombatant targets by subnational groups or clandestine agents.

do not seek so much to influence government as to attack government and society itself.

Methods of unconventional participation, in contrast, are used by disadvantaged groups that resort to them in lieu of more conventional forms of participation used by most citizens. These groups accept government while seeking to influence it. Let us look at both unconventional and conventional political participation in the United States.

Unconventional Participation

On Sunday, March 7, 1965, a group of about six hundred people set out to march fifty miles from Selma, Alabama, to the state capital at Montgomery. The marchers were demonstrating in favor of voting rights for blacks. At the time, Selma had fewer than five hundred registered black voters, out of fifteen thousand who were eligible.[13] Alabama governor George Wallace declared the march illegal and sent state troopers to stop it. The two groups met at the Edmund Pettus Bridge over the Alabama River at the edge of Selma. The peaceful marchers were disrupted and beaten by state troopers and deputy sheriffs—some on horseback—using clubs, bullwhips, and tear gas. The day became known as Bloody Sunday.

The march from Selma was a form of unconventional political participation. Marching fifty miles in a political protest is certainly not common; moreover, the march challenged the existing institutions that prevented blacks from participating conventionally—voting in elections—for many decades. In contrast to some later demonstrations against the Vietnam War, this 1965 civil rights march posed no threat of violence. The brutal response to the marchers helped the rest of the nation understand the seriousness of the civil rights problem in the South. Unconventional participation is stressful and occasionally violent, but sometimes it is worth the risk.

Support for Unconventional Participation

Unconventional political participation has a long history in the United States. The Boston Tea Party of 1773 was the first in a long line of violent protests against British rule that eventually led to revolution. Yet we know less about unconventional political participation than about conventional participation. The reasons are twofold. First, it is easier to collect data on conventional practices, so they are studied more frequently. Second, political scientists are

A Sticky Situation

When the Deepwater Horizon oil rig caught fire and sank in the Gulf of Mexico in April 2010, the disastrous leak that followed became the largest oil spill in history. The drilling rig, owned by the Swiss firm Transocean Ltd., was under contract to oil giant BP. BP mounted a huge effort lasting months to stop the gusher a mile below the ocean's surface. Concerned that BP's financial liability for the disaster might be capped at $75 million under a 1990 law, protestors rallied outside BP's Washington lobbying offices to demand seizure of the company's assets in the United States to guarantee payment for all damages caused by the disaster.

(Alex Wong/Getty Images)

biased toward institutionalized, or conventional, politics. In fact, some basic works on political participation explicitly exclude any behavior that is "outside the system."[14]

One major study of unconventional political action asked people whether they had engaged in or approved of three types of political participation outside of voting: signing petitions, joining boycotts, and attending demonstrations.[15] As shown in Figure 5.1, only signing petitions was clearly regarded as conventional, in the sense that the behavior was widely practiced. In fact, when political activities interfere with people's daily lives (occupying buildings, for example), disapproval is nearly universal. Most Americans would allow public meetings for religious extremists but not for people

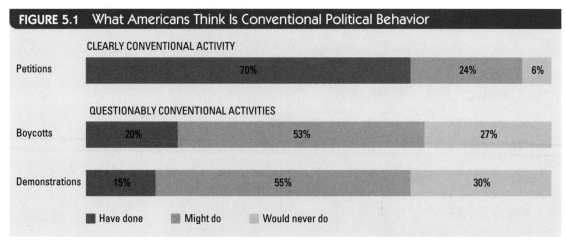

FIGURE 5.1   What Americans Think Is Conventional Political Behavior

CLEARLY CONVENTIONAL ACTIVITY

Petitions — Have done 70% | Might do 24% | Would never do 6%

QUESTIONABLY CONVENTIONAL ACTIVITIES

Boycotts — Have done 20% | Might do 53% | Would never do 27%

Demonstrations — Have done 15% | Might do 55% | Would never do 30%

■ Have done   ■ Might do   ■ Would never do

A survey presented Americans with three forms of political participation outside the electoral process and asked whether they "have done," "might do," or "would never do" any of them. The respondents approved overwhelmingly of signing petitions, which was widely done and rarely ruled out. However, attending demonstrations (a right guaranteed in the Constitution) would "never" be done by 30 percent of the respondents. Boycotting products was slightly less objectionable and more widely practiced. According to this test, attending demonstrations and boycotting products are only marginally conventional forms of political participation in the United States.

Source: 2005–2008 World Values Survey, World Values Survey Association, based in Stockholm, conducts representative surveys in nations across the world. See http://www.worldvaluessurvey.org/.

who want to "overthrow the government."[16] When protesters demonstrating against the Vietnam War disrupted the 1968 Democratic National Convention in Chicago, they were clubbed by the city's police. Although the national television audience saw graphic footage of the confrontations, most viewers condemned the demonstrators, not the police.

The Effectiveness of Unconventional Participation

Vociferous antiabortion protests discourage many doctors from performing abortions but have not led to the outlawing of abortion. Does unconventional participation ever work (even when it provokes violence)? Yes. Antiwar protesters helped convince President Lyndon Johnson not to seek reelection in 1968, and they heightened public concern over U.S. participation in the Vietnam War. The unconventional activities of civil rights workers also produced notable successes. Dr. Martin Luther King, Jr., led the 1955 Montgomery bus boycott that sparked the civil rights movement. He used **direct action** to challenge specific cases of discrimination, assembling crowds to confront businesses and local governments and demanding equal treatment in public accommodations and government.

direct action
Unconventional participation that involves assembling crowds to confront businesses and local governments to demand a hearing.

Denied the usual opportunities for conventional political participation, members of minorities used unconventional politics to pressure Congress to pass a series of civil rights laws in 1957, 1960, 1964, and 1968—each one in some way extending federal protection against discrimination by reason of race, color, religion, or national origin. The 1964 act also prohibited discrimination in employment on the basis of sex. In addition, the Voting Rights Act of 1965 put state electoral procedures under federal supervision, increasing the registration of black voters and the rate of black voter turnout (especially in the South). The civil rights movement shows that social change can occur, even when it is violently opposed at first.

Although direct political action and the politics of confrontation can work, using them takes a special kind of commitment. Studies show that direct action appeals most to those who both (1) distrust the political system and (2) have a strong sense of political efficacy—the feeling that they can do something to affect political decisions.[17] Whether this combination of attitudes produces behavior that challenges the system depends on the extent of organized group activity.[18] The decision to use unconventional behavior also depends on the extent to which individuals develop group consciousness—identification with their group and awareness of its position in society, its objectives, and its intended course of action.[19] These characteristics were present among blacks and young people in the mid-1960s and are strongly present today among blacks and, to a lesser degree, women.

Unconventional Participation in America and the World

Although most Americans may disapprove of using certain forms of participation to protest government policies, U.S. citizens are just as likely as citizens of other countries to express interest in politics, sign a petition, or boycott products. Americans are notably less likely to participate in demonstrations, but compared with citizens in other nations, Americans are not markedly apathetic.[20]

Is something wrong with a political system if citizens resort to unconventional—and widely disapproved of—methods of political participation? To answer this question, we must first learn how much citizens use conventional methods of participation.

Conventional Participation

A practical test of the democratic nature of any government is whether citizens can affect its policies by acting through its institutions: meeting with public officials, supporting candidates, voting in elections. Citizens should not have to risk their life and property to participate in politics, and they should not have to take direct action to force the government to hear their views. The objective of democratic institutions is to make political participation conventional—to allow ordinary citizens to engage in relatively routine, nonthreatening behavior to get the government to heed their opinions, interests, and needs.

In a democracy, a group gathering at a statehouse or city hall to dramatize its position on an issue—say, a tax increase—is not unusual. Such a demonstration is a form of conventional participation. The group is not powerless, and its members are not risking their personal safety. But violence can erupt between opposing groups. Circumstances, then, often determine whether organized protest is or is not conventional. Town hall protests against health care in 2009 certainly threatened Democratic members of Congress enough for some to cancel such meetings. Conventional political behaviors fall into two major categories: actions that show support for government policies and those that try to change or influence policies.

Supportive Behavior

supportive behavior
Actions that express allegiance to government and country.

Supportive behaviors are actions that express allegiance to country and government. When we recite the Pledge of Allegiance or fly the American flag on holidays, we are showing support for the country and, by implication, its political system. Such ceremonial activities usually demand little initiative by citizens. The simple act of turning out to vote is in itself a show of support for the political system. Other supportive behaviors, such as serving as an election judge in a nonpartisan election or organizing a holiday parade, demand greater initiative.

At times, perceptions of patriotism move people across the line from conventional to unconventional behavior. In their eagerness to support the American system, they break up a meeting or disrupt a rally of a group they believe is radical or somehow "un-American." Radical groups may threaten the political system with wrenching change, but superpatriots pose their own threat. Their misguided excess of allegiance denies nonviolent means of dissent to others.[21]

influencing behavior
Behavior that seeks to modify or reverse government policy to serve political interests.

Influencing Behavior

Citizens use **influencing behaviors** to modify or even reverse government policy to serve political interests. Some forms of influencing behavior seek particular benefits from government; other forms have broad policy objectives.

Particular Benefits. Some citizens try to influence government to obtain benefits for themselves, their immediate families, or their close friends. Serving one's self-interest through the voting process is certainly acceptable in democratic theory. Each individual has only one vote, and no single voter can wangle particular benefits from government through voting unless a majority of the voters agrees.

Political actions that require considerable knowledge and initiative are another story. Individuals or small groups that influence government officials to advance their self-interest may secretly benefit without others knowing. Those who quietly obtain particular benefits from government pose a serious challenge to a democracy. Pluralist theory holds that groups ought to be able to make government respond to their special problems and needs. Majoritarian theory holds that government should not do what a majority does not want it to do. A majority of citizens might very well not want the government to do what any particular person or group seeks if it is costly to other citizens.

Citizens often ask for special services from their local government. Such requests may range from contacting the city forestry department to remove a dead tree in front of a house to calling the county animal control center to deal with a vicious dog in the neighborhood. Studies of such "contacting" behavior find that it tends not to be empirically related to other forms of political activity. Contacting behavior is related to socioeconomic status: people of higher socioeconomic status are more likely to contact public officials.[22]

Americans demand much more of their local government than of the national government. Although many people value self-reliance and individualism in national politics, most people expect local government to solve a wide range of social problems. A study of residents of Kansas City, Missouri, found that more than 90 percent thought it was the city's responsibility to provide services in thirteen areas, including maintaining parks, setting standards for new home construction, demolishing vacant and unsafe buildings, ensuring that property owners clean up trash and weeds, and providing bus service. The researcher noted that "it is difficult to imagine a set of federal government activities about which there would [be] more consensus."[23] Citizens can also mobilize against a project. Dubbed the "not-in-my-back-yard," or NIMBY, phenomenon, some citizens pressure local officials to stop undesired projects from being located near their homes.

Contributing money to a candidate's campaign is another form of influencing behavior. Here too the objective can be particular or broad benefits. Because of the potential for abuse, financial contributions are regulated at the national level (see Chapter 6).

Several points emerge from this review of "particularized" forms of political participation. First, approaching government to serve one's particular interests is consistent with democratic theory, because it encourages input from an active citizenry. Second, particularized contact may be a form of participation unto itself, not necessarily related to other forms of participation. Third, such participation tends to be used more by citizens who are advantaged in knowledge and resources. Fourth, particularized participation may serve private interests to the detriment of the majority.

Broad Policy Objectives. We come now to what many scholars have in mind when they talk about political participation: activities that influence the selection of government personnel and policies. Here too we find behaviors that require little initiative (such as voting) and behaviors that require high initiative (attending political meetings, persuading others how to vote). Later in this chapter, we focus on elections as a mechanism for participation. For now, we simply note that voting to influence policy is usually a low-initiative activity. It actually requires more initiative to register to vote in the United States than to cast a vote on election day.

Other types of participation to affect broad policies require high initiative. Running for office requires the most (see Chapter 6). Some high-initiative activities, such as attending party meetings and working in campaigns, are associated with the electoral process; others, such as attending legislative hearings and writing letters to Congress, are not. Studies of citizen contacts in the United States show that about two-thirds deal with broad social issues and only one-third are for private gain.[24]

Few people realize that using the court system is a form of political participation, a way for citizens to press for their rights in a democratic society. Although most people use the courts to serve their particular interests, some also use them, as we discuss shortly, to meet broad objectives. Going to court demands high personal initiative.[25] It also requires knowledge of the law or the financial resources to afford a lawyer.

People use the courts for both personal benefit and broad policy objectives. A person or group can bring **class-action suits** on behalf of other people in similar circumstances. Lawyers for the National Association for the Advancement of Colored People pioneered this form of litigation in the famous school desegregation case, *Brown* v. *Board of Education* (1954).[26] They succeeded in getting the Supreme Court to outlaw segregation in public schools, not just for Linda Brown, one of the children on whose behalf the lawsuit was brought in Topeka, Kansas, but for all others "similarly situated"—that is, for all other black students who wanted to attend desegregated schools. This form of participation has proved to be effective for organized groups, especially those who have been unable to gain their objectives through Congress or the executive branch.

Individual citizens can also try to influence policies at the national level by direct participation in the legislative process. One way is to attend congressional hearings, which are open to the public and occasionally held outside Washington. To facilitate citizen involvement, national government agencies are required to publish all proposed and approved regulations in the daily *Federal Register* and to make government documents available to citizens on request. The Internet certainly facilitates access to information such as the *Federal Register*, and private sites have arisen to give citizens access to policy information from spending in the 2009 economic stimulus legislation to how well President Obama has kept a list of 515 campaign promises.[27]

Conventional Participation in America and the World

How often do Americans contact government officials and engage in other forms of conventional political participation compared with citizens in other countries? The most common political behavior in most industrial democracies is voting for candidates. In the United States, however, voting for candidates is less common than it is in other countries. When voting turnout in the United States over more than half a century was compared with historical patterns of voting in twenty-three other democratic countries, the United States ranked at the *bottom* of the pack. This is a political paradox: Americans are as likely as citizens in other countries to engage in many forms of political participation, but when it comes to voting, Americans rank dead last.[28]

class-action suit
A legal action brought by a person or group on behalf of a number of people in similar circumstances.

Other researchers have noted this paradox and written: "If, for example, we concentrate our attention on national elections we will find that the United States is the least participatory of [all] five nations." But looking at the other indicators, they found that "political apathy, by a wide margin, is lowest in the United States. Interestingly, the high levels of overall involvement reflect a rather balanced contribution of both . . . conventional and unconventional politics."[29] Clearly, low voter turnout in the United States constitutes a puzzle, to which we will return.

Participating Through Voting

The heart of democratic government lies in the electoral process. Whether a country holds elections—and if so, what kind—constitutes the critical difference between democratic and nondemocratic government. Elections institutionalize mass participation in democratic government according to the three normative principles of procedural democracy discussed in Chapter 1: electoral rules specify *who* is allowed to vote, *how much* each person's vote counts, and *how many* votes are needed to win.

Again, elections are formal procedures for making group decisions. *Voting* is the act individuals engage in when they choose among alternatives in an election. **Suffrage** and the **franchise** both mean the right to vote. By formalizing political participation through rules for suffrage and for counting ballots, electoral systems allow large numbers of people, who individually have little political power, to wield great power. Electoral systems decide collectively who governs and, in some instances, what government should do. The simple fact of holding elections is less important than the specific rules and circumstances that govern voting. According to democratic theory, everyone should be able to vote. In practice, however, no nation grants universal suffrage. All countries have age requirements for voting, and all disqualify some inhabitants on various grounds: lack of citizenship, criminal record, mental incompetence, and so forth. What is the record of enfranchisement in the United States?

suffrage
The right to vote. Also called the *franchise.*

franchise
The right to vote. Also called *suffrage.*

Expansion of Suffrage

The United States was the first country to provide for general elections of representatives through mass suffrage, but the franchise was far from universal. When the Constitution was framed, the idea of full adult suffrage was too radical to consider seriously. Instead, the framers left the issue of enfranchisement to the states, stipulating only that individuals who could vote for "the most numerous Branch of the State Legislature" could also vote for their representatives to the U.S. Congress (Article I, Section 2).

Initially, most states established taxpaying or property-holding requirements for voting. Virginia, for example, required ownership of twenty-five acres of settled land or five hundred acres of unsettled land. The original thirteen states began to lift such requirements after 1800. Expansion of the franchise accelerated after 1815 with the admission of new "western" states (Indiana, Illinois, Alabama), where land was more plentiful and widely owned. By the 1850s, the states had eliminated nearly all taxpaying and property-holding requirements, thus allowing the working class—at least its white male members—to vote. Extending the vote to blacks and women took more time.

The Enfranchisement of Blacks. The Fifteenth Amendment, adopted shortly after the Civil War, prohibited the states from denying the right to vote "on account of race, color, or previous condition of servitude." But the states of the old Confederacy worked around the amendment, reestablishing old voting requirements (poll taxes, literacy tests) that worked primarily against blacks. Because the amendment said nothing about voting rights in private organizations, some southern states denied blacks the right to vote in the "private" Democratic primary elections held to choose the party's candidates for the general election. Because the Democratic Party came to dominate politics in the South, the "white primary" effectively disenfranchised blacks despite the Fifteenth Amendment. Also, in many areas of the South, the threat of violence kept blacks from the polls.

The extension of full voting rights to blacks came in two phases, separated by twenty years. In 1944, the Supreme Court decided in *Smith* v. *Allwright* that laws preventing blacks from voting in primary elections were unconstitutional, holding that party primaries are part of the continuous process of electing public officials.[30] The Voting Rights Act of 1965, which followed Selma's Bloody Sunday by less than five months, suspended discriminatory voting tests. It also authorized federal registrars to register voters in seven southern states, where less than half of the voting-age population had registered to vote in the 1964 election. For good measure, in 1966 the Supreme Court ruled in *Harper* v. *Virginia State Board of Elections* that state poll taxes are unconstitutional.[31] Although

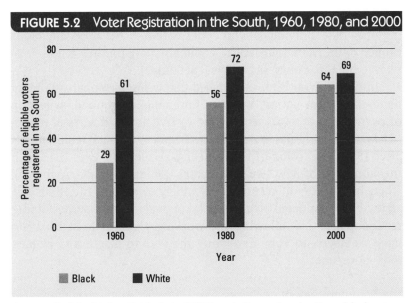

FIGURE 5.2   Voter Registration in the South, 1960, 1980, and 2000

As a result of the Voting Rights Act of 1965 and other national actions, black voter registration in the eleven states of the old Confederacy nearly doubled between 1960 and 1980. In 2000, there was very little difference between the voting registration rates of white and black voters in the Deep South.

Sources: Data for 1960 and 1980 are from U.S. Bureau of the Census, *Statistical Abstract of the United States, 1982–1983* (Washington, D.C.: U.S. Government Printing Office, 1983), p. 488; data for 2000 come from the U.S. Census Bureau, *Current Population Report,* P20-542, Table 3, Internet release, 27 February 2002.

long in coming, these actions by the national government to enforce political equality within the states dramatically increased the registration of southern blacks (see Figure 5.2).

The Enfranchisement of Women. Women also had to fight long and hard to win the right to vote. Until 1869, women could not vote anywhere in the world.[32] Women began to organize to obtain suffrage in the mid-1800s. Known then as *suffragettes,* the early feminists initially had a limited effect on politics. Their first major victory did not come until 1869, when Wyoming, while still a territory, granted women the right to vote. No state followed suit until 1893, when Colorado enfranchised women.

Between 1896 and 1918, twelve other states gave women the vote. Most of these states were in the West, where pioneer women often departed from traditional women's roles. Nationally, the women's suffrage movement intensified, often resorting to unconventional political behaviors (marches, demonstrations), which occasionally

The Fight for Women's Suffrage . . . and Against It

Militant suffragettes demonstrated outside the White House prior to ratification of the Nineteenth Amendment to the Constitution, which gave women the right to vote. Congress passed the proposed amendment in 1919, and it was ratified by the required number of states in time for the 1920 presidential election. Suffragettes' demonstrations were occasionally disrupted by men—and other women—who opposed extending the right to vote to women.

(Courtesy of the Library of Congress)

invited violent attacks from men and even other women. In 1919, Congress finally passed the Nineteenth Amendment, which prohibits states from denying the right to vote "on account of sex." The amendment was ratified in 1920, in time for the November election.

Evaluating the Expansion of Suffrage in America. The last major expansion of suffrage in the United States took place in 1971, when the Twenty-sixth Amendment lowered the voting age to eighteen. For most of its history, the United States has been far from the democratic ideal of universal suffrage. However, compared with other countries, it looks pretty democratic.[33] Women did not gain the vote on equal terms with men until 1921 in Norway; 1922 in the Netherlands; 1944 in France; 1946 in Italy, Japan, and Venezuela; 1948 in Belgium; and 1971 in Switzerland. Women are still not universally enfranchised. While women in Kuwait voted for the first time in 2006, women in Saudi Arabia, for example, still lack the right to vote.[34] Of course, no one at all can vote in the United Arab Emirates. In South Africa, blacks, who outnumber whites by more than four to one, were not allowed to vote freely in elections until 1994. With regard to voting age, 158 of 201 countries (almost 80 percent) allow eighteen-year-olds to vote. Another 34 countries set the minimum age at twenty or twenty-one. Fewer than 12 allow persons under age eighteen to vote—including Austria, which has the lowest voting age, at sixteen.[35]

Voting on Policies

Disenfranchised groups have struggled to gain voting rights because of the political power that comes with suffrage. Belief in the ability of ordinary citizens to make political decisions and to control government through the power of the ballot box was strongest in the United States during the Progressive era, which began around 1900 and lasted until about 1925.

Progressivism was a philosophy of political reform that trusted the goodness and wisdom of individual citizens and distrusted "special interests" (railroads, corporations) and political institutions (traditional political parties, legislatures). Such attitudes resurfaced among followers of the Reform Party and others who share this populist outlook.

The leaders of the Progressive movement were prominent politicians (former president Theodore Roosevelt, Senator Robert La Follette of Wisconsin) and eminent scholars (historian Frederick Jackson Turner, philosopher John Dewey). Not content to vote for candidates chosen by party leaders, the Progressives championed the **direct primary**—an election, run by the state governments, in which the voters chose the party's candidates for the general election. Wanting a mechanism to remove elected candidates from office, the Progressives backed the **recall**, a special election initiated by a petition signed by a specified number of voters. Although eighteen states provide for the recall of state officials, only one state governor had ever been unseated until 2003, when California voters threw out Governor Gray Davis in a bizarre recall election that placed movie actor Arnold Schwarzenegger in the governor's mansion.

The Progressives also championed the power of the masses to propose and pass laws, approximating the citizen participation in policymaking that is the hallmark of direct democracy. They developed two voting mechanisms for policymaking that are still in use:

- A **referendum** is a direct vote by the people on a proposed law or on an amendment to a state constitution. The measures subject to popular vote are known as *propositions*. Twenty-four

progressivism
A philosophy of political reform based on the goodness and wisdom of the individual citizen as opposed to special interests and political institutions.

direct primary
A preliminary election, run by the state government, in which the voters choose each party's candidates for the general election.

recall
The process for removing an elected official from office.

referendum
An election on a policy issue.

states permit popular referenda on laws, and all but Delaware require a referendum for a constitutional amendment. Most referenda are placed on the ballot by legislatures, not voters.

- The **initiative** is a procedure by which voters can propose an issue to be decided by the legislature or by the people in a referendum. The procedure involves gathering a specified number of signatures from registered voters (usually 5 to 10 percent of the total in the state), then submitting the petition to a designated state agency. Twenty-four states currently provide for some form of voter initiative.

Hundreds of propositions have appeared on state ballots in general elections since 2000. In November 2010 alone, voters in thirty-six states cast ballots on 159 propositions, passing almost two-thirds of them. Some of these propositions dealt with the most controversial topics in contemporary politics. Symbolic propositions against President Obama's health care plan were adopted in 2010 by voters in Missouri, Arizona, and Oklahoma, while a similar measure was rejected in Colorado.[36] In California, voters rejected propositions intended to legalize marijuana. Voters in Arizona, Oregon, and South Dakota voted to reject medical marijuana measures.[37]

What conclusion can we draw about the Progressives' legacy of mechanisms for direct participation in government? One seasoned journalist paints an unimpressive picture. He notes that an expensive "industry" developed in the 1980s that makes money by circulating petitions, then managing the large sums of money needed to run a campaign to approve (or defeat) a referendum.[38] In 2006, supporters of a measure to tax oil extracted in California in order to fund alternative energy spent $61.3 million. This huge sum, however, pales in comparison to the $92.9 million spent by oil companies and conservative interests to defeat the measure. The proposition failed.[39]

Clearly, citizens can exercise great power over government policy through the mechanisms of the initiative and referendum. What is not clear is whether these forms of direct democracy improve the policies made by representatives elected for that purpose.

Voting for Candidates

We saved for last the most visible form of political participation: voting to choose candidates for public office. Voting for candidates serves democratic government in two ways. First, citizens can

initiative
A procedure by which voters can propose an issue to be decided by the legislature or by the people in a referendum. It requires gathering a specified number of signatures and submitting a petition to a designated agency.

choose the candidates they think will best serve their interests. Second, voting allows the people to reelect the officials they guessed right about and to kick out those they guessed wrong about. In Chapter 6, we look at the factors that underlie voting choice. Here, we examine Americans' reliance on the electoral process.

In national politics, voters seem content to elect just two executive officers—the president and vice president—and to trust the president to appoint a cabinet to round out his administration. But at the state and local levels, voters insist on selecting all kinds of officials. Every state elects a governor (and forty-five elect a lieutenant governor). Forty-two states elect an attorney general; thirty-nine, a treasurer; and thirty-seven, a secretary of state. The list goes on, down through the superintendent of education, secretary of agriculture, board of education, and public utilities commissioners. Elected county officials commonly include commissioners, a sheriff, a treasurer, a clerk, a superintendent of schools, and a judge (often several). At the local level, voters elect all but about 600 of 15,300 school boards across the nation.[40] Instead of trusting state and local chief executives to appoint lesser administrators (as we do for more important offices at the national level), we expect voters to choose intelligently among scores of candidates they meet for the first time on a complex ballot in the polling booth.

In the American version of democracy, the laws recognize no limit to voters' ability to make informed choices among candidates and thus to control government through voting. The reasoning seems to be that elections are good; therefore, more elections are better, and the most elections are best. By this thinking, the United States clearly has the best and most democratic government in the world because it is the undisputed champion at holding elections. The author of a study that compared elections in the United States with elections in twenty-six other democracies concluded:

> No country can approach the United States in the frequency and variety of elections, and thus in the amount of electoral participation to which its citizens have a right. No other country elects its lower house as often as every two years, or its president as frequently as every four years. No other country popularly elects its state governors and town mayors; no other has as wide a variety of nonrepresentative offices (judges, sheriffs, attorneys general, city treasurers, and so on) subject to election. . . . The average American is

entitled to do far more electing—probably by a factor of three or four—than the citizen of any other democracy.[41]

However, the United States ranks near the bottom of industrialized democracies in voter turnout. (See Compared with What? Voter Turnout in European and American Elections since 1945.) How do we square low voter turnout with Americans' devotion to elections as an instrument of democratic government? To complicate matters further, how do we square low voter turnout with the fact that Americans seem to participate in politics in various other ways?

Explaining Political Participation

As you have seen, political participation can be unconventional or conventional, can require little or much initiative, and can serve to support the government or influence its decisions. This section begins our examination of some factors that affect the most obvious forms of political participation, with particular emphasis on voting. Our first task is to determine how much variation there is in patterns of participation within the United States over time.

Patterns of Participation Over Time

Were Americans more politically apathetic in the 2000s than they were in the 1960s? Generally not, as plots of several measures of participation from 1952 through 2008 show little variation over time in the percentage of citizens who were interested in election campaigns, talked to others about voting, worked for candidates, or attended party meetings. The only substantive dip in participation occurred in voter turnout during the 1970s and 1980s. Turnout returned to 1960s levels in 2004 and 2008, but even then voter turnout was much lower than in most European countries. Other forms of participation have remained stable or even increased. What is going on? Who votes? Who does not? Why? And does it really matter?

The Standard Socioeconomic Explanation

Researchers have found that socioeconomic status is a good indicator of most types of conventional political participation. People with more education, higher incomes, and white-collar or professional occupations tend to be more aware of the impact of politics on their lives, to know what can be done to influence government

Compared with What?

Voter Turnout in European and American Elections since 1945

Compared with turnout rates in sixteen established European nations, voter turnout for American presidential elections ranks at the bottom, and turnout for American congressional elections ranks even lower. The European data show the mean percentages of the registered electorate voting in all 292 parliamentary elections from 1945 through 2008. The American data for all 31 presidential and congressional elections from 1946 to 2008 show voters as percentages of the eligible voting-age population (those eighteen and older, excluding noncitizens and ineligible felons). Turnout in U.S. elections tends to average about fifteen points higher in presidential years than in congressional years. As discussed in the text, low turnout in the United States is partly due to requiring voters to register on their own initiative. The governments in virtually all the other nations automatically register eligible citizens as voters. Note also that the United States has held more elections during that period than any other country.

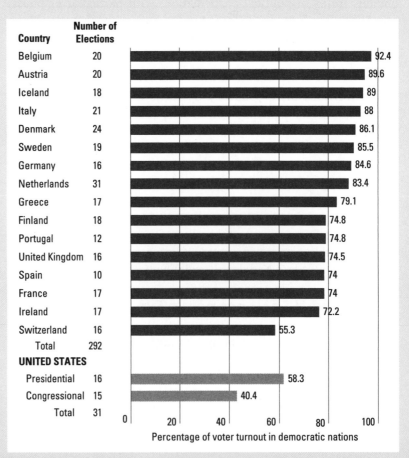

Country	Number of Elections
Belgium	20
Austria	20
Iceland	18
Italy	21
Denmark	24
Sweden	19
Germany	16
Netherlands	31
Greece	17
Finland	18
Portugal	12
United Kingdom	16
Spain	10
France	17
Ireland	17
Switzerland	16
Total	292
UNITED STATES	
Presidential	16
Congressional	15
Total	31

Values shown on bars: Belgium 92.4; Austria 89.6; Iceland 89; Italy 88; Denmark 86.1; Sweden 85.5; Germany 84.6; Netherlands 83.4; Greece 79.1; Finland 74.8; Portugal 74.8; United Kingdom 74.5; Spain 74; France 74; Ireland 72.2; Switzerland 55.3; Presidential 58.3; Congressional 40.4

Percentage of voter turnout in democratic nations

actions, and to have the necessary resources (time and money) to take action. So they are more likely to participate in politics than are people of lower socioeconomic status. This relationship between socioeconomic status and conventional political involvement is called the **standard socioeconomic model** of participation.[42]

Unconventional political behavior is also related to socioeconomic status. Those who protest against U.S. government policies tend to be better educated. Moreover, this relationship holds in other countries too. One scholar notes: "Protest in advanced industrial democracies is not simply an outlet for the alienated and deprived; just the opposite often occurs."[43] In one major way, however, those who engage in unconventional political behavior differ from those who participate more conventionally: protesters tend to be younger.

Younger people are more likely to take part in demonstrations or boycotts, and less likely to participate in conventional politics.[44] Younger people engage in more voluntary and charitable activities, but older Americans are more likely to vote, identify with the major political parties, and contact public officials.[45] Voting rates tend to increase as people grow older, until about age sixty-five, when physical infirmities begin to lower rates again.[46]

Two other variables, race and gender, have been related to participation in the past, but as times have changed, so have those relationships. Blacks, who had very low participation rates in the 1950s, now participate at rates comparable to that of whites, when differences in socioeconomic status are taken into account.[47] Women also exhibited low participation rates in the past, but gender differences in political participation have almost disappeared.[48] (The one exception is in attempting to persuade others how to vote, which women are less likely to do than men.)[49] Research on the social context of voting behavior has shown that married men and women are more likely to vote than those of either sex living without a spouse.[50]

Of all the social and economic variables, education is the strongest single factor in explaining most types of conventional political participation (see Figure 5.3).[51] The strong link between education and electoral participation raises questions about low voter turnout in the United States both over time and relative to other democracies. The fact is that the proportion of individuals with college degrees is greater in the United States than in other countries. Moreover, that proportion has been increasing steadily. Why, then, is voter turnout in elections so low? And why has it dropped over time?

standard socioeconomic model
A relationship between socioeconomic status and conventional political involvement: people with higher status and more education are more likely to participate than those with lower status.

FIGURE 5.3   Effects of Education on Political Participation

Education has a powerful effect on political participation in the United States. These data from a 2008 sample show that level of education is directly related to five forms of conventional political participation. (Respondents tend to overstate whether they voted.)

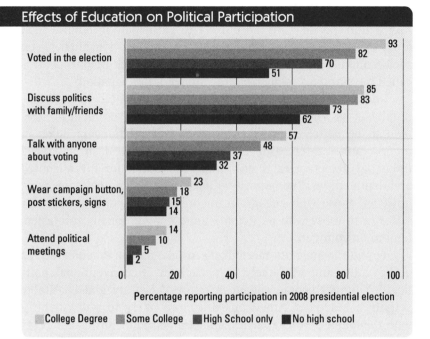

Percentage reporting participation in 2008 presidential election

College Degree   Some College   High School only   No high school

Source: This analysis was based on the 2008 American National Election Time Series Study (Ann Arbor, Mich., and Palo Alto, Calif.: The University of Michigan and Stanford University).

Low Voter Turnout in America

Voting is a low-initiative form of participation that can satisfy all three motives for political participation: showing allegiance to the nation, obtaining particularized benefits, and influencing broad policy. How, then, do we explain the decline in voter turnout in the United States?

The Fluctuation in Voting Over Time. The graph of voter turnout in Figure 5.4 shows that turnout in presidential elections was higher in the 1950s and 1960s than in the 1970s, 1980s, and 1990s, but it increased somewhat in 2004 and 2008.[52] The three-decade downward trend began with a sizable drop between the 1968 and 1972 elections. It was during this period (in 1971, actually) that Congress proposed and the states ratified the Twenty-sixth Amendment, which expanded the electorate by lowering the voting age from twenty-one to eighteen. Because people younger than twenty-one are much less likely to vote, their eligibility reduced the overall national turnout rate (the percentage of those eligible to vote who actually vote). Although young nonvoters inevitably vote more often as they grow older, some observers estimate that the enfranchisement of eighteen-year-olds accounts for about one

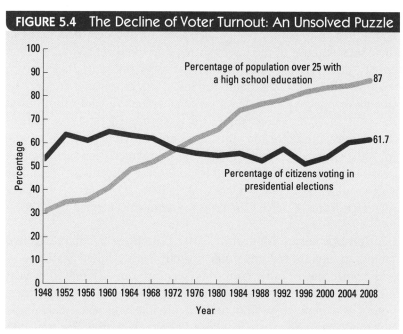

FIGURE 5.4   The Decline of Voter Turnout: An Unsolved Puzzle

Education strongly predicts the likelihood of voting in the United States. The percentage of adult citizens with a high school education or more has grown steadily since the end of World War II, but the overall rate of voter turnout trended downward from 1960 to 1996 and is still below the levels two decades after the war. Why turnout decreased as education increased is an unsolved puzzle in American voting behavior.

Sources: U.S. Census Bureau, *Statistical Abstract 1962* and *Statistical Abstract 2010*, "Table A-1. Years of School Completed by People 25 Years and Over, by Age and Sex: Selected Years 1940 to 2008," at http://www.census.gov/population/www/socdemo/educ-attn.html; and Harold W. Stanley and Richard G. Niemi, *Vital Statistics on American Politics, 2009–2010* (Washington, D.C.: CQ Press, 2009), Table 1.1. The percentage voting in elections is based on the eligible voter population, not the voting-age population.

or two percentage points in the total decline in turnout since 1952, but that still leaves more than ten percentage points to be explained in the lower rates since 1972.[53]

Why has voter turnout declined since 1968, while the level of education has increased? Many researchers have tried to solve this puzzle.[54] Some attribute most of the decline to changes in voters' attitudes toward politics. One major factor is the growing belief that government is not responsive to citizens and that voting does no good. Another is a change in attitude toward political parties, along with a decline in the extent and strength of party identification.[55] This puzzle is compounded by the fact that the decline in turnout is not occurring evenly across the United States. Participation in the South seems to be gradually increasing.

According to the age explanation, turnout in the United States is destined to remain a percentage point or two below its highs of the 1960s because of the lower voting rate of citizens younger than twenty-one. Turnout rates do increase as young people age, which suggests that voting is habit forming.[56] Despite these trends, the Obama campaign stimulated a wave of young voters to turn out at the polls in 2008. Voters under thirty accounted for 17 percent of the votes cast in 2000 and 2004, but they cast 18 percent of the vote in 2008 when over two million more eighteen- to twenty-nine-year-olds turned out. More significantly, the percentage of eligible voters under age thirty who cast ballots is estimated to have increased from 35 percent in 1996 to roughly 50 percent in 2008.

U.S. Turnout Versus Turnout in Other Countries. Scholars cite two factors to explain the low voter turnout in the United States compared with that in other countries. First are the differences in voting laws and administrative machinery.[57] In a few countries, voting is compulsory, and turnout obviously is extremely high. But other methods can encourage voting: declaring election days to be public holidays or providing a two-day voting period. The United States does none of these things.

Furthermore, nearly every other democratic country places the burden of registration on the government rather than on the individual voter. This is important. Voting in the United States is a two-stage process, and the first stage (going to the proper officials to register) requires more initiative than the second stage (going to the polling booth to cast a ballot). In most American states, the registration process is separated from the voting process in both time (usually voters have to register weeks in advance of the election) and geography (often voters have to register somewhere other than their polling place). The seven states that do allow citizens to register and vote on the same day have consistently higher voter participation rates.[58] Turnout is higher in Oregon, where everyone votes by mail.[59] Regardless of voting ease, registration procedures are often obscure, requiring potential voters to call around to find out what to do. People who move (and younger people move more frequently) have to reregister. If we compute voter turnout on the basis of those who are registered to vote, about 80 percent of Americans vote, a figure that moves the United States to the middle (but not the top) of all democratic nations.[60] Since 1995, the so-called motor-voter law has required states to allow citizens to register by mail (similar to renewing drivers' licenses) and at certain agencies that provide public assistance.[61] In the 2001–2002 election cycle, over 42 percent of all voter registration

applications were submitted through state motor vehicle offices.[62] However, a 2009 study showed that half of all voters are unaware that they can register at motor vehicle offices.[63]

The second factor usually cited to explain low turnout in American elections is the lack of political parties that mobilize the vote of particular social groups, especially lower-income and less-educated people. American parties do make an effort to get out the vote, but neither party is as closely linked to specific groups as are parties in many other countries, where certain parties work hand in hand with ethnic, occupational, or religious groups. Research shows that strong party–group links can significantly increase turnout.[64] Similarly, citizens are more likely to turn out to vote when the elections are competitive or close.[65]

To these explanations for low voter turnout in the United States—the traditional burden of registration and the lack of strong party–group links—we add another. Although the act of voting requires low initiative, the process of learning about dozens of candidates on the ballot in American elections requires a great deal of initiative. Some people undoubtedly fail to vote because they feel inadequate to the task of deciding among candidates for the many offices on the ballot in U.S. elections.

Teachers, newspaper columnists, and public affairs groups tend to worry a great deal about low voter turnout in the United States, suggesting that it signifies some sort of political sickness—or at least that it gives us a bad mark for democracy. Others are less concerned.[66] One scholar argues:

> Turnout rates do not indicate the amount of electing—the frequency of occasion, the range of offices and decisions, the "value" of the vote—to which a country's citizens are entitled. . . . Thus, although the turnout rate in the United States is below that of most other democracies, American citizens do not necessarily do less voting than other citizens; most probably, they do more.[67]

Participation and Freedom, Equality, and Order

As we have seen, Americans participate in government in a variety of ways, and to a reasonable extent, compared with citizens of other countries. What is the relationship of political participation to the values of freedom, equality, and order?

Participation and Freedom

From the standpoint of normative theory, the relationship between participation and freedom is clear: individuals should be free to participate in government and politics in the way they want and as much as they want. And they should be free not to participate as well. Ideally, all barriers to participation, such as restrictive voting registration and limitations on campaign expenditures, should be abolished, as should any schemes for compulsory voting. In theory, freedom to participate also means that individuals should be able to use their wealth, connections, knowledge, organizational power (including sheer numbers in organized protests), or any other resource to influence government decisions, provided they do so legally. Of all these resources, the individual vote may be the weakest—and the least important—means of exerting political influence. Obviously, then, freedom as a value in political participation favors those with the resources to advance their own political self-interest.

Participation and Equality

The relationship between participation and equality is also clear. Each citizen's ability to influence government should be equal to that of every other citizen, so that differences in personal resources do not work against the poor or otherwise disadvantaged.[68] Elections, then, serve the ideal of equality better than any other means of political participation. Formal rules for counting ballots—in particular, one person, one vote—cancel differences in resources among individuals.

At the same time, groups of people who have few resources individually can combine their votes to wield political power. Various European ethnic groups exercised this type of power in the late nineteenth and early twentieth centuries, when their votes won them entry to the sociopolitical system and allowed them to share in its benefits (see Chapter 4). More recently, blacks, Hispanics, homosexuals, and people with disabilities have used their voting power to gain political recognition. However, minorities often have had to use unconventional forms of participation to win the right to vote. As two major scholars of political participation put it, "Protest is the great equalizer, the political action that weights intensity as well as sheer numbers."[69]

Participation and Order

The relationship between participation and order is complicated. Some types of participation (pledging allegiance, voting) promote order, and so are encouraged by those who value order; other types promote disorder, and so are discouraged. Many citizens—men and women alike—even resisted giving women the right to vote for fear of upsetting the social order by altering the traditional roles of men and women.

Both conventional and unconventional participation can lead to the ouster of government officials, but the regime—the political system itself—is threatened more by unconventional participation. To maintain order, the government has a stake in converting unconventional participation to conventional participation whenever possible. Think about the student unrest on college campuses during the Vietnam War when thousands of protesting students stopped traffic, occupied buildings, destroyed property, and behaved in other unconventional ways. Confronted by such civil strife and disorder, Congress took action. On March 23, 1971, it enacted and sent to the states the proposed Twenty-sixth Amendment, lowering the voting age to eighteen. Three-quarters of the state legislatures had to ratify the amendment before it became part of the Constitution. Astonishingly, thirty-eight states (the required number) complied by July 1, establishing a new speed record for ratification.[70] As one observer argued, the right to vote was extended to eighteen-year-olds not because young people demanded it but because "public officials believed suffrage expansion to be a means of institutionalizing youths' participation in politics, which would, in turn, curb disorder."[71]

Participation and the Models of Democracy

Ostensibly, elections are institutional mechanisms that implement democracy by allowing citizens to choose among candidates or issues. But elections also serve several other important purposes:[72]

- *Elections socialize political activity.* The opportunity to vote for change encourages citizens to refrain from demonstrating in the streets. Elections transform what might otherwise be sporadic citizen-initiated acts into a routine public function. This helps preserve government stability by containing and channeling away potentially disruptive or dangerous forms of mass political activity.
- *Elections institutionalize access to political power.* They allow ordinary citizens to run for political office or to play an important role in selecting political leaders. Working to elect a candidate encourages the campaign worker to identify problems or propose solutions to the newly elected official.
- *Elections bolster the state's power and authority.* The opportunity to participate in elections helps convince citizens that the government is responsive to their needs and wants, which reinforces its legitimacy.

Participation and Majoritarianism

Although the majoritarian model assumes that government responsiveness to popular demands comes through mass participation in politics, majoritarianism views participation rather narrowly. It favors conventional, institutionalized behavior, primarily voting in elections. Because majoritarianism relies on counting votes to determine what the majority wants, its bias toward equality in political participation is strong. Clearly, better-educated, wealthier citizens are more likely to participate in elections, and get-out-the-vote campaigns cannot counter this distinct bias.[73] Because it favors collective decisions formalized through elections, majoritarianism has little place for motivated, resourceful individuals to exercise private influence over government actions.

Majoritarianism also limits individual freedom in another way: its focus on voting as the major means of mass participation narrows the scope of conventional political behavior by defining which political actions are "orderly" and acceptable. By favoring equality and order in political participation, majoritarianism goes hand in hand with the ideological orientation of communitarianism (see Chapter 1).

Participation and Pluralism

Resourceful citizens who want the government's help with problems find a haven in the pluralist model of democracy. A decentralized and organizationally complex form of government allows many points of access and accommodates various forms of conventional participation in addition to voting. For example, wealthy people and well-funded groups can afford to hire lobbyists to press their interests in Congress. In one view of pluralist democracy, citizens are free to ply and wheedle public officials to further their own selfish visions of the public good. From another viewpoint, pluralism offers citizens the opportunity to be treated as individuals when dealing with the government, to influence policymaking in special circumstances, and to fulfill (insofar as possible in representative government) their social potential through participation in community affairs.

Tying It Together

1. What are the ways citizens can participate in government?
   - Political participation is defined as those actions of citizens that attempt to influence
     - the structure of government.
     - the selection of government officials.
     - the policies of government or to support government and politics.
   - Forms of participation include
     - conventional participation.
     - unconventional participation.

2. What is unconventional participation, and why is it practiced?
   - Unconventional participation is behavior that challenges or defies established institutions and dominant norms.
   - Unconventional participation, such as direct action during the civil rights movement, can be effective.

- Direct action appeals most to those who distrust the political system but have a strong sense of political efficacy.
- Americans are less likely to take part in demonstrations than their European counterparts.

3. How can citizens participate in government in more conventional ways?
   - Conventional behavior falls into two categories:
     - supportive behavior.
     - influencing behavior.
   - Supportive behaviors are actions that express allegiance to country and government. They include
     - pledging allegiance.
     - flying the flag.
     - voting.
     - serving as an election judge.
     - organizing a holiday parade.
   - Influencing behaviors attempt to modify or reverse government policy to serve particular political interests.
   - Particularized forms of participation
     - are consistent with democratic theory.
     - are used more by citizens who are advantaged.
     - can serve private interests to the detriment of the majority.
   - Participation can require high initiative or low initiative.

4. How does society promote participation?
   - Two terms refer to the right to vote: suffrage and the franchise.
   - Progressivism championed participation by
     - the direct primary.
     - recall elections.
     - referendum votes.
     - initiative procedures.
   - Voting to choose candidates for political office is the most visible form of political participation and serves democracy because
     - citizens can choose the candidate they think will best serve their interests.
     - people can reelect officials they want to keep in office and vote out those they do not want to represent them.
   - Americans seem to participate in many political activities at high levels but have low voter turnout.

5. How do Americans participate through voting?
   - Young people are more likely to engage in unconventional participation than other people.
   - Older citizens are more likely to vote than younger citizens.

- Blacks and women are voting at higher rates today than in the past.
- Voting is a low-initiative activity that satisfies all three motives for participation:
  - showing allegiance.
  - obtaining particularized benefits.
  - influencing policy.
- Voter turnout has declined because
  - voters believe government is unresponsive.
  - fewer people identify with political parties.
  - Americans have voter registration procedures that may lower voter participation.
  - parties have not mobilized voters, which may lower participation.

6. What is the relationship of political participation to the values of freedom, equality, and order?
   - Individuals should be free to participate in government and politics in any way they want.
     - Barriers to voting should be abolished.
     - Individuals should be able to use their resources to influence the government legally.
   - Each citizen's influence on government should be the same as another's.
     - Elections serve this ideal.
     - Groups can use their voting power to gain influence.
   - Unconventional participation is a greater threat to order than conventional participation.
   - Government has a stake in promoting conventional participation.

7. What are the purposes of elections, and how do these serve the models of democracy?
   - Elections socialize political activity.
   - Elections institutionalize access to political power.
   - Elections bolster the state's power and authority.
   - Majoritarianism supports conventional participation.
   - Pluralism supports participation as it gives groups many access points to government.

Test Prepper 5.1

Democracy and Political Participation

True or False?

1. Voting is the only legitimate way for citizens to participate in government in a democracy.
2. Elections do not guarantee a democratic government.
3. All demonstrations are considered unconventional participation.

Comprehension

4. What constitutes unconventional participation?
5. List some examples of conventional participation.

Test Prepper 5.2

Unconventional Participation

True or False?

1. Direct action, used in the civil rights movement, is a form of unconventional participation.
2. The Underground Railroad is probably the first example of unconventional participation in the history of the United States.
3. Unconventional participation never works.

Comprehension

4. Who is most likely to engage in unconventional participation?
5. Compare American unconventional participation to that in other countries.

Test Prepper 5.3

Conventional Participation

True or False?

1. Supportive behaviors are forms of unconventional participation.
2. Influencing behaviors are used by citizens when they have exhausted all possible means of participation in their government.
3. *Brown* v. *Board of Education* is an example of a class-action suit.

Comprehension

4. Explain the NIMBY phenomenon.
5. How do supportive and influencing behaviors differ?

Test Prepper 5.4

Participating Through Voting

True or False?

1. Suffrage refers to political persecution.
2. In 1869 Wyoming became the first territory to grant women the right to vote.
3. Progressivism was a political reform philosophy that trusted the ability of voters to make political decisions at the ballot box.

Comprehension

4. How do referenda and initiatives differ?
5. Describe and give examples of how the United States has the most democratic government in the world because of its elections.

Explaining Political Participation

True or False?

1. Voter turnout in the United States has steadily increased over the last half century.
2. Education is the strongest single factor in explaining most types of conventional political participation.
3. Voting is considered a high-effort activity.

Comprehension

4. Why did voter turnout decline after 1968 despite an increase in education?
5. What could the United States do to increase voter turnout?

Participation and Freedom, Equality, and Order

True or False?

1. In the United States, elections serve the ideal of equality better than any other form of political participation.
2. Student unrest on campuses during the Vietnam War led Congress to curtail voting rights for young Americans.

Comprehension

3. How does participation serve the ideal of equality?
4. Describe how the unrest on college campuses during the Vietnam War constituted unconventional participation and the results it produced.

Participation and the Models of Democracy

True or False?

1. Elections institutionalize access to political power.
2. Elections diminish the state's power because they involve citizens in decision making.
3. Resourceful and wealthy people have advantages in both the pluralist and majoritarian models of democracy.

Comprehension

4. How does majoritarianism limit individual freedom?

CourseMate CL Resources:

Visit www.cengagebrain.com/shop/ISBN/1111832587 for flashcards, web quizzes, videos and more!

AP Photo/Ed Reinke

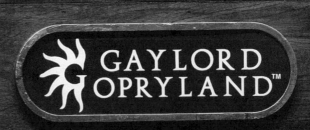

FOCUS QUESTIONS

1. What are political parties, and what are their roles in a democracy?
2. How have U.S. political parties become institutionalized?
3. In what ways does the two-party system function in the United States?
4. How are parties organized?
5. Are American parties consistent with the majoritarian model?
6. What is the party's role in nominating candidates and structuring voter choice?
7. How is the election process structured?
8. How are campaigns organized and executed?
9. Why do people choose one candidate over another?
10. How can campaigns and elections be explained in terms of the two models of democracy?

In 2009, voters in the far northeast region of New York elected a Democrat to Congress for the first time since the Civil War. The story of why the seat changed hands begins with their 2008 reelection of Republican John M. McHugh. After comfortably winning the Twenty-third Congressional District for the fourth straight time, McHugh was appointed Secretary of the Army by President Obama in the summer of 2009. That appointment created a vacancy in Congress to be filled in a special election on November 2, which was expected to produce a Republican replacement.

Republican Party leaders in the district's counties selected as their candidate Republican New York State assemblywoman Dierdre "Dede" Scozzafava,

who held moderate views on abortion and same-sex marriage and supported the federal stimulus package. In keeping with the national party's strategy to expand its base by relaxing ideological purity,[1] local leaders passed over other possibilities, including committed social conservative Douglas Hoffman. The Republican National Committee (RNC) heartily accepted Scozzafava's candidacy and directed almost a million dollars into her campaign. Former House speaker Newt Gingrich backed her as a Republican who could readily defeat the Democratic candidate, Bill Owens, an air force veteran.

Rejected Republican contender Doug Hoffman did not go away, however. He filed to run in November as a candidate of New York's Conservative

Party, claiming that Scozzafava was a "RINO"—Republican in Name Only—and far too liberal to represent the Twenty-third District. Hoffman attracted to his cause prominent conservative Republicans, including 2008 vice-presidential candidate Sarah Palin, Minnesota governor and 2012 presidential hopeful Tim Pawlenty, and former House majority leader Dick Armey. They were joined by conservative talk show host Rush Limbaugh, Fox TV commentator Glenn Beck, and editors of the *Wall Street Journal.* Conservatives poured money into Hoffman's campaign and attacked Scozzafava, whose polls nosedived so that she trailed both Hoffman and Owens less than one week before the election.

On October 31, the official Republican candidate suspended her campaign. Saying she was outspent and unable to address "charges that have been made about my record," she endorsed Owens, her Democratic opponent.[2] The RNC backtracked and said that it would "endorse and support the Conservative candidate, Doug Hoffman." Nevertheless, the surprised Democratic candidate Owens took 49 percent of the vote to Hoffman's 45 percent. Republican Scozzafava (still on the ballot) got 5 percent.

Most observers attributed Hoffman's defeat to voters' resentment of outside intervention in the district. A local Republican Party leader said, "I'm seeing part of the party I never knew existed."[3] Hoffman's conservative supporters preferred losing the seat to electing a Republican who was not sufficiently conservative. Moreover, they think that fielding more conservative candidates will produce more Republican victories. Tom Davis, a former chair of the National Republican Congressional Committee, worried that his party would see more conservative challenges to moderate candidates in primary fights, which could get "very, very ugly."[4]

U.S. politics is dominated by a two-party system. The Democratic and Republican parties have dominated national and state politics for more than 125 years. Their domination is closer to complete than that of any pair of parties in any other democratic government. Although all democracies have some form of multiparty politics, very few have a stable two-party system, Britain being the most notable exception. Most people take our two-party system for granted, not realizing that it is arguably the most distinctive feature of the American government.

Why do we have any political parties? What functions do they perform? How did we become a nation of Democrats and Republicans? Are parties really necessary for democratic government, or do they get in the way of citizens and their government? In this chapter, we answer these questions by examining political parties, perhaps the most misunderstood element of American politics.

And what of the election campaigns conducted by the two major parties? In this chapter, we also consider how those campaigns have changed over time, how candidates are nominated in the United States, what factors are important in election campaigns, and why voters choose one candidate over another. In addition, we address these other important questions: Do election campaigns function more to inform or to confuse voters? How important is money in conducting a winning election campaign? What are the roles of party identification, issues, and candidate attributes in influencing voters' choices and thus election outcomes? How do campaigns, elections, and parties fit into the majoritarian and pluralist models of democracy?

Political Parties and Their Functions

According to democratic theory, the primary means by which citizens control their government is by voting in free elections. Most Americans agree that voting is important. Of those surveyed after the 2008 presidential campaign, 89 percent felt that elections made the government "pay attention to what the people think."[5] Americans are not nearly as supportive of the role that political parties play in elections, however. When asked whether Ross Perot should run for president in 1996 as "head of a third party which would also run candidates in state and local races" or "by himself as an independent candidate," 60 percent of a national sample favored his running without a party.[6]

Nevertheless, Americans are quick to condemn as "undemocratic" countries that do not hold elections contested by political parties. In truth, Americans have a love–hate relationship with political parties. They believe that parties are necessary for democratic government; at the same time, they think parties are somehow "obstructionist" and not to be trusted. This distrust is particularly strong among younger voters. To better appreciate the role of political parties in democratic government, we must understand exactly what parties are and what they do.

What Is a Political Party?

A **political party** is an organization that sponsors candidates for political office *under the organization's name.* The italicized part of this definition is important. True political parties select individuals to run for public office through a formal process of **nomination,** which designates them as the parties' official candidates. This activity distinguishes the Democratic and Republican parties from interest groups. The AFL-CIO and the National Association of Manufacturers are interest groups. They often support candidates in various ways,

political party
An organization that sponsors candidates for political office under the organization's name.

nomination
Designation as an official candidate of a political party.

but they do not nominate them to run as their avowed representatives. If they did, they would be transformed into political parties. In short, the sponsoring of candidates designated as representatives of the organization is what defines an organization as a party. Because the so-called tea party does not nominate its own candidates, it is not a national political party, despite holding a national convention in 2010 and having some candidates on the 2010 ballot at the state level.[7]

Most democratic theorists agree that a modern nation-state cannot practice democracy without at least two political parties that regularly contest elections. In fact, the link between democracy and political parties is so close that many people define *democratic government* in terms of competitive party politics.

Party Functions

Parties contribute to democratic government through the functions they perform for the **political system**—the interrelated institutions that link people with government. Four of the most important party functions are nominating candidates for election to public office, structuring the voting choice in elections, proposing alternative government programs, and coordinating the actions of government officials.

Nominating Candidates. Without political parties, voters would confront a bewildering array of self-nominated candidates, each seeking votes on the basis of personal friendships, celebrity status, or name. Parties can provide a form of quality control for their nominees through the process of peer review. Party insiders, the nominees' peers, usually know the strengths and faults of potential candidates much better than average voters do and thus can judge their suitability for representing the party.

In nominating candidates, parties often do more than pass judgment on potential office seekers. Sometimes they go so far as to recruit talented individuals to become party candidates. In this way, parties help not only to ensure a minimum level of quality among candidates who run for office but also to raise the quality of those candidates.

Structuring the Voting Choice. Political parties also help democratic government by structuring the voting choice—reducing the number of candidates on the ballot to those who have a realistic chance of winning. Established parties—those with experience in contesting elections—acquire a following of loyal voters who guarantee the

political system
A set of interrelated institutions that links people with government.

party's candidates a predictable base of votes. The ability of established parties to mobilize their supporters has the effect of discouraging nonparty candidates from running for office and discouraging new parties from forming. Consequently, the realistic choice is between candidates offered by the major parties, reducing the amount of new information that voters need to make a rational decision.

Proposing Alternative Government Programs. Parties also help voters choose candidates by proposing alternative programs of government action—the general policies their candidates will pursue if they gain office. Even if voters know nothing about the qualities of the parties' candidates, they can vote rationally for candidates of the party that has policies they favor. The specific policies advocated vary from candidate to candidate and from election to election. However, candidates of the same party tend to favor policies that fit their party's underlying political philosophy, or ideology.

In many countries, parties' names, such as *Conservative* and *Socialist,* reflect their political stance. The Democrats and Republicans have issue-neutral names, but many minor parties in the United States have used their names to advertise their policies: the Prohibition Party, the Socialist Party, and even the Reform Party. The neutrality of the two major parties' names suggests that their policies are similar. This is not true. As we shall see, they regularly adopt very different policies in their platforms.

Coordinating the Actions of Government Officials. Finally, party organizations help coordinate the actions of public officials. A government based on the separation of powers, such as that of the United States, divides responsibilities for making public policy. The president and the leaders of the House and Senate are not required to cooperate with one another. Political party organizations are the major means for bridging the separate powers to produce coordinated policies that can govern the country effectively.

A History of U.S. Party Politics

The two major U.S. parties are among the oldest in the world. In fact, the Democratic Party, founded in 1828 but with roots reaching back into the late 1700s, has a strong claim to being the oldest party in existence. Its closest rival is the British Conservative Party, formed in 1832, two decades before the Republican Party was organized in 1854. Several generations of Americans have supported the Democratic and

Republican parties, which have become institutionalized in our political process.

The Emergence of the Party System

Today we think of party activities as normal, even essential, to American politics. It was not always so. The Constitution makes no mention of political parties, and none existed when the Constitution was written in 1787. It was common then to refer to groups pursuing some common political interest as *factions*. Although factions were seen as inevitable in politics, they were also considered dangerous. One argument for adopting the Constitution—proposed in *Federalist No. 10* (see Chapter 2)—was that its federal system would prevent factional influences from controlling the government.

The debate over ratification of the Constitution produced two factions. Those who backed the Constitution were loosely known as *Federalists,* their opponents as *Antifederalists*. At this stage, the groups could not be called parties because they did not sponsor candidates for election. We can classify George Washington as a Federalist because he supported the Constitution, but he was not a factional leader and actually opposed factional politics. During Washington's administration, however, the political cleavage sharpened between those who favored a stronger national government and those who wanted a less powerful, more decentralized national government.

Members of the first group, led by Alexander Hamilton, proclaimed themselves Federalists. Members of the second group, led by Thomas Jefferson, called themselves Republicans. (Although they used the same name, they were *not* the Republicans as we know them today. Indeed, Jefferson's followers were later known as the Democratic Republicans.) Disheartened by the political split in his administration, Washington spoke out against "the baneful effects" of parties in his farewell address in 1796. Nevertheless, parties already existed in the political system. For the most part, from that time to the present, two major political parties have competed for political power.

The Current Party System: Democrats and Republicans

By 1820, the Federalists were no more. In 1828, the Democratic Republican Party split in two. One wing, led by Andrew Jackson, became the Democratic Party. The other later joined forces with several minor parties and formed the Whig Party, which lasted for two decades.

In the early 1850s, antislavery forces (including Whigs and antislavery Democrats) began to organize. They formed a new party, the Republican Party, to oppose the extension of slavery into the Kansas and Nebraska territories. It is this party, founded in 1854, that continues as today's Republican Party. In 1860, the Republicans nominated Abraham Lincoln and successfully confronted a Democratic Party deeply divided over slavery.

The election of 1860 is considered the first of three critical elections under the current party system.[8] A **critical election** is marked by a sharp change in existing patterns of party loyalties among groups of voters. This change, which is called an **electoral realignment,** lasts through several subsequent elections.[9] When one party in a two-party system regularly enjoys support from most of the voters, it is called the *majority party*; the other is called the *minority party*.

The 1860 election divided the country between the northern states, which mainly voted Republican, and the southern states, which were overwhelmingly Democratic. The victory of North over South in the Civil War cemented Democratic loyalties in the South, particularly following the withdrawal of federal troops after the 1876 election. For forty years, from 1880 to 1920, no Republican presidential candidate won even one of the eleven states of the former Confederacy.

A second critical election, in 1896, transformed the Republican Party into a true majority party when, in opposition to the Democrats' inflationary free silver platform, a link was forged between the Republican Party and business. Voters in the heavily populated Northeast and Midwest surged toward the Republican Party, many of them permanently.

A third critical election occurred in 1932, when Franklin Delano Roosevelt led the Democratic Party to majority party status by uniting southern Democrats, northern urban workers, middle-class liberals, Catholics, Jews, and white ethnic minorities in the "Roosevelt coalition." (The relatively few blacks who voted at that time tended to remain loyal to the Republicans, the "party of Lincoln.") Democrats held control of both houses of Congress in most sessions from 1933 until 1995. In 1995, Republicans gained control of Congress for the first time in forty years. They retained control after the 1996 elections—the first time that Republicans took both houses in successive elections since Herbert Hoover's presidency. In 2007,

critical election
An election that produces a sharp change in the existing pattern of party loyalties among groups of voters.

electoral realignment
The change in voting patterns that occurs after a critical election.

Democrats regained control of both the House and the Senate after a decade of Republican dominance.

The North–South coalition of Democratic voters forged by Roosevelt in the 1930s has completely crumbled. Since 1952, in fact, the South has voted more consistently for Republican presidential candidates than for Democrats, and rural voters have become decidedly more Republican.[10] The majority of southern senators and representatives are now Republicans. However, the Democratic coalition of urban workers and ethnic minorities still seems intact, if weakened. Some scholars say that in the 1970s and 1980s we were in a period of **electoral dealignment**, in which party loyalties have become less important to voters as they cast their ballots. Others counter that partisanship increased in the 1990s in a gradual process of realignment not marked by a single critical election.[11] We examine the influence of party loyalty on voting later in this chapter.

The American Two-Party System

The critical election of 1860 established the Democratic and Republican parties as the major parties in our **two-party system**. In a two-party system, most voters are so loyal to one or the other of the major parties that independent candidates or candidates from a third party (which means any minor party) have little chance of winning office. Third-party candidates tend to be most successful at the local or state level. Since the current two-party system was established, relatively few minor-party candidates have won election to the U.S. House; very few have won election to the Senate, and none has won the presidency. However, we should not ignore the special contributions of certain minor parties, among them the Anti-Masonic Party, the Populists, and the Progressives of 1912. In this section, we study the fortunes of minor or third parties in American politics. We also look at why we have only two major parties, explain how federalism helps the parties survive, and describe voters' loyalty to the two major parties today.

Minor Parties in America

Minor parties have always figured in party politics in America. Most true minor parties in our political history have been of four types[12]:

- *Bolter parties* are formed from factions that split off from one of the major parties. Seven times in thirty-six presidential elections since the Civil War, disgruntled leaders "bolted the

electoral dealignment
A lessening of the importance of party loyalties in voting decisions.

two-party system
A political system in which two major political parties compete for control of the government. Candidates from a third party have little chance of winning office.

ticket" and challenged their former parties. Bolter parties have occasionally won significant proportions of the vote. However, with the exception of Teddy Roosevelt's Progressive Party in 1912 and possibly George Wallace's American Independent Party in 1968, bolter parties have not affected the outcome of presidential elections.

- *Farmer-labor parties* represent farmers and urban workers who believe that they, the working class, are not getting their share of society's wealth. The People's Party, founded in 1892 and nick-named the "Populist Party," was a prime example of a farmer-labor party. The Populists won 8.5 percent of the vote in 1892 and became the first third party since 1860 to win any electoral votes. Flushed by success, they endorsed William Jennings Bryan, the Democratic candidate, in 1896. When he lost, the party quickly faded. Farm and labor groups revived many Populist ideas in the Progressive Party in 1924. The party died in 1925.

- *Parties of ideological protest* go further than farmer-labor parties in criticizing the established system. These parties reject prevailing doctrines and propose radically different principles, often favoring more government activism. The Socialist Party has been the most successful party of ideological protest. Even at its high point in 1912, however, it garnered only 6 percent of the vote, and Socialist candidates for president have never won a single state. In recent years, the sound of ideological protest has been heard more from rightist parties, arguing for the radical disengagement of government from society. Such is the program of the Libertarian Party, which stresses freedom over order and equality. In contrast, the Green Party protests from the left, favoring government action to preserve the environment.

- *Single-issue parties* are formed to promote one principle, not a general philosophy of government. The Free Soil Party of the 1840s and 1850s worked to abolish slavery. The Prohibition Party, the most durable example of a single-issue party, opposed the consumption of alcoholic beverages. The party has run candidates in every presidential election since 1884. Recently, however, its platform has grown to include other conservative positions, including right-to-life, limiting immigration, and withdrawal from the World Bank.

Minor parties, then, form primarily to express discontent with the choices offered by the major parties and to work for their own objectives within the electoral system.[13]

How have minor parties fared historically? As vote getters, they have not performed well. However, bolter parties have twice won more than 10 percent of the vote. More significant, the Republican Party originated in 1854 as a single-issue third party opposed to slavery in the nation's new territories; in its first election, in 1856, the party came in second, displacing the Whigs. The age of these exceptions is suggestive: although surveys repeatedly show over half the public saying they want a third major party, voters tend not to support them at the polls.[14]

As policy advocates, minor parties have a slightly better record. At times, they have had a real effect on the policies adopted by the major parties. Women's suffrage, the graduated income tax, and the direct election of senators all originated in third parties.[15]

Most important, minor parties function as safety valves. They allow those who are unhappy with the status quo to express their discontent within the system and contribute to the political dialogue. Surely this was the function of Ralph Nader's candidacy with the Green Party in 2000. If minor parties and independent candidates indicate discontent, what should we make of the numerous minor parties that took part in the 2008 election? Not much. The number of third parties that contest elections is much less important than the total number of votes they receive. Despite the presence of numerous minor parties in every presidential election, the two major parties usually collect over 95 percent of the vote, as they did in 2008.

Why a Two-Party System?

The history of party politics in the United States is essentially the story of two parties that have alternating control of the government. With relatively few exceptions, Americans conduct elections at all levels within the two-party system. This pattern is unusual in democratic countries, where multiparty systems are more common. Why does the United States have only two major parties? The two most convincing answers to this question stem from the electoral system in the United States and the process of political socialization here.

In the typical U.S. election, two or more candidates contest each office, and the winner is the single candidate who collects the most votes, whether those votes constitute a majority or not. When the two principles of *single winners* chosen by a *simple plurality* of votes govern the election of members of a legislature, the system (despite its reliance on pluralities rather than majorities) is known as **majority representation**. Think about how American states choose representatives to Congress. A state entitled to ten representatives is divided into ten congressional districts; each district elects one representative. Majority representation of voters through single-member districts is also a feature of most state legislatures.

Alternatively, a legislature might be chosen through a system of **proportional representation**, which would award legislative seats to a party in proportion to the total number of votes it wins in an election. Under this system, the state might have a single statewide election for all ten seats, with each party presenting a list of ten candidates. Voters could vote for the entire party list they preferred, and the party's candidates would be elected from the top of each list, according to the proportion of votes won by the party. Thus, if a party got 30 percent of the vote in this example, its first three candidates would be elected.

Although this form of election may seem strange, more democratic countries use it than use our system of majority representation. Proportional representation tends to produce (or perpetuate) several parties, because each can win enough seats nationwide to wield some influence in the legislature. In contrast, our system of elections forces interest groups of all sorts to work within the two major parties, for only one candidate in each race stands a chance to be elected under plurality voting. Therefore, the system tends to produce only two parties.

The rules of our electoral system may explain why only two parties tend to form in specific election districts, but why do the same two parties (Democratic and Republican) operate within every state? The contest for the presidency is the key to this question. A candidate can win a presidential election only by amassing a majority of electoral votes from across the entire nation. Presidential candidates try to win votes under the same party label in each state in order to pool their electoral votes in the electoral college. The presidency is a big enough political prize to induce parties to harbor uncomfortable coalitions of voters (southern white Protestants allied with northern Jews and blacks in the Democratic Party, for example) just to win the electoral vote and the presidential election.

The American electoral system may force U.S. politics into a two-party mold, but why do the same two parties reappear from election to election? After more than one hundred years of political

majority representation
The system by which one office, contested by two or more candidates, is won by the single candidate who collects the most votes.

proportional representation
The system by which legislative seats are awarded to a party in proportion to the vote that party wins in an election.

socialization, the Republicans and Democrats today have such a head start in structuring the vote that they discourage challenges from new parties. In addition to political socialization within the public, the two parties in power write laws that make it hard for minor parties to get on the ballot, such as requiring petitions with thousands of signatures.[16]

The Federal Basis of the Party System

Focusing on contests for the presidency is a convenient and informative way to study the history of American parties, but it also oversimplifies party politics to the point of distortion. Even during its darkest defeats for the presidency, a party can still claim many victories for state offices. Victories outside the arena of presidential politics give each party a base of support that keeps its machinery oiled and running for the next contest.[17]

Party Identification in America

The concept of **party identification** is one of the most important in political science. It signifies a voter's sense of psychological attachment to a party, which is not the same as voting for the party in any given election. Scholars measure party identification simply by asking, "Do you usually think of yourself as a Republican, a Democrat, an independent, or what?"[18] Voting is a behavior; identification is a state of mind. For example, millions of southerners voted for Dwight Eisenhower for president in 1952 and 1956 but continued to consider themselves Democrats. The proportions of self-identified Republicans, Democrats, and independents (no party attachment) in the electorate since 1952 are shown in Figure 6.1. Three significant points stand out:

- The number of Republicans and Democrats combined far exceeds the proportion of independents in every year.
- The number of Democrats consistently exceeds that of Republicans.
- The number of Democrats has shrunk over time, to the benefit of independents.

Although party identification predisposes citizens to vote for their favorite party, other factors may cause voters to choose the opposition candidate. If they vote against their party often enough, they may rethink their party identification and eventually switch. Apparently this rethinking has gone on in the minds of many

party identification
A voter's sense of psychological attachment to a party.

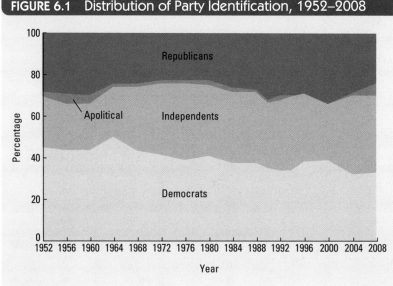

FIGURE 6.1 Distribution of Party Identification, 1952–2008

In every presidential election since 1952, voters across the nation have been asked, "Generally speaking, do you usually think of yourself as a Republican, a Democrat, an independent, or what?" Most voters think of themselves as either Republicans or Democrats, but the proportion of those who think of themselves as independents has increased over time. The size of the Democratic Party's majority has also shrunk. Nevertheless, most Americans today still identify with one of the two major parties, and Democrats still outnumber Republicans.

Sources: National Election Studies, *Guide to Public Opinion and Electoral Behavior*, available at http://www.electionstudies.org/nesguide/nesguide.htm. The 2008 figure is from a PEW Report, "An Even More Partisan Agenda for 2008," 24 January 2008.

southern Democrats over time. In 1952, about 70 percent of white southerners thought of themselves as Democrats, and fewer than 20 percent thought of themselves as Republicans. By 2008, white southerners were only 21 percent Democratic, 39 percent Republican, and 35 percent independent.[19] Much of the nationwide growth in the proportion of Republicans and independents (and the parallel drop in the number of Democrats) stems from changes in party preferences among white southerners and from the migration of northerners, which translated into substantial gains in the number of registered Republicans by 2002.[20]

Who are the self-identified Democrats and Republicans in the electorate? Figure 6.2 shows party identification by various social groups in 2008. The effects of socioeconomic factors are clear. People who have lower incomes and less education are more likely

FIGURE 6.2	Party Identification by Social Groups

Respondents to a 2008 election survey were grouped by seven socioeconomic criteria—income, education, religion, gender, ethnicity, region, and age—and analyzed according to their self-descriptions as Democrats, independents, or Republicans. As income increases, people become more likely to vote Republican. The same is true for education, except for those with advanced degrees. Protestants are far more likely to be Republican than those without religious affiliation, while women, Hispanics, and all nonwhite groups are more likely to be Democrats. Easterners are least likely to be Republican. The main effect of age was to reduce the proportion of independents as respondents grew older. Younger citizens who tend to think of themselves as independents are likely to develop an identification with one party or the other as they mature.

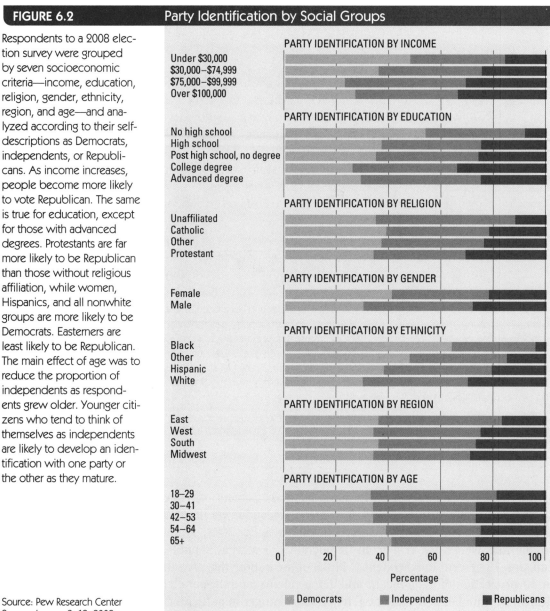

Source: Pew Research Center Survey, January 9–13, 2008.

to think of themselves as Democrats than as Republicans. However, citizens with advanced degrees (such as college faculty) are slightly more Democratic. The cultural factors of religion and race produce even sharper differences between the parties. Jews are strongly Democratic compared with other religious groups, and African Americans are also overwhelmingly Democratic. In addition, American politics has a gender gap: women tend to be more Democratic than men.

The influence of region on party identification has changed over time. Because of the high proportion of blacks in the South, Democrats still outnumber Republicans by a wide margin (in party identity, but not in voting because of lower turnout among low-income blacks). The north-central states have slightly more Republicans than the other regions. Despite the erosion of Democratic strength in the South, we still see elements of Roosevelt's old Democratic coalition of socioeconomic groups. Perhaps the major change in that coalition has been the replacement of white European ethnic groups by blacks, attracted by the Democrats' backing of civil rights legislation in the 1960s.

The ethnic composition of the United States is inexorably becoming less white, and nonwhites today are generally more Democratic than Republican. Estimated at 65 percent in 2010, the non-Latino white population is projected to be only 55 percent in 2030. The Latino and nonwhite share of the population, estimated at 36 percent in 2010, is projected to be 45 percent by 2030.[21] Given that over 70 percent of blacks, Asians, and Latinos voted for Democratic candidates for Congress in 2008, the Republican Party faces problems in the partisan implications of demographic change.

Studies show that about half the citizens in the United States adopt their parents' party. But it often takes time for party identification to develop. The youngest group of voters is most likely to be independent, but people now in their thirties and forties, who were socialized during the Reagan and first Bush presidencies, are heavily Republican. The oldest group is not only strongly Democratic but also shows the greatest partisan commitment (fewest independents), reflecting the fact that citizens become more interested in politics as they mature.

Americans tend to find their political niche and stay there.[22] The enduring party loyalty of American voters tends to structure the vote even before an election is held, even before the candidates are chosen. Later we will examine the extent to which party identification determines voting choice. But first we will look to see whether the Democratic and Republican parties have any significant differences between them.

Party Ideology and Organization

George Wallace, a disgruntled Democrat who ran for president in 1968 on the American Independent Party ticket, complained that "there isn't a dime's worth of difference" between the Democrats and Republicans. Humorist Will Rogers said, "I am not a member of any organized political party–I am a Democrat." Wallace's comment was made in disgust, Rogers's in jest. Wallace was wrong; Rogers was close to being right. Here we will dispel the myth that the parties do not differ significantly on issues and explain how they are organized to coordinate the activities of party candidates and officials in government.

Differences in Party Ideology

George Wallace notwithstanding, there is more than a dime's worth of difference between the two parties. In fact, the difference amounts to many billions of dollars–the cost of the different government programs supported by each party. Democrats are more disposed to government spending to advance social welfare (and hence to promote equality) than are Republicans. And social welfare programs cost money, a lot of money. Republicans, however, are not averse to spending billions of dollars for the projects they consider important. Although President George W. Bush introduced a massive tax cut, he also revived spending on missile defense, backed a $400 billion increase in Medicare, and proposed building a space platform on the moon for travel to Mars. One result was a huge increase in the budget deficit and a rare *Wall Street Journal* editorial against the GOP "spending spree."[23]

Voters and Activists. One way to examine the differences is to compare party voters with party activists. When such a comparison was done in 2008, it was found that 16 percent of those who identified themselves as Democratic voters described themselves as conservatives, compared with 63 percent of those who identified themselves as Republican voters. The ideological gap between the parties is even larger among party activists (see Figure 6.3). Only 3 percent of the delegates to the 2008 Democratic convention considered themselves conservatives compared with 72 percent of the delegates to the Republican convention.

party platform
The statement of policies of a national political party.

Platforms: Freedom, Order, and Equality. For another test of party philosophy, we can look at the **party platforms**–the statements of

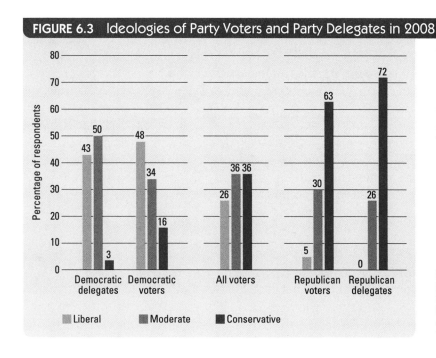

FIGURE 6.3 Ideologies of Party Voters and Party Delegates in 2008

Contrary to what many people think, the Democratic and Republican parties differ substantially in their ideological centers of gravity. When citizens were asked to classify themselves on an ideological scale, more Republicans than Democrats described themselves as conservative. When delegates to the parties' national conventions were asked to classify themselves, the differences between the parties grew even sharper.

Source: *New York Times*/CBS News Poll, 2008 Democratic National Delegate Survey and 2008 Republican National Survey, cited in *The New York Times*, 1 September 2008, p. A14.

policies—adopted in party conventions. Although many people feel that party platforms do not matter very much, several scholars have demonstrated that winning parties tend to carry out much of their platforms when in office.[24] Party platforms also matter a great deal to the parties' convention delegates. The wording of a platform plank often means the difference between victory and defeat for factions within a party.

The platforms adopted by the Democratic and Republican conventions in 2008 were strikingly different in style and substance, and these differences reflected different preferences for freedom, order, and equality. The Republicans mentioned "free" or "freedom" more than twice as frequently (59 to 26), while the Democrats referred to "equal" or "equality" or "inequality" more than twice as much (14 to 6). Republicans talked more about order than Democrats, mentioning "crime" or "criminals" by a wide margin (34 to 18). The 2008 Republican convention also called for several amendments to the Constitution that reflected their values and priorities. Their platform called for a balanced budget amendment, an amendment to guarantee rights for crime victims, an amendment to end abortion and guarantee rights for the unborn, and an amendment to prevent same-sex marriage. In the Democratic Party's platform, the

only amendment proposed was the equal rights amendment to prohibit gender discrimination. While both platforms recognized many
of the same threats facing the United States, the Republicans identified the "gravest threat" as nuclear terrorism. For Democrats, the
"greatest threat" was global climate change.[25]

Different But Similar. Republicans and Democrats have very different
ideological orientations. Yet many observers claim that the parties
are really quite similar in ideology compared with the different parties of other countries. Although both Republicans and Democrats
favor a market economy over a planned economy more than parties
elsewhere, Republicans do so more strongly than Democrats. A
major cross-national study of party positions in Western countries
since 1945 concludes that the United States experiences "a form of
party competition that is as ideologically (or non-ideologically)
driven as the other countries we have studied."[26]

National Party Organization

American parties parallel our federal system: they have separate
national and state organizations (and functionally separate local
organizations). At the national level, each major party has four
main organizational components:

- *National convention.* Every four years, each party assembles thousands of delegates from the states and U.S. territories (such as Puerto Rico and Guam) in a **national convention** for the purpose of nominating a candidate for president. This presidential nominating convention is the supreme governing body of the party. It determines party policy through the platform, formulates rules to govern party operations, and designates a national committee, which is empowered to govern the party until the next convention.
- *National committee.* The **national committee**, which governs each party between conventions, is composed of party officials representing the states and territories, including the chairpersons of their party organizations. The Republican National Committee (RNC) has about 150 members, and the Democratic National Committee (DNC) has approximately 450 elected and appointed members. The chairperson of each national committee is chosen by the party's presidential nominee, then duly elected by the committee. If the nominee loses the presidential election, the national committee usually replaces the nominee's chairperson.
- *Congressional party conferences.* At the beginning of each session of Congress, Republicans and Democrats in each chamber hold separate **party conferences** (the House Democrats call theirs a *caucus*) to select their party leaders and decide committee assignments. The party conferences deal only with congressional matters and have no structural relationship to each other or to their respective national committee.
- *Congressional campaign committees.* Democrats and Republicans in the House and Senate also maintain separate **congressional campaign committees**, each of which raises its own funds to support its candidates in congressional elections. The separation of these organizations from the national committee tells us that the national party structure is loose; the national committee seldom gets involved with the election of any individual member of Congress. Moreover, even the congressional campaign organizations merely supplement the funds that senators and representatives raise on their own to win reelection.

It is tempting to think of the national party chairperson sitting at the top of a hierarchical party organization that not only controls its members in Congress but also issues orders to the state

national convention
A gathering of delegates of a single political party from across the country to choose candidates for president and vice president and to adopt a party platform.

national committee
A committee of a political party composed of party chairpersons and party officials from every state.

party conference
A meeting to select party leaders and decide committee assignments, held at the beginning of a session of Congress by Republicans or Democrats in each chamber.

congressional campaign committee
An organization maintained by a political party to raise funds to support its own candidates in congressional elections.

committees and on down to the local level. Few notions could be more wrong.[27] In fact, the RNC and DNC do not even really direct or control presidential campaigns. Prospective nominees hire their own campaign staffs during the party primaries to win delegates who will support them for nomination at the party conventions. The main role of a national committee is to support the eventual nominee's personal campaign staff in the effort to win the general election.

For many years, the role of the national committees was essentially limited to planning for the next party convention. The committee would select the site, issue the call to state parties to attend, plan the program, and so on.[28] In the 1970s, the roles of the DNC and RNC began to expand—but in different ways.

In 1968, during the Vietnam War, an unpopular President Lyndon Johnson was challenged for renomination by prominent Democrats, including senators Robert Kennedy and Eugene McCarthy. On March 31, after primary elections had begun, Johnson announced he would not run for reelection. Vice President Hubert Humphrey then announced his candidacy. A month later Senator Kennedy was assassinated. Although Humphrey did not enter a single primary, he won the nomination over McCarthy at a riotous convention angry at the war and the role of party bosses in picking Humphrey. In an attempt to open the party to broader participation, a party commission formulated new guidelines for selecting delegates to the next convention in 1972. These guidelines promised party members a "full, meaningful and timely opportunity" to participate in the process and required that state delegations starting in 1972 include women, blacks, and young people "in reasonable relationship to the group's presence in the population of the state."[29]

The DNC threatened to deny seating at the 1972 convention to any state delegation that did not comply with the guidelines. Never before had a national party committee imposed these kinds of rules on a state party organization, but it worked. To comply with the new guidelines, many more states began to use primaries to select convention delegates.

While the Democrats were busy in the 1970s with *procedural* reforms, the Republicans were making *organizational* reforms.[30] Republicans were not inclined to impose quotas on state parties through their national committee. Instead, the RNC strengthened its fundraising, research, and service roles. Republicans acquired their own building and their own computer, and in 1976 they hired the first full-time chairperson of either national party. The new RNC chairman, William Brock, expanded the party's staff, launched new publications, held seminars, conducted election analyses, and advised candidates—things that national party committees in other countries had been doing for years.

The vast difference between the Democratic and Republican approaches to reforming the national committees shows in the funds raised by the DNC and RNC during election campaigns. During Brock's tenure as chairman of the RNC, the Republicans raised three to four times as much money as the Democrats, and they raised more of their funds in small contributions (less than $100) than the Democrats.

Slow to respond to the Republicans' organizational initiatives, the Democrats acquired their own building in the 1990s and enhanced their computer system for fundraising. After former Vermont governor Howard Dean became the new chair of the DNC in 2005, he pushed a program to build the party's strength in all fifty states. His plan clashed with that of Rahm Emanuel (D-Ill.), at that time the new head of the Democratic Congressional Campaign Committee, who favored focusing resources on "winnable" races in selected states. The clash itself showed the dispersion of power in the national party organization, but the party benefited from both efforts. Thanks largely to Emanuel's fervent work with congressional candidates, the Democrats won control of the Congress in the 2006 election, and state party leaders across the nation praised Dean for improving their organizations.[31] Emanuel later served as President Obama's first White House chief of staff.

State and Local Party Organizations

At one time, both major parties were firmly anchored by strong state and local party organizations. Big-city party organizations, such as the Democrats' Tammany Hall in New York City and the Cook County Central Committee in Chicago, were called *party machines*. A **party machine** was a centralized organization that dominated local politics by controlling elections—sometimes by illegal means, often by providing jobs and social services to urban workers in return for their votes. These patronage and social service functions of party machines were undercut when the government expanded its social services. As a result, most local party organizations lost their ability to deliver votes and thus to determine the outcome of elections.

party machine
A centralized party organization that dominates local politics by controlling elections.

The individual state and local organizations of both parties vary widely in strength, but research has found that "neither the Republican nor Democratic party has a distinct advantage with regard to direct campaign activities."[32] Whereas once both the RNC and the DNC were dependent for their funding on "quotas" paid by state parties, now the funds flow the other way. In addition to money, state parties also receive candidate training, poll data and research, and campaigning instruction.[33]

Decentralized But Growing Stronger

The absence of centralized power has always been the most distinguishing characteristic of American political parties. Moreover, the rise in the proportion of citizens who call themselves "independents" suggests that our already weak parties are in further decline.[34] However, there is evidence that our political parties *as organizations* are enjoying a period of resurgence. Indeed, both national parties have globalized their organizations, maintaining branches in over a dozen nations.[35] And more votes in Congress are being decided along party lines. In fact, a specialist in congressional politics has concluded, "When compared to its predecessors of the last half-century, the current majority party leadership is more involved and more decisive in organizing the party and the chamber, setting the policy agenda, shaping legislation, and determining legislative outcomes."[36]

The Model of Responsible Party Government

According to the majoritarian model of democracy, parties are essential to making the government responsive to public opinion. In fact, the ideal role of parties in majoritarian democracy has been formalized in the four principles of **responsible party government**[37]:

1. Parties should present clear and coherent programs to voters.
2. Voters should choose candidates according to the party programs.
3. The winning party should carry out its program once in office.
4. Voters should hold the governing party responsible at the next election for executing its program.

responsible party government
A set of principles formalizing the ideal role of parties in a majoritarian democracy.

How well do these principles describe American politics? You've learned that the Democratic and Republican platforms are different and that they are much more ideologically consistent than many people believe. So the first principle is being met fairly well. To a lesser extent, so is the third principle: once parties gain power, they usually do what they said they would do. As President Obama's attempt to reform health care showed, however, not every party member will necessarily support the party's position. From the standpoint of democratic theory, the real question lies in principles 2 and 4: Do voters really pay attention to party platforms and policies when they cast their ballots? And if so, do voters hold the governing party responsible at the next election for delivering, or failing to deliver, on its pledges? To answer these questions, we must consider in greater detail the parties' role in nominating candidates and structuring the voters' choices in elections. At the conclusion of this chapter, we return to evaluating the role of political parties in democratic government.

Parties and Candidates

An **election campaign** is an organized effort to persuade voters to choose one candidate over others competing for the same office. An effective campaign requires sufficient resources to acquire and analyze information about voters' interests, develop a strategy and matching tactics for appealing to these interests, deliver the candidate's message to the voters, and get voters to cast their ballots.[38]

In the past, political parties conducted all phases of the election campaign. Today, however, candidates seldom rely much on political parties to conduct their campaigns. How do candidates plan their campaign strategy and tactics now? By hiring political consultants to devise clever "sound bites" (brief, catchy phrases) that capture voters' attention on television, not by consulting party headquarters. How do candidates deliver their messages to voters? By conducting media campaigns, not by counting on party regulars to canvass the neighborhoods. Beginning with the 2004 election, presidential and congressional candidates have also relied heavily on the Internet to raise campaign funds and mobilize supporters.[39]

Increasingly, election campaigns have evolved from being party centered to being candidate centered.[40] Whereas the parties virtually ran election campaigns in the past, now they exist mainly to support candidate-centered campaigns by providing services or funds to their candidates. Nevertheless, we will see that the party label is usually a candidate's prime attribute at election time.

election campaign
An organized effort to persuade voters to choose one candidate over others competing for the same office.

Perhaps the most important change in American elections is that candidates do not campaign just to get elected anymore. It is now necessary to campaign for *nomination* as well. Party organizations once controlled that function. For most important offices today, however, candidates are no longer nominated *by* the party organization but are nominated *within* the party. Party leaders seldom choose candidates themselves; they organize and supervise the election process by which party *voters* choose the candidates. Because almost all aspiring candidates must first win a primary election to gain their party's nomination, those who would campaign for election must first campaign for nomination.

The distinguishing feature of the nomination process in American party politics is that it usually involves an election by party voters. Virtually no other political parties in the world nominate candidates to the national legislature through party elections.[41] In more than half the world's parties, local party leaders choose legislative candidates, and their national party organization must usually approve those choices.

Democrats and Republicans nominate their candidates for national and state offices in varying ways across the country because each state is entitled to make its own laws governing the nomination process. (This is significant in itself, for political parties in most other countries are largely free of laws stating how they must select their candidates.) We can classify their nomination practices by the types of party elections held and the level of office sought.

Nomination for Congress and State Offices

In the United States, almost all aspiring candidates for major offices are nominated through a **primary election**, a preliminary election conducted within the party to select its candidates. Forty states use primary elections alone to nominate candidates for all state and national offices, and primaries figure in the nomination process in all the other states. The rules governing primary elections vary greatly by state and can change between elections. Hence, it is difficult to summarize the types of primaries and their incidence. Every state uses primary elections to nominate candidates for statewide office, but about ten states also use party conventions to place names on the primary ballots.[42] The nomination process, then, is highly decentralized, resting on the decisions of thousands, perhaps millions, of the party rank and file who participate in primary elections.

primary election
A preliminary election conducted within a political party to select candidates who will run for public office in a subsequent election.

There are four major types of primary elections, and variants of each type are used about equally across all states to nominate candidates for state and congressional offices.[43] At one end of the spectrum stand **closed primaries**, in which voters must register their party affiliation to vote on that party's potential nominees. At the other end stand **open primaries**, in which any voter, regardless of party registration or affiliation, can choose either party's ballot. In between are **modified closed primaries**, in which individual state parties decide whether to allow those not registered with either party to vote with their party registrants; and **modified open primaries**, in which all those not already registered with a party can choose any party ballot and vote with party registrants.

Nomination for President

The decentralized nature of American parties is readily apparent in how presidential hopefuls must campaign for their party's nomination for president. Each party formally chooses its presidential and vice-presidential candidates at a national convention held every four years in the summer prior to the November election. Until the 1960s, party delegates chose their party's nominee at the convention, sometimes after repeated balloting over several candidates who divided the vote and kept anyone from getting the majority needed to win the nomination. The last time that either party needed more than one ballot to nominate its presidential candidate was in 1952, when the Democrats took three ballots to nominate Adlai E. Stevenson. Since 1972, both parties' nominating conventions have simply ratified the results of the complex process for selecting the convention delegates. Most minor parties, like the Green Party in 2008, still tend to use conventions to nominate their presidential candidates.

Selecting Convention Delegates. No national legislation specifies how state parties must select delegates to their national conventions. Instead, state legislatures have enacted a bewildering variety of procedures, which often differ for Democrats and Republicans in the same state. The most important distinction in delegate selection is between the presidential primary and the local caucus.

A **presidential primary** is a special primary held to select delegates to attend the party's national nominating convention. Party supporters typically vote for the candidate they favor as their party's nominee for president, and candidates win delegates according to a

closed primary
A primary election in which voters must declare their party affiliation before they are given the primary ballot containing that party's potential nominees.

open primary
A primary election in which voters need not declare their party affiliation and can choose either party's primary ballot to take into the voting booth.

modified closed primary
A primary election that allows individual state parties to decide whether they permit independents to vote in their primaries and for which offices.

modified open primary
A primary election that entitles independent voters to vote in a party's primary.

presidential primary
A special primary election used to select delegates to attend the party's national convention, which in turn nominates the presidential candidate.

variety of formulas. Most Democratic presidential primaries are *proportional*, so candidates who win at least 15 percent of the vote divide the delegates from that state in proportion to the percentage of votes they won in the state's primary. Most Republican primaries are *winner-take-all*, so the candidate receiving the most votes in a state primary election takes all of that state's convention delegates.

Delegate selection by **caucus/convention** has several stages. It begins with local meetings, or caucuses, of party supporters to choose delegates to attend a larger subsequent meeting, usually at the county level. Most delegates selected in the local caucuses openly back one of the presidential candidates. The county meetings, in turn, select delegates to a higher level. The process culminates in a state convention, which selects the delegates to the national convention.

Primary elections were first used to select delegates to nominating conventions in 1912. Now parties in about forty states rely on presidential primaries in some form, which generate approximately 80 percent of the delegates.[44] Because nearly all delegates selected in primaries are publicly committed to specific candidates, one can easily tell before a party's summer nominating convention who is going to be its nominee. Indeed, we have been learning the nominee's identity earlier and earlier, thanks to the **front-loading** of primaries. This term describes the tendency during the past two decades for states to move their primaries earlier in the calendar year to gain more attention from the media and the candidates.[45] In 2008 so many states pushed their delegate selection process so far toward the beginning of the year that more than half of the delegates to both conventions were selected by February 5—when twenty-four states held simultaneous primary elections or caucuses to select convention delegates.[46] Prior to 2000, New Hampshire's primary (the first in the nation) had never occurred that early.

caucus/convention
A method used to select delegates to attend a party's national convention. Generally a local meeting selects delegates for a county-level meeting, which in turn selects delegates for a higher-level meeting; the process culminates in a state convention that selects the national convention delegates.

front-loading
States' practice of moving delegate selection primaries and caucuses earlier in the calendar year to gain media and candidate attention.

Campaigning for the Nomination. The process of nominating party candidates for president is a complex, drawn-out affair that has no parallel in any other nation.[47] Would-be presidents announce their candidacy and begin campaigning many months before the first convention delegates are selected. Soon after one election ends, prospective candidates quietly begin lining up political and financial support for their likely race nearly four years later. By historical accident, two small states, Iowa and New Hampshire, have become the testing ground of candidates' early popularity with party voters. Accordingly, each basks in the media spotlight once every four years.

Midnight Madness in New Hampshire

Once every four years, there's something to do after midnight in Dixville Notch, New Hampshire, and in nearby Hart's Landing. Both small towns (each with under forty residents) revel in the tradition of being the first to vote in the nation's first primary. In 2008, Senator Barack Obama crushed his opposition in the Democratic primary, winning seven of the ten votes cast at midnight in Dixville Notch. On the Republican side of the ballot, John McCain picked up four of the seven votes.

The Iowa caucuses and the New Hampshire primary have served different functions in the presidential nominating process.[48] The contest in Iowa has traditionally tended to winnow out candidates who are rejected by the party faithful. The New Hampshire primary, generally held one week later, tests the Iowa front-runners' appeal to ordinary party voters, which foreshadows their likely strength in the general election. Iowa held its 2008 caucuses on January 3 to be first to select delegates. New Hampshire followed with the nation's first primary on January 8.

To combat the pressures of front-loading in 2008, the Democratic National Committee passed a rule in July 2006 allowing only Iowa, New Hampshire, Nevada, and South Carolina to hold primaries before the February 5 Super Tuesday primaries. The major Democratic candidates pledged not to campaign in states that violated the new party rules.

Two key states—Michigan and Florida—defied the party rules. In response, the DNC initially vowed not to seat Michigan's and Florida's delegates at the party's convention, sparking hot controversy between the candidates. Hillary Clinton claimed that the delegates she won in both states should be counted at the convention. Barack Obama objected that this would be unfair, as both he and Clinton had signed a pledge supporting the rule. Indeed, Obama's name did not even appear on the ballot in Michigan. Ultimately, the Democratic National Committee decided to seat the delegations in question with only one-half vote per delegate.[49] Without the extra delegates from Florida and Michigan, Clinton had fallen too far behind in the delegate count to beat Obama, so she suspended her campaign. Obama went on to win the nomination and full votes were restored to Michigan and Florida in August. The Republican Party also penalized several states for front-loading primaries by reducing their number of delegates, but it did not affect the outcome of their nomination process.

Requiring prospective presidential candidates to campaign before many millions of party voters in primaries and hundreds of thousands of party activists in caucus states has several consequences:

- *When no incumbent in the White House is seeking reelection, the presidential nominating process becomes contested in both parties.* This is what occurred in the 2008 elections. With President Bush ineligible to run again in 2008, twelve Republicans and ten Democrats met the Federal Election Commission's requirements for electronic filing of their presidential campaigns.
- *An incumbent president usually encounters little or no opposition for renomination with the party.* That is what happened in 2004, but challenges can occur. In 1992, President George Herbert Walker Bush faced fierce opposition for the Republican nomination from Pat Buchanan.
- *The Iowa caucuses and New Hampshire primaries do matter.* Since the first Iowa caucus in 1972, ten candidates in each party have won presidential nominations. All of the ten Republicans nominees were first in either Iowa or New Hampshire, as were eight of the Democrats.[50]
- *Candidates favored by most party identifiers usually win their party's nomination.* There have been only two exceptions to this rule since 1936, when poll data first became available: Adlai E. Stevenson in 1952 and George McGovern in 1972.[51] Both were Democrats; both lost impressively in the general election.
- *Candidates who win the nomination do so largely on their own and owe little or nothing to the national party organization, which usually does not promote a candidate.* In fact, Jimmy Carter won the nomination in 1976 against a field of

nationally prominent Democrats, although he was a party out-sider with few strong connections in the national party leader-ship. Barack Obama won in 2008, despite the strong ties Hillary Clinton had to Democratic Party leaders.

Elections

By national law, all seats in the House of Representatives and one-third of the seats in the Senate are filled in a **general election** held in early November in even-numbered years. Every state takes advantage of the national election to also fill some of nearly 500,000 state and local offices across the country, which makes the election even more "general." When the president is chosen every fourth year, the election year is identified as a *presidential election*. The intervening years are known as *congressional, mid-term,* or *off-year elections*.

Presidential Elections and the Electoral College

In contrast to almost all other offices in the United States, the presidency does not go automatically to the candidate who wins the most votes. In fact, George W. Bush won the presidency in 2000 despite receiving fewer votes than Al Gore. Instead, a two-stage procedure specified in the Constitution decides elections for president. The president and vice president are chosen by a group of electors representing the states. These electors, known collec-tively as the electoral college, meet in their respective states to cast their ballots.

The Electoral College. The Constitution (Article II, Section 1) says, "Each State shall appoint, in such Manner as the Legislature thereof may direct, a Number of Electors, equal to the whole Num-ber of Senators and Representatives to which the State may be entitled in the Congress." Thus, each state is entitled to one elector for each of its senators (100 total) and one for each of its represen-tatives (435 votes total), totaling 535 electoral votes. In addition, the Twenty-third Amendment to the Constitution awarded three electoral votes to the District of Columbia, although it elects no voting members of Congress. So the total number of electoral votes is 538. The Constitution specifies that a candidate needs a majority of electoral votes, or 270 today, to win the presidency. If no candidate receives a majority when the electoral college votes,

general election
A national election held by law in November of every even-numbered year.

FIGURE 6.4   State Population Change and the Electoral College

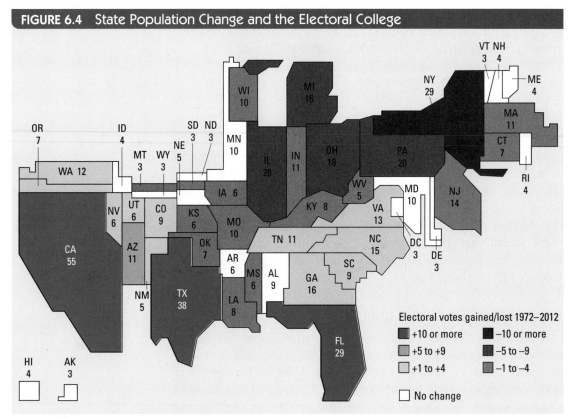

If the states were sized according to their electoral votes, the nation might resemble this map, on which the states are drawn according to their population, based on the census. Each state has as many electoral votes as its combined representation in the Senate (always two) and the House (which depends on population). Although New Jersey is much smaller in area than Montana, it has far more people and is thus bigger in terms of "electoral geography." The shading on this map shows the states that have gained or lost electoral votes since 1972 due to changing population patterns.

(© Cengage Learning 2013)

the election is thrown into the House of Representatives. The House votes by state, with each state casting one vote.*

The 538 electoral votes are apportioned among the states according to their representation in Congress, which depends on their population. Because of population changes recorded by the 2010 census, the distribution of electoral votes among the states changed between the 2008 and 2012 presidential elections. Figure 6.4 shows the distribution of electoral votes for the 2012, 2016,

---

*The candidates in the House election are the top three finishers in the general election. A presidential election has gone to the House only twice in American history, in 1800 and 1824, before a stable two-party system had developed.

and 2020 elections. The distribution will not change again until the 2024 presidential election, which will take population changes identified in the 2020 census into account.

The presidential election is a *federal* election. A candidate is not chosen president by national popular vote but by a majority of the states' electoral votes. In forty-eight states, the candidate who wins a plurality of its popular vote—whether by 20 votes or by 20,000—wins all of the state's electoral votes. (The two exceptions are Maine and Nebraska, where two and three of the states' electoral votes, respectively, are awarded by congressional district. The presidential candidate who carries each district wins a single electoral vote, and the statewide winner gets two additional votes.)

Abolish the Electoral College? Following the controversial 2000 election, letters flooded into newspapers urging that the electoral college system be changed. To evaluate the criticisms, one must first distinguish between the electoral "college" and the "system" of electoral votes. The electoral college is merely the set of individuals empowered to cast a state's electoral votes. In a presidential election, voters do not actually vote for a candidate; they vote for a slate of little-known electors (their names are rarely even on the ballot) pledged to one of the candidates. On rare occasions "faithless electors" break their pledges when they assemble to cast their written ballots at their state capitol in December. This happened in 2004 when a Democratic elector in Minnesota voted for John Edwards for both president and vice president, rather than casting the presidential vote for John Kerry. Such aberrations make for historical footnotes, but they do not affect outcomes.

The more troubling criticism centers on the electoral vote *system,* which makes for a federal rather than a national election. Many reformers favor a majoritarian method for choosing the president: a nationwide direct popular vote. They argue that it is simply wrong to have a system that allows a candidate who wins the most popular votes nationally to lose the election. Until 2000, that situation had not happened since 1888. In fact, the electoral vote generally operated to magnify the margin of victory in the popular vote.

The 2000 election proved that a federal election based on electoral votes does not necessarily yield the same outcome as a national election based on the popular vote. However, three lines of argument support selecting a president by electoral votes rather than by popular vote. First, if one supports a federal form of government as embodied within the Constitution, then one may defend the electoral vote system because it gives small states more weight in the vote: they have two senators, the same as large states. Second, if one favors presidential candidates' campaigning on foot and in rural areas (needed to win most states) rather than campaigning via television to the one hundred most populous market areas, then one might favor the electoral vote system.[52] Third, if one does not want to see a *nationwide* recount in a close election (multiplying by fifty the counting problems in Florida in the 2000 election), then one might want to keep the current system. So switching to selecting the president by popular vote has serious implications, which explains why Congress has not moved quickly to amend the Constitution.

Congressional Elections

The candidates for the presidency are listed at the top of the ballot in a presidential election, followed by the candidates for other national offices and for state and local offices. Voters are said to vote a **straight ticket** when they choose one party's candidates for all the offices. A voter who chooses candidates from different parties is said to vote a **split ticket**. About half of all voters say they split their tickets.[53] A common pattern in the 1970s and 1980s was to elect a Republican as president but send mostly Democrats to Congress, producing divided government (see Chapter 9). This pattern was reversed in the 1994 election, when voters elected a Republican Congress to face a Democratic president. Though Republican president George W. Bush enjoyed a unified government for more than half of his presidency, the 2006 midterm elections brought Democratic majorities to both the House and the Senate. Unified government was restored with the election of Democratic president Barack Obama in 2008.

Heading into the 2010 congressional elections, Republicans hoped to benefit from the historical pattern of the president's party losing seats in fourteen of sixteen midterm elections from 1946 to 2006. The only exceptions to the pattern, Presidents Clinton in 1998 and Bush in 2002, enjoyed approval ratings above 60 percent at election time. President Obama's approval rating had dropped below 50 percent at the end of his first year, unemployment was near historic highs, and more troops were headed to fight an unpopular war in Afghanistan. Although the Democrats held about 60 percent of the seats in both the House and Senate, Republican hopes for 2010 soared when Republican Scott Brown, aided in his campaign by "tea party" activists, won the January election in Massachusetts to replace the late Democratic senator Ted Kennedy. Brown filled the seat held

straight ticket
In voting, a single party's candidates for all the offices.

split ticket
In voting, candidates from different parties for different offices.

by Democrats since the election of 1952. Republican hopes were met in part when the party won control of the House of Representatives in November 2010, but Democrats were able to maintain narrow control in the Senate.[54]

Campaigns

Political scientists Barbara Salmore and Stephen Salmore have developed an analytical framework that emphasizes the political context of an election campaign, the financial resources available for conducting the campaign, and the strategies and tactics that underlie the dissemination of information about the candidate.[55]

The Political Context

The two most important structural factors that face each candidate planning a campaign are the office the candidate is seeking and whether he or she is the *incumbent* (the current officeholder, running for reelection) or the *challenger* (who seeks to replace the incumbent). Incumbents usually enjoy great advantages over challengers, especially in elections to Congress. Incumbents in the House of Representatives are virtually impossible to beat: over 95 percent are reelected.[56] A nonincumbent candidate has a much better chance of winning in an **open election**, which lacks an incumbent as a result of resignation, death, or Constitutional requirement.

Every candidate organizing a campaign must also examine the characteristics of the district, including its physical size and the sociological makeup of its electorate. In general, the bigger and more populous the district and the more diverse the electorate, the more complicated and costly is the campaign.

The party preference of the electorate is an important factor in the context of a campaign. It is easier for candidates to get elected when their party matches the electorate's preference, in part because raising the money needed to conduct a winning campaign is easier. Finally, significant political issues, such as economic recession, personal scandals, and war, not only affect a campaign but also can dominate it and even negate such positive factors as incumbency and the normal inclinations of the electorate.

Financing

Former House Speaker Thomas ("Tip") O'Neill once said, "As it is now, there are four parts to any campaign. The candidate, the issues

open election
An election that lacks an incumbent.

of the candidate, the campaign organization, and the money to run the campaign with. Without money you can forget the other three."[57] Money will buy the best campaign managers, equipment, transportation, research, and consultants, making the quality of the organization largely a function of money.[58] Campaign financing is now heavily regulated by national and state governments, and regulations vary according to the level of the office—national, state, or local. At the national level, new legislation now governs raising and spending money for election campaigns.

Regulating Campaign Financing. In 1971, during a period of party reform, Congress passed the Federal Election Campaign Act (FECA), which imposed stringent new rules for full reporting of campaign contributions and expenditures. FECA has been strengthened several times since 1971. A 1974 amendment created the **Federal Election Commission (FEC)** to enforce limits on financial contributions to national campaigns, require full disclosure of campaign spending, and administer the public financing of presidential campaigns, which began with the 1976 election.

The 1974 legislation imposed limits on contributions by individuals and organizations to campaigns for Congress and the presidency. The FECA targeted so-called **hard money** (direct contributions to candidates' election campaigns) in contrast to **soft money** (donations to party committees for party mailings, voter registration, and get-out-the-vote campaigns). No person could give more than $1,000 per candidate for federal office in a given election.

In reviewing the law, the Supreme Court upheld limits on hard-money contributions; it ruled that wealthy candidates could spend their own money without limit. It also struck down limits on spending by individuals or organizations made independently on behalf of a candidate, ruling that such spending constituted free speech. The 1974 FECA (with minor amendments) governed national elections for almost three decades.

In 2002 Congress passed the **Bipartisan Campaign Reform Act (BCRA)**, introduced by Republican senator John McCain (Ariz.) and Democratic senator Russell Feingold (Wis.). The new law banned soft-money contributions and issue-advocacy ads that favored a given candidate.[59] BCRA was fiercely challenged from several sources, but it was upheld by the Supreme Court in 2003 and took effect for the 2004 election.

In general, BCRA raised the old limits on individual contributions in the 1974 act from $1,000 per federal candidate in an election to

Federal Election Commission (FEC)
A bipartisan federal agency that oversees the financing of national election campaigns.

hard money
Financial contributions given directly to a congressional or presidential campaign.

soft money
Funds raised by parties to be spent on party mailings, voter registration, and get-out-the-vote campaigns rather than for a specific federal election campaign.

Bipartisan Campaign Reform Act (BCRA)
A law passed in 2002 governing campaign financing; the law took effect with the 2004 election.

$2,000 and indexed it for inflation in future years. However, the 2002 law did not raise the $5,000 contribution limit for PACs and did not index PAC contributions for inflation. Here are the major limitations on *individual* contributions for 2009–2010 under BCRA:

- $2,400 to a specific candidate in a separate election during a two-year cycle (primaries, general, and runoff elections count as separate elections)
- $10,000 per year to state, district, and local party committees (combined limit)
- $30,400 per year to any national party committee
- an aggregate limit of $115,500 over a two-year cycle, based on limits to individual candidates and committees

Beginning in 2004, BCRA banned the practice of raising soft money by national party committees, which could now raise and spend only hard money for specific campaigns. However, this ban did not extend to state parties, and BCRA also allowed issue-advocacy groups—called **527 committees** after Section 527 of the Internal Revenue Code, which makes them tax exempt—to raise unlimited amounts of soft money to spend on television commercials and other forms of advertising, as long as they did not expressly advocate a candidate's election or defeat. Scholars studying campaign spending by 527 committees after BCRA found that their contributions increased from $151 million in 2002 to $424 million in 2004.[60]

In 2007, the Supreme Court struck down BCRA's ban on issue ads run before an election, which opened the door to massive independent campaign spending by nonparty groups. Many no longer organized as 527 committees, which were required to report their donors to the FEC, but as 501(c)(4) social welfare organizations, exploiting a legal loophole excusing them from disclosing donors.[61]

In 2010 a bitterly divided Supreme Court departed from its precedents and ruled against BCRA's ban on spending by corporations in candidate elections.[62] Conservatives viewed its decision in *Citizens United* v. *Federal Election Commission* as defending freedom of speech,[63] while liberals saw it as opening the door to the corrupting influence of corporate money.[64] Beginning with the 2010 election, corporations are free to run ads directly advocating a candidate's election for the first time since 1907, when the Congress first banned using general corporate funds in federal election campaigns.[65]

Public Financing of Presidential Campaigns. The 1974 campaign finance law provided public funds for presidential candidates who

527 committees
Political organizations that are organized under Section 527 of the Internal Revenue Code; they enjoy tax-exempt status and may accept unlimited funds from unlimited sources but cannot expressly advocate a candidate's election or defeat.

agreed to abide by an overall campaign spending limit and raised at least $5,000 (in private donations of no more than $250 each) in each of twenty states. The FEC matches these donations up to one-half of a preset spending limit for the primary election campaign. By 2008, the inflation-adjusted spending limit for primary election expenditures had risen to $42.05 million. Candidates who raised up to $21.025 million in private funds would have that amount matched by up to $21.025 million in public funds, subject to the limitation that they could not spend more than $42.05 million in their primary campaigns.

From 1976 through 1992, all major candidates seeking their party's presidential nomination accepted public matching funds for their primary election campaigns and thus adhered to the spending limits. Wealthy publisher Steve Forbes was the first to opt out of the system in 1996. In 2004, Democratic hopefuls Howard Dean and John Kerry and incumbent president George W. Bush (who faced no meaningful opposition for renomination) declined public matching funds and chose to raise their own funds for the primary campaigns, avoiding the spending cap.[66] In 2008, only six of the nineteen candidates who participated in either party's primary debates relied on matching funds.[67] Both Barack Obama and John McCain refused federal matching funds during the primary season, relying on private donations instead. Through March 2008, Obama alone had spent $183 million—far more than the $42 million limit imposed by accepting public funds.

The public funding program for presidential elections in November operates somewhat differently. The campaign spending limit for the general election was roughly $84.1 million in 2008, twice the limit for primary elections. Candidates who accept public funds have no need to raise matching funds privately. They are simply reimbursed by the government up to the spending limit.

From 1976 to 2004, every major party nominee for president accepted public funds and spending limits for the general election. In 2008 Republican John McCain agreed to accept public funds and limit his campaign spending in the general election to $84.1 million. The Democratic nominee, Barack Obama, refused public funds for the general election, becoming the first candidate to do so since the system was established over thirty years earlier. He raised over $745 million in private funds, $150 million in September 2008 alone. If McCain—coauthor of the McCain–Feingold campaign finance reform law (BCRA)—had not been so closely identified with limiting the role of private money in campaigns, he might also have declined public funding and the spending limit it imposed.

Strategies and Tactics

In an election campaign, strategy is the broad approach used to persuade citizens to vote for a candidate, and tactics determine the content of the messages and the way they are delivered. There are three basic strategies, which campaigns may blend in different mixes.[68] A *party-centered strategy* relies heavily on voters' partisan identification as well as on the party's organization to provide the resources necessary to wage the campaign. An *issue-oriented strategy* seeks support from groups that feel strongly about various policies. A *candidate-oriented strategy* depends on the candidate's perceived personal qualities, such as experience, leadership ability, integrity, independence, and trustworthiness.

The campaign strategy must be tailored to the political context of the election. Research suggests that a party-centered strategy is best suited to voters with little political knowledge.[69] How do candidates learn what the electorate knows and thinks about politics, and how can they use this information? Candidates today usually turn to pollsters and political consultants, of whom there are hundreds.[70] Professional campaign managers can use information from such sources to settle on a strategy that mixes party affiliation, issues, and images in its messages.[71] In major campaigns, the mass media disseminate these messages to voters in news coverage, advertising, and the Internet.

Making the News. Campaigns value news coverage by the media for two reasons: the coverage is free, and it seems objective to the audience. If news stories do nothing more than report a candidate's name, that is important, for name recognition by itself often wins elections. Getting free news coverage is yet another advantage that incumbents enjoy over challengers, for incumbents can command attention simply by announcing political decisions.

Advertising the Candidate. In all elections, the first objective of paid advertising is name recognition. The next is to promote the candidates by extolling their virtues. Campaign advertising also can have a negative objective: attacking one's opponent. But name recognition is the most important. Studies show that many voters cannot recall the names of their U.S. senators or representatives but can recognize those names on a list—as on a ballot.

Researchers attribute the high reelection rate for members of Congress mainly to high name recognition (see Chapter 8).

At one time, candidates for national office relied heavily on newspaper advertising; today they overwhelmingly use the electronic media.[72] The media often inflate the effects of prominent ads by reporting them as news, which means that citizens are about as likely to see controversial ads during the news as in the ads' paid time slots.

Using the Internet. The Internet has emerged as a significant tool for fundraising and communicating, particularly with the party faithful.[73] Of the two purposes, fundraising has taken the front seat. In January 2008, the month Barack Obama won contests in Iowa and South Carolina, he raised $32 million from 170,000 new contributors, mostly online.[74] However, candidates need not win stunning victories to raise large sums on the Internet. Republican Ron Paul, who trailed in the polls, raised $4 million online in a single day.[75]

It is more difficult to measure the impact of the Internet in campaign communications. A national survey in December 2008 asked respondents to name two sources for "most of" their news about the presidential campaign. Most people (70 percent) named television. Although about one-third (30 percent) cited newspapers, a larger percentage (40) claimed the Internet over newspapers for the first time.[76] However, because Internet users seek out what they want to view, the best way to reach average voters is still through local broadcast television.[77]

Explaining Voting Choice

Why do people choose one candidate over another? The answer is not easy to determine, but there are ways to approach the question. Individual voting choices may be viewed as products of both long-term and short-term forces. Long-term forces operate throughout a series of elections, predisposing voters to choose certain types of candidates. Short-term forces are associated with particular elections; they arise from a combination of the candidates and the issues at that time. Party identification is by far the most important long-term force affecting U.S. elections. The most important short-term forces are candidates' attributes and their policy positions.

Despite frequent comments in the media about the decline of partisanship in voting behavior, party identification continues to have a substantial effect on the presidential vote, as Figure 6.5

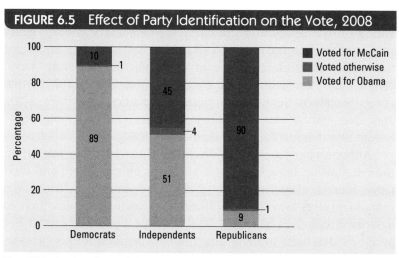

FIGURE 6.5   Effect of Party Identification on the Vote, 2008

■ Voted for McCain
■ Voted otherwise
■ Voted for Obama

The 2008 election showed that party identification still plays a key role in voting behavior, even with an independent candidate in the contest. The chart shows the results of exit polls of thousands of voters as they left hundreds of polling places across the nation on election day. Voters were asked what party they identified with and how they voted for president. Those who identified with one of the two parties voted strongly for their party's candidate.

Source: Data from Bob Davis, "Voters Cast Their Ballots with the Economy in Mind, Exit Polls Indicate," *Wall Street Journal*, November 5, 2008, http://online.wsj.com/article/SB122584499389399483.html#articleTabs%3Dinteractive.

shows. Typically, the winner holds nearly all the voters who identify with his party. The loser holds most of his fellow Democrats or Republicans, but some percentage defects to the winner, a product of short-term forces—the candidates' attributes and the issues— surrounding the election. The winner usually gets most of the independents, who split disproportionately for him, also because of short-term forces.

Candidates' attributes are especially important to voters who lack good information about a candidate's past performance and policy stands—which means most of us. Without such information, voters search for clues about the candidates to try to predict their behavior in office.[78] Some fall back on their personal beliefs about religion, gender, and race in making political judgments. Such stereotypical thinking accounts for the patterns of opposition and support met by a Catholic candidate for president (John Kennedy in 1960) and a woman candidate for vice president (Geraldine Ferraro in 1984). In 2008 Barack Obama tested the stereotype when he became the first African American nominee of a major party.[79]

Voters who choose candidates on the basis of their policies are voting on the issues. Unfortunately for democratic theory, many studies of presidential elections show that issues are less important than either party identification or the candidate's attributes when people cast their ballots. One exception occurred in 1972, when voters perceived George McGovern as too liberal for their tastes, and issue voting exceeded party identification in importance.[80] Recent research has found an increase in policy-based voting.[81]

Although party voting has declined somewhat since the 1950s, the relationship between voters' positions on the issues and their party identification is clearer today. For example, Democratic Party identifiers are now more likely than Republican identifiers to describe themselves as liberal, and they are more likely than Republican identifiers to favor government spending for social security and health care. The more closely party identification is aligned with ideological orientation, the more sense it makes to vote by party. When citizens see differences between parties, they are less likely to vote for incumbents and more likely to justify their voting choice.[82] Similarly, in the absence of detailed information about candidates' positions on the issues, party labels are a handy indicator of those positions.[83]

If party identification is the most important factor in the voting decision and also is resistant to short-term changes, there are definite limits to the capacity of a campaign to influence the outcome of elections.[84] In a close election, however, changing a modest percentage of the votes means the difference between victory and defeat, so a campaign can be decisive even if it has little overall effect. To leverage the impact of their outreach to voters, both presidential candidates in 2008 hired professional consultants to plan their ad campaigns. (As the mother lode for political consultants throughout the world—see "Politics of Global Change: The Americanization of Campaigns"—the United States has plenty to supply.)

Campaigns, Elections, and Parties

Election campaigns today tend to be highly personalized, candidate centered, and conducted outside the control of party organizations. The increased use of electronic media, especially television, has encouraged candidates to personalize their campaign messages; at the same time, the decline of party identification has decreased the power of party-related appeals. Although the party affiliations of

Politics of Global Change

The Americanization of Campaigns

When Americans think about globalization, it is usually in the context of its impact on American politics. Here we consider the effect of the United States on politics and governments in other countries. Foreign scholars have used the term *Americanization of politics* to describe how politics elsewhere has been influenced by political developments in the United States. In no other aspect of politics is "Americanization" more noticeable than in election campaigns, and American influence has grown over time. A 1998 survey identified thirty-five members (half Americans) of the International Association of Political Consultants

(IAPC) who worked outside the United States and Canada. Just two years later, another survey collected responses from almost six hundred campaign consultants in forty-three countries. Based on their responses, this graph shows the extent to which U.S. campaign techniques have been employed in different regions of the world. Of the forty-five IAPC officers and board directors in 2010, nineteen are from the United States. The rest spread over nineteen other countries. In the 2010 Ukrainian presidential election, three different American consulting firms advised the campaigns of the top three contenders.

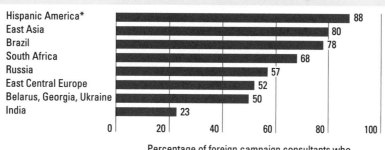

Percentage of foreign campaign consultants who implemented U.S. campaign techniques in their countries

*Argentina, Chile, Colombia, Mexico, and Venezuela

Sources: Shaun Bowler and David M. Farrell, "The Internationalization of Campaign Consultancy," in *Campaign Warriors,* ed. James A. Thurber and Candice J. Nelson (Washington, D.C.: Brookings Institution Press, 2000); Fritz Plasser and Gunda Plasser, *Global Political Campaigning: A Worldwide Analysis of Campaign Professionals and Their Practices* (Westport, Conn.: Praeger, 2002), pp. 41–43, available at http://www.iapc.org; Richard Boudreaux, "Candidates Sought Guidance from American Consultants," *Wall Street Journal,* 9 February 2010, p. A10.

the candidates and the party identifications of the voters jointly explain a good deal of electoral behavior, party organizations are not central to elections in America, and this has implications for democratic government.

Parties and the Majoritarian Model

According to the majoritarian model of democracy, parties link people with their government by making government responsive to public opinion. The Republican and Democratic parties follow the model in that they formulate different platforms and tend to pursue their announced policies when in office. The weak links in this model of responsible party government have been those that connect candidates to voters through campaigns and elections.

You have not read much about the role of the party platform in nominating candidates, conducting campaigns, or explaining voters' choices. Certainly a presidential candidate who wins enough convention delegates through the primaries will be comfortable with any platform that her or his delegates adopt. But House and Senate nominations are rarely fought over the party platform. And thoughts about party platforms usually are absent from campaigning and from voters' minds when they cast their ballots.

Parties and the Pluralist Model

The way parties in the United States operate is more in keeping with the pluralist model of democracy than with the majoritarian model. Our parties are not the basic mechanism through which citizens control their government; instead, they function as two giant interest groups. The parties' interests lie in electing and reelecting their candidates, in enjoying the benefits of public office. In most cases, the parties care little about the positions or ideologies favored by their candidates for Congress and statewide offices.

Some scholars believe that stronger parties would strengthen democratic government even if they could not meet all the requirements of the responsible party model. Our parties already perform valuable functions in structuring the vote along partisan lines and proposing alternative government policies, but stronger parties might also be able to play a more important role in coordinating government policies after elections. At present, the decentralized nature of the nominating process and campaigning for office offers many opportunities for organized groups outside the party to identify and back candidates who favor their interests. Although this is in keeping with pluralist theory, it is certain to frustrate majority interests on occasion.

Tying It Together

1. What are political parties, and what are their roles in a democracy?
   - A political party is an organization that sponsors candidates for political office under the organization's name.
   - Political parties have several functions they perform for the political system, such as
     - nominating candidates.
     - structuring the voting choice.
     - proposing alternative programs of government action.
     - helping coordinate the actions of government officials.

2. How have U.S. political parties become institutionalized?
   - Factions such as the Federalists and Antifederalists were the forerunners of modern political parties.
   - Since 1860 three critical elections have taken place in which a sharp change resulted in electoral realignment:
     - In 1860, the northern states primarily supported the Republicans; the southern states were Democratic.
     - In 1896, the Republican Party was transformed into a true majority party.
     - In 1932, Franklin Roosevelt led the Democratic Party to become the majority party.
   - The party system is likely undergoing an electoral dealignment today as party loyalties are less important.

3. In what ways does the two-party system function in the United States?
   - The critical election of 1860 established Republicans and Democrats as the two major parties.
   - Minor parties have been formed to express discontent with the choices offered by major parties. Four types of minor parties are
     - bolter parties.
     - farmer-labor parties.

- parties of ideological protest.
- single-issue parties.
- The two-party system is maintained by political socialization and the system of majority representation.
- Proportional representation is a system by which legislative seats go to a party based on the proportion of total number of votes the party wins in an election.
- Party identification has changed historically.
  - Socioeconomic factors affect party identification.
  - Regional identification affects party identification.
  - Half of U.S. citizens adopt their parents' party.
  - Voter party identification is generally consistent over time.

4. How are parties organized?
   - Party differences are reflected in party platforms and statements of policies.
   - Parties parallel our federal system with national and state organizations.
   - At the national level, parties have four components:
     - a national convention.
     - a national committee.
     - congressional party conferences.
     - congressional campaign committees.
   - Party machines were centralized organizations that dominated local politics and elections.

5. Are American parties consistent with the majoritarian model?
   - The ideal role of parties in the majoritarian model has been formalized into four principles of responsible party government.
     - Parties should present clear and coherent programs to voters.
     - Voters should choose candidates according to the party programs.
     - The winning party should carry out its program once in office.
     - Voters should hold the governing party responsible at the next election for executing its program.
   - The major U.S. parties meet the requirements of the first and third principles.

6. What is the party's role in nominating candidates and structuring voter choice?
   - To be elected, candidates must conduct election campaigns, which are organized efforts to persuade voters and require strategies and tactics to be successful.

- Party voters nominate candidates through primary elections, of which there are four types:
  - closed primaries.
  - open primaries.
  - modified closed primaries.
  - modified open primaries.
- Delegates chosen through presidential primaries, caucuses, and conventions in each state officially nominate presidential and vice-presidential candidates at a national convention.
  - Republican primaries are generally winner-take-all.
  - Democratic primaries are proportional.
- The process of nominating candidates is complex and has no parallel in any other nation.

7. How is the election process structured?
   - A general election occurs when all seats in the House and one-third of the seats in the Senate are filled in an election held in early November in even-numbered years.
   - A presidential candidate is chosen not by popular vote but by a majority of all the electoral votes awarded by the fifty states and the District of Columbia.
   - The electoral college is the set of individuals who cast electoral votes.
   - Voters vote a straight ticket when they vote solely for their party candidates and split their ticket when they vote for some candidates of each party.

8. How are campaigns organized and executed?
   - When candidates organize their campaigns, they must consider:
     - the great advantages incumbents have in elections.
     - campaign financing, which is heavily regulated by the Federal Election Campaign Act and the Bipartisan Campaign Reform Act, an act that changed spending limits on hard money and soft money.
     - generating news coverage.
     - advertising.
     - using the Internet.

9. Why do people choose one candidate over another?
   - Long-term forces, such as party identification, affect voter choice in elections.
   - Short-term forces, such as issues or a particular candidate's attributes, are secondary factors in elections.

10. How can campaigns and elections be explained in terms of the two models of democracy?
    - Party organizations are not central to elections in America.
    - Republican and Democratic parties follow the majoritarian model as they announce policies and follow them in office.
    - The decentralization of the party system reflects the pluralist model by allowing more input from interest groups.

Test Prepper 6.1

Political Parties and Their Functions

True or False?
1. A political party's only real function is to nominate candidates.
2. Interest groups do not nominate candidates to run as their representatives.
3. The policies of the Democratic and Republican parties are actually quite similar.

Comprehension
4. Explain the difference between political parties and interest groups.
5. What are the roles or functions of political parties?

Test Prepper 6.2

A History of U.S. Party Politics

True or False?
1. The Republican Party was organized in 1828, and the Democratic Party was organized in 1854.
2. The Constitution never mentions political parties.
3. A critical election is one in which an electoral realignment occurs.

Comprehension
4. Were the Federalists and Antifederalists political parties?
5. Explain why 1860, 1896, and 1932 are considered critical elections.

Test Prepper 6.3

The American Two-Party System

True or False?
1. Minor parties often function as safety valves.
2. Majority representation is defined as one office contested by two or more candidates, in which the winner collects the most votes.

3. Based on a 2008 survey, which of the following party identification statements are true?

    a. People in the highest income bracket are most likely to vote Democratic.
    b. African Americans are strongly Republican.
    c. Women tend to be more Democratic than men.
    d. The north-central states have the highest proportion of Republicans.

Comprehension

4. In our history, what have been the four primary types of minor parties?
5. What is party identification, and why is it important?

Test Prepper 6.4

Party Ideology and Organization

True or False?

1. Party platforms are the statements of policies adopted at party conventions and tend to be carried out in office.
2. The Democratic Party reforms of the 1970s focused on inclusion and participation, whereas the Republican Party reforms of that decade focused on organization.
3. Each national party committee has a voice in congressional activity and exercises significant control over state and local campaigns.

Comprehension

4. What are the four main organizational components of each major party at the national level?
5. What is meant by the term *party machine*?

Test Prepper 6.5

The Model of Responsible Party Government

True or False?

1. According to the majoritarian model of democracy, parties are important because they are responsive to special interests.
2. The major American parties present clear and coherent programs to voters.

Comprehension

3. What characterizes the ideal role of parties in a majoritarian democracy?

Test Prepper 6.6

Parties and Candidates

True or False?

1. There are five major types of primary elections: closed primaries, open primaries, modified closed primaries, modified open primaries, and proportional primaries.
2. National party organizations have no voice in when primary elections take place.

3. When no incumbent in the White House is seeking reelection, the presidential nominating process becomes contested in both parties.

Comprehension
4. Why do political parties favor closed rather than open primaries?
5. What is front-loading?

Elections

True or False?
1. Two-thirds of the seats in the House of Representatives and one-third of the seats in the Senate are filled in each general election.
2. The electoral votes are divided among the states based on their representation in Congress, which depends in part on their population.
3. Very few voters split their tickets.

Comprehension
4. When are general elections held?
5. Explain how many electoral votes are required to select a president and why.

Campaigns

True or False?
1. Incumbents enjoy great advantages over challengers in congressional elections.
2. Hard money is the funds raised by parties to be spent on party mailings and voter registration, while soft money is spent on federal election campaigns.
3. Corporations and unions may spend money independently without limit in election campaigns.

Comprehension
4. What is the FEC?
5. Explain the presidential public financing system.

Explaining Voting Choices

True or False?
1. Party identification is the most important long-term force influencing voter choice.
2. Most studies on presidential elections show that campaign issues are less important than party identification and the candidates' attributes.
3. Party voting is more common today than it was in the 1950s.

Comprehension

4. Describe two short-term forces that affect how people vote during an election.
5. What does the strength of party identification mean for the importance of a campaign?

Campaigns, Elections, and Parties

True or False?

1. Increased use of electronic media such as television has depersonalized campaign messages.
2. According to the majoritarian model of democracy, parties link people to their government by making government responsive to public opinion.
3. The decentralized nature of the nominating process and campaigning for office allows organized groups outside the party to identify and support candidates who favor their interests.

Comprehension

4. How do the Democratic and Republican parties relate to the pluralist model?
5. What are the weak links in the majoritarian model of democracy?

CourseMate CL Resources:

Visit www.cengagebrain.com/shop/ISBN/1111832587 for flashcards, web quizzes, videos and more!

CHAPTER
7

Interest Groups

FOCUS QUESTIONS

1. What is the value of interest groups, and what are their roles in a pluralist democracy?

2. Who organizes interest groups, and how are they formed?

3. What resources do interest groups have, and how do they obtain them?

4. What are the types of lobbying tactics used by interest groups?

5. Are the policy decisions made in a pluralistic system fair?

This changing of the guard didn't take place at Buckingham Palace in London. It took place in Washington, D.C., along "K" Street and other areas where lobbyists have their offices. No sooner had Barack Obama been elected president than lobbying firms began beefing up their Democratic credentials.

Firms with a strong Republican orientation, which had done well for clients seeking access to policymakers in the George W. Bush administration, began hunting for Democratic talent. For example, during the Bush years one of the leading lobbying shops around town was BGR Holdings, which represented blue-chip clients such as Citigroup and Pfizer. One of BGR's principals was Haley Barbour, former chair of the Republican National Committee and currently the governor of Mississippi. Now, however, BGR proceeded to purchase a Democratic-leaning firm, the Westin Rinehart Group. Ed Rogers, the chairman of BGR, said, "It looks like there will be more Democrats

running Washington for the foreseeable future." Rogers added, "We've done what we've done to meet that demand."[1] Republicans heading the lobbying offices in Washington of corporations such as Lockheed Martin, Boeing, and Comcast were replaced by Democrats.[2]

With Democrats firmly in control of both houses of Congress and the White House, those firms wanting to hire new lobbyists were most interested in Democrats with many years of experience in Washington and with excellent contacts to those in power. Bud Cramer, a Democrat who had served as a representative from Alabama for 18 years, had no shortage of prospective employers when he retired from Congress in 2008. He became chairman of Wexler & Walker Public Policy Associates, a well-known lobbying group. During his time in the House, Cramer had served on a number of important committees, including the Committee on Transportation and Infrastructure and the Committee on Appropriations. Surely his background is appealing to American Airlines, one of Wexler & Walker's most important clients.[3]

Although connections to policymakers are greatly valued, top lobbyists have broad skill sets. Policymaking is a continuous, long-term process, and those who want to try to influence government must develop appropriate strategies. As Michael Berman, an executive with the Duberstein Group, noted, the job of a lobbyist is "advising people on how to structure their business. . . . It requires knowing what's going on."[4]

Still, whatever skills a lobbyist possesses, having connections to those in power greatly enhances his or her career. Democratic lobbyists are benefiting significantly from this changing of the guard. When the tide turns and Republicans come back to power, lobbyists with ties to the Republicans will be in great demand. In Washington administrations come and go; lobbyists are always there.

In this chapter, we look at the central dynamic of pluralist democracy: the interaction of interest groups and government. In analyzing the process by which interest groups and lobbyists come to speak on behalf of different groups, we focus on several questions. How do interest groups form? Whom do they represent? What tactics do they use to convince policymakers that their views are best for the nation? Is the interest group system biased to favor certain types of people? If it is, what are the consequences?

Interest Groups and the American Political Tradition

An **interest group** is an organized body of individuals who share some political goals and try to influence public policy decisions. Among the most prominent interest groups in the United States are the AFL-CIO (representing labor union members), the American Farm Bureau Federation (representing farmers), the Business Roundtable (representing big business), and Common Cause (representing citizens concerned with reforming government). Interest groups are also called *lobbies*, and their representatives are referred to as **lobbyists**.

interest group
An organized group of individuals that seeks to influence public policy. Also called a *lobby*.

lobbyist
A representative of an interest group.

Interest Groups: Good or Evil?

A recurring debate in American politics concerns the role of interest groups in a democratic society. Are interest groups a threat to the well-being of the political system, or do they contribute to its proper functioning? Alexis de Tocqueville, a French visitor to the United States in the early nineteenth century, marveled at the array of organizations he found. He later wrote that "Americans of all ages, all conditions, and all dispositions, constantly form associations."[5] Tocqueville was suggesting that the ease with which we form organizations reflects a strong democratic culture.

Yet other early observers were concerned about the consequences of interest group politics. Writing in the *Federalist* papers, James Madison warned of the dangers of "factions," the major divisions in American society. In *Federalist* No. 10, written in 1787, Madison said that it was inevitable that substantial differences would develop between factions and that each faction would try to persuade government to adopt policies that favored it at the expense of others.[6] Madison, however, argued against trying to suppress factions. He concluded that they can be eliminated only by removing our freedoms, because "liberty is to faction what air is to fire."[7]

Madison suggested that relief from the self-interested advocacy of factions should come only through controlling the effects of that advocacy. This relief would be provided by a democratic republic in which government would mediate between opposing factions. The size and diversity of the nation as well as the structure of government would also ensure that even a majority faction could never come to suppress the rights of others.[8]

How we judge interest groups—as "good" or "evil"—may depend on how strongly we are committed to freedom or equality (see Chapter 1). In a survey of the American public, almost two-thirds of those polled regarded lobbying as a threat to American democracy.[9] Yet as we will demonstrate, interest groups have enjoyed unparalleled growth in recent years. Apparently we distrust interest groups as a whole, but we like those that speak on our behalf.

The Roles of Interest Groups

The "evil" side of interest group politics is all too apparent: each group pushes its own selfish interests, which, despite the group's claims to the contrary, are not always in the best interest of other Americans. The "good" side of interest group advocacy may not be as clear. How do the actions of interest groups benefit our political system?[10]

Representation. Interest groups represent people before their government. Just as a member of Congress represents a particular constituency, so does a lobbyist. A lobbyist for the National Association of Broadcasters, for example, speaks for the interests of radio and television broadcasters when Congress or a government agency is considering a relevant policy decision.

Whatever the political interest—the cement industry, social security, endangered species—it is helpful to have an active lobby operating in Washington. Members of Congress represent a multitude of interests, some of them conflicting, from their own districts and states. Government administrators, too, are pulled in different directions and have their own policy preferences. Interest groups articulate their members' concerns, presenting them directly and forcefully in the political process.

Participation. Interest groups are also vehicles for political participation. They provide a means by which like-minded citizens can pool their resources and channel their energies into collective political action. One farmer fighting against a new pesticide proposal in Congress probably will not get very far. Thousands of farmers united in an organization will stand a much better chance of getting policymakers to consider their needs.

Education. As part of their efforts to lobby and increase their membership, interest groups try to educate their members, the public at large, and government officials. High-tech companies were slow to set up lobbying offices in Washington and to develop a mind-set within the corporate structure that communicating with people in government was part of their job. As more and more issues affecting the industry received attention from government, high-tech executives began to realize that policymakers did not have a sufficient understanding of the rapidly changing industry. For example, as it began to grow, the Internet search engine Google found it useful to open a Washington office and to hire an outside law firm to help represent its interests before government. To gain the attention of the policymakers they are trying to educate, interest groups need to provide them with information that is not easily obtained from other sources.[11]

agenda building
The process by which new issues are brought into the political limelight.

Agenda Building. In a related role, interest groups bring new issues into the political limelight through a process called **agenda building**. American society has many problem areas, but public officials are not addressing all of them. Through their advocacy, interest groups make the government aware of problems and then try to see that something is done to solve them. Labor unions, for example, have played a key role in gaining attention for problems that were being systematically ignored. As Figure 7.1 shows, however, union membership has declined significantly over the years.

FIGURE 7.1 Labor Pains

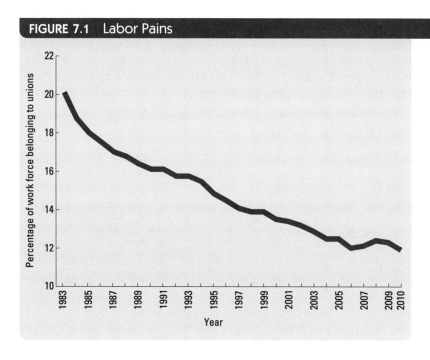

Over the years, many manufacturing jobs in the United States have "migrated" overseas to developing countries with lower wages. That may be good for consumers (cheaper wages mean lower-cost products), but it has been bad for labor unions as workers in heavy industry have traditionally been the most likely to be unionized. Service sector workers (such as restaurant employees) have been much harder for unions to organize.

Source: Bureau of Labor Statistics, "Union Members (Annual)," 21 January 2011, available at http://www.bls.gov/schedule/archives/all_nr.htm#UNION2.

Program Monitoring. Finally, interest groups engage in **program monitoring**. Lobbies follow government programs that are important to their constituents, keeping abreast of developments in Washington and in the communities where the policies are implemented. When a program is not operating as it should, concerned interest groups push administrators to resolve problems in ways that promote the group's goals. They draw attention to agency officials' transgressions and even file suit to stop actions they consider unlawful.

Interest groups do play some positive roles in their pursuit of self-interest. But we should not assume that the positive side of interest groups neatly balances the negative. Questions remain about the overall influence of interest groups on public policymaking. Are the effects of interest group advocacy being controlled, as Madison believed they should be?

How Interest Groups Form

Do some people form interest groups more easily than others? Are some factions represented while others are not? Pluralists assume that when a political issue arises, interest groups with relevant policy concerns begin to lobby. Policy conflicts are ultimately

program monitoring
Keeping track of government programs, usually by interest groups.

resolved through bargaining and negotiation between the involved organizations and the government. Unlike Madison, who dwelled on the potential for harm by factions, pluralists believe that interest groups are a good thing: they further democracy by broadening representation within the system.

Disturbance Theory

An important part of pluralism is the belief that new interest groups form as a matter of course when the need arises. David Truman outlines this idea in his classic work, *The Governmental Process.*[12] He says that when individuals are threatened by change, they band together in an interest group. For example, if government threatens to regulate a particular industry, the firms that compose that industry will start a trade association to protect their financial well-being. Truman sees a direct cause-and-effect relationship: existing groups stand in equilibrium until some type of disturbance (such as falling wages or declining farm prices) forces new groups to form.

Truman's *disturbance theory* paints an idealized portrait of interest group politics in America. In real life, people do not automatically organize when they are adversely affected by some disturbance. A good example of such "nonorganization" can be found in Herbert Gans's book *The Urban Villagers.*[13] Gans, a sociologist, moved into the West End, a low-income neighborhood in Boston, during the late 1950s. The neighborhood had been targeted for urban redevelopment. This meant that the people living there, primarily poor Italian Americans who very much liked their neighborhood, had to move. The people of the West End barely put up a fight to save their neighborhood. They started an organization, but it attracted little support. Despite the threat of eviction, residents remained unorganized. Soon they were moved out, and buildings were demolished.

Disturbance theory fails to explain what happened (or did not happen) in Boston's West End. An adverse condition or change does not automatically result in the formation of an interest group. What, then, is the missing ingredient? Political scientist Robert Salisbury says that the quality of interest group leadership may be the crucial factor.[14]

Interest Group Entrepreneurs

Salisbury likens the role of an interest group leader to the role of an entrepreneur in the business world. A business entrepreneur is someone who starts new enterprises, usually at considerable personal financial risk.

Salisbury says that an **interest group entrepreneur**, or organizer, succeeds or fails for many of the same reasons a business entrepreneur succeeds or fails. The interest group entrepreneur must have something attractive to "market" in order to convince people to join the group.[15] Potential members must be persuaded that the benefits of joining outweigh the costs.

The development of the United Farm Workers shows the importance of leadership in the formation of an interest group. Members of this union are men and women who pick crops in California and other parts of the country. They are predominantly poor, uneducated Mexican Americans. Throughout the twentieth century, various unions tried to organize the pickers, and for many reasons—including distrust of union organizers, intimidation by employers, and lack of money to pay union dues—all failed. Then in 1962, the late Cesar Chavez, a poor Mexican American, began to crisscross the Central Valley of California, talking to workers and planting the idea of a union.

After a strike against grape growers failed in 1965, Chavez changed his tactics of trying to build a strong union merely by recruiting more and more members. Copying the civil rights movement, Chavez and his followers marched 250 miles to the California state capitol in Sacramento to demand help from the governor. This march and other nonviolent tactics began to draw sympathy from people who had no direct involvement in farming. With his stature increased by that support, Chavez called for a grape boycott, and a small but significant number of Americans stopped buying grapes. The growers, who had bitterly fought the union, were hurt economically. Under this and other economic pressures, they eventually agreed to recognize and bargain with the United Farm Workers.

Who Is Being Organized?

Cesar Chavez's success is a good example of the importance of leadership in the formation of a new interest group. But another important element is at work in the formation of interest groups. The residents of Boston's West End and the farm workers in California were economically poor, uneducated or undereducated, and politically inexperienced—factors that made it extremely difficult to organize them into interest groups. If they had been well-off,

interest group entrepreneur
An interest group organizer.

well educated, and politically experienced, they probably would have banded together immediately. People who have money, education, and knowledge of how the system operates are more confident that their actions can make a difference.

Every existing interest group has its own history, but the three variables just discussed can help explain why groups may or may not become fully organized. First, a disturbance or adverse change can heighten people's awareness that they need political representation. However, awareness alone does not ensure that an organization will form, and organizations may form in the absence of a disturbance. Second, the quality of leadership is critical to the organization of interest groups. Third, the higher the socioeconomic level of potential members, the more likely they are to know the value of interest groups and to join them.

The question that remains, then, is *how well* various opposing interests are represented. Or, in terms of Madison's premise in *Federalist* No. 10, are the effects of faction—in this case, the advantages of the wealthy and well educated—being controlled? Before we can answer this question, we need to turn our attention to the resources available to interest groups.

Interest Group Resources

The strengths, capabilities, and influence of an interest group depend in large part on its resources. A group's most significant resources are its members, lobbyists, and money, including funds that can be contributed to political candidates. The sheer quantity of a group's resources is important, and so is the wisdom with which its resources are used.

Members

One of the most valuable resources an interest group can have is a large, politically active membership. If a lobbyist is trying to persuade a legislator to support a particular bill, having a large group of members who live in the legislator's home district or state is tremendously helpful. A legislator who has not already taken a firm position on a bill might be swayed by the knowledge that interest groups are keeping voters back home informed of his or her votes on key issues.

Members give an organization not only the political muscle to influence policy but also financial resources. The more money an organization can collect through dues and contributions, the more people it can hire to lobby government officials and monitor policymaking. Greater resources also allow the organization to communicate with its members more and to inform them better. And funding helps the group maintain its membership and attract new members.

Maintaining Membership. To keep the members it already has, an organization must persuade them that it is a strong, effective advocate. Most lobbies use a newsletter to keep members apprised of developments in government that relate to issues of concern and to inform them about steps the organization is taking to protect their interests.

Business, professional, and labor associations generally have an easier time retaining members than do citizen groups—groups whose basis of organization is a concern for issues not directly related to their members' jobs. In many companies, corporate membership in a trade group constitutes only a minor business expense. Labor unions are helped in states that require workers to affiliate with the union that is the bargaining agent with their employer. In contrast, citizen groups base their appeal on members' ideological sentiments. These groups face a difficult challenge: issues can blow hot and cold, and a particularly hot issue one year may not hold the same interest to citizens the next.

Attracting New Members. All membership groups are constantly looking for new members to expand their resources and clout. Groups that rely on ideological appeals have a special problem because the competition in most policy areas is intense. People concerned about the environment, for example, can join a seemingly infinite number of local, state, and national groups that lobby on environmental issues. One common method of attracting new members is *direct mail*—letters sent to a selected audience to promote the organization and appeal for contributions. The main drawbacks to direct mail are its expense and low rate of return.

The Internet has become an increasingly important means of soliciting new members. Compared to direct mail—an interest group sending a letter and supporting material via old-fashioned "snail mail"—e-mail is much cheaper. E-mail directed to prospects may entice them to go the organization's website to learn more and, possibly, make a contribution. Interest groups also use social networking sites like Facebook for fundraising. These are typically ideological groups, and many try to tap the idealism of the generally youthful clientele of networking sites.

The Free-Rider Problem. The need for aggressive marketing by interest groups suggests that getting people who sympathize with a group's goals to support the group with contributions is difficult. Economists call this difficulty the **free-rider problem**, but we might call it, more colloquially, the "let-George-do-it" problem.[16] Funding for public television stations illustrates this dilemma. Only a fraction of those who watch public television contribute on a regular basis. Why? Because a free rider has the same access to public television as a contributor.

The same problem troubles interest groups. When a lobbying group wins benefits, those benefits are often not restricted to members of the organization. For instance, if the U.S. Chamber of Commerce convinces Congress to enact a policy benefiting business, all businesses will benefit, not just those that pay membership dues to the lobbying group. Thus, some executives may feel that their corporation does not need to spend the money to join the Chamber of Commerce, even though they might benefit from the group's efforts; they prefer to let others shoulder the financial burden.

The free-rider problem increases the difficulty of attracting paying members. Nevertheless, millions of Americans contribute to interest groups because they are concerned about an issue or feel a responsibility to help organizations that work on their behalf. Also, many organizations offer membership benefits that have nothing to do with politics or lobbying. **Trade associations**, for example, are a source of information about industry trends and effective management practices; they organize conventions at which members can learn, socialize, and occasionally find new customers or suppliers.

Lobbyists

free-rider problem
The situation in which people benefit from the activities of an organization (such as an interest group) but do not contribute to those activities.

trade association
An organization that represents firms within a particular industry.

Interest groups use part of the money they raise to pay lobbyists, who represent the organizations before the government. Lobbyists make sure that people in government know what their members want and that their organizations know what the government is doing.[17] Lobbyists can be full-time employees of an interest group or employees of public relations or law firms hired on retainer. When hiring a lobbyist, an interest group looks for someone who knows his or her way around Washington. Karen Ignagni, the chief lobbyist for America's Health Insurance Plans, an industry

You Got Problems? Call Us

If your organization or cause needs representation in Washington, there's no shortage of free-standing lobbying shops and law firms ready to help. These partners in the lobbying firm the c2 Group advertise themselves as offering a "broad range of bipartisan government affairs consulting services." The firm's clients include Home Depot, PepsiCo, Porsche Cars North America, and the National Council of Coal Lessors.

(Scott J. Ferrell/Congressional Quarterly/Getty Images)

trade group, was at the center of the negotiations over the Obama administration's health reform proposal in 2009. Ignagni's experience, knowledge of health care, and bargaining skills made her a formidable presence as Congress struggled to formulate a bill that could pass. The stakes for the insurance companies were enormous: a government-run insurance plan could cost them customers. Her stature is such that she is paid $1.6 million annually.[18]

Lobbyists are valued for their experience and their knowledge of how government operates. Often they are people who have served in the legislative or executive branches and have firsthand experience with government. Many lobbyists have law degrees and find their legal backgrounds useful in bargaining and negotiating over laws and regulations. Because of their location, many Washington law firms are drawn into lobbying. Corporations without Washington offices rely heavily on these law firms to lobby for them before the national government.

The stereotype of lobbyists portrays them as people of dubious ethics because they trade on their connections and may hand out campaign donations to candidates for office. To enhance their access, many lobbyists also raise money for legislators. However, the lobbyist's primary job is not to trade on favors or campaign contributions but to pass on information to policymakers. Lobbyists provide government officials and their staffs with a constant flow of data that support their organizations' policy goals. Lobbyists also try to build a compelling case for their goals, showing that the "facts" dictate that a particular change be made or avoided. What lobbyists are really trying to do, of course, is to convince policymakers that their data deserve more attention and are more accurate than the data presented by other lobbyists.

Political Action Committees

One of the organizational resources that can make a lobbyist's job easier is a **political action committee (PAC)**. PACs pool campaign contributions from group members and donate those funds to candidates for political office. Under federal law, a PAC can give as much as $5,000 to a candidate for Congress for each separate election. PACs have grown much more prevalent since the early 1970s. In the 2007–2008 election cycle, more than 3,600 PACs made donations. They contributed more than $413 million to candidates, almost all of which went to congressional candidates.[19]

The greatest growth came from corporations, most of which had been legally prohibited from operating PACs. There was also rapid growth in the number of nonconnected PACs, largely ideological groups that have no parent lobbying organization and are formed solely for the purpose of raising and channeling campaign funds. Thus, a PAC can be the campaign-wing affiliate of an existing interest group or a wholly independent, unaffiliated group. Although most PACs give less than $50,000 in total contributions during a two-year election cycle, some contribute millions of dollars to campaigns. During the 2007–2008 election cycle, for example, the National Association of Realtors' PAC contributed over $4 million to candidates. It was in good company: there were over twenty PACs whose contributions to candidates exceeded $2 million in that election cycle.[20]

Why do interest groups form PACs? Lobbyists believe that campaign contributions help significantly when they are trying to gain an audience with a member of Congress. Members of

political action committee (PAC)

An organization that pools campaign contributions from group members and donates those funds to candidates for political office.

Congress and their staffers generally are eager to meet with representatives of their constituencies, but their time is limited. However, a member of Congress or a staffer would find it difficult to turn down a lobbyist's request for a meeting if the PAC of the lobbyist's organization had made a significant campaign contribution in the previous election.

Typically, PACs, like most other interest groups, are highly pragmatic organizations; pushing a particular political philosophy takes second place to achieving immediate policy goals. As one lobbyist put it, "Politics are partisan; policy is bipartisan."[21] In recent elections, corporate PACs as a group have given as much as 90 percent of their contributions to incumbents (see Figure 7.2).[22] At the same time, different sectors of the PAC universe may strongly favor one party or the other. Approximately nine out of every ten dollars that unions give go to Democrats, whether they be incumbents, challengers, or open seat candidates.[23]

Critics charge that members of Congress cannot help but be influenced by the PAC contributions they receive. Political scientists, however, have not been able to document any consistent link

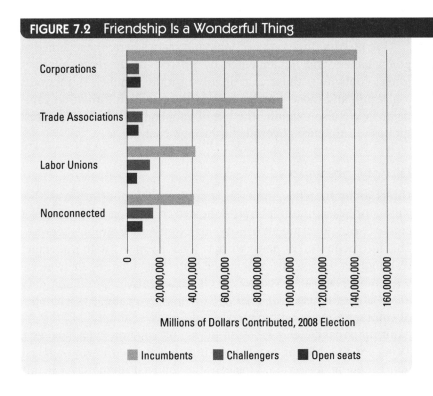

FIGURE 7.2   Friendship Is a Wonderful Thing

Millions of Dollars Contributed, 2008 Election

Incumbents   Challengers   Open seats

Political action committees are more practical than ideological, primarily directing their contributions to incumbents. A modest exception to this trend is so-called nonconnected PACs. These tend to be ideological citizen groups whose primary concern is promoting a broad liberal or conservative perspective. But even nonconnected PACs give roughly 60 percent of their contributions to incumbents.

Source: Federal Elections Commission, "PAC Financial Activity 2007–2008," at www.FEC.gov.

between campaign donations and the way members of Congress vote on the floor of the House and Senate.[24] The problem is this: Do PAC contributions influence votes in Congress, or are they really just rewards for ideologically like-minded legislators who would vote for the group's interests anyway? Some sophisticated research does show that PACs have an advantage in the committee process and appear to gain influence because of the additional access they receive.[25]

Lobbying Tactics

Keep in mind that lobbying extends beyond the legislative branch. Groups can seek help from the courts and administrative agencies as well as from Congress. Moreover, interest groups may have to shift their focus from one branch of government to another. After a bill becomes a law, for example, a group that lobbied for the legislation will probably try to influence the administrative agency responsible for implementing the new law. Some policy decisions are left unresolved by legislation and are settled through regulations. Interest groups try to influence policy through the courts as well, though litigation can be expensive and opportunities to go to court may be narrowly structured.

We discuss three types of lobbying tactics here: those aimed at policymakers and implemented by interest group representatives (direct lobbying), those that involve group members (grassroots lobbying), and those directed toward the public (information campaigns). We also examine the use of cooperative efforts of interest groups to influence government through coalitions.

Direct Lobbying

Direct lobbying relies on personal contact with policymakers. One survey of Washington lobbyists showed that 98 percent use direct contact with government officials to express their group's views.[26] This interaction takes place when a lobbyist meets with a member of Congress, an agency official, or a staff member. In their meetings, lobbyists usually convey their arguments by providing data about a specific issue. If a lobbyist from, for example, a chamber of commerce meets with a member of Congress about a bill the organization backs, the lobbyist does not say (or even suggest), "Vote for this bill, or our people in the district will vote against you in the next election." Instead, the lobbyist might say, "If this

direct lobbying
Attempts to influence a legislator's vote through personal contact with the legislator.

bill is passed, we're going to see hundreds of new jobs created back home." The representative has no trouble at all figuring out that a vote for the bill can help in the next election.

Personal lobbying is a day-in, day-out process. Lobbyists must maintain contact with congressional and agency staffers, constantly providing them with pertinent data. One lobbyist described his strategy in personal meetings with policymakers as rather simple and straightforward: "Providing information is the most effective tool. People begin to rely on you."[27] In their meetings with policymakers, lobbyists also try to frame issues in terms most beneficial to their point of view. Is a gun control bill before the Congress a policy that would make streets and schools safer from violent individuals who should not have access to guns, or is it a bill aimed at depriving law-abiding citizens of their constitutional right to bear arms? Research has shown that once an issue emerges, it is very difficult for lobbyists to reframe it—that is, to influence journalists and policymakers alike to view the issue in a new light.[28]

A tactic related to direct lobbying is testifying at committee hearings when a bill is before Congress. This tactic allows the interest group to put its views on record and make them widely known when the hearing testimony is published. Although testifying is one of the most visible parts of lobbying, it is generally considered window dressing. Most lobbyists believe that testimony usually does little by itself to persuade members of Congress.

Another direct but somewhat different approach is legal advocacy. Using this tactic, a group tries to achieve its policy goals through litigation. Claiming some violation of law, a group will file a lawsuit and ask that a judge make a ruling that will benefit the organization. When the Army Corps of Engineers announced plans to permit coal companies to blast off the top of mountains to facilitate their mining, environmental groups went to court alleging a violation of the Clean Water Act. The judge agreed, since the coal companies' actions would leave waste and rock deposits in adjoining streams.[29]

Grassroots Lobbying

Grassroots lobbying involves an interest group's rank-and-file members and may also include people outside the organization who sympathize with its goals. Grassroots tactics, such as letter-writing campaigns and protests, are often used in conjunction

grassroots lobbying
Lobbying activities performed by rank-and-file interest group members and would-be members.

with direct lobbying by Washington representatives. Policymakers are more concerned about what a lobbyist says when they know that constituents are really watching their decisions.

The Internet facilitates mobilization; an interest group office can communicate instantaneously with its members and followers through e-mail at virtually no cost. It also makes it easy for interest groups to communicate with each other, easing some of the costs in time and money to forming and maintaining coalitions.

If people in government seem unresponsive to conventional lobbying tactics, a group might resort to some form of political protest. A protest or demonstration, such as picketing or marching, is designed to attract media attention to an issue. The main drawback to protesting is that policymaking is a long-term, incremental process, but a demonstration is only short-lived. It is difficult to sustain anger and activism among group supporters—to keep large numbers of people involved in protest after protest. A notable exception was the civil rights demonstrations of the 1960s, which were sustained over a long period. The protests were a major factor in stirring public opinion, which hastened passage of the Civil Rights Act of 1964 and the Voting Rights Act of 1965.

Information Campaigns

Interest groups generally feel that public backing strengthens their lobbying efforts. They believe that they will get that backing if they can make the public aware of their position and the evidence supporting it. To this end, interest groups launch **information campaigns**, organized efforts to gain public backing by bringing a group's views to the public's attention. Various means are used. Some are directed at the larger public, others at smaller audiences with long-standing interest in an issue.

Public relations is one information campaign tactic. A public relations campaign might send speakers to meetings in various parts of the country, produce pamphlets and handouts, take out newspaper advertising, or establish websites. Recently labor unions and progressives initiated a campaign critical of Wal-Mart. The huge retailer pays relatively low wages, offers limited benefits, and aggressively fights any efforts to unionize its work force. Both Wake Up Wal-Mart and Wal-Mart Watch have publicized Wal-Mart's record on its treatment of employees. In turn, Wal-Mart has fought back with a concerted public relations campaign designed to demonstrate that it is a responsible citizen in the communities

information campaign
An organized effort to gain public backing by bringing a group's views to public attention.

where its stores are located. The company's extensive efforts to provide water and other supplies to victims of Hurricane Katrina were particularly effective at burnishing its image.[30]

Sponsoring research is another way interest groups press their cases. When a group believes that evidence has not been fully developed in a certain area, it may commission research on the subject. In the controversy over illegal immigration studies have proliferated as interest groups push their positions forward. Lobbies on opposing sides of the issue have publicized research on matters such as the impact of illegal immigration on the overall economy, whether immigrants drive down wages, and whether undocumented aliens take jobs away from citizens who would otherwise fill them.

Coalition Building

A final aspect of lobbying strategy is **coalition building**, in which several organizations band together for the purpose of lobbying. Such joint efforts conserve or make more effective use of the resources of groups with similar views. Most coalitions are informal, ad hoc arrangements that exist only for the purpose of lobbying on a single issue.

Coalitions form most often among groups that work in the same policy area and have similar constituencies, such as environmental groups or feminist groups. Yet coalitions often extend beyond organizations with similar constituencies and similar outlooks. Some business groups support the same goals as environmental lobbies, because doing so is in their self-interest. For example, companies in the business of cleaning up toxic waste sites have worked with environmental groups.[31] Lobbyists see an advantage in having a diverse coalition. In the words of one lobbyist, "You can't do anything in this town without a coalition. I mean the first question [from policymakers] is, 'Who supports this?'"[32]

Is the System Biased?

As we noted in Chapter 1, our political system is more pluralist than majoritarian. Policymaking is determined more by the interaction of groups with government than by elections. Indeed, among Western democracies, the United States is one of the most pluralistic governments (see "Compared with What? Pluralism

coalition building
The banding together of several interest groups for the purpose of lobbying.

Worldwide"). How, then, do we determine whether policy decisions in a pluralist system are fair?

There is no precisely agreed-on formula, but most people would agree with the following two simple notions. First, all significant interests in the population should be adequately represented by lobbying groups. Second, government should listen to the views of all major interests as it develops policy. We should also recognize that elections inject some of the benefits of majoritarianism into our system, because the party that wins an election will have a larger voice in the making of public policy than its opponent.

Membership Patterns

Who is best represented in the interest group system?[33] Those who work in business or in a profession, those with a high level of education, and those with high incomes are the most likely to belong to interest groups. Even middle-income people are much more likely to join interest groups than people who are poor.

One recent survey of interest groups is revealing, finding that "the 10 percent of adults who work in an executive, managerial, or administrative capacity are represented by 82 percent" of the organizations that in one way or another engage in advocacy on economic issues. In contrast, "organizations of or for the economically needy are a rarity." In terms of membership in interest groups, there is a profound bias in favor of those who are well off financially.[34]

Citizen Groups

Before we reach the conclusion that the interest group system is biased, we should examine another set of data. The actual population of interest groups in Washington surely reflects a class bias in interest group membership, but that bias may be modified in an important way. Some interest groups derive support from sources other than their membership. Thus, although the Center for Budget and Policy Priorities and the Children's Defense Fund have no welfare recipients among their members, they are highly respected Washington lobbies working on the problems of poor people. Poverty groups gain their financial support from philanthropic foundations, government grants, corporations, and wealthy individuals. Such groups have played an important role in influencing policy on poor people's programs. In short, some bias exists in the representation of the poor, but it is not nearly as bad as membership patterns suggest.

Compared with What?

Pluralism Worldwide

A study of democracies around the world measured the degree to which interest groups operated independent of any formal link to government. Interest groups in political systems with low scores in this chart (such as Norway) run the risk of being co-opted by policymakers because of their partnerships with government. These countries tend to have fewer groups, but those groups are expected to work with government in a coordinated fashion. High scores indicate that the interest groups in those systems are clearly in a competitive position with other groups. Thus, countries with high scores (such as the United States) are the most pluralistic.

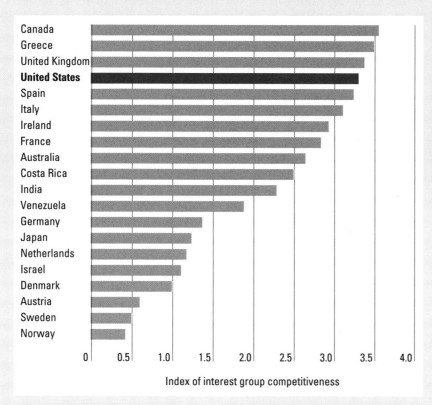

Index of interest group competitiveness

Source: Arend Lijphart, *Patterns of Democracy* (New Haven, Conn.: Yale University Press, 1999), p. 177. Copyright © 1999 Yale University Press. Reproduced by permission.

Another part of the problem of membership bias has to do with free riders. The interests that are most affected by free riders are broad societal problems, such as the environment and consumer protection, in which literally everyone can be considered as having a stake in the outcome. The greater the number of potential members of a group, the more likely it is that individuals will decide to be free riders, because they believe that plenty of others can offer financial support to the organization.

Environmental and consumer interests have been chronically under-represented in the Washington interest group community. In the 1960s, however, a strong citizen group movement emerged. **Citizen groups** are lobbying organizations built around policy concerns unrelated to members' vocational interests. People who join Environmental Defense do so because they care about the environment, not because it lobbies on issues related to their profession. If that group fights for stricter pollution control requirements, it does not further the financial interests of its members. The benefits to members are largely ideological and aesthetic. In contrast, a corporation fighting the same stringent standards is trying to protect its economic interests.

Organizations pursuing environmental protection, consumer protection, good government, family values, and equality for various groups in society have grown in number and collectively attracted millions of members. The national press gives them considerable coverage, reinforcing the ability of these groups to get their issues on the national agenda. One study showed that citizen groups received almost half of all TV network news coverage of interest groups, even though they are a much smaller portion of the interest group universe.[35]

Business Mobilization

Because a strong public interest movement has become an integral part of Washington politics, an easy assumption is that the bias in interest group representation in favor of business has been largely overcome. What must be factored in is that business has become increasingly mobilized as well.[36] The 1970s and 1980s saw a vast increase in the number of business lobbies in Washington. Many corporations opened Washington lobbying offices, and many trade associations headquartered elsewhere either moved to Washington or opened branch offices there.

citizen group
Lobbying organization built around policy concerns unrelated to members' vocational interests.

Usually we think of lobbying as a process in which groups approach a government official. But sometimes the reverse is true: a policymaker might approach an interest group to try to gain its support for a specific proposal or just to promote a good working relationship. Here, Representative Loretta Sanchez (D-Calif.) works the room at a meeting of the Hispanic Leadership Summit.

(© Ted Soqui/Corbis)

This mobilization was partly a reaction to the success of the liberal public interest movement, which business tended to view as hostile to the free-enterprise system. The reaction of business also reflected the expanded scope of the national government. As the Environmental Protection Agency, the Consumer Product Safety Commission, the Occupational Safety and Health Administration, and other regulatory agencies were created, many more companies found they were affected by federal regulations.

The health-care industry is a case in point. As government regulation has become an increasingly important factor in determining health-care profits, more and more health-care trade associations have opened offices in Washington so that they can make more of an effort to influence the government. In 1999 there were already over 2,300 health-care lobbyists working in the city. By 2009 the number had jumped another 50 percent to over 3,600.[37]

The advantages of business are enormous. As Figure 7.3 illustrates, there are more business lobbies (corporations and trade associations) than any other type. Professional associations, such as the American Dental Association, tend to represent business interests as well. Beyond the numbers of groups are the superior resources of business including lobbyists, researchers, campaign contributions,

FIGURE 7.3 | Who Lobbies?

One large-scale study of lobbying in Washington documented the pattern of participation by interest groups on close to one hundred issues before the federal government. Business-related groups (corporations and trade associations) made up the largest segment of all lobbies, while citizen groups constituted roughly a quarter of all organizations.

Source: Frank R. Baumgartner Jeffrey M. Berry, Marie Hojnacki, David C. Kimball, and Beth L. Leech, *Advocacy and Policy Change* (Chicago: University of Chicago Press, 2009), p. 9. Copyright © 2009 University of Chicago Press. Reproduced by permission.

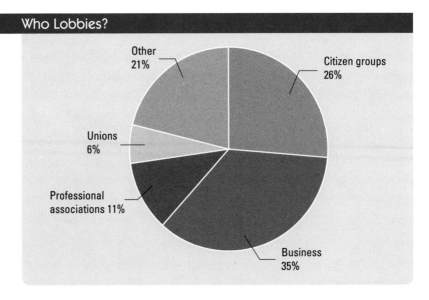

and well-connected CEOs. Whereas citizen groups can try to mobilize their individual members, trade associations can mobilize the corporations that are members of the organization.

Yet the resource advantages of business make it easy to overlook the obstacles business faces in the political arena. To begin with, business is often divided, with companies and industries competing with one another. Cable companies and phone companies have frequently tangled over who will have access to what markets. And even if an industry is unified, it may face strong opposition from labor or citizen groups—sectors that have substantial resources too, even if they do not match up to businesses.[38]

Reform

In an economic system marked by great differences in income, great differences in the degree to which people are organized are inevitable. Moreover, as Madison foresaw, limiting interest group activity is difficult without limiting fundamental freedoms. The First Amendment guarantees Americans the right to petition their government, and lobbying, at its most basic level, is a form of organized petitioning.

Still, if it is felt that the advantages of some groups are so great that they affect the equality of people's opportunity to be heard in the political system, then restrictions on interest group behavior can be justified on the ground that the disadvantaged must be protected. Pluralist democracy is justified on exactly these grounds: all constituencies must have the opportunity to organize, and the competition between groups as they press their case before policymakers must be fair.

Some critics charge that a system of campaign finance that relies so heavily on PACs undermines our democratic system. Close to half of all PAC contributions come from corporations, business trade associations, and professional associations.[39] It is not merely a matter of wealthy interest groups showering incumbents with donations; members of Congress aggressively solicit donations from PACs. Although observers disagree on whether PAC money actually influences policy outcomes, agreement is widespread that PAC donations give donors better access to members of Congress.

In 2002 the Congress enacted a major campaign finance reform. Until passage of the Bipartisan Campaign Reform Act (BCRA), corporations, labor unions, and other organizations could donate unlimited amounts of so-called soft money to the political parties. Before BCRA, a company or union with issues before government could give a six-figure gift to the Democratic or Republican Party, even though the company or union PAC could make only a modest contribution to individual candidates. The 2002 legislation bans soft-money contributions to national party committees.

A serious scandal surrounding a lobbyist named Jack Abramoff (since sent to prison) prompted Congress to tighten its ethical rules. This legislation passed in 2007 bans gifts, travel, and meals paid for by lobbyists. Lobbyists must also now disclose campaign contributions that they solicit on behalf of candidates.[40] During the 2008 presidential campaign Barack Obama promised to "change the culture of Washington." On his second day in office Obama banned lobbyists from working in an agency that they had lobbied anytime during the previous two years. Citizen lobbies were particularly incensed at the president's new rule, believing that since their advocacy did not financially benefit their members and donors, they should not be looked upon with the presumptive suspicion underlying the Obama policy. A coalition of citizen groups formally complained to the administration and in a letter to the White House noted that "The right to petition the government is a constitutionally protected activity."[41]

In January 2010, the Supreme Court ruled that government may not restrict corporations from spending money in candidate elections. (Recall that PAC funds come from individual donations and corporations as well as other PACs that aggregate money and then donate it.) There is considerable concern that the Court's decision will flood the political marketplace with corporations spending unlimited funds to support their allies and oppose their enemies. Incumbents are sure to take heed. Defenders point out that the logic of the decision makes it likely that labor unions, too, can spend freely from their own treasuries, though corporate coffers dwarf labor assets.[42]

Tying It Together

1. What is the value of interest groups, and what are their roles in a pluralist democracy?
   - Interest groups are organized bodies of individuals who share some political goals and try to influence public policy decisions.
   - Lobbyists represent interest groups, often called lobbies.
   - Most Americans distrust interest groups, yet interest groups have grown in recent years.
   - Interest groups have several roles, such as
     - representing people.
     - providing an opportunity for people to participate.
     - providing education on important topics.
     - bringing issues to light through agenda building.
     - engaging in program monitoring.

2. Who organizes interest groups, and how are they formed?
   - Three variables help explain how interest groups form:
     - When individuals are threatened by change, they may band together in an interest group. This is the premise of disturbance theory.
     - The quality of leadership provided by an interest group entrepreneur is critical to the organization of an interest group.
     - The higher the socioeconomic level of potential members, the more likely they are to band together.

3. What resources do interest groups have, and how do they obtain them?
   - Members are a valuable resource. Interest groups must work to maintain and recruit members while trying to avoid the free-rider problem.
   - Lobbyists represent interest groups and promote their policy views.
   - PACs contribute funds to candidates.

4. What are the types of lobbying tactics used by interest groups?
   - Direct lobbying, which relies on personal contact with policy-makers.
   - Grassroots lobbying, which involves an interest group's rank-and-file members and may also include people outside the organization who sympathize with its goals and organize letter-writing campaigns and protests.
   - Information campaigns, such as public relations, to inform the public.
   - Coalition building through banding together with several other organizations.

5. Are the policy decisions made in a pluralistic system fair?
   - All significant interests in the population should be adequately represented by lobbying groups.
   - Government should listen to the views of all major interests as it develops policy.
   - Business groups are the most prevalent form of interest group in Washington.
   - Business groups can mobilize corporate members with their significant financial resources.
   - Citizen groups mobilize individuals based on ideological agreement or on policy concerns.
   - Citizen groups receive the most television news coverage, despite being a small part of the interest group universe.
   - Campaign finance reform has been enacted to limit the role of soft-money contributions in politics.
   - Corporations and unions may now directly engage in campaign spending.

Interest Groups and the American Political Tradition

True or False?

1. The actions of interest groups do not benefit our political system.
2. All interest groups seek to influence public policy.
3. Labor unions have been growing steadily in size, membership, and power over the past twenty years.

Comprehension

4. What are the roles of interest groups?
5. According to James Madison, how should interest groups be controlled?

How Interest Groups Form

True or False?

1. An interest group entrepreneur is an individual who lobbies for the interests of small-business owners.
2. There are two variables that explain why groups organize or fail to organize: a disturbance or adverse change, and the socioeconomic level of the potential members.
3. In 1965, Cesar Chavez led a successful strike against grape growers by simply organizing hundreds of crop pickers into a union.

Comprehension

4. According to the disturbance theory, when are interest groups formed?
5. What nonviolent methods did Cesar Chavez use to improve the situation of the United Farm Workers? Why was this approach so effective?

Interest Group Resources

True or False?

1. On average, PACs contribute more than $100,000 to each candidate they support.
2. The "free-rider problem" refers to a situation in which someone illegally acquires something at another's expense.
3. The primary task of lobbyists is to collect campaign contributions from group members and donate funds to candidates for political office.

Comprehension

4. Why are interest groups always looking for new members?
5. Why do business, professional, and labor associations have an easier time retaining members than citizen groups?

Lobbying Tactics

True or False?

1. Grassroots lobbying is done by "green" groups interested in the environment.
2. The most common direct lobbying tactic involves lobbyists meeting with government officials.
3. Letter-writing campaigns and protests are grassroots lobbying tactics and are often used in conjunction with direct lobbying tactics.

Comprehension

4. What is the purpose of information campaigns?
5. Briefly describe the goals of coalition building.

Is the System Biased?

True or False?

1. Business is better represented in the interest group world than any other type of organization.
2. Middle-income people are more likely to join interest groups than low-income people.
3. PACs receive negative criticism from people who believe that donations from interest groups influence policy outcomes in an undemocratic way.

Comprehension

4. Why do businesses mobilize?
5. What 2002 reform law did Congress pass to eliminate soft-money contributions from interest groups to political parties?

⁊CourseMate CL Resources:

Visit www.cengagebrain.com/shop/ISBN/1111832587 for flashcards, web quizzes, videos and more!

ANTHONY DEPRIMO/Staten Island Advance/Landov

CourseMate

Visit www.cengagebrain.com/shop/ ISBN/1111832587 for flashcards, web quizzes, videos and more!

FOCUS QUESTIONS

1. How did the framers envision the powers of the Congress?
2. In what ways do incumbency and other factors affect the way voters elect members of Congress?
3. How do issues get on the congressional agenda?
4. What is the process by which bills become laws?
5. What are the functions of congressional committees?
6. What is the leadership structure, and what procedures are used to run the House and Senate?
7. What forces in the legislative environment affect decision making in Congress?
8. Are legislators trustees or delegates?
9. How do the models of pluralism and majoritarianism manifest themselves in Congress?

During the 2008 presidential campaign, Barack Obama pledged to close the detention facility at the U.S. military base in Guantánamo Bay, Cuba, which had been used during the George W. Bush administration as a prison for people with suspected ties to international terrorist groups. Many claimed that the prisoners were denied basic legal protections and that the prison itself had become a symbol used to help recruit al Qaeda members overseas.[1]

Obama learned on election day that he would have large majorities in both the House and the Senate to help him follow through on his campaign promises. Just two days after taking office, Obama issued an executive order calling for Guantánamo to be shut down within one year. At the time, Speaker of the House Nancy Pelosi praised the order, saying that closing Guantánamo would "ensure that terrorist suspects held by the United States are treated in ways consistent with our laws and our values."[2] Senate majority leader Harry Reid agreed that closing Guantánamo was the right decision. The Democratic victories certainly suggested that they could do something in Congress to enact this executive order. In theory, at least, that's how majoritarian government should work. The parties present a clear choice on a key issue, and the voters choose one or the other. The winning party then implements its policy objectives. In practice, however, the majority often turns out to be more elusive than it seems.

Indeed, having the support of congressional leadership and having such a large group of fellow partisans controlling the legislature have not made it any easier for Obama to deliver on his promise to close Guantánamo. In June 2009, Congress passed a military spending bill that explicitly prohibited the use of those funds for closing the prison. A few months later, both houses passed a bill that would prohibit the transfer of Guantánamo prisoners to the United States except for prosecution. By the fall of 2009, the administration admitted that it might not be able to close the prison by January 2010 as it had ordered.[3]

Why was it so difficult for Obama to work with Congress and deliver on this campaign promise? First, divisions exist within the Democratic Party on this issue as well as on many other issues. Second, many representatives felt that the president was crafting his detention policy without sufficient input from Congress.[4] Third, several members of Congress, including Democrats, were less than enthusiastic about the possibility of detainees being relocated to their states.[5] Finally, many Democrats in the House were concerned about being portrayed as soft on terrorism by Republican challengers in the 2010 election. Being the majority party rarely means that the party has smooth sailing in enacting its agenda.

In this chapter we examine majoritarian politics through the prism of the two congressional parties, looking at how the forces of pluralism work against majoritarian policymaking. We then explore the procedures and norms that facilitate bargaining and compromise in the Congress. We will also focus on Congress's relations with the executive branch and analyze how the legislative process affects public policy. A starting point is to ask how the framers envisioned Congress.

The Origin and Powers of Congress

The framers of the Constitution wanted to prevent the concentration of power in the hands of a few, but they also wanted to create a union strong enough to overcome the weaknesses of the government created by the Articles of Confederation. They argued passionately about the structure of the new government and in the end produced a legislative body that was as much of an experiment as the new republic itself.

The Great Compromise

The U.S. Congress has two separate and powerful chambers: the House of Representatives and the Senate. A bill cannot become law unless it is passed in identical form by both chambers. When the framers were drafting the Constitution during the summer of 1787, "the fiercest struggle for power" centered on representation in the legislature.[6] The small states wanted all the states to have equal representation. The more populous states wanted representation based on population; they did not want their power diluted. The Great Compromise broke the deadlock: the small states would receive equal representation in the Senate, but the number of each state's representatives in the House would be based on population, and the House would have the sole right to originate revenue-related legislation.

As the Constitution specifies, each state has two senators, and senators serve six-year terms of office. Terms are staggered, so that one-third of the Senate is elected every two years. When it was ratified, the Constitution directed that senators should be chosen by the state legislatures. However, the Seventeenth Amendment, adopted in 1913, provided for the direct election of senators by popular vote. From the beginning, the people have directly elected members of the House of Representatives. They serve two-year terms, and all House seats are up for election at the same time.

There are 435 members in the House of Representatives. Because each state's representation in the House is in proportion to its population, the Constitution provides for a national census every ten years. Population shifts are handled by the **reapportionment** (redistribution) of seats among the states after each census is taken. Since recent population growth has been centered in the Sunbelt, California, Texas, and Florida have gained seats, and northeastern and midwestern states like New York and Illinois have lost them. Each representative is elected from a particular congressional district within his or her state, and each district elects only one representative. The districts within a state must be roughly equal in population.

Duties of the House and Senate

Although the Great Compromise provided for considerably different schemes of representation for the House and Senate, the Constitution gives them essentially similar legislative tasks. They share many important powers, among them the powers to declare war, raise an army and navy, borrow and coin money, regulate interstate commerce, create federal courts, establish rules for the naturalization of immigrants, and "make all Laws which shall be necessary and proper for carrying into Execution the foregoing Powers."

Of course, the constitutional duties of the two chambers are different in at least a few important ways. As noted in Chapter 2,

reapportionment
Redistribution of representatives among the states, based on population change. Congress is reapportioned after each census.

the House alone has the right to originate revenue bills, a right that apparently was coveted at the Constitutional Convention. In practice, this power is of limited consequence because both House and Senate must approve all bills, including revenue bills. The House also has the power of **impeachment**: the power to charge the president, vice president, or other "civil Officers" of the national government with "Treason, Bribery, or other high Crimes and Misdemeanors." The Senate is empowered to act as a court to try impeachments; a two-thirds majority vote of the senators present is necessary for conviction. Prior to President Clinton's impeachment in 1998, only one president, Andrew Johnson, had been impeached, and in 1868 the Senate came within a single vote of finding him guilty. Clinton was accused of both perjury and obstruction of justice concerning his relationship with a White House intern, Monica Lewinsky, but was acquitted by the Senate as well. The House Judiciary Committee voted to impeach President Richard Nixon for his role in the Watergate scandal, but he resigned (in August 1974) before the full House could vote.

The Constitution gives the Senate the power to approve major presidential appointments (such as to federal judgeships, ambassadorships, and cabinet posts) and treaties with foreign nations. The president is empowered to make treaties but must submit them to the Senate for approval by a two-thirds majority. Because of this requirement, the executive branch generally considers the Senate's sentiments when it negotiates a treaty.[7]

Despite the long list of congressional powers in the Constitution, the question of what powers are appropriate for Congress has generated substantial controversy. For example, although the Constitution gives Congress the sole power to declare war, many presidents have initiated military action on their own. And at times, the courts have found that congressional actions have usurped the rights of the states.

Electing the Congress

impeachment
The formal charging of a government official with "treason, bribery, or other high crimes and misdemeanors."

incumbent
A current officeholder.

If Americans are not happy with the job Congress is doing, they can use their votes to say so. With a congressional election every two years, the voters have frequent opportunities to express themselves.

The Incumbency Effect

Congressional elections offer voters a chance to show their approval of Congress's performance by reelecting **incumbents** or to

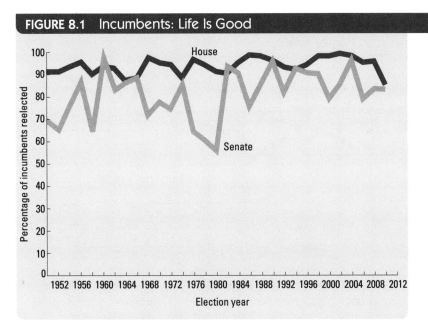

FIGURE 8.1   Incumbents: Life Is Good

Despite the public's dissatisfaction with Congress in general, incumbent representatives win reelection at an exceptional rate. Incumbent senators are not quite as successful but still do well in reelection races. Voters seem to believe that their own representatives and senators do not share the same foibles that they attribute to the other members of Congress.

Sources: Various sources for 1950–2006. For 2008, Harold W. Stanley and Richard G. Niemi (eds.), *Vital Statistics on American Politics, 2009–2010* (Washington, D.C.: CQ Press, 2010), pp. 39–40. For 2010, Larry J. Sabato, *Pendulum Swing* (Boston: Longman, 2011), pp. 16–19.

demonstrate their disapproval by "throwing the rascals out."[8] The voters seem to do more reelecting than rascal throwing. The reelection rate is astonishingly high; in the majority of elections since 1950, more than 90 percent of all House incumbents have held on to their seats (see Figure 8.1). In the 2010 congressional elections, fifty-eight incumbents in the House of Representatives were defeated by challengers, but 85 percent of those running for reelection won. In recent elections, over 70 percent of House incumbents have won reelection by margins of greater than 60 percent of the vote.[9] Senate elections are usually somewhat more competitive, but incumbents still have a high reelection rate.

These findings may seem surprising, since the public does not hold Congress as a whole in particularly high esteem. In the past few years Americans have been particularly critical of the Congress, and some polls have showed less than one in five approving its performance (see Figure 8.2). One reason Congress is held in disdain is that Americans regard it as overly influenced by interest groups. A declining economy, the wars in Iraq and Afghanistan, and persistent partisan disagreements within the Congress have also reduced the people's confidence in the institution. In short, voters tend to support their own representatives while being contemptuous of the rest of the membership.

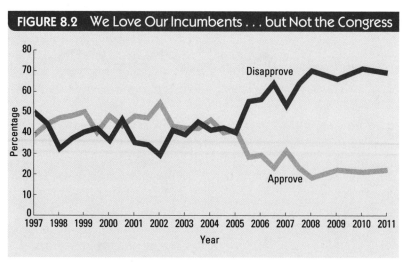

FIGURE 8.2   We Love Our Incumbents . . . but Not the Congress

Despite the reelection rate of incumbents reflected in Figure 8.1, public approval of Congress is far less positive. Confidence scores have never been particularly high, but opinion has turned decidedly negative in recent years. Citizens do not believe that the House and Senate are addressing the nation's problems.

Source: NBC News/*Wall Street Journal* polls, accessed at http://www.pollingreport.com/ CongJob1.htm. The question used asks respondents, "In general, do you approve or disapprove of the job that Congress is doing?"

Redistricting. One explanation for the incumbency effect centers on redistricting—the way state legislatures redraw House districts after a census-based reapportionment. It is entirely possible for them to draw the new districts to benefit the incumbents of one or both parties. Altering district lines for partisan advantage is commonly called **gerrymandering.** Of course, a state legislature can redraw district boundaries to harm incumbents as well. Of the seven incumbents in the U.S. House of Representatives who lost their seats on Election Day in 2004, four were Texas Democrats whose districts' boundaries had been altered in a controversial redistricting plan supported by Republicans in the state legislature.[10]

Gerrymandering contributes to the increasing pattern of polarization between the two parties in the House. In a district with a disproportionate number of liberals or conservatives, the representative will be pulled more toward a pole of the ideological spectrum than the moderate center.[11]

gerrymandering
Redrawing a congressional district to intentionally benefit one political party.

Name Recognition. Holding office brings with it some important advantages. First, incumbents develop significant name recognition among voters simply by being members of Congress. Congressional press secretaries promote name recognition through their efforts to get publicity for the activities and speeches of their bosses. The primary focus of such publicity seeking is on the local media back in the home district, where the votes are.[12] The local press, in turn, is eager to cover what members of Congress are saying about the issues.

Another resource available to members of Congress is the *franking privilege*–the right to send mail free of charge. Mailings work to make constituents aware of their legislators' names, activities, and accomplishments. In 2007 House members sent out 98 million pieces of mail, "many of them glossy productions filled with flattering photos and lists of the latest roads and bridges the lawmaker has brought home to the district."[13] Under current franking regulations, information about the representative's personal life and political campaign cannot be included in official mailings, but no such rules exist to govern communication with constituents via social media such as Twitter. Currently, 38 percent of representatives have Twitter accounts and have used them to send information about campaign events, policies, and even their shopping trips.[14]

Casework. Much of the work performed by the large staffs of members of Congress is **casework**–services for constituents such as tracking down a social security check or directing the owner of a small business to the appropriate federal agency. Legislators devote much of their office budget to casework because they assume that when they provide assistance to a constituent, that constituent will be grateful. Not only will this person probably vote for the legislator next time, he or she will be sure to tell family members and friends how helpful the representative or senator was.

Campaign Financing. Anyone who wants to challenge an incumbent needs solid financial backing. But here, too, the incumbent has the advantage. In the 2009–2010 campaign cycle, House incumbents running for reelection received approximately 57 percent of all money contributed to all candidates for the House. Challengers received only 31 percent of the contributions, with the remainder going to candidates in open races where there was no incumbent running for reelection.[15] Challengers find raising campaign funds difficult because they have to overcome contributors' doubts about whether they can win. PACs show a strong preference for incumbents (see Chapter 7). They tend not to want to risk offending an incumbent by giving money to a long-shot challenger. In the 2009–2010 House

casework
Solving problems for constituents, especially problems involving government agencies.

and Senate campaigns in which an incumbent was running for reelection, PACs gave over 88 percent of their contributions to incumbents.[16]

Successful Challengers. Clearly the deck is stacked against challengers to incumbents. Yet some challengers do beat incumbents. How? The opposing party and unsympathetic PACs may target incumbents who seem vulnerable because of age, lack of seniority, a scandal, or unfavorable redistricting.

Senate challengers have a higher success rate than House challengers, in part because they are generally higher-quality candidates. Often they are governors or members of the House who enjoy high name recognition and can attract significant campaign funds because they are regarded as credible candidates.[17]

The party controlling the White House almost always loses House seats in the midterm election as voters take out their disappointments with the president on candidates from his party. The president's party usually loses seats in the Senate too. This was the case in 2006, when the Republicans lost enough seats to give the Democrats control of both the House and the Senate.

2010 Election

A similar pattern emerged in the next midterm election. When President Obama's health-care bill was adopted into law in 2009, public opposition was widespread. Coupled with concerns over the nation's persistent economic struggles, the size of the economic stimulus package, and the explosive growth of the nation's debt, Democratic incumbents faced a vexing political climate in the midterm elections. With the support of tea party conservatives, Republican candidates in 2010 won five dozen seats formerly held by Democrats to seize firm control of the House of Representatives, bringing an end to Nancy Pelosi's tenure as Speaker. Even though the Democrats lost seats in the Senate, they maintained narrow control of that chamber. Prospects for President Obama's legislative agenda plunged after the election.

Whom Do We Elect?

The people we elect (and then reelect) to Congress are not a cross-section of American society. Most members of Congress are professionals—primarily lawyers and businesspeople—and at last count, 44 percent are millionaires.[18] Although nearly a third of the American labor force works in blue-collar jobs, a person employed as a

The Millionaires' Club

In 2010, Representative Darrell Issa (R-Calif.) was the richest lawmaker in the House, with an estimated net worth of $160 million. While 44 percent of lawmakers are millionaires, only about 1 percent of Americans can say the same.

Source: Jennifer Yachnin, Paul Singer, Melanie Zanona, Rachael Bade, and Jessica Estepa, "The 50 Richest Members of Congress," *Roll Call*, 16 September 2010, http://www.rollcall.com/features/Guide-to-Congress_2010/guide/-49892-1.html. *Photo*: Alex Wong/Getty Images.

blue-collar worker rarely wins a congressional nomination. Women and minorities also have long been underrepresented in elective office, although both groups have recently increased their representation in Congress significantly. In the 112th Congress, elected in November 2010, seventy-one representatives and seventeen senators were women, forty-two representatives (but no senators) were African Americans, and twenty-seven representatives and two senators were Hispanic.[19] Yet many women and minorities believe that only members of their own group—people who have experienced what they have experienced—can truly represent their interests. This is a belief in **descriptive representation**—the view that a legislature should resemble the demographic characteristics of the population it represents.[20]

When Congress amended the Voting Rights Act in 1982, it encouraged the states to draw districts that concentrated minorities together so that African Americans and Hispanic Americans would have a better chance of being elected to office. Supreme Court decisions also pushed the states to concentrate minorities in House districts.[21] After the 1990 census, states redrew House boundaries with the intent of creating districts with majority or near-majority minority populations. Some districts were very oddly shaped, snaking through their state to pick up black neighborhoods in various cities but leaving adjacent white neighborhoods to other districts. This effort led to a roughly 50 percent increase in the number of blacks elected to the House.

descriptive representation
A belief that constituents are most effectively represented by legislators who are similar to them in such key demographic characteristics as race, ethnicity, religion, or gender.

The effort to draw boundaries to promote the election of minorities has been considerably less effective for Hispanics. Hispanic representation is only about two-thirds that of African Americans, even though there are slightly more Hispanics in the United States than African Americans. Part of the reason for this inequity is that Hispanics tend not to live in such geographically concentrated areas as do African Americans. This makes it harder to draw boundaries that will likely lead to the election of a Hispanic. Another reason is that 37 percent of adult Hispanics living in the United States are ineligible to vote because they are not American citizens.[22]

In a decision that surprised many, the Supreme Court ruled in 1993 that states' efforts to increase minority representation through **racial gerrymandering** could violate the rights of whites. In *Shaw* v. *Reno,* the majority ruled in a split decision that a North Carolina district that meandered 160 miles from Durham to Charlotte was an example of "political apartheid." In effect, the Court ruled that racial gerrymandering segregated blacks from whites instead of creating districts built around contiguous communities.[23] In a later decision, the Supreme Court ruled that the "intensive and pervasive use of race" to protect incumbents and promote political gerrymandering violated the Fourteenth Amendment and Voting Rights Act of 1965.[24] In 2001, just before the redistricting from the 2000 census was to begin in the individual states, the Court modified its earlier decisions by declaring that race was not an illegitimate consideration in drawing congressional boundaries as long as it was not the "dominant and controlling" factor.[25]

Although this movement over time to draw districts that work to elect minorities has clearly increased the number of black and Hispanic legislators, almost all of whom are Democrats, it has also helped the Republican Party. As more Democratic voting minorities have been packed into selected districts, their numbers in other districts have fallen. This has left the remaining districts not merely "whiter" but also more Republican than they would have otherwise been.[26]

How Issues Get on the Congressional Agenda

racial gerrymandering
The drawing of a legislative district to maximize the chances that a minority candidate will win election.

The formal legislative process begins when a member of Congress introduces a *bill*—a proposal for a new law. In the House, members drop new bills in the "hopper," a mahogany box near the rostrum where the Speaker presides. Senators give their bills to one of the

Senate clerks or introduce them from the floor.[27] But before a bill can be introduced to solve a problem, someone must perceive that a problem exists or that an issue needs to be resolved. In other words, the problem or issue somehow must find its way onto the congressional agenda. Many of the issues Congress is working on at any one time seem to have been around forever, yet all issues have a beginning point. Foreign aid, the national debt, and social security have come up in just about every recent session of Congress. Other issues emerge more suddenly, especially those that are the products of technological change.[28] The issue of "cyberbullying" is one example. Just a few years ago, the term did not even exist, but in 2009, a bill was introduced in the House that would make it a federal crime to "coerce, intimidate, harass, or cause substantial emotional distress to another person, using electronic means to support severe, repeated, and hostile behavior."[29] The bill, known as the Megan Meier Cyberbullying Prevention Act, was drafted after national attention was drawn to the case of a thirteen-year-old girl in St. Louis who committed suicide after being taunted by an adult neighbor who pretended to be a teenage boy on the social networking site MySpace.[30]

Sometimes a highly visible event focuses national attention on a problem. When it became evident that the September 11 hijackers had little trouble bringing box cutters that they would use as weapons on board the planes, Congress quickly took up the issue of airport screening procedures. It decided to create a federal work force to conduct passenger and luggage screening at the nation's airports. Presidential support can also move an issue onto the agenda quickly. Media attention gives the president enormous opportunity to draw the nation's attention to problems he believes need some form of governmental action.

Within Congress, party leaders and committee chairs have the opportunity to influence the political agenda. At times, the efforts of an interest group spark awareness of an issue.

The Dance of Legislation: An Overview

The process of writing bills and getting them passed is relatively simple, in the sense that it follows a series of specific steps. What complicates the process is the many different ways legislation can be treated at each step. Here, we examine the straightforward process by which laws are made. In the next few sections, we discuss some of the complexities of that process.

After a bill is introduced in either house, it is assigned to the committee with jurisdiction over that policy area (see Figure 8.3). A banking bill, for example, is assigned to the Banking and Finance Services Committee in the House or the Banking, Housing, and Urban Affairs Committee in the Senate. When a committee actively considers a piece of legislation assigned to it, the bill is usually referred to a specialized subcommittee. The subcommittee may hold hearings, and legislative staffers may do research on the bill. The original bill usually is modified or revised. If passed in some form, it is sent to the full committee. A bill approved by the full committee is reported (that is, sent) to the entire membership of the chamber, where it may be debated, amended, and either passed or defeated.

Bills coming out of House committees go to the Rules Committee before going before the full House membership. The Rules Committee attaches a rule to the bill that governs the coming floor debate, typically specifying the length of the debate and the types of amendments House members may offer. The Senate does not have a comparable committee, although restrictions on the length of floor debate can be reached through unanimous consent agreements (see the "Rules of Procedure" section later in the chapter).

Even if both houses of Congress pass a bill on the same subject, the Senate and House versions usually differ. If neither chamber amends its bill to match the bill passed in the other chamber, a conference committee, composed of legislators from both houses, works out the differences and develops a compromise version. This version goes back to each house for another floor vote. If both chambers approve the bill, it is then sent to the president for his signature (approval) or **veto** (rejection).

When the president signs a bill, it becomes law. When the president vetoes a bill, it is sent back to Congress with his reasons for rejecting it. The bill becomes law only if Congress overrides the president's veto by a two-thirds vote in each house. If the president neither signs nor vetoes the bill within ten days of receiving it (Sundays excepted), the bill becomes law. But if Congress adjourns within that ten-day period, the president can let the bill die through a **pocket veto** by not signing it.

The content of a bill can be changed at any stage of the process and in either house. Lawmaking (and thus policymaking) in Congress has many access points for those who want to influence

veto
The president's rejection of a bill that has been passed by both houses of Congress. Congress can override a veto with a two-thirds vote in each house.

pocket veto
A means of killing a bill that has been passed by both houses of Congress, in which the president neither signs the bill nor returns it to Congress and Congress adjourns within ten days of the bill's passage.

FIGURE 8.3   The Legislative Process

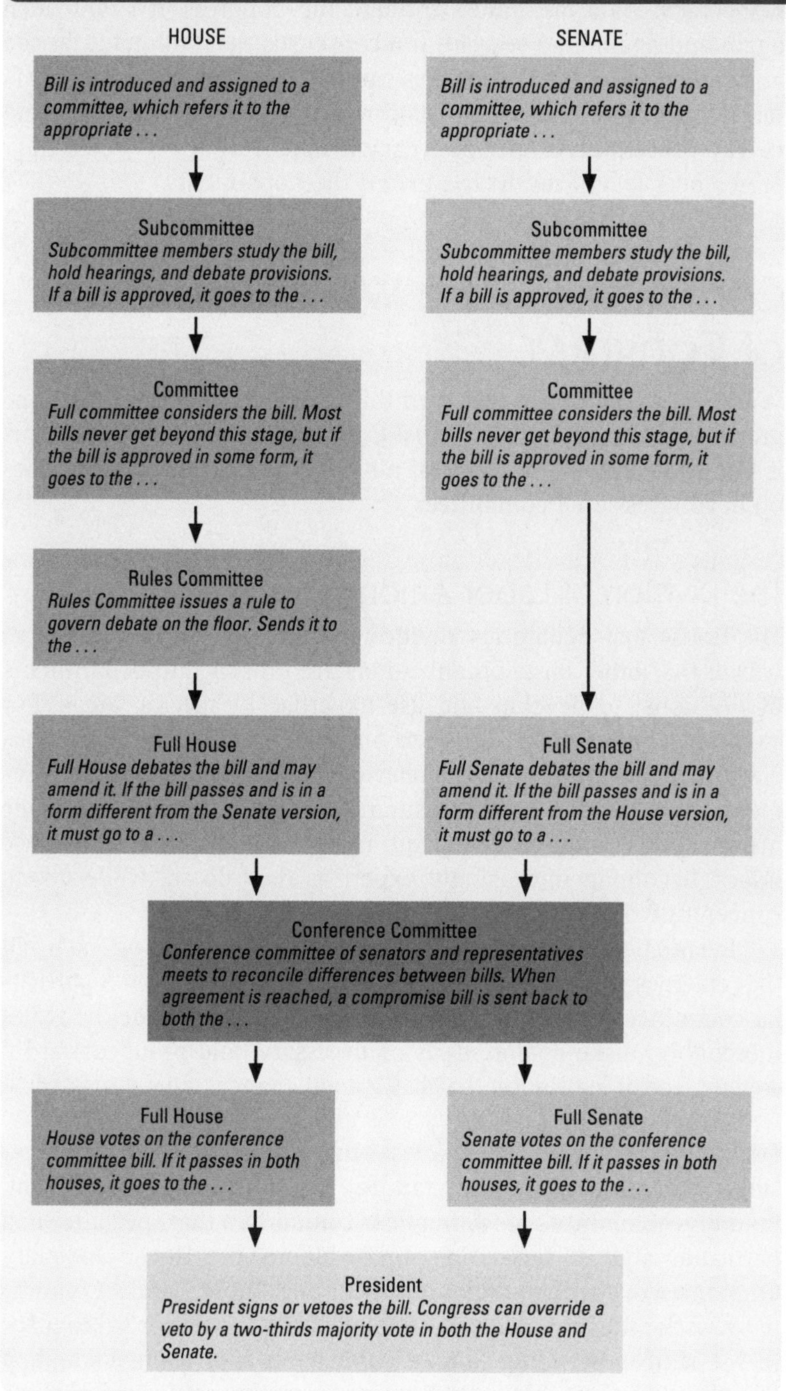

HOUSE

Bill is introduced and assigned to a committee, which refers it to the appropriate . . .

↓

Subcommittee
Subcommittee members study the bill, hold hearings, and debate provisions. If a bill is approved, it goes to the . . .

↓

Committee
Full committee considers the bill. Most bills never get beyond this stage, but if the bill is approved in some form, it goes to the . . .

↓

Rules Committee
Rules Committee issues a rule to govern debate on the floor. Sends it to the . . .

↓

Full House
Full House debates the bill and may amend it. If the bill passes and is in a form different from the Senate version, it must go to a . . .

SENATE

Bill is introduced and assigned to a committee, which refers it to the appropriate . . .

↓

Subcommittee
Subcommittee members study the bill, hold hearings, and debate provisions. If a bill is approved, it goes to the . . .

↓

Committee
Full committee considers the bill. Most bills never get beyond this stage, but if the bill is approved in some form, it goes to the . . .

↓

Full Senate
Full Senate debates the bill and may amend it. If the bill passes and is in a form different from the House version, it must go to a . . .

↓

Conference Committee
Conference committee of senators and representatives meets to reconcile differences between bills. When agreement is reached, a compromise bill is sent back to both the . . .

↓

Full House
House votes on the conference committee bill. If it passes in both houses, it goes to the . . .

Full Senate
Senate votes on the conference committee bill. If it passes in both houses, it goes to the . . .

↓

President
President signs or vetoes the bill. Congress can override a veto by a two-thirds majority vote in both the House and Senate.

The process by which a bill becomes law is subject to much variation. This diagram depicts the typical path a bill might follow. It is important to remember that a bill can fail at any stage because of lack of support.

(© Cengage Learning 2013)

legislation. This openness tends to fit within the pluralist model of democracy. As a bill moves through the Congress, it is amended again and again, in a search for a consensus that will get it passed and signed into law. The process can be tortuously slow, and it often is fruitless. Derailing legislation is much easier than enacting it. The process gives groups frequent opportunities to voice their preferences and, if necessary, thwart their opponents.

Committees: The Workhorses of Congress

Woodrow Wilson once observed that "Congress in session is Congress on public exhibition, whilst Congress in its committee-rooms is Congress at work."[31] The real nuts and bolts of lawmaking goes on in congressional committees.

The Division of Labor Among Committees

The House and Senate are divided into committees for the same reason that other large organizations are broken into departments or divisions: to develop and use expertise in specific areas. For example, congressional decisions on weapons systems require special knowledge that is of little relevance to decisions on reimbursement formulas for health insurance. It makes sense for some members of Congress to spend more time examining defense issues, becoming increasingly expert as they do so, while others concentrate on health matters.

Eventually all members of Congress have to vote on each bill that emerges from the committees. Those who are not on a particular committee depend on committee members to examine the issues thoroughly, make compromises as necessary, and bring forward a sound piece of legislation that has a good chance of being passed.

Standing Committees. There are several different kinds of congressional committees, but the **standing committee** is predominant. Standing committees are permanent committees that specialize in a particular area of legislation–for example, the House Judiciary Committee or the Senate Environment and Public Works Committee. Most of the day-to-day work of drafting legislation takes place in the sixteen standing Senate committees and twenty standing House committees. Typically from sixteen to twenty senators serve

standing committee
A permanent congressional committee that specializes in a particular legislative area.

on each standing Senate committee, and on average forty-two members serve on each standing committee in the House. The proportion of Democrats and Republicans on a standing committee generally reflects party proportions in the full Senate or House.

With a few exceptions, standing committees are further broken down into subcommittees. The House Agriculture Committee, for example, has six subcommittees, among them one on livestock, dairy, and poultry, and another one on horticulture and organic agriculture.

Other Congressional Committees. Members of Congress can also serve on joint, select, and conference committees. **Joint committees** are made up of members of both House and Senate. Like standing committees, they are concerned with particular policy areas. The Joint Economic Committee, for instance, analyzes the country's economic policies. Joint committees are much weaker than standing committees because they are almost always restricted from reporting bills to the House or Senate.

A **select committee** is usually a temporary committee created for a specific purpose. Congress establishes select committees to deal with special circumstances or with issues that either overlap or fall outside the areas of expertise of standing committees. The Senate committee that investigated the Watergate scandal was a select committee, created for that purpose only. These committees typically disband after their work is completed. However, some select committees, such as the Senate Select Committee on Intelligence and the House Permanent Select Committee on Intelligence, are granted permanent status and function much like standing committees.

A **conference committee** is also a temporary committee, created to work out differences between House and Senate versions of a specific piece of legislation. Its members are appointed from the standing committees or subcommittees from each house that originally handled and reported the legislation. Depending on the nature of the differences and the importance of the legislation, a conference committee may meet for hours or for weeks on end. When the conference committee agrees on a compromise, it reports the bill to both houses, which must then either approve or disapprove the compromise; they cannot amend or change it in any way. Conference committees are not always used, however, to reconcile differing bills. Often, informal negotiations between committee leaders in the House and Senate resolve differences. The increasing partisan conflict between Democrats and Republicans has often resulted in a

joint committee
A committee made up of members of both the House and the Senate.

select committee
A congressional committee created for a specific purpose and, usually, for a limited time.

conference committee
A temporary committee created to work out differences between the House and Senate versions of a specific piece of legislation.

compromise bill devised solely by the majority party (when a single party controls both chambers).

Congressional Expertise and Seniority

Once appointed to a committee, a representative or senator has great incentive to remain on it in order to gain increasing expertise and influence. Influence also grows in a more formal way—with **seniority**, or years of consecutive service, on a committee. In their quest for expertise and seniority, members tend to stay on the same committees. However, sometimes they switch places when they are offered the opportunity to move to one of the high-prestige committees (such as Ways and Means in the House or Finance in the Senate) or to a committee that handles legislation of vital importance to their constituents.

Within each committee, the senior member of the majority party usually becomes the committee chair. Other senior members of the majority party become subcommittee chairs; their counterparts from the minority party gain influence as ranking minority members. The numerous subcommittees in the House and Senate offer multiple opportunities for power and status.

The seniority norm was weakened in the 1990s when the Republic Party leadership established six-year term limits for committee and subcommittee chairs. This was a sharp break with the tradition of unlimited tenure as a committee chair. The Speaker of the House at that time, Newt Gingrich, also rejected three Republicans who were in line to become committee chairs in favor of other committee members who he thought would best promote the Republican program. Speakers had not appointed House committee chairs in this fashion since "Uncle Joe" Cannon ruled the chamber with an iron fist as Speaker from 1903 to 1911.[32] Democratic Party leaders have largely adhered to the seniority system, though they have also worked to increase the representation of women, minorities, and junior members of Congress on the most prestigious congressional committees.

The way in which committees and subcommittees are led and organized within Congress is significant because much public policy decision making takes place there. The first step in drafting legislation is to collect information on the issue. Committee staffers research the problem, and hearings may be held to take testimony from witnesses who have special knowledge on the subject.

The meetings at which subcommittees and committees actually debate and amend legislation are called *markup sessions*. The process

seniority
Years of consecutive service on a particular congressional committee.

by which committees reach decisions varies. In many committees, there is a strong tradition of decision by consensus. The chair, the ranking minority member, and others on these committees work hard, in formal committee sessions and in informal negotiations, to find a middle ground on issues that divide committee members. In other committees, members exhibit strong ideological and partisan sentiments. However, committee and subcommittee leaders prefer to find ways to overcome inherent ideological and partisan divisions so that they can build compromise solutions that will appeal to the broader membership of their house. The skill of committee leaders in assembling coalitions that produce legislation that can pass on the floor of their house is critically important.

Oversight: Following Through on Legislation

It is often said in Washington that "knowledge is power." For Congress to retain its influence over the programs it creates, it must be aware of how the agencies responsible for them are administering them. To that end, legislators and their committees engage in **oversight**, the process of reviewing agency operations to determine whether the agency is carrying out policies as Congress intended.

Congress performs its oversight function in several different ways. The most visible is the hearing. Hearings may be part of a routine review or the byproduct of information that reveals a major problem with a program or with an agency's administrative practices. After the disastrous federal response to Hurricane Katrina, a storm that destroyed much of New Orleans in 2005, congressional committees held hearings to understand why the government failed. Another way Congress keeps track of what departments and agencies are doing is by requesting reports on specific agency practices and operations. After the Democrats captured the Congress in the 2006 election, committees in both houses became much more aggressive in investigating activities in the Bush administration. A good deal of congressional oversight takes place informally. There is ongoing contact between committee and subcommittee leaders and agency administrators and between committee staffers and top agency staffers.

Oversight is often stereotyped as a process in which angry legislators bring some administrators before the television cameras at a hearing and proceed to dress them down for some recent scandal or mistake. Some of this does go on, but at least some members of a committee are advocates of the programs they oversee because

oversight
The process of reviewing the operations of an agency to determine whether it is carrying out policies as Congress intended.

those programs serve their constituents back home. Members of the House and Senate agriculture committees, for example, both Democrats and Republicans, want farm programs to succeed. Most oversight is aimed at finding ways to improve programs, not discredit them.[33] In the last analysis, Congress engages in oversight because it is an extension of its efforts to control public policy.[34]

Majoritarian and Pluralist Views of Committees

Government by committee vests a tremendous amount of power in the committees and subcommittees of Congress, and especially in their leaders. This is particularly true of the House, which has more decentralized patterns of influence than the Senate and is more restrictive about letting members amend legislation on the floor. Committee members can bury a bill by not reporting it to the full House or Senate. The influence of committee members extends even further, to the floor debate. Many of them also make up the conference committees charged with developing compromise versions of bills.

In some ways, the committee system enhances the force of pluralism in American politics. Representatives and senators are elected by the voters in particular districts and states, and they tend to seek membership on the committees that make the decisions most important to their constituents. Members from farm areas, for example, want membership on the House and Senate agriculture committees. As a result, committees with members who represent constituencies with an unusually strong interest in their policy area are predisposed to write legislation favorable to those constituencies.

The committees have a majoritarian aspect as well. The membership of most committees tends to resemble the general ideological profiles of the two parties' congressional contingents. Even if a committee's views are not in line with the views of the full membership, the committee is constrained in the legislation it writes because bills cannot become law unless they are passed by the parent chamber and the other house. Consequently, in formulating legislation, committees anticipate what other representatives and senators will accept. The parties within each chamber also have means of rewarding the members who are most loyal to party priorities. Party committees and the party leadership within each chamber make committee assignments and respond to requests for transfers from less prestigious to more prestigious committees. Those whose voting is most in line with the party get the best assignments.[35]

Leaders and Followers in Congress

Above the committee chairs is another layer of authority in the organization of the House and Senate. The Democratic and Republican leaders in each house work to maximize the influence of their own party while trying to keep their chamber functioning smoothly and efficiently. The operation of the two houses is also influenced by the rules and norms that each chamber has developed over the years.

The Leadership Task

Each of the two parties elects leaders in each of the two houses. In the House of Representatives, the majority party's leader is the **Speaker of the House**, who, gavel in hand, chairs sessions from the ornate rostrum at the front of the chamber. The Speaker's counterpart in the opposing party is the House *minority leader.* The Speaker is a constitutional officer, but the Constitution does not list the Speaker's duties. The majority party in the House also has a majority leader, who helps the Speaker guide the party's policy program through the legislative process, and a majority whip, who keeps track of the vote count and rallies support for legislation on the floor. The minority party is led by a minority leader who is assisted by the minority whip.

The Constitution makes the vice president of the United States the president of the Senate. But in practice, the vice president rarely visits the Senate chamber unless there is a possibility of a tie vote, in which case he can break the tie. The *president pro tempore* (president "for the time"), elected by the majority party, is supposed to chair the Senate in the vice president's absence. By custom this constitutional position is entirely honorary and occupied by the senator of the majority party with the longest continuous tenure. The real power in the Senate resides with the **majority leader**. The top position in the opposing party is Senate *minority leader.* Technically, the majority leader does not preside over Senate sessions (members rotate in the president pro tempore's chair). But the majority leader does schedule legislation in consultation with the minority leader.

Party leaders play a critical role in getting bills through Congress. Their most significant function is steering the bargaining and negotiating over the content of legislation. When an issue divides their party, their house, the two houses, or their house and the White House, the leaders must take the initiative to work out a compromise.

speaker of the house
The presiding officer of the House of Representatives.

majority leader
The head of the majority party in the Senate; the second-highest-ranking member of the majority party in the House.

Day in and day out, much of what they do is to meet with other members of their house to try to strike deals that will yield a majority on the floor. Beyond trying to engineer tradeoffs that will win votes, the party leaders must persuade others (often powerful committee chairs) that theirs is the best deal possible. Former Speaker of the House Dennis Hastert used to say, "They call me the Speaker, but . . . they really ought to call me the Listener."[36]

It is often difficult for party leaders to control rank-and-file members because they have independent electoral bases in their districts and states and receive the vast bulk of their campaign funds from nonparty sources. Contemporary party leaders are coalition builders, not autocrats. Yet party leaders can be aggressive about enforcing party discipline. When an energy bill was being developed in the House in 2007, Speaker Pelosi found herself at odds with Michigan Democrat John Dingell, chair of the Energy and Commerce Committee. Dingell believed that a proposed increase in fuel consumption standards would be bad for the automobile industry, key to his home state's economy. Advised of an initiative pushing for high fuel economy standards, the gruff Dingell dismissed it. "Let them try," he said. But Pelosi persuaded enough members of the committee to go against Dingell, and the chastised chair was forced to go along with the Speaker's wishes.[37]

Rules of Procedure

The operations of the House and Senate are structured by both formal rules and informal norms of behavior. Rules in each chamber are mostly matters of parliamentary procedure. For example, they govern the scheduling of legislation, outlining when and how certain types of legislation can be brought to the floor.

An important difference between the two chambers is the House's use of its Rules Committee to govern floor debate. Lacking a similar committee to act as a "traffic cop" for legislation approaching the floor, the Senate relies on unanimous consent agreements to set the starting time and length of the debate. If only one senator objects to an agreement, it does not take effect. Senators do not routinely object to unanimous consent agreements, however, because they know they will need them when bills of their own await scheduling by the leadership.

A senator who wants to stop a bill badly enough may start a **filibuster** and (in its classic form) try to talk the bill to death. By historical tradition, the Senate gives its members the right of unlimited

filibuster
A delaying tactic, used in the Senate, that often involves speech making to prevent action on a piece of legislation.

debate. The record for holding the floor belongs to the late Republican senator Strom Thurmond of South Carolina, for a twenty-four-hour, eighteen-minute marathon.[38] In the House, no member is allowed to speak for more than an hour without unanimous consent.

After a 1917 filibuster by a small group of senators killed President Wilson's bill to arm merchant ships, a bill favored by a majority of senators, the Senate finally adopted **cloture**, a means of limiting debate. A petition signed by sixteen senators initiates a cloture vote. It now takes the votes of sixty senators to invoke cloture, which creates a time limit for the debate. Since the 1960s the filibuster has taken on a variety of new forms that do not actually require a senator to occupy the floor and speak continuously. Today the term *filibuster* is also applied to a parliamentary device in the Senate that blocks action on a bill (as if a senator were speaking), but still allows business on other issues to take place. Because a senator can now filibuster without actually occupying the floor and speaking continuously about a bill, it is much easier to maintain filibusters, and they have become much more common. In today's Congress, the mere threat of a filibuster is extremely common, which means that a bill often needs the support of sixty senators instead of a simple majority in order to pass. This era of the "sixty-vote Senate" is often criticized for its ability to obstruct the principle of majority rule and to make the legislative process even slower than was intended by Madison and his fellow framers.[39]

Norms of Behavior

Both houses have codes of behavior that help keep them running. These codes are largely unwritten norms, although some have been formally adopted as rules. Members of Congress recognize that they must eliminate personal conflict, lest Congress dissolve into bickering factions unable to work together. One of the most celebrated norms is that members show respect for their colleagues in public deliberations. During floor debate, bitter opponents have traditionally referred to one another in such terms as "my good friend, the senior senator from . . ." or "my distinguished colleague." There are no firm measures of civility in Congress, but it seems to have declined in recent years.[40]

Probably the most important norm of behavior in Congress is that individual members should be willing to bargain with one another. Policymaking is a process of give-and-take; it demands compromise. Members of Congress are not expected to violate

cloture
The mechanism by which a filibuster is cut off in the Senate.

their consciences on policy issues simply to strike a deal. Rather, they are expected to listen to what others have to say and to make every effort to reach a reasonable compromise. Obviously, if they all stick rigidly to their own views, they will never agree on anything. Moreover, few policy matters are so clear-cut that compromise destroys one's position.

Some important norms have changed in recent years, most notably the notion that junior members of the House and Senate should serve apprenticeships and defer to their party and committee elders during their first couple of years in Congress. Aggressive, impatient, and ambitious junior legislators of both parties chafed under this norm, and it has weakened considerably in the past few decades.

The Legislative Environment

In this section, we examine the broader legislative environment that affects decision making in Congress. More specifically, we look at the influence on legislators of political parties, the president, constituents, and interest groups. The first two influences push Congress toward majoritarian democracy. The other two are pluralist influences on congressional policymaking.

Political Parties

The national political parties might appear to have limited resources at their disposal to influence lawmakers. They do not control the nominations of House and Senate candidates. Candidates receive the bulk of their funds from individual contributors and political action committees, not from the national parties. Nevertheless, the parties are strong forces in the legislative process. The party leaders and various party committees within each house can help or hinder the efforts of rank-and-file legislators to get on the right committees, get their bills and amendments considered, and climb onto the leadership ladder themselves. Moreover, party members on a committee tend to act as agents of their party as they search for solutions to policy problems.[41]

The most significant reason that the parties are important in Congress is that Democrats and Republicans have different ideological views. Both parties have diversity, but as Figure 8.4 illustrates, Democrats increasingly tend to vote one way and Republicans the other. The main reason that partisanship has been rising is that each

FIGURE 8.4   Rising Partisanship

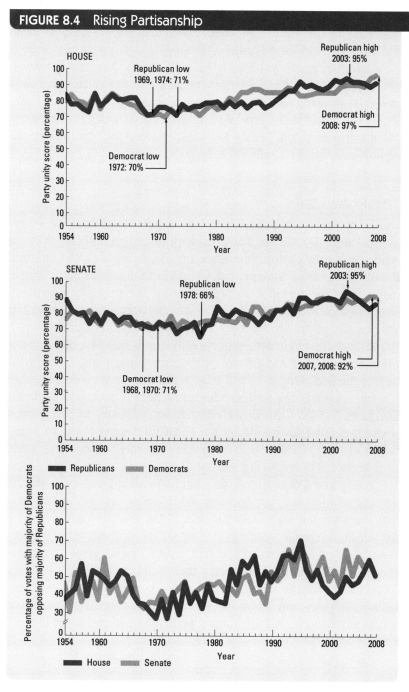

Congress long relied on bipartisanship—the two parties working together—in policymaking. This often meant that the moderates of both parties were central to the development of legislation as they coalesced around the most workable compromise. More recently, behavior has turned more partisan. Increasingly, members of each party vote with one another and against the position of the other party.

Sources: Harold W. Stanley and Richard G. Niemi (eds.), *Vital Statistics on American Politics, 2009–2010* (Washington, D.C.: CQ Press, 2010), p. 204. Copyright © 2010 CQ Press, a division of Sage Publications, Inc. Reprinted by permission of the publisher, CQ Press.

party is becoming more homogeneous.[42] The liberal wing of the Republican Party has practically disappeared, and the party is unified around a conservative agenda for America. Likewise, the conservative wing of the Democratic Party has declined. Republicans tend to be dominant in the South and West; Democrats control more seats in the Northeast and West Coast.

Majoritarianism was clearly at work when Congress convened after the 2010 election. House Republicans, having just captured control of that chamber, moved immediately to repeal the health care legislation passed in the previous Congress. Even though the House bill could not pass in the Senate (which Democrats still controlled), the action demonstrated resolve to Republican voters.

The President

Unlike members of Congress, the president is selected by voters across the entire nation. The president has a better claim, then, to representing the nation than does any single member of Congress. But it can also be argued that Congress as a whole has a better claim than the president to representing the majority of voters. Nevertheless, presidents capitalize on their national constituency and usually act as though they are speaking for the majority.

During the twentieth century, public expectations of what the president can accomplish in office grew enormously. We now expect the president to be our chief legislator: to introduce legislation on major issues and use his influence to push bills through Congress.[43] This is much different from our early history, when presidents felt constrained by the constitutional doctrine of separation of powers and had to have members of Congress work confidentially for them during legislative sessions.[44]

Today the White House is openly involved not only in the writing of bills but also in their development as they wind their way through the legislative process. If the White House does not like a bill, it tries to work out a compromise with key legislators to have the legislation amended. On issues of the greatest importance, the president himself may meet with individual legislators to persuade them to vote a certain way. To monitor daily congressional activities and lobby for the administration's policies, there are hundreds of legislative liaison personnel who work for the executive branch.

Although members of Congress grant presidents a leadership role in proposing legislation, they jealously guard the power of Congress to debate, shape, and pass or defeat any legislation the president proposes. Congress often clashes sharply with the president when his proposals are seen as ill advised.

Constituents

Constituents are the people who live and vote in a legislator's district or state. As much as members of Congress want to please their party's leadership or the president by going along with their preferences, they have to think about what the voters back home want. If the way members vote displeases enough people, they might lose their seats in the next election.

Constituents' influence contributes to pluralism, because the diversity of America is mirrored in the geographical basis of representation in the House and Senate. A representative from Los Angeles, for instance, may need to be sensitive to issues of particular concern to constituents whose backgrounds are Korean, Vietnamese, Hispanic, Indian, African American, or Jewish. A representative from Montana may have few such constituents but must pay particular attention to issues involving minerals and mining. A senator from Nebraska will give higher priority to agricultural issues than to urban issues. Conversely, a senator from New York will be hypersensitive to issues related to cities. All these constituencies, enthusiastically represented by legislators who want to do a good job for the people back home, push and pull Congress in many different directions.

Interest Groups

As we pointed out in Chapter 7, interest groups offer constituents one way to influence Congress. Because they represent a vast array of vocational, regional, and ideological groupings within the population, interest groups exemplify pluralist politics. They press members of Congress to take a particular course of action, believing sincerely that what they prefer is also best for the country. Legislators, in turn, are attentive to interest groups because these organizations represent citizens, some of whom live in their home district or state. Lobbies are also sources of useful information and potentially of political support (and, in some instances, campaign contributions) for members of Congress.

With all these strong forces pushing and constraining legislators, it is easy to believe that they function solely in response to these external pressures. Legislators, however, bring their own views and own life experiences to Congress. The issues they choose to work on and the way they vote reflect these personal values too.[45] But to the degree that the four external sources of influence on Congress—parties, the president, constituents, and interest groups—do influence legislators, they push them in both majoritarian and pluralist directions. We will

constituents
People who live and vote in a government official's district or state.

return to the conflict between pluralism and majoritarianism at the end of this chapter.

The Dilemma of Representation: Trustees or Delegates?

When candidates for the House and Senate campaign for office, they routinely promise to work hard for their district's or state's interests. When they get to Washington, though, they all face a troubling dilemma: what their constituents want may not be what the people across the nation want. Members of Congress are often criticized for being out of touch with the people they are supposed to represent. This charge does not seem justified. A typical week in the life of a representative means working in Washington, then boarding a plane and flying back to the home district. There the representative spends time meeting with individual constituents and talking to civic groups, church gatherings, business associations, labor unions, and the like. A survey of House members during a nonelection year showed that each made an average of thirty-five trips back to his or her district, spending an average of 138 days there.[46] Legislators work extraordinarily hard at keeping in touch with voters and finding out what is on their constituents' minds. The problem is how to act on that knowledge.

Are members of Congress bound to vote the way their constituents want them to vote, even if doing so means voting against their consciences? Some say no. They argue that legislators must be free to vote in line with what they think is best. This view is associated with the English political philosopher Edmund Burke (1729–1797). Burke, who served in Parliament, told his constituents in Bristol that "you choose a member, indeed; but when you have chosen him, he is not a member of Bristol, but he is a member of *Parliament.*"[47] Burke reasoned that representatives are sent by their constituents to vote as they think best. As **trustees**, representatives are obligated to consider the views of constituents, but they are not obligated to vote according to those views if they think they are misguided.

Others disagree. They hold that legislators are duty-bound to represent the majority view of their constituents. They maintain that legislators are **delegates** with instructions from the people at home on how to vote on critical issues, and they insist that delegates, unlike trustees, must be prepared to vote against their own policy preferences.

trustee
A representative who is obligated to consider the views of constituents but is not obligated to vote according to those views if he or she believes they are misguided.

delegate
A legislator whose primary responsibility is to represent the majority view of his or her constituents, regardless of his or her own view.

Although the interests of their districts encourage them to act as delegates, their interpretation of the larger national interest calls on them to be trustees.[48] Given these conflicting role definitions, it is not surprising that Congress is not clearly either a body of delegates or a body of trustees. Research has shown, however, that members of Congress are most likely to assume the delegate role on issues that are of great concern to their constituents.[49] But much of the time, what constituents really want is not clear. Many issues are not highly visible back home, they cut across the constituency to affect it in different ways, or constituents only partially understand them. For such issues, no delegate position is obvious.

Pluralism, Majoritarianism, and Democracy

The dilemma that individual members of Congress face in adopting the role of either delegate or trustee has broad implications for the way our country is governed. If legislators tend to act as delegates, congressional policymaking is more pluralistic, and policies reflect the bargaining that goes on among lawmakers who speak for different constituencies. If, instead, legislators tend to act as trustees and vote their consciences, policymaking becomes less tied to the narrower interests of districts and states. But even here there is no guarantee that congressional decision making reflects majority interests.

We end this chapter with a short discussion of pluralism versus majoritarianism in Congress. But first, to establish a frame of reference, we need to take a quick look at a more majoritarian type of legislature: the parliament.

Parliamentary Government

In our system of government, the executive and legislative functions are divided between a president and a congress, each elected separately. Most other democracies—for example, Britain and Japan—have parliamentary governments. In a **parliamentary system**, the chief executive is the legislative leader whose party holds the most seats in the legislature after an election or whose party forms a major part of the ruling coalition. For instance, in Great Britain, voters do not cast a ballot for prime minister. They vote only for their member of Parliament and thus influence the choice of prime minister only indirectly, by voting for the party they favor in the local district

parliamentary system
A system of government in which the chief executive is the leader whose party holds the most seats in the legislature after an election or whose party forms a major part of the ruling coalition.

Politics of Global Change

Creating a Legislature

After the fall of Saddam Hussein in 2003, Iraqis faced a daunting challenge: how to create a democratically elected legislature with free and fair elections that Iraqis see as legitimate. The problem was that the country consisted of a population marked by deep and enduring divisions over religion, ethnicity, and territory.

One of the first decisions they needed to make was on the kind of legislature to establish. An American-style Congress with single-member districts elected by plurality rule seemed appealing at first because such a system would likely minimize the chances for extremist parties to gain seats and produce representatives committed to their local constituency as well as to their party. But advocates for proportional representation

(PR), including most of the major political factions in Iraq, prevailed. Under PR, each politically organized group can expect to be represented roughly in proportion to its support in society.

Iraqis held three successful elections in 2005. The first established a transitional Iraqi government, the second was a referendum for the new Iraqi constitution, and the third elected the first representatives to the new permanent government. This new government is federal in nature, with eighteen provinces. Its unicameral legislature, the Council of Representatives, had 275 seats after the first election; it has since been increased to 325. Most of the seats are divided among the provinces, much as delegations to the House of Representatives in the United States are apportioned among the

election. Parties are unified, and in Parliament, legislators vote for their party's position, giving voters a strong and direct means of influencing public policy. Where there is a multiple-party system (as opposed to just two parties), a governing coalition must sometimes be formed out of an alliance of several parties. (See "Politics of Global Change: Creating a Legislature.")

In a parliamentary system, government power is highly concentrated in the legislature, because the leader of the majority party is also the head of the government. Moreover, parliamentary legislatures are usually composed of only one house or have a second chamber that is much weaker than the other. And parliamentary governments usually do not have a court that can invalidate acts of the parliament. Under such a system, the government is in the hands of the party that controls the parliament. Over all, these governments fit the majoritarian model of democracy to a much greater extent than a separation-of-powers system.

states. But Iraq does not assign representatives to districts within the provinces; each province comprises a multimember district. In the 2005 election, voters voted for parties, not individual candidates. The party leadership determined which individuals would be seated.

Seventy-seven percent of registered voters voted in 2005. They gave a near majority to a coalition of Shiite groups called the United Iraqi Alliance. Kurdish and Sunni coalitions came in second and third, respectively. A total of twelve parties or coalitions won seats.

Despite the seeming success of the 2005 elections, the Iraqi parliament remains a work in progress. The second national parliamentary election was held in March 2010, this time with a revised set of election rules to address a number of disputes. The most notable change was to allow voters to vote for individual candidates instead of voting for parties. Many Iraqis, including Shiite religious leader Grand Ayatollah Ali al-Sistani, argued that people should have the power to vote directly for candidates. Party leaders, however,

had wanted to keep control over who gets seated in parliament.

While some Iraqi leaders were unconcerned about delaying the elections until these disputes were resolved, American officials wanted the elections to occur quickly; the pace of the withdrawal of U.S. troops will be based in part on whether the country successfully conducts a second round of parliamentary elections. The verdict is still out. The March 2010 elections have been called the most open and democratic in that nation's history, with an estimated turnout of 62 percent. But the day was still met with violence and at least 38 deaths. Almost 500 candidates were barred from the ballot because of ties to the former Baath Party of Saddam Hussein. In addition, no party won an outright majority. The results were subject to an extended and bitter recount. It took a world-record setting nine months of intense negotiation before Prime Minister Maliki was officially granted a second term in office on December 21. Ironically, this record for a country operating without a government fell just three months later . . . to Belgium.

Pluralism Versus Majoritarianism in Congress

The U.S. Congress is often criticized for being too pluralistic and not majoritarian enough. The federal budget deficit provides a case in point. Americans are deeply concerned about the big deficits that have plagued national budgets in recent years. And both Democrats and Republicans in Congress have repeatedly called for reductions in those deficits. But when spending bills come before Congress, legislators' concerns turn to what the bills will or will not do for their district or state. Appropriations bills usually include **earmarks**, pork barrel projects that benefit specific districts or states and further add to any deficit. Recent earmarks include $349,000 for swine and other waste management in North Carolina, $1.45 million to study mosquito trapping in Florida, and $2.9 million for shrimp aquaculture research in Louisiana.[50] More expensive earmarks abound too. Mississippi senator Thad Cochran, a top earmark recipient for the 2010 fiscal year, has snagged an

earmarks
Federal funds appropriated by Congress for use on specific local projects.

astonishing $490 million in earmarks for 240 projects.[51] Members of Congress try to win projects and programs that will benefit their constituents and thus help them at election time.

Projects such as these get into the budget through bargaining among members. Members of Congress try to win projects and programs that will benefit their constituents and thus help them at election time. To win approval of such projects, members must be willing to vote for other legislators' projects in turn. Such a system obviously promotes pluralism (and spending).

It is easy to conclude that the consequence of pluralism in Congress is a lot of unnecessary spending and tax loopholes. Yet many different constituencies are well served by an appropriations process that takes pluralism into account. When Congress included $50 million for the Iowa Environmental/Education Project, was it one more example of frivolous pork barrel spending? The Iowa economy has been hit hard in recent years, and the new tourist attraction is to be built on a former industrial site in Coralville. When it is finished, tourists will be able to enter replicas of different ecosystems, including a 4.5-acre indoor rain forest. One estimate—possibly optimistic—is that when it is up and running, the new facility will generate $120 million a year for the state's economy. It will provide jobs too, replacing at least some of those lost when factories shut down.[52] The people of Iowa pay taxes to Washington, so shouldn't Washington send some of that money back to the district in the form of economic development projects?

Proponents of pluralism also argue that the makeup of Congress generally reflects that of the nation, that different members of Congress represent farm areas, oil and gas areas, low-income inner cities, industrial areas, and so on. They point out that America itself is pluralistic, with a rich diversity of economic, social, religious, and racial groups, and that even if one's own representatives and senators do not represent one's particular viewpoint, it is likely that someone else in Congress does.[53]

Whatever the shortcomings of pluralism, broad-scale institutional reform aimed at reducing legislators' concern for individual districts and states is difficult. Members of Congress resist any structural changes that might weaken their ability to gain reelection. Certainly, maintaining the prerogatives of the committee system and the dominant influence of committees over legislation and pork barrel spending has proven stubbornly resistant to significant reform.[54] Nevertheless, the growing partisanship in the Congress illustrated in Figure 8.4 represents a trend toward greater majoritarianism. As noted earlier, as both parties have become more ideologically homogeneous, there is greater unity around policy preferences. To the degree that voters

Earmark Question Mark

Distributional policies allocate resources to a specific constituency, sometimes through congressional earmarks. One such earmark went to support the Drake Well Museum in Venango County, Pennsylvania. The museum contains artifacts of the oil discovery there in 1859, including the oil rig pictured here. Earmarks such as these are controversial as many believe that they are a poor use of taxpayers' money.

(Superstock)

correctly recognize the differences between the parties and are willing to cast their ballots on that basis, the more majoritarianism will act as a constraint on pluralism in the Congress. Ironically, once in office, legislators can weaken the incentive for their constituents to vote on the basis of ideology. The congressional system is structured to facilitate casework for voters with a problem and to fund a certain amount of pork barrel spending. Both of these characteristics of the modern Congress work to boost each legislator's reputation in his or her district or state. In short, the modern Congress is characterized by strong elements of both majoritarianism and pluralism.

Tying It Together

1. How did the framers envision the powers of the Congress?
   - The framers wanted to prevent the concentration of power but create a strong union.
   - Each state has two senators serving six-year terms that are staggered and a certain number of representatives based on population as determined by the census.

- The House and Senate share similar powers to declare war, raise an army and navy, borrow and coin money, regulate interstate commerce, create federal courts, establish rules for the naturalization of immigrants, and make all laws.
- Both the House and Senate must approve all bills.
- The House has the power to initiate revenue bills and to impeach. The Senate has the power to confirm presidential appointees, ratify treaties, and try cases of impeachment.

2. In what ways do incumbency and other factors affect the way voters elect members of Congress?
- Voters usually reelect incumbents.
- There are several explanations for the incumbency effect:
  - gerrymandering during redistricting.
  - name recognition developed over time and maintained through media coverage, the franking privilege, and technology such as websites.
  - provision of casework or problem solving for constituents.
  - campaign contributions, which go predominantly to incumbents.
- Many believe descriptive representation is important, and laws have been enacted to encourage minority representation.

3. How do issues get on the congressional agenda?
- The congressional agenda is the broad, imprecise, and unwritten set of all the issues that Congress is considering.
- Sometimes a highly visible event causes issues to be put on the agenda by legislators.
- Interest groups can bring an issue to the attention of legislators who move it to the agenda.
- The formal legislative process begins when a member introduces a bill, which is a proposal for a new law.

4. What is the process by which bills become laws?
- Bills introduced to either house are assigned to the committee with jurisdiction over that area.
- Subcommittees often hold a hearing, research the bill, and then modify the bill.
- If passed by a subcommittee, bills are sent for a vote by the full committee. If approved, they report to the entire membership for a vote.
- In the House, bills go to the Rules Committee for rules regarding debate and amendments.

- If both chambers pass the bill, it goes to the president for his signature (approval) or veto (rejection).
  - If signed, the bill is law.
  - If the president does not act on a bill within ten days, the bill becomes law if Congress is still in session.
  - If Congress adjourns within that ten-day period, the president can let the bill die through a pocket veto.

5. What are the functions of congressional committees?
   - Standing committees are the predominant committees. They specialize in a particular area of legislation.
     - They complete the day-to-day work.
     - They have subcommittees.
     - Party representation is proportional to the full Senate or House.
   - Joint committees are made up of members of both houses.
   - Select committees are generally temporary committees that are created for a specific purpose.
   - Conference committees are temporary committees created to work out differences between House and Senate versions of legislation.
   - Committees collect information on an issue, hold hearings, and debate and amend legislation in markup sessions.
   - Legislators engage in oversight to review the operations of agencies, which are charged with carrying out policies to be sure they are acting as Congress intended. Oversight is performed in several ways:
     - holding hearings.
     - requesting reports on practices and operations.
     - maintaining informal contact between committees and agency administration.

6. What is the leadership structure, and what procedures are used to run the House and Senate?
   - Each of the two parties elects leaders in each of the two houses.
     - In the House, the majority party's leader is the Speaker of the House, a constitutional officer, who actively shapes the House agenda and leadership.
     - The minority party leader is not an officer but nevertheless is important.
     - The vice president of the United States is the president of the Senate but rarely appears in this capacity unless there is a tie vote.
     - The Senate majority leader has the most power in the Senate.

- The House and Senate have formal rules regarding
  - parliamentary procedure.
  - scheduling of legislation.
  - movement of legislation to the floor.
  - filibusters (allowed in the Senate only).
- Informal rules historically included norms of behavior to
  - maintain civility.
  - bargain.
  - compromise.
  - require junior members to follow the lead of experienced legislators.

7. What forces in the legislative environment affect decision making in Congress?
   - Political parties are strong forces on legislators due to increasing partisanship based on party ideology.
   - Presidents today use their support from the public to initiate legislation and to influence members of Congress to vote along party lines.
   - Constituents influence legislators who wish to be reelected.
   - Interest groups also influence legislators by representing a wide variety of interests.

8. Are legislators trustees or delegates?
   - As trustees, representatives are obligated to consider the views of constituents, but they are not obligated to vote according to those views if they think they are misguided.
   - As delegates, legislators are sent to Congress with instructions from the people at home on how to vote on critical issues and are expected to vote against their own views if necessary.
   - Members of Congress are subject to both these forces, but research shows they most often act as trustees.

9. How do the models of pluralism and majoritarianism manifest themselves in Congress?
   - In a parliamentary system, government power is concentrated in the legislature. These systems are more majoritarian than separation-of-powers systems.
   - The U.S. Congress is often criticized for being too pluralistic and not majoritarian enough.
   - Majoritarianism is growing in the Congress due to the rise in party unity.

The Origin and Powers of Congress

True or False?

1. The Supreme Court is the only governmental institution with the power to impeach.
2. Because Congress has sole power to declare war, no president has ever initiated military action on his own.
3. The founders established a publicly elected House and Senate through the U.S. Constitution to give citizens a strong voice in government.

Comprehension

4. How is the number of congressional representatives who are elected from each state determined?
5. How does the impeachment process work?

Electing the Congress

True or False?

1. Gerrymandering means altering district lines for partisan advantage.
2. Much of Congress is composed of blue-collar workers.
3. Challengers and incumbents receive approximately equal financial contributions during congressional campaigns.

Comprehension

4. What is meant by descriptive representation?
5. Why, despite a general disdain for Congress, do Americans tend to reelect their own representatives?

How Issues Get on the Congressional Agenda

True or False?

1. Bills are introduced automatically in Congress as problems and issues arise.
2. The "hopper" is a staff member who carries bills back and forth between committees and the Senate floor.

Comprehension

3. What might bring an issue to the forefront of the political agenda so legislators will consider it?

The Dance of Legislation: An Overview

True or False?

1. After a bill is introduced, the next step is to assign it to a committee with jurisdiction over that policy area.

2. Once a bill leaves its assigned Senate committee, it then goes directly to the Rules Committee.

3. When House and Senate versions of a bill differ, a conference committee develops a compromise version.

Comprehension

4. What happens to bills that are vetoed by the president?

5. Why is lawmaking a complicated process?

Committees: The Workhorses of Congress

True or False?

1. The standing committees of Congress are predominant, as they are permanent, specialized committees in which most of the day-to-day legislative work occurs.

2. Select committees are generally temporary because they are created for a specific purpose and usually disbanded after the purpose is fulfilled.

3. Committee members do not stay on a committee for any great length of time but instead move from committee to committee.

Comprehension

4. How do legislators make sure the agencies that administer their programs are carrying out the policies as Congress intended?

5. How does the committee system enhance the force of pluralism in American politics?

Leaders and Followers in Congress

True or False?

1. Today, it is easier to maintain a filibuster in the Senate than it was fifty years ago.

2. Cloture requires the vote of sixty senators and creates a time limit for debate.

3. The Speaker of the House and the majority leader in that chamber come from the same party.

Comprehension

4. Who serves as the Speaker of the House?

5. What are the norms or "codes of behavior" in Congress?

The Legislative Environment

True or False?

1. Constituents are staffers who work for members of Congress.

2. The four external sources of influence on Congress are parties, the president, constituents, and interest groups.

Comprehension

3. Which influences push Congress toward majoritarian democracy?

The Dilemma of Representation: Trustees or Delegates?

True or False?

1. Edmund Burke promoted the idea that representatives are trustees.
2. The view that legislators are duty-bound to represent the majority view of their constituents, even if it contradicts their own preferences, is most closely linked with the delegate perspective.

Comprehension

3. What is the difference between a trustee and a delegate?

Pluralism, Majoritarianism, and Democracy

True or False?

1. Parliaments reflect the majoritarian model more than the pluralist model because power is concentrated in the legislature.
2. The U.S. Congress is often criticized for being too majoritarian and not pluralistic enough.

Comprehension

3. Why are pork barrel projects and earmarks associated with the pluralist model?

CourseMate CL Resources:

Visit www.cengagebrain.com/shop/ISBN/1111832587 for flashcards, web quizzes, videos and more!

CHAPTER 9 The Presidency

CHAPTER OUTLINE

Lee Craker/DoD/Handout/CORBIS

FOCUS QUESTIONS

1. What are the origins of the powers of the president?
2. How have the powers of the president changed over time?
3. What staff and other resources make up the Executive Office of the President?
4. What factors affect the public's perception of a president's leadership?
5. How does a president implement his vision and policy preferences?
6. In what ways does a president fulfill his role as a leader on the world stage?

The not-so-secret secret war in Pakistan is one largely fought by remote control. Predator drones piloted remotely fly over the country, providing live feeds from their cameras to U.S. military intelligence at bases in other countries. When instructed, the drones also fire Hellfire guided missiles on terrorist targets below them.[1] Despite the fact that the drones are controlled remotely so their American pilots are not at risk, the Predator war is a dangerous one. Since 2004 these missiles have killed an estimated 1,400 to 2,200 people.

Although the intended targets on the ground are high-ranking officials in either the Taliban or al Qaeda, civilians have also been killed. After he came into office, President Obama decided to increase the Predator strikes. As a result, the number of civilian casualties is increasing. In the first two years since he took office, somewhere in the neighborhood of 130 to 280 civilians were killed by drone-launched missiles.[2]

Since being forced from power in Afghanistan, the Taliban have used northwestern Pakistan (the so-called tribal areas) as a safe haven.[3] Until recently the Pakistani government has allowed them to operate freely, as the government has little control over these areas. The Predator war is aimed at killing Taliban leaders, creating instability in their leadership, and possibly activating rivalries among competing factions trying to replace deceased leaders. The same strategy is aimed at al Qaeda, which pursues a global vision of *jihad* (holy war) against the Western powers.

Pakistan's fragile government, fearful of the terrorism that plagues the country, has been hesitant to take on al Qaeda and other insurgents in its northern provinces. At the same time, Pakistan desperately needs the U.S. foreign aid it receives. Moreover, as an ostensible ally of the United States, it needs to give some appearance of fighting terrorism.

During the Obama administration, the pressure on Pakistan to do more has mounted. With the surge of U.S. troops committed to Afghanistan, it became intolerable to the U.S. military to have the Taliban ensconced just across the border in Pakistan. At some point Pakistani leaders decided that al Qaeda and its allies inside the country were a growing threat to the government itself. Publicly, the government condemns the increasing Predator strikes; privately, it supplies the U.S. military with intelligence about the location of Taliban and al Qaeda leaders.

This intelligence has been useful not only for targeting high-tech drone strikes, but for putting American boots on the ground to kill Osama bin Laden, the head of al Qaeda. Nearly a decade after 9/11, intelligence was able to pinpoint bin Laden's location in a compound in Abbottabad,

Pakistan. On May 2, 2011, American forces conducted a lightning raid and killed bin Laden and other al Qaeda personnel.[4]

Although bin Laden's death was a major victory for President Obama, questions loom before him. What is the long-term strategy for this war in Pakistan? Since no one in the military believes that bin Laden's death or continued Predator attacks will put an end to terrorism, what other steps need to be taken and can be taken? Drone-launched missiles are increasingly effective at killing leaders, but they also inflame the local population when innocent civilians die. Insurgents use this anger to recruit new members. And terrorism has increased inside of Pakistan. Destabilization of the Pakistani government would have serious implications, particularly if Pakistan's nuclear arsenal were to fall into the hands of al Qaeda.[5]

Like all presidents Barack Obama faces a daunting set of challenges. American presidents are expected to offer solutions to national problems, whether fighting crime or reviving a failing economy. As the nation's major foreign diplomat and commander in chief of the armed forces, they are held responsible for the security and status of America in the world. Our presidents are the focal point for the nation's hopes and disappointments.

This chapter analyzes presidential leadership, looking at how presidents try to muster majoritarian support for their domestic goals and how presidents must function today as global leaders. What are the powers of the presidency? How is the president's advisory system organized? What are the ingredients of strong presidential leadership: character, public relations, or a friendly Congress? Finally, what are the issues and problems that presidents face in foreign affairs?

The Constitutional Basis of Presidential Power

When the presidency was created, the thirteen former colonies had just fought a war of independence; their reaction to British domination had focused on the autocratic rule of King George III. Thus, delegates to the Constitutional Convention were extremely wary of unchecked power and were determined not to create an all-powerful, dictatorial presidency. The delegates' fear of a powerful presidency was counterbalanced by their desire for strong leadership. The Articles of Confederation, which did not provide for a single head of state, had failed to bind the states together into a unified nation (see Chapter 2). The delegates knew they had to create some type of effective executive office. Their task was to provide national leadership without allowing any opportunity for tyranny.

Initial Conceptions of the Presidency

Debates over the nature of the office began. Should there be one president or a presidential council or committee? Should the president be chosen by Congress and remain subservient to that body?

The final structure of the presidency reflected the "checks and balances" philosophy that shaped the entire Constitution. The delegates believed they had imposed important limits on the presidency through the powers specifically delegated to Congress and the courts. Those counterbalancing powers would act as checks, or controls, on presidents who might try to expand the office beyond its proper bounds.

The Powers of the President

The requirements for the presidency are set forth in Article II of the Constitution. The president must be a U.S.-born citizen, at least thirty-five years old, who has lived in the United States for a minimum of fourteen years. Article II also sets forth the responsibilities of presidents. In view of the importance of the office, the constitutional description of the president's duties is surprisingly brief and vague. This vagueness has led to repeated conflict about the limits of presidential power.

The major presidential duties and powers listed in the Constitution can be summarized as follows:

- *Serve as administrative head of the nation.* The Constitution gives little guidance on the president's administrative duties. It states merely that "the executive Power shall be vested in a President of the United States of America" and that "he shall take Care that the Laws be faithfully executed." These imprecise directives have been interpreted to mean that the president is to supervise and offer leadership to various departments,

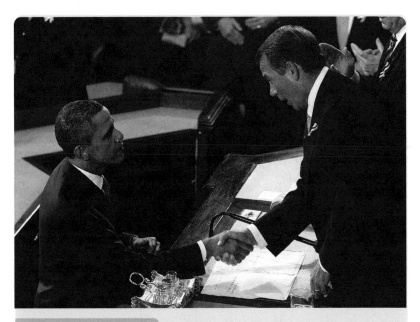

Welcome to my House

A key decision during the constitutional convention was to establish a chief executive separate from the legislative branch. Although the president has a unique ability to focus attention on issues and propose policies, he lacks authority in the legislative process. When his party holds the majority of congressional seats, as was the case during the first two years of President Obama's administration, members of his party can often push presidential proposals through. When the Republicans took control of the House after the 2010 elections, Rep. John Boehner became the new Speaker of the House. President Obama now must seek support from both sides of the aisle.

(Chip Somodevilla/Getty Images)

agencies, and programs created by Congress. In practice, a chief executive spends much more time making policy decisions for his cabinet departments and agencies than enforcing existing policies.

- *Act as commander in chief of the military.* In essence, the Constitution names the president as the highest-ranking officer in the armed forces. But it gives Congress the power to declare war. The framers no doubt intended Congress to control the president's military power; nevertheless, presidents have initiated military action without the approval of Congress.[6]
- *Convene Congress.* The president can call Congress into special session on "extraordinary Occasions," although this has rarely

been done. He must also periodically inform Congress of "the State of the Union."

- *Veto legislation.* The president can **veto** (reject) any bill or resolution enacted by Congress, with the exception of joint resolutions that propose constitutional amendments. Congress can override a presidential veto with a two-thirds vote in each house.
- *Appoint various officials.* The president has the authority to appoint federal court judges, ambassadors, cabinet members, other key policymakers, and many lesser officials. Many appointments are subject to Senate confirmation.
- *Make treaties.* With the "Advice and Consent" of at least two-thirds of those senators voting at the time, the president can make treaties with foreign powers. The president is also to "receive Ambassadors," a phrase that presidents have interpreted to mean the right to formally recognize other nations.
- *Grant pardons.* The president can grant pardons to individuals who have committed "Offenses against the United States, except in Cases of Impeachment."

The Expansion of Presidential Power

The framers' limited conception of the president's role has given way to a considerably more powerful interpretation. In this section, we discuss how presidential power has expanded as presidents have exercised their explicit constitutional responsibilities and boldly interpreted the ambiguities of the Constitution. First, we look at the ways in which formal powers, such as the veto power, have been increasingly used over time. Second, we turn to claims that presidents make about "inherent" powers implicit in the Constitution. Finally, we discuss congressional grants of power to the executive branch.

Formal Powers

The Constitution clearly involves the president in the policymaking process through his veto power, ability to report to Congress on the state of the union, and role as commander in chief. Over time, presidents have been increasingly aggressive in their use of these formal powers. Vetoes, for instance, have become much more frequent, particularly when presidents face a Congress dominated by

veto
The president's rejection of a bill that has been passed by both houses of Congress. Congress can override a veto with a two-thirds vote in each house.

the opposing political party. The first sixteen presidents, from Washington to Lincoln, issued a total of 59 vetoes. Dwight Eisenhower issued 181 vetoes over the course of his two terms in office; Ronald Reagan vetoed legislation 78 times.[7] At least during the first part of his presidency, Barack Obama made little use of the veto as his party had firm control of both houses of Congress. Yet the ability to veto legislation gives the president power even when he does not issue many vetoes. Veto threats shape legislation because members of Congress anticipate vetoes and modify legislation to avoid them.[8]

Modern presidents have also taken a much more active role in setting the nation's policy agenda. The Constitution states that the president shall give Congress information on the state of the Union "from time to time." For the most part, nineteenth-century presidents sent written messages to Congress and did not publicly campaign for the passage of legislation.[9] Early twentieth-century presidents like Woodrow Wilson began to deliver their State of the Union speeches in person before Congress, personalizing and fighting for their own policy agendas. It is now expected that the president will enter office with clear policy goals and work with his party in Congress to pass legislation.

Modern presidents have used their power as commander in chief to enter into foreign conflicts without appealing to Congress for a formal declaration of war.[10] The entire Vietnam War was fought without a congressional declaration of war. When President Bush ordered retaliatory military strikes and the bombing of Taliban strongholds in Afghanistan after the September 11 terrorist attacks, Congress never formally declared war. In 2002 the House and Senate passed a joint resolution authorizing President Bush to use military force "as he determined necessary and appropriate" in order to enforce United Nations Security Council resolutions regarding Iraq, but they did not declare war.[11]

The Inherent Powers

inherent powers
Authority claimed by the president that is not clearly specified in the Constitution. Typically these powers are inferred from the Constitution.

Several presidents have expanded the power of the office by taking actions that exceeded commonly held notions of the president's proper authority. These men justified what they had done by saying that their actions fell within the **inherent powers** of the presidency. From this broad perspective, presidential power derives not only from those duties clearly outlined in Article II but also from inferences that may be drawn from the Constitution.

When a president claims a power that has not been considered part of the chief executive's authority, he forces Congress and the courts to either acquiesce to his claim or restrict it. For instance, President Bush unilaterally established a military commission to try alleged enemy combatants held at the U.S. naval base at Guantánamo Bay, Cuba. In 2006, the U.S. Supreme Court ruled that the military commissions as established were illegal. The Bush administration was forced to go to Congress for the authorization to establish new commissions with new trial procedures.[12]

Claims of inherent powers often come at critical points in the nation's history. During the Civil War, for example, Abraham Lincoln issued several orders that exceeded the accepted limits of presidential authority and usurped powers constitutionally conferred on Congress. Lincoln said the urgent nature of the South's challenge to the Union forced him to act without waiting for congressional approval. His rationale was simple: "Was it possible to lose the nation and yet preserve the Constitution?"[13] In other words, Lincoln circumvented the Constitution in order to save the nation. Subsequently, Congress and the Supreme Court approved Lincoln's actions. That approval gave added legitimacy to the theory of inherent powers, a theory that has transformed the presidency over time.

Today presidents routinely issue **executive orders**, presidential directives that carry the force of law.[14] The Constitution does not explicitly grant the president the power to issue an executive order. Sometimes presidents use them to see that the laws are "faithfully executed." This was the case when Dwight Eisenhower ordered the Arkansas National Guard into federal service in Little Rock, Arkansas, to enforce court orders to desegregate the schools. But many times presidents issue executive orders by arguing that they may take actions in the best interest of the nation so long as the law does not directly prohibit these actions. Executive orders are issued for a wide variety of purposes, from administrative reorganization to civil rights.

The boundaries of the president's inherent powers have been sharply debated since the September 11, 2001, attacks upon the United States. In response to an ongoing threat of terrorism, President Bush secretly authorized the National Security Agency (NSA) to wiretap telephone calls, without a warrant, between people within the United States and people overseas with suspected links to terrorism.[15] The 1978 Foreign Intelligence Surveillance Act (FISA), however, requires intelligence agencies like the NSA to obtain a

executive orders
Presidential directives to the executive branch that create or modify public policies, without the direct approval of Congress.

warrant from a panel of judges before wiretapping the calls of U.S. persons. When the wiretapping was revealed, critics accused Bush of putting himself above the law. Bush argued that the Constitution designates the president as the commander in chief of the armed forces; he said he could disregard FISA requirements if they hindered his ability to collect the foreign intelligence necessary to protect the nation from another terrorist attack. Criticism of warrantless wiretapping eventually led Bush to request this power from Congress, which passed legislation that essentially authorized what the NSA had been doing.[16]

Congressional Delegation of Power

Presidential power grows when presidents successfully challenge Congress, but in many instances, Congress willingly delegates power to the executive branch. As the American public pressures the national government to solve various problems, Congress, through a process called **delegation of powers**, gives the executive branch more responsibility to administer programs that address those problems. One example of delegation of congressional power occurred in the 1930s, during the Great Depression, when Congress gave Franklin Roosevelt's administration wide latitude to do what it thought was necessary to solve the nation's economic ills.

When Congress concludes that the government needs flexibility in its approach to a problem, the president is often given great freedom in how or when to implement policies. Richard Nixon was given discretionary authority to impose a freeze on wages and prices in an effort to combat escalating inflation. If Congress had been forced to debate the timing of this freeze, merchants and manufacturers would surely have raised their prices in anticipation of it. Instead, Nixon was able to act suddenly, and the freeze was imposed without warning. (We discuss congressional delegation of authority to the executive branch in more detail in Chapter 10.)

At other times, Congress believes that too much power has accumulated in the executive branch, and it enacts legislation to reassert congressional authority. During the 1970s, many representatives and senators agreed that presidents were exercising power that rightfully belonged to the legislative branch and that Congress's role in the American political system was declining. The most notable reaction was passage of the War Powers Resolution (1973), directed toward ending the president's ability to pursue armed conflict without explicit congressional approval.

delegation of powers
The process by which Congress gives the executive branch the additional authority needed to address new problems

The Executive Branch Establishment

Although we elect a single individual as president, it would be a mistake to ignore the extensive staff and other resources of the executive branch of government. The president has a White House staff that helps him formulate policy. The vice president is another resource; his duties within the administration vary according to his relationship with the president. The president's cabinet secretaries—the heads of the major departments of the national government—play several roles, including the critical function of administering the programs that fall within their jurisdictions.

The Executive Office of the President

The president depends heavily on his key aides. They advise him on crucial political choices, devise the general strategies the administration will follow in pursuing congressional and public support, and control access to the president to ensure that he has enough time for his most important tasks. Consequently, he needs to trust and respect these top staffers; many in a president's inner circle of assistants are long-time associates. The president's personal staff constitutes the White House Office.

Presidents typically have a chief of staff, who may be first among equals or, in some administrations, the unquestioned leader of the staff. There also is a national security adviser to provide daily briefings on foreign and military affairs and longer-range analyses of issues confronting the administration. Similarly, the Council of Economic Advisers and the National Economic Council advise the president on the best way to promote economic growth. Senior domestic policy advisers help determine the administration's basic approach to such areas as health, education, and social services.

Below these top aides are the large staffs that serve them and the president. These staffs are organized around certain specialties. For example, President Obama's Assistant to the President for National Security Affairs, Tom Donilon, oversees the National Security Council staff, which provides analysis and logistical support to the president on foreign affairs. Some staff members work on political matters, such as liaison with interest groups, relations with ethnic and religious minorities, and party affairs. One staff deals exclusively with the media, and a legislative liaison staff lobbies Congress for the administration. The large Office of Management and Budget (OMB) analyzes budget requests, is involved in the policymaking process, and also examines agency management practices. This extended White House executive establishment, including the White House Office, is known as the **Executive Office of the President (EOP)**. The Executive Office employs close to 1,700 individuals and has an annual budget outlay of approximately $800 million.[17]

No one agrees about a "right way" for a president to organize his White House staff, but scholars have identified three major advisory styles.[18] Franklin Roosevelt exemplified the first system: a competitive management style. He organized his staff so that his advisers had overlapping authority and differing points of view. Roosevelt used this system to ensure that he would get the best possible information, hear all sides of an argument, and still be the final decision maker in any dispute. Dwight Eisenhower, a former general, best exemplifies a hierarchical staff model. His staff was arranged with clear lines of authority and a hierarchical structure that mirrored a military command. This places fewer demands on presidential time and energy, since the president does not participate in the details of policy discussion. Bill Clinton had more of a collegial staffing arrangement, a loose staff structure that gave many top staffers direct access to him, particularly early in his first administration. Clinton himself was immersed in the details of the policymaking process, brainstorming with his advisers. He was much less likely to delegate authority to others. Presidents tend to choose the advisory systems that best suit their personality. Most presidents use a combination of styles, learning from their predecessors.

Above all, a president must ensure that staff members feel comfortable telling him things he may not want to hear. Telling the president of the United States he is misguided on something is not an easy thing to do. The term *groupthink* has been used to refer to situations in which staffers reach consensus without properly considering all sides of an issue.[19] Several analysts have argued that the Johnson administration suffered from group-think when making decisions about the Vietnam War.

The Vice President

The vice president's most important duty is to take over the presidency in the event of presidential death, disability, impeachment, or resignation. Traditionally, vice presidents were not used in any important advisory capacity. Instead, presidents tended to give

Executive Office of the President (EOP)
The president's executive aides and their staffs; the extended White House executive establishment.

them political chores: campaigning, fundraising, and "stroking" the party faithful. This is often the case because vice-presidential candidates are chosen for reasons that have more to do with the political campaign than with governing the nation. Presidential candidates often choose vice-presidential candidates who appeal to a different geographic region or party coalition. Sometimes they even join forces with a rival from their political primary campaign. New Englander John Kennedy chose Texan Lyndon Johnson. Conservative Ronald Reagan selected George H. W. Bush, his more moderate rival in the Republican primaries. Texas governor George W. Bush chose Washington insider Dick Cheney as his vice-presidential running mate, who brought experience as a former member of the House of Representatives, presidential chief of staff to Richard Nixon, and secretary of defense to Bush's father.[20] The incumbent vice president, Joe Biden, is an important adviser within the Obama administration. He brought a wealth of foreign policy experience from years on the Senate Foreign Relations Committee to the administration. Despite a propensity for verbal gaffes, Vice President Biden has emerged as a forceful spokesman for administration policy.[21]

The Cabinet

The president's **cabinet** is composed of the heads of the departments in the executive branch and a small number of other key officials, such as the head of the Office of Management and Budget and the

cabinet
A group of presidential advisers; the heads of the executive department and other key officials.

U.S. Trade Representative. The cabinet has expanded greatly since George Washington formed his first cabinet: an attorney general and the secretaries of state, treasury, and war. Clearly, the growth of the cabinet to fifteen departments reflects the growth of government responsibility and intervention in areas such as energy, housing, and, most recently, homeland security.

In theory, the members of the cabinet constitute an advisory body that meets with the president to debate major policy decisions. In practice, however, cabinet meetings have been described as "vapid non-events in which there has been a deliberate non-exchange of information as part of a process of mutual non-consultation."[22] Why is this so?

First, the cabinet has become rather large. Counting department heads, other officials of cabinet rank, and presidential aides, it is a body of at least twenty people—a size that many presidents find unwieldy for the give-and-take of political decision making. Second, most cabinet members have limited areas of expertise and cannot contribute much to deliberations in policy areas they know little about. The secretary of defense, for example, would probably be a poor choice to help decide important issues of agricultural policy. Third, although cabinet members have impressive backgrounds, they may not be personally close to the president or easy for him to work with. The president often chooses cabinet members because of their reputations, or he may be guided by a need to give his cabinet some racial, ethnic, geographic, gender, or religious balance.

Finally, modern presidents do not rely on the cabinet to make policy because they have such large White House staffs, which offer most of the advisory support they need. And in contrast to cabinet secretaries, who may be pulled in different directions by the wishes of the president and those of their clientele groups, staffers in the White House Office are likely to see themselves as being responsible to the president alone. Thus, despite periodic calls for the cabinet to be a collective decision-making body, cabinet meetings seem doomed to be little more than academic exercises. In practice, presidents prefer the flexibility of ad hoc groups, specialized White House staffs, and the advisers and cabinet secretaries with whom they feel most comfortable.

More broadly, presidents use their personal staffs and the large Executive Office of the President to centralize control over the entire executive branch. The vast size of the executive branch and the number and complexity of decisions that must be made each day pose a challenge for the White House. Each president must be careful to appoint to top administrative positions people who are passionate about the president's goals and skillful enough to lead others in the executive branch to fight for the president's program instead of for their own agendas.[23]

Presidential Leadership

A president's influence in office comes not only from his assigned responsibilities but also from his political skills and from how effectively he uses the resources of his office. His leadership also depends on perceptions of his character and the political environment in which he finds himself. Table 9.1 provides two rankings of presidents. One is based on a Gallup poll of ordinary Americans; the other is based on a C-SPAN survey of fifty-eight prominent historians and professional observers of the presidency. In this section, we look at the factors that affect presidential performance. Why do some presidents rank higher than others?

Presidential Character

How does the public assess which presidential candidate has the best judgment and a character suitable to the office? Americans must make a broad evaluation of the candidates' personalities and leadership styles. Although it is difficult to judge, character matters. One of Lyndon Johnson's biographers argues that Johnson had trouble extricating the United States from Vietnam because of insecurities about his masculinity. Johnson wanted to make sure he "was not forced to see himself as a coward, running away from Vietnam."[24] It is hard to know for sure whether this psychological interpretation is valid. Clearer, surely, is the tie between President Nixon's character and Watergate. Nixon had such an exaggerated fear of what his "enemies" might try to do to him that he created a climate in the White House that nurtured the Watergate break-in and subsequent cover-up.

Presidential character was at the forefront of national politics when it was revealed that President Clinton engaged in a sexual relationship with Monica Lewinsky, a White House intern half his age.[25] Many argued that presidential authority is irreparably damaged when the president is perceived as personally untrustworthy or immoral. Yet despite the disgust and anger that Clinton's actions provoked among many Americans, most remained unconvinced that his behavior constituted an impeachable offense. The buoyant

TABLE 9.1	Presidential Greatness

This table provides two "top twelve" lists of the American presidents. The first ranking comes from a 2007 Gallup poll that asked ordinary Americans to name whom they regarded as the greatest U.S. president. The second ranking comes from a survey of historians and observers of the presidency, who rated presidents according to their abilities such as public persuasion, crisis leadership, economic management, moral authority, and relations with Congress. Although the rank order is different, nine presidents appear on both lists. Ordinary Americans are more likely to name recent presidents with whom they have had direct experience.

Gallup Poll Ratings		Historians' Ratings	
Rank	President	Rank	President
1	Abraham Lincoln	1	Abraham Lincoln
2	Ronald Reagan	2	Franklin Roosevelt
3	John F. Kennedy	3	George Washington
4	Bill Clinton	4	Theodore Roosevelt
5	Franklin Roosevelt	5	Harry Truman
6	George Washington	6	Woodrow Wilson
7	Harry Truman	7	Thomas Jefferson
8	George W. Bush	8	John F. Kennedy
9	Theodore Roosevelt	9	Dwight Eisenhower
10	Dwight Eisenhower	10	Lyndon Johnson
11	Thomas Jefferson	11	Ronald Reagan
12	Jimmy Carter	12	James K. Polk

Sources: The historians' ranking is reported by the C-SPAN Survey of Presidential Leadership 2000, http://www.americanpresidents .org/survey/historians/. Copyright 2000 C-SPAN. Gallup Poll results are reported by Lydia Saad, "Lincoln Resumes Position as Americans' Top-Rated President," 19 February 2007, available at http://www.gallup.com.

economy and the public's general satisfaction with Clinton's leadership strongly influenced the country's views on the matter. A majority of the House of Representatives voted to impeach him, on the grounds that he had committed perjury when testifying before a federal grand jury and that he had obstructed justice by concealing evidence and encouraging others to lie about his relationship with Lewinsky. But the Senate did not have the two-thirds majority necessary to convict Clinton, so he remained in office.

Scholars have identified personality traits such as strong self-esteem and emotional intelligence that are best suited to leadership positions like the American presidency.[26] In the media age, it often proves difficult to evaluate a candidate's personality when everyone tries to present himself or herself in a positive light. Even so, voters repeatedly claim that they care about traits such as leadership, integrity, and competence when casting their ballots.[27]

The President's Power to Persuade

In addition to desirable character traits, individual presidents must have the interpersonal and practical political skills to get things done. A classic analysis of the use of presidential resources is offered by Richard Neustadt in his book *Presidential Power,* which discusses how presidents gain, lose, or maintain their influence. Neustadt's initial premise is simple: "Presidential power is the power to persuade."[28] Presidents, for all their resources—a skilled staff, extensive media coverage of presidential actions, the great respect the country holds for the office—must depend on others' cooperation to get things done. Harry Truman echoed Neustadt's premise when he said, "I sit here all day trying to persuade people to do the things they ought to have sense enough to do without my persuading them. . . . That's all the powers of the President amount to."[29]

Ability in bargaining, dealing with adversaries, and choosing priorities, according to Neustadt, separates above-average presidents from mediocre ones. A president must make wise choices about which policies to push and which to put aside until he can find more support. He must decide when to accept compromises and when to stand on principles. He must know when to go public and when to work behind the scenes.

A president's political skills can be important in affecting outcomes in Congress. The chief executive cannot intervene in every legislative struggle. He must choose his battles carefully, then try to use the force of his personality and the prestige of his office to forge an agreement among differing factions. In terms of getting members to vote a certain way, presidential influence is best described as taking place "at the margins." Presidents do not have the power to consistently move large numbers of votes one way or the other. They can, however, affect some votes—possibly enough to affect the fate of a closely fought piece of legislation.[30] Neustadt stresses that a president's influence is related to his professional reputation and public prestige. When a president pushes hard for a bill that Congress eventually defeats or emasculates, the president's reputation is hurt. Washington insiders perceive him as weak or as showing poor judgment, and Congress becomes even less likely to cooperate with him in the future.

The President and the Public

Neustadt's analysis suggests that a popular president is more persuasive than an unpopular one. A popular president has more power to persuade because he can use his public support as a resource in the bargaining process.[31] Members of Congress who know that the president is highly popular back home have more incentive to cooperate with the administration.

A familiar aspect of the modern presidency is the effort presidents devote to mobilizing public support for their programs. A president uses televised addresses (and the press coverage surrounding them), remarks to reporters, and public appearances to speak directly to the American people and convince them of the wisdom of his policies. Scholars have coined the phrase "going public" to describe situations where the president "forces compliance from fellow Washingtonians by going over their heads to appeal to their constituents."[32] Rather than bargain exclusively with a small number of party and committee leaders in Congress, the president rallies broad coalitions of support as though undertaking a political campaign.

Since public opinion is a resource for modern presidents, they pay close attention to their standing in the polls. Presidential popularity is typically at its highest during a president's first year in office. This "honeymoon period" usually affords the president a particularly good opportunity to use public support to get some of his programs through Congress.[33]

Several factors generally explain the rise and fall in presidential popularity. First, public approval of the job done by a president is affected by economic conditions, such as inflation and unemployment. Second, a president is affected by unanticipated events of all types that occur during his administration.[34] A third factor that affects approval ratings, however, is that presidents typically lose popularity when involved in a war with heavy casualties.[35]

Barack Obama entered office with very high approval ratings and great expectations. His most important domestic initiative, health-care reform, was not put front and center immediately after his inauguration as he first had to address the dire straits of the nation's banking system and the deepening recession. Even though the $700 billion Troubled Asset Relief Program (TARP) introduced under the Bush administration succeeded in stabilizing the faltering banking system, it was unpopular. Many saw it as a taxpayer "bailout" of banks that deserved to go out of business because of their role in the subprime mortgage collapse that contributed so strongly to the recession. The $787 billion economic stimulus package Obama supported drew widespread criticism of its own as the nation's deficit soared, and Obama's popularity began to decline.

Throughout the spring, summer, and fall of 2009, Obama tried to rally public opinion around his health proposal. His goal was to extend health insurance to 30 million Americans who could not afford it. To pay for this expansion of health care, the Obama plan also included regulatory measures designed to reduce health-care costs and placed a tax on the top 5 percent of earners. The plan was expansive, expensive, and complex. Despite Obama's energetic campaigning for the legislation, its support among the American people dropped steadily, and entering 2010, a majority of the public opposed the plan.

With substantial Democratic majorities in Congress, the legislation was eventually passed roughly a year after Obama began pushing for it. At the time the bill became law Obama's popularity had dropped very low, with roughly as many Americans saying they approved of the president's job performance as saying they disapproved (see Figure 9.1).[36] Unemployment and the continuing recession were probably more responsible for the president's decline in popularity than his health-care plan, but it contributed too. As political scientist George Edwards concludes, "Presidents cannot

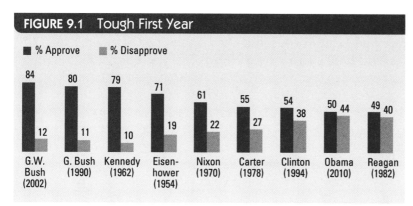

FIGURE 9.1 Tough First Year

The terrible recession and the controversy over his plan to expand health-care coverage to the uninsured drove down Barack Obama's approval ratings. At the end of his first year, his rating was the second lowest among modern presidents. Yet Obama can take heart from this comparison. Bill Clinton and Ronald Reagan recovered from their low ratings to win easy reelection. In contrast George H. W. Bush, who had the second-highest rating, was defeated for reelection. George W. Bush, who had the highest end-of-first-year rating, did win reelection, albeit in a close race.

Source: Lydia Saad, "Obama Starts 2010 with 50% Approval," Gallup Poll, 6 January 2010. Available at Gallup.com. Copyright © 2010 Gallup, Inc. All rights reserved. Reproduced by permission.

Compared with What?

Hatoyama Goes Down

Barack Obama can certainly sympathize. Like Obama, Japan's new prime minister, Yukio Hatoyama, saw his popularity drop considerably after taking office. Hatoyama's descent, however, was quicker and more destructive. Starting with approval ratings of over 70 percent, he dropped 30 points in just four months. Six months into office he had the approval of only about a third of the electorate. Not much of a honeymoon.

Hatoyama came into office in a blaze of glory. After more than a half century of rule by the Liberal Democratic Party (LDP), Hatoyama's Democratic Party of Japan (DPJ) crushed the LDP in the August 2009 parliamentary elections. The DPJ won more than 60 percent of the seats in the lower house of the parliament, the Diet. The country had grown weary of the Liberal Democrats, who had ruled uninterrupted for more than fifty years. The LDP's troubles led to instability, and after three LDP prime ministers in just three years, the country finally broke with the LDP and voted for the DPJ. The real source of dissatisfaction was the Japanese economy, which has slumped badly. The DPJ seemed to offer a fresh approach.

Unfortunately, Hatoyama stumbled right out of the gate, becoming embroiled in an embarrassing campaign finance scandal. For some time his mother, a wealthy heiress, had been sending 15 million yen ($167,000) a month to the DPJ. But a high-ranking Hatoyama aide had recorded these donations as coming from many different contributors, making the party look more popular and keeping Hatoyama from looking as though his success was due to an allowance from his mother. Hatoyama said he had no knowledge of the contributions and was not indicted. Still, the episode was damaging. His popularity sagged again when he went back on his campaign promise to cut taxes as the country's budget pressures made it impossible to give up revenue.

A squabble with the United States did not help. The issue involved a possible relocation of an air base on the island of Okinawa, close to the

reshape the contours of the political landscape to pave the way for change."[37] Still, Obama's leadership did play a role in persuading members of his own party in Congress to vote for the plan despite widespread public opposition.[38]

Presidents' obsessive concern with public opinion can be defended as a means of furthering majoritarian democracy: the president tries to main Japanese islands. Okinawa was the last island where the Americans fought ground battles with Japanese troops in World War II before the United States dropped the atomic bombs on Hiroshima and Nagasaki. Even though the United States and Japan are now close allies, the presence of U.S. forces on Okinawa remains a touchy subject.

The economy was Hatoyama's biggest problem. Japanese unemployment has risen along with the national deficit. The growing debt led to serious discussion of raising the nation's sales tax, hardly a step someone who campaigned on cutting taxes would have been interested in taking. Japan, of course, was caught in the same worldwide economic slowdown that plagued the United States, Europe, and other nations of the world.

It was Okinawa that proved to be the final straw. In May 2010 Hatoyama came to an agreement with President Obama to extend U.S. rights to the air base. His decision sparked a firestorm of criticism. Seen as weak and irreparably damaged, members of his own party began to ask for Hatoyama's resignation. In protest a partner in the parliament, the Social Democratic Party, withdrew from the ruling coalition. Within a few days a tearful Hatoyama addressed the nation to announce that he was resigning. LDP legislators quickly elected veteran politician Naoto Kan as the new prime minister. He had his work cut out for himself.

In addition to budget woes, Japan was hit by a series of crises in March 2011. An earthquake off the Japanese coast measuring 9.0 on the Richter scale produced a devastating tsunami. The twin natural disasters caused more than 10,000 deaths and a multi-reactor nuclear crisis in the Fukushima province. Kan faces hundreds of thousands of displaced citizens, the worst nuclear disaster since Chernobyl, and calls to resign.

Sources: Martin Fackler, "Doubts Grow in Japan about Premier Amid Money Scandal," *New York Times*, 19 December 2009; Takashi Nakamichi, Alison Tudor, and Takashi Mochizuki, "Funding Scandal, Economy Weigh Down Hatoyama," *Wall Street Journal*, 26–27 December 2009; "Nagasaki Fallout," *Economist*, 25 February 2010; Blaine Harden, "Japanese Prime Minister Yukio Hatoyama Resigns," *Washington Post*, 2 June 2010; Chico Harlan, "In Tokyo, an Already Unpopular Leader Struggles with Response," *Washington Post*, 21 March 2010, p. A10; and various polls from Angus Reid Global Monitor.

gauge what the people want so that he can offer policies that reflect popular preferences. Responsiveness to the public's views is a bedrock principle of democracy, and presidents should respond to public opinion as well as try to lead it.[39] Some believe that presidents are too concerned about their popularity and are unwilling to champion unpopular causes or take principled stands that may affect their poll ratings. Commenting on the presidential polls that first became widely used during his term, Harry Truman said, "I wonder how far Moses would have gone if he'd taken a poll in Egypt?"[40]

The Political Context

Although character and political skill are important, the president's popularity and legislative success also depend on the wider political environment.

Partisans in Congress. Presidents vary considerably in their ability to convince Congress to enact the legislation they send to Capitol Hill. Generally presidents have their greatest success in Congress during the period immediately following their inauguration, which we noted is also the peak of their popularity. One of the best predictors of presidential success in Congress is the number of fellow partisans in Congress, particularly whether the president's party has a majority in each chamber.[41]

Presidential success in Congress is measured by how often the president wins his way on congressional roll call votes on which he takes a clear position. George W. Bush's success rate hovered around 75 percent during his first six years in office with a Republican Congress. After the Democrats won control of Congress in 2006, his success rate fell to 38 percent.[42] With large majorities in both the House and the Senate during his first two years in office, Barack Obama did very well with the Congress and got major pieces of legislation such as the economic stimulus package and the health-care plan enacted. (See Figure 9.2.)

The American political system poses a challenge for presidents and their policy agendas because the president is elected independent of Congress. Often this leads to **divided government**, with one party controlling the White House and the other party controlling at least one house of Congress. This outcome may seem politically schizophrenic, with the electorate saying one thing by electing a president and another by electing a majority in Congress that opposes his policies. This does not appear to bother the American people, however, as divided government is fairly common.

Scholars are divided on the impact of divided government. Despite these differences in the scholarly literature, political scientists generally do not believe that divided government produces **gridlock**, a situation in which government is incapable of acting on important policy issues.[43] In recent years, however, there has been a pattern of increasingly partisan voting in Congress: Republicans voting

divided government
The situation in which one party controls the White House and the other controls at least one house of Congress.

gridlock
A situation in which government is incapable of acting on important issues, usually because of divided government.

FIGURE 9.2 Congress: Friend or Foe?

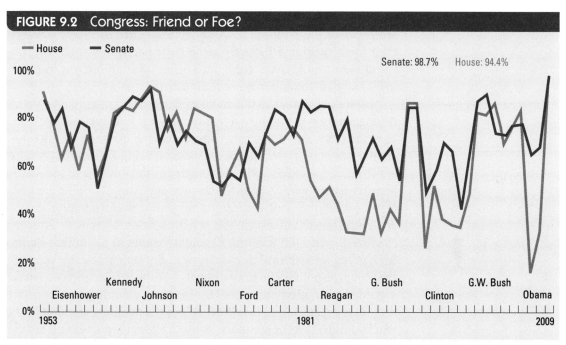

The scales here measure the success rate of presidents in Congress when they had a clearly stated preference on a bill. As is evident, the success rate varies considerably over time. This reflects each president's skill to be sure, but the partisan makeup of the Congress is critical. Obama's exceptional success during his first year was built on large Democratic majorities in the House and Senate; losing the House in 2010 makes his job harder. George W. Bush's success dropped precipitously after Republicans lost majorities in both houses in the 2006 elections.

Source: The data is from CQ and the graphic representation from Don Gonyea, "CQ: Obama's Winning Streak on Hill Unprecedented," January 11, 2010.

in a relatively unified pattern while Democrats also vote in an increasingly unified manner.[44]

Elections. In his farewell address, Jimmy Carter lashed out at the interest groups that had plagued his presidency. Interest groups, he said, "distort our purposes because the national interest is not always the sum of all our single or special interests." Carter noted the president's singular responsibility: "The president is the only elected official charged with representing all the people."[45] Like all other presidents, Carter quickly recognized the dilemma of majoritarianism versus pluralism after he took office. The president must try to please countless separate constituencies while trying to do what is best for the whole country.

It is easy to stand on the sidelines and say that presidents should always try to follow a majoritarian path, pursuing policies that reflect the preferences of most citizens. However, simply by running for office, candidates align themselves with particular segments of the population. As a result of their electoral strategy, their identification with activists in their party, and their own political views, candidates come into office with an interest in pleasing some constituencies more than others.

Each candidate tries to win votes from different groups of voters through his or her stand on various issues. Because issue stances can cut both ways—attracting some voters but driving others away—candidates may try to finesse an issue by being deliberately vague. However, a candidate who is noncommittal on too many issues appears wishy-washy. And future presidents do not build their political careers without working strongly for and becoming associated with important issues and constituencies. Moreover, after the election is over, the winning candidate wants to claim that he has been given an **electoral mandate,** or endorsement, by the voters to carry out the policies he campaigned on. New presidents try to make a majoritarian interpretation of the election, claiming that their victory is an expression of the direct will of the people. Candidates who win by large margins are more likely to claim mandates and ask for major policy changes.

Political Party Systems. American political history is marked by eras in which one of the major political parties tends to dominate national-level politics, consistently capturing the presidency and majorities in the Senate and House of Representatives. Presidential leadership is determined in part by whether the president is a member of the dominant political party and whether the public policies and political philosophy associated with his party have widespread support. A president will have a greater opportunity to change public policy when he is in the majority and the opposing political party is perceived as unable to solve major national problems.

Some presidents inherit a political climate ripe for change; others do not. Presidents who come to power right after critical elections have the most favorable environment for exerting strong presidential leadership. Franklin Roosevelt, for instance, came to office when the Republican Party was unable to offer solutions to the economic crisis of the Great Depression. He enjoyed a landslide victory and large Democratic majorities in Congress, and he proposed fundamental changes in government and public policy. The weakest presidents are those, like Herbert Hoover, who are constrained by their affiliation with a political party that is perceived to stand for worn-out ideas.

electoral mandate
An endorsement by voters. Presidents sometimes argue they have been given a mandate to carry out policy proposals.

George W. Bush envisioned an evolution of party fortunes in which his party would become newly dominant. In the half-century since 1950 neither party had dominated the presidency, but the September 2001 terrorist attacks on the United States changed the political landscape. Bush saw an opportunity for the Republican Party on security issues, believing that the Republicans' traditional emphasis on defense would help the party's long-term fortunes. Conversely, he believed the Democratic Party would be seen as weaker since it was divided over the decision to invade Iraq. But the increasingly unpopular Iraq War and the faltering economy devastated Republican fortunes in the 2006 and 2008 elections.[46]

Barack Obama envisioned a changing party landscape when he took office, and he believes that the Democrats have an opportunity to emerge as the dominant party. Democrats see demographic change helping them, as the growing proportion of minorities in the country strongly prefers the Democrats. Young voters have strongly moved toward the Democrats, there is continuing strength among urban dwellers, and the party is faring better in the suburbs than in the past. But this optimism may be premature, as the Democrats have been hurt by the faltering economy, growing deficits, and public controversies over health care legislation and the stimulus package. The result? In 2010 Republicans won the biggest swing of congressional seats since 1948.

The President as National Leader

With an election behind him and the resources of his office at hand, a president is ready to lead the nation. Each president enters office with a general vision of how government should approach policy issues. During his term, he spends much of his time trying to get Congress to enact legislation that reflects his general philosophy and specific policy preferences.

From Political Values . . .

Presidents differ greatly in their views of the role of government. Lyndon Johnson had a strong liberal ideology concerning domestic affairs. He believed that government has a responsibility to help disadvantaged Americans. In describing his vision of justice in his inaugural address, Johnson used the words *justice* and *injustice* as code words for *equality* and *inequality*. They were used six times in his speech; *freedom* was used only twice. Johnson used his popularity, his skills, and the resources of his office to press for a "just" America—a "Great Society."[47]

To achieve his Great Society, Johnson sent Congress an unprecedented package of liberal legislation. He launched such projects as the Job Corps (which created centers and camps offering vocational training and work experience to youths aged sixteen to twenty-one), Medicare (which provided medical care for the elderly), and the National Teacher Corps (which paid teachers to work in impoverished neighborhoods). Supported by huge Democratic majorities in Congress during 1965 and 1966, he had tremendous success in getting his proposals through. Liberalism was in full swing.

In 1985, exactly twenty years after Johnson's inaugural speech, Ronald Reagan took his oath of office for the second time. Addressing the nation, Reagan reasserted his conservative philosophy. He emphasized *freedom,* using the term fourteen times, and failed to mention justice or equality even once. He turned Johnson's philosophy on its head, declaring that "government is not the solution to our problem. Government is the problem." During his presidency, Reagan worked to undo many welfare and social service programs, and he cut funding for such programs as the Job Corps and food stamps. By the end of his term, there had been a fundamental shift in federal spending, with sharp increases in defense spending and "decreases in federal social programs [which] served to defend Democratic interests and constituencies."[48]

. . . to Policy Agenda

The roots of particular policy proposals can be traced to the more general political ideology of the president. Presidential candidates outline that philosophy of government during their campaigns for the White House. But when the hot rhetoric of the presidential campaign meets the cold reality of what is possible in Washington, the newly elected president must make some hard choices about what to push for during the coming term. These choices are reflected in the bills the president submits to Congress, as well as in the degree to which he works for their passage. The president's bills, introduced by his allies in the House and Senate, always receive a good deal of initial attention. In the words of one Washington lobbyist, "When a president sends up a bill, it takes first place in the queue. All other bills take second place."[49]

The president's role in legislative leadership began primarily in the twentieth century. Not until the Budget and Accounting Act of

1921 did executive branch departments and agencies have to clear their proposed budget bills with the White House. Before this, the president did not even coordinate proposals for how much the executive branch would spend on all the programs it administered. Later, Franklin D. Roosevelt required that the White House clear all major legislative proposals by an agency or department. No longer could a department submit a bill without White House support.[50]

Roosevelt's influence on the relationship between the president and Congress went far beyond this new administrative arrangement. With the nation in the midst of the Great Depression, Roosevelt began his first term in 1933 with an ambitious array of legislative proposals. During the first hundred days Congress was in session, it enacted fifteen significant laws, including the Agricultural Adjustment Act, the act creating the Civilian Conservation Corps, and the National Industrial Recovery Act. Never before had a president demanded—and received—so much from Congress. Roosevelt's legacy was that the president would henceforth provide aggressive leadership for Congress through his own legislative program.

Chief Lobbyist

When Franklin D. Roosevelt and Harry Truman first became heavily involved in preparing legislative packages, political scientists typically described the process as one in which "the president proposes and Congress disposes." In other words, once the president sends his legislation to Capitol Hill, Congress decides on its own what to do with it. Over time, though, presidents have become increasingly active in all stages of the legislative process. The president is expected not only to propose legislation but also to make sure that it passes.

The president's efforts to influence Congress are reinforced by the work of his legislative liaison staff. All departments and major agencies have legislative specialists who work with the White House liaison staff to coordinate the administration's lobbying on major issues. The **legislative liaison staff** is the communications link between the White House and Congress. As a bill slowly makes its way through Congress, liaison staffers advise the president on the problems that emerge. They specify what parts of a bill are in trouble and may have to be modified or dropped. They tell their boss what amendments are likely to be offered, which members of Congress

legislative liaison staff
Those people who act as the communications link between the White House and Congress, advising the president or cabinet secretaries on the status of pending legislation.

need to be lobbied, and what the bill's chances for passage are with or without certain provisions. Decisions on how the administration will respond to such developments must then be reached. For example, when the Reagan White House realized that it was still a few votes short of victory on a budget bill in the House, it reversed its opposition to a sugar price support bill. This attracted the votes of representatives from Louisiana and Florida, two sugar-growing states, for the budget bill. The White House would not call what happened a deal, but it noted that "adjustments and considerations" had been made.[51]

A certain amount of the president's job consists of stereotypical arm twisting—pushing reluctant legislators to vote a certain way. During President Obama's first four months in office, 400 representatives and senators were brought to the White House to speak with him or to attend meetings or other events.[52] Yet most day-in, day-out interactions between the White House and Congress tend to be more subtle, with the liaison staff trying to build consensus by working cooperatively with legislators. The White House also works directly with interest groups in its efforts to build support for legislation.[53] Interest groups can quickly reach the constituents who are most concerned about a bill, using their communications network to quickly mobilize members to write, call, or e-mail their members of Congress.

Although much of the liaison staff's work with Congress is done in a cooperative spirit, agreement cannot always be reached. When Congress passes a bill that the president opposes, he may veto it and send it back to Congress. As we noted earlier, Congress can override a veto with a two-thirds majority of those voting in each house. Presidents use their veto power sparingly, but the threat that a president will veto an unacceptable bill increases his bargaining leverage with members of Congress. We have also seen that a president's leverage with Congress is enhanced when he is riding high in the public opinion polls and hindered when the public is critical of his performance.[54]

Party Leader

Part of the president's job is to lead his party.[55] This is very much an informal duty, with no prescribed tasks. In this respect, American presidents are considerably different from European prime ministers, who are the formal leader of their party in the national legislature, as well as the head of their government. In the American system, a president and members of his party in Congress can clearly take very different positions on the issues before them. As Congress has turned more partisan, presidents have focused more on leading their own party rather than trying to bridge differences between the two parties.[56] With less of a moderate middle to work with in Congress, a president needs to work hard to unify his party around his priorities.

The president himself has become the "fundraiser in chief" for his party. Since presidents have a vital interest in more members of their party being elected to the House and Senate, they have a strong incentive to spend time raising money for congressional candidates. All incumbent presidents travel frequently to fundraising dinners in different states where they are the main attraction. In addition to helping elect more members of his party, the president gains the gratitude of legislators. It is a lot harder to say no to a president's request for help on a bill when he spoke at your fundraiser during the previous election.

The President as World Leader

The president's leadership responsibilities extend beyond Congress and the nation into the international arena. Each administration tries to advance what it sees as the country's best interests in its relations with allies, adversaries, and the developing countries of the world. In this role, the president must be ready to act as diplomat and crisis manager.

Foreign Relations

From the end of World War II until the late 1980s, presidents were preoccupied with containing communist expansion around the globe. After the collapse of communism in the Soviet Union and Eastern Europe, American presidents entered a new era in international relations, but they are still concerned with three fundamental objectives.

First is national security: the direct protection of the United States and its citizens from external threats. National security has been highlighted since the September 11 terrorist attacks. Indeed, George W. Bush called the global war against terrorism his number one priority, sending military troops to both Afghanistan and Iraq.[57]

Second, and related, is fostering a peaceful international environment. Presidents work with international organizations like the

United Nations and the North Atlantic Treaty Organization (NATO) to seek an end to regional conflicts throughout the world.

A third objective is the protection of U.S. economic interests. The new presidential job description places much more emphasis on managing economic relations with the rest of the world. Trade relations are an especially difficult problem, because presidents must balance the conflicting interests of foreign countries (many of them U.S. allies), the interests of particular American industries, the overall needs of the American economy, and the demands of the legislative branch.

Each president must decide the extent to which the United States should use its power to promote American ideals abroad.

Crisis Management

Periodically the president faces a grave situation in which conflict is imminent or a small conflict threatens to explode into a larger war. Handling such episodes is a critical part of the president's job. Thus, citizens may vote for candidates who project careful judgment and intelligence.

A president must be able to exercise good judgment and remain cool in crisis situations. John Kennedy's behavior during the Cuban missile crisis of 1962 has become a model of effective crisis management. When the United States learned that the Soviet Union had placed missiles containing nuclear warheads in Cuba, Kennedy sought the advice of a group of senior aides, Pentagon officials, cabinet secretaries, and other trusted advisers. An armed invasion of Cuba and air strikes against the missiles were two options considered. In the end, Kennedy decided on a more flexible response: a naval blockade of Cuba. Faced with this challenge and a secret, back-channel overture from Kennedy, the Soviet Union agreed to remove its missiles. For a short time, though, the world held its breath over the very real possibility of a nuclear war.

What guidelines determine what a president should do in times of crisis? Drawing on a range of advisers and opinions is one.[58] Not acting in unnecessary haste is another. A third is having a well-designed, formal review process that promotes thorough analysis and open debate.[59] A fourth guideline is rigorously examining the reasoning underlying each option to ensure that its assumptions are valid. Still, these are rather general rules and provide no assurance that mistakes will not be made. Each crisis is a unique event. In the crisis after September 11, 2001, President Bush resisted calls for immediate retaliation.

Instead, he planned a concerted attack against the al Qaeda terrorist network in Afghanistan. The first air strikes, conducted jointly with Britain, did not occur until October 7. Two months later, the defeated Taliban government surrendered its last stronghold. Though coalition allies praised Bush's patience, they levied criticism when he named North Korea, Iran, and Iraq terrorist regimes that constitute an "axis of evil." They feared where Bush was heading.

Tying It Together

1. What are the origins of the powers of the president?
   - The president of the United States must be
     - a U.S.-born citizen.
     - at least thirty-five years of age.
     - a resident of the United States for a minimum of fourteen years.
   - The Constitution empowers the president to
     - serve as administrative head of the nation.
     - act as commander in chief of the military.
     - convene Congress.
     - veto legislation.
     - appoint various officials.
     - make treaties.
     - grant pardons.

2. How have the powers of the president changed over time?
   - Presidential power has expanded as presidents have exercised their explicit constitutional responsibilities and interpreted the Constitution.
   - Formal powers have increased.
     - Vetoes have become more frequent.
     - Presidents have taken a more active role in setting the policy agenda.
     - Presidents have used their power as commander in chief to enter conflicts without a congressional declaration of war.
   - Inherent powers have increased.
     - When the president takes advantage of inherent powers inferred from the Constitution, Congress and the courts are forced to respond.

- Presidents issue executive orders, which are presidential directives to the executive branch that carry the force of law.
- Congress can, by legislation, delegate power to the president or reassert control over the presidency.

3. What staff and other resources make up the Executive Office of the President?
- Presidents rely on their aides to advise, develop strategies, and control access to the president.
- The extended White House executive establishment, which includes the White House Office (the president's personal staff), is known as the Executive Office of the President (EOP).
- The three major advisory styles used by presidents are
  - the competitive management model.
  - the hierarchical staff model.
  - the collegial staff model.
- The vice president's main duty is to take over in the event of presidential death, disability, impeachment, or resignation. Vice presidents are usually selected to strengthen the electoral chances of the presidential candidate.
- The president's cabinet is composed of the heads of the departments in the executive branch as well as other key officials.

4. What factors affect the public's perception of a president's leadership?
- A president's influence in office comes from power and skill as well as effective use of resources.
- Scholars have identified strong self-esteem and emotional intelligence as important personality traits for leadership roles such as the presidency.
- The abilities to bargain, deal effectively with adversaries, and prioritize are important.
- Factors that affect presidential popularity include
  - economic conditions.
  - unanticipated events.
  - American involvement in war.
- The political environment affects presidential popularity:
  - When a divided government exists, one party controls the White House and the other controls at least one house of Congress, which can be challenging for presidents.
  - Gridlock, the situation in which government cannot act on policy issues, is less typical than the public may believe.

- Presidents who come to office in critical elections have the most favorable environment for exerting strong leadership.

5. How does a president implement his vision and policy preferences?
   - The president sends bills to Congress based on his ideological agenda.
   - The president keeps track of Congressional action through a legislative liaison staff, which is the communications link between the White House and Congress.
   - The president is the informal leader and chief fundraiser of his party.

6. In what ways does a president fulfill his role as a leader on the world stage?
   - The president must act as a diplomat as well as a crisis manager.
   - Today, the president's foreign policies must be concerned with three fundamental objectives:
     - national security.
     - fostering a peaceful international environment.
     - the protection of U.S. economic interests.
   - The model for crisis management should include
     - a range of advisers and opinions.
     - calm consideration, not unnecessary haste.
     - a well-designed, formal review process for analysis and debate, including rigorous consideration of the underlying reasoning and assumptions upon which decisions are made.

Test Prepper 9.1

The Constitutional Basis of Presidential Power

True or False?
1. There was no individual serving as head of state under the Articles of Confederation.
2. The powers of the presidency are set forth in Article III of the Constitution.
3. The president has the authority to formally recognize other nations.

Comprehension
4. Name three requirements for the presidency.
5. What are the major presidential duties?

The Expansion of Presidential Power

True or False?

1. Presidential power today is much greater than originally envisioned by the founders.
2. In recent years presidents have generally waged war without a congressional declaration of war.
3. The War Powers Resolution Act (1973) was intended to give the president more power to pursue armed conflict.

Comprehension

4. What are presidential executive orders?
5. Explain the purpose of a congressional delegation of power.

The Executive Branch Establishment

True or False?

1. Vice-presidential candidates are generally chosen because of their close friendship with a presidential candidate.
2. The president's cabinet is the advisory group that formulates policies for the president.
3. The president's personal staff is called the White House Office.

Comprehension

4. Describe the three major advisory systems used to organize the White House staff, and identify a president commonly associated with each style.
5. Is the vice president the president's chief adviser?

Presidential Leadership

True or False?

1. Richard Neustadt's theory of presidential power states that power comes from boldness, creativity, and the ability to command.
2. A divided government inevitably leads to gridlock.
3. Presidents who come to power immediately following critical elections have the best environment for demonstrating strong leadership.

Comprehension

4. What factors explain presidential popularity?
5. Explain the different criteria used by voters to choose a president versus a congressional representative.

The President as National Leader

True or False?

1. The Budget and Accounting Act of 1921 required executive departments and agencies to clear their proposed budgets with the White House.
2. The legislative liaison staff advises the president as problems emerge when a bill makes its way through Congress.
3. Like their European counterparts, American presidents fulfill the formal role of leader of their party.

Comprehension

4. Describe the differences between Lyndon Johnson's and Ronald Reagan's views of the role of government.
5. How did the role of the president in the legislative process change after Franklin D. Roosevelt's administration?

The President as World Leader

True or False?

1. A key goal of presidents is pursuing foreign policy unilaterally, without involving international organizations.
2. John F. Kennedy's handling of the Cuban missile crisis of 1962 is an example of poor crisis management.

Comprehension

3. What are the three fundamental objectives for the president when it comes to international relations?
4. What are the guidelines for the president during times of crisis or other important junctures?

CourseMate CL Resources:

Visit www.cengagebrain.com/shop/ISBN/1111832587 for flashcards, web quizzes, videos and more!

CHAPTER 10

The Bureaucracy

FOCUS QUESTIONS

1. Who administers the nation's laws and policies?
2. How did the current bureaucratic state come about, and should it be cut back?
3. What is the organizational structure of the bureaucracy?
4. How do government agencies operate?
5. How are administrative decisions made and implemented by the government?
6. What problems are encountered in the implementation of governmental policies?
7. Does the bureaucracy need to be controlled?

Harry Markopolos was angry. The investment adviser had been asked by his boss why the investment vehicle that Markopolos directed was producing lower earnings than a similar investment fund directed by financier Bernard Madoff. Markopolos was suspicious of the Madoff fund because year after year it consistently yielded returns of about 12 percent. Given that the stock market fluctuates and sometimes has years when it declines significantly, such steady positive returns looked highly improbable.

Markopolos began to study Madoff's stated investment strategy and eventually uncovered what turned out to be a "Ponzi scheme." This is essentially a swindle in which new investors are drawn by the promise of very high returns. The fund manager, however, pockets the money and creates fictitious returns. If an existing investor wants to withdraw some money, he or she is paid with money coming in from new investors.

Markopolos continued to investigate, but without access to Madoff's books, he could not definitively prove that the fund was a Ponzi scheme. In the spring of 2000 Markopolos turned over the evidence he had collected to the Securities and Exchange Commission (SEC), the government's regulatory agency for overseeing financial markets. The SEC responded to Markopolos's detailed and well-documented complaint by doing nothing.

While the SEC slept, Madoff continued to take in money from both new and continuing investors. His Ponzi scheme would not collapse until late in 2008. Many of his investors—individuals, schools, banks, churches, synagogues, even charities—were ruined financially by his scam. It's not clear how much money was lost in the Madoff scandal.

Estimates go as high as $65 billion, but some of this money may have never truly existed beyond the fantasy profits entered into the doctored financial statements mailed to clients.

When the scandal broke, questions immediately emerged as to how Madoff got away with his fraud for so long and why the SEC had failed to uncover it. Harry Markopolos was not the only one who filed a complaint about Madoff with the SEC. Over a sixteen-year period the agency received six substantive complaints about him. The SEC launched investigations in response to some of these complaints but, remarkably, failed to turn up anything untoward. Looking back from his jail cell in 2009, Madoff said all the SEC had to do to determine if his fund was operating honestly was check to see that the stock trades he said he was making were actually carried out. Had the SEC taken this simple step, the Ponzi scheme "would have been easy for them to see," said Madoff.

The SEC launched an exhaustive review of its failures in the Madoff case—a failure that had cat-astrophic consequences for Madoff's investors. Its 2009 report concluded that its earlier investigations were marred by the inexperience of the staffers assigned to inspect Madoff's operations. When Madoff failed to give investigators the information they requested, they didn't follow up and insist upon it or subpoena the documents. Outside analysts looking at the SEC point out that the agency is understaffed and overwhelmed by the size of the financial markets it is meant to supervise.

The Madoff case is a painful reminder of how we depend on regulatory agencies to protect us. When those agencies fail, our health, safety, and financial well-being can be compromised. The SEC's errors in the Madoff case are surely not typical of the government's performance. However, this case does suggest that we cannot take government competence for granted and we must always look for ways to reform and improve the performance of the bureaucracy.[1]

Despite the shortcomings of bureaucracies, we must rely on them to administer government. In this chapter we examine how bureaucracies operate and address many of the central dilemmas of American political life. Bureaucracies represent what Americans dislike about government, yet our interest groups lobby them to provide us with more of the services we desire. We say we want smaller, less intrusive government, but different constituencies value different agencies of government and fight fiercely to protect those bureaucracies' budgets. This enduring conflict once again represents the majoritarian and pluralist dimensions of American politics.

Organization Matters

In the American system, the legislative branch passes laws, but it does not actually administer them. A nation's laws and policies are administered, or put into effect, by a variety of executive branch departments, agencies, bureaus, offices, and other government units that together are known as the *bureaucracy.* **Bureaucracy** actually means any large, complex organization in which employees have very specific job responsibilities and work within a hierarchy of authority. The employees of these government units have become known, somewhat derisively, as **bureaucrats.**

Bureaucracies play a central role in the governments of modern societies, and the organization of modern governmental bureaucracies reflects their need to survive. The environment of modern bureaucracies is filled with conflicting political demands and the ever-present threat of budget cuts. The way a given government bureaucracy is organized also reflects the needs of its clients. The bottom line, however, is that the manner in which any bureaucracy is organized affects how well it can accomplish its tasks.

Unfortunately, "if organization matters, it is also the case that there is no one best way of organizing."[2] Although centralizing the control and analysis of information might improve the ability of the intelligence community to detect potential attacks, that might not be the best approach to solving every bureaucratic performance problem. A common complaint against Washington bureaucracies is that they devise one-size-fits-all solutions to problems. The study of bureaucracy, then, centers on finding solutions to the many different kinds of problems that large government organizations face.

Bureaucratic Growth

A common complaint voiced by Americans is that the national bureaucracy is too big and tries to accomplish too much. To the average citizen, the federal government may seem like an octopus—its long arms reach just about everywhere. Ironically, compared to other Western democracies, the size of the U.S. government is proportionally smaller.

The Growth of the Bureaucratic State

American government seems to have grown unchecked during the twentieth century. As one observer noted wryly, "The assistant administrator for water and hazardous materials of the Environmental Protection Agency presided over a staff larger than Washington's entire first administration."[3] Yet even during George Washington's time, bureaucracies were necessary. No one argued then about the

bureaucracy
A large, complex organization in which employees have specific job responsibilities and work within a hierarchy of authority.

bureaucrat
An employee of a bureaucracy, usually meaning a government bureaucracy.

need for a postal service to deliver mail or a treasury department to maintain a system of currency.

However, government at all levels (national, state, and local) grew enormously in the twentieth century.[4] There are several major reasons for this growth. A principal cause of government expansion is the increasing complexity of society. George Washington did not have an assistant administrator for water and hazardous materials because there was no need for one. A National Aeronautics and Space Administration (NASA) was not necessary until rockets were invented.

Another reason government has grown is that the public's attitude toward business has changed. Throughout most of the nineteenth century, business was generally autonomous, and government intervention in the economy that might limit that autonomy was considered inappropriate. This attitude began to change toward the end of the nineteenth century, as more Americans became aware that a laissez-faire approach did not always create competitive markets that benefited consumers. Gradually government intervention came to be accepted as necessary to protect the integrity of markets.[5] And if government was to police unfair business practices effectively, it needed administrative agencies.

During the twentieth century, new bureaucracies were organized to regulate specific industries. Among them are the Securities and Exchange Commission (SEC), which oversees securities trading, and the Food and Drug Administration (FDA), which tries to protect consumers from unsafe food, drugs, and cosmetics. Through bureaucracies such as these, government has become a referee in the marketplace, developing standards of fair trade, setting rates, and licensing individual businesses for operation. As new problem areas have emerged, government has added new agencies, further expanding the scope of its activities.

General attitudes about government's responsibilities in the area of social welfare have changed too. An enduring part of American culture is the belief in self-reliance. People are expected to overcome adversity on their own, to succeed because of their own skills and efforts. Yet certain segments of our population are believed to deserve government support, because we so value their contribution to society or have come to believe that they cannot realistically be expected to overcome adversity on their own.[6] This belief dates back to the nineteenth century. The government provided pensions to Civil War veterans. Later, programs to help mothers and children were developed.[7] In the wake of the Great Depression, the Social Security Act became law, creating a fund that workers pay into and then collect income from during old age. In the 1960s, the government created programs designed to help minorities. As the government made these new commitments, it also created new bureaucracies or expanded existing ones.

Also, government has grown because ambitious, entrepreneurial agency officials have expanded their organizations and staffs to take on added responsibilities. Each new program that is developed leads to new authority. Larger budgets and staffs, in turn, are necessary to support that authority.

Can We Reduce the Size of Government?

Even incumbent candidates for Congress and the presidency typically "run against the government." Government is unpopular: most Americans have little confidence in its capabilities and feel that it wastes money and is out of touch with ordinary people. Americans want a smaller government that costs less and performs better.

If government is to become smaller, bureaucracies will have to be eliminated or reduced in size. Serious budget cuts also require serious reductions in programs. Not surprisingly, presidents and members of Congress face a tough job when they try to cut specific programs. One strategy the national government uses is to modestly reduce the number of bureaucrats (which is popular) without reducing government programs (which is politically risky). This is done by hiring nonprofit or private contractors who do the same job as bureaucrats but are not technically government employees.[8]

Efforts to shrink the bureaucracy have varied considerably. During the 1980s, President Reagan preached smaller government and made a concerted effort to reduce domestic social programs. He had only modest success, and his most ambitious proposals, like abolishing the Department of Education, did not come close to passage by Congress. Though George W. Bush was a conservative in many ways, he worked to enlarge the government. Most significantly, the 9/11 attacks and the continuing threat of terrorism led to the creation of the Department of Homeland Security and the expansion of defense and other security-related agencies. But the new programs and bureaucracies went far beyond security threats. Bush also worked to expand social welfare through a prescription drug benefit for senior citizens. He understood that it was not always good politics to try to downsize government and that there is an upside to providing a benefit to citizens.

President Obama proposed an expanded bureaucracy to protect the country's economy and individual consumers from the kinds of irresponsibility demonstrated by financial institutions in creating a housing bubble based on unsound mortgages. Speculators bid up the prices of real estate, assuming that prices would continue to rise, allowing quick, profitable sales. When that bubble burst, it accelerated a deep and damaging recession beginning in 2008. Obama's proposed plan called for a consumer protection agency to regulate various financial products. The financial services industry opposed the proposal, believing that the government would introduce inefficiencies and higher costs into the market for financial services.[9]

Reagan and Obama represent two polar philosophies. To Reagan, small government enhanced personal freedom; to Obama, a larger government is a means of promoting equality and protecting citizens.

The tendency for big government to endure reflects the tension between majoritarianism and pluralism. Even when the public as a whole wants a smaller national government, that sentiment can be undermined by the strong desire of different segments of society for government to continue performing some valuable function for them. Lobbies that represent these segments work strenuously to convince Congress and the administration that certain agencies' funding is vital and that any cuts ought to come out of other agencies' budgets.

Bureaus and Bureaucrats

We often think of the bureaucracy as a monolith. In reality, the bureaucracy in Washington is a disjointed collection of departments, agencies, bureaus, offices, and commissions, each a bureaucracy in its own right.

The Organization of Government

By examining the basic types of government organizations, we can better understand how the executive branch operates. In our discussion, we pay particular attention to the relative degree of independence of these organizations and to their relationship with the White House.

department
The biggest unit of the executive branch, covering a broad area of government responsibility. The heads of the departments, or secretaries, form the president's cabinet.

Departments. **Departments** are the biggest units of the executive branch, covering broad areas of government responsibility. As noted

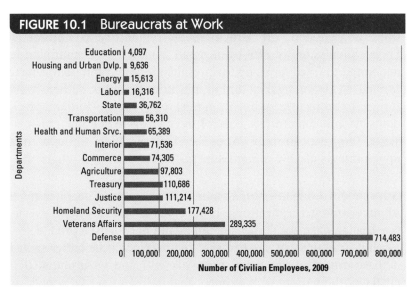

FIGURE 10.1   Bureaucrats at Work

The size of cabinet departments varies dramatically. As this graph indicates, the Department of Defense is by far the largest cabinet-level bureaucracy within the federal government. That more than 1 million civilian workers are employed in the departments of Defense, Veterans Affairs, and Homeland Security is a reflection of the centrality of national security and war in recent American history. At the opposite end of the spectrum is the tiny Department of Education, with fewer than 5,000 employees.

Source: U.S. Census Bureau, Statistical Abstract of the United States: 2011 (Washington, D.C.: U.S. Government Printing Office, 2010), Table 497: Federal Civilian Employment by Branch and Agency: 1990 to 2009, http://www.census.gov/compendia/statab/2011/tables/11s0497.pdf.

in Chapter 9, the secretaries (heads) of the departments, along with a few other key officials, form the president's cabinet. The current cabinet departments are State, Treasury, Defense, Interior, Agriculture, Justice, Commerce, Labor, Health and Human Services, Housing and Urban Development, Transportation, Energy, Education, Veterans Affairs, and Homeland Security. Each of these massive organizations is broken down into subsidiary agencies, bureaus, offices, and services. The largest of the cabinet-level departments is the Department of Defense, with over 714,000 civilian employees supporting and providing policy direction for over 1.4 million active duty military personnel.[10] (See Figure 10.1.)

Independent Agencies. Within the executive branch, there are also many **independent agencies**, which are not part of any cabinet department. They stand alone and are controlled to varying degrees by the president. Some, among them the CIA, are under

independent agency
An executive agency that is not part of a cabinet department.

the president's control. Others, such as the Federal Communications Commission, are structured as **regulatory commissions**. Each commission is run by a small number of commissioners appointed to fixed terms by the president. Some commissions were formed to guard against unfair business practices. Others were formed to protect the public from unsafe products. Although presidents do not have direct control over these regulatory commissions, they can strongly influence their direction through their appointments of new commissioners.

Government Corporations. Congress has created a small number of **government corporations**. In theory, the services these executive branch agencies perform could be provided by the private sector, but Congress has decided that the public will be better served if these organizations have some link with the government. For example, the national government maintains the postal service as a government corporation because it feels that Americans need low-cost, door-to-door service for all kinds of mail, not just for profitable routes or special services. In some instances, the private sector does not have enough financial incentive to provide an essential service. This is the case with the financially troubled Amtrak passenger train line.[11]

The Civil Service

The national bureaucracy is staffed by about 2.8 million civilian employees, who account for about 2 percent of the U.S. work force.[12] Most of those government workers are hired under the requirements of the **civil service**. The civil service was created by the Pendleton Act (1883). The objective of the act was to reduce *patronage*—the practice of filling government positions with the president's political allies or cronies. The civil service fills jobs on the basis of merit and sees to it that workers are not fired for political reasons.

The vast majority of the national government's workers (85 percent) are employed outside the Washington area.[13] One reason for this decentralization is to make government offices accessible to the people they serve. Decentralization is also a way to distribute jobs and income across the country. Members of Congress, of course, are only too happy to place some of this "pork" back home, so that their constituents will credit them with the jobs and money that government installations create.

regulatory commission
An agency of the executive branch of government that controls or directs some aspect of the economy.

government corporation
A government agency that performs services that might be provided by the private sector but that involve either insufficient financial incentive or are better provided when they are somehow linked with government.

civil service
The system by which most appointments to the federal bureaucracy are made, to ensure that government jobs are filled on the basis of merit and that employees are not fired for political reasons.

Presidential Control Over the Bureaucracy

Civil service and other reforms have effectively insulated the vast majority of government workers from party politics. An incoming president can appoint about three thousand people to jobs in the administration, less than 1 percent of all executive branch employees. Still, presidential appointees fill the top policymaking positions in government, and about 1,100 of his appointees require Senate confirmation.[14] Each new president establishes an extensive personnel review process to find appointees who are both politically compatible and qualified in their field. Although the president selects some people from his campaign staff, cabinet secretaries, assistant secretaries, and agency heads tend to be drawn directly from business, universities, and government itself.

Presidents find that the bureaucracy is not always as responsive as they might like, for several reasons. Principally, pluralism can pull agencies in a direction other than that favored by the president. The Department of Transportation may want to move toward more support for mass transit, for example, but politically it cannot afford to ignore the preferences of highway builders. An agency administrator must often try to broker a compromise between conflicting groups rather than pursue a position that holds fast and true to the president's ideology. Bureaucracies must also follow—at least in general terms—the laws governing the programs they are entrusted with, even if the president does not agree with some of those statutes.

Congress always has the prerogative to pass new laws overriding regulations that it feels distort its intent. Whatever party controls Congress, the White House and agency administrators have an incentive to consult with committee chairs to minimize conflict and gain a sense of what might provoke a hostile response on the part of a committee overseeing a particular agency.[15] A committee can punish an agency by cutting its budget, altering a key program, or (for Senate committees) holding up confirmation of a nominee to a top agency post.

Administrative Policymaking: The Formal Processes

Many Americans wonder why agencies sometimes make policy rather than merely carry it out. Administrative agencies are, in fact, authoritative policymaking bodies, and their decisions on substantive issues are legally binding on the citizens of this country.

Administrative Discretion

What are executive agencies set up to do? Cabinet departments, independent agencies, and government corporations are creatures of Congress. Congress creates a new department or agency by enacting a law that describes the organization's mandate, or mission. As part of that mandate, Congress grants to the agency the authority to make certain policy decisions. Congress long ago recognized that it has neither the time nor the technical expertise to make all policy decisions. Ideally, it sets general guidelines for policy and expects agencies to act within those guidelines. The latitude that Congress gives agencies to make policy in the spirit of their legislative mandate is called **administrative discretion.**

Critics of the bureaucracy frequently complain that agencies are granted too much discretion.[16] Congress often is vague about its intent when setting up a new agency or program. At times a problem is clear cut but the solution is not, yet Congress is under pressure to act. So Congress creates an agency or program to show that it is concerned and responsive, but it leaves the development of specific solutions to agency administrators. For example, the 1934 enabling legislation that established the Federal Communications Commission (FCC) recognized a need for regulation in the burgeoning radio industry. But Congress avoided tackling several sticky issues by giving the FCC the ambiguous directive that broadcasters should "serve the public interest, convenience, and necessity."[17] In other cases, several obvious solutions to a problem may be available, but lawmakers cannot agree on which one is best. Compromise wording is thus often ambiguous, papering over differences and ensuring conflict over administrative regulations as agencies try to settle lingering policy disputes.

Congress grants the broadest discretion to those agencies involved in domestic and global security. Both the FBI and the CIA have enjoyed a great deal of freedom from formal and informal congressional constraints because of the legitimate need for secrecy in their operations. The National Security Agency (NSA) was formed to centralize the work of breaking foreign codes and protecting sensitive government information systems. It also monitors foreign communications. After September 11, President Bush directed the NSA to wiretap telephone conversations between people within the United States and people overseas who have suspected links with terrorists, without first obtaining a warrant as required by the 1978 Foreign Intelligence Surveillance Act. NSA bureaucrats followed the secret orders of the president, often without the knowledge of

administrative discretion
The latitude that Congress gives agencies to make policy in the spirit of their legislative mandate.

most members of Congress.[18] Congress has since amended the law, actually expanding the authority of the government to eavesdrop.[19]

The wide latitude Congress gives administrative agencies often leads to charges that the bureaucracy is out of control. But such claims are frequently exaggerated. Congress has the power to express its displeasure by reining in agencies with additional legislation. If Congress is unhappy with an agency's actions, it can pass laws invalidating specific policies, reducing discretion, or providing more guidance to the bureaucracy.[20] A second powerful tool is Congress's control over the budget. Congress can threaten an agency through its power to cut budgets and can reorder agency priorities through its detailed appropriations legislation.

Rule Making

Agencies make policy through formal administrative procedures, usually **rule making**, the administrative process that results in regulations.[21] **Regulations** are rules that govern the operation of government programs. When an agency issues regulations, it is using the discretionary authority granted to it by Congress to implement a program or policy.

Rule making itself follows procedural guidelines requiring that proposed regulations first be published so that interested parties—typically interest groups—have a chance to comment on them, making any recommendations they see as appropriate.[22]

Because they are authorized by congressional statutes, regulations have the effect of law. When Congress created the Department of Transportation in 1966 it was given authority to write regulations relevant to the safety, accessibility, and efficiency of various transportation industries. Controversy has swirled for years around a practice of airlines to keep passengers on board an aircraft that has pulled away from the gate but cannot take off (usually due to inclement weather). In August 2009, an ExpressJet flight with forty-seven passengers on board stayed overnight on the tarmac at the airport in Rochester, New York. It does not take long before a plane runs out of food and water and bathrooms become fouled.

Whenever Congress threatened to enact a "passenger bill of rights" to forbid such unconscionable tarmac delays, the airlines promised to improve their service. At the end of 2009, however, the Department of Transportation announced a new set of rules, limiting tarmac waits to no more than three hours. If that much time elapses, the plane must return to the gate and give passengers the option of deplaning. Airlines claimed there would be even longer delays as

rule making
The administrative process that results in the issuance of regulations by government agencies.

regulations
Administrative rules that guide the operation of a government program.

Politics of Global Change

And Now for a Real Challenge, Regulate the World

It is difficult for a government to regulate its own country, and an effort by an international body to try to regulate the world seems like an impossible task in all but the direst of emergencies.

Yet many scientists believe that global warming is, indeed, an emergency with dire consequences for the planet. The suspected culprit is industrialization. As countries develop they build

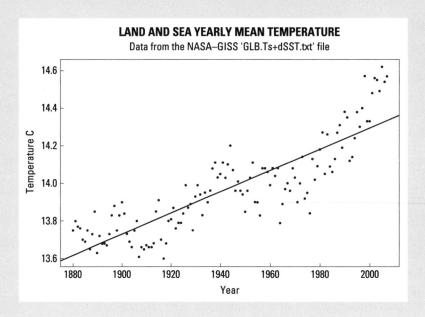

ground crews searched for bags belonging to deplaning passengers, but passenger rights organizations were ecstatic.[23]

The regulatory process is controversial because regulations often require individuals and corporations to act against their own self-interest. (On regulating across nations and the problem of self-interest, see "Politics of Global Change: And Now for a Real Challenge, Regulate the World.") The airline regulations are a classic case of freedom versus order. The airline companies believed they needed greater freedom to conduct business in a way that they found most efficient. Consumer groups preferred that the government put more factories, use automobiles for transportation, and heat residences and buildings with carbon-based fuels. All these sources emit greenhouse gases into the atmosphere. Data collected by NASA show a general rise in global surface temperature since 1880, but there is considerable annual variation in temperature. These variations support those who argue that the world has always undergone periods of warming and cooling. Other observers acknowledge the reality of warming but throw doubt on the long-term implications.

International cooperation is necessary to fight global warming because greenhouse gas emissions know no borders. Pollution goes into the atmosphere, where it can cross political boundaries with impunity.

Some countries have tried to reduce greenhouse gases on their own, but their efforts have been insufficient as the amount of carbon-based emissions continues to grow. Thus, over the years there have been attempts to negotiate a global reduction in greenhouse gases. An agreement of sorts was reached at the summit in Kyoto, Japan,

in 1997, but it had no enforcement mechanism and the United States refused to implement it.

The nub of the political problem is this: poorer, developing countries don't want to limit industrialization because they believe doing so will hinder efforts to improve the standard of living for their citizens. Yet developed nations are often reluctant to require their citizens to make changes in their lifestyles in order to reduce greenhouse gas emissions if the developing world is just going to pollute more as it industrializes.

Expectations were high when the heads of state of 115 countries met in Copenhagen, Denmark, in 2009 to try to hammer out a new agreement. The equity problem was partially addressed by the developed countries' pledge of $100 billion in aid to poorer countries. But the sticking point in a broad treaty was an enforcement provision for implementing any agreed-on reductions. Copenhagen represents a small step forward for those concerned with limiting greenhouse gases. On the other hand, there is no assurance that any country will take actual steps to curb emissions.

Sources: John Whalley and Sean Walsh, "Bringing the Copenhagen Global Climate Change Negotiations to Conclusion," *CESifo Economic Studies* 55 (April 2009): 255–285; Michele B. Battig and Thomas Bernauer, "National Institutions and Global Public Goods: Are Democracies More Cooperative in Climate Change Policy?" *International Organization* 63 (Spring 2009): 281–308; Darren Samuelsohn and Lisa Freeman, "Obama Tries to Rally U.N. Climate Conference, but Deadlock Persists," *New York Times*, 18 December 2009; Anthony Faiola, Juliet Eilperin, and John Pomfret, "Copenhagen Talks Show U.S., China May Shape Future," *Washington Post*, 20 December 2009, p. A01; "Global Warming Statistics" at http://www.theglobalwarmingoverview.com/index.php/Global-Warming-Statistics.html.

emphasis on maintaining order (preserving the well-being of passengers). Administrative rule making gives agencies flexibility as they try to find a balance between conflicting pressures.

Administrative Policymaking: Informal Politics

When an agency is considering a new regulation and all the evidence and arguments have been presented, how does an administrator reach a decision? Because policy decisions typically address complex problems that lack a single satisfactory solution, they rarely exhibit mathematical precision and efficiency.

The Science of Muddling Through

In his classic analysis of policymaking, "The Science of Muddling Through," Charles Lindblom compared the way policy might be made in the ideal world with the way it is formulated in the real world.[24] The ideal rational decision-making process, according to Lindblom, would begin with an administrator tackling a problem by ranking values and objectives. After the objectives were clarified, the administrator would thoroughly consider all possible solutions to the problem. The administrator would comprehensively analyze alternative solutions, taking all relevant factors into account. Finally, the administrator would choose the alternative that is seen as the most effective means of achieving the desired goal and solving the problem.

Lindblom claims that this "rational-comprehensive" model is unrealistic. Policymakers have great difficulty defining precise values and goals. Administrators at the U.S. Department of Energy, for example, want to be sure that supplies of home heating oil are sufficient each winter, but at the same time they want to reduce dependence on foreign oil. Obviously the two goals are not fully compatible. How do administrators decide which is more important? And how do they relate those goals to the other goals of the nation's energy policy?

Real-world decision making parts company with the ideal in another way: the policy selected cannot always be the most effective means to the desired end. Even if a tax at the pump is the most effective way to reduce gasoline consumption during a shortage, motorists' anger would make this theoretically "right" decision politically difficult. The "best" policy is often the one on which most people can agree. However, political compromise may mean that the government is able to solve only part of a problem.

Finally, critics of the rational-comprehensive model point out that policymaking can never be based on truly comprehensive analysis. Time is of the essence, and many problems are too pressing to wait for a complete study.

In short, policymaking tends to be characterized by **incrementalism**: policies and programs change bit by bit, step by step.[25] Decision makers are constrained by competing policy objectives, opposing political forces, incomplete information, and the pressures of time. They choose from a limited number of feasible options that are almost

incrementalism
Policymaking characterized by a series of decisions, each instituting modest change.

always modifications of existing policies rather than wholesale departures from them. Although Lindblom offered a more realistic portrayal of the policymaking process, incrementalism is not ubiquitous. There are a minority of cases in which decisions are made that move a policy in a significantly new direction. It is certainly true that virtually all policy changes have antecedents in current policy, but some changes are considerable in scope.[26]

The Culture of Bureaucracy

How an agency makes decisions and performs its tasks is greatly affected by the people who work there: the bureaucrats. Americans often find their interactions with bureaucrats frustrating because bureaucrats are inflexible (they go by the book) or lack the authority to get things done. Top administrators too can also become frustrated with the bureaucrats who work for them.

Why do people act bureaucratically? Individuals who work for large organizations cannot help but be affected by the culture of bureaucracy.[27] Modern bureaucracies develop explicit rules and standards in order to make operations more efficient and to guarantee fair treatment of their clients. Within each organization, **norms** (informal, unwritten rules of behavior) also develop and influence the way people act on the job.

Bureaucracies are often influenced in their selection of policy options by the prevailing customs, attitudes, and expectations of the people working within them. Departments and agencies commonly develop a sense of mission, which emphasizes a particular objective. The Army Corps of Engineers, for example, is dominated by engineers who define the agency's objective as protecting citizens from floods by building dams. There could be other objectives, and there are other methods of achieving flood protection, but the engineers promote the solutions that fit their conception of what the agency should be doing. Bureaucrats are often criticized for being rigid, for going by the book when some flexibility might be a better option. Bureaucrats go by the book because the "book" is actually the law they administer, and they are obligated to enforce the law. The regulations under those laws are often broad standards intended to cover a range of behaviors. Bureaucratic caution and close adherence to agency rules ensure a measure of consistency. It would be unsettling if government employees interpreted rules as they pleased. Americans expect to be treated equally before the law, and bureaucrats work with that expectation in mind.

norms
An organization's informal, unwritten rules that guide individual behavior.

Problems in Implementing Policy

The development of policy in Washington marks the end of one phase of the policymaking cycle and the beginning of another. After policies are developed, they must be implemented. **Implementation** is the process of putting specific policies into operation. It is important to study implementation because policies do not always do what they were designed to do.

Implementation may be difficult because the policy to be carried out is not clearly stated. Policy directives to bureaucrats sometimes lack specificity and leave them with too much discretion.

Implementation can also be problematic because of the complexity of some government endeavors. Toxic cleanups, for example, pose complicated engineering, political, and financial problems. On April 20, 2010, an oil rig named the *Deepwater Horizon* experienced an explosion and fire that killed eleven workers. Two days later, it sank off the Louisiana coast. As the rig collapsed, the mile-long pipe connecting it to the floor of the ocean below crumpled, broke, and fell to the seabed. Oil gushed out of the pipe, starting what would become the worst environmental disaster in American history. The oil giant BP, which leased the drilling platform; Transocean, which owned and operated the *Deepwater Horizon;* and Halliburton, which provided the cement seal in the drilling shaft that appeared to have failed, all blamed each other for the disaster.

The Minerals Management Service (MMS) of the Department of the Interior and the U.S. Coast Guard are the key regulators of offshore drilling activity and rig safety.[28] The MMS was harshly criticized for what appeared to have been a half-hearted review of the required safety plans submitted by the companies that leased and operated the drilling rig. Though environmental reviews, safety plans, and accident contingency action plans are all required before rigs are allowed to operate, important elements were overlooked. Six weeks after the spill, the head of the MMS was forced to resign.[29]

Implementing multiple simultaneous plans to cap the well, recover the oil, and protect coastal areas was an extraordinary technical challenge requiring expertise that the government lacked. No government agency was equipped to stop an oil gusher a mile below the ocean's surface pumping tens of thousands of barrels of oil into the ocean each day. Although President Obama appointed Coast Guard Admiral Thad Allen as the national incident commander to

implementation
The process of putting specific policies into operation.

Bureaucratic Boots on the Ground

As head of the executive branch, the president sits at the top of a vast bureaucratic pyramid responsible for implementing the laws and regulations of the United States, including those related to environmental protection and offshore drilling. Here President Obama is briefed by Coast Guard Admiral Thad Allen and LaFourche Parish President Charlotte Randolph on the federal response to BP's massive oil spill in the Gulf of Mexico in 2010.

(JIM WATSON/AFP/Getty Images)

coordinate all efforts to address the disaster, Allen and the government bureaucracies involved had to rely on BP both to invent a solution (multiple strategies failed as months passed) and to pay for the economic and ecological consequences of the disaster.[30] As months went by without stopping the flow of oil, tension between the states on the Gulf Coast affected by the disaster, the federal government, and BP increased. The more agencies, organizations, and levels of government that are involved in handling anything, the more difficult it is to coordinate implementation. Even after the well was effectively capped in July 2010, BP continued drilling relief wells to install a permanent plug under the seabed. BP also faced the more daunting long-term challenge of restoring the damaged ecosystems of the Gulf Coast. Elements of the federal bureaucracy faced not only the responsibility of supervising the ongoing clean-up, but also the complex task of reviewing their regulations to minimize the likelihood of such disasters in the future.

Obstacles to effective implementation can create the impression that nothing the government does succeeds, but programs can and do work. Problems in implementation demonstrate why patience and continual analysis are necessary ingredients of successful policymaking. Implementation is an *incremental* process in which trial and error eventually lead to policies that work.

Reforming the Bureaucracy: More Control or Less

As we saw at the beginning of this chapter, organization matters. How bureaucracies are designed directly affects how effective they are in accomplishing their tasks.[31] Administrative reforms have taken many different approaches in recent years as the criticism of government has mounted.

Deregulation

Many people believe that government is too involved in **regulation**, intervention in the natural workings of business markets to promote some social goal. For example, government might regulate a market to ensure that products pose no danger to consumers. Through **deregulation**, the government reduces its role and lets the natural market forces of supply and demand take over.

Considerable deregulation took place in the 1970s and 1980s, notably in the airline, trucking, financial services, and telecommunications industries. In telecommunications, for example, consumers before 1982 had no choice of long-distance vendors: they could call on AT&T's Bell System or not call at all. After an out-of-court settlement broke up the Bell System in 1982, AT&T was awarded the right to sell the long-distance services that Bell had been providing, but it now had to face competition from new long-distance carriers. Deregulation for local phone service followed some years later, and consumers have benefited from the vigorous competition for their business.

Deciding on an appropriate level of deregulation is particularly difficult for health and safety issues. Companies within an industry may legitimately claim that health and safety regulations are burdensome, making it difficult for them to earn sufficient profits or compete effectively with foreign manufacturers. But the drug-licensing procedures used by the FDA illustrate the potential danger of deregulating in such policy areas. The thorough and lengthy process the FDA uses to evaluate drugs has as its ultimate validation the thalidomide case in the 1960s. Dr. Frances Kelsey, who was assigned to evaluate the sedative, demanded that all FDA drug-testing requirements be met, despite the fact that the drug was already in use in other countries. Before the tests were completed, news came pouring in from Europe that some women who

regulation
Government intervention in the workings of business to promote some socially desired goal.

deregulation
A bureaucratic reform by which the government reduces its role as a regulator of business.

had taken thalidomide during pregnancy were giving birth to babies without arms, legs, or ears. Strict adherence to FDA regulation protected Americans from the same tragic consequences. In 1997, the FDA reversed course and decided to permit the use of thalidomide to treat leprosy, but the dangers to pregnant women remain. To avert a catastrophe, the FDA includes stickers on the drug's packaging to warn women of the consequences of taking this drug during pregnancy.

Some agencies have tried to move beyond rules that simply increase or decrease the amount of government control to regulatory processes that offer firms flexibility in meeting standards while at the same time protecting health and safety concerns. For example, the Environmental Protection Agency (EPA) has instituted

The Politics of Thalidomide

The United States avoided the thalidomide disaster because of the skepticism of Frances Kelsey, a Food and Drug Administration doctor who refused to allow thalidomide to be prescribed here. Across the Atlantic, patients were not so fortunate. Thalidomide victims in Europe have created an international organization that has mounted lobbying and protest efforts to win compensation from the German government and Grunenthal, a German pharmaceutical company. This 2008 demonstration took place outside the German embassy in London.

(Leon Neal/AFP/Getty Images)

flexible caps on air pollution at some manufacturing plants. Instead of having to request permits on new equipment and processes, plants are given an overall pollution cap and can decide on their own how to meet that limit. Although such "cap and trade" provisions for power plants were struck down by a federal appeals court in 2008, they illustrate the creativity that bureaucracies can at times bring to the regulatory process.[32]

Another regulatory approach gaining favor is the effort to make organizations, typically corporations, more transparent and accountable in their actions. For example, food manufacturers are now required to disclose the quantity of trans-fats in a product on its label. Regulations do not limit the amount of trans-fatty acids but, rather, give consumers the information and then let them decide how much is too much.[33]

A strong case can be made for deregulated business markets, in which free and unfettered competition benefits consumers and promotes productivity. The strength of capitalist economies comes from the ability of individuals and firms to compete freely in the marketplace, and the regulatory state places restrictions on this freedom. But without regulation, nothing ensures that marketplace participants will act responsibly.

Competition and Outsourcing

Conservative critics of government have long complained that bureaucracies should act more like businesses, meaning they should try to emulate private sector practices that promote efficiency and innovation. Many recent reformers advocate something more drastic: unless bureaucracies can demonstrate that they are as efficient as the private sector, turn those agencies' functions over to the private sector. Underlying this idea is the belief that competition will make government more dynamic and more responsive to changing environments.[34]

One widespread adaptation of competitive bidding to administer government programs has come in the area of social services. Over time government welfare programs have increasingly emphasized social services—giving people training and noncash support—rather than income maintenance (cash support). State and local governments have found it efficient to outsource programs to nonprofit organizations like community health centers and day-care centers for elderly people. Recently, for-profit companies have started to compete for the grants and contracts that the government awards through competitive grants or bidding.[35] This movement toward **competition and outsourcing** continues to grow. More and more government jobs

competition and outsourcing
Procedures that allow private contractors to bid for jobs previously held exclusively by government employees.

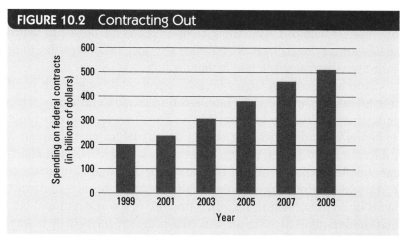

FIGURE 10.2   Contracting Out

An explosive growth in contracting out government programs and services to non-profits and for-profit organizations is changing the face of government. In a recent six-year period, contracting out almost doubled. Although competitive bidding theoretically gives the government the lowest prices, only half of all contracts are subject to full and open competition. Government officials claim that national security concerns often lead them to seek out a single contractor rather than opening the process to all potential bidders.

Source: Federal Procurement Reports 1999–2009, Federal Procurement Data System – Next Generation, available at http://www.fpdsng.com/fpdsng_cms/index.php/reports.

are open to bidding from nongovernment competitors, and sometimes a government bureau or office competes for the jobs and programs that they used to "own." (See Figure 10.2.)

Performance Standards

Another approach to improving the bureaucracy's performance is to hold it accountable for reaching quantifiable goals each year or budget cycle. A major initiative to hold agencies accountable for their performance is the **Government Performance and Results Act**. This law requires each agency to identify specific goals, adopt a performance plan, and develop quantitative indicators of agency progress in meeting its goals.[36] The law further requires that agencies begin to publish reports with performance data on each measure established.

A case in point is the Healthy Start program funded by the Health Resources and Services Administration (HRSA) and intended to improve infant mortality rates and infant health generally. Among the specific goals are increasing the number of mothers receiving prenatal care during the first trimester and reducing the number of low-weight births. These are measurable, and the hospitals and health

Government Performance and Results Act

A law requiring each government agency to implement quantifiable standards to measure its performance in meeting stated program goals.

centers receiving federal funding for Healthy Start must report the appropriate data to HRSA. More complicated is the degree to which these various programs make a difference since infant health can be influenced by many different factors.[37]

Another challenge arises because agencies set their own goals and know they will be judged on meeting them, so they may select indicators where they know they'll do best.[38] Or if standards prove to be too difficult to achieve, standards may be lowered, sometimes under the guise of "reform," to make them work better. The Department of Education intended the No Child Left Behind program to force underperforming schools to raise students' reading and math skills up to prescribed standards. Although this was a national law, states were allowed to implement the program in their own way. Over time many states reduced their standards because their schools could not improve enough to meet the model guidelines of a national test of students. Between 2005 and 2007, fifteen states lowered the bar for student performance. Other states had already lowered their standards. In short, performance-based management runs the risk of perverting an agency's incentives toward what it can achieve rather than what would be most valuable to achieve.[39]

Despite the relative appeal of these different approaches to improving the bureaucracy, each has serious shortcomings. The commitment of the government to solve a problem is far more important than management techniques.[40] Still, to return to a theme that we began with, organization does matter. Trying to find ways of improving the bureaucracy is important because bureaucracies affect people's lives, and enhancing their performance, even at the margins, has real consequences.

Tying It Together

1. Who administers the nation's laws and policies?
   - The nation's laws and policies are administered by a variety of executive branch departments, agencies, bureaus, offices, and other governmental units, all of which are known collectively as the bureaucracy.
   - Bureaucracies exist in all modern governments.

- Bureaucracies face conflicting demands when attempting to accomplish their tasks.

2. How did the current bureaucratic state come about, and should it be cut back?
   - Bureaucracies have been part of the U.S. government since George Washington's administration.
   - Attitudes about government's responsibilities regarding social welfare have changed, and the government has grown to respond to these changing attitudes.
   - Ambitious government bureaucrats have increased the scope of their authority and responsibility.
   - Due to a lack of confidence in its performance, Americans want to reduce the size of government.
   - For government to become smaller, budget cuts would require curtailment of services or contracts with private organizations.
   - The tendency for big government to continue reflects the tension between majoritarianism and pluralism.

3. What is the organizational structure of the bureaucracy?
   - There are several types of government organizations.
     - Departments: the biggest units of the executive branch covering broad areas of responsibility.
     - Independent agencies: stand-alone units controlled to varying degrees by the president, including regulatory commissions.
     - Government corporations: agencies that are created by Congress to provide services to the public that could be provided by private organizations.
   - The Pendleton Act started the modern civil service, which is designed to reduce patronage by requiring bureaucracies to hire employees based on merit.

4. How do government agencies operate?
   - Administrative agencies have the authority to make policy decisions on important issues that are legally binding to citizens.
   - Congress creates new departments or agencies by passing laws.
   - When Congress passes laws, it generally grants an agency the authority to administer or enforce those laws.
   - Agencies make policy through formal administrative procedures known as rule making, which results in regulations.
   - Regulations, which have the effect of law, govern the operation of government programs.

5. How are administrative decisions made and implemented by the government?
   - Agencies are required to seek broad input from the public before deciding on a course of action.
   - Ideally, administrators would set rational objectives and values, consider all possible solutions, analyze alternative solutions, and choose the best alternative to solve the problems.
     - This "rational-comprehensive" model is unrealistic for government because of the difficulty administrators have in setting precise goals and values.
     - Most decisions in government are made by a process of gradual change called incrementalism, but there are exceptions.
   - Bureaucrats are obliged to operate according to the rules enacted for their agencies.

6. What problems are encountered in the implementation of governmental policies?
   - Implementation is the process of putting specific policies into operation.
     - Implementation is made difficult by a lack of clarity in policies.
     - Implementation is problematic because of the complexity of government endeavors.
     - The involvement of multiple organizations, agencies, and levels of government complicates implementation.
   - Obstacles often make it appear that government is unsuccessful, but this is not always true.

7. Does the bureaucracy need to be controlled?
   - By deregulation, government reduces its role and lets market forces work.
   - The conflict between regulation and deregulation reflects the conflict between freedom and order: capitalists want a free market, but there is no guarantee they will act responsibly.
   - One way to reduce government size is through competition and outsourcing, by allowing private contractors to bid for jobs previously held exclusively by government employees.
   - Increasingly, government agencies have integrated competition and outsourcing into their approaches for policy implementation.

Organization Matters

True or False?

1. The U.S. national government is the only true bureaucracy in the world.
2. A bureaucracy is any large, complex organization in which employees have specific responsibilities and work within a hierarchy.

Comprehension

3. What is the role of the bureaucracy in government?

Bureaucratic Growth

True or False?

1. All levels of government grew enormously during the twentieth century because society became more complex.
2. The Securities and Exchange Commission (SEC) and Food and Drug Administration (FDA) are examples of interest groups.

Comprehension

3. Explain why some segments of the American public believe they deserve government support.
4. What actions would be required to decrease the size of government?

Bureaus and Bureaucrats

True or False?

1. The largest department in government is the Department of Defense.
2. Government corporations are the largest units of the executive branch.
3. The CIA is an example of an independent agency.

Comprehension

4. Why was the civil service created?
5. Explain why bureaucracies may not be as responsive as presidents would like them to be.

Administrative Policymaking: The Formal Processes

True or False?

1. Agencies make policy decisions because Congress recognized it has neither the time nor the technical expertise to make all policy decisions.

2. Administrative discretion is the inability of agencies to make policy without Congress's approval.
3. Rule making is the administrative process that results in regulations.

Comprehension
4. Describe the broadest discretion given to agencies by Congress. Which agencies enjoy this latitude?
5. How does Congress control administrative agencies?

Administrative Policymaking: Informal Politics

True or False?
1. Policymakers often have difficulty defining precise values and goals for policies.
2. Policymaking tends to be shaped by incrementalism and not the rational-comprehensive model.
3. Norms are formal, written rules of behavior.

Comprehension
4. What is incrementalism?
5. Describe how different bureaucracies are influenced by the different types of people who work for them.

Problems in Implementing Policy

True or False?
1. Implementation of policies is difficult if directives are not specific and they leave bureaucrats with too much discretion.
2. The example of the Gulf oil leak in 2010 shows that government bureaucracies generally have technical expertise that private sectors lack.
3. Implementation consists of gathering feedback to assess policies.

Comprehension
4. What are some of the obstacles to implementing policy?

Reforming the Bureaucracy: More Control or Less?

True or False?
1. When the government deregulates, it is trying to reduce its role and let the market forces of supply and demand prevail.
2. The case of thalidomide illustrates the benefits that occur with deregulation of industry.
3. Recent approaches to regulation include a focus on making corporations more transparent and accountable in their actions.

Comprehension

4. Give an example of how deregulation is especially difficult in the health and medical sector.

5. Why would government try to stimulate competition through outsourcing services?

CourseMate CL Resources:

Visit www.cengagebrain.com/shop/ISBN/1111832587 for flashcards, web quizzes, videos and more!

The Courts

iStockphoto.com/lillisphotography

FOCUS QUESTIONS

1. What is the concept of judicial review, and how did it come about?
2. How is the American court system organized at the national and state levels?
3. How does the Supreme Court reach decisions?
4. How are judges appointed to the courts?
5. How are judicial rulings implemented, and what is their effect on public opinion?
6. Do the courts reflect the majoritarian or pluralist models of democracy?

When Chief Justice Fred M. Vinson died unexpectedly in September 1953, his colleague Associate Justice Felix Frankfurter commented, "This is the first solid piece of evidence I've ever had that there really is a God."[1] Frankfurter despised Vinson as a leader and disliked him as a person. Vinson's sudden death would bring a new colleague—and perhaps new hope—to the school desegregation cases known collectively as *Brown* v. *Board of Education*. The issue of segregated schools had arrived in the Supreme Court in late 1951. Although the Court had originally scheduled oral argument for October 1952, the justices elected a postponement until December and merged several similar cases. When a law clerk expressed puzzlement at the delay, Frankfurter explained that the Court was holding the cases for the outcome of the national election in 1952. "I thought the Court was supposed to decide without regard to elections," declared the clerk. "When you have a major social political issue of this magnitude," replied Frankfurter, "we do not think this is the time to decide it."[2]

The justices were at loggerheads following the December argument, with Vinson unwilling to invalidate racial segregation in public education. Because the justices were not ready to reach a decision, they scheduled the cases for reargument the following year. The justices asked the attorneys to address the history of the Fourteenth Amendment and the potential remedies if the Court ruled against segregation.

Frankfurter's caustic remark about Vinson's death reflected the critical role Vinson's replacement would play when the Court again tackled the desegregation issue. In his first appointment to the nation's highest court, President Dwight D. Eisenhower chose California's Republican governor, Earl Warren, as chief justice. The president would later regret his choice.

When the Court heard the reargument of *Brown v. Board of Education* in late 1953, the new chief justice led his colleagues from division to unanimity on the issue of public school segregation. Unlike his predecessor, Warren began the secret conference to decide the segregation issue with a strong statement: that segregation was contrary to the Thirteenth, Fourteenth, and Fifteenth Amendments to the Constitution. "Personally," remarked the new chief justice, "I can't see how today we can justify segregation based solely on race."[3] Moreover, if the Court were to uphold segregation, he argued, it could do so only on the theory that blacks were inherently inferior to whites. As the discussion proceeded, Warren's opponents were cast in the awkward position of appearing to support racism.

Five justices were clearly on Warren's side, making six votes; two were prepared to join the majority if Warren's reasoning satisfied them. With only one clear holdout, Warren set about the task of responding to his colleagues' concerns. In the months that followed, he met with them individually in their chambers, reviewing the decision and the justification that would accompany it. Finally, in April 1954, Warren approach Justice Stanley Reed, whose vote would make the opinion unanimous. "Stan," said the Chief Justice, "you're all by yourself in this now. You've got to decide whether it's really the best thing for the country." Ultimately, Reed joined the others. On May 17, 1954, the Supreme Court unanimously ruled against racial segregation in public schools, signaling the end of legally created or government-enforced segregation of the races in the United States.[4]

Judges confront conflicting values in the cases before them, and in crafting their decisions judges—especially Supreme Court justices—make policy. Their decisions become the precedents other judges use to rule in similar cases. One judge in one court makes public policy to the extent that she or he influences other decisions in other courts.

The power of the courts to shape public policy creates a difficult problem for democratic theory. According to that theory, the power to make law resides only in the people or their elected representatives.

Court rulings—especially Supreme Court rulings—extend far beyond any particular case. Judges are students of the law, but they remain human beings. They have their own opinions about the values of freedom, order, and equality. And although all judges are constrained by statutes and precedents from expressing their personal beliefs in their decisions, some judges are more prone than others to interpret laws in the light of those beliefs. America's courts are deeply involved in the life of the country and its people. Some courts, such as the Supreme Court, make fundamental policy decisions vital to the preservation of freedom, order, and equality. Through checks and balances, the elected branches link the courts to democracy, and the courts link the elected branches to the Constitution. But does this arrangement work? Can the courts exercise political power within the pluralist model? Or are judges simply sovereigns in black robes, making decisions independent of popular control? This chapter seeks to answer these questions by exploring the role of the judiciary in American political life.

National Judicial Supremacy

Section 1 of Article III of the Constitution creates "one supreme Court." The founders were divided on the need for other national courts, so they deferred to Congress the decision to create a national court system. Those who opposed the creation of national courts believed that such a system would usurp the authority of the state courts.[5] Congress considered the issue in its first session and, in the Judiciary Act of 1789, gave life to a system of federal (that is, national) courts that would coexist with the courts in each state but be independent of them. Federal judges would also be independent of popular influences because the Constitution provided for their potentially lifetime appointment.

In the early years of the Republic, the federal judiciary was not a particularly powerful branch of government. It was especially difficult to recruit and keep Supreme Court justices. They spent much of their time as individual traveling judges ("riding circuit"), and disease and transportation were everyday hazards. The justices met as the Supreme Court for only a few weeks in February and August.[6] John Jay, the first chief justice, refused to resume his duties in 1801 because he concluded that the Court could not muster the "energy, weight, and dignity" to contribute to national affairs.[7] But a period of profound change began in 1801 when President John Adams appointed his secretary of state, John Marshall, to the position of chief justice.

Judicial Review of the Other Branches

Shortly after Marshall's appointment, the Supreme Court confronted a question of fundamental importance to the future of the new republic: If a law enacted by Congress conflicts with the Constitution, which should prevail? The question arose in the case of *Marbury* v. *Madison* (1803), which involved a controversial series of last-minute political appointments.

The case began in 1801, when an obscure Federalist, William Marbury, was designated a justice of the peace in the District of Columbia. Marbury and several others were appointed to government posts created by Congress in the last days of John Adams's presidency, but the appointments were never completed. Though the Senate had approved their appointment, the official documents of appointment were not delivered to several of the judicial appointments, including Marbury. The newly arrived Jefferson administration had little interest in delivering the required documents; qualified Jeffersonians would welcome the jobs.

To secure their jobs, Marbury and the other disgruntled appointees invoked an act of Congress to obtain the papers. The act authorized the Supreme Court to issue orders against government officials. Marbury and the others sought such an order in the Supreme Court against the new secretary of state, James Madison, who held the crucial documents.

Chief Justice John Marshall observed that the act of Congress that Marbury invoked to sue in the Supreme Court conflicted with Article III of the U.S. Constitution, which did not authorize such suits. In February 1803, the Court delivered its opinion.

Must the Supreme Court follow the law or the Constitution? The Court held, in Marshall's forceful argument, that the Constitution was "the fundamental and paramount law of the nation" and that "an act of the legislature repugnant to the constitution is void." In other words, when an act of the legislature conflicts with the Constitution—the nation's highest law—that act is invalid. Marshall's argument vested in the judiciary the power to weigh the validity of congressional acts:

> It is emphatically the province and duty of the judicial department to say what the law is. Those who apply the rule to particular cases, must of necessity expound and interpret that rule. . . . If a law be in opposition to the constitution, if both the law and the constitution apply to a particular case, so that the court must either decide that case conformably to the law, disregarding the constitution; or conformably to the constitution, disregarding the law; the court must determine which of these conflicting rules governs the case. This is the very essence of judicial duty.[8]

The decision in *Marbury* v. *Madison* established the Supreme Court's power of **judicial review**—the power to declare congressional acts invalid if they violate the Constitution.* Subsequent cases extended the power to cover presidential acts as well.[9]

judicial review
The power to declare congressional and presidential acts invalid because they violate the Constitution.

---

*The Supreme Court had earlier upheld an act of Congress in *Hylton* v. *United States,* 3 Dallas 171 (1796). *Marbury* v. *Madison* was the first exercise of the power of a court to invalidate an act of Congress.

Marshall expanded the potential power of the Supreme Court to equal or exceed the power of the other branches of government. Should a congressional act (or, by implication, a presidential act) conflict with the Constitution, the Supreme Court claimed the power to declare the act void. The judiciary would be a check on the legislative and executive branches, consistent with the principle of checks and balances embedded in the Constitution. Judicial review gave the Supreme Court the final word on the meaning of the Constitution.

The exercise of judicial review—an appointed branch's checking of an elected branch in the name of the Constitution—appears to run counter to democratic theory. But in over two hundred years of practice, the Supreme Court has invalidated only about 160 provisions of national law. Only a small number have had great significance for the political system.[10] However, since 1994 the Court has struck down more than 30 acts of Congress. Moreover, there are mechanisms to override judicial review (constitutional amendment) and to control the excesses of the justices (impeachment). In addition, the Court can respond to the continuing struggle among competing interests (a struggle that is consistent with the pluralist model) by reversing itself.

Judicial Review of State Government

The establishment of judicial review of national laws made the Supreme Court the umpire of the national government. When acts of the national government conflict with the Constitution, the Supreme Court can declare those acts invalid. But suppose state laws conflict with the Constitution, national laws, or federal treaties? Can the U.S. Supreme Court invalidate them as well?

The Court answered in the affirmative in 1796. The case involved a British creditor who was trying to collect a debt from the state of Virginia.[11] Virginia law canceled debts owed British subjects, yet the Treaty of Paris (1783), in which Britain formally acknowledged the independence of the colonies, guaranteed that creditors could collect such debts. The Court ruled that the Constitution's supremacy clause (Article VI), which embraces national laws and treaties, nullified the state law.

The states continued to resist the yoke of national supremacy. Advocates of strong states' rights conceded that the supremacy clause obligates state judges to follow the Constitution when state law conflicts with it; however, they maintained that the states were bound only by their own interpretation of the Constitution. The Supreme Court said no, ruling that it had the authority to review state court decisions that called for the interpretation of national law.[12] National supremacy required the Supreme Court to impose uniformity on federal law; otherwise, the Constitution's meaning would vary from state to state. The people, not the states, had ordained the Constitution, and the people had subordinated state power to it in order to establish a viable national government. In time, the Supreme Court would use its judicial review power in nearly 1,300 instances to invalidate state and local laws on issues as diverse as abortion, the death penalty, the rights of the accused, and reapportionment.[13]

The Exercise of Judicial Review

These early cases, coupled with other historic decisions, established the components of judicial review:

- The power of the courts to declare national, state, and local laws invalid if they violate the Constitution
- The supremacy of national laws or treaties when they conflict with state and local laws
- The role of the Supreme Court as the final authority on the meaning of the Constitution

This political might—the power to undo decisions of the representative branches of the national and state governments—lay in the hands of appointed judges, people not accountable to the electorate. Did judicial review square with democratic government?

Alexander Hamilton had foreseen and tackled the problem in *Federalist* No. 78. Writing during the ratification debates surrounding the adoption of the Constitution (see Chapter 2), Hamilton maintained that despite the power of judicial review, the judiciary would be the weakest of the three branches of government because it lacked "the strength of the sword or the purse." The judiciary, wrote Hamilton, had "neither force nor will, but only judgment."

Although Hamilton was defending legislative supremacy, he argued that judicial review was an essential barrier to legislative oppression.[14] He recognized that the power to declare government acts void implied the superiority of the courts over the other branches. But this power, he contended, simply reflects the will of the people declared in the Constitution as opposed to the will of the legislature expressed in its statutes. Judicial independence, guaranteed by lifetime tenure and protected salaries, frees judges from executive and legislative control, minimizing the risk of their deviating from the law established in the Constitution. If judges make a mistake, the people or their elected representatives have the means to correct the error, through constitutional amendments and impeachment.

Nevertheless, lifetime tenure does free judges from the direct influence of the president and Congress. And although mechanisms to check judicial power are in place, they require extraordinary majorities and are rarely used. When judges exercise the power of judicial review, then, they can and occasionally do operate counter to majoritarian rule by invalidating the actions of the people's elected representatives.

The Organization of Courts

The American court system is complex, partly as a result of our federal system of government. Each state runs its own court system, and no two states' courts are identical. In addition, we have a system of courts for the national government. The national, or federal, courts coexist with the state courts (see Figure 11.1). Individuals fall under the jurisdiction of both court systems. They can sue or be sued in either system, depending mostly on what their case is about. Litigants file nearly all cases (99 percent) in the state courts.[15]

Some Court Fundamentals

Criminal and Civil Cases. A crime is a violation of a law that forbids or commands an activity. Criminal laws are set forth in each state's penal code, as are punishments for violations. Because crime is a violation of public order, the government prosecutes **criminal cases**. Maintaining public order through the enforcement of criminal law is largely a state and local function. Criminal cases brought by the national government represent only a small fraction of all criminal cases prosecuted in the United States. Courts decide both criminal and civil cases. **Civil cases** stem from disputed claims to something of value. Disputes arise from accidents, contractual obligations, and divorce, for example. Often the parties disagree over tangible issues (possession of property, custody of children), but civil cases can involve more abstract issues too (the right to equal accommodations, damages for pain and suffering). The government can be a party to civil disputes, called on to defend its actions or to allege wrongdoing.

criminal case
A court case involving a crime, or violation of public order.

civil case
A court case that involves a private dispute arising from such matters as accidents, contractual obligations, and divorce.

FIGURE 11.1   The Federal and State Court Systems, 2008–2009

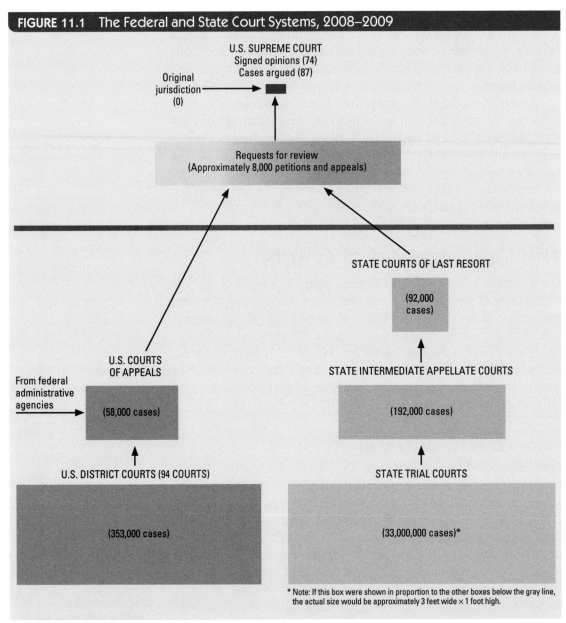

The federal courts have three tiers: district courts, courts of appeals, and the Supreme Court. The Supreme Court was created by the Constitution; all other federal courts were created by Congress. State courts dwarf federal courts, at least in terms of caseload. There are more than one hundred state cases for every federal case filed. The structure of state courts varies from state to state; usually there are minor trial courts for less serious cases, major trial courts for more serious cases, intermediate appellate courts, and supreme courts. State courts were created by state constitutions.

Sources: John Roberts, "The 2009 Year-End Report on the Federal Judiciary," 31 December, 2009, http://www.supremecourt.gov/publicinfo/year-end/2009year-endreport.pdf; *Federal Court Management Statistics 2009*, http://www.uscourts.gov/fcmstat/index.html; Court Statistics Project, *State Court Case-load Statistics, 2007* (Williamsburg, Va.:National Center for State Courts, 2007), Table 10, p. 153, http://www.ncsconline.org/D_Research/csp/CSP_Main_Page.html.

Procedures and Policymaking. Most civil and criminal cases never go to trial. In a criminal case, a defendant's lawyer and the prosecutor might **plea-bargain**, which means they negotiate about the severity and number of charges facing the accused. The defendant pleads guilty to a lesser charge in exchange for the promise of less severe punishment. In a civil case, one side may use a lawsuit as a threat to exact a concession from the other. Often the parties settle their dispute. When parties do not settle, cases end with *adjudication,* a court judgment resolving the parties' claims and ultimately enforced by the government. When trial judges adjudicate cases, they may offer written reasons to support their decisions. When the issues or circumstances of cases are novel, judges may publish *opinions,* explanations justifying their rulings.

Judges make policy in two different ways. Occasionally, in the absence of legislation, they use rules from prior decisions. We call this body of rules **common, or judge-made, law.** The roots of common law lie in the English legal system. Contracts, property, and torts (an injury or wrong to the person or property of another) are common law domains. The second area of judicial lawmaking involves the application of statutes enacted by legislatures. The judicial interpretation of legislative acts is called *statutory construction.* To determine how a statute should be applied, judges look for the legislature's intent, reading reports of committee hearings and debates. If these sources do not clarify the statute's meaning, the court does so. With or without legislation to guide them, judges look to the relevant opinions of higher courts for authority to decide the issues before them.

The federal courts are organized in three tiers, as a pyramid. At the bottom of the pyramid are **U.S. district courts,** where litigation begins. In the middle are **U.S. courts of appeals.** At the top is the Supreme Court of the United States. To *appeal* means to take a case to a higher court. The courts of appeals and the Supreme Court are appellate courts; with few exceptions, they review only cases already decided in lower courts.

The U.S. District Courts

There are ninety-four federal district courts in the United States. Each state has at least one district court, and no district straddles more than one state.[16] In 2010 there were 678 authorized federal district judgeships with 590 active judges.[17] These judges received approximately 353,000 new criminal and civil cases.[18]

plea-bargain
A defendant's admission of guilt in exchange for a less severe punishment.

common, or judge-made, law
Legal precedents derived from previous judicial decisions.

U.S. district court
A court within the lowest tier of the three-tiered federal court system; the trial court in which litigation begins.

U.S. courts of appeals
Courts within the second tier of the three-tiered federal court system, to which decisions of the district courts and federal agencies may be appealed for review.

The district courts are the entry point to the federal court system. When trials occur in the federal system, they take place in the federal district courts. Here is where witnesses testify, lawyers conduct cross-examinations, and judges and juries decide the fate of litigants. More than one judge may sit in each district court, but each case is tried by a single judge, sitting alone. Federal magistrates assist district judges, but they lack independent judicial authority. In 2010 there were 527 full-time magistrate positions and 41 part-time magistrate positions.[19]

Sources of Litigation. Today the authority of U.S. district courts extends to the following types of cases:

- Federal criminal cases as defined by national law (for example, robbery of a federally insured bank or interstate transportation of stolen securities)
- Civil cases brought by individuals, groups, or government alleging violation of national law (for example, failure of a municipality to implement pollution-control regulations required by a national agency)
- Civil cases brought against the national government (for example, a vehicle manufacturer sues the motor pool of a government agency for its failure to take delivery of a fleet of new cars)
- Civil cases between citizens of different states when the amount in controversy exceeds $75,000 (for example, when a citizen of New York sues a citizen of Alabama in a U.S. district court in Alabama for damages stemming from an auto accident that occurred in Alabama)

The U.S. Courts of Appeals

All cases resolved in a U.S. district court and all decisions of federal administrative agencies can be appealed to one of the twelve regional U.S. courts of appeals. These courts, with 167 authorized judgeships, received nearly 56,000 new cases in 2010.[20] Each appeals court hears cases from a geographic area known as a *circuit*. The United States is divided into twelve circuits.*

Appellate Court Proceedings. Appellate court proceedings are public, but they usually lack courtroom drama. There are no jurors,

---

*A thirteenth court, the U.S. Court of Appeals for the Federal Circuit, is not a regional court. It specializes in appeals involving patents, contract claims against the national government, and federal employment cases.

witnesses, or cross-examinations; these are features of the trial courts. Appeals are based strictly on the rulings made and procedures followed in the trial courts.

Suppose that in the course of a criminal trial, a U.S. district judge allows the introduction of evidence that convicts a defendant but was obtained under questionable circumstances. The defendant can appeal on the grounds that the evidence was obtained in the absence of a valid search warrant and so was inadmissible. The issue on appeal is the admissibility of the evidence, not the defendant's guilt or innocence. If the appellate court agrees with the trial judge's decision to admit the evidence, the conviction stands. If the appellate court disagrees with the trial judge and rules that the evidence is inadmissible, the defendant must be retried without the incriminating evidence or must be released.

It is common for litigants to try to settle their dispute while it is on appeal. Occasionally litigants abandon their appeals for want of resources or resolve. Most of the time, however, appellate courts adjudicate the cases.

The courts of appeals are regional courts. They usually convene in panels of three judges to render judgments. The judges receive written arguments known as *briefs* (which are also sometimes submitted in trial courts). Often the judges hear oral arguments and question the lawyers to probe their arguments.

Precedents and Making Decisions. When an appellate opinion is published, its influence can reach well beyond the immediate case. For example, a lawsuit turning on the meaning of the Constitution produces a ruling that serves as a **precedent** for subsequent cases—that is, the decision becomes a basis for deciding similar cases in the same way. At the appellate level, precedent requires that opinions be written.

Making decisions according to precedent is central to the operation of our legal system, providing continuity and predictability. The bias in favor of existing decisions is captured by the Latin expression *stare decisis*, which means "let the decision stand." But the use of precedent and the principle of *stare decisis* do not make lower-court judges cogs in a judicial machine. "If precedent clearly governed," remarked one federal judge, "a case would never get as far as the Court of Appeals: the parties would settle."[21]

Judges on courts of appeals direct their energies to correcting errors in district court proceedings and interpreting the law (in the course of writing opinions). When judges interpret the law, they

precedent
A judicial ruling that serves as the basis for the ruling in a subsequent case.

stare decisis
Literally, "let the decision stand"; decision making according to precedent.

often modify existing laws. In effect, they are making policy. Judges are politicians in the sense that they exercise political power, but the black robes that distinguish judges from other politicians signal constraints on their exercise of power.

Uniformity of Law. Decisions by the courts of appeals ensure a measure of uniformity in the application of national law. The courts of appeals harmonize the decisions of district judges within their region so that laws are applied uniformly.

Nevertheless, the regional character of the courts of appeals undermines uniformity somewhat because the courts are not bound by the decisions of other circuits. The percolation of cases up through the federal system of courts practically guarantees that at some point, two or more courts of appeals, working with similar sets of facts, are going to interpret the same law differently. However, the problem of conflicting decisions in the intermediate federal courts can be corrected by review in the Supreme Court, where policymaking, not error correction, is the paramount goal.

The Supreme Court

Above the west portico of the Supreme Court Building are inscribed the words EQUAL JUSTICE UNDER LAW. At the opposite end of the building, above the east portico, are the words JUSTICE THE GUARDIAN OF LIBERTY. These mottoes reflect the Court's difficult task: achieving a just balance among the values of freedom, order, and equality. Consider how those values came into conflict in two controversial issues the Court has faced: flag burning and school desegregation.

Flag burning as a form of political protest pits the value of order, or the government's interest in maintaining a peaceful society, against the value of freedom, including the individual's right to vigorous and unbounded political expression. In two flag-burning cases, the Supreme Court affirmed constitutional protection for unbridled political expression, including the emotionally charged act of desecrating a national symbol.[22]

School desegregation pits the value of equality against the value of freedom. In *Brown* v. *Board of Education,* the Supreme Court carried the banner of racial equality by striking down state-mandated segregation in public schools. The justices recognized the disorder their decision would create in a society accustomed to racial bias, but in this case, equality clearly outweighed freedom.

The Supreme Court, 2010 Term: The Lineup

The justices of the Supreme Court of the United States. Seated are (left to right) Clarence Thomas, Antonin Scalia, Chief Justice John G. Roberts, Jr., Anthony Kennedy, and Ruth Bader Ginsburg. Standing are Sonia Sotomayor, Stephen J. Breyer, Samuel A. Alito, and Elena Kagan.

(Steve Petteway, Collection of the Supreme Court of the United States)

Twenty-four years later, the Court was still embroiled in controversy over equality when it ruled that race could be a factor in university admissions (to diversify the student body), in *Regents of the University of California* v. *Bakke* (1978).[23] Having secured equality for blacks, the Court in 2003 faced the charge by white students who sought admission to the University of Michigan that it was denying whites the freedom to compete for admission. A slim Court majority concluded that the equal protection clause of the Fourteenth Amendment did not prohibit the narrowly tailored use of race as a factor in law school admissions but rejected the automatic use of racial categories to award fixed points toward undergraduate admissions.[24]

The use of race in assigning students to public schools was narrowed significantly in *Parents Involved in Community Schools* v. *Seattle School Dist. No. 1* (2007). In a deeply divided decision that addressed parallel cases in Seattle, Washington, and Louisville, Kentucky, the Court struck down two desegregation plans that classified students by race and used that information to determine where students would go to school to achieve racial balance. Though the plans were intended to integrate students rather than segregate them, the majority ruled that race was inappropriately used by the school district in plans that were not narrowly tailored. Though district administrators may consider race in the context of broader goals and issues, the broad and blunt use of race as a determining factor was struck down.[25]

The Supreme Court makes national policy. Because its decisions have far-reaching effects on all of us, it is vital that we understand how it reaches those decisions.

Access to the Court

There are rules of access that must be followed to bring a case to the Supreme Court. Also important is sensitivity to the justices' policy and ideological preferences. The notion that anyone can take a case all the way to the Supreme Court is true only in theory, not in fact.

The Supreme Court's cases come from two sources. A few arrive under the Court's **original jurisdiction**, conferred by Article III, Section 2, of the Constitution, which gives the Court the power to hear and decide "all Cases affecting Ambassadors, other public Ministers and Consuls, and those in which a State shall be a Party." Cases

original jurisdiction
The authority of a court to hear a case before any other court does.

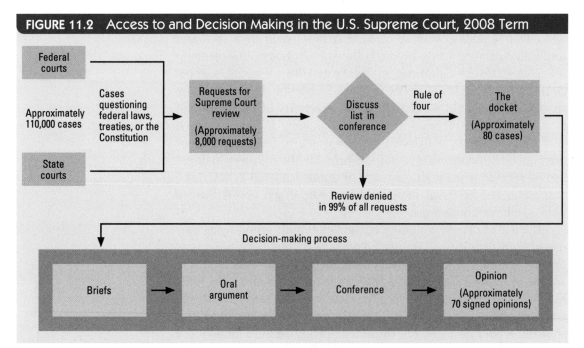

FIGURE 11.2 Access to and Decision Making in the U.S. Supreme Court, 2008 Term

State and national appeals courts churn out thousands of decisions each year. Only a fraction ends up on the Supreme Court's docket. This chart sketches the several stages leading to a decision from the High Court.

Source: John Roberts, "The 2009 Year-End Report on the Federal Judiciary," 31 December, 2009, http://www.supremecourt.gov/publicinfo/year-end/2009year-endreport.pdf

falling under the Court's original jurisdiction are tried and decided in the Court itself; the cases begin and end there. For example, the Court is the first and only forum in which legal disputes between states are resolved. Most cases enter the Supreme Court from the U.S. courts of appeals or the state courts of last resort. These cases are within the Court's **appellate jurisdiction.** They have been tried, decided, and reexamined as far as the law permits in other federal or state courts. The Supreme Court exercises judicial power under its appellate jurisdiction because Congress gives it the authority to do so. Congress may change (and perhaps eliminate) the Court's appellate jurisdiction. This is a powerful but rarely used weapon in the congressional arsenal of checks and balances.

Litigants in state cases who invoke the Court's appellate jurisdiction must satisfy two conditions. First, the case must reach the end of the line in the state court system. Litigants cannot jump at will from state to federal arenas of justice. Second, the case must raise a **federal question,** an issue covered under the Constitution, federal laws, or national treaties. However, even most cases that meet these conditions do not reach the Supreme Court.

Since 1925, the Court has exercised substantial (today, nearly complete) control over its **docket,** or agenda. The Court selects a handful of cases (fewer than one hundred) for consideration from the seven thousand or more requests filed each year. These requests take the form of petitions for *certiorari,* in which a litigant seeking review asks the Court "to become informed" of the lower-court proceedings. For the vast majority of cases, the Court denies the petition for *certiorari,* leaving the decision of the lower court undisturbed. No explanations accompany cases that are denied review, so they have little or no value as Court rulings.

The Court grants a review only when four or more justices agree that a case warrants full consideration. This unwritten rule is known as the **rule of four.** With advance preparation by their law clerks, who screen petitions and prepare summaries, all nine justices make these judgments at conferences held twice a week.[26] During these conferences, justices vote on previously argued cases and consider which new cases to add to the docket.

Business cases represent a substantial portion of the Court's docket, though they receive far less attention than cases addressing social issues such as the death penalty, affirmative action, or school prayer. Business disputes are less emotional and the issues more technical. But business cases involve billions of dollars, have enormous consequences for the economy, and affect people's lives

appellate jurisdiction
The authority of a court to hear cases that have been tried, decided, or reexamined in other courts.

federal question
An issue covered by the U.S. Constitution, national laws, or U.S. treaties.

docket
A court's agenda.

rule of four
An unwritten rule that requires at least four justices to agree that a case warrants consideration before it is reviewed by the Supreme Court.

more often than the social issues that tend to dominate public debate and discussion.[27]

The Solicitor General

Why does the Court decide to hear certain cases but not others? The best evidence scholars have adduced suggests that agenda setting depends on the individual justices, who vary in their decision-making criteria and the issues raised by the cases. Occasionally, justices weigh the ultimate outcome of a case when granting or denying review. At other times, justices grant or deny review based on disagreement among the lower courts or because delay in resolving the issues would impose alarming economic or social costs.[28] The solicitor general plays a vital role in the Court's agenda setting.

The **solicitor general** represents the national government before the Supreme Court. Appointed by the president, the solicitor general is the third-highest-ranking official in the U.S. Department of Justice (after the attorney general and the deputy attorney general). The solicitor general's duties include determining whether the government should appeal lower-court decisions; reviewing and modifying, when necessary, the briefs filed in government appeals; and deciding whether the government should file an **amicus curiae brief*** in any appellate court.[29] The objective is to create a cohesive program for the executive branch in the federal courts. Solicitors general are a "formidable force" in the setting of the Supreme Court's agenda.[30] Their influence in bringing cases to the Court and arguing them there has earned the solicitor general the informal title of "the tenth justice."

Decision Making

Once the Court grants review, attorneys submit written arguments (briefs). Oral arguments, limited to thirty minutes for each side, usually follow. From October through April, the justices spend two to three hours a day, five or six days a month, hearing arguments. They reach no collective decision at oral argument. A tentative decision is reached only after they have met in conference.

solicitor general
The third-highest-ranking official of the U.S. Department of Justice, and the one who represents the national government before the Supreme Court.

amicus curiae brief
A brief filed (with the permission of the court) by an individual or group that is not a party to a legal action but has an interest in it.

Amicus curiae is Latin for "friend of the court." Amicus briefs can be filed with the consent of the Court. They allow groups and individuals who are not parties to the litigation but have an interest in it to influence the Court's thinking and, perhaps, its decision.

Only the justices attend the Court's Wednesday and Friday conferences. After the justices shake hands, the chief justice begins the presentation of each case with a discussion of it and his vote, which is followed by a discussion and vote from each of the other justices, in order of their seniority on the Court. As Justice Antonin Scalia once remarked, "To call our discussion of a case a conference is really something of a misnomer. It's much more a statement of the views of each of the nine Justices, after which the totals are added and the case is assigned" for an opinion.[31] Votes remain tentative until the opinion announcing the Court's judgment is issued.

Judicial Restraint and Judicial Activism. How do the justices decide how to vote on a case? According to some scholars, legal doctrines and past decisions explain their votes. This explanation, which is consistent with the majoritarian model, anchors the justices closely to the law and minimizes the contribution of their personal values. This view is embodied in the concept of **judicial restraint**, which maintains that legislators, not judges, should make the laws. Judges are said to exercise judicial restraint when they defer to the decisions of elected representatives. Other scholars contend that the value preferences and resulting ideologies of the justices provide a more powerful interpretation of their voting.[32] This view is embodied in the concept of **judicial activism**, which maintains that judges should not give deference to the elected branches but should use their judicial power to promote their preferred social and political goals. Essentially, judges act as activists when they substitute their own judgment for the judgment of the people's representatives. By interjecting personal values into court decisions, activist judging is more consistent with the pluralist model.

Judgment and Argument. The voting outcome is the **judgment**, the decision on who wins and who loses. The justices often disagree, not only on winners and losers but also on the reasons for their judgments. After voting, a justice in the majority must draft an opinion setting out the reasons for their decision. The **argument** is the kernel of the opinion—its logical content, as distinct from facts, rhetoric, and procedure. If all justices agree with the judgment and the reasons supporting it, the opinion is unanimous. Agreement with a judgment for reasons different from those set forth in the majority opinion is called a **concurrence**. Or a justice can **dissent** if she or he disagrees with a judgment. Both concurring and dissenting opinions may be drafted in addition to the majority opinion.

judicial restraint
A judicial philosophy in which judges tend to defer to decisions of the elected branches of government.

judicial activism
A judicial philosophy in which judges tend not to defer to decisions of elected branches of government, resulting in the invalidation or emasculation of those decisions.

judgment
The judicial decision in a court case.

argument
The heart of a judicial opinion; its logical content separated from facts, rhetoric, and procedure.

concurrence
The agreement of a judge with the court's majority decision, for a reason other than the majority reason.

dissent
The disagreement of a judge with a majority decision.

The Opinion. After the conference, the chief justice writes the majority opinion or assigns that responsibility to another justice in the majority. If the chief justice is not in the majority, the writing or assigning responsibility rests with the most senior associate justice in the majority. The writing justice distributes a draft opinion to all the justices, who then read it and circulate their criticisms and suggestions. An opinion may have to be rewritten several times to accommodate colleagues who remain unpersuaded by the draft. Justices can change their votes, and perhaps alter the judgment, at any time before the decision is officially announced.

Justices in the majority frequently try to muffle or stifle dissent in order to encourage institutional cohesion. Since the mid-1940s, however, unity has been more difficult to obtain.[33] Gaining agreement from the justices today is akin to negotiating with nine separate law firms. Nevertheless, the justices must be keenly aware of the slender foundation of their authority, which rests largely on public respect. That respect is tested whenever the Court ventures into areas of controversy. Freedom of speech and religion, racial equality, the right to privacy, and the extent of presidential power have led the Court into controversy in the past half-century.

Strategies on the Court

If we start with the assumption that the justices attempt to stamp their own policy views on the cases they review, we should expect typical political behavior from them. Because the justices are grappling with conflict on a daily basis, they probably have well-defined ideologies that reflect their values.

Scholars and journalists have attempted to pierce the veil of secrecy that shrouds the Court from public view and analyze the justices' ideologies.[34] The beliefs of most justices can be located on the two-dimensional model of political values discussed in Chapter 1 (see Figure 1.2). Liberal justices, such as Ruth Bader Ginsburg, choose freedom over order and equality over freedom. Conservative justices—Antonin Scalia, for example—choose order over freedom and freedom over equality. These choices translate into policy preferences as the justices struggle to win votes or retain coalitions.

As in any other group of people, the justices also vary in intellectual ability, advocacy skills, social graces, temperament, and other characteristics. They argue for the support of their colleagues, offering information in the form of drafts and memoranda to explain the advantages and disadvantages of voting for or against an issue. And the justices make occasional, if not regular, use of friendship, ridicule, and appeals to patriotism to mold their colleagues' views.

The Chief Justice

The chief justice is only one of nine justices, but he has several important functions based on his authority. Apart from his role in forming the docket and directing the Court's conferences, the chief justice can also be a social leader, generating solidarity within the group. Sometimes a chief justice can embody intellectual leadership. The chief justice also can provide policy leadership, directing the Court toward a general policy position.

When presiding at the conference, the chief justice can control the discussion of issues, although independent-minded justices are not likely to acquiesce to his views. Moreover, justices today rarely engage in a debate of the issues in the conference. Rather, they communicate by written memoranda (not e-mail). Members of the Court use their law clerks as ambassadors between justices' chambers and, in effect, "run the Court without talking to one another."[35]

Judicial Recruitment

Neither the Constitution nor national law imposes formal requirements for appointment to the federal courts. Once appointed, district court and appeals judges must reside in the district or circuit to which they are appointed. The president appoints judges to the federal courts, and all nominees must be confirmed by the Senate. Congress sets, but cannot lower, a judge's compensation.

State courts operate somewhat similarly. Governors appoint judges in more than half the states, often in consultation with judicial nominating commissions. In many of these states, voters decide whether judges should be retained in office. In some states, nominees must be confirmed by the state legislature. Contested elections for judgeships are relatively unusual, but in 2010, there were thirty-four state supreme court seats up for grabs in contestable elections throughout the United States. Given the emphasis in federal courts on an independent judiciary free of electoral pressures and perceived conflicts of interest, it should come as no surprise that there are many critics of state judicial elections.[36] In most other countries, judges are appointed, not elected (see "Compared with What? Selecting Judges Around the World").

Compared with What?

Selecting Judges Around the World

In at least half of the U.S. states, judges run for election. In fact, nearly 90 percent of all state judges face the voters. This practice is in stark contrast to the rest of the world, where judges are appointed, either by the executive branch (with or without recommendations from a judicial selection commission), by the judicial selection commission itself, or by the legislative branch. In a few countries the civil service offers a professional career path leading to a judgeship. In these countries judges are selected through examinations and school programs. In only two nations—Switzerland and Japan—judicial elections hold sway, but only in a very limited way: (1) Some smaller Swiss cantons (subnational units) elect judges, and (2) appointed justices of the Japanese Supreme Court may face retention elections, though scholars regard the practice as a mere formality. Hans A. Linde, a retired justice of the Oregon Supreme Court, captured the essence of the American exception when he observed, "To the rest of the world, American adherence to judicial elections is as incomprehensible as our rejection of the metric system."

The table here shows the judicial selection process used in countries around the world. Some countries use more than one method; the table lists the primary one.

Executive Appointment without Commission	Executive Appointment with Commission	Appointment by Commission	Legislative Appointment	Career Judiciary
Afghanistan	Albania	Algeria	China	Czech Republic
Argentina	Canada	Andorra	Cuba	France
Australia	Dominican Republic	Angola	Laos	Germany
Bangladesh	England	Bulgaria	Macedonia	Italy
Belarus	Greece	Croatia	Montenegro	Japan
Belgium	Namibia	Cyprus		Poland
Cambodia	Russia	Israel		Portugal
Chad	Scotland	Lebanon		Spain
Egypt	South Africa	Mexico		Turkey
New Zealand	Ukraine	Rwanda		
Uzbekistan	Zimbabwe	Yemen		

Source: Based on Adam Liptak, "American Exception: Rendering Justice, with One Eye on Re-election," *New York Times*, 25 May 2008, http://www.nytimes.com/2008/05/25/us/25exception.html?pagewanted=1&_r=1.

The Appointment of Federal Judges

The Constitution states that federal judges hold their commission "during good Behaviour," which in practice means for life.* A president's judicial appointments, then, are likely to survive his administration, providing a kind of political legacy. The appointment power assumes that the president is free to identify candidates and appoint judges who favor his policies.

Judicial vacancies occur when sitting judges resign, retire, or die. Vacancies also arise when Congress creates new judgeships to handle increasing caseloads. In both cases, the president nominates a candidate, who must be confirmed by the Senate. The president has the help of the Justice Department, which screens candidates before the formal nomination, subjecting serious contenders to FBI investigation. The White House and the Justice Department have formed a Judicial Selection Committee as part of this vetting process. The White House and the Senate vie for control in the appointment of district and appeals judges.

The "Advice and Consent" of the Senate. For district and appeals vacancies, a practice called **senatorial courtesy** forces presidents to share the nomination power with members of the Senate. The Senate will not confirm a nominee who is opposed by the senior senator from the nominee's state if that senator is a member of the president's party. The Judicial Selection Committee searches for acceptable candidates and polls the appropriate senator for her or his reaction to them. The Senate does not actually reject the candidate. Instead, the chair of the Senate Judiciary Committee, which reviews all judicial nominees, will not schedule a confirmation hearing, effectively killing the nomination.

The Senate Judiciary Committee conducts a hearing for each judicial nominee. The chair exercises a measure of control in the appointment process that goes beyond senatorial courtesy. If a nominee is objectionable to the chair, he or she can delay a hearing or hold up other appointments until the president and the Justice Department find an alternative.

The American Bar Association. The American Bar Association (ABA), the biggest organization of lawyers in the United States,

senatorial courtesy
A practice whereby the Senate will not confirm for a lower federal court judgeship a nominee who is opposed by the senior senator in the president's party in the nominee's state.

*As of 2010, fourteen federal judges have been impeached. Of these, seven were convicted in the Senate and removed from office. Judge Thomas Porteous was impeached by the House in 2010; his trial is pending in the Senate.

Justice Thomas & Company

Justice Clarence Thomas meets with his law clerks in his chambers at the Supreme Court. Justices assign a range of responsibilities to their clerks, from memo preparation to opinion drafting. The typical clerkship lasts a year, though it may seem longer at times because of the demanding work schedule. Despite the absence of overtime pay, there is no shortage of applications from the best graduates of the best law schools.

(© David Hume Kennerly/Getty Images)

has been involved in evaluating candidates for the federal bench since 1946.[37] Its role is defined by custom, not law. The ABA's Standing Committee on the Federal Judiciary routinely rates the professional qualifications of prospective appointees, using a three-value scale: "well qualified," "qualified," and "not qualified." The association does not always have advance notice of nominees. The George W. Bush administration considered the ABA too liberal, posing an unnecessary impediment to the confirmation of conservative judges.[38] President Obama restored the ABA's prenomination review in March 2009.

Recent Presidents and the Federal Judiciary

Since the presidency of Jimmy Carter, presidents have tended to make appointments to the federal courts that are more diverse in racial, ethnic, and gender terms than in previous administrations.

President Bill Clinton took the lead on diversity. For the first time in history, more than half of a president's judicial appointments were women or minorities. In his first term in office, George W. Bush appointed more Hispanics to the bench (9 percent) than any of his predecessors. Twenty-two percent of the president's confirmed judicial nominees were women.[39]

The racial and ethnic composition of the parties themselves helps to explain much of the variation between the appointments of presidents of different parties. It seems clear that political ideology, not demographics, lies at the heart of judicial appointments. A review of more than 25,000 federal court decisions from 1968 to 1995 concluded that Carter-appointed judges were the most liberal, whereas judges appointed by Ronald Reagan and George H. W. Bush were the least liberal.[40] George W. Bush's judges are among the most conservative when it comes to civil rights and civil liberties.[41] One general rule seems clear: presidents like to appoint judges who share similar values.

Appointment to the Supreme Court

The president is not shackled by senatorial courtesy when it comes to nominating a Supreme Court justice. However, appointments to the Court attract more intense public scrutiny than do lower-level appointments, effectively narrowing the president's options and focusing attention on the Senate's advice and consent.

Presidents have sent the Senate 160 nominations for the Supreme Court, including nominations for the chief justice. Of these nominations, 124 were confirmed by the Senate (though 7 of those ultimately declined to serve). Eleven names were withdrawn, and the other 25 failed to receive Senate confirmation.[42] The most important factor in the rejection of a nominee is partisan politics.

Nineteen of the twenty-six successful Supreme Court nominees since 1950 have had prior judicial experience in federal or state courts. This tendency toward "promotion" from within the judiciary may be based on the idea that judges' previous opinions are good predictors of their future opinions on the Supreme Court. After all, a president is handing out a powerful lifetime appointment; it makes sense to want an individual who is sympathetic to his views.

In the 2006 term—the first full term with George W. Bush appointees John Roberts and Samuel Alito on the bench—the Court moved in a decidedly conservative direction. One-third of all the cases were decided by a vote of 5–4, almost triple the proportion of close votes from the previous term. In each case, Justice Anthony Kennedy cast the deciding vote. He joined the majority in all twenty-four 5–4 decisions, siding more often with his conservative colleagues. In fact, Kennedy has been in the majority more than any other justice since joining the court in 1988.[43]

The retirement of Justice David H. Souter in the summer of 2009 gave President Obama the opportunity to appoint federal judge Sonia Sotomayor of New York to the Supreme Court. Sotomayor, the first Latina to be nominated to the Court, possessed a sterling résumé with a compelling personal story. Raised by her widowed mother in a Bronx housing project, Sotomayor went on to distinction at Yale Law School. She spent years as a federal prosecutor and in private legal practice before she was appointed by Republican president George H. W. Bush to the federal district court in 1992. President Bill Clinton appointed her to the federal appellate court in 1998.

Republicans on the Senate Judiciary Committee tried to derail Sotomayor's nomination, pouring over everything she had written or said. Some senators focused on a comment she made in 2001, that "a wise Latina woman . . . would more often than not reach a better conclusion than a white male who hasn't lived that life."[44] Sotomayor deflected the attacks and stuck to her well-rehearsed script, declaring that her core guiding principle was "fidelity to the law." In the end, she was confirmed by a vote of 68 to 31, largely along party lines.

Liberal justice John Paul Stevens retired in the summer of 2010, giving President Obama the opportunity to nominate Elena Kagan, his solicitor general, to the Supreme Court. In a departure from recent practice, Obama did not find his choice in the minor leagues of the federal judiciary. Rather, Kagan made her mark as a law professor and law school administrator (and a coveted clerkship with Supreme Court Justice Thurgood Marshall). Lacking the typical paper trail of controversial judicial decisions authored by most nominees, during confirmation hearings senators sought unsuccessfully to elicit evidence of Kagan's likely positions on controversial issues likely to come before the Supreme Court. Though many challenged her lack of judicial experience and her decision as Dean of Harvard Law School to limit the access of military recruiters on campus, the Senate approved Kagan 63–37 in a largely partisan vote. Having served as President Obama's solicitor general, Kagan recused herself from several cases she worked on when the Court heard them during her first term.

The Consequences of Judicial Decisions

Of all the lawsuits begun in the United States, the overwhelming majority end without a court judgment. Many civil cases are settled, or the parties give up, or the courts dismiss the suits because they are beyond the legitimate bounds of judicial resolution. Most criminal cases end with a plea bargain, the defendant's admission of guilt in exchange for a less severe punishment. Only about 10 percent of criminal cases in the federal district courts are tried; an equally small percentage of civil cases are adjudicated.

Furthermore, the fact that a judge sentences a criminal defendant to ten years in prison or a court holds a company liable for $11 billion in damages does not guarantee that the defendant will lose his or her freedom or the company will give up any assets. In the cases of criminal defendants, the road of appeal following trial and conviction is well traveled, and if it accomplishes nothing else, an appeal delays the day when a defendant must go to prison. In civil cases as well, an appeal may be filed to delay the day of reckoning.

Supreme Court Rulings: Implementation and Impact

When the Supreme Court makes a decision, it relies on others to implement it, to translate policy into action. How a judgment is implemented rests in good measure on how it was crafted. Remember that the justices, in preparing their opinions, must work to hold their majorities together to gain greater, if not unanimous, support for their arguments. This forces them to compromise in their opinions and to moderate their arguments, and it introduces ambiguity into many of the policies they articulate. Ambiguous opinions affect the implementation of policy. For example, when the Supreme Court issued its order in 1955 to desegregate public school facilities "with all deliberate speed,"[45] judges who opposed the Court's policy dragged their feet in implementing it.

Because the Supreme Court confronts issues freighted with deeply felt social values or fundamental political beliefs, its decisions have an impact beyond the immediate parties in a dispute. The Court's decision in *Roe* v. *Wade* legalizing abortion generated heated public reaction. Groups opposing abortion vowed to overturn the decision; groups favoring the freedom to obtain an abortion

Which Way to the Entrance?

Chief Justice John G. Roberts, Jr., walks down the west steps of the Supreme Court with the newest associate justice, Elena Kagan. Until 2010, this was the primary entrance for visitors to the Court, who walked under the motto "Equal Justice Under Law" as they entered the Great Hall of the Court. Visitors were barred from entering through the bronze doors for security reasons and must now enter through a much smaller side doorway, where they go through a security screening process.

(© PAUL J. RICHARDS/AFP/Getty Images)

moved to protect the right they had won. Within eight months of the decision, more than two dozen constitutional amendments had been introduced in Congress, but none managed to carry the extraordinary majority required for passage.

Public Opinion and the Supreme Court

Democratic theorists have a difficult time reconciling a commitment to representative democracy with a judiciary that is not accountable to the electorate yet has the power to undo legislative and executive acts. This difficulty may simply be a problem for theorists, however. Policies coming from the Supreme Court, though lagging years behind public opinion, rarely seem out of line with the public's ideological choices.[46] Surveys in several controversial areas reveal that the Court seldom departs from majority sentiment or trends.[47]

"What history shows," wrote Professor Barry Friedman in the most recent and thorough study in this area, "is assuredly not that Supreme Court decisions always are in line with popular opinion, but rather that they come into line with one another over time."[48] That alignment has yet to materialize nearly five decades later on the issue of school prayer, since the Court struck down the recitation of a nondenominational public school prayer in 1961.[49] A majority of Americans then and now do not agree with the Court's position. And so long as much of the public continues to want prayer in schools, the controversy will continue.

However, as recently as 2009, the Gallup Poll showed that nearly six out of ten Americans are much more likely to approve than disapprove of the job the Supreme Court is doing.[50] Following the 2000 presidential election, polling organizations documented a large gap in the Court's approval ratings between Democrats and Republicans. Oddly, the gap flip-flopped in 2009. Court approval surged for Democrats and declined for Republicans even as the Court continued its conservative direction.[51]

The Courts and Models of Democracy

How far should judges stray from existing statutes and precedents? Supporters of the majoritarian model argue that judges must refrain from injecting their own values into their decisions. If the law places too much (or not enough) emphasis on equality or order, the elected legislature, not the courts, can change the law. In contrast, those who support the pluralist model maintain that the courts are a policymaking branch of government. It is thus legitimate for the individual values and interests of judges to mirror group interests and preferences and for judges to consciously attempt to advance group interests as they see fit. However, when, where, and how to proceed are difficult for judges at all levels to determine.

The argument that our judicial system fits the pluralist model gains support from a legal procedure called a **class action**. A class

class action
A procedure by which similarly situated litigants may be heard in a single lawsuit.

action is a device for assembling the claims or defenses of similarly situated individuals so that they can be tried in a single lawsuit. A class action makes it possible for people with small individual claims and limited financial resources to aggregate their claims and resources in order to make a lawsuit viable. Since the 1940s, class action suits have been the vehicles through which groups have asserted claims involving civil rights, legislative apportionment, and environmental problems. For example, schoolchildren have sued (through their parents) under the banner of class action to rectify claimed racial discrimination by school authorities, as in *Brown v. Board of Education.*

Abetting the class action is the resurgence of state supreme courts' fashioning policies consistent with group preferences. State courts may serve as the staging areas for legal campaigns to change the law in the nation's highest court. They also exercise substantial influence over policies that affect citizens daily, including the rights and liberties enshrined in their state constitutions, statutes, and common law.[52]

Furthermore, a state court can avoid review by the U.S. Supreme Court by basing its decision solely on state law or by plainly stating that its decision rests on both state and federal law. If a state court chooses to rely solely on national law in deciding a case, that case is reviewable by the U.S. Supreme Court. If the U.S. Supreme Court is likely to render a restrictive view of a constitutional right and the judges of a state court are inclined toward a more expansive view, the state judges can use the state ground to avoid Supreme Court review. In a period when the nation's highest court is moving in a conservative direction, some state courts have become safe havens for liberal values.

When judges reach decisions, they pay attention to the views of other courts, and not just courts above them in the judicial hierarchy. State and federal court opinions are the legal storehouse from which judges regularly draw their ideas. Often the issues that affect individual lives—property, family, contracts—are grist for state courts, not federal courts. State courts have become arenas for political conflict with litigants, individually or in groups, vying for their preferred policies. The multiplicity of the nation's court system, with overlapping state and federal responsibilities, provides alternative points of access for individuals and groups to present and argue their claims. This description of the courts fits the pluralist model of government.

Tying It Together

1. What is the concept of judicial review, and how did it come about?
   - The Constitution initially established only the Supreme Court.
     - Congress gave life to a federal court system in the Judiciary Act of 1789.
     - *Marbury* v. *Madison* established the Supreme Court's power of judicial review: the power to declare congressional acts invalid if they violate the Constitution.
   - Judicial review checks the power of the elected branches in the name of the Constitution and gives the Supreme Court power over state laws that conflict with the Constitution, national laws, and federal treaties.
   - Mechanisms exist to override judicial review: constitutional amendment and impeachment of justices.
   - The components of judicial review include
     - the power of the courts to declare laws invalid if they violate the Constitution.
     - the supremacy of national laws or treaties when they conflict with state or local laws.
     - the role of the Supreme Court as the final authority on the Constitution.

2. How is the American court system organized at the national and state levels?
   - Judges make policy by
     - reviewing rules from prior decisions, known as common or judge-made law.
     - interpreting legislative acts, known as statutory construction.
     - considering relevant opinions from higher courts.
   - Federal courts are organized in three tiers: U.S. district courts (trial courts where litigation begins), U.S. courts of appeals, and the U.S. Supreme Court.
   - U.S. district courts
     - are the entry point to the federal court system and exist in all states.
     - have judges or magistrates hearing four types of trials: (1) federal criminal cases in violation of national law; (2) civil cases brought

by individuals, groups, or government in violation of national law; (3) civil cases brought against the national government; (4) civil cases between citizens of different states when the controversy exceeds $75,000.

- The U.S. courts of appeals
  - hear any case appealed through the U.S. district courts system or based on decisions of federal administrative agencies.
  - are organized into twelve geographic areas known as circuits.
  - review past rulings and procedures of lower courts.
  - interpret the meaning of the Constitution, which acts as a precedent for future cases (known as *stare decisis*).
  - ensure uniformity within the circuit in the application of national law.

3. How does the Supreme Court reach decisions?
   - Specific rules of access must be followed to bring a case before the Court.
     - Very few cases arrive under the Court's original jurisdiction. Those that affect ambassadors, public ministers and consuls, or disputes among states are tried in the Court itself.
     - Most cases arrive through the Court's appellate jurisdiction.
   - The Court hears only those cases that four or more justices agree warrant full consideration (the rule of four).
   - The solicitor general represents the national government before the Supreme Court and influences which cases are heard.
   - Judges sometimes embrace the principle of judicial restraint when making decisions (so that personal values are minimized) or the principle of judicial activism (in which judges interpret laws loosely, promoting their personal goals).
   - The chief justice's functions are to
     - form the docket and direct Court conferences.
     - be a social leader, intellectual leader, or policy leader.
     - preside at conferences and control the discussion of issues.

4. How are judges appointed to the courts?
   - With the help of the Justice Department, the president appoints judges to the federal courts with confirmation by the Senate.
   - For federal district and appeals court vacancies, the president is forced to share nomination power with the Senate (senatorial courtesy).
   - The Senate Judiciary Committee conducts hearings and can influence the process.

- In more than half of state courts, governors appoint judges, who are then approved by judicial nominating commissions. In some states, judges and even state supreme court justices are elected in contested partisan elections.

5. How are judicial rulings implemented, and what is their effect on public opinion?
   - Most criminal cases end with a plea bargain.
   - The Supreme Court relies on others to implement its decisions.
   - The Supreme Court seldom influences public opinion, as it enjoys only moderate popularity with the public.

6. Do the courts reflect the majoritarian or pluralist model of democracy?
   - The majoritarian model suggests that judges should refrain from injecting their own values into their decisions and that law should be changed by the elected legislature.
   - The pluralist model
     - suggests that as the courts are policymaking branches of government, it is legitimate for judges to vote their values and to consciously attempt to advance group interests.
     - supports the judicial system because of the opportunity for class action.
   - The multiplicity of courts provides many access points for citizens to influence government.

Test Prepper 11.1

National Judicial Supremacy

True or False?
1. The Supreme Court can use its power of judicial review to invalidate laws that violate the Constitution.
2. The Judiciary Act of 1789 determined that federal court rulings would be superior to those of state courts.
3. Chief Justice John Marshall's opinion in *Marbury* v. *Madison* (1803) was the first exercise of judicial review to strike down a national law.

Comprehension
4. Why might the Supreme Court's ability to invalidate unconstitutional laws be construed as undemocratic?
5. Name two strategies for overriding judicial review.

The Organization of Courts

True or False?

1. Litigants file nearly all cases in the federal courts.
2. When a court adjudicates a case, it means the case will be retried at a higher court.
3. The principle of *stare decisis* refers to the bias in favor of precedents, or previously made court decisions, when trying future cases.

Comprehension

4. What differentiates a criminal case from a civil case?
5. What are the three levels of the U.S. federal court system?

The Supreme Court

True or False?

1. The solicitor general represents the federal government before the Supreme Court and influences the Court's agenda.
2. The person who directs the discussion at the Supreme Court's judicial conference is the solicitor general.

Comprehension

3. What is the "rule of four"?
4. When may a state case be brought before the U.S. Supreme Court?

Judicial Recruitment

True or False?

1. Before the president nominates a person to serve as a federal judge, he or she is screened by the Justice Department and is investigated by the FBI.
2. Senatorial courtesy means that when the Senate cannot decide which judge to appoint for a district or appeals court, that body passes the decision to the president.

Comprehension

3. What does the Constitution mean in stating that federal judges hold their commission "during good Behaviour"?
4. How are appointments to state courts similar and different from appointments to federal courts?

The Consequences of Judicial Decisions

True or False?

1. Most lawsuits in the United States end in a court ruling.
2. A plea bargain is a defendant's appeal to retry the case at a higher level of court.

Comprehension

3. How do Supreme Court rulings usually relate to public opinion?
4. Why do justices on the Supreme Court have to compromise when drafting an opinion?

The Courts and Models of Democracy

True or False?

1. Class action lawsuits give individuals a means to assemble their claims or defenses about a similar situation to be heard in a single lawsuit.
2. Supporters of the majoritarian judiciary model maintain that judges should inject their personal values into their decision-making process.
3. A state court can avoid review by the U.S. Supreme Court by basing its decision solely on state law or by clearly stating it based its decision on both state law and federal law.

Comprehension

4. What is the pluralist notion of judicial responsibility?
5. How was a class action lawsuit used in *Brown* v. *Board of Education*?

CourseMate CL Resources:

Visit www.cengagebrain.com/shop/ISBN/1111832587 for flashcards, web quizzes, videos and more!

Order and Civil Liberties

© Michael Greenlar/The Image Works

FOCUS QUESTIONS

1. How has the Bill of Rights evolved?
2. In what ways does the First Amendment guarantee freedom of religion?
3. How does the First Amendment guarantee freedom of speech?
4. What right does the Second Amendment protect?
5. How does the Constitution limit states with regard to citizens' rights?
6. How does the Ninth Amendment protect citizens?

The Pledge of Allegiance has been part of classroom culture since 1892, when President Benjamin Harrison issued a proclamation celebrating the 400th anniversary of Christopher Columbus's discovery of America. In January 2010, a middle school student in Germantown, Maryland, was sent to a school counselor's office and threatened with detention after she refused to stand, salute, and say the Pledge of Allegiance. She returned to school the next day and again refused to participate and was escorted to the counselor's office by two school police officers. Her mother objected, demanding an apology from the teacher. He refused. The assistant principal countered, suggesting that the student apologize to the teacher. As a last straw, the mother contacted the local chapter of the American Civil Liberties Union (ACLU).[1]

The ACLU intervened, explaining that the law has been crystal clear since 1943 when the U.S. Supreme Court ruled that students with religious objections are not required to recite the Pledge or salute the flag.[2] Subsequent decisions have clarified further that a student's rights to free expression—as well as freedom from forced expression—are protected by the Constitution, regardless of the source of a student's beliefs.[3] This student exercised her freedom of expression, though to be more exact, it was her freedom not to speak or participate that was at issue. But the price of her exercise was steep: she was humiliated and embarrassed repeatedly by her Pledge-reciting classmates.[4]

Can school officials suppress or require student expression? More generally, how well do the courts respond to clashes that pit freedom against order in some cases and freedom against equality in others? Are freedom, order, and equality ever unconditional? In this chapter, we explore some value conflicts that the judiciary has resolved. You will be able to judge from the decisions in these cases whether American government has met the challenge of democracy by finding the appropriate balance between freedom and order and between freedom and equality.

The value conflicts described in this chapter revolve around claims or entitlements that rest on law. Although we concentrate on conflicts over constitutional issues, the Constitution is not the only source of people's rights. Government at all levels can—and does—create rights through laws written by legislatures and regulations issued by bureaucracies.

We begin this chapter with the Bill of Rights and the freedoms it protects. Then we take a closer look at the role of the First Amendment in the original conflict between freedom and order. Next we explore how the Bill of Rights applies to the states under the Fourteenth Amendment. Then we examine the Ninth Amendment and its relationship to issues of personal autonomy.

The Bill of Rights

You may remember from Chapter 2 that the omission of a bill of rights was the most important obstacle to the adoption of the Constitution by the states. Eventually the First Congress approved twelve amendments and sent them to the states for ratification. In 1791, ten were ratified, and the nation had a bill of rights.

The Bill of Rights imposed limits on the national government but not on the state governments.* During the next seventy-seven years, litigants pressed the Supreme Court to extend the amendments' restraints to the states, but the Court refused until well after the adoption of the Fourteenth Amendment in 1868. Before then, protection from repressive state government had to come from state bills of rights.

The U.S. Constitution guarantees Americans numerous liberties and rights. In this chapter, we explore several of them. We will define and distinguish between *civil liberties* and *civil rights* (although on some occasions, we use the terms interchangeably). **Civil liberties** are freedoms that are guaranteed to the individual. The guarantees take the form of restraints on government. For

civil liberties
Freedoms guaranteed to individuals.

---

*Congress considered more than one hundred amendments in its first session. One that was not approved would have limited the power of the states to infringe on the rights of conscience, speech, press, and jury trial in criminal cases. James Madison thought this amendment was the "most valuable" of the list, but it failed to muster a two-thirds vote in the Senate.

example, the First Amendment declares that "Congress shall make no law . . . abridging the freedom of speech." Civil liberties declare what the government cannot do. In contrast, civil rights declare what the government must do or provide.

Civil rights are powers or privileges that are guaranteed to the individual and protected against arbitrary removal at the hands of the government or other individuals. The right to vote and the right to a jury trial in criminal cases are civil rights embedded in the Constitution. Today, civil rights also embrace laws that further certain values. The Civil Rights Act of 1964, for example, furthered the value of equality by establishing the right to nondiscrimination in places of public accommodation and the right to equal employment opportunity.

The Bill of Rights lists both civil liberties and civil rights. When we refer to the "rights and liberties" of the Constitution, we mean the protections enshrined in the Bill of Rights and the first section of the Fourteenth Amendment.[5] The list includes freedom of religion, freedom of speech and of the press, the right to assemble peaceably and to petition the government, the right to bear arms, the rights of the criminally accused, the requirement of due process, and the equal protection of the laws.

Freedom of Religion

> Congress shall make no law respecting an establishment of religion, or prohibiting the free exercise thereof.

Religious freedom was very important to the colonies, and later to the states. That importance is reflected in its position in the Bill of Rights: the first amendment. The First Amendment guarantees freedom of religion in two clauses: the **establishment clause** prohibits laws establishing religion, and the **free-exercise clause** prevents the government from interfering with the exercise of religion. Together they ensure that the government can neither promote nor inhibit religious beliefs or practices.

At the time of the Constitutional Convention, many Americans, especially in New England, maintained that government could and should foster religion, specifically Protestantism. However, many more Americans agreed that this was an issue for state governments; the national government had no authority to meddle in religious affairs. The religion clauses were drafted in this spirit.[6]

The Supreme Court has refused to interpret the religion clauses definitively. The result is an amalgam of rulings, the cumulative

civil rights
Powers or privileges guaranteed to individuals and protected from arbitrary removal at the hands of government or individuals.

establishment clause
The first clause in the First Amendment, which forbids government establishment of religion.

free-exercise clause
The second clause in the First Amendment, which prevents the government from interfering with the exercise of religion.

effect of which is the idea that freedom to believe is unlimited but freedom to practice a belief can be limited. Religion cannot benefit directly from government actions (for example, government cannot make contributions to churches or synagogues), but it can benefit indirectly from government actions (for example, government can supply books on secular subjects for use in all schools–public, private, and parochial).

The Establishment Clause

The provision that "Congress shall make no law respecting an establishment of religion" bars government sponsorship or support of religious activity. The Supreme Court has consistently held that the establishment clause requires government to maintain a position of neutrality toward religions and maintain that position in cases that involve choices between religion and nonreligion. However, the Court has never interpreted the clause as barring all assistance that incidentally aids religious institutions.

Government Support of Religion. In 1879, the Supreme Court contended, quoting Thomas Jefferson, that the establishment clause erected "a wall of separation between church and state."[7] That wall was breached somewhat in 1947, when the justices upheld a local government program that provided free transportation to parochial school students.[8] The breach seemed to widen in 1968, when the Court held constitutional a government program in which parochial school students borrowed state-purchased textbooks.[9] The objective of the program, reasoned the majority, was to further educational opportunity. The students, not the schools, borrowed the books, and the parents, not the church, realized the benefits.

But in 1971, in *Lemon* v. *Kurtzman,* the Court struck down a state program that would have helped pay the salaries of teachers hired by parochial schools to give instruction in secular subjects.[10] The justices proposed a three-pronged test for determining the constitutionality of government programs and laws under the establishment clause:

- They must have a secular purpose (such as lending books to parochial school students).
- Their primary effect must not be to advance or inhibit religion.
- They must not entangle the government excessively with religion.

A program or law missing any prong would be unconstitutional.

The program at issue in *Lemon* failed on the last ground. To be sure that the secular teachers did not include religious instruction in their lessons, the government would have needed to constantly monitor them. However, in a 1997 test of the establishment clause, the Court held that "a federally funded program providing supplemental, remedial instruction to disadvantaged children on a neutral basis is not invalid under the Establishment Clause when such instruction is given on the premises of sectarian schools by government employees pursuant to a program containing safeguards," such as that of a New York program that, in the eyes of the Court, did not "run afoul of the three primary criteria" cited in *Lemon*.[11]

The issue of neutrality has taken on great significance in recent years. Writing for the Court in *Zelman* v. *Simmons-Harris* (2002), Chief Justice William Rehnquist summarized this principle:

> Where a government aid program is neutral with respect to religion, and provides assistance directly to a broad class of citizens who, in turn, direct government aid to religious schools wholly as a result of their own genuine and independent private choice, the program is not readily subject to challenge under the Establishment Clause.[12]

Using this logic, the Court ruled that it was constitutional for the state of Ohio to provide poor students with tuition vouchers they could use at the school of their choice. In fact, a large number of voucher recipients chose to use the state funds to attend parochial schools, but this was merely an option along with public schools, magnet schools, community schools, and secular private schools.

School Prayer. The Supreme Court has consistently equated organized prayer in public schools with government support of religion. In *Engel* v. *Vitale* (1962), it struck down the daily reading of a twenty-two-word nondenominational prayer in New York's public schools. In the years since that decision, new challenges on the issue of school prayer have continued to find their way to the Supreme Court. In 1985, the Court struck down a series of Alabama statutes requiring a moment of silence for meditation or voluntary prayer in elementary schools.[13] In 1992, the Court ruled 5–4 that public schools may not include nondenominational prayers in graduation ceremonies.[14] By a 6–3 vote, the Court went further in 2000 by striking down the practice of organized, student-led prayer at public high school football games.[15]

Religious training during public school is out of bounds, but this does not mean that students may not participate in religious activities on school property. In 2001 the Supreme Court ruled that public schools must open their doors to after-school religious activities on the same basis as other after-school programs such as the debate club.[16] To do otherwise would constitute viewpoint discrimination in violation of the free speech clause of the First Amendment.

The establishment clause creates a problem for government. Support for all religions at the expense of nonreligion seems to pose the least risk to social order. Tolerance of the dominant religion at the expense of other religions risks minority discontent, but support for no religion (neutrality between religion and nonreligion) risks majority discontent.

The Free-Exercise Clause

The free-exercise clause of the First Amendment states that "Congress shall make no law . . . prohibiting the free exercise [of religion]." The Supreme Court has struggled to avoid absolute interpretations of this restriction so as not to violate its complement, the establishment clause. An example: suppose Congress grants exemptions from military service to individuals who have religious scruples against war. These exemptions could be construed as a violation of the establishment clause because they favor some religious groups over others. But if Congress forces conscientious objectors to fight—to violate their religious beliefs—the government would run afoul of the free-exercise clause. In fact, Congress has granted military draftees such exemptions. But the Supreme Court has avoided a conflict between the establishment and free-exercise clauses by equating religious objection to war with any deeply held humanistic opposition to it.[17]

In the free-exercise cases, the justices have distinguished religious beliefs from actions based on those beliefs. Beliefs are inviolate, beyond the reach of government control. But the First Amendment does not protect antisocial actions. Consider conflicting values about working on the Sabbath and using drugs in religious sacraments.

Working on the Sabbath. The modern era of free-exercise thinking begins with *Sherbert* v. *Verner* (1963). Adeil Sherbert was a Seventh-Day Adventist who was disqualified from receiving unemployment benefits after declining a job that required working on Saturday, which is the Adventist Sabbath. In a 7–2 decision, the Supreme Court

The Eyes Have It

In 2003, Sultaana Freeman wore a veil for her Florida driver's license photo. When Florida officials denied her a license, she took her case to court. Freeman contended that the government interfered with her free exercise of religion, since her Muslim faith requires the wearing of the veil. Florida argued, and prevailed, that the government has a compelling interest in identifying drivers.

(AP Photo/Red Huber, Pool)

ruled that the disqualification imposed an impermissible burden on Sherbert's free exercise of religion. The First Amendment, declared the majority, protected observance as well as belief. A neutral law that burdens the free exercise of religion is subject to **strict scrutiny**. This means the law may be upheld only if the government can demonstrate that the law is justified by a "compelling governmental interest," narrowly tailored, and the least restrictive means for achieving that interest.[18]

Using Drugs as Religious Sacraments. Partaking of illegal substances as part of a religious sacrament forces believers to violate the law. For example, Rastafarians and members of the Ethiopian Zion Coptic Church smoke marijuana in the belief that it is the body and blood of Christ. Taken to an extreme the freedom to practice religion can result in license to engage in illegal conduct. The inevitable result is a clash between religious freedom and social order.

The courts used the compelling-government-interest test for many years and on that basis invalidated most laws restricting free exercise. But in 1990, the Supreme Court abruptly and unexpectedly rejected its longstanding rule, tipping the balance in

strict scrutiny
A standard used by the Supreme Court in deciding whether a law or policy is to be adjudged constitutional. To pass strict scrutiny, the law or policy must be justified by a "compelling governmental interest," must be narrowly tailored, and must be the least restrictive means for achieving that interest.

favor of social order. In *Employment Division* v. *Smith,* two members of the Native American Church sought an exemption from an Oregon law that made the possession or use of peyote a crime.[19] (Peyote is a cactus that contains the hallucinogen mescaline. Native Americans have used it for centuries in their religious ceremonies.) Oregon rejected the two church members' applications for unemployment benefits after they were dismissed from their drug-counseling jobs for using peyote. Oregon believed it had a compelling interest in proscribing the use of certain drugs according to its own drug laws.

Justice Antonin Scalia, writing for the 6–3 majority, examined the conflict between freedom and order through the lens of majoritarian democratic thought. He observed that the Court has never held that an individual's religious beliefs excuse him or her from compliance with an otherwise valid law prohibiting conduct that government is free to regulate. Allowing exceptions to every state law or regulation affecting religion "would open the prospect of constitutionally required exemptions from civic obligations of almost every conceivable kind." Scalia cited as examples compulsory military service, payment of taxes, vaccination requirements, and child-neglect laws. The Court ruled that laws indirectly restricting religious practices are acceptable; only laws aimed at religious groups are constitutionally prohibited.

The political response to *Employment Division* v. *Smith* was an example of pluralism in action. A coalition of religious and nonreligious groups organized to restore the more restrictive strict scrutiny test. The alliance regained in Congress what it had lost in the Supreme Court. In 1993, President Bill Clinton signed into law the Religious Freedom Restoration Act (RFRA). The law once again required federal, state, and local government to satisfy the strict-scrutiny standard before it could institute measures that interfere with religious practices. However, the Supreme Court struck back in 1997, declaring the act's attempt to impose the strict scrutiny standard on states unconstitutional in *City of Boerne* v. *Flores.* The 6–3 Supreme Court decision means that RFRA no longer binds state and local government actions.[20] However, in a unanimous 2006 opinion, the Court upheld RFRA limitations over federal law. The national government sought to control the sacramental use of a hallucinogenic tea by a small religious sect in New Mexico. The Court held that the government was unable to detail a compelling interest in barring the use of the tea under the strict scrutiny that RFRA imposes on federal laws and regulations.[21]

Freedom of Expression

> Congress shall make no law . . . abridging the freedom of
> speech, or of the press; or the right of the people peaceably
> to assemble, and to petition the government for a redress
> of grievances.

James Madison introduced the initial versions of the speech clause
and the press clause of the First Amendment in the House of Representatives in June 1789. One of these proposals was merged with
the religion and peaceable assembly clauses to yield the First
Amendment.

The sparse language of the First Amendment seems perfectly
clear: "Congress shall make no law . . . abridging the freedom of
speech, or of the press." Yet a majority of the Supreme Court has
never agreed that this "most majestic guarantee" is absolutely invio-
lable.[22] Historians have long debated the framers' intentions regarding these **free-expression clauses**. The dominant view is that the
clauses confer the right to unrestricted discussion of public affairs.[23]
Other scholars, examining much the same evidence, conclude that
few, if any, of the framers clearly understood the clause; moreover,
they insist that the First Amendment does not rule out prosecution
for seditious statements (statements inciting insurrection).[24]

Today the clauses are deemed to bar not only most forms of **prior
restraint**—censorship before publication—but also after-the-fact
prosecution for political and other discourse. The Supreme Court
has evolved two approaches to the resolution of claims based on the
free-expression clauses. First, government can regulate or punish the
advocacy of ideas, but only if it can prove an intent to promote lawless action and demonstrate that a high probability exists that such
action will occur.[25] Second, government may impose reasonable
restrictions on the means for communicating ideas, which can incidentally discourage free expression.

Suppose that a political party advocates nonpayment of personal
income taxes. Government cannot regulate or punish that party for
advocating nonpayment, because the standards of proof—that the act
be directed to inciting or producing imminent lawless action and that
the act be judged likely to produce such action—do not apply. But
government can impose restrictions on the way the party's candidates
communicate what they are advocating. Government can bar them
from blaring messages from loudspeakers in residential neighborhoods at 3:00 A.M., for example.

free-expression clauses
The press and speech
clauses of the First
Amendment.

prior restraint
Censorship before
publication.

Freedom of Speech

The starting point for any modern analysis of free speech is the **clear and present danger** test formulated by Justice Oliver Wendell Holmes in the Supreme Court's unanimous decision in *Schenck* v. *United States* (1919). Charles T. Schenck and his fellow defendants were convicted under a federal criminal statute for attempting to disrupt World War I military recruitment by distributing leaflets claiming that conscription was unconstitutional. The government believed this behavior threatened the public order. At the core of the Court's opinion, as Holmes wrote, was the view that

> the character of every act depends upon the circumstances in which it is done. . . . The most stringent protection of free speech would not protect a man in falsely shouting fire in a theatre and causing a panic. . . . The question in every case is whether the words used are used in such circumstances and are of such a nature as to create a *clear and present danger* that they will bring about the substantive evils that Congress has a right to prevent. It is a question of proximity and degree. When a nation is at war many things that might be said in time of peace are such a hindrance to its effort that their utterance will not be endured so long as men fight and that no Court could regard them as protected by any constitutional right. [Emphasis added.][26]

Because the actions of the defendants in *Schenck* were deemed to create a clear and present danger to the United States at that time, the Supreme Court upheld the defendants' convictions. The clear and present danger test helps to distinguish the advocacy of ideas, which is protected, from incitement, which is not.

In 1925, the Court issued a landmark decision in *Gitlow* v. *New York*.[27] Benjamin Gitlow was arrested for distributing copies of a "left-wing manifesto" that called for the establishment of socialism through strikes and class action of any form. Gitlow was convicted under a state criminal anarchy law; Schenck had been convicted under a federal law. For the first time, the Court assumed that the First Amendment speech and press provisions applied to the states through the due process clause of the Fourteenth Amendment. Still, a majority of the justices affirmed Gitlow's conviction.

The protection of advocacy faced yet another challenge in 1948, when eleven members of the Communist Party were charged with violating the Smith Act, a federal law making the advocacy of force or violence against the United States a criminal offense. The leaders were convicted, although the government introduced

clear and present danger test
A means by which the Supreme Court has distinguished between speech as the advocacy of ideas, which is protected by the First Amendment, and speech as incitement, which is not protected.

no evidence that they actually had urged people to commit specific violent acts. The Supreme Court mustered a majority for its decision to uphold the convictions under the Smith Act, but it could not get a majority to agree on the reasons in support of that decision. Four justices announced the plurality opinion in 1951, arguing that the government's interest was substantial enough to warrant criminal penalties.[28] The justices interpreted the threat to government to be the gravity of the advocated action "discounted by its improbability." In other words, a single soap-box orator advocating revolution stands a low chance of success, and a well-organized, highly disciplined political movement advocating revolution in the tinderbox of unstable political conditions stands a greater chance of success. In broadening the meaning of "clear and present danger," the Court held that the government was justified in acting preventively rather than waiting until revolution was about to occur.

By 1969, the pendulum had swung back in the other direction. That year, in *Brandenburg* v. *Ohio,* a unanimous decision extended the freedom of speech to new limits.[29] Clarence Brandenburg, the leader of the Ohio Ku Klux Klan, had been convicted under a state law for advocating racial strife at a Klan rally. His comments, filmed by a television crew, included threats against government officials. The Court reversed Brandenburg's conviction because the government had failed to prove that the danger was real. The Court went even further and declared that threatening speech is protected by the First Amendment unless the government can prove that such advocacy is "directed to inciting or producing imminent lawless action and is likely to produce such action."

The United States stands virtually alone when it comes to protection for hateful speech. Several democratic nations—including Canada, England, France, Germany, the Netherlands, South Africa, Australia, and India—have laws or have signed international conventions banning such speech. Nazi swastikas and flags are forbidden for sale in Israel and France but not in the United States. Anyone who denies the Holocaust in Canada, Germany, and France is subject to criminal prosecution but not in the United States. Some scholars have begun to urge a relaxation of our stringent speech protections because we now live "in an age when words have inspired acts of mass murder and terrorism."[30]

Symbolic Expression. Symbolic expression, or nonverbal communication, generally receives less protection than pure speech. But the courts have upheld certain types of symbolic expression. *Tinker* v. *Des*

Moines Independent County School District (1969) involved three public school students who wore black armbands to school to protest the Vietnam War. Principals in their school district had prohibited the wearing of armbands on the grounds that such conduct would provoke a disturbance; the district suspended the students. The Supreme Court overturned the suspensions. Justice Abe Fortas declared for the majority that the principals had failed to show that the forbidden conduct would substantially interfere with appropriate school discipline:

> Undifferentiated fear or apprehension is not enough to overcome the right to freedom of expression. Any departure from absolute regimentation may cause trouble. Any variation from the majority's opinion may inspire fear. Any word spoken, in class, in the lunchroom, or on the campus, that deviates from the views of another person may start an argument or cause a disturbance. But our Constitution says we must take this risk.[31]

The Supreme Court does allow school administrators some leeway in limiting expression advocating the use of illegal drugs. In *Morse* v. *Frederick* (2007), the Court ruled that a principal had the authority to suspend a student who unfurled a banner reading "Bong Hits 4 Jesus" at a school event. Unlike political speech, advocating illegal drug use in school is not protected by the First Amendment.[32]

Free Speech Versus Order: Obscenity. The Supreme Court has always viewed obscene material—words, music, books, magazines, films—as outside the bounds of constitutional protection, which means that states may regulate or even ban obscenity. However, difficulties arise in determining what is obscene and what is not.

In *Miller* v. *California* (1973), its most recent major attempt to clarify constitutional standards governing obscenity, the Court declared that a work—play, film, or book—is obscene and may be regulated by government if (1) the work taken as a whole appeals to prurient interest ("prurient" means having a tendency to excite lustful thoughts), (2) the work portrays sexual conduct in a patently offensive way, and (3) the work taken as a whole lacks serious literary, artistic, political, or scientific value.[33] Local community standards govern application of the first and second prongs of the *Miller* test.

In 1996, Congress passed the Communications Decency Act, which made it a crime for a person knowingly to circulate "patently offensive" sexual material to Internet sites accessible to those under eighteen years old. Is this an acceptable way to protect children from offensive material, or is it a muzzle on free speech? A federal court quickly declared the act unconstitutional. In an opinion of over two hundred pages, the court observed that "just as the strength of the Internet is chaos, so the strength of our liberty depends on the chaos and cacophony of the unfettered speech the First Amendment protects."[34]

The Supreme Court upheld the lower court's ruling in June 1997 in *Reno* v. *ACLU*.[35] The Court's nearly unanimous opinion was a broad affirmation of free speech rights in cyberspace, arguing that the Internet was more analogous to print media than to television, and thus even indecent material on the Internet was entitled to First Amendment protection. Following the *Reno* decision, Congress enacted the Child Online Protection Act (COPA) to achieve similar goals in a more carefully targeted fashion. District and appellate courts granted a preliminary injunction blocking enforcement of the new law, because the law was not the least restrictive means to protect children. In *Ashcroft* v. *ACLU* (2004), the Supreme Court agreed that COPA did not appear to represent the least restrictive means possible for a compelling governmental interest. The Court remanded the case to the lower courts for further consideration, where in *ACLU* v. *Gonzales,* COPA was declared unconstitutional in March 2007, in part because COPA "prohibits much more speech than is necessary to further Congress' compelling interest."[36] However, in 2008 the Supreme Court upheld a national law established to punish those who offered or sought child pornography, whether pornographic materials actually existed or not. In a 7–2 decision written by Associate Justice Antonin Scalia, the Court declared, "We hold that offers to provide or requests to obtain child pornography are categorically excluded from the First Amendment."[37]

Despite the lack of protection for obscenity, the protection of free expression remains quite broad. In 2010 the Supreme Court struck down on free-expression grounds a federal law that banned depictions of animal cruelty. While torturing animals may be illegal, distributing videos of it is not.[38]

Freedom of the Press

The First Amendment guarantees that government "shall make no law . . . abridging the freedom . . . of the press." Although it originally was adopted as a restriction on the national government, since

1931 the Supreme Court has held the free press guarantee to apply to state and local governments as well.

The ability to collect and report information without government interference was (and still is) thought to be essential to a free society. The print media continue to use and defend the freedom conferred on them by the framers. However, the electronic media have had to accept some government regulation stemming from the scarcity of broadcast frequencies (see Chapter 4).

Defamation of Character. Libel is the written defamation of character.* A person who believes his or her name and character have been harmed by false statements in a publication can institute a lawsuit against the publication and seek monetary compensation for the damage. Such a lawsuit can impose limits on freedom of expression; at the same time, false statements impinge on the rights of individuals. In a landmark decision in *New York Times* v. *Sullivan* (1964), the Supreme Court declared that freedom of the press takes precedence—at least when the defamed individual is a public official.[39] The Court unanimously agreed that the First Amendment protects the publication of all statements, even false ones, about the conduct of public officials except when statements are made with actual malice (with knowledge that they are false or in reckless disregard of their truth or falsity). Citing John Stuart Mill's 1859 treatise *On Liberty,* the Court declared that "even a false statement may be deemed to make a valuable contribution to public debate, since it brings about the clearer perception and livelier impression of truth, produced by its collision with error."

Three years later, the Court extended this protection to apply to suits brought by any public figures, whether a government official or not. **Public figures** are people who assume roles of prominence in the affairs of society or thrust themselves to the forefront of public controversy—officials, actors, writers, television personalities, and others. These people must show actual malice on the part of the publisher that prints false statements about them. Because the burden of proof is so great, few plaintiffs prevail.

Prior Restraint and the Press. In the United States, freedom of the press has primarily meant protection from prior restraint, or censorship. The Supreme Court's first encounter with a law imposing

public figures
People who assume roles of prominence in society or thrust themselves to the forefront of public controversy.

---

*Slander is the oral defamation of character. The durability of the written word usually means that libel is a more serious accusation than slander.

prior restraint on a newspaper was in *Near* v. *Minnesota* (1931).[40] In Minneapolis, Jay Near published a scandal sheet in which he attacked local officials, charging that they were in league with gangsters.[41] Minnesota officials obtained an injunction to prevent Near from publishing his newspaper under a state law that allowed such action against periodicals deemed "malicious, scandalous, and defamatory."

The Supreme Court struck down the law, declaring that prior restraint is an unacceptable burden on a free press. Chief Justice Charles Evans Hughes forcefully articulated the need for a vigilant, unrestrained press: "The fact that the liberty of the press may be abused by miscreant purveyors of scandal does not make any the less necessary the immunity of the press from previous restraint in dealing with official misconduct." Although the Court acknowledged that prior restraint may be permissible in exceptional circumstances, it did not specify those circumstances, nor has it yet done so.

Consider another case, which occurred during a war, a time when the tension between government-imposed order and individual freedom is often at a peak. In 1971, Daniel Ellsberg, a special assistant in the Pentagon, delivered portions of a classified U.S. Department of Defense study to the *New York Times* and the *Washington Post*. By making the documents public, he hoped to discredit the Vietnam War and thereby end it. The U.S. Department of Justice sought to restrain the *Times* and the *Post* from publishing the documents, contending that publication would prolong the war and embarrass the government. The case was quickly brought before the Supreme Court.

Three days later, in a 6–3 decision in *New York Times* v. *United States* (1971), the Court concluded that the government had not met the heavy burden of proving that immediate, inevitable, and irreparable harm would follow publication.[42] The majority expressed its view in a brief unsigned opinion; individual and collective concurring and dissenting views added nine opinions to the decision. Two justices maintained that the First Amendment offers absolute protection against government censorship, no matter what the situation. But the other justices left the door ajar for the imposition of prior restraint in the most extreme and compelling of circumstances.

Freedom of Expression Versus Maintaining Order. The courts have consistently held that freedom of the press does not override the requirements of law enforcement. A grand jury called a Louisville, Kentucky, reporter, who had researched and written an article about drug-related activities, and asked him to identify people he had seen in possession of marijuana or in the act of processing it. The reporter refused to testify, maintaining that freedom of the press shielded him from inquiry. In a closely divided decision, the Supreme Court in 1972 rejected this position.[43] The Court declared that no exception exists to the rule that all citizens have a duty to give their government whatever testimony they are capable of giving.[44]

Consider the 1988 case of a St. Louis high school principal who deleted articles on divorce and teenage pregnancy from the school's newspaper on the grounds that the articles invaded the privacy of the individuals who were the focus of the stories.[45] Three student editors claimed that the principal's censorship interfered with the newspaper's function as a public forum, a role protected by the First Amendment. The principal maintained that the newspaper was an extension of classroom instruction and was thus not protected by the First Amendment.

In a 5–3 decision, the Court upheld the principal's actions in sweeping terms. Educators may limit speech within the confines of the school curriculum and speech that might seem to bear the approval of the school, provided their actions serve a "valid educational purpose."

The Rights to Assemble Peaceably and to Petition the Government

The final clause of the First Amendment states that "Congress shall make no law . . . abridging . . . the right of the people peaceably to assemble, and to petition the Government for a redress of grievances." The framers meant that the people have the right to assemble peaceably *in order to* petition the government. Today, however, the right to assemble peaceably is equated with the right of free speech and a free press, independent of whether the government is petitioned. Precedent has merged these rights and made them equally indivisible.[46] Government cannot prohibit peaceful political meetings and cannot brand as criminals those who organize, lead, and attend such meetings.[47]

The Right to Bear Arms

The Second Amendment declares:

> A well-regulated militia being necessary to the security of a free State, the right of the people to keep and bear arms shall not be infringed.

Gun-control advocates assert that the amendment protects the right of the states to maintain *collective* militias. Gun-use advocates assert that the amendment protects the right of *individuals* to own and use guns. There are good arguments on both sides.

Federal firearms regulations did not come into being until Prohibition, so the Supreme Court had little to say on the matter. In 1939, however, a unanimous Court upheld a 1934 federal law requiring the taxation and registration of machine guns and sawed-off shotguns. The Court held that the Second Amendment protects a citizen's right to own ordinary militia weapons; sawed-off shotguns did not qualify for protection.[48]

In 2008, the Court considered whether the Second Amendment protects an individual's right to gun ownership or is simply a right tied to service in a militia. Opponents of gun control challenged the strictest gun-control statute in the country, a District of Columbia law that barred private possession of handguns and required the disassembly or use of trigger locks on rifles and shotguns. In *District of Columbia* v. *Heller,* the Supreme Court struck down the District of Columbia's statute, established gun ownership as an individual right, and clarified that the Second Amendment forbids outright bans on gun ownership. Writing for a 5–4 majority, Associate Justice Antonin Scalia declared that the Second Amendment "surely elevates above all other interests the right of law-abiding, responsible citizens to use arms in defense of hearth and home." Despite the expansive sweep of the decision, Scalia was careful to point out that nothing in the decision overturned previous prohibitions on the "possession of firearms by felons and the mentally ill, or laws forbidding the carrying of firearms in sensitive places such as schools and government buildings, or laws imposing conditions and qualifications on the commercial sale of arms."[49]

In *McDonald* v. *Chicago* (2010) the Court addressed the question of whether the individual right to keep and bear arms should apply to the states. Writing for a 5–4 Court, Justice Alito concluded that the "Framers and ratifiers of the Fourteenth Amendment counted the right to keep and bear arms among those fundamental rights necessary to our system of ordered liberty." Repeating Scalia's caveats in the *Heller* decision, the Court declared the Second Amendment "fully applicable to the states" under the Fourteenth Amendment. While a four-member plurality expressly invoked the language of the due process clause to justify the incorporation, Justice Thomas wrote a concurring opinion in which he argued that the "privileges or immunities clause" of the

Fourteenth Amendment would have been the best justification for the Court's decision.[50]

Applying the Bill of Rights to the States

The major purpose of the Constitution was to structure the division of power between the national government and the state governments. Even before it was amended, the Constitution set some limits on both the nation and the states with regard to citizens' rights. It barred both governments from passing **bills of attainder**, laws that make an individual guilty of a crime without a trial. Both were also prohibited from enacting **ex post facto laws**, laws that declare an action a crime after it has been performed. And it barred both nation and states from impairing the **obligation of contracts**, the obligation of the parties in a contract to carry out its terms.

Although initially the Bill of Rights seemed to apply only to the national government, various litigants pressed the claim that its guarantees also applied to the states. In response to one such claim, Chief Justice John Marshall affirmed that the provisions of the Bill of Rights served only to limit national authority: "Had the framers of these amendments intended them to be limitations on the powers of the state governments," wrote Marshall, "they would have . . . expressed that intention."[51]

Change came with the Fourteenth Amendment, which was adopted in 1868. The due process clause of that amendment is the linchpin that holds the states to the provisions of the Bill of Rights.

The Fourteenth Amendment: Due Process of Law

Section 1 . . .
No State shall make or enforce any law which shall abridge the privileges or immunities of citizens of the United States; nor shall any State deprive any person of life, liberty, or property, without due process of law.

Most freedoms protected in the Bill of Rights today apply as limitations on the states. And many of the standards that limit the national government serve equally to limit state governments. These changes have been achieved through the Supreme Court's interpretation of the due process clause of the Fourteenth Amendment: "nor shall any

bills of attainder
A law that pronounces an individual guilty of a crime without a trial.

ex post facto law
A law that declares an action to be criminal after it has been performed.

obligation of contracts
The obligation of the parties to a contract to carry out its terms.

State deprive any person of life, liberty, or property, without due process of law." The clause has two central meanings. First, it requires the government to adhere to appropriate procedures. Second, it forbids unreasonable government action. The Supreme Court has used the first meaning of the due process clause as a sponge, absorbing or incorporating the procedural specifics of the Bill of Rights and spreading or applying them to the states.

The Fundamental Freedoms

In 1897, the Supreme Court declared that the states are limited by the Fifth Amendment's prohibition on taking private property without providing just compensation.[52] The Court accomplished its goal by absorbing that prohibition into the due process clause of the Fourteenth Amendment, which applies to the states. Thus, one Bill of Rights protection—but only that one—applied to both the states and the national government. In 1925, the Court assumed that the due process clause protected the First Amendment speech and press liberties from impairment by the states.[53]

The inclusion of other Bill of Rights guarantees within the due process clause faced a critical test in *Palko* v. *Connecticut* (1937).[54] Frank Palko had been charged with homicide in the first degree. He was convicted of second-degree murder, however, and sentenced to life imprisonment. The state of Connecticut appealed and won a new trial; this time Palko was found guilty of first-degree murder and sentenced to death. Palko appealed the second conviction on the grounds that it violated the protection against double jeopardy guaranteed to him by the Fifth Amendment. This protection applied to the states, he contended, because of the Fourteenth Amendment's due process clause.

The Supreme Court upheld Palko's second conviction. Justice Benjamin N. Cardozo, in his opinion for the majority, formulated principles that were to direct the Court's actions for the next three decades. He noted that some Bill of Rights guarantees, such as freedom of thought and speech, are fundamental, and that these fundamental rights are absorbed by the Fourteenth Amendment's due process clause and are therefore applicable to the states. These rights are essential, argued Cardozo, because "neither liberty nor justice would exist if they were sacrificed." Trial by jury and other rights, though valuable and important, are not essential to liberty and justice and therefore are not absorbed by the due process clause. "Few would be so narrow or provincial," Cardozo claimed, "as to maintain that a fair and enlightened system of justice would be impossible" without these other rights. In other words, only some provisions of the Bill of Rights—the "fundamental" provisions—were absorbed into the due process clause and made applicable to the states (see Figure 12.1). Because protection against double jeopardy was not one of them, Palko died in Connecticut's gas chamber in April 1938.

The next thirty years saw slow but perceptible change in the standard for determining whether a Bill of Rights guarantee was fundamental. The reference point changed from the idealized "fair and enlightened system of justice" in *Palko* to the more realistic "American scheme of justice" thirty years later.[55] Case after case tested various guarantees that the Court found to be fundamental. By 1969, when *Palko* was finally overturned, the Court had found most of the Bill of Rights applicable to the states.

Criminal Procedure: The Meaning of Constitutional Guarantees

"The history of liberty," remarked Justice Felix Frankfurter, "has largely been the history of observance of procedural safeguards."[56] The safeguards embodied in the Fourth through Eighth Amendments

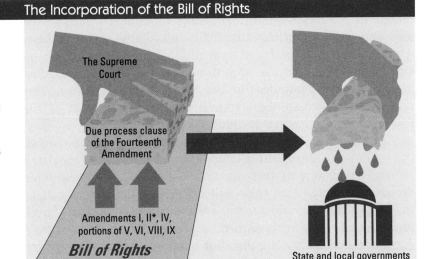

FIGURE 12.1	The Incorporation of the Bill of Rights

The Supreme Court has used the due process clause of the Fourteenth Amendment as a sponge, absorbing most—but not all—of the provisions in the Bill of Rights and applying them to state and local governments. All provisions in the Bill of Rights apply to the national government.

(© Cengage Learning 2013)

The Supreme Court

Due process clause of the Fourteenth Amendment

Amendments I, II*, IV, portions of V, VI, VIII, IX

Bill of Rights

State and local governments

*While a majority of the Court agreed in *McDonald* v. *Chicago* (2010) that the Fourteenth Amendment incorporated the Second Amendment, only a plurality of four cited the due process clause. In a concurring opinion, Justice Thomas wrote that the Second Amendment applied to the states because of the "privileges or immunities" clause of the Fourteenth Amendment.

to the Constitution specify how government must behave in criminal proceedings. Their application to the states has reshaped American criminal justice in the previous four decades in two steps. The first step is the judgment that a guarantee asserted in the Bill of Rights also applies to the states. The second step requires that the judiciary give specific meaning to the guarantee. If the rights are fundamental, their meaning cannot vary from state to state. But life is not quite so simple under the U.S. Constitution. The concept of federalism is sewn into the constitutional fabric, and the Supreme Court recognizes that there may be more than one way to prosecute the accused while heeding fundamental rights.

Consider, for example, the right to a jury trial in criminal cases, which is guaranteed by the Sixth Amendment. This right was made obligatory on the states in *Duncan* v. *Louisiana* (1968). The Supreme Court later held that the right applied to all nonpetty criminal cases—those in which the penalty for conviction was more than six months' imprisonment.[57] But the Court did not require that state juries have twelve members, the number required for federal criminal proceedings. The Court permits jury size to vary from state to state, although it set the minimum number at six. Furthermore, it has not imposed on the states the federal requirement of a unanimous jury verdict.

In contrast, the Court left no room for variation in its definition of the fundamental right to an attorney, also guaranteed by the Sixth Amendment. Clarence Earl Gideon was a penniless vagrant accused of breaking into and robbing a pool hall. Because Gideon could not afford a lawyer, he asked the state to provide him with legal counsel for his trial. The state refused, and Gideon was subsequently convicted and sentenced to five years in the Florida State Penitentiary. From his cell, Gideon appealed to the U.S. Supreme Court, claiming that his conviction should be struck down because the state had denied him his Sixth Amendment right to counsel.[58]

In its landmark decision in *Gideon* v. *Wainwright* (1963), the Court set aside Gideon's conviction and extended to the states the Sixth Amendment right to counsel.[59] The state retried Gideon, who this time had the assistance of a lawyer, and the court found him not guilty. In subsequent rulings that stretched over more than a decade, the Court specified at what points in the course of criminal proceedings a defendant is entitled to a lawyer (from arrest to trial, appeal, and beyond). These pronouncements are binding on all states.

During this period, the Court also came to grips with another procedural issue: informing suspects of their constitutional rights.

Ernesto Miranda was arrested in Arizona in connection with the kidnapping and rape of an eighteen-year-old woman. After the police questioned him for two hours and the woman identified him, Miranda confessed to the crime. An Arizona court convicted him based on that confession—although he was never told he had the right to counsel and the right not to incriminate himself. Miranda appealed his conviction, which the Supreme Court overturned in 1966.[60]

The Court based its decision in *Miranda* v. *Arizona* on the Fifth Amendment privilege against self-incrimination. According to the Court, warnings are necessary to dispel the coercion that is inherent in custodial interrogation without counsel. The Court does not require warnings if a person is only in custody without questioning or subject to questioning without arrest. But in *Miranda,* the Court found the combination of custody and interrogation sufficiently intimidating to require warnings before questioning. These statements are known today as the *Miranda* **warnings.**

- You have the right to remain silent.
- Anything you say can be used against you in court.
- You have the right to talk to a lawyer of your own choice before questioning.
- If you cannot afford to hire a lawyer, a lawyer will be provided without charge.

In one of its most important cases in 2000, the Court reaffirmed this protection in a 7–2 decision, holding that *Miranda* had "announced a constitutional rule" that Congress could not undermine through legislation.[61] In 2004, the Court underscored this status by ruling unconstitutional a police tactic of questioning suspects before they were informed of their *Miranda* rights, and then, after informing suspects of their rights, questioning them again until they obtained the same answers.[62]

However, a suspect's *Miranda* rights are not invoked automatically. In 2010 the Court ruled that police may continue to interrogate a suspect who simply remains silent without "unambiguously invoking" his rights. In *Berghuis* v. *Thompkins,* Justice Kennedy wrote for a 5–4 majority that even after a suspect remains silent for hours of interrogation, an uncoerced statement from that suspect can be considered an implicit waiver of the right to remain silent. In order to end interrogation, suspects must unambiguously state that they wish to remain silent or request that interrogation stop and a lawyer be provided.[63]

Miranda **warnings**
Statements concerning rights that police are required to make to a person before he or she is subjected to in-custody questioning.

The Fourth Amendment guarantees that "the right of the people to be secure in their persons, houses, papers, and effects, against unreasonable searches and seizures, shall not be violated." The Court made this right applicable to the states in *Wolf* v. *Colorado* (1949).[64] But although the Court found that protection from illegal searches by state and local government was a fundamental right, it refused to apply to the states the **exclusionary rule** that evidence obtained from an illegal search and seizure cannot be used in a trial.

The justices considered the exclusionary rule again in *Mapp* v. *Ohio* (1961).[65] An Ohio court had found Dolree Mapp guilty of possessing obscene materials after an admittedly illegal search of her home for a fugitive. The Ohio Supreme Court affirmed her conviction, and she appealed to the U.S. Supreme Court. In a 6–3 decision, the Court declared, "all evidence obtained by searches and seizures in violation of the Constitution is, by [the Fourth Amendment], inadmissible in a state court." The decision was historic. It placed the exclusionary rule within the confines of the Fourth Amendment and required all levels of government to operate according to the provisions of that amendment.

The struggle over the exclusionary rule took a new turn in 1984, when the Court reviewed *United States* v. *Leon*.[66] In this case, a judge had issued a search warrant without "probable cause" having been firmly established. The police, relying on the warrant, found large quantities of illegal drugs.

The Court, by a 6–3 vote, established the **good faith exception** to the exclusionary rule. The justices held that the state could introduce at trial evidence seized on the basis of a mistakenly issued search warrant. The exclusionary rule, argued the majority, is not a right but a remedy justified by its ability to deter illegal police conduct. Such a deterrent effect was not a factor in *Leon*: the police acted in good faith. Hence, the Court decided, there is a need for an exception to the rule.

The USA-PATRIOT Act

More than fifty years ago, Justice Robert H. Jackson warned that exceptional protections for civil liberties might convert the Bill of Rights into a suicide pact. The national government decided, after the September 11, 2001, terrorist attacks, to forgo some liberties to secure greater order, through bipartisan passage of the USA-PATRIOT Act. This landmark law greatly expanded the ability of law enforcement and intelligence agencies to tap phones, monitor

exclusionary rule
The judicial rule that states that evidence obtained in an illegal search and seizure cannot be used in trial.

good faith exception
An exception to the Supreme Court exclusionary rule, holding that evidence seized on the basis of a mistakenly issued search warrant can be introduced at trial if the mistake was made in good faith, that is, if all the parties involved had reason at the time to believe that the warrant was proper.

Politics of Global Change

Wiretapping in the Digital Age

In the pre-Internet world, telephone calls followed a continuous path between two parties. Investigators with a search warrant could select a point somewhere along the wire to tap the call. But with the advent of the Internet, calls can be placed online. The emergence of VoIP (Voice over Internet Protocol) has dropped the cost of long-distance and international telephone calls to all-time lows. Some services like Skype provide such services for free. Lawbreakers have reason to rejoice.

Congress passed the Communications Assistance for Law Enforcement Act (CALEA) in 1994 to govern wiretap requests. Enacted at the dawn of the Internet, the law requires telecom companies to cooperate with lawful intercepts. The early growth

of VoIP telephony left the FBI, the Drug Enforcement Administration, and the Department of Justice powerless. These agencies successfully lobbied the Federal Communications Commission (the agency that oversees implementation of CALEA) to extend the rules to cover VoIP telecoms.

Civil libertarians cried foul, claiming that CALEA targeted only traditional telephone wiretaps. But the fight against terrorism trumped these objections. Today, all broadband-Internet and VoIP providers must comply with the new rules. These firms are required to intercept calls such that suspects cannot tell that they are under surveillance. That's no easy task for at least three reasons.

First, complying with CALEA is complicated because the device at the end of the line today is

Internet traffic, and conduct other forms of surveillance in pursuit of terrorists.

Shortly after the bill became law, then attorney general John Ashcroft declared: "Let the terrorists among us be warned: If you overstay your visas, even by one day, we will arrest you. If you violate a local law, we will hope that you will, and work to make sure that you are put in jail and kept in custody as long as possible. We will use every available statute. We will seek every prosecutorial advantage. We will use all our weapons within the law and under the Constitution to protect life and enhance security for America."[67]

The USA-PATRIOT Act ran over 300 pages. Some parts engendered strong opposition; others were benign. Consider one of the key provisions: Section 215 dealing with rules for searching private records such as you might find in the library, video store, telephone company, or doctor's office. Prior to the act, the government needed, a computer, not a telephone. A sophisticated caller can tell if her calls are intercepted by simply measuring the "latency" of the connection, that is, the time taken for a single packet of data to travel from a local machine to a computer elsewhere on the Internet. To address this problem, Internet companies now leave lawful-intercept equipment permanently in place to be activated as required.

A second challenge posed by VoIP telephony is the enormous volume of data passing along the Internet. Traditional telephone taps entailed an agent switching on a voice recorder to collect evidence. Today's digital eavesdropping requires collecting hundreds upon hundreds of gigabytes of digital data and then making sense of the material. Standards for formatting and delivering data to investigators still need resolution to work across national borders.

Third, perhaps the biggest issue remains encryption. Not all VoIP calls are encrypted. But telecoms that do encrypt their calls must provide law enforcement agencies with the appropriate decryption keys. The one exception is Skype, the most

popular VoIP service, with over 663 million users by 2011. Skype is a "peer-to-peer" system, routing calls entirely over the public Internet. Skype cannot provide investigators with access to a suspect's calls because Skype does not handle any of the traffic itself. Even if law enforcement investigators could intercept a Skype call, they would still face the task of unraveling the strong encryption used for those calls. While the National Security Agency (NSA) has the computing power to unravel Skype packets, the NSA's resources focus on intelligence gathering, not law enforcement.

In a world made ever smaller by technology, eavesdropping on criminals today will require governments to be nimble in lawmaking and persuasive in their efforts to secure cooperation from other nations.

Sources: "Bugging the Cloud," *Economist Technology Quarterly*, 8 March 2008, pp. 28–30; Skype S.à r.l., Amendment No. 2 to United States Securities and Exchange Commission Form S-1 Registration Statement, filed 4 March 2011. Available at http://www.sec.gov/Archives/edgar/data/1498209/00011931 2511056174/ds1a.htm.

---

at minimum, a warrant issued by a judge and probable cause to access such records. Now, under the USA-PATRIOT Act, the government need certify without substantiation only that its search protects against terrorism, which turns judicial oversight into a rubber stamp. To complicate matters, a gag order barred the person turning over the records from disclosing the search to anyone. The USA-PATRIOT Act was reauthorized in 2006, at which time Congress made many of its temporary provisions permanent. The reauthorizing legislation also tightened up the definition of domestic terrorism and modified Section 215 to explicitly allow individuals to consult their attorneys when they receive a request to turn over records to the government.

Detainees and the War on Terrorism

An important debate has arisen over whether suspected terrorists held by the U.S. government overseas are guaranteed access to attorneys and to the judicial system under the Constitution.

President Bush maintained that detainees held as "enemy combatants" were not entitled to basic legal requirements such as attorneys or hearings and that his actions could not be reviewed in the courts. In 2004 the Supreme Court handed down two decisions rejecting that view. In *Rasul* v. *Bush,* the Court ruled that U.S. judges have the jurisdiction to consider the legality of detaining foreign nationals captured abroad and held at the Guantánamo Bay detention facility in Cuba.[68]

In *Hamdi* v. *Rumsfeld,* the Court considered the case of a Saudi Arabian resident who was born in the United States and was thus a citizen. Hamdi was picked up on an Afghan battlefield and detained as an enemy combatant. In the 8–1 vote, the Court declared that he is entitled by the due process clause of the Fifth Amendment to a "meaningful opportunity" to contest the basis for his detention. In blunt language, Justice Sandra Day O'Connor, speaking for herself and three other justices, rebuffed the president's claim: "We have long since made clear that a state of war is not a blank check for the President when it comes to the rights of the Nation's citizens."[69]

The Supreme Court issued a third critical decision in *Hamdan* v. *Rumsfeld* in July 2006. Hamdan was a Yemeni citizen captured on the battlefield in Afghanistan and held at Guantánamo Bay, Cuba, in anticipation of prosecution before a military commission. In a 5–4 decision, the Court ruled that the military commissions were not authorized by federal law and would violate the Uniform Code of Military Justice and the Geneva Convention because of the lack of procedural rights for the defendants.[70]

The detainee debate took on added layers of complexity when President Bush confirmed news accounts that the Central Intelligence Agency (CIA) had been running secret prisons abroad, in which "high-value" terrorism suspects had been kept and interrogated. The president announced the CIA's high-value detainees had been transferred from their secret prisons abroad to Guantánamo Bay to await trial by tribunal. While the ruling in *Hamdan* v. *Rumsfeld* was initially a setback for the Bush administration, Bush's transfer of the high-value detainees to Guantánamo Bay put the Congress under pressure to explicitly authorize military tribunals.

In October 2006 the Congress passed the Military Commission Act of 2006, authorizing the establishment of the commissions, limiting the use of habeas corpus petitions from noncitizen detainees, eliminating some traditional defendant rights associated with military prosecutions, and authorizing the CIA to continue detainment and tough interrogation techniques.[71] In 2008 the Supreme Court responded by striking down these limits on habeas corpus petitions. In its narrow 5–4 decision in *Boumediene* v. *Bush,* the Court ruled again that detainees have a right to challenge their imprisonment in courts of law.[72] While the Constitution does allow Congress to formally (and temporarily) suspend habeas rights "when in Cases of Rebellion or Invasion the public Safety may require it," legislation simply banning federal judges from hearing detainee habeas cases did not meet the constitutional standard.[73]

The Ninth Amendment and Personal Autonomy

> The enumeration in the Constitution, of certain rights, shall not be construed to deny or disparage others retained by the people.

The wording and history of the Ninth Amendment remain an enigma. The evidence supports two different views: the amendment may protect rights that are not enumerated, or it may simply protect state governments against the assumption of power by the national government.[74] The meaning of the amendment was not an issue until 1965, when the Supreme Court used it to protect privacy, a right that is not enumerated in the Constitution.

Controversy: From Privacy to Abortion

In *Griswold* v. *Connecticut* (1965), the Court struck down, by a 7–2 vote, a seldom-used Connecticut statute that made the use of birth control devices a crime.[75] Justice William Douglas, writing for the majority, asserted that the "specific guarantees in the Bill of Rights have penumbras [partially illuminated regions surrounding fully lit areas]" that give "life and substance" to broad, unspecified protections in the Bill of Rights. Several specific guarantees in the First, Third, Fourth, and Fifth amendments create a zone of privacy, Douglas argued, and this zone is protected by the Ninth Amendment and is applicable to the states by the due process clause of the Fourteenth Amendment.

Griswold established a zone of personal autonomy, protected by the Constitution, which was the basis of a 1973 case that sought to invalidate state antiabortion laws. In *Roe* v. *Wade* (1973), the Court in a

7–2 decision declared unconstitutional a Texas law making it a crime to obtain an abortion except for the purpose of saving the woman's life.[76]

Justice Harry A. Blackmun, who authored the majority opinion, based the decision on the right to privacy protected by the due process clause of the Fourteenth Amendment. The Court declared that in the first three months of pregnancy, the abortion decision must be left to the woman and her physician. In the interest of protecting the woman's health, states may restrict but not prohibit abortions in the second three months of pregnancy. Finally, in the last three months of pregnancy, states may regulate or even prohibit abortions to protect the life of the fetus except when medical judgment determines that an abortion is necessary to save the woman's life. In all, the Court's ruling affected the laws of forty-six states.

The dissenters—Justices Byron White and William Rehnquist— were quick to assert what critics have frequently repeated since the decision: the Court's judgment was directed by its own dislikes, not by any constitutional compass. In the absence of guiding principles, they asserted, the majority justices simply substituted their views for the views of the state legislatures whose abortion regulations they invalidated.[77]

There was a perceptible shift away from abortion rights in *Webster* v. *Reproductive Health Services* (1989). In *Webster,* the Court upheld the constitutionality of a Missouri law that denied the use of public employees or publicly funded facilities in the performance of an abortion unless the woman's life was in danger.[78] Furthermore, the law required doctors to perform tests to determine whether fetuses twenty weeks and older could survive outside the womb. This was the first time the Court upheld significant government restrictions on abortion.

The Court has since moved cautiously down the road toward greater government control of abortion. In 1990, the justices split on two state parental notification laws. Since then, the Court has reaffirmed *Roe* while tolerating additional restrictions on abortion. In *Planned Parenthood* v. *Casey* (1992), the Court opted for O'Connor's test that restrictions must not place "an undue burden" on a woman's ability to choose an abortion. Although the Court struck down a Nebraska law in 2000 that had banned partial-birth abortions in that state in a 5–4 decision, it upheld a more narrowly tailored federal law banning the procedure in *Gonzales* v. *Carhart* (2007) in another 5–4 vote. The Court remains deeply divided on abortion.[79]

Personal Autonomy and Sexual Orientation

The right-to-privacy cases may have opened a Pandora's box of divisive social issues. Does the right to privacy embrace private homosexual acts between consenting adults? Consider the case of Michael Hardwick, who was arrested in 1982 in his Atlanta bedroom while having sex with another man. In a standard approach to prosecuting homosexuals, Georgia charged him under a state criminal statute with the crime of sodomy, which means oral or anal intercourse. Hardwick sued to challenge the law's constitutionality. He won in the lower courts. However, in a bitterly divided ruling in 1986, the Supreme Court held in *Bowers* v. *Hardwick* that the Constitution does not protect homosexual relations between consenting adults, even in the privacy of their own homes.[80]

Justice White's majority opinion was reconsidered in 2003 when the Supreme Court considered a challenge to a Texas law that criminalized homosexual but not heterosexual sodomy. This time, in *Lawrence and Garner* v. *Texas,* a new coalition of six justices viewed the issue in a different light. Speaking through Justice Kennedy, the Court observed "an emerging awareness that liberty gives substantial protection to adult persons in deciding how to conduct their private lives in matters pertaining to sex." Since the Texas law furthered no legitimate state interest but intruded into the intimate personal choices of individuals, the law was void. Kennedy, along with four other justices, then took the unusual step of reaching back in time to declare that the *Bowers* decision was wrong and therefore should be overruled.[81]

Justice Antonin Scalia, joined by Chief Justice Rehnquist and Justice Clarence Thomas, issued a stinging dissent. Scalia charged the majority with "signing on to the homosexual agenda" aimed at eliminating moral opprobrium traditionally attached to homosexual conduct. The consequence is that the Court would be departing from its role of ensuring that the democratic rules of engagement are observed. He continued:

> What Texas has chosen to do is well within the range of traditional democratic action, and its hand should not be stayed through the invention of a brand-new "constitutional right" by a Court that is impatient of democratic change. It is indeed true that "later generations can see that laws once thought necessary and proper in fact serve only to oppress," . . . and when that happens, later generations can repeal

those laws. But it is the premise of our system that those judgments are to be made by the people, and not imposed by a governing caste that knows best.[82]

The challenge of democracy calls for the democratic process to sort out value conflicts whenever possible. And according to Scalia, the Court's majority has moved from its traditional role of umpiring the system to favoring one side over another in the struggle between freedom and order.

Issues around sexual orientation have shifted toward the states, where various groups continue to assert their political power. Some states have been innovators in legitimizing homosexuality. Same-sex couples may now marry in six states (Connecticut, Iowa, Massachusetts, New Hampshire, New York and Vermont) plus the District of Columbia. Additional states have recognized same-sex "unions" but not same-sex marriages. The difference between a union and a marriage may prove to be a distinction without a difference.

Same-sex marriage still remains a flash point for political conflict. In 2008, the California Supreme Court struck down a law limiting marriage to opposite-sex couples, declaring that under the state constitution marriage is a basic civil right guaranteed to all Californians. But opponents struck back six months later with an initiative—known as Proposition 8—asking voters to ban same-sex marriage. It passed with 52 percent of the vote.[83] In the interim, 18,000 couples married and their marriages are duly recognized by the state. When Proposition 8 was challenged in a federal district court, Judge Vaughn Walker declared it unconstitutional in 2010. The case has been appealed.[84]

In 2009, Maine voters, relying on a public referendum, became the thirty-first state to ban same-sex marriages. About the same time, the New York State legislature failed to adopt a same-sex marriage law despite a concerted campaign to assure passage.

The pluralist model provides one solution for groups dissatisfied with rulings from the nation's highest court. State courts and state legislatures have demonstrated their receptivity to positions that are probably untenable in the federal courts. Pluralist mechanisms like the initiative and referendum offer counterweights to judicial intervention.

Tying It Together

1. How has the Bill of Rights evolved?
   - The Bill of Rights was ratified with ten amendments in 1791.
   - Liberties and rights are guaranteed by the Constitution.
     - Civil liberties are freedoms that are guaranteed to the individual by restraint of government.
     - Civil rights are powers or privileges that are guaranteed to the individual, must be provided equally, and are protected against arbitrary removal by the government or other individuals.
   - Both liberties and rights are enshrined in the Bill of Rights and in the first section of the Fourteenth Amendment.

2. In what ways does the First Amendment guarantee freedom of religion?
   - The establishment clause prohibits laws establishing religion.
   - The free-exercise clause prevents the government from interfering with the exercise of religion.
   - The Court has interpreted the religion clauses to mean
     - freedom to believe is unlimited but practicing a belief can be limited.
     - religion may not benefit directly from government actions but it may benefit indirectly.
   - In *Lemon* v. *Kurtzman*, the Court proposed a three-pronged test for determining the constitutionality of government programs and laws.
     - They must have a secular purpose.
     - Their primary effect must not be to advance or inhibit religion.
     - They must not entangle the government excessively with religion.
   - Historically, neutral laws were subject to strict scrutiny; they could be upheld only if the government could demonstrate the law was justified by a compelling governmental interest and the least restrictive means for achieving that interest.
   - After *Employment Division* v. *Smith,* neutral state laws that indirectly infringe on religious exercise are usually constitutional if they apply to the public and do not target religious observance.
   - RFRA reestablished the strict scrutiny test for evaluating federal laws that infringe upon religious exercise.

3. How does the First Amendment guarantee freedom of speech?
   - The Court recognizes a limited number of permissible limitations on free expression:
     – The government can regulate or punish the advocacy of ideas if they promote "imminent lawless action" with a high likelihood of success.
     – The government can impose reasonable restrictions on the means for communicating ideas.
     – Symbolic expression or nonverbal communication receives less protection than pure speech.
     – Obscene material is outside the bounds of constitutional protection.
     – Freedom of the press is essential to a free society so the print media has enjoyed great freedoms, whereas the electronic media has accepted limitations because of limited broadcast frequencies.
   - The right to assemble peaceably and petition the government cannot be prohibited by the government nor can those who organize, lead, or attend such meetings be branded as criminals.

4. What right does the Second Amendment protect?
   - Gun-control advocates assert the Second Amendment protects the right of the states to maintain collective militias.
   - Gun-use advocates assert the amendment protects the right of individuals to own and use guns.
   - Restrictions on gun ownership have been found to be constitutional; general prohibitions on gun ownership have not.

5. How does the Constitution limit states with regard to citizens' rights?
   - The Constitution bars both state and national governments from
     – passing bills of attainder (laws that make an individual guilty of a crime without a trial).
     – passing ex post facto laws (laws that declare an action a crime after it has been performed).
     – impairing the obligation of contracts (the obligation of the parties in a contract to carry out its terms).
   - The Fourteenth Amendment introduced the linchpin that holds the states to the provisions of the Bill of Rights.
     – The due process clause requires the government to adhere to appropriate procedures.
     – The due process clause forbids unreasonable government action.
   - *Miranda* warnings include the following:
     – You have the right to remain silent.

- Anything you say can be used against you in court.
- You have the right to talk to a lawyer of your own choice before questioning.
- If you cannot afford a lawyer, a lawyer will be provided without charge.
- The Court found that the Fourth Amendment protected citizens from illegal searches by state and local governments and required that all levels of government must apply the exclusionary rule: evidence obtained from an illegal search and seizure cannot be used in a trial unless subject to the good faith exception.
- The USA-PATRIOT Act limited freedoms in a shift toward order after September 11, 2001, and has caused various groups to bring litigation, charging violations of constitutionally guaranteed freedoms.

6. How does the Ninth Amendment protect citizens?
   - The Ninth Amendment has two interpretations:
     - The amendment may protect rights that are not enumerated.
     - It may protect state governments against the assumption of power by the national government.
   - Since 1965, the Supreme Court has used the Ninth Amendment to protect privacy, a right that is not enumerated in the Constitution.

KEY CASES

Lemon v. *Kurtzman*
Engel v. *Vitale*
Sherbert v. *Verner*
Brandenburg v. *Ohio*
Tinker v. *Des Moines Independent County School District*
Miller v. *California*
New York Times v. *Sullivan*
New York Times v. *United States*
District of Columbia v. *Heller*
McDonald v. *Chicago*
Palko v. *Connecticut*
Gideon v. *Wainwright*
Miranda v. *Arizona*
Griswold v. *Connecticut*
Roe v. *Wade*
Gonzales v. *Carhart*
Lawrence and Garner v. *Texas*

The Bill of Rights

True or False?

1. The Bill of Rights was adopted in 1776 and refers to the first twelve amendments to the Constitution.
2. The "rights and liberties" guaranteed by the Constitution are all found in the Bill of Rights.

Comprehension

3. How are civil liberties and civil rights different?
4. What rights did the Civil Rights Act of 1964 establish?

Freedom of Religion

True or False?

1. The Supreme Court does not support religious training in public schools during regular school hours but allows students to participate voluntarily in after-school religious activities and clubs in public schools.
2. If the Supreme Court hears a case in which a neutral state law supposedly burdens the free exercise of religion indirectly, the Court must apply the strict scrutiny test to the law to determine its constitutionality.
3. The First Amendment protects religious observance as well as belief.

Comprehension

4. Identify and describe the two clauses in the First Amendment that guarantee freedom of religion.
5. Based on the establishment clause, what three criteria must be considered under the *Lemon* test to determine the constitutionality of government programs and laws as they relate to religion?

Freedom of Expression

True or False?

1. The free-expression clauses concern freedom of speech and the press and can be found in the Constitution's Second Amendment.
2. Under the First Amendment, symbolic expression, or nonverbal communication, generally receives less protection than pure speech.
3. If a journalist researches and writes an article about unlawful activities such as illegal drug use, the First Amendment protects him or her from revealing the names of informants.

Comprehension

4. What is the clear and present danger test?
5. What is the *Miller* test? What are its three components?

The Right to Bear Arms

True or False?

1. Since 1939, the Second Amendment has protected a citizen's right to carry guns such as sawed-off shotguns.
2. The Constitution permits restrictions, but not federal prohibitions, on gun ownership.

Comprehension

3. What are the primary differences between gun-control advocates and gun-use advocates regarding the intent of the Second Amendment?

Applying the Bill of Rights to the States

True or False?

1. Bills of attainder assume that an individual is innocent until proven guilty.
2. Originally, the Bill of Rights served to limit national authority, and state laws were not bound to it.
3. *Miranda* warnings protect citizens by advising them of certain rights when they are held in custody and interrogated.

Comprehension

4. What is the exclusionary rule?
5. Why is the USA-PATRIOT Act controversial among many civil libertarians?

The Ninth Amendment and Personal Autonomy

True or False?

1. The Ninth Amendment can be interpreted to mean that states are protected from the national government taking over their powers.
2. The Ninth Amendment can be interpreted to mean that rights that are not enumerated in the Constitution, such as the right to privacy, can still be protected.
3. Each state is responsible for determining its stance on the validation of same-sex unions and marriages.

Comprehension

4. What was the *Bowers* v. *Hardwick* decision, and when was it overturned?
5. In *Roe* v. *Wade*, what was the opinion of the majority of the justices? What was the argument of the two dissenters?

CourseMate CL Resources:

Visit www.cengagebrain.com/shop/ISBN/1111832587 for flashcards, web quizzes, videos and more!

Equality and Civil Rights

AP Photo/Danny Moloshok

FOCUS QUESTIONS

1. How do Americans define equality?
2. What freedoms do the Civil War amendments protect?
3. How and why was segregation eliminated?
4. How did the civil rights movement result in new legislation?
5. How have civil rights been achieved for other groups?
6. How did the women's movement change gender equality?
7. Does affirmative action work?

"When we want you, we'll call you; when we don't, git."[1] A rancher's sentiment toward his Mexican workers summarizes the treatment of illegal immigrants, many of them Mexicans or Latin Americans, who routinely cross our southern border in search of better wages and the possibility of a better life.

The swings of the economy often signal whether illegal immigrants will be welcomed or sent packing. To be sure, illegal immigrants have provided the United States with cheap labor for a hundred years, undertaking tasks that few, if any, Americans would care to shoulder and providing goods and services at a far lower price than we would otherwise have to pay. They pick our fruit and vegetables, butcher our meat and poultry, clean our homes, flip our burgers, and mow our lawns. But illegal immigrants have also taken up jobs and better pay in other trades, including construction and manufacturing. "Better pay" is relative; it may be better for the illegal, but it is likely to drive down wages for everyone else.

All governments provide for the general welfare, which embraces health, education, and fire and police protection. For example, public hospitals cannot decline care, and public schools must admit and educate every student. These services ensure a measure of equality, a floor beneath which no one need fall. But does the floor exist for illegal immigrants and their children? Should illegal immigrants or their children be denied public education or health care?

In this chapter, we will consider the different ideals of equality and the quest to realize them through government action. We begin with the struggle for racial equality, which continues to cast a long shadow in government policies. This struggle has served as a model for the diverse groups that chose to follow in the same path.

Two Conceptions of Equality

Most Americans support **equality of opportunity**—the idea that people should have an equal chance to develop their talents and that effort and ability should be rewarded equitably. This form of equality glorifies personal achievement and free competition, and it allows everyone to play on a level field where the same rules apply to all. Special recruitment efforts aimed at identifying qualified minority or female job applicants, for example, ensure that everyone has the same chance starting out. Low-bid contracting illustrates equality of opportunity because every bidder has the same chance to compete for work.

Americans are far less committed to **equality of outcome**, which means greater uniformity in social, economic, and political power among different social groups. Equality of outcome can occur only with restrictions on the free competition that is the basis of equality of opportunity. For example, schools and businesses aim at equality of outcome when they allocate admissions or jobs on the basis of race, gender, or disability—factors that are unrelated to ability. Some observers refer to these allocations as *quotas*; others call them *goals*. The difference is subtle. A quota *requires* that a specified, proportional share of some benefit go to a favored group. A goal *aims* for a proportional allocation of benefits, but without requiring it. The government seeks equality of outcome when it adjusts the rules to handicap some bidders and favor others. The vast majority of Americans, however, consistently favor low-bid contracting and merit-based admissions and employment over preferential treatment.[2] Quota- or goal-based policies muster only modest support.

Quota policies generate the most opposition because they confine competition. Quotas limit advancement for some individuals and ensure advancement for others by taking into account factors unrelated to ability. Quotas seem to be at odds with individual initiative. In other words, equality clashes with freedom. To understand the ways government resolves this conflict, we have to understand the evolution of civil rights in this country. The struggle of blacks has been a beacon lighting the way for Native Americans, Hispanic

equality of opportunity
The idea that each person is guaranteed the same chance to succeed in life.

equality of outcome
The concept that society must ensure that people are equal, and governments must design policies to redistribute wealth and status to achieve economic and social equality.

Americans, women, and people with disabilities. Each of these groups has confronted **invidious discrimination**. Discrimination is simply the act of making or recognizing distinctions. When making distinctions among people, discrimination may be benign (that is, harmless) or invidious (harmful).

Remember that **civil rights** are powers or privileges guaranteed to the individual and protected from arbitrary removal at the hands of the government or other individuals. Sometimes people refer to civil rights as "positive rights." In this chapter, we concentrate on the rights guaranteed by the constitutional amendments adopted after the Civil War and by laws passed to enforce those guarantees. Prominent among them is the right to equal protection under the law.

The Civil War Amendments

The Civil War amendments were adopted to provide freedom and equality to black Americans. The Thirteenth Amendment, ratified in 1865, provided that

> neither slavery nor involuntary servitude . . . shall exist within the United States, or any place subject to their jurisdiction.

The Fourteenth Amendment, adopted three years later, provides first that freed slaves are citizens:

> All persons born or naturalized in the United States, and subject to the jurisdiction thereof, are citizens of the United States and of the State wherein they reside.

It also prohibits the states from abridging the "privileges or immunities of citizens of the United States" or depriving "any person of life, liberty, or property, without due process of law." The Fourteenth Amendment then goes on to protect equality under the law, declaring that no state shall

> deny to any person within its jurisdiction the equal protection of the laws.

The Fifteenth Amendment, adopted in 1870, added a measure of political equality:

> The right of citizens of the United States to vote shall not be denied or abridged by the United States or by any State on account of race, color, or previous condition of servitude.

invidious discrimination
Discrimination against persons or groups that works to their harm and is based on animosity.

civil rights
Powers or privileges guaranteed to individuals and protected from arbitrary removal at the hands of government or individuals.

American blacks were thus free and politically equal—at least according to the Constitution. But for many years, the courts sometimes thwarted the efforts of other branches to protect these constitutional rights.

Congress and the Supreme Court: Lawmaking Versus Law Interpreting

In the years after the Civil War, Congress went to work to protect the rights of black citizens. In 1866, lawmakers passed a civil rights act that granted all citizens, white and black, the right to make and enforce contracts; sue or be sued; give evidence; and inherit, purchase, lease, sell, hold, or convey property. Later, in the Civil Rights Act of 1875, Congress attempted to guarantee blacks equal access to public accommodations (streetcars, inns, parks, theaters, and the like).

Although Congress enacted laws to protect the civil rights of black citizens, the Supreme Court weakened some of those rights. In 1873, the Court ruled that the Civil War amendments had not changed the relationship between the state and national governments.[3] State citizenship and national citizenship remained separate and distinct. According to the Court, the Fourteenth Amendment did not obligate the states to honor the rights guaranteed by U.S. citizenship. In effect, the Court stripped the amendment of its power to secure for black citizens the freedoms guaranteed by the Bill of Rights.

In 1883, the Court struck down the public accommodations section of the Civil Rights Act of 1875.[4] The justices declared that the national government could prohibit only government action that discriminated against blacks. Private acts of discrimination or acts of omission by a state, they maintained, were beyond the reach of the national government. The Court refused to see racial discrimination as an act that the national government could prohibit. By tolerating racial discrimination, the justices abetted **racism**, the belief that there are inherent differences among the races that determine people's achievement and that one's own race is superior to, and thus has a right to dominate, others.

The Court's decisions gave the states ample room to maneuver around civil rights laws. In the matter of voting rights, for example, states that wanted to bar black men from the polls simply used nonracial means to do so. One popular tool was the **poll tax**, first imposed by Georgia in 1877. This was a tax of $1 or $2 on every citizen who wanted to vote. The tax was not a burden for most whites. But many blacks were tenant farmers who did not have any extra

racism
The belief that there are inherent differences among the races that determine people's achievement and that one's own race is superior to, and thus has a right to dominate, others.

poll tax
A tax of $1 or $2 on every citizen who wished to vote, first instituted in Georgia in 1877. Although it was no burden on most white citizens, it effectively disenfranchised blacks.

money for voting. Other bars to black suffrage included literacy tests, minimum education requirements, and a grandfather clause that restricted suffrage to men who could establish that their grandfathers were eligible to vote before 1867 (three years before the Fifteenth Amendment declared that race could not be used to deny individuals the right to vote).[5] Intimidation and violence were also used to keep blacks from the polls.

The Roots of Racial Segregation

Well before the Civil War, **racial segregation** was a way of life in the South: blacks lived and worked separately from whites. After the war, southern states began to enact Jim Crow laws that enforced segregation (*Jim Crow* was a derogatory term for a black person). Once the Supreme Court took the teeth out of the Civil Rights Act of 1875, such laws proliferated. They required blacks to live in separate (generally inferior) areas and restricted them to separate sections of hospitals, separate cemeteries, separate schools, and separate sections of streetcars, trains, jails, and parks. Each day, in countless ways, blacks were reminded of the inferior status accorded them by white society.

In 1892, Homer Adolph Plessy, who was seven-eighths Caucasian, took a seat in a "whites only" car of a Louisiana train. He refused to move to the car reserved for blacks and was arrested. Plessy argued that Louisiana's law mandating racial segregation on its trains was an unconstitutional infringement on the privileges and immunities guaranteed by the Fourteenth Amendment and its equal protection clause. The Supreme Court disagreed. The majority in *Plessy* v. *Ferguson* (1896) upheld state-imposed racial segregation.[6] They based their decision on the **separate-but-equal doctrine**, which held that separate facilities for blacks and whites satisfied the Fourteenth Amendment so long as they were equal.

Three years later, the Supreme Court extended the separate-but-equal doctrine to schools.[7] The justices ignored the fact that black educational facilities (and most other "colored-only" facilities) were far from equal to those reserved for whites.

By the end of the nineteenth century, racial segregation was firmly and legally entrenched in the American South. Although constitutional amendments and national laws to protect equality under the law were in place, the Supreme Court's interpretation of those amendments and laws rendered them ineffective. Several decades passed before any change was discernible.

racial segregation
Separation from society because of race.

separate-but-equal doctrine
The concept that providing separate but equivalent facilities for blacks and whites satisfies the equal protection clause of the Fourteenth Amendment.

The Dismantling of School Segregation

By the middle of the twentieth century, public attitudes toward race relations were slowly changing. Black troops had fought with honor, albeit in segregated military units, in World War II. Blacks and whites were working together in unions and in service and religious organizations. Social change and court decisions suggested that government-imposed segregation was vulnerable.

President Harry S. Truman risked his political future with his strong support of blacks' civil rights. In 1947, he established the President's Committee on Civil Rights. The committee's report, issued later that year, became the agenda for the civil rights movement over the next two decades. It called for national laws prohibiting racially motivated poll taxes, segregation, and brutality against minorities and for guarantees of voting rights and equal employment opportunity. In 1948, Truman ordered the **desegregation** (the dismantling of authorized racial segregation) of the armed forces.

In 1947, the U.S. Department of Justice had begun to submit briefs to the courts in support of civil rights. Perhaps the department's most important intervention came in *Brown* v. *Board of Education.*[8] This case was the culmination of twenty years of planning and litigation by the National Association for the Advancement of Colored People (NAACP) to invalidate racial segregation in public schools.

Linda Brown was a black child whose father tried to enroll her in a white public school in Topeka, Kansas. Brown's request was refused because of Linda's race. A federal district court found that the black public school was, in all major respects, equal in quality to the white school; therefore, according to the *Plessy* doctrine, Linda was required to go to the black public school. Brown appealed the decision.

Brown v. *Board of Education* reached the Supreme Court in late 1951. The justices delayed argument on the sensitive race issue, placing the case beyond the 1952 national election. *Brown* was merged with four similar cases into a class action (see Chapter 11). The class action was supported by the NAACP and coordinated by Thurgood Marshall, who later became the first black justice to sit on the Supreme Court. The five cases squarely challenged the separate-but-equal doctrine. By all tangible measures (standards for teacher licensing, teacher–pupil ratios, library facilities), the two school

desegregation
The ending of authorized segregation, or separation by race.

systems in each case—one white, the other black—were equal. The issue was legal separation of the races.

On May 17, 1954, Chief Justice Earl Warren, who had recently joined the Court, delivered a single opinion covering four of the cases. Warren spoke for a unanimous Court when he declared that "in the field of public education the doctrine of 'separate but equal' has no place. Separate educational facilities are inherently unequal,"[9] depriving the plaintiffs of the equal protection of the laws. Segregated facilities generate in black children "a feeling of inferiority . . . that may affect their hearts and minds in a way unlikely ever to be undone."[10] In short, the nation's highest court found that state-imposed public school segregation violated the equal protection clause of the Fourteenth Amendment.

The Court deferred implementation of the school desegregation decisions until 1955. Then, in *Brown* v. *Board of Education II,* it ruled that school systems must desegregate "with all deliberate speed," and it assigned the process of supervising desegregation to the lower federal courts.[11]

Some states quietly complied with the *Brown* decree. Others did little to desegregate their schools. Many communities in the South defied the Court, sometimes violently. This resistance, along with the Supreme Court's "all deliberate speed" order, placed a heavy burden on federal judges to dismantle what was the fundamental social order in many communities.[12] Gradual desegregation under *Brown* was in some cases no desegregation at all. By 1969, a unanimous Supreme Court ordered that the operation of segregated school systems must stop "at once."[13]

Two years later, the Court approved several remedies to achieve integration, including busing, racial quotas, and the pairing or grouping of noncontiguous school zones. But these remedies applied only to **de jure segregation**, government-imposed segregation (for example, government assignment of whites to one school and blacks to another within the same community). Court-imposed remedies did not apply to **de facto segregation**, segregation that is not the result of government influence (for example, racial segregation resulting from residential patterns).

Public opinion strongly opposed the busing approach, and Congress sought limits on busing as a remedy. In 1974, a closely divided Court ruled that lower courts could not order busing across school district boundaries unless each district had practiced racial discrimination or unless school district lines had been deliberately drawn to achieve racial segregation.[14]

de jure segregation
Government-imposed segregation.

de facto segregation
Segregation that is not the result of government influence.

Anger Erupts in Little Rock

In 1957, the Little Rock, Arkansas, school board attempted to implement court-ordered desegregation: nine black teenagers were to be admitted to Little Rock Central High School. Governor Orval Faubus ordered the National Guard to bar their attendance. A mob blocked a subsequent attempt by the students. Finally, President Dwight D. Eisenhower ordered federal troops to escort the students to the high school. Among them was fifteen-year-old Elizabeth Eckford (*right*). Hazel Brown (*left*) angrily taunted her from the crowd. This image seared the nation's conscience. The violence and hostility led the school board to seek a postponement of the desegregation plan. The Supreme Court, meeting in special session, affirmed the decision in *Brown* v. *Board of Education* and ordered the plan to proceed. Fifty years later, a federal judge declared Little Rock's schools desegregated.

(ullstein bild/The Image Works)

The Civil Rights Movement

The NAACP concentrated on school desegregation but made headway in other areas as well. The Supreme Court responded to NAACP efforts in the late 1940s by outlawing the whites-only primary elections in the South, declaring them to be in violation of the Fifteenth Amendment. The Court also declared segregation on interstate bus routes to be unconstitutional, and it desegregated restaurants and hotels in the District of Columbia. Despite these and other decisions that chipped away at existing barriers to equality, the realization of equality required the political mobilization of the people—black and white—into what is now known as the **civil rights movement**.

Civil Disobedience

Rosa Parks, a black woman living in Montgomery, Alabama, sounded the first call to action. That city's Jim Crow ordinances required blacks to sit in the back of the bus and empowered drivers to order blacks to vacate an entire row of seats to make room for one white or to order blacks to stand even when some seats were vacant. In December 1955, Parks boarded a city bus on her way home from work and took an available seat near the front of the bus. She refused to give up her seat when the driver asked her to do so and was arrested and fined $10 for violating the city ordinance.

Under the leadership of a charismatic twenty-six-year-old Baptist minister named Martin Luther King, Jr., Montgomery's black community responded to Parks's arrest with a boycott of the city's bus system. A **boycott** is a refusal to do business with a company or individual, as an expression of disapproval or a means of coercion. A year after the boycott began, the federal courts ruled that segregated transportation systems violated the equal protection clause of the Constitution.

In 1957, King helped organize the Southern Christian Leadership Conference (SCLC) to coordinate civil rights activities. King was totally committed to nonviolent action to bring racial issues into the light. To that end, he advocated **civil disobedience**, the willful but nonviolent breach of unjust laws.

Martin Luther King, Jr., had risen to worldwide prominence by August 1963, when he joined in a march on Washington, D.C., called "A March for Jobs and Freedom." More than 250,000 people, black and white, gathered peaceably at the Lincoln Memorial to hear King speak. "I have a dream," he told them, "that my little children will one day live in a nation where they will not be judged by the color of their skin but by the content of their character."[15]

The Civil Rights Act of 1964

President Lyndon B. Johnson considered civil rights his top legislative priority. Within months after he assumed office, Congress

civil rights movement
The mass mobilization during the 1960s that sought to gain equality of rights and opportunities for blacks in the South and to a lesser extent in the North, mainly through nonviolent unconventional means of participation. Martin Luther King, Jr., was the leading figure and symbol of the civil rights movement, but it was powered by the commitment of great numbers of people, black and white, of all sorts and stations in life.

boycott
A refusal to do business with a firm, individual, or nation as an expression of disapproval or as a means of coercion.

civil disobedience
The willful but nonviolent breach of laws that are regarded as unjust.

passed the Civil Rights Act of 1964, the most comprehensive legislative attempt ever to erase racial discrimination in the United States. Among its many provisions, the act:

- Entitled all persons to "the full and equal enjoyment" of goods, services, and privileges in places of public accommodation without discrimination on the grounds of race, color, religion, or national origin
- Established the right to equality in employment opportunities
- Strengthened voting rights legislation
- Created the Equal Employment Opportunity Commission (EEOC) and charged it with hearing and investigating complaints of job discrimination*
- Provided that funds could be withheld from federally assisted programs that were administered in a discriminatory manner

President Johnson's goal was a "great society." Soon a constitutional amendment and a series of civil rights laws were in place to help him meet his goal:

- The Twenty-fourth Amendment, ratified in 1964, banned poll taxes in primary and general elections for national office.
- The Economic Opportunity Act of 1964 focused on education and training to combat poverty.
- The Voting Rights Act of 1965 empowered the attorney general to send voter registration supervisors to areas in which fewer than half the eligible minority voters had been registered. This act has been credited with doubling black voter registration in the South in only five years.[16]
- The Fair Housing Act of 1968 banned discrimination in the rental or sale of most housing.

The Continuing Struggle Over Civil Rights

Civil rights laws on the books do not ensure civil rights in action. While Congress has tried to expand civil rights enforcement, the Supreme Court has weakened it in recent years. In 1989, the Court restricted minority contractor **set-asides** of state public works funds, an arrangement it had approved in 1980. (A *set-aside* is a purchasing or contracting provision that reserves a certain percentage of funds for minority-owned contractors.) The five-person

set-aside
A purchasing or contracting provision that reserves a certain percentage of funds for minority-owned contractors.

---

*Since 1972, the EEOC has had the power to institute legal proceedings on behalf of employees who allege that they have been victims of illegal discrimination.

majority held that past societal discrimination alone cannot serve as the basis for rigid quotas.[17]

Buttressed by Republican appointees, the Supreme Court continued to narrow the scope of national civil rights protections in a string of decisions that suggested the ascendancy of a new conservative majority concerned more with freedom than with equality.[18] To counter the Court's changing interpretations of civil rights laws, liberals turned to Congress to restore and enlarge earlier Court decisions by writing them into law. The result was a comprehensive new civil rights bill. The Civil Rights Act of 1991 reversed or altered twelve Court decisions that had narrowed civil rights protections. The new law clarified and expanded earlier legislation and increased the costs to employers for intentional, illegal discrimination. Continued resentment generated by equal outcomes policies moved the battle back to the courts, however.

Civil Rights for Other Minorities

Recent civil rights laws and court decisions protect members of all minority groups. The Supreme Court underscored the breadth of this protection in an important decision in 1987.[19] The justices ruled unanimously that the Civil Rights Act of 1866 (known today as "Section 1981") offered broad protection against discrimination to all minorities. Previously, members of white ethnic groups could not invoke the law in bias suits. The 1987 decision allows members of *any* ethnic group—Italian, Iranian, Norwegian, or Chinese, for example—to recover money damages if they prove they were denied a job, excluded from rental housing, or subjected to another form of discrimination prohibited by the law. The 1964 Civil Rights Act offers similar protections but specifies strict procedures for filing suits that tend to discourage litigation.

Clearly, the civil rights movement has had an effect on all minorities. Here we examine the civil rights struggles of three groups: Native Americans, immigrant groups, and persons with disabilities.

Native Americans

During the eighteenth and nineteenth centuries, the U.S. government took Indian lands, isolated Native Americans on reservations, and denied them political and social rights. The government's dealings with the Indians were often marked by violence and broken promises.

The national government switched policies at the beginning of the twentieth century, promoting assimilation instead of separation. The government banned the use of native languages and religious rituals; it sent Indian children to boarding schools and gave them non-Indian names. In 1924, Indians received U.S. citizenship. Until that time, they were considered members of tribal nations whose relations with the U.S. government were determined by treaties. The agencies responsible for administering Indian reservations kept Native Americans poor and dependent on the national government. And Indian lands continued to shrink through the 1950s and into the 1960s—despite signed treaties and the religious significance of portions of the lands they lost.

Anger bred of poverty, unemployment, and frustration with an uncaring government exploded into militant action in November 1969, when several Indians seized Alcatraz Island, an abandoned island in San Francisco Bay. The group cited an 1868 Sioux treaty that entitled them to unused federal lands; they remained on the island for a year and a half. In 1973, armed members of the American Indian Movement seized eleven hostages at Wounded Knee, South Dakota, the site of an 1890 massacre of two hundred Sioux (Lakota) by U.S. cavalry troops. They remained there, occasionally exchanging gunfire with federal marshals, for seventy-one days until the government agreed to examine the treaty rights of the Oglala Sioux.[20]

In 1946, Congress enacted legislation establishing an Indian claims commission to compensate Native Americans for land that had been taken from them. In the 1970s, the Native American Rights Fund and other groups used that legislation to win important victories in the courts. The tribes won the return of lands in the Midwest and in the states of Oklahoma, New Mexico, and Washington. In 1980, the Supreme Court ordered the national government to pay the Sioux $117 million plus interest for the Black Hills of South Dakota, which had been stolen from them a century before. Other cases, involving land from coast to coast, are still pending.

The special status accorded Indian tribes in the Constitution has proved attractive to a new kind of Indian leader. Some of the 565 federally recognized tribes have successfully instituted casino gambling on their reservations, even in the face of state opposition.[21] Congress allows these developments provided that the tribes spend their profits on Indian assistance programs. The wealth created by casino gambling and other ventures funded with gambling profits may prove to be Native Americans' most effective weapon for retaining and regaining their heritage.

Immigrant Groups

For most of the first half of the twentieth century, immigration rules established a strict quota system that gave a clear advantage to Northern and Western Europeans and guaranteed that few Southern or Eastern Europeans, Asians, Africans, and Jews would enter the country by legal means. In 1965, President Lyndon Johnson signed a new immigration bill into law. Henceforth, the invidious quota system was gone; everyone was supposed to have an equal chance of immigrating to the United States. One purpose of the new law was to reunite families. Another provision gave preference in much smaller numbers to immigrants with needed skills, such as doctors and engineers.

The demand for cheap labor in agriculture and manufacturing proved an enticing lure to many of the poor with access to America's southern border. The personal risk in crossing the border illegally was often outweighed by the possible gain in employment and a new, though illegal, start. In 1986 Congress placed the burden of enforcement on employers by imposing fines for hiring undocumented workers and then by offering amnesty to resident illegal immigrants who were in the United States for at least five years.

Frustration brought about by hard economic times tends to make illegal immigrants easy targets. This is especially the case in Arizona, which experiences the greatest number of illegal border crossings from Mexico and has a large Hispanic population. With a surge in violence resulting from drug smuggling and human trafficking at its border, the Arizona legislature—backed by strong public opinion—adopted the strictest state immigration law in the nation in 2010. The Support Our Law Enforcement and Safe Neighborhoods Act makes it a crime for an alien to be in Arizona without carrying legal documents and obligates the police to determine a person's immigration status if there's a reasonable suspicion that the person is an illegal alien. It also steps up state and local law enforcement of federal immigration laws and cracks down on those sheltering, hiring, and transporting illegal aliens. As noted in Chapter 3, parts of the law were struck down by a federal judge in July 2010, including the requirement that police check the immigration status of those arrested or stopped.

Many Latinos have a rich and deep-rooted heritage in America, but until the 1920s that heritage was largely confined to the southwestern states and California. Then unprecedented numbers of Mexican immigrants came to the United States in search of employment

Sí, Se Puede! No, You Can't!

Though a majority of the American public supports the controversial bill, passage of the Support Our Law Enforcement and Safe Neighborhoods Act in Arizona prompted protests in over 70 cities across the United States in May 2010. More than 50,000 people protested in Los Angeles. Protestors carried American and Mexican flags and chanted "Sí, se puede" ("Yes, we can"), while a few supporters of the Arizona bill held their own counterprotests. A federal judge held key provisions void on federalism grounds shortly before the law was to take effect.

(AP Photo/Matt York)

and a better life. Businesspeople who saw in them a source of cheap labor welcomed them. Many Mexicans became farm workers, but a good number also settled mainly in crowded, low-rent, inner-city districts. Like blacks who had migrated to northern cities, most of them met poverty and discrimination. During the Great Depression in the 1930s, about one-third of the Mexican American population (mainly those who had been migratory farm workers) returned to Mexico.

World War II gave rise to another influx of Mexicans, this time primarily courted to work on farms in California. But by the late 1950s, most farm workers—blacks, whites, and Hispanics—were living in poverty. Latinos who lived in cities fared little better. Yet millions of Mexicans continued to cross the border into the United States, both legally and illegally. The effect was to depress wages for farm labor in California and the Southwest.

The Latino population continues to grow. The 20 million Latinos living in the United States in the 1970s were still mainly Puerto Rican and Mexican American, but they were joined by immigrants from the Dominican Republic, Colombia, Cuba, Ecuador, and elsewhere. Although civil rights legislation helped them to some extent, they are among the poorest and least-educated groups in the United States.

One effect of the language barrier is that voter registration and voter turnout among Hispanic citizens are lower than among other groups. Also, voter turnout depends on effective political advertising, and Hispanics are not targeted as often as other groups with political messages that they can understand. But despite these stumbling blocks, Latinos have started to exercise a measure of political power.

Hispanics or Latinos constitute over 16 percent of the U.S. population and account for 56 percent of all growth between the 2000 and 2010 censuses. Yet they comprise only 5 percent of the Congress. The 112th Congress (2011–2012) convened with a group of twenty-seven Hispanic House members and two Hispanic senators. Eleven members—nine in the House and two in the Senate—are of Asian, Native Hawaiian, or Pacific Island heritage. Eight U.S. representatives and one senator were born outside the United States.[22] The appointment of Sonia Sotomayor to the U.S. Supreme Court in 2009 and the growing number of Hispanics appointed to the lower federal courts signal other milestones in the quest for equality for America's largest minority group.

Americans with Disabilities

Minority status is not confined to racial and ethnic groups. Forty-three million Americans with disabilities gained recognition in 1990 as a protected minority with the enactment of the Americans with Disabilities Act (ADA). The law extends the protections embodied in the Civil Rights Act of 1964 to people with physical or mental disabilities, including people with AIDS, recovering alcoholics, and drug abusers. It guarantees them access to employment, transportation, public accommodations, and communication services.

Advocates for people with disabilities found a ready model in the existing civil rights laws. Opponents argued that the changes mandated by the 1990 law (such as access for those confined to wheelchairs) could cost billions of dollars, but supporters replied that the costs would be offset by an equal or greater reduction in federal aid to people with disabilities, who would rather be working.

The law's enactment set off an avalanche of job discrimination complaints filed with the national government's discrimination watchdog agency, the Equal Employment Opportunity Commission (EEOC). By 2011, the EEOC had received over 319,000 ADA-related complaints. Most complaints charged that employers failed to provide reasonable accommodations as required by the law.[23]

A change in the law, no matter how welcome, does not ensure a change in attitudes. Laws that end racial discrimination do not extinguish racism, and laws that ban biased treatment of persons with disabilities cannot mandate their acceptance. But civil rights advocates predict that bias against people with disabilities, like similar attitudes toward other minorities, will wither away as they become full participants in society.

Gender and Equal Rights: The Women's Movement

The Supreme Court has expanded the array of legal weapons available to all minorities to help them achieve social equality. Women, too, have benefited from this change.

Political Equality for Women

Until the early 1970s, laws that affected the civil rights of women were based on traditional views of the relationship between men and women. At the heart of these laws was **protectionism**–the notion that women must be sheltered from life's harsh realities. And protected they were, through laws that discriminated against them in employment and other areas. With few exceptions, women were also "protected" from voting until early in the twentieth century.

In 1878, Susan B. Anthony, a women's rights activist, persuaded a U.S. senator from California to introduce a constitutional amendment requiring that "the right of citizens of the United States to vote shall not be denied or abridged by the United States or by any State on account of sex." The amendment was introduced and voted down a number of times over the next twenty years. Meanwhile, a number of states, primarily in the Midwest and West, granted limited suffrage to women.

By the early 1900s, the movement for women's suffrage had become a political battle to amend the Constitution. The battle was won in 1920 when the **Nineteenth Amendment** gave women the right to vote in the wording first suggested by Anthony.

Prohibiting Sex-Based Discrimination

The movement to provide equal rights to women advanced a step with the passage of the Equal Pay Act of 1963. That act requires equal pay for men and women doing similar work. However, to remove the restrictions of protectionism, women needed equal opportunity for employment. They got it in the Civil Rights Act of 1964 and later legislation. The EEOC, which had been created by that law, was empowered to act on behalf of victims of invidious sex discrimination, or **sexism**.

protectionism
The notion that women must be protected from life's cruelties, the basis, until the 1970s, for laws affecting women's civil rights.

Nineteenth Amendment
The amendment to the Constitution, adopted in 1920, that assures women of the right to vote.

sexism
Invidious sex discrimination.

Stereotypes Under Scrutiny

After nearly a century of protectionism, the Supreme Court began to take a closer look at gender-based distinctions. In 1971, it struck down a state law that gave men preference over women in administering the estate of a person who died without naming an administrator.[24] Two years later, the justices declared that paternalism operated to "put women not on a pedestal, but in a cage."[25] They then proceeded to strike down several gender-based laws that either prevented or discouraged departures from "proper" sex roles. In 1976, the Court finally developed a workable standard for reviewing these kinds of laws. Gender-based distinctions are justified only if they serve some important government purpose.[26]

The courts have not been reluctant to extend to women the constitutional guarantees won by blacks. In 1994, the Supreme Court extended the Constitution's equal protection guarantee by forbidding the exclusion of potential jurors on the basis of their sex.[27] The 1994 decision completed a constitutional revolution in jury selection that began in 1986 with a bar against juror exclusions based on race.

In 1996, the Court spoke with uncommon clarity when it declared that the men-only admissions policy of the Virginia Military Institute (VMI), a state-supported military college, violated the equal protection clause of the Fourteenth Amendment. In an effort to meet women's demands to enter VMI—and to stave off continued legal challenges—Virginia had established a separate-but-equal institution, the Virginia Women's Institute for Leadership (VWIL). Writing for a six-member majority in *United States* v. *Virginia*, Justice Ruth Bader Ginsburg applied a demanding test she labeled "skeptical scrutiny" to official acts that deny individuals rights or responsibilities based on their sex. "Parties who seek to defend gender-based government action," she wrote, "must demonstrate an 'exceedingly persuasive justification' for that action." Ginsburg declared that "women seeking and fit for a VMI-quality education cannot be offered anything less, under the State's obligation to afford them genuinely equal protection."[28] The upshot is that distinctions based on sex are now almost as suspect as distinctions based on race.

Despite the lack of a Constitutional amendment explicitly guaranteeing equal rights for both genders, the Supreme Court has largely implemented that principle through its decisions. It has struck down distinctions based on sex and held that stereotyped generalizations of sexual differences must fall.[29] In recent rulings, the Court has held that states may require employers to guarantee job reinstatement to women returning from maternity leave, sexual harassment in the workplace is illegal, and a hostile work environment will be judged by a reasonable perception of abuse rather than a demonstration of psychological injury.[30]

Affirmative Action: Equal Opportunity or Equal Outcome?

In his vision of the Great Society, President Johnson linked economic rights with civil rights and equality of outcome with equality of opportunity. "Equal opportunity is essential, but not enough," he declared. "We seek not just legal equity but human ability, not just equality as a right and a theory but equality as a fact and equality as a result."[31] This commitment led to affirmative action programs to expand opportunities for women, minorities, and those who are disabled.

Affirmative action is a commitment by a business, employer, school, or other public or private institution to expand opportunities for women, blacks, Hispanic Americans, and members of other minority groups. It embraces a range of public and private programs, policies, and procedures, including special recruitment, preferential treatment, and quotas in job training and professional education, employment, and the awarding of government contracts. The point of these programs is to move beyond equality of opportunity to equality of outcome.

Arguments for affirmative action programs (from increased recruitment efforts to quotas) tend to use the following reasoning. Certain groups have historically suffered invidious discrimination, denying them educational and economic opportunities. To eliminate the lasting effects of such discrimination, the public and private sectors must take steps to provide access to good education and jobs. If the majority once used discrimination to hold groups back, discriminating to benefit those groups is fair. Therefore, quotas are a legitimate means to provide a place on the ladder of success.[32]

Affirmative action opponents maintain that quotas for designated groups necessarily create invidious discrimination (in the form of reverse discrimination) against individuals who are themselves blameless. Moreover, they say, quotas lead to the admission, hiring, or promotion of the less qualified at the expense of the well

affirmative action
Any of a wide range of programs, from special recruitment efforts to numerical quotas, aimed at expanding opportunities for women and minority groups.

qualified. In the name of equality, such policies thwart individuals' freedom to succeed. Do preferential policies in other nations offer lessons for us? (See "Compared with What? How India Struggles with Affirmative Action.")

Reverse Discrimination

The Supreme Court confronted an affirmative action quota program for the first time in *Regents of the University of California* v. *Bakke*.[33] Allan Bakke, a thirty-five-year-old white man, had twice applied for admission to the University of California Medical School at Davis. He was rejected both times. The school had reserved sixteen places in each entering class of one hundred for qualified minority applicants as part of the university's affirmative action program. Bakke's qualifications (college grade point average and test scores) exceeded those of any of the minority students admitted in the two years his applications were rejected. Bakke contended, first in the California courts and then in the Supreme Court, that he was excluded from admission solely on the basis of race. He argued that the equal protection clause of the Fourteenth Amendment and the Civil Rights Act of 1964 prohibited this reverse discrimination.

The Court's decision in *Bakke* contained six opinions and spanned 154 pages. But even after careful analysis of the decision, discerning what the Court had decided was difficult. No opinion had a majority. One bloc of four justices opposed the medical school's plan; a second bloc of four justices supported the plan. Justice Lewis F. Powell, Jr., agreed with parts of both arguments. With the first bloc, he argued that the school's rigid use of racial quotas violated the equal protection clause of the Fourteenth Amendment. With the second bloc, he contended that the use of race was permissible as one of several admissions criteria. Powell cast the deciding vote ordering the medical school to admit Bakke. Despite the confusing multiple opinions, the Court signaled its approval of affirmative action programs in education that use race as a *plus* factor (one of many such factors) but not as *the* factor (one that alone determines the outcome).

True to the pluralist model, groups opposed to affirmative action continued their opposition in federal courts and state legislatures. They met with some success. In 1995, the Supreme Court struck down government mandated set-aside programs in the U.S. Department of Transportation, declaring that such programs must be

Compared with What?

How India Struggles with Affirmative Action

Americans are not alone in their disagreements over affirmative action. Controversies, even bloodshed, have arisen around the world where governments treat certain groups of citizens preferentially. One study found several common patterns among countries that had enacted preferential policies. Although begun as temporary measures, preferential policies tended to persist and even to expand to include more groups. The policies usually sought to improve the situation of disadvantaged groups as a whole, but they often benefited the better-off members of such groups more than the worse-off members. Finally, preferential policies tended to increase antagonisms among different groups within a country.

Of course, there were variations across countries in terms of who benefited from such policies, what types of benefits were bestowed, and even the names the policies were given. Although India is the world's largest democracy, its society is rigidly stratified into groups called castes. The government forbids caste-based discrimination, but members of the lower castes (the lowest being the Dalits, or "untouchables") were historically restricted to the least prestigious and lowest-paying jobs. To improve their status, India has set aside government jobs for the lower castes, who make up half of India's population of 1 billion. India now reserves 27 percent of government jobs for the lower castes and an additional 23 percent for untouchables and remote tribe members. Gender equality has also

subject to the most searching judicial inquiry ("strict scrutiny") and must be "narrowly tailored" to achieve a "compelling government interest."[34]

By 2003, twenty-five years after *Bakke,* the Supreme Court was ready to weigh in again on affirmative action in two cases that challenged aspects of the University of Michigan's racial preference policies. In *Gratz* v. *Bollinger,* the Court considered the university's undergraduate admissions policy, which conferred 20 points automatically to members of favored groups (100 points guaranteed admission). In a 6–3 opinion, Chief Justice William H. Rehnquist argued that such a policy violated the equal protection clause because it lacked the narrow tailoring required for permissible racial improved since a 1993 constitutional amendment set aside one-third of all seats in local government councils for women. By 2004, 900,000 women had been elected to public office, and 80,000 of them now lead local governing bodies. These efforts have intensified tensions between the lower and upper castes. A 2010 proposal to create a one-third set-aside for women in the parliament and state legislatures has met stiff resistance from the political parties representing the lower castes. The Dalits view the proposal as a threat to their monopoly quota. Lower-caste women oppose the idea while feminists from higher-caste parties support it. The issue is not the use of quotas but which group should benefit from quotas. No longer considered temporary, quotas have become a fact of life in the world's largest democracy.

Under a majoritarian model, group demands could lead quickly to conflict and instability because majority rule leaves little room for compromise. By parceling out benefits, pluralism mitigates disorder in the short term. But in the long term, repeated demands for increased benefits can spark instability. A vigorous pluralist system should provide acceptable mechanisms to vent such frustrations and yield new allocations of benefits.

Sources: Trudy Rubin, "Will Democracy Survive in India?" *Record* (Bergen County, N.J.), 19 January 1998, p. A12; Alex Spillius, "India's Old Warriors to Launch Rights Fight," *Daily Telegraph,* 20 October 1997, p. 12; Robin Wright, "World's Leaders: Men, 187, Women, 4," *Los Angeles Times,* 30 September 1997, p. A1; "Indian Eunuchs Demand Government Job Quotas," *Agence France Presse,* 22 October 1997; Juergen Hein and M. V. Balaji, "India's First Census of New Millennium Begins on February 9," *Deutsche Presse-Agentur,* 7 February 2001; Gillian Bowditch, "You Can Have Meritocracy or Equality, but Not Both," *Sunday Times,* Features Section: Scotland News, 19 January 2003, p. 21; Press Trust of India, "About a Million Women Elected to Local Bodies in India," 10 February 2004; Somini Sengupta, "Quotas to Aid India's Poor vs. Push for Meritocracy," *New York Times,* 23 May 2006, p. A3; "Caste in Doubt," *Economist,* 12 June 2010, p. 46; Shikha Dalmia, "India's Government by Quota," *Wall Street Journal,* 1–2 May 2010, p. A13.

preferences and it failed to provide for individualized consideration of each candidate.[35] In the second case, *Grutter* v. *Bollinger,* the Court considered the University of Michigan's law school admissions policy, which gave preference to minority applicants. The school defended its policy on the ground that it served a "compelling interest in achieving diversity among its student body." This time, the Court, in a 5–4 decision, held that the equal protection clause did not bar the school's narrowly tailored use of racial preferences to further a compelling interest that flowed from a racially diverse student body.[36] Since each applicant is judged individually on his or her merits, race remains only one among many factors that enter into the admissions decision.

The issue of race-based classification in education arose again in *Parents Involved in Community Schools* v. *Seattle School District No. 1,* in which a group of parents brought suit against a Washington school district policy concerning voluntary school integration plans based on race.[37] When multiple students applied to transfer to an oversubscribed school, one of the district's tie-breaking factors was to consider which students would help create a racial balance in that particular school. In 2007, a slim majority of the Supreme Court struck down the school board's policy, ruling that there was no compelling interest for school districts to use race as a basis to assign seats in schools. In effect, the Court's decision meant that integrating public schools is not a compelling interest if de jure segregation is not present as it was in the case of *Brown* v. *Board of Education.*

The Politics of Affirmative Action

A comprehensive review of nationwide surveys conducted over the past twenty years reveals an unsurprising truth: blacks favor affirmative action programs, and whites do not. Women and men do not differ on this issue. The gulf between the races was wider in the 1970s than it is today, but the moderation results from shifts among blacks, not whites. Perhaps the most important finding is that "whites' views have remained essentially unchanged over twenty-five years."[38]

How do we account for the persistence of equal outcomes policies? A majority of Americans have consistently rejected explicit race or gender preferences for the awarding of contracts, employment decisions, and college admissions, regardless of the groups such preferences benefit. Nevertheless, preference policies have survived and thrived under both Democrats and Republicans. The list of protected groups has expanded beyond African Americans to include Hispanic Americans, Native Americans, Asian Pacific Americans, Subcontinental Asian Americans, and women. Politicians have a powerful motive—votes—to expand the number of protected groups and the benefits such policies provide.

The conflict between freedom and equality will continue as other individuals and groups press their demands through litigation and legislation. The choice the country makes will depend on whether and to what extent Americans are prepared to change their minds on these thorny issues.

Tying It Together

1. How do Americans define equality?
   - Most Americans support equality of opportunity, which is the idea that people should have an equal chance to develop their talents and be rewarded equally.
   - Americans are less committed to equality of outcomes, which is the idea that different groups should have greater uniformity of social, economic, and political power.

2. What freedoms do the Civil War amendments protect?
   - The Thirteenth Amendment, ratified in 1865, ended slavery.
   - The Fourteenth Amendment, ratified in 1868, granted former slaves citizenship.
   - The Fifteenth Amendment, adopted in 1870, asserted that citizens could not be denied their rights on the basis of race, color, or previous condition of servitude.
     - In the following years, the Supreme Court struck down some provisions of early civil rights laws, thus tolerating racial discrimination or racism. Some examples are the imposition of poll taxes (imposing a fee to vote) and racial segregation.
     - In 1896 the Court upheld state-imposed separate-but-equal doctrines that asserted that rights under the Fourteenth Amendment were met with separate yet comparable facilities.

3. How and why was segregation eliminated?
   - Attitudes toward segregation began to change after World War II, during which blacks served in the military with valor.
   - President Harry S. Truman established the President's Committee on Civil Rights and desegregated the armed forces.
   - In *Brown* v. *Board of Education,* the Supreme Court ruled that schools must be desegregated.
   - The Court has continued to approve remedies to achieve integration and end de jure segregation (supported by law) but has pulled back from challenging de facto segregation (not the result of government action).

4. How did the civil rights movement result in new legislation?
   - The civil rights movement used civil disobedience and boycotts to draw attention to the injustice of segregation and discrimination.

- The Civil Rights Act of 1964 set forth the following provisions:
  - entitled all to full and equal enjoyment of goods, services, and privileges in public accommodation.
  - established equal opportunity in employment.
  - strengthened voting rights.
  - created the Equal Employment Opportunity Commission, a government agency, to oversee that laws were carried out.
  - created provisions whereby federal funds could be withheld from programs that discriminated.
- The Equal Opportunity Act focused on programs that attempted to end poverty.

5. How have civil rights been achieved for other groups?
   - Native Americans were
     - granted citizenship in 1924.
     - subjected to broken treaties and promises as well as violence.
     - returned their land in a few cases, and the government ordered reparations to be paid to the Sioux for damages suffered.
     - empowered to develop casinos on tribal land to provide economic incentives.
   - Hispanic Americans have immigrated from Mexico and Central and South America and now live throughout the United States.
     - Despite legislation, poverty is widespread. A large number of noncitizens and a common language barrier lead to very low voter participation.
     - Political representation for Latinos is improving.
   - Americans with disabilities also face discrimination.
     - In 1990, the Americans with Disabilities Act was passed to extend protections from the Civil Rights Act to people with disabilities.
     - The EEOC processes complaints when employers do not provide reasonable accommodations for people with disabilities as required by law.

6. How did the women's movement change gender equality?
   - Women were discriminated against by laws that limited their participation in society. Early laws were protectionist in that they were based on the notion that women needed to be sheltered from life's realities.
   - In 1920, after much lobbying by the suffrage movement led by Susan B. Anthony, the Nineteenth Amendment was ratified, guaranteeing women the right to vote.
   - The Civil Rights Act was advanced by the Equal Pay Act of 1963, which guaranteed equal pay for equal work regardless of gender.

7. Does affirmative action work?
   - Affirmative action is a commitment by a business, employer, school, or other public or private institution to expand opportunities for women, blacks, Hispanic Americans, and members of other minority groups.
   - Arguments in favor of affirmative action programs state that protected groups have suffered from generations of discrimination that require concerted effort—even preferences—to overcome.
   - Arguments against affirmative action programs maintain that quotas create reverse discrimination against individuals who are blameless, leading to admission, hiring, or promotion of the less qualified at the expense of the well qualified.
   - While Americans do not support equal outcomes policies, preference policies have persisted and the number of protected groups has grown.

KEY CASES

Plessy v. *Ferguson*
Brown v. *Board of Education*
Brown v. *Board of Education II*
United States v. *Virginia*
Regents of the University of California v. *Bakke*
Gratz v. *Bollinger*
Grutter v. *Bollinger*
Parents Involved in Community Schools v. *Seattle School District No. 1*

Test Prepper 13.1

Two Conceptions of Equality

True or False?
1. Americans of different social groups are far less committed to greater uniformity in social and economic power than they are to equality of opportunity.
2. Invidious discrimination is the limitation of freedoms due to economics.

Comprehension
3. What is equality of outcome?
4. Describe the difference between a quota and a goal.

The Civil War Amendments

True or False?

1. The Fifteenth Amendment states that all persons born or naturalized in the United States, and subject to the jurisdiction thereof, are citizens of the United States and of the state wherein they reside.
2. In the Civil Rights Act of 1875, Congress attempted to guarantee blacks equal access to public accommodations.
3. Poll taxes and literacy tests were instituted to prevent blacks from voting.

Comprehension

4. What was the separate-but-equal doctrine?
5. Who is Homer Adolph Plessy, and what famous court case is he known for?

The Dismantling of School Segregation

True or False?

1. President Harry Truman opposed black civil rights and all desegregation.
2. *Brown* v. *Board of Education* was a key factor in the 1952 national election.
3. De facto and de jure segregation mean essentially the same thing.

Comprehension

4. What is the significance of the Supreme Court case *Brown* v. *Board of Education* with regard to civil rights?

The Civil Rights Movement

True or False?

1. Civil disobedience is the refusal to do business with a company or individual as an expression of disapproval or a means of coercion.
2. The Twenty-fourth Amendment banned poll taxes in primary and general elections for national office.

Comprehension

3. What was Martin Luther King, Jr.'s, role in the civil rights movement?
4. How did the Civil Rights Act of 1991 come about?

Civil Rights for Other Minorities

True or False?

1. In 1987 the Supreme Court ruled that *any* ethnic group could recover monetary damages if it could prove it was denied a job, excluded from rental housing, or discriminated unlawfully in another way.

2. Native Americans do not hold U.S. citizenship.
3. The protections guaranteed by the Americans with Disabilities Act extend to recovering alcoholics and people with AIDS as well as other physical and mental disabilities.

Comprehension
4. How does the language barrier prevent some Hispanics from participating in government?
5. Describe the progress persons with disabilities have made with equality and protection.

Test Prepper 13.6

Gender and Equal Rights

True or False?
1. Laws affecting the civil rights of women were based on protectionism until the 1970s.
2. The Nineteenth Amendment guaranteed women the right to vote.

Comprehension
3. What was Susan B. Anthony's role in women's right to vote?

Test Prepper 13.7

Affirmative Action

True or False?
1. Affirmative action is the requirement that a business must hire a certain number of minorities.
2. In *Gratz* v. *Bollinger* the Supreme Court held that the University of Michigan violated the equal protection clause because its undergraduate admissions policies were not individualized or narrowly tailored enough.
3. Over the past twenty years, surveys have revealed that whites favor affirmative action and blacks do not.

Comprehension
4. Who is Allan Bakke, and what court case is he associated with?
5. What is the central argument behind affirmative action?

CourseMate CL Resources:
Visit www.cengagebrain.com/shop/ISBN/1111832587 for flashcards, web quizzes, videos and more!

Brendan Smialowski/Getty Images

FOCUS QUESTIONS

1. How and why does the government create policies?
2. What forces work against coherent problem solving in government?
3. How is the national budget created?

Providing affordable health care for all. That goal was a central theme of Barack Obama's presidential campaign. He told one audience, "We'll guarantee health care for anyone who needs it [and] make it affordable for anyone who wants it. And we're not going to do it 20 years from now or 10 years from now; we're going to do it by the end of my first term as president."[1] Why the urgency? For starters, rising health-care costs and insurance premiums for private coverage in recent years have far outpaced inflation and increases in income.[2] About 16 percent of America's gross domestic product is currently spent on health care, a number that experts say will continue to rise.[3]

Then there's the human side of this issue. According to one study, "an American family filed for bankruptcy in the aftermath of illness every 90 seconds" in 2007. Over 60 percent of all personal bankruptcies that year were attributed to medical costs. Most of those debtors actually had health insurance and were considered to be solidly middle class, but once they became ill, either they discovered that their insurance plans were inadequate or their illnesses kept them out of work for so long that they lost their jobs and the health insurance that came along with it.[4]

Then there's the issue of the uninsured, who accounted for over 15 percent of the population, or about 46.3 million people, at any given time in 2009.[5] One study found that nearly 87 million people—almost 1 in 3 Americans under sixty-five years old—went without insurance at some point during 2007 and 2008.[6] Among their ranks were countless people who tried to purchase private health insurance but were denied coverage due to preexisting health conditions, whether severe (e.g., heart disease) or less dramatic (e.g., acne, bunions, and toenail fungus).[7]

Addressing the health-care problem in America is not straightforward. Americans support government aid for those in need but have a long-standing aversion to "big government." In March 2010, Democrats in Congress passed the Patient Protection and Affordable Care Act, a major overhaul of the American health-care system that attempted to address many of the challenges noted above. The bill squeaked through the House 219–212, without a single Republican vote.

Under the law, children with preexisting conditions may not be denied coverage (adults will be eligible for coverage as well, though initially in special pools). Lifetime caps on health-care payments are banned, and annual caps will be eliminated by 2014. The law also allows many young adults to stay on their parents' insurance until the age of twenty-six and improves prescription drug coverage for seniors. Small businesses with less than fifty employees will receive tax credits to defray the cost of providing insurance. Most dramatic, however, is the requirement that most Americans purchase health insurance or pay a fine.[8] The cost of all this? In May 2010, the Congressional Budget Office (CBO) estimated it will exceed a trillion dollars over the next decade. The CBO estimate increased $115 billion within two months of passage.[9] Over thirty states filed suit in an attempt to escape some of the requirements of the health-care bill. With mixed decisions in lower courts over its constitutionality, years of litigation lie ahead.[10]

Previous chapters have focused on individual institutions of government. Here we focus on government more broadly and ask how policymaking takes place across institutions. We first identify different types of public policies and then analyze the stages in the policymaking process. We examine how policy is made when many competing interest groups are trying to influence the outcome and how relationships between those groups, and between such groups and different parts of government, structure the policymaking process. Finally, we take a closer look at budgeting and policies relating to the economy.

Government Purposes and Public Policies

In Chapter 1, we noted that nearly all citizens are willing to accept limitations on their personal freedom in return for various benefits of government. We defined the major purposes of government as maintaining order, providing public benefits, and promoting equality. Different governments place different values on each broad purpose, and those differences are reflected in their public policies. A **public policy** is a general plan of action adopted by a government to solve a social problem, counter a threat, or pursue an objective.

Whatever their form and effectiveness, all policies have this in common: they are the means by which government pursues certain goals in specific situations. People disagree about public policies

public policy
A general plan of action adopted by the government to solve a social problem, counter a threat, or pursue an objective.

because they disagree about one or more of the following elements: the goals that government should have, the means it should use to achieve goals, and the perception of the situation at hand.

When people inside and outside government disagree on goals, that disagreement is often rooted in a basic difference in values. As emphasized throughout this book, such value conflict is often manifested as disputes pitting freedom versus order or freedom versus equality. The roots of the values we hold can run deep, beginning with childhood socialization as the values of parents are transmitted to their children. Disputes involving values are in many ways the hardest to bridge since they reflect a basic worldview and go to the core of one's sense of right and wrong.

The problem of illegal drugs illustrates how different core values lead us to prefer different public policies. Everyone is in agreement that government should address the problems created by drugs. Yet there are sharply contrasting views of what should be done. Recall from Chapter 1 that libertarians put individual freedom above all else and want to limit government as much as possible. Many libertarians argue that drugs should be decriminalized; if people want to take drugs, they should be free to do so, just as they are free to drink alcohol if they want. If drugs were decriminalized, they could be sold openly, the prices would fall dramatically, and the crime associated with illegal drugs would largely evaporate. Conservatives' value system places considerable emphasis on order. In their mind, a decent, safe, and civilized society does not allow people to debase themselves through drug abuse. Pointing to the broad costs to society brought on through alcoholism, such as drunk driving accidents, conservatives argue that government should punish those who violate the law rather than decriminalize the behavior. Liberals place greater emphasis on treatment as a policy option. They regard drug addiction as a medical or emotional problem and believe that government should offer the services that addicts can use to stop their self-destructive behavior. Liberals value equality, and their view on this issue is that government should be expansive so that it can help people in need. Many drug offenders are impoverished because of their spending on drugs and cannot pay for private treatment.

Types of Policies

Although values underlie choices, analysis of public policy does not usually focus explicitly on core beliefs. Political scientists often try to categorize public policy choices by their objectives. That is, in the broad scheme of things, what are policymakers trying to do by choosing a particular policy direction? One common purpose is to allocate resources so that some segment of society can receive a service or benefit. We can call these **distributive policies**. Democratic Representative John Murtha was known as the "King of Pork" for his ability to write grants and contracts into bills that were restricted to specific companies in his economically depressed Pennsylvania district. Some of these contracts worked out well. Concurrent Technologies got off the ground thanks to Murtha's earmarks and now employs 800 workers. On the other hand, despite more than $150 million in grants, Caracal, Inc., never employed more than 10 people and went out of business.[11]

Distributional policies are not all projects or new buildings. Some are social programs designed to help a disadvantaged group in society. What distributional policies have in common is that all of us pay through our taxes to support those who receive the benefit, presumably because that benefit works toward the common good, such as enhanced security, a better-trained work force, or a cleaner environment. In contrast, **redistributional policies** are explicitly designed to take resources from one sector of society and transfer them to another (reflecting the core value of greater equality). In a rather unusual redistributional proposal in Seattle, Washington, in 2003, proponents of early childhood education programs succeeded in getting an initiative on a citywide ballot that would have added a 10-cent tax on every cup of espresso sold in the city. The new revenues brought in by this tax were to fund early childhood programs and, as such, the plan was to redistribute revenues from espresso drinkers to families with small children. The voters rejected the initiative, and no such redistribution took place.[12]

Another basic policy approach is **regulation**. In Chapter 10, we noted that regulations are the rules that guide the operation of government programs. When regulations apply to business markets, they are an attempt to structure the operations of that market in a particular way. Government intersperses itself as a referee, setting rules as to what kinds of companies can participate in what kinds of market activities. Trucking is a case in point. The United States used to restrict the entrance of Mexican trucks into this country, barring them from traveling more than 20 miles into the United States. Thus, they would have to unload their cargo at a transfer station, where it would be placed on an American carrier that would take the merchandise to its destination. The United States

distributive policies
Government policies designed to confer a benefit on a particular institution or group.

redistributional policies
Policies that take government resources, such as tax funds, from one sector of society and transfer them to another.

regulation
Rules that guide the operation of government programs and business markets.

said it forbade Mexican trucks from traveling on their own to wherever their cargo was headed because they were not always safe and they polluted more than American trucks did. An international trade panel determined, however, that these regulatory rules violated the North American Free Trade Agreement. In response, Congress passed a new law providing for inspection stations at border crossings to ensure that the Mexican trucks were safe and that their drivers met the same licensing standards as American drivers. In the case of the Mexican trucks, the restrictive regulations were largely the product of lobbying by American trucking firms and the Teamsters union, which wanted to preserve business for themselves.[13]

This framework of distributional, redistributional, and regulatory policies is rather general, and there are surely policy approaches that do not fit neatly into one of these categories.[14] Nevertheless, this framework is a useful prism to examine public policymaking. Understanding the broad purposes of public policy allows a better evaluation of the tools necessary to attain these objectives.

A Policymaking Model

Not only do political scientists distinguish among the different types of policies, they also distinguish among different stages of the policymaking process and try to identify patterns in the way people attempt to influence decisions and in the way decisions are reached. We can separate the policymaking process into four stages: agenda setting, policy formulation, implementation, and policy evaluation.[15] Figure 14.1 shows the four stages in sequence. As the figure indicates, policymaking is a circular process: the end of one phase is the beginning of another.

Agenda setting is the stage at which problems are defined as political issues. Many problems confront Americans in their daily lives, but government is not actively working to solve them all. For example, the problem of poverty among the elderly did not suddenly arise during the 1930s, but that is when inadequate income for the elderly was defined as a political problem. When the government begins to consider acting on an issue it has previously ignored, we say that the issue has become part of the political agenda.

Why does an existing social problem become redefined as a political problem? There is no single reason; many factors can stimulate new thinking about a problem. Sometimes highly visible events or developments push issues onto the agenda. Issues may also reach the agenda through the efforts of scholars and activists to get more

agenda setting
The stage of the policymaking process during which problems get defined as political issues.

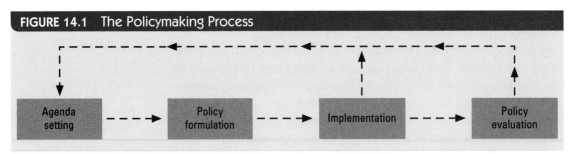

FIGURE 14.1   The Policymaking Process

This model, one of many possible ways to depict the policymaking process, shows four stages. Feedback on program operations and on performance from the last two stages stimulates new cycles of the process.

(© Cengage Learning 2013)

people to pay attention to a condition about which the general public seems unaware. The likelihood that a certain problem will move onto the agenda is also affected by who controls the government and by broad ideological shifts. Agenda building also may involve redefining old issues so that people look at them in different ways.[16]

Policy formulation is the stage of the policymaking process in which formal policy proposals are developed and officials decide whether to adopt them. The most obvious kind of policy formulation is the proposal of a measure by the president or the development of legislation by Congress. Administrative agencies also formulate policy through the regulatory process. Courts too formulate policy when their decisions establish new interpretations of the law.

Policies are not self-executing; **implementation** is the stage at which they are carried out. When agencies in Washington issue regulations, some government bodies must put those policies into effect. In the case of the Americans with Disabilities Act, for example, the owners of office buildings probably would not have repositioned their water fountains simply because Washington had published new regulations. Administrative bodies at the regional, state, or local level had to inform them of the rules, give them a timetable for compliance, communicate the penalties for noncompliance, answer questions, and report to Washington on how well the regulations were working.

As pointed out in Chapter 10, one of the biggest problems at the implementation stage of policymaking is coordination. After officials in Washington enact a law and write the new regulations, people outside Washington typically are designated to implement the policy. The agents may be local officials, state administrators, or federal bureaucrats headquartered in regional offices around the country. Although implementation may sound highly technical, it is very much a political

policy formulation
The stage of the policymaking process during which formal proposals are developed and adopted.

implementation
The process of putting specific policies into operation.

process calling for a great deal of bargaining and negotiation among different groups of people in and out of government.

Policy evaluation is the analysis of how well a policy is working. Evaluation tends to draw heavily on approaches used by academics, including cost-effectiveness analysis and statistical methods designed to provide quantitative measurements of program outcomes. Technical studies can be quite influential in decisions about whether to continue, expand, alter, reduce, or eliminate programs.

Evaluation is part of the policymaking process because it helps to identify problems and issues arising from current policy. In other words, evaluation studies provide **feedback** about program performance. The dotted line in Figure 14.1 represents a feedback loop. Feedback can be positive or negative.[17] Consider abstinence-only sex education programs, which generally teach students to "wait until marriage." Some research indicates that these programs, whose message can be moralistic in tone, are ineffective. One study of four programs aimed at students at either the elementary or middle school level revealed that they had no impact on rates of sexual activity when researchers gathered data from those students four to six years after their courses. Students from the abstinence-only programs were just as likely to engage in sexual activity as those from the control group of students who were not exposed to these programs.[18] Concluding that abstinence-only programs were ineffective, the Obama administration eliminated funding for them in its first budget.

To the surprise of critics, a study published in early 2010 demonstrated that a certain type of abstinence approach was effective. This program differed from others, however. It was not moralistic and did not tell students that they needed to wait until marriage. Rather, the message was "wait until you're ready." There were other differences as well, but this evaluation demonstrated something important: subtle differences in the design of programs can be the difference between success and failure.[19] The end of the policy process—evaluating whether the policy is being implemented as it was envisioned when it was formulated—marks the beginning of a new cycle of public policymaking.

Fragmentation and Coordination

The policymaking process encompasses many different stages and includes many different participants at each stage. Here we examine some forces that pull the government in different directions

policy evaluation
Analysis of a public policy so as to determine how well it is working.

feedback
Information received by policymakers about the effectiveness of public policy.

and make problem solving less coherent than it might otherwise be. In the next section, we look at some structural elements of American government that work to coordinate competing and sometimes conflicting approaches to the same problems.

Multiplicity and Fragmentation

A single policy problem may be attacked in different and sometimes competing ways by government for many reasons. At the heart of this **fragmentation** of policymaking is the fundamental nature of government in America. The separation of powers divides authority among the branches of the national government, and federalism divides authority among national, state, and local levels of government. These multiple centers of power are, of course, a primary component of pluralist democracy. Within any issue area, a number of interest groups try to influence different parts of government. No one entity completely controls policy decisions.

Fragmentation is often the result of many different agencies being created at different times to address different problems. Over time, however, as those problems evolve and change, they can become more closely related even as the different agencies do little or nothing to try to coordinate their efforts. Many of the intelligence and operational failures associated with the September 11 terrorist attacks can be traced in part to the lack of coordination among various security-related agencies. In the area of border and transportation security, for example, responsibility was split among the Immigration and Naturalization Service, the Customs Service, the Coast Guard, the Federal Protective Services, and other agencies.

The formation of the Department of Homeland Security in 2002 was an attempt to overcome fragmentation in this area by creating a centralized administrative structure.[20] To coordinate the efforts of the sixteen-member intelligence community, Congress passed a separate law in 2004 to create a new director of national intelligence (DNI).[21] Yet fragmentation still plagues homeland security. On Christmas Day 2009, a Nigerian member of al Qaeda, Umar Farouk Abdulmutallab, boarded a flight from Amsterdam to Detroit with an explosive hidden in his underwear. Fortunately, when he tried to set off the device while the plane was in flight, it failed to detonate. Months earlier, U.S. intelligence had learned that Abdulmutallab was a potential terrorist, but his name was never put on the no-fly list. A furious President Obama vented that "This was not a failure to collect intelligence, it was a failure to integrate and understand the intelligence."[22] The DNI at the time, Dennis Blair, was forced to resign.

fragmentation
In policymaking, the phenomenon of attacking a single problem in different and sometimes competing ways.

Congress is characterized by the same diffusion of authority. At the time the Department of Homeland Security was created, sixty-one House and Senate committees and subcommittees possessed some degree of jurisdiction over the twenty-two agencies that were incorporated into the new organization.[23]

The Pursuit of Coordination

How does the government overcome fragmentation so that it can make its public policies more coherent? One common response to the problem of coordination is the formation of interagency task forces within the executive branch. Their common goal is to develop a broad policy response that all relevant agencies will endorse. Such task forces include representatives of all agencies claiming responsibility for a particular issue. They attempt to forge good policy as well as goodwill among competing agencies.

As illustrated with the case of homeland security, reorganization of disparate parts of government working in related areas is a fundamental approach to enhancing coordination. Despite the obstacles that administrators trying to protect their turf put up, reorganization across agencies is possible. The involvement and commitment of the president is often critical, as his status and willingness to expend political capital can put reorganizations on the agenda and push them forward.

The White House uses the Office of Management and Budget (OMB) to foster coordination within the executive branch. OMB can do much more than review budgets and look for ways to improve management practices. Since the Reagan administration, presidents have used this office to clear regulations before they were proposed publicly by the administrative agencies. OMB's regulatory review role centralizes control of the executive branch.[24]

In a decentralized, federal system of government with large numbers of interest groups, fragmentation is inevitable. Beyond the structural factors is the natural tendency of people and organizations to defend their base of power. Government officials understand, however, that mechanisms of coordination are necessary so that fragmentation does not overwhelm policymaking. Mechanisms such as interagency task forces, reorganizations, and White House review can bring some coherence to policymaking.

Government by Policy Area

Policy formulation takes place across different institutions. Participants from these institutions do not patiently wait their turn as policymaking proceeds from one institution to the next. Rather, they try to influence policy at whatever stage they can. Suppose that Congress is considering amendments to the Clean Air Act. Because Congress does not function in a vacuum, the other parts of government that will be affected by the legislation participate in the process too. The Environmental Protection Agency (EPA) has an interest in the outcome because it will have to administer the law. The White House is concerned about any legislation that affects such vital sectors of the economy as the steel and coal industries. As a result, officials from both the EPA and the White House work with members of Congress and the appropriate committee staffs to try to ensure that their interests are protected. At the same time, lobbyists representing corporations, trade associations, and environmental groups do their best to influence Congress, agency officials, and White House aides. Trade associations might hire public relations firms to sway public opinion toward their industry's point of view. Experts from think tanks and universities might be asked to testify at hearings or to serve in an informal advisory capacity in regard to the technical, economic, and social effects of the proposed amendments.

The various individuals and organizations that work in a particular policy area form a loosely knit community. The boundaries and membership of an **issue network** are hardly precise, but participants share expertise in a policy domain and interact frequently.[25] In general terms, such networks include members of Congress, committee staffers, agency officials, lawyers, lobbyists, consultants, scholars, and public relations specialists. This makes for a large number of participants. One study identified over twelve hundred interest groups that had some contact with government officials in Washington in relation to health care over a five-year period.[26] Not all of the participants in an issue network have a working relationship with all the others. Indeed, some may be chronic antagonists. Others tend to be allies.

The common denominator in a network is not the same political outlook; it is policy expertise. One must have the necessary expertise to enter the community of activists and politicians who influence policymaking in an issue area. Consider Medicare, for example. The program is crucial to the health of the elderly, and with millions of baby boomers rapidly approaching retirement age, it needs to be restructured to make sure there will be enough money available to care for them all. But to enter the political debate on this issue requires specialized knowledge. What is the difference between "global capitation"

issue network
A shared-knowledge group consisting of representatives of various interests involved in some particular aspect of public policy.

and "fee for service"? What's the "doughnut hole" in Medicare Part D? "Advance directives" and "withholds for never events" may be grating jargon to the uninitiated, but they are meaningful terms to those in this network.

The members of an issue network speak the same language. They can participate in the negotiation and compromise of policymaking because they can offer concrete, detailed solutions to the problems at hand. They understand the substance of policy, the way Washington works, and one another's viewpoints.

In a number of ways, issue networks promote pluralist democracy. They are open systems, populated by a wide range of interest groups. Decision making is not centralized in the hands of a few key players; policies are formulated in a participatory fashion. But there is still no guarantee that all relevant interests are represented, and those with the greatest financial resources have an advantage. Nevertheless, issue networks provide access to government for a diverse set of competing interests and thus further the pluralist ideal.[27]

Those who prefer majoritarian democracy, however, see issue networks as an obstacle to achieving their vision of how government should operate. The technical complexity of contemporary issues makes it especially difficult for the public at large to exert control over policy outcomes. However, although issue networks promote pluralism, keep in mind that majoritarian influences on policymaking are still significant. The broad contours of public opinion can be a dominant force on highly visible issues. Elections, too, send messages to policymakers about the most widely discussed campaign issues. What issue networks have done, however, is facilitate pluralist politics in policy areas in which majoritarian influences are weak.

Economic Policy and the Budget

While the Washington policy community includes thousands of actors scattered throughout many issue networks, their issues share one thing in common. Whether large or small, there are economic and budgetary consequences to the acceptance of their policy proposals. Policymakers must consider not only the direct costs of a new antipollution measure or health program, but also the broader impact that starting such programs might have on the nation's economy. Tinkering with the economy is not a task to be undertaken lightly. Economists often disagree about the budgetary impact of various programs and whether they would help or hurt broader efforts to control the ups and downs of the nation's economy.

Economic Theory

Government efforts to control the economy rely on theories about how the economy responds to government taxing and spending policies and its control of the money supply. How policymakers tax and spend, or loosen and tighten interest rates, depends on their beliefs about how the economy functions and the proper role of government in the economy.

Keynesian theory
An economic theory stating that the government can stabilize the economy—that is, can smooth business cycles—by controlling the level of aggregate demand, and that the level of aggregate demand can be controlled by means of fiscal and monetary policies.

fiscal policies
Economic policies that involve government spending and taxing.

deficit financing
The Keynesian technique of spending beyond government income to combat an economic slump. Its purpose is to inject extra money into the economy to stimulate aggregate demand.

monetary policies
Economic policies that involve control of, and changes in, the supply of money.

inflation
An economic condition characterized by price increases linked to a decrease in the value of the currency.

Federal Reserve System
The system of banks that acts as the central bank of the United States and controls major monetary policies.

Keynesian theory, developed by John Maynard Keynes, a British economist, holds that government can stabilize the economy through a combination of fiscal and monetary policies.[28] **Fiscal policies**, which are enacted by the president and Congress, involve changes in government spending and taxing. When demand for goods and services is too low, according to Keynes, government should either spend more itself—hiring people and thus giving them money—or cut taxes, leaving people more of their own money to spend. When demand is too great, the government should either spend less or raise taxes, leaving people less money to spend. Governments frequently use the Keynesian technique of **deficit financing**—spending in excess of tax revenues. Most deficits are financed with funds borrowed through the issuing of government bonds, notes, or other securities. President Obama's $787 billion stimulus package in 2009 drew heavy fire, but even conservative economists credit it with saving millions of jobs and contributing to 5.7 percent economic growth by the end of the year.[29]

Monetary policies involve changes in the money supply and operate less directly on the economy. Increasing the amount of money in circulation increases demand and thus increases **inflation**, price increases that decrease the value of currency. Decreasing the money supply decreases aggregate demand and inflationary pressures. Monetary policies in the United States are under the control of the **Federal Reserve System**, which acts as the country's central bank. At the top of the system is the board of governors, seven members who are appointed by the president for staggered terms of fourteen years. The president designates one member of the board to be its chairperson, serving a four-year term that extends beyond the president's term of office.

Budgeting for Public Policy

To most people the national budget is B-O-R-I-N-G. To national politicians, it is an exciting script for high drama. The numbers, categories, and percentages that numb normal minds cause politicians' nostrils to flare and their hearts to pound. The budget is a battlefield on which politicians wage war over the programs they support.

Today, the president proposes the budget before Congressional deliberation. This was not always the case. Before 1921, Congress prepared the budget under its constitutional authority to raise taxes and appropriate funds. The budget was formed piecemeal by enacting a series of laws that originated in the many committees involved in the highly decentralized process of raising revenue, authorizing expenditures, and appropriating funds.

Congressional budgeting (such as it was) worked well enough for a nation of farmers but not for an industrialized nation with a growing population and an increasingly active government. Soon after World War I, Congress realized that the budget-making process needed to be centralized. With the Budget and Accounting Act of 1921, it thrust the responsibility for preparing the budget onto the president. The act established the Bureau of the Budget to prepare the president's budget for submission to Congress each January. Congress retained its constitutional authority to raise and spend funds, but now it would begin its work with the president's budget as its starting point. And all executive agencies' budget requests had to be funneled for review through the Bureau of the Budget (which became the Office of Management and Budget in 1970); requests that were consistent with the president's overall economic and legislative program were incorporated into the president's budget.

The Nature of the Budget

The national budget is complex, but its basic elements are not beyond understanding. We begin with some definitions. The *Budget of the United States Government* is the annual financial plan that the president is required to submit to Congress at the start of each year. It applies to the next **fiscal year (FY)**, the interval the government uses for accounting purposes. Currently, the fiscal year runs from October 1 to September 30. The budget is named for the year in which it *ends*, so the FY 2012 budget applies to the twelve months from October 1, 2011, to September 30, 2012.

Broadly, the budget defines **budget authority** (how much government agencies are authorized to spend on current and future programs); **budget outlays**, or expenditures (how much agencies are expected to spend this year); and **receipts** (how much is expected in taxes and other revenues). President Obama's FY 2012 budget proposal contained *authority* for expenditures of $3.685 trillion, but it

fiscal year (FY)
The twelve-month period from October 1 to September 30 used by the government for accounting purposes. A fiscal year budget is named for the year in which it ends.

budget authority
The amounts that government agencies are authorized to spend for current and future programs.

budget outlays
The amounts that government agencies are expected to spend in the fiscal year.

receipts
For a government, the amount expected or obtained in taxes and other revenues.

called for outlays of $3.729 trillion. His budget also anticipated receipts of $2.627 trillion, leaving an estimated *deficit* of $1.101 trillion—the difference between receipts and outlays in a single fiscal year.[30] A deficit is different from the **public debt**, which represents the accumulated sum of borrowing (mainly to finance past annual deficits) that remains to be paid. The total public debt on May 1, 2011, was a staggering $14.3 *trillion,* over 50 percent more than it had been a mere three years earlier.[31] However, about $4.6 trillion of that total public debt is in "intragovernmental holdings"—money that one part of the government owes to another part. An example of intragovernmental holding would be when the Treasury Department borrows money from the Social Security Trust Fund. The money might be used to pay for highway construction, but it is still owed to the Social Security Trust Fund and is part of the public debt. Of the portion of the public debt actually owed to the public, almost half is held by institutions or individuals in other countries (see "Politics of Global Change").

Preparing the President's Budget

The budget that the president submits to Congress each winter is the end product of a process that begins the previous spring under the supervision of the **Office of Management and Budget (OMB).** OMB is located within the Executive Office of the President and is headed by a director appointed by the president with the approval of the Senate. The OMB, with a staff of more than five hundred, is the most powerful domestic agency in the bureaucracy, and its director, who attends meetings of the president's cabinet, is one of the most powerful figures in government.

Thousands of pages long, the president's budget contains more than numbers. It also explains individual spending programs in terms of national needs and agency objectives, and it analyzes proposed taxes and other receipts.

The OMB initiates the budget process each spring by meeting with the president to discuss the economic situation and his budgetary priorities. It then sends broad budgeting guidelines to every government agency and requests their initial projection of how much money they will need for the next fiscal year. The OMB assembles this information and makes recommendations to the president, who then develops more precise guidelines describing how much each is likely to get. By summer, the agencies are asked to prepare budgets based on the new guidelines. By fall, they submit their formal

public debt
The accumulated sum of past government borrowing that remains to be paid.

Office of Management and Budget (OMB)
The budgeting arm of the Executive Office; prepares the president's budget.

Politics of Global Change

We Buy More, and We Borrow More

Globalization produces economic interdependence among nations. Over the past four decades, Americans have been buying more goods and services from other countries than we are selling to them. Foreigners have been using their profits to buy U.S. government securities, thus acquiring increasing shares of our public debt. Excluding the 4.5 trillion in intragovernmental holdings, the publicly held portion of the debt totaled over $7.5 trillion at the end of 2009, of which foreign individuals, institutions, and governments held almost half. In effect, foreigners have been lending us money to buy their goods and services.

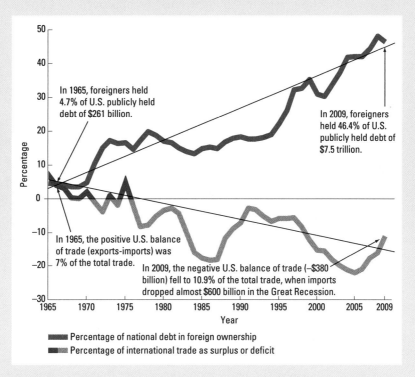

In 1965, foreigners held 4.7% of U.S. publicly held debt of $261 billion.

In 2009, foreigners held 46.4% of U.S. publicly held debt of $7.5 trillion.

In 1965, the positive U.S. balance of trade (exports-imports) was 7% of the total trade.

In 2009, the negative U.S. balance of trade (–$380 billion) fell to 10.9% of the total trade, when imports dropped almost $600 billion in the Great Recession.

■■■ Percentage of national debt in foreign ownership
■■■ Percentage of international trade as surplus or deficit

Sources: Office of Management and Budget, "Table 6-7: Foreign Holdings of Federal Debt," in *Analytical Perspectives: Budget of the U.S. Government, Fiscal Year 2011* (Washington, D.C.: U.S. Government Printing Office, 2010); U.S. Census Bureau, Foreign Trade Division, "U.S. Trade in Goods and Services, Balance of Payments (BOP) Basis," http://www.census.gov/foreign-trade/statistics/historical/gands.txt, and "Historical Series," http://www.census.gov/foreign-trade/statistics/historical/index.html.

budgets to the OMB, where budget analysts scrutinize agency requests, considering both their costs and their consistency with the president's legislative program. A lot of politicking goes on at this stage as agency heads try to circumvent the OMB by pleading for their pet projects with presidential advisers and perhaps even with the president himself.

Political negotiations over the budget may extend into the early winter, often until it goes to the printer. The voluminous document looks very much like a finished product, but the figures it contains are not final. In giving the president the responsibility for preparing the budget in 1921, Congress simply provided itself with a starting point for its own work.

Passing the Congressional Budget

The president's budget must be approved by Congress. Its process for doing so is a creaky conglomeration of traditional procedures overlaid with structural reforms from the 1970s, external constraints from the 1980s, and changes introduced by the 1990 Budget Enforcement Act. The cumbersome process has had difficulty producing a budget according to Congress's own timetable.

The Traditional Procedure: The Committee Structure. Traditionally, the tasks of budget making were divided among a number of committees, a process that has been retained. Three types of committees are involved in budgeting:

tax committees
The two committees of Congress responsible for raising the revenue with which to run the government.

authorization committees
Committees of Congress that can authorize spending in their particular areas of responsibility.

appropriations committees
Committees of Congress that decide which of the programs passed by the authorization committees will actually be funded.

- **Tax committees** are responsible for raising the revenues to run the government. The Ways and Means Committee in the House and the Finance Committee in the Senate consider all proposals for taxes, tariffs, and other receipts contained in the president's budget.
- **Authorization committees** (such as the House Armed Services Committee and the Senate Banking, Housing, and Urban Affairs Committee) have jurisdiction over particular legislative subjects. The House has about twenty committees that can authorize spending and the Senate about fifteen. Each pores over the portions of the budget that pertain to its area of responsibility. However, in recent years, power has shifted from the authorization committees to the appropriations committees.
- **Appropriations committees** decide which of the programs approved by the authorization committees will actually be

funded (that is, given money to spend). For example, the House Armed Services Committee might propose building a new line of tanks for the army, and it might succeed in getting this proposal enacted into law. But the tanks will never be built unless the appropriations committees appropriate funds for that purpose. Thirteen distinct appropriations bills are supposed to be enacted each year to fund the nation's spending.

Two serious problems are inherent in a budgeting process that involves three distinct kinds of congressional committees. First, the two-step spending process (first authorization, then appropriation) is complex; it offers wonderful opportunities for interest groups to get into the budgeting act in the spirit of pluralist democracy. Second, because one group of legislators in each house plans for revenues and many other groups plan for spending, no one is responsible for the budget as a whole.

Three Decades of Budgetary Reforms. Congress surrendered considerable authority in 1921 when it gave the president the responsibility of preparing the budget. During the next fifty years, attempts by Congress to regain control of the budgeting process failed because of jurisdictional squabbles between the revenue and appropriations committees.

In the 1970s, Congress added a new committee structure to combat the pluralist politics inherent in the old procedures and to make budget choices in a more majoritarian manner, by roll-call votes in both chambers. The Budget and Impoundment Control Act of 1974 fashioned a typically political solution to the problems of wounded egos and competing jurisdictions that had frustrated previous attempts to change the budget-making process. All the tax and appropriations committees (and chairpersons) were retained, but new House and Senate budget committees were superimposed over the old committee structure. The **budget committees** supervise a comprehensive budget review process, aided by the Congressional Budget Office. The **Congressional Budget Office (CBO)**, with a staff of more than two hundred, has acquired a budgetary expertise equal to that of the president's OMB, so it can prepare credible alternative budgets for Congress.

The 1974 reforms also set up a timetable for the congressional budgeting process—that is, certain steps were to be taken by certain dates. This process worked reasonably well for the first few years, but it broke down when President Reagan submitted annual budgets heavy with military spending and huge deficits. The

budget committees
One committee in each house of Congress that supervises a comprehensive budget review process.

Congressional Budget Office (CBO)
The budgeting arm of Congress, which prepares alternative budgets to those prepared by the president's OMB.

Democratic Congress refused to propose a tax increase to reduce the deficit without the president's cooperation, and Congress encountered increasing difficulty in enacting its budget resolutions according to its own timetable.

In the 1980s, Congress tried to force itself to balance the budget by setting annual targets. If Congress did not meet the deficit level in any year, a law would trigger across-the-board budget cuts. Unable to make the deficit meet the targets in 1986 or 1987, Congress and the president simply changed the law to match the deficit, demonstrating that Congress lacked the will to force itself to balance the budget by an orderly plan of deficit reduction.

In the 1990s, Congress introduced some belt-tightening reforms and passed important tax increases that led to a balanced budget. Threatened by another huge deficit for FY 1991, Congress and President George H. W. Bush agreed on a new package of reforms and deficit targets in the **Budget Enforcement Act (BEA)** of 1990. Instead of defining annual deficit targets, the BEA defined two types of spending: **mandatory spending** and **discretionary spending**. Spending is mandatory for **entitlement** programs (such as Social Security and veterans' pensions) that provide benefits to individuals legally entitled to them and cannot be reduced without changing the law. Discretionary spending entails expenditures authorized by annual appropriations, such as for the military. The law also established pay-as-you-go restrictions—called **pay-go**—on mandatory spending: any proposed expansion of an entitlement program must be offset by cuts to another program or by a tax increase. Similarly, any tax cut must be offset by a tax increase somewhere else or by spending cuts.[32] The law also imposed limits, or "caps," on discretionary spending.

To get the Democratic Congress to pass the BEA, President George H. W. Bush accepted some modest tax increases—despite having vowed at the 1988 Republican National Convention: "Read my lips: no new taxes." The tax hike may have cost him reelection in 1992. Nevertheless, the 1990 law did limit discretionary spending and slowed unfinanced entitlements and tax cuts. The 1993 Deficit Reduction Act under President Bill Clinton made even more progress in reducing the deficit by cutting spending and raising taxes. By 1997, the deficit declined to $22 billion.[33]

The 1990 and 1993 budget agreements, both of which encountered strong opposition in Congress, helped pave the way for the historic **Balanced Budget Act (BBA)** that President Clinton and Congress negotiated in 1997. Empowered by strong tax revenues

---

Budget Enforcement Act (BEA)
A 1990 law that distinguished between mandatory and discretionary spending.

mandatory spending
In the Budget Enforcement Act of 1990, expenditures required by previous commitments.

discretionary spending
In the Budget Enforcement Act of 1990, authorized expenditures from annual appropriations.

entitlement
A benefit to which every eligible person has a legal right and that the government cannot deny without changing the law.

pay-go
In the Budget Enforcement Act of 1990, the requirement that any tax cut or expansion of an entitlement program must be offset by a tax increase or other savings.

Balanced Budget Act (BBA)
A 1997 law that promised to balance the budget by 2002.

during a long period of economic growth, the BBA accomplished what most observers thought was beyond political possibility. It not only led to the balanced budget it promised but actually produced a budget surplus ahead of schedule—the first surplus since 1969.

The End of Budgetary Reform, 2000–Present. In the early 2000s, President Bush and Republicans in Congress advocated using the budget surplus for large across-the-board tax cuts to return money to taxpayers.[34] Although the caps on discretionary spending and pay-go requirements, established by the 1990 Budget Enforcement Act, helped balance the budget entering 2000, many members of Congress in both parties resented its restrictions on their freedom to make fiscal decisions. Accordingly, Congress allowed the caps on discretionary spending and the pay-go requirements to expire at the end of 2002.[35] Since 2002, the government has run budget deficits, not surpluses. Congress reinstituted the pay-go rules in 2010. Ironically, Congress passed pay-go as part of a measure that also raised the government's borrowing limit (called the "debt ceiling") from $12.4 to $14.3 trillion.[36]

Taxing and Spending Decisions

Ultimately, the budget is a policy document in which programs are funded in an effort to achieve policy objectives and address national problems. Decisions on how to raise and spend government funds are inherently political, because members of the public, governmental leaders, and the political parties all hold diverse and competing perspectives on what policies should be adopted. Many of these policy decisions are shaped by circumstances outside the government's immediate control.

Tax Policies. Tax policy is designed to provide a continuous flow of income. A major text on government finance says that tax policy is sometimes changed to accomplish one or more of several objectives:

- To adjust overall revenue to meet budget outlays
- To make the tax burden more equitable for taxpayers
- To help control the economy by raising taxes (thus decreasing demand) or lowering taxes (thus increasing demand)[37]

In 1986 Congress passed one of the most sweeping tax reform laws in history. The new policy reclaimed a great deal of revenue

We Gave at the Bureaucracy

One of many clerks working at the Cincinnati Internal Revenue Service Center in Covington, Kentucky, one of the ten centers operated by the Internal Revenue Service to process tax forms and taxpayer requests. Each processes millions of forms each year.

(© Mike Simons/Getty Images)

progressive taxation
A system of taxation whereby the rich pay proportionately higher taxes than the poor; used by governments to redistribute wealth and thus promote equality.

by eliminating many deductions for corporations and wealthy citizens. By eliminating many tax brackets, the new tax policy approached the idea of a flat tax—one that requires everyone to pay at the same rate. A flat tax has the appeal of simplicity, but it violates the principle of **progressive taxation**, under which the rich pay proportionately higher taxes than the poor. Governments can rely on progressive taxation to redistribute wealth and thus promote economic equality.

After the 1986 tax reform, there were only two tax rates: 15 and 28 percent. In 1990 George H. W. Bush was forced to violate his pledge of "no new taxes" by creating a third tax rate, 31 percent. Clinton created a fourth level, 39.6 percent in 1993, moving toward a more progressive tax structure.

Soon after his election, George W. Bush got Congress to pass a complex $1.35 trillion tax cut, with a top personal tax rate of 35 percent. Intended to stimulate the economy, the tax cuts also reduced the government's tax revenue needed to match spending.[38] Budget deficits quickly returned under Bush, owing to reduced revenue, a downturn in the stock market, and unanticipated expenses for homeland security and military action following the September 11 attacks on the United States. The recession that began at the end of 2007 significantly reduced government tax revenues. One study showed that from December 2007 to May 2008, approximately one-third of the adults in the work force were unemployed at some point, and 55 percent of the adults in the work force either were unemployed, had wages cut, or had their hours reduced involuntarily.[39] All of these events reduce tax revenue. The deficit zoomed to over a trillion dollars in Bush's last budget, which reflected costs of his $168 billion stimulus package and his $700 billion Troubled Assets Relief Program (TARP). The deficit grew further with Obama's $787 billion stimulus package in 2009.

Spending Policies. The FY 2012 budget projects spending over $3,700,000,000,000—that's almost four *trillion* dollars (or four thousand billion, if you prefer). Where does the money go? Figure 14.2 shows the relative size of eighteen categories of budget outlays proposed in President Obama's budget for FY 2012.

To understand current expenditures, it is a good idea to examine national expenditures over time, as shown in Figure 14.3. The effect of World War II is clear: spending for national defense rose sharply after 1940, peaked at about 90 percent of the budget in 1945, and fell to about 30 percent in peacetime. The percentage allocated to defense rose again in the early 1950s, reflecting rearmament during the Cold War with the Soviet Union. Thereafter, the share of the budget devoted to defense decreased steadily (except for the bump during the Vietnam War in the late 1960s). This trend was reversed by the Carter administration in the 1970s but shot up during the Reagan presidency. Defense spending significantly decreased under George H. W. Bush and continued to fall under Clinton. Following the September 11 terrorist attacks, however, defense spending rose sharply. President George W. Bush's proposed FY 2009 budget estimated outlays for national defense more than double the national defense budget for FY 2001. Even taking inflation into account, this represented a 59.5 percent increase in constant dollars over the course of his administration.[40] The Iraq war alone cost an estimated $600 billion over the first five years.[41]

Government payments to individuals (Social Security checks) consistently consumed less of the budget than national defense until 1971. Since then, payments to individuals have accounted for the largest portion of the national budget, and they have been increasing. Net interest payments also increased substantially during the years of budget deficits. Pressure from payments for

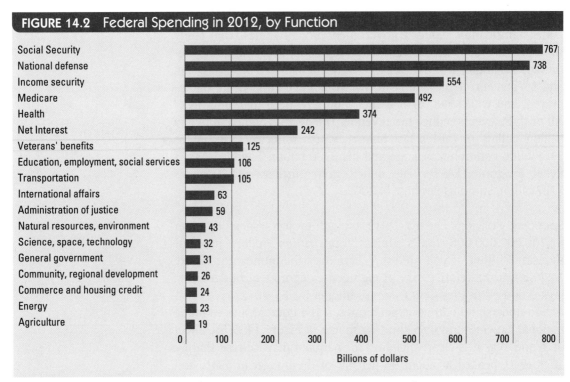

FIGURE 14.2 Federal Spending in 2012, by Function

Federal budget authorities and outlays are organized into about twenty categories, some of which are mainly for bookkeeping purposes. This graph shows expected outlays for each of eighteen substantive functions in President Obama's FY 2012 budget. The final budget differed somewhat from this distribution because Congress amended some of the president's spending proposals. The graph makes clear the huge differences among spending categories. Although the nation is engaged in wars abroad and military spending accounts for 19 percent of the budget, about 35 percent of government outlays are for payments to individuals through Social Security and income security programs. Taken together, health costs (including Medicare) account for almost 25 percent (more than national defense), and net interest consumes just under 7 percent of all outlays. This leaves relatively little for transportation, agriculture, justice, science, and energy—matters often regarded as important centers of government activity—which fall under the heading of "discretionary spending."

Source: Executive Office of the President, *Budget of the United States Government, Historical Tables, Fiscal Year 2012* (Washington, D.C.: U.S. Government Printing Office, 2011), Table 3.1.

national defense, individuals, and interest on the public debt has squeezed all other government outlays.

National spending has increased from about 15 percent of gross domestic product (GDP) soon after World War II to over 20 percent, for many years at the price of a growing national deficit. There are two major explanations for this steady increase in government spending. One is bureaucratic, the other political.

The bureaucratic explanation for spending increases involves **incremental budgeting**. When compiling their funding requests for

incremental budgeting
A method of budget making that involves adding new funds (an increment) onto the amount previously budgeted (in last year's budget).

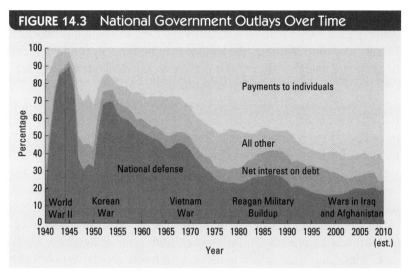

FIGURE 14.3 National Government Outlays Over Time

This chart plots the percentage of the annual budget devoted to four major expense categories over time. It shows that significant changes have occurred in national spending since 1940. During World War II, defense spending consumed more than 80 percent of the national budget. Defense again accounted for most national expenditures during the Cold War of the 1950s. Since then, the military's share of expenditures has declined, while payments to individuals (mostly in the form of Social Security benefits) have increased dramatically. Although recent defense spending to support wars in Iraq and Afghanistan consumes more constant dollars (adjusted to eliminate the effects of inflation) than defense spending at any time since 1945, this chart shows that as a proportion of the budget, defense has been dwarfed by the even more rapidly growing payments to individuals.

Source: Executive Office of the President, *Budget of the United States Government, Fiscal Year 2011: Historical Tables* (Washington, D.C.: U.S. Government Printing Office, 2010), Table 6-1.

the coming year, bureaucrats traditionally ask for the amount they received in the current year, plus some increment to fund new projects. Because Congress already approved the agency's budget for the current year, it pays little attention to the agency's current size (the largest part of its budget) and focuses instead on the extra money (the increment) requested for the next year. As a result, few agencies are ever cut back, and spending continually goes up.

Incremental budgeting produces a sort of bureaucratic momentum that continually pushes up spending. Once an agency is established, it attracts a clientele that defends its existence and supports the agency's requests for extra funds to do more year after year. Because budgeting is a two-step process, agencies that get cut back in the authorizing committees sometimes manage (assisted by their interest group clientele) to get funds restored in the appropriations committees—and if not in the House, then perhaps in the Senate. So incremental budgeting and the congressional budget-making process itself are ideally suited to pluralist politics.

Certain government programs are effectively immune to budget reductions, because they have been enacted into law and enshrined in politics. For example, Social Security legislation guarantees certain benefits to program participants when they retire. Medicare and veterans' benefits also entitle citizens to certain payments. Because these payments have to be made under existing law, they represent **mandatory outlays**. In Obama's FY 2012 budget, about 64 percent of all budget outlays were uncontrollable or relatively uncontrollable—mainly payments to individuals under Social Security, Medicare, Medicaid, and public assistance; interest on the public debt; and farm price supports. About 65 percent of the rest went for "security" (national defense, homeland security), leaving less than 13 percent of the total outlays in "nonsecurity" discretionary spending.[42] To be sure, Congress could change the laws to abolish entitlement payments. But politics argues against large-scale reductions.

What spending cuts would be acceptable to the public? In the abstract, voters favor cutting government spending, but they tend to favor maintaining "government programs that help needy people and deal with important national problems."[43] In fact, when a national poll asked whether respondents thought federal spending should be "increased, decreased, or kept about the same" for twelve different purposes—highways, welfare, public schools, crime, child care, border security, terrorism, aid to the poor, Social Security, science and technology, the environment, and foreign aid—respondents favored increasing or keeping about the same level of spending for *every* purpose!"[44] A perplexed Congress, trying to reduce the budget deficit, faces a public that favors funding programs at even higher levels than those favored by most lawmakers.[45] Moreover, spending for the most expensive of these programs—Social Security and Medicare—is uncontrollable.

mandatory outlay
A payment that government must make by law.

Social Security
Social insurance that provides economic assistance to persons faced with unemployment, disability, or old age; it is financed by taxes on employers and employees.

Social Security. The largest entitlement program is **Social Security**, a social insurance program that provides economic assistance to people faced with unemployment, disability, or old age; it is financed by taxes on employers and employees. Initially, Social Security benefits were distributed only to the aged, the unemployed, and surviving spouses—most of whom were widows—with dependent children.

Today, Social Security also provides medical care for the elderly and income support for the disabled.

The Social Security taxes collected today pay the benefits of today's retirees, with surpluses held over, in theory at least, to help finance the retirement of future generations. Thus, Social Security is not a form of savings; it is a pay-as-you-go tax system. Today's workers support today's elderly.

When the program began, it had many contributors and few beneficiaries. The program could thus provide relatively large benefits with low taxes. In 1937, for example, the tax rate was 1 percent, and the Social Security taxes of nine workers supported each beneficiary. As the program matured and more people retired or became disabled, the ratio of workers to recipients decreased.

In FY 2010, the Social Security system paid old age, survivor, and disability benefits of a little over $696 billion to 54 million people and collected tax revenue from 157 million, a ratio of roughly 2.9 workers for every beneficiary.[46] On February 12, 2008, the first baby boomer, Kathleen Casey Kirschling, received her first benefit check from Social Security. The problem is that there are 80 million other baby boomers in line behind her.[47] As the bulk of the baby boom generation retires between 2010 and 2030, the number of retirees will grow at a much faster rate than the number of workers. By 2030, the ratio will decline to approximately two workers for every beneficiary.

To minimize the impact of the aging population and the impending retirement of the large baby boomer generation, the government has been collecting substantially more taxes each year than it needs to pay out in current benefits. The surplus has been put into a trust fund account. Due in part to the effects of the Great Recession, Social Security tax revenues fell below program costs in 2010, six years earlier than previously expected, and trust fund interest receipts were necessary to cover expenses. Though tax revenues are expected to rebound from 2012 to 2014, by 2015, benefit payments will permanently exceed tax receipts unless significant structural changes are made to the program. Ultimately, the Social Security Administration will need to tap into not only the interest revenue, but the trust fund itself to help cover monthly payments.[48] That will create a new challenge. The money in the trust fund has been invested in government securities. In other words, the Social Security funds for the future have been borrowed by the Treasury Department (and spent) to finance part of the government's general debt. (See Figure 14.4.)

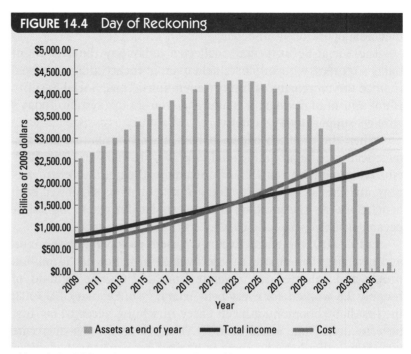

FIGURE 14.4   Day of Reckoning

Billions of 2009 dollars

Year

■ Assets at end of year   ▬ Total income   ▬ Cost

Although Social Security tax revenues dipped below program costs in 2010, taken together with interest income from the trust fund, total revenues still exceed benefits paid out. But after 2014, benefits paid out will permanently exceed revenues flowing into the program from taxes. With bankruptcy of the system looming so predictably, the debate over change boils down to two questions that politicians politely decline to answer: How soon will the national government change the current system, and how much will it change it?

Source: Social Security Administration, "Operations of the Combined OASI and DI Trust Funds, in Current Dollars," in *The 2010 Annual Report of the Board of Trustees of the Federal Old-Age and Survivors Insurance and Federal Disability Insurance Trust Funds* (Washington, D.C.: U.S. Government Printing Office, 9 August 2010), http://www.ssa.gov/OACT/TR/2010/lr6f8.html.

Social Security Act
The law that provided for Social Security and is the basis of modern American social welfare.

Medicare
A health insurance program for all persons older than sixty-five, as well as for some younger individuals with disabilities.

Politicians will face an inevitable dilemma: whether to reduce benefits and generate the ire of retirees or to raise taxes and generate the ire of taxpayers. As a group, older Americans exercise enormous political power. People at or approaching retirement age now make up over 30 percent of the potential electorate, and voter turnout among older Americans is reported to be about twice that of younger people.[49]

Medicare and Medicaid. The **Social Security Act** was amended in 1965 to provide **Medicare**, health care for all people aged sixty-five or older. Fearful of the power of the American Medical Association (AMA), which then opposed any form of government-provided medical care, the Democrats confined their efforts to a compulsory hospitaliza-tion insurance plan for the elderly (this is known today as Part A of Medicare). In addition, the bill contained a version of an alternative Re-publican plan that called for voluntary government-subsidized insur-ance to cover physicians' fees (this is known today as Part B of Medicare). A third program, added a year later, is called Medicaid; it provides medical aid to the poor through federally assisted state health programs. **Medicaid** is a need-based comprehensive medical and hospi-talization program; those who are very poor qualify. Finally, in 2003, the Congress passed the Medicare Prescription Drug, Improvement, and Modernization Act to provide beneficiaries with prescription drug cov-erage. By 2009, 10 percent of government spending on Medicare was devoted to the prescription plan.[50]

Medicare and Medicaid costs continue to increase at rates in excess of the cost of living. According to one author, "Medicaid has now overtaken Medicare in both enrollment and spending to become the largest health insurance program in the United States. It insures one-fifth of the nation's children and pays for one-third of all childbirths. It finances nearly 40 percent of all long-term care expenses, more than one-sixth of all drug costs, and half of states' mental health services. It is . . . the 'workhorse' of the U.S. health system."[51] Unlike Medicare, which is solely a federal program, Medicaid is jointly run and financed by the federal government and the states. In 2010, for instance, the federal share of Medicaid costs was $273 billion, just 59 percent of the total cost.[52] Since Medicaid is one of the most expensive items in state budgets, rising health-care costs and declining tax revenues in a recession place enormous economic pressures on states as well as the national government.[53]

Medicaid
A need-based comprehensive medical and hospitalization program.

Tying It Together

1. How and why does the government create policies?
   - A public policy is a general plan of action adopted by a govern-ment to solve a social problem, counter a threat, or pursue an objective.
   - The government sets policies in three categories:
     - distributive policies: allocate resources so that some segment of society can receive a service or benefit.

- redistributional policies: are explicitly designed to take resources from one sector of society and transfer them to another, which reflects the core value of greater equality.
- regulations: are applied to business markets in an attempt to make the market operate in a way that the government wants.
- The policymaking process can be separated into four stages:
  - agenda setting: the stage at which problems are defined as political issues; problems can be considered sources of policies for many reasons.
  - policy formulation: the stage at which formal policy proposals are developed and officials decide to adopt them; this can occur through a measure proposed by the president or legislation.
  - implementation: the stage at which the policy is carried out and coordination is critical.
  - policy evaluation: analysis of policy performance through feedback gathered by studies that measure the success of the policy.

2. What forces work against coherent problem solving in government?
   - Forces that work against cohesiveness include
     - fragmentation, as when a single policy problem is attacked in different and competing ways by government.
     - the separation of power, which divides authority and causes fragmentation.
     - federalism, which enables both states and the national government to legislate on an issue.
     - different agencies working on different aspects of a problem within different jurisdictions.
   - Forces that create coordination include
     - interagency task forces within the executive branch whose goal it is to develop a broad policy response that all relevant agencies can endorse.
     - the Office of Management and Budget (OMB), which acts as a coordinator.
     - reorganizations and White House reviews.
   - Issue networks provide opportunities for compromise and negotiation in order to create solutions and promote pluralist democracy. These are based on shared expertise rather than ideological similarity.

3. How is the national budget created?
   - The national budget defines
     - budget authority, or how much government agencies are authorized to spend on programs.

- budget outlays, or actual expenditures by agencies in a fiscal year.
  - receipts, or how much is expected in tax and other revenues.
- The OMB supervises the budget process in the executive branch by
  - initiating the process by meeting with the president and ascertaining his priorities.
  - assembling information and making recommendations to the president.
  - receiving budgets from other agencies and negotiating the budget.
- Approving budgets in Congress is cumbersome because
  - there are opportunities for special interest groups to get into the process.
  - it is an uncoordinated process in which one group of legislators in each house reviews the budget while others plan for spending.
- The Balanced Budget Act (BBA) was passed in 1997, and a balanced budget was delivered.
- A serious economic downturn, increased defense spending after 9/11, and skyrocketing entitlement programs have brought back enormous deficits.
- Tax policies are designed to provide a continuous flow of income.
- Entitlement programs (Social Security, Medicare, Medicaid) are mandatory outlays because they are required under current law and continue to increase.
- Most of the budget now consists of either defense and homeland security spending, which is difficult to cut, or mandatory programs of one form or another. Nonsecurity discretionary spending is less than 15 percent of the budget.

Test Prepper 14.1

Government Purposes and Public Policies

True or False?

1. Redistributional policies are designed to transfer government resources from one sector of society to another.
2. Policy evaluation always precedes policy implementation in the policymaking process.
3. Once old issues are resolved, there is no need to reconsider them.

Comprehension

4. How do policies originate?
5. Is the feedback from the policy evaluation stage always consistent? Give an example.

Test Prepper 14.2

Fragmentation and Coordination

True or False?

1. An issue network is made up of policy actors united by a common ideological perspective on an issue.
2. Fragmentation occurs when different parts of the government attack a problem in different ways.
3. Majoritarians do not value the role of issue networks in the policymaking process.

Comprehension

4. How does the separation of powers lead to fragmentation in policymaking?
5. How does the Office of Management and Budget (OMB) foster coordination within the executive branch?

Test Prepper 14.3

Economic Policy and the Budget

True or False?

1. The federal income tax generally brings in adequate revenue to cover government outlays.
2. The fiscal year (FY) runs from December 1 to November 30.
3. Social Security taxes bring in more money each year than is needed for current retirees.

Comprehension

4. What is the objective of tax policies?
5. Why would some argue that a flat tax is not a fair tax?

CourseMate CL Resources:

Visit www.cengagebrain.com/shop/ISBN/1111832587 for flashcards, web quizzes, videos and more!

Appendix

The Declaration of Independence, July 4, 1776

The Constitution of the United States of America

The Declaration of Independence, July 4, 1776

The unanimous Declaration of the thirteen United States of America
When in the course of human events, it becomes necessary for one people to dissolve the political bands which have connected them with another, and to assume, among the powers of the earth the separate and equal station to which the Laws of Nature and of Nature's God entitle them, a decent respect to the opinions of mankind requires that they should declare the causes which impel them to the separation.

We hold these truths to be self-evident, that all men are created equal, that they are endowed by their Creator with certain unalienable rights, that among these are life, liberty, and the pursuit of happiness. That to secure these rights, governments are instituted among men, deriving their just powers from the consent of the governed. That whenever any form of government becomes destructive of these ends, it is the right of the people to alter or to abolish it, and to institute new government, laying its foundation on such principles, and organizing its power in such form, as to them shall seem most likely to effect their safety and happiness. Prudence, indeed, will dictate that governments long established should not be changed for light and transient causes; and accordingly all experience hath shown, that mankind are more disposed to suffer, while evils are sufferable, than to right themselves by abolishing the forms to which they are accustomed. But when a long train of abuses and usurpations, pursuing invariably the same object evinces a design to reduce them under absolute despotism, it is their right, it is their duty, to throw off such government, and to provide new guards for their future security. Such has been the patient sufferance of these Colonies;

and such is now the necessity which constrains them to alter their former systems of government. The history of the present King of Great Britain is a history of repeated injuries and usurpations, all having in direct object the establishment of an absolute tyranny over these States. To prove this, let facts be submitted to a candid world.

He has refused his assent to laws, the most wholesome and necessary for the public good.

He has forbidden his governors to pass laws of immediate and pressing importance, unless suspended in their operation till his assent should be obtained; and, when so suspended, he has utterly neglected to attend to them.

He has refused to pass other laws for the accommodation of large districts of people, unless those people would relinquish the right of representation in the legislature, a right inestimable to them, and formidable to tyrants only.

He has called together legislative bodies at places unusual, uncomfortable, and distant from the depository of their public records, for the sole purpose of fatiguing them into compliance with his measures.

He has dissolved representative houses repeatedly, for opposing, with manly firmness, his invasions on the rights of the people.

He has refused for a long time, after such dissolutions, to cause others to be elected; whereby the legislative powers, incapable of annihilation, have returned to the people at large for their exercise; the State remaining, in the meantime exposed to all the dangers of invasions from without and convulsions within.

He has endeavored to prevent the population of these States; for that purpose obstructing the laws for naturalization of foreigners; refusing to pass others to encourage their migration hither, and raising the conditions of new appropriations of lands.

He has obstructed the administration of justice, by refusing his assent to laws for establishing judiciary powers.

He has made judges dependent on his will alone, for the tenure of their offices, and the amount and payment of their salaries.

He has erected a multitude of new offices, and sent hither swarms of officers to harass our people, and eat out their substance.

He has kept among us, in times of peace, standing armies, without the consent of our legislatures.

He has affected to render the military independent of and superior to the civil power.

He has combined with others to subject us to a jurisdiction foreign to our constitution, and unacknowledged by our laws; giving his assent to their acts of pretended legislation:

For quartering large bodies of armed troops among us;

For protecting them, by a mock trial, from punishment for any murders which they should commit on the inhabitants of these states;

For cutting off our trade with all parts of the world;

For imposing taxes on us without our consent;

For depriving us, in many cases, of the benefits of trial by jury;

For transporting us beyond seas, to be tried for pretended offenses;

For abolishing the free system of English laws in a neighboring province, establishing therein an arbitrary government, and enlarging its boundaries, so as to render it at once an example and fit instrument for introducing the same absolute rule into these Colonies;

For taking away our Charters, abolishing our most valuable laws, and altering fundamentally the forms of our governments;

For suspending our own Legislatures, and declaring themselves invested with power to legislate for us in all cases whatsoever.

He has abdicated government here, by declaring us out of his protection and waging war against us.

He has plundered our seas, ravaged our coasts, burned our towns, and destroyed the lives of our people.

He is at this time transporting large armies of foreign mercenaries to complete the works of death, desolation, and tyranny, already begun with circumstances of cruelty and perfidy scarcely paralleled in the most barbarous ages, and totally unworthy the head of a civilized nation.

He has constrained our fellow-citizens taken captive on the high seas to bear arms against their country, to become the executioners of their friends and brethren, or to fall themselves by their hands.

He has excited domestic insurrection among us, and has endeavored to bring on the inhabitants of our frontiers the merciless Indian savages, whose known rule of warfare is an undistinguished destruction of all ages, sexes, and conditions.

In every stage of these oppressions we have petitioned for redress in the most humble terms: our repeated petitions have been answered only by repeated injury. A prince whose character is thus marked by every act which may define a tyrant, is unfit to be the ruler of a free people.

Nor have we been wanting in our attentions to our British brethren. We have warned them, from time to time, of attempts by their Legislature to extend an unwarrantable jurisdiction over us. We have reminded them of the circumstances of our emigration and settlement here. We have appealed to their native justice and magnanimity, and we have conjured them by the ties of our common kindred to disavow these usurpations, which would inevitably interrupt our connections and correspondence. They too have been deaf to the voice of justice and of consanguinity. We must, therefore, acquiesce in the necessity, which denounces our separation, and hold them, as we hold the rest of mankind, enemies in war, in peace friends.

We, therefore, the Representatives of the United States of America, in General Congress assembled, appealing to the Supreme Judge of the world for the rectitude of our intentions, do, in the name, and by the authority of the good people of these Colonies, solemnly publish and declare, That these United Colonies are, and of right ought to be, FREE AND INDEPENDENT STATES; that they are absolved from all allegiance to the British Crown, and that all political connection between them and the State of Great Britain is, and ought to be, totally dissolved; and that, as Free and Independent States they have full power to levy war, conclude peace, contract alliances, establish commerce, and do all other acts and things which independent States may of right do. And for the support of this declaration, with a firm reliance on the protection of Divine Providence, we mutually pledge to each other our lives, our fortunes and our sacred honor.

JOHN HANCOCK
and fifty-five others

The Constitution of the United States of America*
[Preamble: outlines goals and effect]

We the people of the United States, in order to form a more perfect Union, establish Justice, insure domestic Tranquility, provide for the common defence, promote the general Welfare, and secure the Blessings of Liberty to ourselves and our Posterity, do ordain and establish this Constitution for the United States of America.

Article I
[The legislative branch]

[Powers vested]

Section 1 All legislative Powers herein granted shall be vested in a Congress of the United States, which shall consist of a Senate and a House of Representatives.

[House of Representatives: selection, term, qualifications, apportionment of seats, census requirement, exclusive power to impeach]

Section 2 The House of Representatives shall be composed of Members chosen every second Year by the people of the several States, and the Electors in each State shall have the Qualifications requisite for Electors of the most numerous Branch of the State Legislature.

No person shall be a Representative who shall not have attained to the Age of twenty five Years, and been seven Years a Citizen of the United States, and who shall not, when elected, be an Inhabitant of that State in which he shall be chosen.

Representatives and direct Taxes shall be apportioned among the several States which may be included within this Union, according to their respective numbers, *which shall be determined by adding to the whole Number of free Persons, including those bound to Service for a Term of Years and excluding Indians not taxed, three-fifths of all other Persons.* The actual Enumeration shall be made within three Years after the first Meeting of the Congress of the United States, and within every subsequent Term of ten Years, in such Manner as they shall by Law direct. The number of Representatives shall not exceed one for every thirty Thousand, but each State shall have at Least one Representative;

*Passages no longer in effect are printed in italic type.

and until such enumeration shall be made, the State of New Hampshire shall be entitled to choose three, Massachusetts eight, Rhode Island and Providence Plantations one, Connecticut five, New York six, New Jersey four, Pennsylvania eight, Delaware one, Maryland six, Virginia ten, North Carolina five, South Carolina five, and Georgia three.

When vacancies happen in the Representation from any State, the Executive Authority thereof shall issue Writs of Election to fill such Vacancies.

The House of Representatives shall chuse their Speaker and other Officers; and shall have the sole Power of Impeachment.

[Senate: selection, term, qualifications, exclusive power to try impeachments]

Section 3 The Senate of the United States shall be composed of two Senators from each State, *chosen by the Legislature thereof,* for six years; and each Senator shall have one Vote.

Immediately after they shall be assembled in Consequence of the first Election, they shall be divided as equally as may be into three Classes. The Seats of the Senators of the first Class shall be vacated at the Expiration of the second Year, of the second Class at the expiration of the fourth Year, and of the third Class at the expiration of the sixth Year, so that one-third may be chosen every second Year; *and if Vacancies happen by Resignation or otherwise, during the Recess of the Legislature of any State, the Executive thereof may make temporary Appointments until the next meeting of the legislature, which shall then fill such Vacancies.*

No person shall be a Senator who shall not have attained to the Age of thirty Years, and been nine Years a Citizen of the United States, and who shall not, when elected, be an Inhabitant of that State for which he shall be chosen.

The Vice President of the United States shall be President of the Senate, but shall have no Vote, unless they be equally divided.

The Senate shall choose their other officers, and also a President pro tempore, in the absence of the Vice President, or when he shall exercise the Office of President of the United States.

The Senate shall have the sole Power to try all impeachments. When sitting for that purpose, they shall be on Oath or Affirmation. When the President of the United States is tried, the Chief Justice shall preside: and no Person shall be convicted without the Concurrence of two-thirds of the members Present.

Judgment in Cases of Impeachment shall not extend further than to removal from the Office, and disqualification to hold and enjoy any Office of honor, Trust or Profit under the United States: but the Party convicted shall nevertheless be liable and subject to Indictment, Trial, Judgment and Punishment, according to Law.

[Elections]

Section 4 The Times, Places and Manner of holding Elections for Senators and Representatives shall be prescribed in each State by the

Legislature thereof; but the Congress may at any time by Law make or alter such regulations, except as to the Places of chusing Senators.

The Congress shall assemble at least once in every Year, and such meeting *shall be on the first Monday in December, unless they shall by Law appoint a different Day.*

[Powers and duties of the two chambers: rules of procedure, power over members]

Section 5 Each House shall be the Judge of the Elections, Returns and Qualifications of its own Members, and a Majority of each shall constitute a Quorum to do Business; but a smaller Number may adjourn from day to day, and may be authorized to compel the Attendance of absent Members, in such Manner, and under such Penalties as each House may provide.

Each House may determine the Rules of its proceedings, punish its Members for disorderly behaviour, and with the Concurrence of two thirds, expel a Member.

Each House shall keep a Journal of its Proceedings, and from time to time publish the same, excepting such Parts as may in their Judgment require Secrecy; and the Yeas and Nays of the Members of either House on any question shall, at the Desire of one fifth of those Present, be entered on the Journal.

Neither House, during the Session of Congress, shall, without the Consent of the other, adjourn for more than three days, nor to any other Place than that in which the two Houses shall be sitting.

[Compensation, privilege from arrest, privilege of speech, disabilities of members]

Section 6 The Senators and Representatives shall receive a Compensation for their services, to be ascertained by Law, and paid out of the Treasury of the United States. They shall in all Cases, except Treason, Felony and Breach of the Peace, be privileged from Arrest during their Attendance at the Session of their respective Houses, and in going to and returning from the same; and for any Speech or Debate in either House, they shall not be questioned in any other Place.

No Senator or Representative shall, during the Time for which he was elected, be appointed to any civil Office under the Authority of the United States, which shall have been created, or the Emoluments whereof shall have been increased, during such time; and no Person holding any Office under the United States, shall be a Member of either House during his Continuance in Office.

[Legislative process: revenue bills, approval or veto power of president]

Section 7 All bills for raising Revenue shall originate in the House of Representatives; but the Senate may propose or concur with Amendments as on other Bills.

Every Bill which shall have passed the House of Representatives and the Senate, shall, before it become a Law, be presented to the President of the United States; if he approve he shall sign it, but if not he shall return it with Objections to that House in which it originated, who shall enter the Objections at large on their journal, and proceed to reconsider it. If after such Reconsideration two thirds of that House shall agree to pass the Bill, it shall be sent, together with the Objections, to the other House, by which it shall likewise be reconsidered, and, if approved by two thirds of that house, it shall become a Law. But in all such Cases the Votes of both houses shall be determined by yeas and Nays, and the Names of the Persons voting for and against the Bill shall be entered on the journal of each House respectively. If any Bill shall not be returned by the President within ten Days (Sundays excepted) after it shall have been presented to him, the Same shall be a Law, in like Manner as if he had signed it, unless the Congress by their Adjournment prevent its Return, in which Case it shall not be a Law.

Every Order, Resolution, or Vote to which the Concurrence of the Senate and House of Representatives may be necessary (except on a question of Adjournment) shall be presented to the President of the United States; and before the Same shall take Effect, shall be approved by him, or being disapproved by him, shall be re-passed by two thirds of the Senate and House of Representatives, according to the Rules and Limitations prescribed in the Case of a Bill.

[Powers of Congress enumerated]

Section 8 The Congress shall have Power

To lay and collect Taxes, Duties, Imposts, and Excises, to pay the Debts and provide for the common Defence and general Welfare of the United States; but all Duties, Imposts and Excises shall be uniform throughout the United States;

To borrow Money on the credit of the United States;

To regulate Commerce with foreign Nations, and among the several States, and with the Indian tribes;

To establish an uniform Rule of Naturalization, and uniform Laws on the subject of Bankruptcies throughout the United States;

To coin Money, regulate the Value thereof, and of foreign Coin, and fix the Standard of Weights and Measures;

To provide for the Punishment of counterfeiting the Securities and current Coin of the United States;

To establish Post Offices and post Roads;

To promote the Progress of Science and useful Arts by securing for limited Times to Authors and Inventors the exclusive Right to their respective Writings and Discoveries;

To constitute Tribunals inferior to the supreme Court;

To define and punish Piracies and Felonies committed on the high Seas, and offenses against the Law of Nations;

To declare War, grant Letters of Marque and Reprisal, and make Rules concerning Captures on Land and Water;

To raise and support Armies, but no Appropriation of Money to that Use shall be for a longer Term than two Years;

To provide and maintain a Navy;

To make rules for the Government and Regulation of the land and naval Forces;

To provide for calling forth the Militia to execute the Laws of the Union, suppress Insurrections, and repel Invasions;

To provide for organizing, arming, and disciplining the Militia, and for governing such Part of them as may be employed in the Service of the United States, reserving to the States respectively the Appointment of the Officers, and the Authority of training the Militia according to the discipline prescribed by Congress;

To exercise exclusive Legislation in all Cases whatsoever, over such District (not exceeding ten Miles square) as may, by cession of particular States, and the Acceptance of Congress, become the Seat of Government of the United States, and to exercise like Authority over all places purchased by the Consent of the Legislature of the State in which the Same shall be, for Erection of Forts, Magazines, Arsenals, dock-Yards, and other needful Buildings;—And

[Elastic clause]

To make all Laws which shall be necessary and proper for carrying into Execution the foregoing Powers, and all other powers vested by this Constitution in the Government of the United States, or in any Department or Officer thereof.

[Powers denied Congress]

Section 9 *The Migration or Importation of such persons as any of the States now existing shall think proper to admit, shall not be prohibited by the Congress prior to the Year 1808; but a Tax or duty may be imposed on such Importation, not exceeding $10 for each Person.*

The Privilege of the Writ of Habeas Corpus shall not be suspended, unless when in Cases of Rebellion or Invasion the public Safety may require it.

No Bill of Attainder or ex post facto Law shall be passed.

No Capitation, or other direct, Tax shall be laid, unless in Proportion to the Census or Enumeration herein before directed to be taken.

No Tax or Duty shall be laid on Articles exported from any State.

No Preference shall be given by any Regulation of Commerce or Revenue to the Ports of one State over those of another; nor shall Vessels bound to, or from, one State, be obliged to enter, clear, or pay Duties in another.

No Money shall be drawn from the Treasury, but in Consequence of Appropriations made by Law; and a regular Statement and Account of the receipts and Expenditures of all public Money shall be published from time to time.

No Title of Nobility shall be granted by the United States: And no Person holding any Office or Profit or trust under them, shall, without the Consent of the Congress, accept of any present, Emolument, Office, or Title, of any kind whatever, from any King, Prince, or foreign State.

[Powers denied the states]

Section 10 No State shall enter into any Treaty, Alliance, or Confederation; grant Letters of Marque and Reprisal; coin Money; emit Bills of Credit; make any Thing but gold and silver Coin a Tender in Payment of Debts; pass any Bill of Attainder, ex post facto law, or Law impairing the obligation of Contracts, or grant any Title of Nobility.

No State shall, without the Consent of Congress, lay any Imposts or Duties on Imports or Exports, except what may be absolutely necessary for executing its inspection Laws: and the net Produce of all duties and imposts, laid by any State on Imports or Exports, shall be for the Use of the Treasury of the United States; and all such Laws shall be subject to the Revision and Controul of the Congress.

No State shall, without the consent of Congress, lay any Duty of Tonnage, keep Troops or Ships of War in time of Peace, enter into any Agreement or Compact with another State, or with a foreign Power, or engage in War, unless actually invaded, or in such imminent Danger as will not admit of delay.

Article II
[The executive branch]

[The president: power vested, term, electoral college, qualifications, presidential succession, compensation, oath of Office]

Section 1 The executive Power shall be vested in a President of the United States of America. He shall hold his Office during the Term of four Years, and, together with the Vice President, chosen for the same Term, be elected as follows:

Each State shall appoint, in such Manner as the Legislature thereof may direct, a Number of Electors, equal to the whole Number of Senators and Representatives to which the State may be entitled in the Congress; but no Senator or Representative, or Person holding an Office of Trust or Profit under the United States, shall be appointed an Elector.

The Electors shall meet in their respective States, and vote by Ballot for two Persons, of whom one at least shall not be an inhabitant of the same State with themselves. And they shall make a List of all the Persons voted for, and of the Number of Votes for each: which List they shall sign and certify, and transmit sealed to the Seat of Government of the United States, directed to the President of the Senate. The President of the Senate shall, in the presence of the Senate and House of Representatives, open all the Certificates, and the Votes shall then be counted. The Person having the greatest Number of Votes shall be the President, if such Number be a Majority of the whole number of Electors appointed; and if there be more than one who have such Majority, and have an equal Number of Votes, then the House of Representatives shall immediately chuse by Ballot one of them for President; and if no Person have a Majority, then from the five highest on the List said House shall in like Manner chuse the President. But in chusing the President the

Votes shall be taken by States, the Representation from each State having one Vote; a quorum for this purpose shall consist of a Member or Members from two thirds of the States, and a Majority of all the States shall be necessary to a Choice. In every Case, after the Choice of the President, the person having the greatest Number of Votes of the Electors shall be the Vice President. But if there should remain two or more who have equal Votes, the Senate shall chuse from them by Ballot the Vice President.

The Congress may determine the Time of chusing the Electors and the Day on which they shall give their Votes; which Day shall be the same throughout the United States.

No person except a natural born Citizen, or a Citizen of the United States at the time of the Adoption of this Constitution, shall be eligible to the Office of President; neither shall any Person be eligible to that Office who shall not have attained to the age of thirty-five Years, and been fourteen Years a Resident within the United States.

In cases of the Removal of the President from Office or of his Death, Resignation, or Inability to discharge the Powers and Duties of the said Office, the same shall devolve on the Vice President, and the Congress may by law provide for the case of Removal, Death, Resignation, or inability, both of the President and Vice President, declaring what Officer shall then act as President, and such Officer shall act accordingly, until the Disability be removed, or a President shall be elected.

The President shall, at stated Times, receive for his Services, a Compensation, which shall neither be increased nor diminished during the Period for which he shall have been elected, and he shall not receive within that Period any other emolument from the United States, or any of them.

Before he enter on the Execution of his Office, he shall take the following Oath or Affirmation:—"I do solemnly swear (or affirm) that I will faithfully execute the Office of the President of the United States, and will to the best of my Ability preserve, protect and defend the Constitution of the United States."

[Powers and duties: as commander in chief, over advisers, to pardon, to make treaties and appoint officers]

Section 2 The President shall be Commander in Chief of the Army and Navy of the United States, and of the Militia of the several States, when called into the actual service of the United States; he may require the Opinion, in writing, of the principal Officer in each of the executive Departments, upon any Subject relating to the Duties of their respective Offices, and he shall have Power to grant Reprieves and Pardons for Offences against the United States, except in Cases of Impeachment.

He shall have Power, by and with the Advice and Consent of the Senate, to make Treaties, provided two-thirds of the Senators present concur; and he shall nominate, and by and with the Advice and Consent of the Senate, shall appoint Ambassadors, other public Ministers and Consuls, Judges of the supreme Court, and all other Officers of the United States, whose Appointments are not herein otherwise provided for, and which shall be established by Law: but Congress may by Law vest the Appointment of such inferior Officers, as they think proper, in the President alone, in the courts of Law, or in the Heads of Departments.

The President shall have Power to fill up all Vacancies that may happen during the Recess of the Senate, by granting Commissions which shall expire at the end of their next Session.

[Legislative, diplomatic, and law-enforcement duties]

Section 3 He shall from time to time give to the Congress Information of the State of the Union, and recommend to their Consideration such Measures as he shall judge necessary and expedient; he may, on extraordinary Occasions, convene both Houses, or either of them, and in Case of Disagreement between them, with Respect to the Time of Adjournment, he may adjourn them to such Time as he shall think proper; he shall receive Ambassadors and other public Ministers; he shall take Care that the Laws be faithfully executed, and shall Commission all the Officers of the United States.

[Impeachment]

Section 4 The President, Vice President and all civil Officers of the United States shall be removed from Office on Impeachment for, and on Conviction of, Treason, Bribery, or other high Crimes and Misdemeanors.

Article III
[The judicial branch]

[Power vested; Supreme Court; lower courts; judges]

Section 1 The judicial Power of the United States shall be vested in one supreme Court, and in such inferior Courts as the Congress may from time to time ordain and establish. The Judges, both of the supreme and inferior Courts, shall hold their Offices during good Behaviour, and shall, at stated Times, receive for their Services a Compensation which shall not be diminished during their Continuance in Office.

[Jurisdiction; trial by jury]

Section 2 The judicial Power shall extend to all Cases, in Law and Equity, arising under this Constitution, the Laws of the United States, and Treaties made, or which shall be made, under their Authority;—to all Cases affecting Ambassadors, other public Ministers and Consuls;—to all Cases of admiralty and maritime Jurisdiction;—to Controversies to which the United States shall be a Party;—to controversies between two or more States;—*between a State and Citizens of another State;*—between Citizens of different States—between Citizens of the same State claiming Lands under grants of different States, and between a State, or the Citizens thereof, and foreign States, Citizens or Subjects.

In all cases affecting Ambassadors, other public Ministers and Consuls, and those in which a State shall be Party, the supreme Court shall have original Jurisdiction. In all the other Cases before mentioned, the supreme

Court shall have appellate Jurisdiction, both as to Law and Fact, with such Exceptions, and under such Regulations, as the Congress shall make.

The Trial of all Crimes, except in cases of Impeachment, shall be by Jury; and such Trial shall be held in the State where said Crimes shall have been committed; but when not committed within any State, the Trial shall be at such Place or Places as the Congress may by Law have directed.

[Treason: definition, punishment]

Section 3 Treason against the United States shall consist only in levying War against them, or in adhering to their Enemies, giving them Aid and Comfort. No Person shall be convicted of Treason unless on the Testimony of two Witnesses to the same overt Act, or on confession in open Court.

The Congress shall have power to declare the Punishment of Treason, but no Attainder of Treason shall work Corruption of Blood, or Forfeiture except during the Life of the Person attainted.

Article IV
[States' relations]

[Full faith and credit]

Section 1 Full Faith and Credit shall be given in each State to the public Acts, Records, and judicial Proceedings of every other State. And the Congress may by general laws prescribe the Manner in which such Acts, Records, and Proceedings shall be proved, and the Effect thereof.

[Interstate comity, rendition]

Section 2 The Citizens of each State shall be entitled to all Privileges and Immunities of Citizens in the several States.

A Person charged in any State with Treason, Felony, or other Crime, who shall flee from Justice, and be found in another State, shall on Demand of the executive Authority of the State from which he fled, be delivered up, to be removed to the State having Jurisdiction of the Crime.

No person held to Service or Labor in one State, under the Laws thereof, escaping into another, shall, in consequence of any Law or Regulation therein, be discharged from such Service or Labor, but shall be delivered up on Claim of the Party to whom such Service or Labor may be due.

[New states]

Section 3 New States may be admitted by the Congress into this Union; but no new State shall be formed or erected within the Jurisdiction of any other State; nor any State be formed by the Junction of two or more States, or parts of States, without the Consent of the Legislatures of the States concerned as well as of the Congress.

The Congress shall have Power to dispose of and make all needful Rules and Regulations respecting the Territory or other Property belonging to the United States; and nothing in this Constitution shall be so construed as to Prejudice any Claims of the United States, or of any particular State.

[Obligations of the United States to the states]

Section 4 The United States shall guarantee to every State in this Union a Republican Form of Government, and shall protect each of them against Invasion; and on Application of the Legislature, or of the Executive (when the Legislature cannot be convened), against domestic Violence.

Article V
[Mode of amendment]

The Congress, whenever two-thirds of both Houses shall deem it necessary, shall propose Amendments to this Constitution, or, on the Application of the Legislatures of two-thirds of the several States, shall call a Convention for proposing Amendments, which, in either Case, shall be valid to all Intents and Purposes, as part of this Constitution, when ratified by the legislatures of three-fourths of the several States, or by Conventions in three-fourths thereof, as the one or the other Mode of Ratification may be proposed by the Congress; Provided *that no Amendment which may be made prior to the Year One thousand eight hundred and eight shall in any Manner affect the first and fourth clauses in the Ninth Section of the first Article;* and that no State, without its Consent, shall be deprived of its equal suffrage in the Senate.

Article VI
[Prior debts, supremacy of Constitution, oaths of Office]

All Debts contracted and Engagements entered into, before the Adoption of this Constitution, shall be as valid against the United States under this Constitution, as under the Confederation.

This Constitution, and the Laws of the United States which shall be made in Pursuance thereof; and all Treaties made, or which shall be made, under the Authority of the United States, shall be the supreme Law of the Land; and the judges in every State shall be bound thereby, anything in the Constitution or Laws of any State to the Contrary notwithstanding.

The Senators and Representatives before mentioned, and the Members of the several State Legislatures, and all executive and judicial Officers, both of the United States and of the several States, shall be bound by Oath or Affirmation to support this Constitution; but no religious test shall ever be required as a Qualification to any Office or public Trust under the United States.

Article VII
[Ratification]

The ratification of the Conventions of nine States shall be sufficient for the Establishment of this Constitution between the States so ratifying the Same.

Done in Convention by the Unanimous Consent of the States present, the seventeenth day of September in the Year of our Lord one thousand seven hundred and eighty-seven and of the Independence of the United States of America the twelfth. In WITNESS whereof We have hereunto subscribed our Names.

GEORGE WASHINGTON
and thirty-seven others

Amendments to the Constitution
[The first ten amendments—the Bill of Rights—were adopted in 1791.]

Amendment I
[Freedom of religion, speech, press, assembly]

Congress shall make no law respecting an establishment of religion, or prohibiting the free exercise thereof; or abridging the freedom of speech, or of the press; or the right of the people peaceably to assemble, and to petition the Government for a redress of grievances.

Amendment II
[Right to bear arms]

A well-regulated militia being necessary to the security of a free State, the right of the people to keep and bear arms shall not be infringed.

Amendment III
[Quartering of soldiers]

No Soldier shall, in time of peace, be quartered in any house without the consent of the Owner, nor in time of war, but in a manner to be prescribed by law.

Amendment IV
[Searches and seizures]

The right of the people to be secure in their persons, houses, papers, and effects, against unreasonable searches and seizures, shall not be violated, and no Warrants shall issue but upon probable cause, supported by Oath or affirmation, and particularly describing the place to be searched, and the persons or things to be seized.

Amendment V
[Rights of persons: grand juries, double jeopardy, self-incrimination, due process, eminent domain]

No person shall be held to answer for a capital, or otherwise infamous crime, unless on a presentment or indictment of a Grand Jury, except in cases arising in the land or naval forces, or in the Militia, when in actual service in time of War or public danger; nor shall any person be subject for the same offense to be twice put in jeopardy of life or limb; nor shall be compelled in any criminal case to be a witness against himself, nor be deprived of life, liberty, or property, without due process of law; nor shall private property be taken for public use without just compensation.

Amendment VI
[Rights of accused in criminal prosecutions]

In all criminal prosecutions, the accused shall enjoy the right to a speedy and public trial, by an impartial jury of the State and district wherein the crime shall have been committed, which district shall have been previously ascertained by law, and to be informed of the nature and cause of the accusation; to be confronted with the witnesses against him; to have compulsory process for obtaining Witnesses in his favor, and to have the assistance of counsel for his defence.

Amendment VII
[Civil trials]

In Suits at common law, where the value in controversy shall exceed twenty dollars, the right of trial by jury shall be preserved, and no fact tried by a jury shall be otherwise reexamined in any Court of the United States, than according to the rules of the common law.

Amendment VIII
[Punishment for crime]

Excessive bail shall not be required, nor excessive fines imposed, nor cruel and unusual punishments inflicted.

Amendment IX
[Rights retained by the people]

The enumeration in the Constitution, of certain rights, shall not be construed to deny or disparage others retained by the people.

Amendment X
[Rights reserved to the states]

The powers not delegated to the United States by the Constitution, nor prohibited by it to the States, are reserved to the States respectively, or to the people.

Amendment XI
[Suits against the states; adopted 1798]

The Judicial power of the United States shall not be construed to extend to any suit in law or equity, commenced or prosecuted against one of the United States by Citizens of another state, or by Citizens or Subjects of any Foreign State.

Amendment XII
[Election of the president; adopted 1804]

The electors shall meet in their respective States, and vote by ballot for President and Vice President, one of whom, at least, shall not be an inhabitant of the same state with themselves; they shall name in their ballots the person voted for as President, and in distinct ballots the person voted for as Vice President, and they shall make distinct lists of all persons voted for as President, and of all persons voted for as Vice President, and of the number of votes for each, which lists they shall sign and certify, and transmit sealed to the seat of government of the United States, directed to the President of the Senate;–the President of the Senate shall, in the presence of the Senate and House of Representatives, open all the certificates and the votes shall then be counted;–the person having the greatest number of votes for President shall be the President, if such number be a majority of the whole number of electors appointed; and if no person have such majority, then from the persons having the highest numbers not exceeding three on the list of those voted for as President, the House of Representatives shall choose immediately, by ballot, the President. But in choosing the President, the votes shall be taken by States, the representation from each State having one vote; a quorum for this purpose shall consist of a member or members from two-thirds of the States, and a majority of all the States shall be necessary to a choice. And if the House of Representatives shall not choose a President whenever the right of choice shall devolve upon them, before *the fourth day of March* next following, then the Vice President shall act as President, as in the case of the death or other constitutional disability of the President.–The person having the greatest number of votes as Vice President shall be the Vice President, if such number be a majority of the whole number of electors appointed; and if no person have a majority, then from the two highest numbers on the list the Senate shall choose the Vice President; a quorum for the purpose shall consist of two-thirds of the whole number of Senators, and a majority of the whole number shall be necessary to a choice. But no person constitutionally ineligible to the Office of President shall be eligible to that of Vice President of the United States.

Amendment XIII
[Abolition of slavery; adopted 1865]

Section 1 Neither slavery nor involuntary servitude, except as a punishment for crime whereof the party shall have been duly convicted, shall exist within the United States, or any place subject to their jurisdiction.

Section 2 Congress shall have power to enforce this article by appropriate legislation.

Amendment XIV
[Adopted 1868]

[Citizenship rights; privileges and immunities; due process; equal protection]

Section 1 All persons born or naturalized in the United States, and subject to the jurisdiction thereof, are citizens of the United States and of the State wherein they reside. No State shall make or enforce any law which shall abridge the privileges or immunities of citizens of the United States; nor shall any State deprive any person of life, liberty, or property, without due process of law; nor deny to any person within its jurisdiction the equal protection of the laws.

[Apportionment of representation]

Section 2 Representatives shall be apportioned among the several States according to their respective numbers, counting the whole number of persons in each State, excluding Indians not taxed. But when the right to vote at any election for the choice of Electors for President and Vice President of the United States, Representatives in Congress, the Executive and Judicial officers of a State, or the members of the Legislature thereof, is denied to any of the male inhabitants of such State, being twenty-one years of age and citizens of the United States, or in any way abridged, except for participation in rebellion, or other crime, the basis of representation therein shall be reduced in the proportion which the number of such male citizens shall bear to the whole number of male citizens twenty-one years of age in such State.

[Disqualification of Confederate officials]

Section 3 No person shall be a Senator or Representative in Congress, or Elector of President and Vice President, or hold any Office, civil or military, under the United States, or under any State, who, having previously taken an oath, as a member of Congress, or as an Officer of the United States, or as a member of any State legislature, or as an executive or judicial Officer of any State, to support the Constitution of the United States, shall have engaged in insurrection or rebellion against the same, or given aid or comfort to the enemies thereof. Congress may, by a vote of two-thirds of each house, remove such disability.

[Public debts]

Section 4 The validity of the public debt of the United States, authorized by law, including debts incurred for payment of pensions and bounties for services in suppressing insurrection or rebellion, shall not be questioned. But neither the United States nor any State shall assume or pay any debt or obligation incurred in aid of insurrection or rebellion against the United States, or any claim for the loss of emancipation of any slave; but all such debts, obligations, and claims shall be held illegal and void.

[Enforcement]

Section 5 The Congress shall have power to enforce, by appropriate legislation, the provisions of this article.

Amendment XV
[Extension of right to vote; adopted 1870]

Section 1 The right of citizens of the United States to vote shall not be denied or abridged by the United States or by any State on account of race, color, or previous condition of servitude.

Section 2 The Congress shall have power to enforce this article by appropriate legislation.

Amendment XVI
[Income tax; adopted 1913]

The Congress shall have power to lay and collect taxes on incomes, from whatever source derived, without apportionment among the several States, and without regard to any census or enumeration.

Amendment XVII
[Popular election of senators; adopted 1913]

Section 1 The Senate of the United States shall be composed of two Senators from each State, elected by the people thereof, for six years; and each Senator shall have one vote. The electors in each State shall have the qualifications requisite for electors of the most numerous branch of the State legislatures.

Section 2 When vacancies happen in the representation of any State in the Senate, the executive authority of such State shall issue writs of election to fill such vacancies: Provided, that the Legislature of any State may empower the executive thereof to make temporary appointments until the people fill the vacancies by election as the Legislature may direct.

Section 3 This amendment shall not be so construed as to affect the election or term of any Senator chosen before it becomes valid as part of the Constitution.

Amendment XVIII
[Prohibition of intoxicating liquors; adopted 1919, repealed 1933]

Section 1 After one year from the ratification of this article the manufacture, sale or transportation of intoxicating liquors within, the importation thereof into, or the exportation thereof from the United States and all territory subject to the jurisdiction thereof, for beverage purposes, is hereby prohibited.

Section 2 The Congress and the several States shall have concurrent power to enforce this article by appropriate legislation.

Section 3 This article shall be inoperative unless it shall have been ratified as an amendment to the Constitution by the legislatures of the several States, as provided by the Constitution, within seven years from the date of the submission thereof to the States by the Congress.

Amendment XIX
[Right of women to vote; adopted 1920]

Section 1 The right of citizens of the United States to vote shall not be denied or abridged by the United States or by any State on account of sex.

Section 2 The Congress shall have power to enforce this article by appropriate legislation.

Amendment XX
[Commencement of terms of Office; adopted 1933]

Section 1 The terms of the President and Vice President shall end at noon on the 20th day of January, and the terms of Senators and Representatives at noon on the 3d day of January, of the years in which such terms would have ended if this article had not been ratified; and the terms of their successors shall then begin.

Section 2 The Congress shall assemble at least once in every year, and such meetings shall begin at noon on the 3d day of January, unless they shall by law appoint a different day.

[Extension of presidential succession]

Section 3 If, at the time fixed for the beginning of the term of the President, the President-elect shall have died, the Vice President elect shall become President. If a President shall not have been chosen before the time fixed for the beginning of his term, or if the President elect shall have failed to qualify, then the Vice President elect shall act as President until a President shall have qualified; and the Congress may by law provide for the case wherein neither a President-elect nor a Vice President elect shall have qualified, declaring who shall then act as President, or the manner in which one who is to act shall be selected, and such persons shall act accordingly until a President or Vice President shall have qualified.

Section 4 The Congress may by law provide for the case of the death of any of the persons from whom the House of Representatives may choose a President whenever the right of choice shall have devolved upon them, and for the case of the death of any of the persons from whom the Senate may choose a Vice President whenever the right of choice shall have devolved upon them.

Section 5 Sections 1 and 2 shall take effect on the 15th day of October following the ratification of this article.

Section 6 This article shall be inoperative unless it shall have been ratified as an amendment to the Constitution by the Legislatures of three-fourths of the several States within seven years from the date of its submission.

Amendment XXI
[Repeal of Eighteenth Amendment; adopted 1933]

Section 1 The eighteenth article of amendment to the Constitution of the United States is hereby repealed.

Section 2 The transportation or importation into any State, Territory, or Possession of the United States for delivery or use therein of intoxicating liquors, in violation of the laws thereof, is hereby prohibited.

Section 3 This article shall be inoperative unless it shall have been ratified as an amendment to the Constitution by conventions in the several States, as provided in the Constitution, within seven years from the date of submission thereof to the States by the Congress.

Amendment XXII
[Limit on presidential tenure; adopted 1951]

Section 1 No person shall be elected to the Office of President more than twice, and no person who has held the Office of President, or acted as President, for more than two years of a term to which some other person was elected President shall be elected to the Office of President more than once. But this article shall not apply to any person holding the Office of President when this article was proposed by the Congress, and shall not prevent any person who may be holding the Office of President, or acting as President, during the term within which this article becomes operative from holding the Office of President or acting as President during the remainder of such term.

Section 2 This article shall be inoperative unless it shall have been ratified as an amendment to the Constitution by the legislatures of three-fourths of the several States within seven years from the date of its submission to the States by the Congress.

Amendment XXIII
[Presidential electors for the District of Columbia; adopted 1961]

Section 1 The District constituting the seat of Government of the United States shall appoint in such manner as the Congress may direct:

A number of electors of President and Vice President equal to the whole number of Senators and Representatives in Congress to which the District would be entitled if it were a State, but in no event more than the least populous State; they shall be in addition to those appointed by the States, but they shall be considered for the purposes of the election of President and Vice President, to be electors appointed by a State; and they shall meet in the District and perform such duties as provided by the twelfth article of amendment.

Section 2 The Congress shall have the power to enforce this article by appropriate legislation.

Amendment XXIV
[Poll tax outlawed in national elections; adopted 1964]

Section 1 The right of citizens of the United States to vote in any primary or other election for President or Vice President, for electors for President or Vice President, or for Senator or Representative in Congress, shall not be denied or abridged by the United States or any State by reason of failure to pay any poll tax or other tax.

Section 2 The Congress shall have the power to enforce this article by appropriate legislation.

Amendment XXV
[Presidential succession; adopted 1967]

Section 1 In case of the removal of the President from Office or of his death or resignation, the Vice President shall become President.

[Vice-presidential vacancy]
Section 2 Whenever there is a vacancy in the Office of the Vice President, the President shall nominate a Vice President who shall take Office upon confirmation by a majority vote of both Houses of Congress.

Section 3 Whenever the President transmits to the President pro tempore of the Senate and the Speaker of the House of Representatives his written declaration that he is unable to discharge the powers and duties of his Office, and until he transmits to them a written declaration to the contrary, such powers and duties shall be discharged by the Vice President as Acting President.

[Presidential disability]
Section 4 Whenever the Vice President and a majority of either the principal officers of the executive departments or of such other body as Congress may by law provide, transmit to the President pro tempore of the Senate and the Speaker of the House of Representatives their written declaration that the President is unable to discharge the powers and

duties of his Office, the Vice President shall immediately assume the powers and duties of the Office as Acting President.

Thereafter, when the President transmits to the President pro tempore of the Senate and the Speaker of the House of Representatives his written declaration that no inability exists, he shall resume the powers and duties of his Office unless the Vice President and a majority of either the principal officers of the executive department(s) or of such other body as Congress may by law provide, transmit within four days to the President pro tempore of the Senate and the Speaker of the House of Representatives their written declaration that the President is unable to discharge the powers and duties of his Office. Thereupon Congress shall decide the issue, assembling within forty-eight hours for that purpose if not in session. If the Congress, within twenty-one days after receipt of the latter written declaration, or, if Congress is not in session, within twenty-one days after Congress is required to assemble, determines by two-thirds vote of both Houses that the President is unable to discharge the powers and duties of his Office, the Vice President shall continue to discharge the same as Acting President; otherwise, the President shall resume the powers and duties of his Office.

Amendment XXVI
[Right of eighteen-year-olds to vote; adopted 1971]

Section 1 The right of citizens of the United States, who are eighteen years of age or older, to vote shall not be denied or abridged by the United States or by any State on account of age.

Section 2 The Congress shall have power to enforce this article by appropriate legislation.

Amendment XXVII
[Congressional pay raises; adopted 1992]

No law, varying the compensation for the services of the Senators and Representatives shall take effect, until an election of Representatives shall have intervened.

Test Prepper Answers

Chapter 1

1.1: Globalization of American Government
1. True. The principle of national sovereignty has been used to define a national government's right to self-determination since 1648.
2. True. Government is also defined as the organization or agency authorized to exercise that force.
3. True. Globalization threatens national sovereignty when international actors intervene in the internal affairs of other states.
4. The United States opposes an international court because it poses a challenge to sovereignty. U.S. soldiers stationed abroad might be arrested and tried in such a court, and the government fears it would be pressured to abolish capital punishment as many other countries have done.
5. International politics and world opinion have an impact on U.S. politics for many reasons, including the fact that the United States is closely tied to former enemies through trade and is also thoroughly embedded in a worldwide economic, social, and political network.

1.2: Purpose of Government
1. False. Governments can legitimately use their coercive powers to promote order or to tax citizens for the purposes of spending on public goods such as parks and education.
2. True. Karl Marx rejected the notion of private property, giving rise to the theory of communism (a complex theory that gives ownership of all land and productive facilities to the people).
3. True. Consider, for example, the debates between Republicans and Democrats in Congress over raising the minimum wage.
4. Communist ideology gives ownership of all land and productive facilities to the people.
5. The government can promote social equality through policies that redistribute income and through other means such as enacting civil rights laws.

1.3: Conceptual Framework
1. True. New laws passed after September 11, 2001, dramatically increased government police power.
2. False. Ideologies are complex sets of consistent values and beliefs about the proper purpose and scope of government.
3. False. Liberals believe it is necessary and appropriate for the government to use its power to promote equality.
4. The original dilemma of government was the tradeoff between freedom and order. The modern dilemma of government is the tension between freedom and equality.
5. The labels *liberal* and *conservative* are often inadequate to capture the way modern Americans want to resolve the original and modern dilemmas of government. While there are still liberals and conservatives, many people would be more accurately characterized as communitarians or libertarians. See Figure 1.2.

1.4: Majoritarian or Pluralist?
1. False. Participatory democracy is the system in which people rule themselves directly rather than electing representatives.
2. True. According to the procedural theory, the principle of government responsiveness states that elected representatives should follow the general contours of public opinion.
3. True. This is one characteristic that distinguishes elite theory from pluralist theory.
4. The pluralistic model of democracy interprets "government by the people" to mean people operating through competing interest groups.

5. The word *democracy* originated in Greek writings around the fifth century B.C.; *demos* refers to the masses; *kratos* means "power." The Greeks originally associated democracy with mob rule, although clearly that connotation has changed dramatically.

1.5: Democracy and Globalization
1. False. Until recently, fewer than twenty countries qualified as true democracies.
2. True. Market economies (i.e., capitalism) give people substantial freedoms, which authoritarian rulers see as a threat to their regime.
3. True. Internal conflict raises significant challenges for the global community.
4. The U.S. government more closely fits the pluralistic model.
5. The establishment of democratic governments is challenging, and countries often face many obstacles when attempting to begin and maintain a democracy, particularly if ethnic and religious conflict is present.

Chapter 2

2.1: The Revolutionary Roots of the Constitution
1. True. In 1763, the colonists and British reached a compromise between imperial control and self-government.
2. True. John Locke's writings, including his belief that people have inalienable, God-given, natural rights, were very influential in the writing of the Declaration of Independence.
3. False. The War of Independence lasted from April 19, 1775, to October 19, 1781.
4. The Coercive Acts were Britain's attempt to impose order on disobedient colonists. The imposition of these laws, which impinged on colonial rights, caused Massachusetts and Virginia to call for the First Continental Congress to speak on behalf of the people.
5. The major dilemma for the delegates of the Second Continental Congress was whether they should prepare for war or try to reconcile with Britain.

2.2: From Revolution to Confederation
1. False. A republic is a government without a monarch but does not require democracy.
2. False. In a confederation, states retain their sovereignty, which means that each has supreme powers within its borders.
3. True. The goal of the delegates who drew up the Articles of Confederation was to maintain state sovereignty.
4. The inability of the confederation to secure funds from the states to maintain order in domestic emergencies like Shays's Rebellion and similar insurrections pointed out the impotence of the confederation and the need for a different form of government.
5. The Articles of Confederation ultimately failed because the national government was too weak. It lacked the power to tax and had to plead for money, the nation was left without a leader because there was no provision for an independent leadership position, the national government could not regulate interstate and foreign commerce, the national government could not respond effectively to domestic instability, and the articles could not be amended without unanimous agreement of Congress and the state legislatures.

2.3: From Confederation to Constitution
1. True. The small states at the convention initially supported the New Jersey Plan, an effort to preserve state sovereignty and the equal votes they had under the Articles of Confederation.
2. True. The Great Compromise was also known as the Connecticut Compromise, as it was proposed by Roger Sherman of the Connecticut delegation.
3. False. The electoral college eliminated the fear of a presidential candidate winning by popular vote.
4. The Great Compromise gave the smaller states equal representation in the Senate and thus freed them from the fear that they would be dominated by the larger states.
5. A president could be impeached on the grounds of treason, bribery, or other high crimes and misdemeanors.

2.4: The Final Product

1. True. The power of Congress to override a president's veto with an extraordinary majority is one way to establish a "check on a check."
2. False. In addition to the Preamble, the Constitution includes seven articles.
3. True. Judicial review is the power of the courts to declare government acts such as laws or executive branch regulations invalid because they violate the Constitution.
4. The supremacy clause asserts that national laws take precedence over state and local laws when they conflict. This allows the federal government to act in the interests of all states.
5. The motives of those who framed the Constitution were primarily to protect their homes, families, and means of livelihood from anarchy.

2.5: Selling the Constitution

1. False. The Bill of Rights provided assurances that the national government would be constrained from limiting basic civil liberties.
2. False. James Madison argued that the Constitution would prevent a "tyranny of the majority" by creating a large and diverse republic in which no one faction would be able to seize power.
3. False. While only nine states were required to officially ratify the Constitution, its success was not ensured until later when the large and powerful states of Virginia and New York ratified it after lengthy debate.
4. The *Federalist* papers were a series of eighty-five newspaper articles reprinted during the ratification process. These articles were widely read throughout the states and served to inform and persuade the citizens by explaining the theories that were used to develop the Constitution.
5. Prominent citizens such as Thomas Jefferson were unhappy that the Constitution did not list basic civil liberties because the colonists had recently rebelled against the British for their freedom. Not including a Bill of Rights seemed irresponsible. However, federalists argued that the national government was not allowed to limit people's liberties, so a list was not necessary.

2.6: Constitutional Change

1. False. With only one exception, all constitutional amendments to date were proposed by a two-thirds vote in both the House of Representatives and the Senate and ratified by three-fourths of the state legislatures.
2. True. Congress chooses the method of ratification for amendments it proposes.
3. True. Chances of ratifying an amendment are high after an amendment has successfully passed the proposal stage.
4. Over time, some actions within the government have fallen out of use, such as the deliberative role of the electors of the electoral college. Thus, significant changes have occurred without a formal amendment to the Constitution.
5. In the proposal stage there must be a two-thirds vote in both houses of Congress, or a national convention called by Congress must be held. Ratification includes a vote by three-fourths of the state legislatures or constitutional conventions in three-fourths of the states.

2.7: An Evaluation of the Constitution

1. False. State constitutions are written with much greater specificity than the U.S. Constitution and thus are significantly more complex.
2. False. The generality of the U.S. Constitution is its greatest strength because it has allowed flexibility to address new developments over the last two centuries.
3. True. Social equality is never mentioned in the U.S. Constitution.
4. While the initial values that motivated the framers of the Constitution dealt with the balance between order and freedom, over time the Constitution has been amended to incorporate the concept of social equality.
5. Answers may vary; however, the Constitution fits the pluralist model of democracy because a republic was created, and the founders avoided a single center of government power by separating the powers and integrating checks and balances.

Chapter 3

3.1: Theories and Metaphors

1. False. Federalism divides power between a central government and state or regional governments.
2. False. Dual federalism holds that the Constitution was a compact among sovereign states, emphasizing states' rights and a limited national government.
3. False. In marble-cake federalism, state and national governmental powers are often intermingled and shared.
4. In cooperative federalism, state and national government responsibilities are intermingled, so there must be a means by which the national government's power can supersede that of the states when it is necessary. That is the role of the supremacy clause.
5. Article I, Section 8, contains the elastic clause that gives Congress the power to make all necessary and proper laws, but the Tenth Amendment reserves powers for the states and the people. Cooperative federalism emphasizes the former, while dual federalism stresses the latter.

3.2: The Dynamics of Federalism

1. True. The two general forms of grants-in-aid are block and categorical grants. Categorical grants come in two types: formula grants and project grants.
2. False. For nearly sixty years, from 1937 to 1995, the Supreme Court almost always supported the national government in contests between state and national authority.
3. True. State governments are more capable policy actors now than they were before 1960.
4. From the late 1930s through the mid-1990s, the Supreme Court interpreted the Constitution's commerce clause broadly; it allowed Congress to legislate in virtually any policy area in which interstate commerce took place.
5. Answers will vary. An example of the use of the elastic clause during a national crisis may be during the Great Depression, when the states could not handle the problems that arose. Congress provided economic relief by helping the unemployed and stimulating the economy. Another example may be when the USA-PATRIOT Act was signed after September 11, 2001, allowing surveillance and giving new investigative powers to the Department of Justice.

3.3: Ideology, Policymaking, and American Federalism

1. False. In 1960 states received less than 10 percent of the federal budget, but they receive approximately 20 percent of the federal budget today.
2. False. President Richard Nixon wanted to decentralize national policies with *New Federalism.*
3. False. Despite a law to reduce the practice, the national government can issue mandates without providing necessary funds to the states.
4. Common arguments used by conservatives in support of maintaining power at the state level are that different states have different problems, the national government is too remote and too tied to special interests to serve the public at large, and the national government overregulates.
5. In theory, conservatives favor states' rights and liberals love the national government. In practice, however, individual policies may often be more important to members of Congress than the ideologies associated with liberals and conservatives.

3.4: Federalism and Electoral Politics

1. False. Candidates for national office do benefit greatly from experience gained in state office as state office is an excellent proving ground to learn about the federal system and to gain recognition on the national level.
2. True. Redistricting is redrawing electoral jurisdictions.
3. False. Redistricting occurs once every ten years following the national census.
4. Advantages of previous political experience include (1) learning the craft, (2) gaining a network of contacts, (3) garnering supportive constituents, and (4) developing potential fundraisers.

5. Federalism has become increasingly intertwined with congressional redistricting. Under the Voting Rights Act, some states must submit their congressional redistricting plans to the U.S. Department of Justice to ensure that they do not dilute minority voting strength.

3.5: Federalism and the American Intergovernmental System

1. False. Municipal governments are the governments of cities and towns.
2. True. Special districts are set up by state government to oversee activities that act across jurisdictional boundaries.
3. False. Voter turnout tends to be lower in local elections, although the impact of a local election is greater on the everyday lives of voters.
4. The large number of different governments helps politicians to be more responsive because diversity is recognized and particular local needs can be addressed quickly.
5. Answers will vary, but one weakness of smaller governments or units is that they may not have the resources or money to respond to and resolve issues. They also face low voter turnout.

3.6: Federalism and Pluralism

1. True. The layer-cake analogy of dual federalism aims to decentralize government and shift power to the states.
2. True. Marble cake federalism allows individuals and interest groups to petition government officials at whichever level offers them the best chance of success.
3. Both of the models of federalism recognize diversity and the importance of putting power in the hands of the states; thus, they promote pluralism.
4. Answers will vary.

Chapter 4

4.1: Public Opinion and the Models of Democracy

1. False. At times, such as in the case of capital punishment, the Supreme Court has denied the constitutionality of laws supported by the public.
2. False. Although they are not perfect, they are fairly accurate. See Figure 4.1 for a comparison of Gallup Poll predictions and election results over the past fifty years.
3. True. The advent of computers made survey methodology an easy-to-use and comprehensive research tool.
4. Today, opinion polling of a random sample of the public is used to gather information on citizens' collective attitudes.
5. In 1948, the poll predicted Republican candidate Thomas Dewey would defeat Harry Truman—underestimating Truman's vote by 5.4 percentage points. A larger magnitude error occurred in 1992, except in that case it did identify the winner (Bill Clinton). Such significant errors are rare.

4.2: Political Socialization

1. False. Political opinions change as people grow older and gain perspective on government.
2. True. Many factors influence how a person forms political opinions, including family, school, community, peers, and the mass media.
3. False. Political socialization is a rather complicated process.
4. People acquire their values through the political socialization process: an awareness of politics, facts, and forming political values.
5. Older Americans are more likely to rely on newspaper and television news to gather information on politics; younger Americans are more likely to turn to radio, magazines, or the Internet.

4.3: Social Groups and Political Values

1. False. Regional effects on public opinion are weaker than a century ago.
2. False. Trends show that, when confronted with a choice between personal freedom and equality, college-educated individuals tend to choose freedom.

3. True. For example, women tend to identify with the Democratic Party more than men do; women are also consistently more supportive than men of both affirmative action and government spending on social programs.
4. Yes, opinions in the United States do differ according to religion.
5. Answers may vary. Overall, these two terms do not adequately describe opinions such as the belief that abortion should be permitted only in certain cases such as incest, rape, or when the woman's life is in danger.

4.4: From Values to Ideology

1. False. Voters tend to identify liberals using terms such as "open-minded" and conservatives with terms such as "fiscally conservative," rather than by invoking explicitly political language.
2. False. As shown in to Figure 4.3, respondents to two questions presenting choices between freedom and order and between freedom and equality showed no correlation. These value choices are better analyzed according to the four different ideological types.
3. False. Both groups do value freedom, but liberals are more willing to trade freedom for equality, and conservatives are more willing to trade it for order.
4. Voters often find it hard to identify themselves with one political ideology because they act as liberals on some issues and conservatives on others.
5. Roosevelt's policies expanded the interventionist role of the national government in order to promote greater economic equality, distinguishing liberals from conservatives for decades to come.

4.5: Forming Political Opinions

1. True. Education is the factor that best predicts political knowledge.
2. False. Researchers have not found any meaningful relationship between political sophistication and self-placement on the liberal–conservative scale.
3. The self-interest principle states that people choose what benefits them personally when making decisions in politics.
4. Politicians appeal to the public on the basis of shared political ideology and self-interest. Their ability to reach the public has been greatly enhanced by the growth of broadcast media.

4.6: The Media in America

1. False. The Supreme Court has limited freedom of the press in times of crisis such as wartime.
2. True. The first form of the Internet was launched with the support from the U.S. Defense Department's Advanced Research Projects Agency.
3. True. A story is judged by its potential impact on readers or listeners, its degree of sensationalism, its treatment of familiar people or life situations, its close-to-home character, and its timeliness.
4. The equal opportunities rule is important because it ensures all candidates will have an opportunity to get media time.
5. The FCC is the Federal Communications Commission, which was created by the Federal Communications Act of 1934. It regulates the television, radio, telephone, telegraph, cable, and satellite industries.

4.7: Reporting and Following the News

1. True. Americans do believe the media exert a strong influence on public opinion.
2. True. Eighty percent of Americans read or hear the news each day, but it is thought less than 80 percent absorb and retain the information.
3. True. Gatekeepers include media executives, news editors, and prominent reporters.
4. *Horse race journalism* occurs when the media present news stories that have to do with who is winning an election rather than candidates' opinions on issues.
5. Scholars believe that the media's greatest impact on politics is their ability to set the political agenda. The media can do this by focusing on some problems and ignoring others.

4.8: Evaluating the Media in Government

1. False. The media also let the government know what people are thinking about the decisions being made and laws being enacted.
2. True. While this is the net effect of polls, they have also been known to create public opinion just by asking questions.
3. The mass media are the source of knowledge for most voters, which is essential in a majoritarian model of democracy.
4. The media have advanced women's rights and the rights of other disadvantaged groups. One example would be the reporting of instances of sexual discrimination exposed by groups working for sexual equality.

Chapter 5

5.1: Democracy and Political Participation

1. False. There are many forms of legitimate participation, such as contacting elected officials or volunteering in a campaign,
2. True. Elections do not guarantee a democratic government.
3. False. Demonstrations may be either conventional or unconventional. Lawful picketing is conventional behavior, whereas civil disobedience or the use of violence would be considered unconventional behavior.
4. Unconventional participation activities include those that challenge or defy established institutions or the dominant culture.
5. Some examples of conventional participation are voting, writing letters to public officials, and displaying campaign posters.

5.2: Unconventional Participation

1. True. Martin Luther King, Jr., used a form of unconventional participation, direct action, in the civil rights movement.
2. False. The Boston Tea Party is probably the first example of unconventional participation in the history of the United States.
3. False. Unconventional participation does work.
4. Groups that distrust the government but have a strong sense of political efficacy are most likely to engage in unconventional participation.
5. Answers may vary, but Americans are less likely to take part in demonstrations than citizens in other nations. It is commonly thought that Americans are apathetic about politics, but this is not the case.

5.3: Conventional Participation

1. False. Supportive behaviors are examples of conventional participation.
2. False. Influencing behaviors are a conventional form of participation in government in which citizens seek to modify or reverse government policy.
3. True. *Brown* v. *Board of Education* is an example of a class-action suit to challenge segregation in public schools.
4. "NIMBY" stands for "not in my backyard" and describes citizens' participation to prevent undesired projects from being located near their neighborhoods. This is an attempt to influence government to serve one's particular interests rather than the collective interests of society. Particular interests can include benefits to individual people, immediate families, or close friends.
5. Influencing behavior is an attempt to shape public policy. Supportive behavior consists of actions that demonstrate allegiance to the political system itself, apart from any particular policy.

5.4: Participating through Voting

1. False. Suffrage means the right to vote. It is also called the franchise.
2. True. Wyoming became the first territory to grant women the right to vote.
3. True. Progressivism was a political reform philosophy that sought to give more control of government and policy to votes at the ballot box. It was based on trust in the goodness and wisdom of individual citizens.
4. A referendum is a vote by the public on a proposed law or amendment to a state constitution. An initiative is a procedure through which citizens collect signatures on a petition to put an issue on the ballot (in a referendum) or send it to the legislature for decision.
5. The United States has the most democratic government because it holds the most frequent elections for the most public offices. Our House of Representatives is elected every two years; our president is elected every four years; our senators are elected every six years; and state governors, mayors, as well as city and county officials are popularly elected. In many states even judges stand for election.

5.5: Explaining Political Participation

1. False. Voter turnout in the United States dipped in the 1970s, 1980s, and 1990s before nudging upward again in the 2000s.
2. True. Education is the strongest single factor in explaining most types of conventional political participation.
3. False. Voting is not considered a high-effort activity.
4. Voter turnout declined after 1968 despite an increase in education. The reasons include an influx of younger voters after the Twenty-seventh Amendment, the growing belief that the government is not responsive, a change in attitude toward political parties, and a decline in the strength and extent of political parties.
5. The United States could make voting compulsory, declare election days as holidays or provide a two-day voting period, allow registration on election day, and make it easier to cast absentee ballots.

5.6: Participation and Freedom, Equality, and Order

1. True. In the United States, each citizen's ability to influence the government is equal when measured by the concept of one person, one vote.
2. False. In reaction to student unrest during the Vietnam War, Congress proposed an amendment to the Constitution, lowering the voting age from twenty-one to eighteen.
3. Elections, as a form of participation, serve the ideal of equality better than any other form of participation because the concept of one person, one vote gives everyone an equal influence in government.
4. The unrest on college campuses during the Vietnam War constituted unconventional participation because students stopped traffic, protested, occupied buildings, and destroyed property. The result was that on March 23, 1971, the Twenty-sixth Amendment was proposed, lowering the voting age to eighteen.

5.7: Participation and the Models of Democracy

1. True. Elections institutionalize access to political power.
2. False. Elections bolster the state's power because they involve citizens in decision making.
3. True. Resourceful and wealthy people have advantages in a majoritarian system because they are more likely to vote. They have advantages in a pluralist system because they are more able to hire lobbyists and organize groups.
4. One way that majoritarianism limits freedom is by favoring collective decisions formalized through elections, which does not give motivated individuals the kind of influence they might wish to have.

Chapter 6

6.1: Political Parties and Their Functions

1. False. Political parties also structure the voting choice, propose alternative programs of government action, and help coordinate the actions of government officials.

2. True. Interest groups do not nominate candidates to run as their representatives.
3. False. Despite their neutral names, the Democratic and Republican parties regularly adopt very different policies.
4. The difference between political parties and interest groups is that true political parties nominate individuals to run for office under the party's name. Interest groups may support candidates in various ways but do not nominate them.
5. Four of the most important party functions are nominating candidates, structuring the voters' choices, proposing alternative government programs, and coordinating the actions of government officials.

6.2: A History of U.S. Party Politics

1. False. The Republican Party was organized in 1854, and the Democratic Party was organized in 1828.
2. True. The Constitution never mentions political parties.
3. True. A critical election is one in which an electoral realignment occurs: a sharp change in existing patterns of party loyalties among groups of voters that lasts through several subsequent elections.
4. The Federalists and the Antifederalists were factions and did not nominate candidates. The terms initially referred to supporters and opponents of the Constitution. Later, a political party called the Federalist Party formed.
5. The elections of 1860, 1896, and 1932 are considered critical elections because they mark a sharp change in existing voting patterns that endured for many years. In 1860, the northern states voted mainly Republican and the southern states voted mainly Democratic, and the victory of the North over the South in the Civil War solidified this pattern. In 1896, business and the Republican Party joined forces in opposition to the Democrats' inflationary free silver platform. In 1932, President Roosevelt united southern Democrats, northern urban workers, middle-class liberals, Catholics, Jews, and white ethnic minorities in the "Roosevelt coalition."

6.3: The American Two-Party System

1. True. Minor parties have served throughout history as safety valves for people with opinions not represented by the major parties.
2. True. Majority representation is defined as one office contested by two or more candidates, in which the winner collects the most votes.
3. Based on a 2008 survey, the following party identifications can be made:
   a. False. People with lower incomes are more likely to vote Democrat.
   b. False. African Americans are strongly Democratic.
   c. True. Women tend to be more Democratic than men.
   d. True. The north-central states have a higher proportion of Republicans than other regions.
4. The four types of minor parties in U.S. political history are bolter parties, farmer-labor parties, parties of ideological protest, and single-issue parties.
5. Party identification is a voter's sense of psychological attachment to a party, and it is important because it predisposes voters to vote for their party's candidates.

6.4: Party Ideology and Organization

1. True. Party platforms are the statements of policies adopted at party conventions, and the winning party tends to carry out much of the platform in office.
2. True. The Democratic Party reforms of the 1970s focused on inclusion and participation, whereas the Republican Party reforms of that decade focused on organization.
3. False. The national committee has no voice in congressional activity and exercises very little direction or control over state and local campaigns.
4. The four main organizational components of each major party at the national level are the national convention, the national committee, the congressional party conferences, and the congressional campaign committees.

5. Party machines were prevalent during the time when major parties were firmly anchored by state and local organizations. The term means a centralized organization that dominates local politics by controlling elections, often through patronage.

6.5: The Model of Responsible Party Government
1. False. Parties fit the majoritarian model of democracy if they make the government responsive to public opinion. The pluralist model emphasizes the role of interest groups.
2. Generally true. Although there are some ideological consistencies between the parties, there are also very clear differences in what the parties value and advocate.
3. According to the principles of responsible party government, parties should present clear and coherent programs to voters, voters should choose candidates according to party programs, the winning party should carry out its program in office, and voters should hold the governing party responsible at the next election for its performance.

6.6: Parties and Candidates
1. False. There are four major types of primary elections: closed primaries, open primaries, modified closed primaries, and modified open primaries.
2. False. The national committees lay out the rules for their party conventions and can, for example, refuse to seat delegates selected in primaries held before the dates established by the party.
3. True. When no incumbent in the White House is seeking reelection, the presidential nominating process becomes contested in both parties.
4. Political parties favor closed primaries because voters must be registered with a particular party to cast their vote, so large numbers of opposing party voters do not have a voice in selecting the nominee as they might in an open primary.
5. Front-loading is scheduling delegate selection primaries and caucuses earlier in the year to get extra media coverage.

6.7: Elections
1. False. All of the seats in the House of Representatives and one-third of the seats in the Senate are filled in a general election.
2. True. The electoral votes are divided among the states based on their representation in the House and Senate. House representation is based on population.
3. False. About half of voters split their tickets.
4. A general election is held in early November in even-numbered years.
5. Each state has the same number of electors as it has senators and representatives. There are 435 representatives and 100 senators, and the District of Columbia has 3 electors. That comes to a total of 538 electors. A candidate must win an absolute majority (270) of the electoral votes to become president.

6.8: Campaigns
1. True. Incumbents enjoy great advantages over challengers in congressional elections.
2. False. Hard money refers to funds raised for federal election campaigns.
3. True. The Supreme Court ruled in 2010 that corporations and unions may spend money independently without limit in election campaigns.
4. The FEC is the Federal Election Commission, which enforces the rules of the Federal Election Campaign Act.
5. Presidential candidates who demonstrate widespread support are eligible to receive matching funds from the government during the primary election season if they agree to an overall spending limit. In the general election, the government pays for the nominees' campaigns if they agree not to exceed a spending limit. If candidates

can raise significantly more money on their own without government funds, they may opt out and are not subject to spending limits.

6.9: Explaining Voting Choice

1. True. Party identification is the most significant long-term force influencing voter choice.
2. True. Most studies on presidential elections show that campaign issues are less important than party identification and the candidates' attributes.
3. False. Party voting is less common today than it was in the 1950s.
4. Two short-term forces that affect how people vote during an election are the candidates' attributes, such as personal beliefs, and the issues surrounding the election.
5. The more important the role of long-term party identification, the less likely a campaign is to influence the outcome of the election. However, short-term issues do matter, particularly when a race is close, when wooing independents, and when ideology seems unconnected to party.

6.10: Campaigns, Elections, and Parties

1. False. Increased use of electronic media such as television has personalized campaign messages.
2. True. According to the majoritarian model of democracy, parties link people to their government by making government responsive to public opinion.
3. True. The decentralized nature of the nominating process and campaigning for office allows organized groups outside the party to identify and support candidates who favor their interests.
4. The Democratic and Republican parties relate to the pluralist model because the decentralized nature of the nominating process and campaigning for office offers many opportunities for organized groups outside the party to identify and back candidates who favor their interests.
5. The weak links in the majoritarian model of democracy have been those that connect candidates to voters through campaigns and elections.

Chapter 7

7.1: Interest Groups and the American Political Tradition

1. False. Interest groups do benefit our political system by giving citizens a means to make their voices heard.
2. True. The desire to influence public policy is the characteristic that distinguishes interest groups from other organizations or clubs.
3. False. Though labor unions have succeeded in putting several issues on the political agenda, their membership has declined dramatically over the past twenty years.
4. Interest group roles include representation, participation, education, agenda building, and program monitoring.
5. James Madison believed the government should not remove freedom to prevent factions from forming. He argued that in a large republic, geography would dilute the effects of factions, and the representative institutions of government would require factions to compromise with one another.

7.2: How Interest Groups Form

1. False. Interest group entrepreneurs are individuals who start and organize interest groups by attracting members with a common interest.
2. False. There are three variables that help to explain why groups may or may not become organized: in addition to a disturbance or adverse change and the socioeconomic level of those affected most by those circumstances, the quality of leadership is a crucial factor.
3. False. Cesar Chavez's strike against the grape growers failed until he adopted the tactics of the civil rights movement and appealed to the sympathy of people outside the agricultural community.

4. According to disturbance theory, interest groups are formed when individuals come together because they are threatened by change.

5. Chavez led crop pickers on a 250-mile march to Sacramento, California, to demand help from the governor. His nonviolent tactics drew sympathy from many Americans who supported the United Farm Workers by not purchasing grapes until the grape growers recognized and negotiated with the union.

7.3: Interest Group Resources

1. False. PACs are limited to a maximum contribution of $5,000 per candidate per election.

2. False. The "free-rider problem" is a situation in which people benefit from an organization's activities without contributing to those activities.

3. False. Lobbyists are mainly responsible for convincing policymakers that their goals are worth supporting. PACs are responsible for pooling campaign contributions from group members and donating funds to candidates for political office.

4. Interest groups are always looking for new members because they want to expand their resources and power.

5. Business, professional, and labor associations have an easier time retaining members than citizen groups because the latter are primarily based on ideological sentiments. Furthermore, the "hot issues" that citizen groups are concerned with vary year to year. Job-related associations, on the other hand, are directly concerned with peoples' employment status and income, which are ongoing concerns.

7.4: Lobbying Tactics

1. False. Grassroots lobbying can be done on behalf of any cause, involves an interest group's rank-and-file members, and may also include people outside the organization.

2. True. The most common direct lobbying tactic involves lobbyists meeting with government officials.

3. True. Letter-writing campaigns and protests are grassroots lobbying tactics and are often used in conjunction with direct lobbying tactics.

4. Interest groups launch information campaigns to bring certain views to the public's attention and to secure public support.

5. Groups participate in lobbying coalitions to share costs, to present a united front to lawmakers, and to demonstrate the breadth of support for a particular policy goal.

7.5: Is the System Biased?

1. True. Business is better represented in the interest group world than any other type of organization.

2. True. Middle-income people are more likely to join interest groups than low-income people.

3. True. PACs receive negative criticism from people who believe that donations from interest groups influence policy outcomes in an undemocratic way.

4. Businesses mobilize to ensure that government decisions and policies will favor their companies.

5. The Bipartisan Campaign Reform Act (BCRA) prevents soft-money gifts from organizations to political parties.

Chapter 8

8.1: The Origin and Powers of Congress

1. False. Only the House of Representatives has the power to impeach officers of the national government.

2. False. Even though the Constitution has granted that power solely to Congress, many presidents have initiated military action on their own.

3. False. Until the Seventeenth Amendment was adopted in 1913, the Constitution specified that senators would be chosen by their state legislatures rather than by voters.

4. The number of representatives from each state is determined by the population of that state and is reapportioned every ten years.
5. The House has the power to bring formal charges against certain federal officers. The Senate then acts as a court to try impeachments; a two-thirds majority vote of the senators present is required for a conviction.

8.2: Electing the Congress
1. True. Gerrymandering means altering the district lines for partisan advantage.
2. False. Most members of Congress are professionals—primarily lawyers, businesspeople, and educators.
3. False. Most money in congressional elections goes to incumbents.
4. Descriptive representation is a belief that a legislature should resemble the demographic characteristics of the population it represents.
5. Most Americans distinguish between Congress as a whole and their own representatives. Incumbents often benefit from high name recognition, weak challengers, and the ability to carry out casework for constituents, among other things.

8.3: How Issues Get on the Congressional Agenda
1. False. Before a bill is introduced, members of Congress must notice the issue or perceive a problem, decide that action is warranted, and draft a written bill to bring to their respective chamber.
2. False. The "hopper" is a mahogany box in which House members place bills they want to introduce.
3. Significant events, party leaders, committee chairs, and interest groups can bring an issue to the forefront of the political agenda in Congress.

8.4: The Dance of Legislation: An Overview
1. True. After a bill is introduced, it goes to its respective committee.
2. False. The Rules Committee assigns rules for floor debate to bills in the House of Representatives, not the Senate.
3. True. The conference committee, composed of legislators from both houses, works out the differences between the Senate and House versions of a passed bill and comes to a compromise.
4. When a bill is vetoed by the president, it is sent back to Congress with the reasons for rejecting it. Congress may override the veto with a two-thirds vote in each house.
5. Throughout the process, the content of a bill can be changed at any time by either the Senate or the House. The bill itself can be tabled or killed at any stage of the process. The search for consensus often slows down the enacting of legislation.

8.5: Committees: The Workhorses of Congress
1. True. The standing committees are the predominant committees.
2. True. Select committees are generally temporary because they are created for a specific purpose, and once that purpose is served, the committee no longer has a function.
3. False. Many members tend to stay on the same committees in order to gain seniority and influence within that committee. However, they are sometimes offered the opportunity to move to a higher-prestige committee or one that handles legislation of importance to their constituents.
4. Legislators and their committees engage in oversight to ensure their policies are being carried out as intended.
5. The committee system enhances the force of pluralism in American politics because representatives and senators are elected by the voters in particular districts and states. Also, they tend to seek membership on the committees that will make decisions that are important to their constituents.

8.6: Leaders and Followers in Congress

1. True. Today it is easier to maintain a filibuster in the Senate because it is not necessary to be physically present and talk continuously.
2. True. Cloture requires the vote of sixty senators and creates a time limit for a debate.
3. True. The Speaker of the House and the majority leader are both from the majority party.
4. The Speaker of the House is the head of the majority party and is a constitutional officer.
5. The norms, or "codes of behavior," in Congress are for the most part unwritten. They include showing respect for colleagues in public deliberations and remaining willing to bargain with one another. The old norms of having junior members of the House and Senate serve apprenticeships and defer to senior members of Congress during their first few years of service have declined.

8.7: The Legislative Environment

1. False. Constituents are the people who live in and vote in a government official's district or state.
2. True. The four external sources of influence on Congress are parties, the president, constituents, and interest groups.
3. Political parties and the president push Congress toward majoritarianism, and constituents and interest groups are pluralist influences on congressional policymaking.

8.8: The Dilemma of Representation: Trustees or Delegates?

1. True. Burke served in Parliament in the eighteenth century and believed, once elected, representatives were trustees.
2. True. The delegate view holds that legislators act with instructions from the people at home and must be prepared to vote against their own policy preferences.
3. A trustee is a representative who, once elected, votes as he or she thinks best on issues. A delegate is a legislator who represents the views of his or her constituents.

8.9: Pluralism, Majoritarianism, and Democracy

1. True. Parliaments reflect the majoritarian model more than the pluralist model because the leader of the majority party is the head of the government, the second house or chamber is usually weaker than the other, and often there is not a court to invalidate acts of parliament.
2. False. Pluralism is much more prevalent in Congress. For example, virtually every possible viewpoint is represented by representatives and senators who try to win projects and programs for their constituents.
3. A focus on local projects desired by interest groups rather than on the national interest as identified by a majority of the public is indicative of pluralism.

Chapter 9

9.1: The Constitutional Basis of Presidential Power

1. True. The Articles of Confederation did not provide for a single head of state.
2. False. The powers of the presidency are set forth in Article II of the Constitution.
3. True. Presidents interpret their power to "receive Ambassadors" as a grant of authority to formally recognize other nations.
4. Three requirements of the presidency are that one must be a U.S.-born citizen, at least thirty-five years old, and a resident of the United States for at least fourteen years.
5. The major presidential duties are to serve as administrative head of the nation, act as commander in chief of the military, convene Congress, veto legislation, appoint various officials, make treaties, and grant pardons.

9.2: The Expansion of Presidential Power

1. True. Presidential power today is much greater than originally envisioned by the founders.
2. True. Modern presidents have used their power as commander in chief to enter into foreign conflicts without appealing to Congress for a formal declaration of war.
3. False. The War Powers Resolution Act (1973) was directed toward limiting the president's ability to pursue armed conflict without explicit congressional approval.
4. Presidential executive orders are presidential directives to the executive branch that carry the force of law.
5. Congress often delegates power to the executive branch to administer programs and address problems that are difficult to address in a legislative setting.

9.3: The Executive Branch Establishment

1. False. Presidential candidates often choose vice-presidential candidates who appeal to a different geographic region or party coalition.
2. False. The president's cabinet is an advisory group that rarely meets with the president and has little impact as a group.
3. True. The president's personal staff is called the White House Office.
4. Franklin Roosevelt used a competitive management style so his managers had overlapping authority. Dwight Eisenhower used a hierarchical style that mirrored a military command. Bill Clinton used a collegial staffing arrangement, a loose structure that allowed him to be immersed in details and less likely to delegate authority to others.
5. The vice president is not the president's chief adviser. The chief adviser may be the chief of staff or other policy advisers. The vice president is often chosen as a candidate for reasons that have to do more with the campaign than with governing the nation.

9.4: Presidential Leadership

1. False. According to Neustadt, presidential power is the power to persuade, which is based upon his professional reputation and public prestige.
2. False. Political scientists generally disagree with this statement, although rising partisanship in Congress may make divided government more of a challenge.
3. True. Presidents who come to power immediately following critical elections have the most favorable environment for exerting leadership.
4. Presidential popularity is shaped by three major factors. First, public approval is affected by economic conditions. Second, it is affected by unanticipated events. Third, involvement in a war may initially boost a president's popularity, but heavy casualties tend to lower it over time.
5. Voters choose presidents based on their views of national issues and their ability to deal with national problems. Congressional candidates are more likely to be chosen based on their personal character, experience, and devotion to local issues.

9.5: The President as National Leader

1. True. The Budget and Accounting Act of 1921 required executive departments and agencies to clear their proposed budget bills with the White House.
2. True. The legislative liaison staff advises the president as problems emerge when a bill makes its way through Congress.
3. False. American presidents informally lead their party, while European prime ministers are the formal leaders of their party.
4. Lyndon Johnson created a package of liberal legislation, launching programs to help disadvantaged Americans. Ronald Reagan, conversely, worked to cut taxes, shift federal spending to defense, and emphasize freedom over equality.

5. Franklin D. Roosevelt established a precedent that the president would aggressively lead Congress through his own legislative programs. Prior to this period, agencies could submit bills without approval of the White House and the executive branch did not approve budgets. During Roosevelt's presidency, he required that all major proposals be cleared by the White House before moving on.

9.6: The President as World Leader

1. False. The United States often pursues foreign policy goals through international organizations such as NATO and the U.N.
2. False. John F. Kennedy's handling of the Cuban missile crisis of 1962 is a model of effective crisis management.
3. The three fundamental objectives for the president with regard to international relations are national security, fostering a peaceful international environment, and protecting U.S. economic interests.
4. Some guidelines for the president are to first draw on the knowledge of his advisers, not make hasty decisions, have a formal review process that promotes analysis and debate, and evaluate the reasoning behind options to guarantee their validity.

Chapter 10

10.1: Organization Matters

1. False. Bureaucracies play a central role in the governments of modern societies.
2. True. A bureaucracy is any large, complex organization with employees with specific responsibilities who work within a hierarchy.
3. The role of the bureaucracy in government is to administer laws and put them into effect.

10.2: Bureaucratic Growth

1. True. Government at all levels grew during the twentieth century because society became more complex. New bureaucracies were created to regulate specific industries. There was also a change in public attitudes toward business and the government's responsibility for social welfare.
2. False. The Securities and Exchange Commission (SEC) and Food and Drug Administration (FDA) are examples of bureaucracies.
3. Some segments of the American population believe they deserve government support because of their value to society or because they do not believe they can overcome adversity on their own.
4. To decrease the size of government, bureaucracies would have to be eliminated or reduced in size. Serious budget cuts will require reductions in programs.

10.3: Bureaus and Bureaucrats

1. True. The department with the most employees is the Department of Defense.
2. False. Departments are the largest units of the executive branch.
3. True. The CIA is an example of an independent agency; it is not part of a department but is under the president's control.
4. The civil service was created to reduce the filling of government positions with the president's political allies. It fills jobs on the basis of merit and makes sure that employees are not fired for political reasons.
5. Bureaucracies may not be as responsive as the president wishes because agencies can be pulled in many directions by the powers of pluralism and because Congress has a powerful influence on executive branch agencies, which must follow the laws governing the programs they run.

10.4: Administrative Policymaking: The Formal Processes

1. True. Agencies make policy decisions because Congress recognized it has neither the time nor the technical expertise to make all policy decisions.
2. False. Administrative discretion is the latitude that Congress gives agencies to make policy in the spirit of their legislative mandate.
3. True. Rule making is the administrative process that results in regulations.
4. The broadest discretion given by Congress is generally to those agencies involved in domestic and global security, like the CIA and FBI, because of their legitimate need for secrecy.
5. Congress controls agencies by passing legislation limiting bureaucratic discretion, by providing advice and direction during hearings, and through threats to cut or reprioritize budgets.

10.5: Administrative Policymaking: Informal Politics

1. True. Policymakers often have difficulty defining values and goals, deciding which values and goals are most important, and relating them to other national goals.
2. True. Policymaking tends to be shaped by incrementalism, a step-by-step process of modest change.
3. False. Norms are informal, unwritten rules of behavior.
4. Incrementalism characterizes policymaking that occurs when policies and programs change slowly; new policies are generally modifications of existing policies.
5. Different bureaucracies are influenced by the different types of people who work for them because they develop a sense of mission and a particular objective. For example, the Army Corps of Engineers is dominated by engineers, and their solutions fit their conception of what their agency should be doing.

10.6: Problems in Implementing Policy

1. True. Implementation of policies may be difficult because directives are not specific and they leave bureaucrats with too much discretion.
2. False. While government bureaucracies sometimes have special technical expertise that private companies lack, the Gulf oil leak shows that this is not always the case.
3. False. Implementation is the process of putting specific policies into operation.
4. Some of the obstacles to implementing policy are that the policy is not clear enough, directives are not specific enough, some government issues are very complex—such as toxic cleanups—and multiple organizations, agencies, and levels of government increase the challenges.

10.7: Reforming the Bureaucracy: More Control or Less?

1. True. When the government deregulates, free competition can benefit customers and promote productivity.
2. False. The case of thalidomide illustrates the beneficial role that bureaucracy and regulation can play in public health.
3. True. Recent approaches to regulation include a focus on making corporations more transparent and accountable in their actions.
4. Although drug companies feel that health and safety regulations are burdensome and impinge on their ability to make a profit, strict regulation is often necessary because health and well-being are immediately affected by products that do not meet strict standards. For example, in the 1960s a sedative, thalidomide, was required to pass tests in the United States, even though it was already in use in Europe. As a result of these precautionary measures, a crisis was prevented here. Europe later reported birth defects in children born to mothers who took thalidomide.
5. Underlying the principle of competition and outsourcing is the belief held by conservatives that government should emulate private sector practices. This view holds that competition will make government more dynamic and responsive to changing conditions.

Chapter 11

11.1: National Judicial Supremacy

1. True. The Supreme Court can use its power of judicial review to invalidate laws that violate the Constitution.
2. False. The Judiciary Act of 1789 created federal courts that independently coexist with the courts in each state.
3. True. *Marbury* v. *Madison* (1803) was the first case in which the Supreme Court exercised judicial review to strike down a law of Congress.
4. The Supreme Court's ability to invalidate unconstitutional laws might be construed as undemocratic because judges, who are appointed to their position and are not accountable to the electorate, are given the power to strike down laws passed by elected officials.
5. Two strategies for overriding judicial review are constitutional amendments and the impeachment of justices.

11.2: The Organization of Courts

1. False. Litigants file nearly all cases in the state courts.
2. False. When a court adjudicates a case, it means the court makes a government-enforced judgment that resolves the parties' claims.
3. True. The principle of *stare decisis* refers to the bias in favor of precedents, or previously made court decisions, when trying future cases.
4. A criminal case involves a crime or violation of public order, whereas a civil case involves a private dispute between parties over tangible issues (e.g., property ownership) or more abstract issues (e.g., damages for pain and suffering).
5. The three levels of the U.S. federal court system, from bottom to top, are the U.S. district courts, the U.S. courts of appeals, and the Supreme Court of the United States. The courts of appeals and the Supreme Court are appellate courts.

11.3: The Supreme Court

1. True. The solicitor general represents the federal government before the Supreme Court and influences the Court's agenda.
2. False. The person who directs the discussion at the judicial conference is the chief justice.
3. The "rule of four" is an unwritten rule that requires at least four justices to agree that a case warrants consideration before it is reviewed by the Supreme Court.
4. State cases may be brought to the U.S. Supreme Court only if they reach the end of the line in the state court system and raise a federal question (one that is covered under the Constitution, federal laws, or national treaties).

11.4: Judicial Recruitment

1. True. Before federal judges are appointed, they are screened by the Justice Department and are investigated by the FBI.
2. False. *Senatorial courtesy* means that the Senate will not confirm a nominee who is opposed by the senior senator from a nominee's state if that senator is in the president's party.
3. The Constitution implies that federal judges hold their positions for life unless they retire or are impeached.
4. Judges on many state courts are often appointed by governors in a system similar to the appointment of federal judges by the president. However, several states also have competitive elections for judges, even at the state supreme court level. That system differs starkly from the federal system of life appointment, which is intended to insulate federal judges from political pressures.

11.5: The Consequences of Judicial Decisions

1. False. Most lawsuits are settled outside of court, dismissed, or dropped by the litigants.
2. False. A plea bargain is a defendant's admission of guilt in exchange for a less severe punishment.

3. A majority of the public approves of the Supreme Court's overall performance. While there are important examples of the Supreme Court taking unpopular stances, the Court's positions often align with public opinion over time.

4. Justices on the Supreme Court have to compromise when drafting an opinion because they must hold their majority together.

11.6: The Courts and Models of Democracy

1. True. Class action lawsuits give individuals a means to assemble their claims or defenses about a similar situation to be heard in a single lawsuit.

2. False. Supporters of the majoritarian judiciary model maintain that judges should not inject their personal values into their decision-making process.

3. True. A state court can avoid review by the U.S. Supreme Court by basing its decision solely on state law or by basing its decision on both state law and federal law.

4. The pluralist model maintains that the courts are a policymaking branch of government and that judges can consciously promote specific groups' interests and preferences as they see fit.

5. In *Brown* v. *Board of Education,* schoolchildren (through their parents) used class action to assemble and rectify claimed racial discrimination by school authorities.

Chapter 12

12.1: The Bill of Rights

1. False. The Bill of Rights was adopted in 1791 and refers to the first ten amendments to the Constitution.

2. False. The "rights and liberties" guaranteed by the Constitution can be found in the Bill of Rights as well as the first section of the Fourteenth Amendment.

3. Civil liberties are freedoms that are guaranteed to the individual and limit action by the government, whereas civil rights declare what the government must do or provide for all people.

4. The Civil Rights Act of 1964 established the right to nondiscrimination in places of public accommodations and the right to equal employment opportunity.

12.2: Freedom of Religion

1. True. The Supreme Court does not support religious training in public schools during regular school hours but allows voluntary after-school religious activities and clubs on the same basis as any other extracurricular activity.

2. False. Strict scrutiny is no longer required for state laws that may burden free exercise. Since *Employment Division* v. *Smith,* neutral laws that indirectly restrict religious practices are acceptable; only laws aimed at religious groups are constitutionally prohibited.

3. True. The First Amendment protects religious observance as well as belief.

4. The two clauses in the First Amendment that guarantee freedom of religion are the establishment clause, which prohibits laws establishing religion, and the free-exercise clause, which prevents the government from interfering with the exercise of religion.

5. Based on the establishment clause, the *Lemon* test proposes that government programs and laws are constitutional if they have a secular purpose, if their primary effect does not advance or inhibit religion, and if they do not entangle the government excessively with religion.

12.3: Freedom of Expression

1. False. The free-expression clauses concern freedom of speech and the press, but they are found in the Constitution's First Amendment.

2. True. Under the First Amendment, symbolic expression, or nonverbal communication, generally receives less protection than pure speech.

3. False. The Constitutional guarantee of freedom of the press does not override the requirements of law enforcement.

4. The clear and present danger test was a test enabling the Supreme Court to distinguish between speech as an advocacy of ideas and speech as incitement or a disruption of the social order.

5. The *Miller* test determines whether a particular work is obscene, and its components are interpreted by local community standards. The components of the test are as follows: whether the work as a whole appeals to prurient (lustful) interest; whether the work portrays sexual conduct in a patently offensive way; and whether the work as a whole lacks serious literary, artistic, political, or scientific value.

12.4: The Right to Bear Arms

1. False. Sawed-off shotguns do not qualify for protection.

2. True. The Constitution permits restrictions, but not federal prohibitions, on gun ownership.

3. Gun-control advocates assert that the Second Amendment protects the right of the states to maintain militias, and gun-use advocates assert that it protects the right of individuals to own and use guns.

12.5: Applying the Bill of Rights to the States

1. False. Bills of attainder are laws that make an individual guilty of a crime without a judicial trial. The Constitution barred such bills so that an individual is innocent until proven guilty.

2. True. The Supreme Court more recently has used the Fourteenth Amendment to apply the Bill of Rights to state laws.

3. True. *Miranda* warnings protect citizens by advising them of certain rights when they are held in custody and interrogated.

4. The exclusionary rule is a judicial rule that states that evidence obtained in an illegal search and seizure cannot be used in trial. There are exceptions to this rule for mistakes made in good faith by law enforcement officials.

5. The USA-PATRIOT Act allows the government to search private, personal records without a judge-issued warrant and bars the person who turns over the records from disclosing the search to anyone other than his or her attorney.

12.6: The Ninth Amendment and Personal Autonomy

1. True. The Ninth Amendment can be interpreted to mean that states are protected from the national government taking over their powers.

2. True. The Ninth Amendment can be interpreted to mean that rights that are not enumerated in the Constitution, such as the right to privacy, can still be protected.

3. True. Each state is responsible for determining its stance on the validation of same-sex unions and marriages.

4. In *Bowers* v. *Hardwick* the Supreme Court ruled that the Constitution did not protect homosexual relations between consenting adults, even in the privacy of their own homes. It was overturned in 2003 when the Supreme Court considered a challenge to a Texas law that criminalized homosexual but not heterosexual sodomy.

5. In *Roe* v. *Wade*, the majority of the justices argued that the right to privacy established a zone of personal autonomy and that during the first trimester of a pregnancy, abortion decisions fell within this zone and were to be determined by the woman and her physician. The dissenters believed that the majority opinion was based on the justices' own views, not the views of the Constitution or the state legislatures whose abortion regulations they invalidated.

Chapter 13

13.1: Two Conceptions of Equality

1. True. Americans are far less committed to equality of outcome because this requires restrictions such as quotas.

2. False. Invidious discrimination is discrimination against persons or groups that harms them and is based on animosity.

3. Equality of outcome is greater uniformity in social, economic, and political power among different social groups. This can occur only with restrictions on the free competition that is the basis of equality of opportunity.

4. A quota requires that a specified, proportional share of some benefit goes to a favored group. A goal also aims for a proportional allocation of benefits but does not require it.

13.2: The Civil War Amendments

1. False. The Fifteenth Amendment states that the right of citizens of the United States to vote shall not be denied or abridged by the United States or by any state on account of race, color, or previous condition of servitude.

2. True. The Civil Rights Act of 1875 attempted to guarantee equal access to streetcars, inns, parks, theaters, and other places.

3. True. Poll taxes and literacy tests were a nonracial means instituted to prevent blacks from voting.

4. The separate-but-equal doctrine held that separate facilities were legal for blacks and whites as long as they were equal.

5. Homer Adolph Plessy was seven-eighths Caucasian and one-eighth black and took a "whites only" seat in a train. He refused to move to a seat reserved for blacks and was arrested. Plessy argued that racial segregation on trains was unconstitutional, and the Supreme Court disagreed. The Court case, *Plessy* v. *Ferguson*, upheld state-imposed racial segregation with the "separate-but-equal" doctrine.

13.3: The Dismantling of School Segregation

1. False. President Harry Truman supported black civil rights and ordered desegregation of the armed forces.

2. False. *Brown* v. *Board of Education* was not a key factor in the 1952 national election because the Supreme Court chose to hear the case after the election.

3. False. De facto and de jure segregation do not mean the same thing. De facto segregation is not a result of government influence, but de jure segregation is government-imposed segregation.

4. The case *Brown* v. *Board of Education* was the culmination of twenty years of planning and litigation by the NAACP to invalidate racial segregation in public schools. The case consisted of five individual cases, all of which challenged the separate-but-equal doctrine. In 1954 the Supreme Court ruled that separate but equal has no place in public education and that separate educational facilities are inherently unequal.

13.4: The Civil Rights Movement

1. False. Civil disobedience is the willful but nonviolent breach of unjust laws.

2. True. The Twenty-fourth Amendment banned poll taxes in primary and general elections and was part of Johnson's goal of a "great society."

3. Martin Luther King, Jr.'s, role in the civil rights movement was monumental. He led a boycott of the Montgomery, Alabama, bus system; helped organize the Southern Christian Leadership Conference to coordinate civil rights activities; joined in the march on Washington, D.C.; and promoted nonviolent protests.

4. The Civil Rights Act of 1991 came about after the narrowing of civil right protections in many court decisions that resulted in an emphasis on freedom and not equality. Liberals countered with a new civil rights bill that reversed or altered twelve court decisions, expanding and clarifying earlier legislation.

13.5: Civil Rights for Other Minorities

1. True. In 1987 the Supreme Court ruled that *any* ethnic group could recover monetary damages if it could prove it had been denied a job, excluded from rental housing, or discriminated unlawfully in another way.

2. False. In 1924 Native Americans received U.S. citizenship.

3. True. The ADA protects those with physical or mental disabilities, including people with AIDS, recovering alcoholics, and drug abusers.

4. The language barrier prevents some Hispanics from participating in government because political advertising is not targeted toward Hispanics as often as other groups, meaning they do not always receive political messages they can understand. Voter registration and voter turnout is particularly low among Hispanics.

5. Persons with disabilities have capitalized on gains from the civil rights laws by gaining recognition as minorities and demanding changes such as equal access to buildings and public transportation as well as job equality.

13.6: Gender and Equal Rights

1. True. The notion of protectionism guided laws that affected the civil rights of women until the 1970s.
2. True. The Nineteenth Amendment guaranteed women the right to vote in state and national elections.
3. In 1878 Susan B. Anthony persuaded a senator to introduce a constitutional amendment to allow women to vote. Some states began to allow limited suffrage to women, but it took until 1920 before the Nineteenth Amendment passed.

13.7: Affirmative Action

1. False. Affirmative action is a commitment by a business, employer, school, or other institution to expand opportunities for women, blacks, Hispanic Americans, and members of other minority groups. Most forms of affirmative action do not involve quotas at all.
2. True. In *Gratz* v. *Bollinger* the Supreme Court held that the University of Michigan violated the equal protection clause because its policies were not individualized or tailored enough.
3. False. Over the past twenty years, surveys have revealed that blacks favor affirmative action much more than whites do.
4. Allan Bakke, a white man, was twice denied admission to the University of California Medical School at Davis, despite his grade point average and test scores exceeding those of minority applicants admitted in both years he applied. He argued that he was denied admission because of his race, and his court case *Regents of California* v. *Bakke* changed affirmative action programs to use race as a *plus* factor and not the only factor.
5. The central argument behind affirmative action is that certain groups have historically suffered discrimination and to eliminate the effects of this, private and public sectors must provide access to good education and jobs.

Chapter 14

14.1: Government Purposes and Public Policy

1. True. Redistributional policies are explicitly designed to take resources from one sector of society and transfer them to another, reflecting the core value of greater equality.
2. False. Implementation precedes evaluation.
3. False. Agenda building sometimes involves redefining older issues so that people look at them in different ways, and feedback from the implementation and evaluation stages of the policymaking process both stimulate new cycles of the process.
4. Policies originate only after issues enter the political agenda through the process called agenda setting. Policy measures then might be proposed by the president or developed by legislation passed in Congress in the policy formulation stage.
5. No—feedback from policy evaluation can be inconsistent. Multiple studies may point in different directions. For example, in examining abstinence-based sex education, studies differed in their conclusions about effectiveness. Comparing disparate conclusions may give hints about what elements of a program are important to its success or failure.

14.2: Fragmentation and Coordination

1. False. Issue networks are shared-knowledge groups consisting of those with various interests in a public policy. They may differ in ideological perspectives, but they share expertise in the subject matter.

2. True. Fragmentation in the policymaking process develops when a single problem is attacked in different and sometimes competing ways by government.
3. True. Majoritarians see issue networks as an obstacle to achieving their vision of how government should operate.
4. Because the separation of powers divides authority among the branches of the national government, multiple actors can exercise influence in the policy process and fragmentation is the natural outcome.
5. The OMB fosters coordination within the executive branch, as its power reaches beyond reviewing budgets and seeking ways to improve management practices. The OMB's regulatory review role centralizes control of the executive branch, and has since the Reagan administration.

14.3: Economic Policy and the Budget
1. False. The U.S. government has rarely had a balanced budget. In most years it has a deficit because revenue falls far short of outlays.
2. False. A fiscal year (FY) is the twelve-month period from October 1 to September 30 and is named for the year in which it ends.
3. True in the past, but rapidly changing. For decades Social Security ran a surplus, which was put into a trust fund to meet future demands. However, due in part to reduced tax revenue during the Great Recession, tax revenues were expected to fall short of benefit expenses in 2010 and 2011. A small surplus is predicted to return in 2012–2014, but with the baby boom generation's retirement, taxes will be inadequate to cover retirees after that unless the program is significantly restructured.
4. Tax policies are designed to provide a continuous flow of revenue to government.
5. Some argue that a flat tax is not a fair tax because it violates the principle of progressive taxation. Under a flat tax, everyone, regardless of income bracket or disposable income, must pay the same percentage of their income in taxes.

CourseMate CL Resources:
Visit www.cengagebrain.com/shop/ISBN/1111832587 for flashcards, web quizzes, videos and more!

References

Chapter 1 / Dilemmas of Democracy / pages 2–41

1. The transcript of President Obama's speech is available at http://www.whitehouse.gov/the-press-office/2011/02/11/remarks-president-egypt.

2. Michael Slackman, "Egyptians' Fury Has Smoldered Beneath the Surface for Decades," *New York Times*, 29 January 2011, p. A11.

3. The non-governmental organization, Freedom House, has rated Egypt "Not Free" in its recent annual surveys. See http://www.freedomhouse.org/template.cfm?page=70&release=1334.

4. Richard Boudreaux, "A Man Needed Abroad, Reviled at Home," *Wall Street Journal*, 12 February 2011, p. A8.

5. Helene Cooper, "The United States Supports, um, Well … When It Comes to Diplomacy in Egypt, Words Often Fail," *New York Times*, 30 January 2011, p. WK 1.

6. Margaret Coker, "Tunisians Oust President," *Wall Street Journal*, 15 January 2011, p. 1; Though we focus on Tunisia and Egypt in this vignette, consider that similar demonstrations swept through many other countries in the Middle East, including Libya, Bahrain, Jordan, Yemen, and Syria within a matter of months of the events in Tunisia. See Marc Fisher, "The Spark That Ignited a Revolution," *Washington Post*, 26 March 2011, pp. A1, A10–A11.

7. David D. Kirkpatrick, "President of Tunisia Flees, Capitulating to Protesters," *New York Times*, 15 January 2011, pp. A1 and A6.

8. Lauren A. E. Schuker, "Al-Jazeera Gets Brunt of Anger at Reports," *Wall Street Journal*, 5 February 2011, p. A10.

9. David D. Kirkpatrick, "Clashes Go on as Power Shifts Again in Tunis," *New York Times*, 16 January 2011, pp. A1 and A11.

10. Jennifer Preston, "Movement Began with Outrage and a Facebook Page That Gave It an Outlet," *New York Times*, 2 February 2011, p. 10.

11. Christopher Rhoads and Geoffrey A. Fowler, "Government Shuts Down Internet, Cellphone Services," *Wall Street Journal*, 29 January 2011, p. A11.

12. David D. Kirkpatrick and Kareen Fahim, "Mubarak's Allies and Foes Clash in Egypt," *New York Times*, 3 February 2011, p. A1.

13. Schuker, "Al-Jazeera Gets Brunt of Anger at Reports."

14. Mark Andreas Kayser, "How Domestic Is Domestic Politics? Globalization and Elections," *Annual Review of Political Science* 10 (2007): 341–362.

15. David Easton, *The Political System* (New York: Knopf, 1953), p. 65.

16. Thomas Biersteker and Cynthia Weber (eds.), *State Sovereignty as Social Construct* (Cambridge: Cambridge University Press, 1996), p. 12. For a definition of sovereignty at the national level, see Bernard Crick, "Sovereignty," in *International Encyclopedia of the Social Sciences,* vol. 15 (New York: Macmillan and the Free Press, 1968), p. 77. In the same encyclopedia, David Apter, "Government," vol. 6, links sovereignty to "a national autonomous community," p. 215.

17. Safeer Tariq Bhatti, "How Has the Conflict in Darfur Impacted Notions of Sovereignty" (unpublished paper, Berkeley Electronic Press, 2007). Available at http://works.bepress.com/safeer_bhatti/1.

18. Nick Timiraos, "Arctic Thaw Defrosts a Sea Treaty," *Wall Street Journal*, 3 November 2007, p. 11.

19. Jess Bravin, "U.S. to Pull Out of World Court on War Crimes," *Wall Street Journal*, 6 May 2002, p. A4.

20. Charles M. Madigan and Colin McMahon, "A Slow, Painful Quest for Justice," *Chicago Tribune,* 7 September 1999, pp. 1, 8.

21. Tom Hundley, "Europe Seeks to Convert U.S. on Death Penalty," *Chicago Tribune,* 26 June 2000, p. 1; Salim Muwakkil, "The Capital of Capital Punishment," *Chicago Tribune,* 12 July 1999, p. 18.

22. Joseph Winter, "Living in Somalia's Anarchy," BBC News, 18 November 2004, http://news.bbc.co.uk/2/hi/4017147.stm; Alemayehu Fentaw, "Anarchy, Terrorism, and Piracy in Somalia: New Rules of Engagement for the International Community," *American Chronicle,* 27 May 2009, http://www.americanchronicle.com/articles/view/103942.

23. 1977 Constitution of the Union of Soviet Socialist Republics, Article 11, in *Constitutions of Countries of the World,* ed. A. P. Blaustein and G. H. Flanz (Dobbs Ferry, N.Y.: Oceana, 1971).

24. Edward Cody, "Chinese Lawmakers Approve Measure to Protect Private Property Rights," *Washington Post,* 17 March 2007, p. A10.

25. Karl Marx and Friedrich Engels, *Critique of the Gotha Programme* (New York: International Publishers, 1938), p. 10. Originally written in 1875 but published in 1891.

26. Abby Goodnough, "Gay Rights Rebuke May Bring Change in Tactics," *New York Times,* 5 November 2009, pp. A1, A4.

27. One scholar holds that freedom came from northern European languages, liberty from Latin, and they originally had opposite meanings. Liberty meant separation and freedom meant connection. See David Hackett Fischer, *Liberty and Freedom: A Visual History of America's Founding Ideas* (New York: Oxford University Press, 2005), pp. 1–15.

28. See the argument in Amy Gutman, *Liberal Equality* (Cambridge: Cambridge University Press, 1980), pp. 9–10.

29. Transportation Security Administration, "Imaging Technology: Innovation & Technology," n.d., available at http://www.tsa.gov/approach/tech/imaging_technology.shtm (accessed 9 May 2010).

30. See John H. Schaar, "Equality of Opportunity and Beyond," in *Nomos IX: Equality,* ed. J. Roland Pennock and John W. Chapman (New York: Atherton Press, 1967), pp. 228–249.

31. Gallup Poll, 1–4 October 2009, http://www.gallup.com/poll/1603/Crime.aspx.

32. See generally Milton Friedman, *Capitalism and Freedom* (Chicago: University of Chicago Press, 1962).

33. Joseph Kahn, "Anarchism, the Creed That Won't Stay Dead," *New York Times,* 5 August 2000, p. A15.

34. For a similar approach, see Scott Keeter and Gregory A. Smith, "In Search of Ideologues in America," Pew Research Center for the People & the Press, 11 April 2006, http://pewresearch.org/pubs/17/in-search-of-ideologues-in-america.

35. The communitarian category was labeled "populist" in early editions of this book. We have relabeled it for two reasons. First, we believe that *communitarian* is more descriptive of the category. Second, we recognize that the term *populist* has been used increasingly to refer to the political styles of candidates such as Pat Buchanan and Ralph Nader. In this sense, a populist appeals to mass resentment against those in power. Given the debate over what *populist* really means, we have decided to use *communitarian,* a less familiar term with fewer connotations. For a discussion of definitions in print, see Michael Kazin, *The Populist Persuasion: An American History* (New York: Basic Books, 1995).

36. Keeter and Smith call this grouping "Populist."

37. The communitarian movement was founded by a group of ethicists and social scientists who met in Washington, D.C., in 1990 at the invitation of sociologist Amitai Etzioni and political theorist William Galston to discuss the declining state of morality and values in the United States. Etzioni became the leading spokesperson for the movement. See his *Rights and the Common Good: The Communitarian Perspective* (New York: St. Martin's Press, 1995), pp. iii–iv. The communitarian political movement should be distinguished from communitarian thought in political philosophy, which is associated with theorists such as Alasdair MacIntyre, Michael Sandel, and Charles Taylor, who wrote in the late 1970s and early 1980s. In essence, communitarian theorists criticized liberalism, which stressed freedom and individualism, as excessively individualistic. Their fundamental critique was that liberalism slights the values of community life. See Allen E. Buchanan, "Assessing the Communitarian Critique of Liberalism," *Ethics*

99 (July 1989): 852–882; and Patrick Neal and David Paris, "Liberalism and the Communitarian Critique: A Guide for the Perplexed," *Canadian Journal of Political Science* 23 (September 1990): 419–439. Communitarian philosophers attacked liberalism over the inviolability of civil liberties. In our framework, such issues involve the trade-off between freedom and order. Communitarian and liberal theorists differ less concerning the trade-off between freedom and equality. See William R. Lund, "Communitarian Politics and the Problem of Equality," *Political Research Quarterly* 46 (September 1993): 577–600. But see also Susan Hekman, "The Embodiment of the Subject: Feminism and the Communitarian Critique of Liberalism," *Journal of Politics* 54 (November 1992): 1098–1119.

38. Etzioni, *Rights and the Common Good,* p. iv; Etzioni, "Communitarian Solutions/What Communitarians Think," *Journal of State Government* 65 (January–March): 9–11. For a critical review of the communitarian program, see Jeremiah Creedon, "Communitarian Manifesto," *Utne Reader* (July–August 1992): 38–40.

39. Etzioni, "Communitarian Solutions/What Communitarians Think," p. 10. See also Lester Thurow, "Communitarian vs. Individualistic Capitalism," in Etzioni, *Rights and the Common Good,* pp. 277–282. Note, however, that government's role in dealing with issues of social and economic inequality is far less developed in communitarian writings than is its role in dealing with issues of order. In the same volume, an article by David Osborne, "Beyond Left and Right: A New Political Paradigm" (pp. 283–290), downplays the role of government in guaranteeing entitlements.

40. Etzioni, *Rights and the Common Good,* p. 17.

41. Jonathan Martin and Carol E. Lee, "Obama to GOP: 'I Won,'" *Politico,* 23 January 2009.

42. Jackie Calmes, "House Passes Stimulus Plan with No G.O.P. Votes," *New York Times,* 29 January 2009; David M. Herszenhorn, "Senate Approves Stimulus Plan," *New York Times,* 11 February 2009.

43. Kenneth Janda, "What's in a Name? Party Labels across the World," in *The CONTA Conference: Proceedings of the Conference of Conceptual and Terminological Analysis of the Social*

Sciences, ed. F. W. Riggs (Frankfurt: Indeks Verlage, 1982), pp. 46–62.

44. See James A. Stimson, Michael B. MacKuen, and Robert S. Erikson, "Dynamic Representation," *American Political Science Review* 89 (September 1995): 543–565; G. Bingham Powell, Jr., "The Chain of Responsiveness," *Journal of Democracy* 15 (October 2004): 91–105.

45. See the discussion in Dietrich Rueschemeyer, "Addressing Inequality," *Journal of Democracy* 15 (October 2004): 76–90.

46. Thomas E. Cronin, *Direct Democracy* (Cambridge, Mass.: Harvard University Press, 1989), p. 47.

47. Deborah Ball and Nicholas Birch, "Swiss Ban Minarets in Controversial Vote," *Wall Street Journal,* 30 November 2009.

48. Gallup Poll, "More Americans Plugged Into Political News," 28 September 2009, http://www.gallup.com/poll/123203/Americans-Plugged-Into-Political-News.aspx.

49. John R. Hibbing and Elizabeth Theiss-Morse, *Stealth Democracy: Americans' Beliefs about How Government Should Work* (Cambridge: Cambridge University Press, 2002), p. 7.

50. See Robert A. Dahl, *Dilemmas of Pluralist Democracy* (New Haven, Conn.: Yale University Press, 1982), p. 5.

51. Jeffrey M. Berry, *The New Liberalism* (Washington, D.C.: The Brookings Institution, 1999).

52. Robert D. Putnam, *Bowling Alone* (New York: Simon & Schuster, 2000).

53. The classic statement on elite theory is C. Wright Mills, *The Power Elite* (New York: Oxford University Press, 1956).

54. Jeffrey A. Winters and Benjamin I. Page, "Oligarchy in the United States?" *Perspectives on Politics* 7 (December 2009): 731–751.

55. Peter Bachrach and Morton S. Baratz, "Two Faces of Power," *American Political Science Review* 56 (December 1962): 947–952; John Gaventa, *Power and Powerlessness* (Urbana: University of Illinois Press, 1980).

56. Frank R. Baumgatner et al., *Lobbying and Policy Change* (Chicago: University of Chicago Press, 2009).

57. See, for example, International Institute for Democracy and Electoral Assistance, *Assessing the Quality of Democracy: A Practical Guide* (Stockholm, Sweden: International IDEA, 2008),

available at http://www.idea.int/publications/aqd/index.cfm.

58. *Freedom in the World 2009* (Washington, D.C.: Freedom House, 2009).

59. The classic treatment of the conflict between freedom and order in democratizing countries is Samuel P. Huntington, *Political Order in Changing Societies* (New Haven: Yale University Press, 1968).

60. E. E. Schattschneider, *The Semi-Sovereign People* (New York: Holt, Rinehart, & Winston, 1960), p. 35.

Chapter 2 / The Constitution / pages 42–79

1. Introductory speech by President V. Giscard d'Estaing to the Convention on the Future of Europe, 28 February 2002, http://european-convention.eu.int/docs/speeches/1.pdf.

2. Letter from George Washington to James Madison, 31 March 1787, http://gwpapers.virginia.edu/documents/constitution/1787/madison3.html.

3. Center for Political Studies, Institute for Social Research, *American National Election Study, 2000* (Ann Arbor: University of Michigan, 2001).

4. Kevin Sullivan, "Ireland Shoots Down Plan for a More Unified E.U.," *Washington Post,* 14 June 2008, p. A8; Charles Forelle and Quentin Fottrell, "Irish Vote Decisively to Support EU Reform," *Wall Street Journal,* 4 October 2009, http://online.wsj.com/article/SB12545618452 1661679.html?mod=WSJ_hps_LEFTWhatsNews (accessed 4 October 2009).

5. Samuel Eliot Morison, *Oxford History of the American People* (New York: Oxford University Press, 1965), p. 172.

6. John Plamentz, *Man and Society,* rev. ed., ed. M. E. Plamentz and Robert Wokler, vol. 1, *From the Middle Ages to Locke* (New York: Longman, 1992), pp. 216–218.

7. Jack N. Rakove (ed.), *The Annotated U.S. Constitution and Declaration of Independence* (Boston: Belknap Press of Harvard University Press, 2009), p. 23.

8. Extrapolated from U.S. Department of Defense, *Selected Manpower Statistics, FY 1982* (Washington, D.C.: U.S. Government Printing Office,

1983), Table 2-30, p. 130; and U.S. Bureau of the Census, *1985 Statistical Abstract of the United States* (Washington, D.C.: U.S. Government Printing Office, 1985), Tables 1 and 2, p. 6.

9. Joseph T. Keenan, *The Constitution of the United States* (Homewood, Ill.: Dow-Jones-Irwin, 1975).

10. Rakove, p. 30.

11. David P. Szatmary, *Shays' Rebellion: The Making of an Agrarian Insurrection* (Amherst: University of Massachusetts Press, 1980), pp. 82–102.

12. Robert H. Jackson, *The Struggle for Judicial Supremacy* (New York: Knopf, 1941), p. 8.

13. Forrest McDonald, *Novus Ordo Seclorum: The Intellectual Origins of the Constitution* (Lawrence: University Press of Kansas, 1985), pp. 205–209.

14. U.S. Constitution, Article V.

15. Donald S. Lutz, "The Preamble to the Constitution of the United States," *This Constitution* 1 (September 1983): 23–30.

16. Richard E. Neustadt, *Presidential Power: The Politics of Leadership* (New York: Wiley, 1960), p. 33.

17. Robert A. Goldwin, letter to the editor, *Wall Street Journal,* 30 August 1993, p. A11.

18. Herbert J. Storing (ed.), *The Complete Anti-Federalist,* 7 vols. (Chicago: University of Chicago Press, 1981).

19. Alexis de Tocqueville, *Democracy in America, 1835–1839,* ed. J. P. Mayer and Max Lerner (New York: Harper & Row, 1966), p. 102.

20. Jerold L. Waltman, *Political Origins of the U.S. Income Tax* (Jackson: University Press of Mississippi, 1985), p. 10.

Chapter 3 / Federalism / pages 80–109

1. Alan Dean Foster, "Garden Variety Javelinas," *New York Times,* 7 Aug 2010, p. WK10.

2. Daniel B. Wood, "Opinion polls show broad support for tough Arizona immigration law," *The Christian Science Monitor,* 30 April 2010, http://www.csmonitor.com/USA/Society/2010/0430/Opinion-polls-show-broad-support-for-tough-Arizona-immigration-law.

3. Compare 8 U.S.C. § 1302 and § 1304(e) with Arizona's SB1070, http://www.azleg.gov/legtext/49leg/2r/bills/sb1070s.pdf.

4. Randal C. Archibold, "Arizona Law Is Stoking Unease Among Latinos," *New York Times,* 28 May 2010, p. A11.

5. *United States of America* v. *Arizona,* CV 10-1413-PHX-SRB (USDC AZ)(28 July 2010), http://www.azd.uscourts.gov/azd/courtinfo.nsf/983700DFEE44B56B0725776E005D6CCB/$file/10-1413-87.pdf.

6. William H. Stewart, *Concepts of Federalism* (Lanham, Md.: University Press of America, 1984).

7. Edward Corwin, "The Passing of Dual Federalism," *University of Virginia Law Review* 36 (1950): 4.

8. See Daniel J. Elazar, *The American Partnership* (Chicago: University of Chicago Press, 1962); Morton Grodzins, *The American System* (Chicago: Rand McNally, 1966).

9. James T. Patterson, *The New Deal and the States: Federalism in Transition* (Princeton, N.J.: Princeton University Press, 1969).

10. For more information on the USA-PATRIOT Act, see http://thomas.loc.gov/cgi-bin/bdquery/z?d107:h.r.03162:. For the Department of Homeland Security, see http://www.dhs.gov/dhspublic.

11. John Dinan and Shama Gamkhar, "The State of American Federalism 2008–2009: The Presidential Election, the Economic Downturn, and the Consequences for Federalism," *Publius: The Journal of Federalism* 39, no. 3 (2009): 369–407.

12. *McCulloch* v. *Maryland,* 4 Wheat. 316 (1819).

13. *Gibbons* v. *Ogden,* 22 U.S. 1 (1824).

14. *Dred Scott* v. *Sanford,* 19 How. 393, 426 (1857).

15. Jeff Shesol, *Supreme Power: Franklin Roosevelt vs. the Supreme Court* (New York: W.W. Norton, 2010).

16. *United States* v. *Lopez,* 514 U.S. 549 (1995).

17. *Printz* v. *United States,* 521 U.S. 98 (1997).

18. *United States* v. *Morrison,* 120 S. Ct. 1740 (2000).

19. *Lawrence and Garner* v. *Texas,* 539 U.S. 558 (2003). This decision overturned *Bowers* v. *Hardwick,* 478 U.S. 186 (1986).

20. *United States* v. *Comstock,* 560 U.S. _____ (2010).

21. Brandy Anderson, "Congress Passes National .08 BAC Law," *DRIVEN* (Fall 2000).

22. Terry Sanford, *Storm over the States* (New York: McGraw-Hill, 1967).

23. Quoted in Cynthia J. Bowling and Deil S. Wright, "Public Administration in the Fifty States: A Half-Century Administrative Revolution," *State and Local Government Review* 30 (Winter 1998): 52.

24. David M. Hedge, *Governance and the Changing American States* (Boulder, Colo.: Westview Press, 1998).

25. Bureau of Labor Statistics, U.S. Department of Labor, "State and Local Government, Excluding Education and Hospitals," in *Career Guide to Industries, 2008–09 Edition,* http://www.bls.gov/oco/cg/cgs042.htm.

26. Paul Manna, *School's In: Federalism and the National Education Agenda* (Washington D.C.: Georgetown University Press, 2006).

27. Ronald Reagan, "Statement on Signing Executive Order Establishing the Presidential Advisory Committee on Federalism," 1981 *Public Papers of the President* 341, 8 April 1981.

28. Dinan and Gamkhar, "The State of American Federalism 2008–2009," p. 370.

29. Joseph F. Zimmerman, *Contemporary American Federalism: The Growth of National Power* (New York: Praeger, 1992), Chap. 4.

30. Internet Tax Nondiscrimination Act of 2004.

31. Joseph Zimmerman, "Congressional Preemption during the George W. Bush Administration," *Publius* 37, no. 3 (2007): 432–452.

32. Ibid., 436.

33. Ibid., 432.

34. John Kincaid, "From Cooperative to Coercive Federalism," *Annals of the American Academy of Political and Social Science* 509 (May 1990): 139–152.

35. "Unfunded Federal Mandates," *Congressional Digest* (March 1995): 68.

36. Paul Posner, "The Politics of Coercive Federalism," *Publius* 37, no. 3 (2007): 390–412.

37. National Conference of State Legislatures, "States Legislatures Face Unsettled Conditions in 2008," *NCSL News,* 14 December 2007. Available at http://www.ncsl.org/default.aspx?tabid=16893.

38. National Conference of State Legislatures Budget and Reform Committee, "Introduction to UMRA," *Mandate Monitor 7,* no. 1 (January 2010): http://www.ncsl.org/default.aspx?tabid=19450.

39. U.S. Department of Justice, "Guidance Concerning Redistricting in Retrogression under Section 5 of the Voting Rights Act of 1965," 42 U.S.C. 1973c, 66 *Federal Register* 5411, 5413, 18 January 2001. David E. Rosenbaum, "Fight over Political Map Centers on Race," *New York Times,* 21 February 2002, p. A20.

40. U.S. Bureau of the Census, *Statistical Abstract of the United States: 2010* (Washington, D.C.: U.S. Government Printing Office, 2009), Table 416: "Number of Governmental Units by Type, 1962–2007." Available at http://www.census.gov/prod/2009pubs/10statab/stlocgov.pdf.

41. *U.S. Term Limits* v. *Thornton,* 514 U.S. 779 (1995).

Chapter 4 / Public Opinion, Political Socialization, and the Media / pages 110–151

1. "A Three Drug Cocktail," *Washington Post,* 26 September 2007, http://www.washingtonpost.com/wp-dyn/content/graphic/2007/09/26/GR2007092600116.html.

2. Ian Urbina, "Ohio Killer Is First Inmate in U.S. to Be Executed with a Single Drug," *New York Times,* 9 December 2009, p. A16.

3. Ian Urbina, "Ohio Is First to Change to One Drug in Executions," *New York Times,* 14 November 2009, p. A10.

4. *Baze and Bowling* v. *Rees,* http://www.oyez.org/cases/2000-2009/2007/2007_07_5439.

5. Ian Urbina, "Ohio Finds Itself Leading the Way to a New Execution Method," *New York Times,* 18 November 2009, p. A21.

6. Tony Rizzo, "Ohio Uses Single-Drug Execution for Second Time," *St. Paul Pioneer Press,* 8 January 2010, p. 16.

7. Frank Newport, "In U.S., Two-Thirds Continue to Support Death Penalty: Little Change in Recent Years despite International Opposition," Gallup Poll Report, 13 October 2009, http://www.gallup.com/poll/123638/in-u.s.-two-thirds-continue-support-death-penalty.aspx.

8. Infoplease, "The Death Penalty World Wide," http://www.infoplease.com/ipa/A0777460.html.

9. Amnesty International, "The Death Penalty in 2008," n.d., http://www.amnesty.org/en/death-penalty/death-sentences-and-executions-in-2008.

10. John Schwartz and Emma G. Fitzsimmons, "Illinois Governor Signs Capital Punishment Ban," *New York Times,* 10 March 2011, p. A18.

11. Warren Weaver, Jr., "Death Penalty a 300-Year Issue in America," *New York Times,* 3 July 1976.

12. *Furman* v. *Georgia,* 408 U.S. 238 (1972).

13. *Gregg* v. *Georgia,* 248 U.S. 153 (1976).

14. U.S. Department of Justice, Bureau of Justice Statistics, "Number of Persons Executed in the U.S. 1930–2006," http://www.ojp.usdoj.gov/bjs/glance/tables/exetab.htm.

15. Seventy percent of whites favor the death penalty, while 56 percent of African Americans oppose it. Lydia Saad, "Racial Disagreement over Death Penalty Has Varied Historically," Gallup News Service, 30 July 2007, available at http://www.gallup.com. For a discussion of the effects of the disenfranchisement of felons, see Jeff Manza and Christopher Uggen, *Locked Out: Felon Disenfranchisement and American Democracy* (New York: Oxford University Press, 2006).

16. Newport, "In U.S., Two-Thirds Continue to Support Death Penalty," p. 1.

17. Death Penalty Information website, "Facts about the Death Penalty," 9 March 2011, http://www.deathpenaltyinfo.org/documents/FactSheet.pdf.

18. David Masci, "An Impassioned Debate: An Overview of the Death Penalty in America," Pew Forum on Religion and Public Life, 19 December 2007, http://pewforum.org/docs/?DocID=270.

19. U.S. Department of Justice, Bureau of Justice Statistics, "Key Facts at a Glance: Executions," 9 March 2011, http://bjs.ojp.usdoj.gov/content/glance/tables/exetab.cfm.

20. See Roberta S. Sigel (ed.), *Political Learning in Adulthood: A Sourcebook of Theory and Research* (Chicago: University of Chicago Press, 1989).

21. One study found that additional media coverage of political issues did not change the impact of education on political knowledge. See Benjamin Highton, "Political Knowledge Gaps and Changes in the Information Environment: The Case of Education" (paper presented

at the annual meeting of the Midwest Political Science Association, Chicago, Ill., 2008).

22. Pew Research Center, "The Internet's Broader Role in Campaign 2008," 11 January 2008, available at http://www.pewresearch.org.

23. The American National Election Studies are jointly done by Stanford University and the University of Michigan, with funding by the National Science Foundation.

24. Other scholars have analyzed opinion on abortion using six questions from the General Social Survey. See R. Michael Alvarez and John Brehm, "American Ambivalence toward Abortion Policy," *American Journal of Political Science* 39 (1995): 1055–1082; and Elizabeth Adell Cook, Ted G. Jelen, and Clyde Wilcox, *Between Two Absolutes: Public Opinion and the Politics of Abortion* (Boulder, Colo.: Westview Press, 1992).

25. Although some people view the politics of abortion as single-issue politics, the issue has broader political significance. In their book on the subject, Cook et al. say, "Although embryonic life is one important value in the abortion debate, it is not the only value at stake." They contend that the politics is tied to alternative sexual relationships and traditional roles of women in the home, which are "social order" issues. See *Between Two Absolutes,* pp. 8–9.

26. Russell J. Dalton, *The Good Citizen* (Washington, D.C.: Congressional Quarterly Press, 2008), Chap. 5.

27. Ibid., p. 50.

28. For years, scholars have been debating whether the increasing wealth in industrialized societies is replacing class conflict with conflict over values. See the exchange between Ronald Inglehart and Scott C. Flanagan, "Value Change in Industrial Societies," *American Political Science Review* 81 (December 1987): 1289–1319.

29. Earl Black and Merle Black, *The Vital South* (Cambridge, Mass.: Harvard University Press, 1992), and *The Rise of Southern Republicans* (Cambridge, Mass.: Harvard University Press, 2002); David Lublin, *The Republican South: Democratization and Partisan Change* (Princeton, N.J.: Princeton University Press, 2004); Nicholas Valentino and David O. Sears, "Old

Times There Are Not Forgotten: Race and Partisan Realignment in the Contemporary South," *American Journal of Political Science* 49 (2005): 672–688.

30. Nathan Glazer, "The Structure of Ethnicity," *Public Opinion* 7 (October–November 1984): 4.

31. Population Division, U.S. Census Bureau, "Summary Table 6: Percent of the Projected Population by Race and Hispanic Origin for the United States: 2010 to 2050 (NP2008-T6)," 14 August 2008, available at http://www.census .gov/population/www/projections/summary tables.html.

32. U.S. Census Bureau, *Statistical Abstract of the United States: 2010* (Washington, D.C.: U.S. Government Printing Office, 2009), online data for "Table 19: Resident Population by Race, Hispanic Origin, and State: 2008," available at http://www.census.gov/compendia/ statab/2010/tables/10s0019.xls.

33. See U.S. Census Bureau, "State and County Quick Facts," for up-to-date population statistics for the states. Available at http://quick facts.census.gov/qfd/index.html.

34. Michael Dawson, *Black Visions: The Roots of Contemporary African American Political Ideologies* (Chicago: University of Chicago Press, 2001) and *Behind the Mule* (Princeton, N.J.: Princeton University Press, 1994); John Garcia, *Latino Politics in America* (Lanham, Md.: Rowman and Littlefield, 2003); Peite Lien, *The Making of Asian America through Political Participation* (Philadelphia: Temple University Press, 2001); Wendy Tam, "Asians—A Monolithic Voting Bloc?" *Political Behavior* 17 (1995): 223–249; Katherine Tate, *Black Faces in the Mirror: African Americans and Their Representatives in the U.S. Congress* (Princeton, N.J.: Princeton University Press, 2003).

35. Glazer, "Structure of Ethnicity," p. 5; Dennis Chong and Dukhong Kim, "The Experiences and Effects of Economic Status among Racial and Ethnic Minorities," *American Political Science Review* 100 (August 2006): 335–351.

36. Frank Newport, "This Christmas, 78% of Americans Identify as Christian," Gallup Poll Report, 24 December 2009.

37. Some scholars have argued that Americans are not as polarized as the news media would have

us think. See Morris P. Fiorina, *Culture Wars? The Myth of a Polarized America* (White Plains, N.Y.: Longman, 2004).

38. Jeffrey M. Jones, "Understanding Americans' Support for the Death Penalty," Gallup News Service, 3 June 2003.

39. Center for American Women and Politics, Eagleton Institute of Politics, "Gender Gap Persists in the 2004 Election," press release, 5 November 2004, http://www.cawp.rutgers.edu/press_room/news/documents/PressAdvisory_GG2004_11-05-04.pdf.

40. John Robinson, "The Ups and Downs and Ins and Outs of Ideology," *Public Opinion* 7 (February–March 1984): 12.

41. For a more positive interpretation of ideological attitudes within the public, see William G. Jacoby, "The Structure of Ideological Thinking in the American Electorate" (paper presented at the annual meeting of the American Political Science Association, Washington, D.C., September 1993). Jacoby applies a new method to survey data for the 1984 and 1988 elections and concludes "that there is a systematic, cumulative structure underlying liberal-conservative thinking in the American public" (p. 1).

42. When asked to describe the parties and candidates in the 1956 election, only about 12 percent of respondents volunteered responses that contained ideological terms (such as *liberal, conservative,* and *capitalism*). Most respondents (42 percent) evaluated the parties and candidates in terms of "benefits to groups" (farmers, workers, or business people, for example). Others (24 percent) spoke more generally about "the nature of the times" (for example, inflation, unemployment, and the threat of war). Finally, a good portion of the sample (22 percent) gave answers that contained no classifiable issue content. See Angus Campbell et al., *The American Voter* (New York: Wiley, 1960), Chap. 10.

43. Marjorie Connelly, "A 'Conservative' Is (Fill in the Blank)," *New York Times,* 3 November 1996, sec. 4, p. 5.

44. Ibid.

45. Pew Research Center for the People & the Press, "Opinion of State Governments Drops with the Economy, Budget Gaps: New Administration Changes Partisan Views of Federal Government," 11 August 2009, http://pewresearch.org/pubs/1307/state-government-favorability-falls-partisan-split-federal-government.

46. A relationship between liberalism and political tolerance was found by John L. Sullivan et al., "The Sources of Political Tolerance: A Multivariate Analysis," *American Political Science Review* 75 (March 1981): 102. See also Robinson, "Ups and Downs," pp. 13–15.

47. Herbert Asher, *Presidential Elections and American Politics* (Homewood, Ill.: Dorsey, 1980), pp. 14–20. Asher also constructs a two-dimensional framework, distinguishing between "traditional New Deal" issues and "new lifestyle" issues.

48. John E. Jackson, "The Systematic Beliefs of the Mass Public: Estimating Policy Preferences with Survey Data," *Journal of Politics* 45 (November 1983): 840–865.

49. Milton Rokeach also proposed a two-dimensional model of political ideology grounded in the terminal values of freedom and equality. See *The Nature of Human Values* (New York: Free Press, 1973), especially Chap. 6. Rokeach found that positive and negative references to the two values permeate the writings of socialists, communists, fascists, and conservatives and clearly differentiate the four bodies of writing from one another (pp. 173–174). However, Rokeach built his two-dimensional model around only the values of freedom and equality; he did not deal with the question of freedom versus order.

50. In our framework, opposition to abortion is classified as a communitarian position. However, the communitarian movement led by Amitai Etzioni adopted no position on abortion. Personal communication from Vanessa Hoffman by e-mail, in reply to a query of 5 February 1996.

51. See W. Russell Neuman, *The Paradox of Mass Politics: Knowledge and Opinion in the American Electorate* (Cambridge, Mass.: Harvard University Press, 1986), p. 81. See also Aaron Wildavsky, "Choosing Preferences by Constructing Institutions: A Cultural Theory of Preference Formation," *American Political Science Review* 81 (March 1987): 13.

52. The same conclusion was reached in a major study of British voting behavior. See Hilde T. Himmelweit et al., *How Voters Decide* (New York: Academic Press, 1981), pp. 138–141. See also Wildavsky, "Choosing Preferences," p. 13; and Stanley Feldman and Christopher Johnston, "Understanding Political Ideology" (paper presented at the annual meeting of the American Political Science Association, Toronto, Canada, 2009).

53. Two researchers who compared the public's knowledge on various topics in 1989 with its knowledge of the same topics in the 1940s and 1950s found similar levels of knowledge across the years. They point out, however, "that knowledge has been stable during a period of rapid changes in education, communication, and the public role of women seems paradoxical." They suspect, but cannot demonstrate, that the expected increase in knowledge did not materialize because of a decline in the public's interest in politics over time. See Michael X. Delli Carpini and Scott Keeter, "Stability and Change in the U.S. Public's Knowledge of Politics," *Public Opinion Quarterly* 55 (Winter 1991): 607.

54. Michael X. Delli Carpini and Scott Keeter, *What Americans Know about Politics and Why It Matters* (New Haven, Conn.: Yale University Press, 1996).

55. Ibid., p. 269. See also Scott L. Althaus, *Collective Preferences in Democratic Politics: Opinion Surveys and the Will of the People* (New York: Cambridge University Press, 2003).

56. There is evidence that the educational system and parental practices hamper the ability of women to develop their political knowledge. See Linda L. M. Bennett and Stephen Earl Bennett, "Enduring Gender Differences in Political Interests," *American Politics Quarterly* 17 (January 1989): 105–122.

57. Pew Research Center for the People & the Press, "Public Knowledge of Current Affairs Little Changed by News and Information Revolution: What Americans Know 1989–2007," 15 April 2007, http://people-press.org/reports/display.php3?ReportID=319.

58. W. Russell Neuman, *The Paradox of Mass Politics: Knowledge and Opinion in the American Electorate* (Cambridge, Mass.: Harvard University Press, 1986), p. 81.

59. Pew Research Center for the People & the Press, "Who Knows News? What You Read or View Matters, but Not Your Politics," 15 October 2008, http://pewresearch.org/pubs/993/who-knows-news-what-you-read-or-view-matters-but-not-your-politics.

60. Stephan Lewandowsky et al., "Memory for Fact, Fiction, and Misinformation: The Iraq War 2003," *Psychological Science* 16 (March 2005): 190–195.

61. A significant literature exists on the limitations of self-interest in explaining political life. See Jane J. Mansbridge (ed.), *Beyond Self-Interest* (Chicago: University of Chicago Press, 1990).

62. Aaron Wildavsky, "Choosing Preferences by Constructing Institutions: A Cultural Theory of Preference Formation," *American Political Science Review* 81 (March 1987): 3–21.

63. Henry Brady and Paul Sniderman, "Attitude Attribution: A Group Basis for Political Reasoning," *American Political Science Review* 79 (1985): 1061–1078; Samuel Popkin, *The Reasoning Voter*, 2nd ed. (Chicago: University of Chicago Press, 1994); Paul M. Sniderman, Richard A. Brody, and Philip E. Tetlock, *Reasoning and Choice* (Cambridge: Cambridge University Press, 1991). Psychologists have tended to emphasize the distorting effects of heuristics. See Daniel Kahneman, Paul Slovic, and Amos Tversky (eds.), *Judgment under Uncertainty: Heuristics and Biases* (Cambridge: Cambridge University Press, 1982); and Richard Nisbett and Lee Ross, *Human Inference: Strategies and Shortcomings of Social Judgment* (Englewood Cliffs, N.J.: Prentice-Hall, 1980).

64. Political psychologists refer to beliefs that guide information processing as opinion "schemas." See Pamela Johnston Conover and Stanley Feldman, "How People Organize the Political World: A Schematic Model," *American Journal of Political Science* 28 (February 1984): 95–127; and Milton Lodge and Kathleen M. McGraw, *Political Judgment: Structure and Process* (Ann Arbor: University of Michigan Press, 1995). For an excellent review of schema structures in contemporary psychology, especially as they relate to

political science, see Reid Hastie, "A Primer of Information-Processing Theory for the Political Scientist," in *Political Cognition,* ed. Richard R. Lau and David O. Sears (Hillsdale, N.J.: Erlbaum, 1986), pp. 11–39.

65. Pew Research Center for the People & the Press, "Religion and Politics: Contention and Consensus," 24 July 2003, http://people-press. org//reports/display.php3?ReportID=189.

66. J. Kuklinski and N. L. Hurley, "On Hearing and Interpreting Political Messages," *Journal of Politics* 56 (1994): 729–751.

67. On framing, see William Jacoby, "Issue Framing and Public Opinion on Government Spending," *American Journal of Political Science* 44 (October 2000): 750–767; and James N. Druckman, "The Implications of Framing Effects for Citizen Competence," *Political Behavior* 23 (September 2001): 225–253. On political spin, see Lawrence Jacobs and Robert Y. Shapiro, *Politicians Don't Pander* (Chicago: University of Chicago Press, 2000).

68. Benjamin I. Page, Robert Y. Shapiro, and Glenn R. Dempsey, "What Moves Public Opinion?" *American Political Science Review* 81 (March 1987): 23–43.

69. Michael Margolis and Gary A. Mauser, *Manipulating Public Opinion: Essays on Public Opinion as a Dependent Variable* (Pacific Grove, Calif.: Brooks/Cole, 1989).

70. John December, Neil Randall, and Wes Tatters, *Discover the World Wide Web with Your Sportster* (Indianapolis, Ind.: Sams.net Publishing, 1995), pp. 11–12.

71. Marsha Walton, "Web Reaches New Milestone: 100 Million Sites," CNN, 1 November 2006, http://www.cnn.com/2006/TECH/internet/11/ 01/100millionwebsites/index.html. Netcraft conducts a monthly survey of Internet host registrations and active websites. A summary of their data is available at http://news .netcraft.com/archives/category/web-server-survey.

72. Pew Project for Excellence in Journalism, *The State of the News Media: 2011,* http:// www.stateofthemedia.org/2011/newspapers-essay/; Newspaper Association of America, "Advertising Expenditures," http://www .naa.org/TrendsandNumbers/Advertising-Expenditures.aspx. Bloomberg News, "Seattle Newspaper Ends Print Edition," 17 March 2009, http://www.boston.com/business/ articles/2009/03/17/seattle_newspaper_end-s_print_edition; Michael Liedke and Andrew Vanacore, "Newspaper Upheaval Seen with Filings," Associated Press, 24 February 2009, http://www.boston.com/ae/media/articles/ 2009/02/24/newspaper_upheaval_seen_-with_filings; Lynn DeBruin and Lisa Ryckman, "Rocky Mountain News to Close, Publish Final Edition Friday," *Rocky Mountain News,* 26 February 2009, http://www.rockymountain-news.com/news/2009/feb/26/rocky-moun-tain-news-closes-friday-final-edition.

73. Kathryn Zickuhr, "Generations 2010," Pew Internet and American Life Project, 16 December 2010, http://www.pewinternet.org/~/ media//Files/Reports/2010/PIP_Generations_and_Tech10.pdf.

74. Pew Research Center for the People & the Press, "Internet News Audience Highly Critical of News Organizations," 9 August 2007, available at http://people-press.org.

75. Ed Pilkington, "Obama Angers Midwest Voters with Guns and Religion Remark," *The Guardian,* 14 April 2008, http://www.guardian .co.uk/world/2008/apr/14/barackobama .uselections2008.

76. Doris A. Graber, *Mass Media and American Politics,* 6th ed. (Washington, D.C.: Congressional Quarterly Press, 2002), pp. 107–109. See also W. Lance Bennett, *News: The Politics of Illusion,* 3rd ed. (White Plains, N.Y.: Longman, 1996), Chap. 2.

77. Gannett, "A Brief Company History," May 2009, http://www.gannett.com/about/history .htm.

78. Bill Carter and Brian Shelter, "In NBC Universal Bid, Comcast Seeks an Empire," *New York Times,* 1 October 2009, http://www.nytimes .com/2009/10/02/business/media/02nbc.html.

79. Frank Ahrens, "At *Wall Street Journal,* Change of Accents," *Washington Post,* 5 March 2008, p. D01.

80. Paige Albiniak, "Court Scraps Reply Rules," *Broadcasting and Cable,* 16 October 2000, pp. 6–7; Stephen Labaton, "In Test F.C.C. Lifts Requirements on Broadcasting Political Replies," *New York Times,* 5 October 2000, pp. A1, A27.

81. For the point of view of a reporter who covered Washington for over sixty years, see Helen Thomas, *Watch-dogs of Democracy? The Waning Washington Press Corps and How It Has Failed the Public* (New York: Scribner, 2006).

82. Richard Davis, *Typing Politics: The Role of Blogs in American Politics* (New York: Oxford University Press, 2009).

83. Pew Research Center for the People & the Press, "Summary of Findings: Modest Interest in 2008 Campaign News," 23 October 2007, available at http://people-press.org.

84. Stephen J. Farnsworth and S. Robert Lichter, "The Nightly News Nightmare Revisited: Network Television's Coverage of the 2004 Presidential Election" (paper presented at the annual meeting of the American Political Science Association, Washington, D.C., 2005); "Contest Lacks Content," *Media Tenor* 1 (2005): 12–15.

85. Pew Project for Excellence in Journalism, "Online: Key Questions Facing Digital News," in *The State of the News Media: 2011*, http://stateofthemedia.org/2011/online-essay/#audience.

86. Kristen Purcell et al., *Understanding the Participatory News Consumer* (Washington, D.C.: Pew Internet and American Life Project, 1 March 2010), p. 2. Available at http://www.pewinternet. org/Reports/2010/Online-News .aspx.

87. Ibid., p. 9.

88. Zogby International, "Zogby Poll: Online News Sources Top All Other Outlets," 15 June 2009, http://www.zogby.com/news/ReadNews .cfm?ID=1710.

89. Pew Project for Excellence in Journalism, "Survey: Mobile News and Paying Online," in *The State of the News Media: 2011*, http://stateofthemedia.org/2011/mobile-survey/.

90. Pew Research Center for the People & the Press, "Public Knows Basic Facts about Politics, Economics, but Struggles with Specifics," 18 November 2010, http://people-press.org/report/677/.

91. William P. Eveland, Jr., and Dietram A. Scheufele, "Connecting News Media Use with Gaps in Knowledge and Participation," *Political Communication* 17 (July–September, 2000): 215–237.

92. W. Russell Neuman, Marion R. Just, and Ann N. Crigler, *Common Knowledge: News and the Construction of Political Meaning* (Chicago: University of Chicago Press, 1992), p. 10. For a more optimistic assessment of television's instructional value, see Doris A. Graber, *Processing Politics: Learning from Television in the Internet Age* (Chicago: University of Chicago Press, 2001), esp. pp. 120–128. Another negative note is sounded by Alan B. Krueger, "Economic Scene," *New York Times*, 1 April 2004, p. C2.

93. Doris A. Graber, *Processing the News: How People Tame the Information Tide*, 2nd ed. (New York: Longman, 1988), pp. 166–169.

94. Neuman et al., *Common Knowledge*, p. 113.

95. Laurence Parisot, "Attitudes about the Media: A Five-Country Comparison," *Public Opinion* 10 (January–February 1988): 60.

96. The statistical difficulties in determining media effects owing to measurement error are discussed in Larry M. Bartels, "Messages Received: The Political Impact of Media Exposure" (paper presented at the annual meeting of the American Political Science Association, Washington, D.C., September 1993). According to Bartels, "More direct and convincing demonstrations of significant opinion changes due to media exposure will require data collections spanning considerably longer periods of time" (p. 27).

97. Doris Graber, *Media Power in Politics* (Washington, D.C.: Congressional Quarterly Press, 2007), pp. 278–279.

98. Daniel J. Wakin, "Report Calls Networks' Election Night Coverage a Disaster," *New York Times*, 3 February 2001, p. A8.

99. Shanto Iyengar and Donald R. Kinder, *News That Matters: Television and American Opinion* (Chicago: University of Chicago Press, 1987), p. 33.

100. Ibid., p. 60.

101. W. Russell Neuman, "The Threshold of Public Attention," *Public Opinion Quarterly* 54 (Summer 1990): 159–176.

102. Robert Entman, *Democracy without Citizens: Media and the Decay of American Politics* (New York: Oxford University Press, 1989), p. 86.

103. Doris Graber reviews some studies of socially undesirable effects on children and adults in *Processing Politics*, pp. 91–95.

104. John J. O'Connor, "Soothing Bromides? Not on TV," *New York Times,* 28 October 1990, Arts and Leisure section, pp. 1, 35.

105. James Fallows, *Breaking the News: How the Media Undermine American Democracy* (New York: Pantheon Books, 1996).

106. See Bernard Goldberg, *Bias: A CBS Insider Exposes How the Media Distort the News* (Washington, D.C.: Regnery Publishing, 2002); and Ann Coulter, *Slander: Liberal Lies about the American Right* (New York: Crown, 2002).

107. See Eric Alterman, *What Liberal Media? The Truth about Bias and the News* (New York: Basic Books, 2003); and Al Franken, *Lies (and the Lying Liars Who Tell Them): A Fair and Balanced Look at the Right* (New York: Penguin, 2003).

108. Pew Research Center of the People & the Press, "Financial Woes Now Overshadow All Other Concerns for Journalists," 17 March 2007, http://people-press.org/reports/pdf/403.pdf.

109. Farnsworth and Lichter, "The Nightly News Nightmare Revisited," p. 31.

110. *The People, the Press, and Their Leaders* (Washington, D.C.: Times-Mirror Center for the People & the Press, 1995).

111. Harold W. Stanley and Richard G. Niemi, *Vital Statistics on American Politics, 2007–2008* (Washington, D.C.: CQ Press, 2010); Greg Mitchell, "Barack the Vote: 2008 Broke with Tradition," *Editor & Publisher,* 1 December 2008.

112. Maura Clancey and Michael J. Robinson, "General Election Coverage: Part I," *Public Opinion* 7 (December–January 1985): 54. Some journalists take their watchdog role seriously. See Pew Research Center, "Striking the Balance, Audience Interests, Business Pressures and Journalists' Values," 30 March 1999, http://people-press.org/reports/display.php3?ReportID=67.

113. Center for Media and Public Affairs, "Election Watch: Campaign 2008 Final," *Media Monitor* 23, no. 1 (Winter 2009): http://www.cmpa.com/pdf/media_monitor_jan_2009.pdf.

114. W. Lance Bennett and William Serrin, "The Watchdog Role," in *Institutions of American Democracy: The Press,* ed. Geneva Overholser and Kathleen Hall Jamieson (Oxford: Oxford University Press, 2005), pp. 169–188.

115. For a critique of the press on these grounds, see W. Lance Bennett et al., *When the Press Fails* (Chicago: University of Chicago Press, 2007).

116. William Schneider and I. A. Lewis, "Views on the News," *Public Opinion* 8 (August/September 1985): 11. For similar findings from a 1994 study, see Times-Mirror Center for the People & the Press, "Mixed Message about Press Freedom on Both Sides of the Atlantic," press release, 16 March 1994, p. 65. See also Thomas E. Patterson and Wolfgang Donsbach, "News Decisions: Journalists as Partisan Actors," *Political Communication* 13, no. 4 (October–December 1996): 455–468.

117. Pew Research Center for the People & the Press, "Bush a Drag on Republican Midterm Prospects," 9 February 2006, http://people-press.org/reports/display.php3?ReportID=270.

Chapter 5 / Participation and Voting / pages 152–185

1. Janet Adamy and Naftali Bendavid, "Lawmakers Rethink Town Halls," *Wall Street Journal,* 8 August 2009, p. A5.

2. Ian Urbina, "Beyond Beltway, Health Debate Turns Hostile," *New York Times,* 8 August 2009, pp. A1, A10.

3. Ibid.

4. Jeff Zeleny, "Thousands Attend Broad Protest of Government," *New York Times,* 13 September 2009, p. 33.

5. Adamy and Bendavid, "Lawmakers Rethink Town Halls."

6. Michael M. Phillips, "FreedomWorks Harnesses Growing Activism on the Right," *Wall Street Journal,* 5 October 2009, p. A4.

7. Rob Jordan, "FreedomWorks Launches Nationwide 'Tea Party Tour,'" 9 March 2009, http://www.freedomworks.org/publications/freedomworks-launches-nationwide-"teaparty"-tour.

8. Justin Quinn, "A Tea Party Revival," About.com Guide to US Conservative Politics, 16 December 2009, http://usconservatives.about.com/b/2009/12/16/a-tea-party-revival.htm.

9. Naftali Bendavid, "Tea-Party Activists Complicate Republican Comeback Strategy," *Wall Street Journal,* 16 October 2009, p. 1.

10. Lester W. Milbrath and M. L. Goel, *Political Participation* (Chicago: Rand McNally, 1977), p. 2.

11. U.S. Department of State, *Patterns of Global Terrorism 2001* (Washington, D.C.: U.S. Department of State, May 2002), p. 17. The definition is contained in Title 22 of the U.S. Code, Section 2656f(d). On the problem of defining terrorism, see Walter Laqueur, *No End to War: Terrorism in the 21st Century* (New York: Continuum International, 2003), esp. the appendix.

12. Lou Nichel and Dan Herbeck, *American Terrorist: Timothy McVeigh and the Oklahoma City Bombing* (New York: HarperCollins, 2001), pp. 350–354.

13. William E. Schmidt, "Selma Marchers Mark 1965 Clash," *New York Times,* 4 March 1985.

14. See Sidney Verba and Norman H. Nie, *Participation in America: Political Democracy and Social Equality* (New York: Harper & Row, 1972), p. 3.

15. 2005–2008 World Values Survey. The World Values Survey Association, based in Stockholm, conducts representative surveys in nations across the world. See http://www.worldvaluessurvey.org.

16. International Social Survey Programme, "ISSP 2004: Citizenship (No. 3950)," 25 April 2007, available at http://zacat.gesis.org.

17. Stephen C. Craig and Michael A. Magiotto, "Political Discontent and Political Action," *Journal of Politics* 43 (May 1981): 514–522. But see Mitchell A. Seligson, "Trust Efficacy and Modes of Political Participation: A Study of Costa Rican Peasants," *British Journal of Political Science* 10 (January 1980): 75–98, for a review of studies that came to different conclusions.

18. Philip H. Pollock III, "Organizations as Agents of Mobilization: How Does Group Activity Affect Political Participation?" *American Journal of Political Science* 26 (August 1982): 485–503. Also see Jan E. Leighley, "Social Interaction and Contextual Influence on Political Participation," *American Politics Quarterly* 18 (October 1990): 459–475.

19. Arthur H. Miller et al., "Group Consciousness and Political Participation," *American Journal of Political Science* 25 (August 1981): 495. See also Susan J. Carroll, "Gender Politics and the Socializing Impact of the Women's Movement," in *Political Learning in Adulthood: A Sourcebook of Theory and Research,* ed. Roberta S. Sigel (Chicago: University of Chicago Press, 1989), p. 307.

20. Arend Lijphart, *Patterns of Democracy* (New Haven, Conn.: Yale University Press, 1999), p. 177.

21. See James L. Gibson, "The Policy Consequences of Political Intolerance: Political Repression during the Vietnam War Era," *Journal of Politics* 51 (February 1989): 13–35. Gibson found that individual state legislatures reacted quite differently in response to antiwar demonstrations on college campuses, but the laws passed to discourage dissent were not related directly to public opinion within the state.

22. See Verba and Nie, *Participation in America,* p. 69. See also John Clayton Thomas, "Citizen-Initiated Contacts with Government Agencies: A Test of Three Theories," *American Journal of Political Science* 26 (August 1982): 504–522; Elaine B. Sharp, "Citizen-Initiated Contacting of Government Officials and Socioeconomic Status: Determining the Relationship and Accounting for It," *American Political Science Review* 76 (March 1982): 109–115.

23. Elaine B. Sharp, "Citizen Demand Making in the Urban Context," *American Journal of Political Science* 28 (November 1984): 654–670, esp. pp. 654, 665.

24. Verba and Nie, *Participation in America,* p. 67; Sharp, "Citizen Demand Making," p. 660.

25. See Joel B. Grossman et al., "Dimensions of Institutional Participation: Who Uses the Courts and How?" *Journal of Politics* 44 (February 1982): 86–114; and Frances Kahn Zemans, "Legal Mobilization: The Neglected Role of the Law in the Political System," *American Political Science Review* 77 (September 1983): 690–703.

26. *Brown* v. *Board of Education,* 347 U.S. 483 (1954).

27. The government provides access to the *Federal Register* at http://www.gpoaccess.gov/fr. A private site keeps track of campaign promises and other claims in politics at http://www.politifact.com/truth-o-meter.

28. Jan-Erik Lane and Svante Ersson, *Democracy: A Comparative Approach* (New York: Routledge, 2003), p. 238; International Institute for Democracy and Educational Assistance, "Voter Turnout," online database available at http://www.idea.int/vt/index.cfm.

29. Max Kaase and Alan Marsh, "Political Action: A Theoretical Perspective," in *Political Action: Mass Participation in Five Western Democracies,* ed. Samuel H. Barnes and Max Kaase (Beverly Hills, Calif.: Sage, 1979), p. 168.

30. *Smith* v. *Allwright,* 321 U.S. 649 (1944).

31. *Harper* v. *Virginia State Board of Elections,* 383 U.S. 663 (1966).

32. Everett Carll Ladd, *The American Polity* (New York: Norton, 1985), p. 392.

33. Ivor Crewe, "Electoral Participation," in *Democracy at the Polls: A Comparative Study of Competitive National Elections,* ed. David Butler, Howard R. Penniman, and Austin Ranney (Washington, D.C.: American Enterprise Institute, 1981), pp. 219–223.

34. Faiza Saleh Ambah, "For Women in Kuwait, a Landmark Election," *Washington Post,* 29 June 2006, p. A20.

35. Central Intelligence Agency, "Suffrage," in *The World Factbook 2010 Online* (Washington, D.C.: CIA, 2010). Available at https://www.cia.gov/library/publications/the-world-factbook/fields/2123.html.

36. Initiative and Referendum Institute, "Election Results 2010: Tea Party Spillover?," *Ballot Watch* (November 2010), available at http://www.iandrinstitute.org/ballotwatch.htm.

37. Ibid.

38. David B. Magleby, *Direct Legislation: Voting on Ballot Propositions in the United States* (Baltimore: Johns Hopkins University Press, 1984), p. 59. See also Ernest Tollerson, "In 90's Ritual, Hired Hands Carry Democracy's Petitions," *New York Times,* 9 July 1996, p. 1.

39. Expenditure data on California's Proposition 87 is available at http://www.cal-access.ss.ca.gov/; search for 1282414 and 1282352.

40. Data on individual states may be found at http://www.census.gov/census2000/states.

41. Crewe, "Electoral Participation," p. 232. A rich literature has grown to explain turnout across nations. See Pippa Norris, *Democratic Phoenix: Reinventing Political Activism* (Cambridge: Cambridge University Press, 2002), Chap. 3; and Mark N. Franklin, "The Dynamics of Electoral Participation," in *Comparing Democracies 2: New Challenges in the Study of Elections and Voting,* ed. Lawrence LeDuc, Richard G. Niemi, and Pippa Norris (London: Sage, 2002), pp. 148–168.

42. Verba and Nie, *Participation in America,* p. 13.

43. Russell J. Dalton, *Citizen Policies,* 3rd ed. (New York: Seven Bridges, 2002), pp. 67–68. For the argument that greater economic inequality leads to greater political inequality, see Frederick Solt, "Economic Inequality and Democratic Political Engagement," *American Journal of Political Science* 52, no. 1 (January 2008): 48–60.

44. Russell J. Dalton, *The Good Citizen: How a Younger Generation Is Reshaping American Politics* (Washington, D.C.: Congressional Quarterly Press, 2008).

45. Cliff Zukin et al., *A New Engagement?* (New York: Oxford University Press, 2006), pp. 188–191.

46. For a concise summary of the effect of age on voting turnout, see William H. Flanigan and Nancy H. Zingale, *Political Behavior of the American Electorate,* 11th ed. (Washington, D.C.: Congressional Quarterly Press, 2005).

47. Richard Murray and Arnold Vedlitz, "Race, Socioeconomic Status, and Voting Participation in Large Southern Cities," *Journal of Politics* 39 (November 1977): 1064–1072; Verba and Nie, *Participation in America,* p. 157. See also Flanigan and Zingale, pp. 46–47.

48. M. Margaret Conway, Gertrude A. Steuernagel, and David W. Ahern, *Women and Political Participation: Cultural Change in the Political Arena* (Washington, D.C.: CQ Press, 1997), pp. 79–80.

49. Ronald B. Rapoport, "The Sex Gap in Political Persuading: Where the 'Structuring Principle' Works," *American Journal of Political Science* 25 (February 1981): 32–48.

50. Bruce C. Straits, "The Social Context of Voter Turnout," *Public Opinion Quarterly* 54 (Spring 1990): 64–73.

51. See Sidney Verba, Kay Lehman Scholzman, and Henry E. Brady, *Voice and Equality: Civic Voluntarism in American Politics* (Cambridge, Mass.: Harvard University Press, 1995), p. 433.

52. Associated Press, "Voter Turnout Tops Since 1968," *St. Paul Pioneer Press,* 14 December 2008, p. A4.

53. Stephen D. Shaffer, "A Multivariate Explanation of Decreasing Turnout in Presidential Elections, 1960–1976," *American Journal of Political*

Science 25 (February 1981): 68–95; Paul R. Abramson and John H. Aldrich, "The Decline of Electoral Participation in America," *American Political Science Review* 76 (September 1981): 603–620. However, one scholar argues that this research suffers because it looks at voters and nonvoters only in a single election. When the focus shifts to people who vote only sometimes, the models do not fit so well. See M. Margaret Conway and John E. Hughes, "Political Mobilization and Patterns of Voter Turnout" (paper presented at the annual meeting of the American Political Science Association, Washington, D.C., September 1993).

54. Apparently Richard A. Brody was the first scholar to pose this problem as a puzzle. See his "The Puzzle of Political Participation in America," in *The New American Political System,* ed. Anthony King (Washington, D.C.: American Enterprise Institute, 1978), pp. 287–324. Since then, a sizable literature has attempted to explain the decline in voter turnout in the United States. Some authors have claimed to account for the decline with just a few variables, but their work has been criticized for being too simplistic. See Carol A. Cassel and Robert C. Luskin, "Simple Explanations of Turnout Decline," *American Political Science Review* 82 (December 1988): 1321–1330. They contend that most of the post-1960 decline is still unexplained. If it is any comfort, voter turnout in Western European elections has seen a somewhat milder decline. See International Institute for Democracy and Electoral Assistance, *Voter Turnout in Western Europe* (Stockholm, Sweden: IDEA, 2004).

55. Abramson and Aldrich, "Decline of Electoral Participation," p. 519; Shaffer, "Multivariate Explanation," pp. 78, 90.

56. See Eric Pultzer, "Becoming a Habitual Voter: Inertia, Resources, and Growth in Young Adulthood," *American Political Science Review* (March 2002): 41–56; Alan S. Gerber, Donald P. Green, and Ron Shachar, "Voting May Be Habit-Forming: Evidence from a Randomized Field Experiment," *American Journal of Political Science* (July 2003): 540–550; and David Dreyer Lassen, "The Effect of Information on Voter Turnout: Evidence from a Natural Experiment," *American Journal of Political Science* 49 (January 2005): 103–111. For the argument that turnout

may be genetic, see "The Genetics of Politics," *Scientific American* (November 2007): 18–21.

57. The negative effect of registration laws on voter turnout is argued in Frances Fox Piven and Richard Cloward, "Government Statistics and Conflicting Explanations of Nonvoting," *PS: Political Science and Politics* 22 (September 1989): 580–588. Their analysis was hotly contested in Stephen Earl Bennett, "The Uses and Abuses of Registration and Turnout Data: An Analysis of Piven and Cloward's Studies of Nonvoting in America," *PS: Political Science and Politics* 23 (June 1990): 166–171. Bennett showed that turnout declined 10 to 13 percent after 1960, despite efforts to remove or lower legal hurdles to registration. For their reply, see Frances Fox Piven and Richard Cloward, "A Reply to Bennett," *PS: Political Science and Politics* 23 (June 1990): 172–173. You can see that reasonable people can disagree on this matter.

58. Nonprofit Voter Engagement Network, "America Goes to the Polls: A Report on Voter Turnout in the 2006 Election," available at http://www .nonprofitvote.org.

59. Ruth Goldway, "The Election Is in the Mail," *New York Times,* 6 December 2006; Randal C. Archibold, "Mail-In Voters Become the Latest Prize," *New York Times,* 14 January 2008.

60. David Glass, Peverill Squire, and Raymond Wolfinger, "Voter Turnout: An International Comparison," *Public Opinion* 6 (December–January 1984): 52. Wolfinger says that because of the strong effect of registration on turnout, most rational choice analyses of voting would be better suited to analyzing turnout of only registered voters. See Raymond E. Wolfinger, "The Rational Citizen Faces Election Day," *Public Affairs Report* 6 (November 1992): 12.

61. Civil Rights Division, U.S. Department of Justice, "About the National Voter Registration Act," 28 June 2010. Available at http://www.justice.gov/ crt/voting/nvra/activ_nvra.php.

62. Federal Election Commission, "NVRA Report Submitted to Congress: Almost 148 Million Registered to Vote in States Covered by Act," press release, 1 July 2003, http://www.fec.gov/press/ 20030701nvrareport.html.

63. Pew Center on the States, "Bringing Elections into the 21st Century: Voter Registration Modernization," Issue Brief (August 2009), p. 2.

64. Recent research finds that "party contact is clearly a statistically and substantively important factor in predicting and explaining political behavior." See Peter W. Wielhouwer and Brad Lockerbie, "Party Contacting and Political Participation, 1952–1990" (paper presented at the annual meeting of the American Political Science Association, Chicago, 1992), p. 14. Of course, parties strategically target the groups that they want to vote in elections. See Peter W. Wielhouwer, "Strategic Canvassing by Political Parties, 1952–1990," *American Review of Politics* 16 (Fall 1995): 213–238.

65. Nonprofit Voter Engagement Network, "America Goes to the Polls: A Report on Voter Turnout in the 2006 Election," available at http://www .nonprofitvote.org.

66. See Charles Krauthammer, "In Praise of Low Voter Turnout," *Time,* 21 May 1990, p. 88. Krauthammer says, "Low voter turnout means that people see politics as quite marginal to their lives, as neither salvation nor ruin.... Low voter turnout is a leading indicator of contentment." A major study in 1996 that compared one thousand likely nonvoters with twenty-three hundred likely voters found that 24 percent of the nonvoters said they "hardly ever" followed public affairs versus 5 percent of likely voters. See Dwight Morris, "No-Show '96: Americans Who Don't Vote," summary report to the Medill News Service and WTTW Television, Northwestern University School of Journalism, 1996.

67. Crewe, "Electoral Participation," p. 262.

68. For research showing that economic inequality depresses political engagement of the citizenry, see Frederick Solt, "Economic Inequality and Democratic Political Engagement," *American Journal of Political Science* 52 (2008): 48–60.

69. Barnes and Kaase, *Political Action,* p. 532.

70. *1971 Congressional Quarterly Almanac* (Washington, D.C.: Congressional Quarterly Press, 1972), p. 475.

71. Benjamin Ginsberg, *The Consequences of Consent: Elections, Citizen Control, and Popular Acquiescence* (Reading, Mass.: Addison-Wesley, 1982), pp. 13–14.

72. Ibid., pp. 6–7.

73. Some people have argued that the decline in voter turnout during the 1980s served to increase the class bias in the electorate because people of lower socioeconomic status stayed home. But others have concluded that "class bias has not increased since 1964." Jan E. Leighley and Jonathan Nagler, "Socioeconomic Class Bias in Turnout, 1964–1988: The Voters Remain the Same," *American Political Science Review* 86 (September 1992): 734. Nevertheless, Rosenstone and Hansen say, "The economic inequalities in political participation that prevail in the United States today are as large as the racial disparities in political participation that prevailed in the 1950s. America's leaders today face few incentives to attend to the needs of the disadvantaged." Steven J. Rosenstone and John Mark Hansen, *Mobilization, Participation, and Democracy in America* (New York: Macmillan, 1993), p. 248.

Chapter 6 / Political Parties, Campaigns, and Elections / pages 186–235

1. Alan K. Ota, "Will Cornyn's 'Big Tent' Strategy Collapse?" CQ Today Online News, 5 November 2009, available at http://www.cqpolitics.com.

2. Jeremy W. Peters and Adam Nagourney, "G.O.P. Candidate Pressed by Right, Ends Upstate Bid," *New York Times,* 1 November 2009, pp. 1, 34.

3. Jonathan Weisman and Naftali Bendavid, "Late Moves Jumble House Race," *Wall Street Journal,* 2 November 2009, p. A3.

4. Charles Mahtesian and Alex Isenstadt, "Uncivil War: Conservatives to Challenge a Dozen GOP Candidates," *Politico,* 3 November 2009, available at http://www.politico.com.

5. American National Election 2008 Time Series Study, available at http://www.electionstudies .org.

6. The Tea Party qualified to appear on the Florida ballot in 2010. See Ballot Access News 25 (1 March 2010): 6; and a U.S. Senate candidate in Nevada qualified to run under the Tea Party of Nevada.

7. However, a self-identified Tea Party candidate qualified to appear on the Florida ballot in 2010. See *Ballot Access News* 25 (1 March 2010): 6.

8. See Jerome M. Clubb, William H. Flanigan, and Nancy H. Zingale, *Partisan Realignment: Voters, Parties, and Government in American History* (Beverly Hills, Calif.: Sage, 1980), p. 163.

9. See Gerald M. Pomper, "Classification of Presidential Elections," *Journal of Politics* 29 (August 1967): 535–566.

10. Seth C. McKeen, "Rural Voters and the Polarization of American Presidential Elections," *PS: Political Science and Politics* 41 (January 2008): 101–108.

11. Jeffrey M. Stonecash, *Political Parties Matter: Realignment and the Return of Partisan Voting* (Boulder, Colo.: Lynne Rienner, 2006), pp. 129–130.

12. The discussion that follows draws heavily on Austin Ranney and Willmoore Kendall, *Democracy and the American Party System* (New York: Harcourt, Brace, 1956), Chaps. 18–19.

13. J. David Gillespie, *Politics at the Periphery: Third Parties in a Two-Party America* (Columbia: University of South Carolina Press, 1993). For an analysis of third-party presidential campaigns in 2008, see Brian J. Brox, "Running Nowhere: Third Party Presidential Campaigns in 2008" (paper presented at the annual meeting of the Midwest Political Science Association, Chicago, Ill., 3–6 April 2008). See Steven J. Rosenstone, Roy L. Behr, and Edward H. Lazarus, *Third Parties in America: Citizen Response to Major Party Failure* (Princeton, N.J.: Princeton University Press, 1984), pp. 5–6.

14. In an 18–29 June 2008 Pew Research Center Poll, 56 percent of the respondents agreed that "we should have a third major political party in this country in addition to the Democrats and Republicans." See also Shigeo Hirano and James M. Snyder, Jr., "The Decline of Third-Party Voting in the United States," *Journal of Politics* 69 (February 2007): 1–16.

15. See Rosenstone et al., p. 8.

16. Samuel Issacharoff, Pamela S. Karlan, and Richard H. Pildes, *The Law of Democracy,* rev. 2nd ed. (New York: Foundation Press, 2002), pp. 417–436.

17. See James Gimpel, *National Elections and the Autonomy of American State Party Systems* (Pittsburgh, Pa.: University of Pittsburgh Press, 1996).

18. Measuring the concept of party identification has had its problems. See R. Michael Alvarez, "The Puzzle of Party Identification," *American Politics Quarterly* 18 (October 1990): 476–491; and Donald Philip Green and Bradley Palmquist, "Of Artifacts and Partisan Instability," *American Journal of Political Science* 34 (August 1990): 872–902.

19. American National Election 2008 Time Series Study, available at http://www.electionstudies.org.

20. Rhodes Cook, "GOP Shows Dramatic Growth, Especially in the South," *Congressional Quarterly Weekly Report,* 13 January 1996, pp. 97–100.

21. Population Division, U.S. Census Bureau, "Summary Table 6: Percent of the Projected Population by Race and Hispanic Origin for the United States: 2010 to 2050 (NP2008-T6)," 14 August 2008, available at http://www.census.gov/population/www/projections/summarytables.html.

22. Two scholars on voting behavior describe partisanship as "the feeling of sympathy for and loyalty to a political party that an individual acquires—sometimes during childhood—and holds through life, often with increasing intensity." See William H. Flanigan and Nancy H. Zingale, *Political Behavior of the American Electorate,* 10th ed. (Washington, D.C.: Congressional Quarterly Press, 2002), p. 60.

23. "The GOP's Spending Spree," *Wall Street Journal,* 25 November 2003, p. A18.

24. See, for example, Gerald M. Pomper, *Elections in America* (New York: Dodd, Mead, 1968); Benjamin Ginsberg, "Election and Public Policy," *American Political Science Review* 70 (March 1976): 41–50; and Jeff Fishel, *Presidents and Promises* (Washington, D.C.: Congressional Quarterly Press, 1985).

25. The platforms are available at http://www.gop.com/2008Platform and http://www.democrats.org/a/party/platform.html.

26. Ian Budge et al., *Mapping Policy Preferences: Estimates for Parties, Electors, and Governments 1945–1998* (Oxford: Oxford University Press, 2001), p. 49.

27. See Ralph M. Goldman, *The National Party Chairmen and Committees: Factionalism at the Top* (Armonk, N.Y.: Sharpe, 1990). The subtitle is revealing.

28. Cornelius P. Cotter and Bernard C. Hennessy, *Politics without Power: The National Party Committees* (New York: Atherton Press, 1964).

29. William Crotty and John S. Jackson III, *Presidential Primaries and Nominations* (Washington, D.C.: Congressional Quarterly Press, 1985), p. 33.

30. Phillip A. Klinkner, "Party Culture and Party Behavior," in *The State of the Parties,* ed. Daniel M. Shea and John C. Green (Lanham, Md.: Rowman & Littlefield, 1994), pp. 275–287; Philip A. Klinkner, *The Losing Parties: Out-Party National Committees, 1956–1993* (New Haven, Conn.: Yale University Press, 1994).

31. Jeff Zeleny, "His Meteoric Days Behind Him, a Less Fiery Dean Leads Party," *New York Times,* 21 October 2007, pp. 1, 16; Naftali Bendavid, "The House That Rahm Built," *Chicago Tribune,* special report, 12 November 2007.

32. John Frendreis et al., "Local Political Parties and Legislative Races in 1992," in Shea and Green, *The State of the Parties,* p. 139.

33. Robert Biersack, "Hard Facts and Soft Money: State Party Finance in the 1992 Federal Elections," in Shea and Green, *The State of the Parties,* p. 114.

34. Martin P. Wattenberg, *The Decline of American Political Parties, 1952–1994* (Cambridge, Mass.: Harvard University Press, 1996).

35. Taylor Dark III, "The Rise of the Global Party? American Party Organizations Abroad," *Party Politics* 9 (March 2003): 241–255.

36. Barbara Sinclair, "The Congressional Party: Evolving Organizational, Agenda-Setting, and Policy Roles," in *The Parties Respond: Changes in American Parties and Campaigns,* 3rd ed., ed. L. Sandy Maisel (Boulder, Colo.: Westview Press, 1998), p. 227.

37. The model is articulated most clearly in a report by the American Political Science Association, "Toward a More Responsible Two-Party System," *American Political Science Review* 44 (September 1950): pt. II. See also Gerald M. Pomper, "Toward a More Responsible Party System? What, Again?" *Journal of Politics* 33 (November 1971): 916–940. See also the seven essays in the symposium "Divided Government and the Politics of Constitutional Reform," *PS: Political Science and Politics* 24 (December 1991): 634–657.

38. This is essentially the framework for studying campaigns set forth in Barbara G. Salmore and Stephen A. Salmore, *Candidates, Parties, and Campaigns: Electoral Politics in America,* 2nd ed. (Washington, D.C.: Congressional Quarterly Press, 1989).

39. Adam Nagourney, "Internet Injects Sweeping Change into U.S. Politics," *New York Times,* 2 April 2006, pp. 1, 17.

40. Martin P. Wattenberg, *The Rise of Candidate-Centered Politics: Presidential Elections of the 1980s* (Cambridge, Mass.: Harvard University Press, 1991).

41. Michael Gallagher, "Conclusion," in *Candidate Selection in Comparative Perspective: The Secret Garden of Politics,* ed. Michael Gallagher and Michael Marsh (London: Sage, 1988), p. 238.

42. *The Book of the States, 2003* (Lexington, Ky.: Council of State Governments, 2003), pp. 295–296. See also Federal Election Commission, "2004 Presidential and Congressional Primary Dates," 26 May 2004, http://www.fec.gov/pubrec/fe2004/2004pdates.pdf.

43. Talar Aslanian et al., "Recapturing Voter Intent: The Nonpartisan Primary in California" (capstone seminar report, Pepperdine University, April 2003), Appendix C.

44. Harold W. Stanley and Richard G. Niemi, *Vital Statistics on American Politics, 1788–2008* (Washington, D.C.: Congressional Quarterly Press, 2008). According to state-by-state delegate totals in "The Green Papers" website, about 15 percent of the delegates to each party's 2008 presidential nominating convention were selected through the caucus/convention system.

45. William G. Mayer and Andrew E. Busch, *The Front-Loading Problem in Presidential Nominations* (Washington, D.C.: The Brookings Institution, 2004).

46. On the front-loading controversy, see the symposium "Reforming the Presidential Nomination Process," *PS: Political Science & Politics* 42 (January 2009): 27–79.

47. See Rhodes Cook, *The Presidential Nominating Process: A Place for Us?* (Lanham, Md.: Rowman & Littlefield, 2004), Chap. 5. Nations that have copied the American model have experienced mixed results. See James A. McCann, "The Emerging International Trend toward Open Presidential Primaries," in *The Making of the Presidential Candidates 2004,* ed. William G. Mayer (Lanham, Md.: Rowman & Littlefield, 2004), pp. 265–293.

48. Gary R. Orren and Nelson W. Polsby (eds.), *Media and Momentum: The New Hampshire Primary and Nomination Politics* (Chatham, N.J.: Chatham House, 1987), p. 23.

49. Dan Balz, "Fla., Mich. Delegates Each Get Half a Vote," *Washington Post,* 1 June 2008, p. A1.

50. In general, Democratic winners are less predictable. See Wayne P. Steger, "Who Wins Nominations and Why? An Updated Forecast of the Presidential Primary Vote," *Political Research Quarterly* 60 (March 2007): 91–99.

51. See James R. Beniger, "Winning the Presidential Nomination: National Polls and State Primary Elections, 1936–1972," *Public Opinion Quarterly* 40 (Spring 1976): 22–38.

52. See Alexis Simendinger, James A. Barnes, and Carl M. Cannon, "Pondering a Popular Vote," *National Journal,* 18 November 2000, pp. 3650–3656.

53. Harold W. Stanley and Richard G. Niemi, *Vital Statistics on American Politics, 2008* (Washington, D.C.: Congressional Quarterly Press, 2009), Table 3.10.

54. Dan Balz, "GOP Seizes Control of House: Economy Drives Party Gains," *Washington Post,* 3 November 2010, p. A1.

55. Salmore and Salmore, *Candidates, Parties, and Campaigns.*

56. See Edward I. Sidlow, *Challenging the Incumbent: An Underdog's Undertaking* (Washington, D.C.: CQ Press, 2004), for an engaging look at what challengers face.

57. Quoted in E. J. Dionne, Jr., "On the Trail of Corporation Donations," *New York Times,* 6 October 1980.

58. Salmore and Salmore, *Candidates, Parties, and Campaigns,* p. 11. See also David Himes, "Strategy and Tactics for Campaign Fund-Raising," in *Campaigns and Elections: American Style,* ed. James A. Thurber and Candice J. Nelson (Boulder, Colo.: Westview Press, 1995), pp. 62–77.

59. For tactical reasons in Congress, the bill that actually passed was the Shays–Meehan bill, sponsored by representatives Christopher Shays (R-Conn.) and Martin Meehan (D-Mass.), but it became known as McCain–Feingold for the early work done by both senators.

60. Steve Weissman and Ruth Hassan, "BCRA and the 527 Groups," in *The Election After Reform,* ed. Michael J. Malbin (Lanham, Md.: Rowman & Littlefield, 2006).

61. Brody Mullins, "Stealthy Groups Shake Up Races," *Wall Street Journal,* 4 February 2008, p. A12.

62. Adam Liptak, "Justices, 5–4, Reject Corporate Campaign Spending Limit," *New York Times,* 22 January 2010, pp. A1, A16.

63. Editorial, "A Free Speech Landmark," *Wall Street Journal,* 22 January 2010, p. A18.

64. Editorial, "The Court's Blow to Democracy," *New York Times,* 22 January 2010, p. A20.

65. "Changing the Rules," *Wall Street Journal,* 22 January 2010, p. A6.

66. Federal Election Commission, "2004 Presidential Campaign Financial Activity Summarized," news release, 3 February 2005.

67. James A. Barnes, "Matching Funds, R.I.P.," *National Journal Magazine,* 26 April 2008, http://www.nationaljournal.com/njmagazine/pi_20080426_9817.php.

68. Salmore and Salmore, *Candidates, Parties, and Campaigns,* p. 11.

69. David Moon, "What You Use Depends on What You Have: Information Effects on the Determinants of Electoral Choice," *American Politics Quarterly* 18 (January 1990): 3–24.

70. See the "Marketplace" section in monthly issues of the magazine *Campaigns and Elections,* which contains scores of names, addresses, and telephone numbers of people who supply "political products and services"—from "campaign schools" to "voter files and mailing lists."

71. Bruce I. Newman, "A Predictive Model of Voter Behavior," in *Handbook of Political Marketing,* ed. Bruce I. Newman (Thousand Oaks, Calif.: Sage, 1999), pp. 259–282. For studies on campaign consultants at work, see James A. Thurber and Candice J. Nelson (eds.), *Campaign Warriors: The Role of Political Consultants in Elections* (Washington, D.C.: Brookings Institution, 2000).

72. See Darrell M. West, *Air Wars: Television Advertising in Election Campaigns, 1952–2004,* 4th ed. (Washington, D.C.: Congressional Quarterly Press, 2005).

73. Lee Rainie, Michael Cornfield, and John Horrigan, *The Internet and Campaign 2004* (Washington, D.C.: Pew Internet and American Life Project, 6 March 2005), p. i, available at http://www.pewinternet.org/~/media//Files/Reports/2005/PIP_2004_Campaign.pdf.

74. Leslie Wayne and Jeff Zeleny, "Enlisting New Donors, Obama Reaped $32 Million in January," *New York Times,* 1 February 2008, pp. A1, A14.

75. Katharine Q. Seelye and Leslie Wayne, "The Web Finds Its Man, and Takes Him for a Ride," *New York Times,* 11 November 2007, p. 22.

76. Pew Research Center for the People & the Press, "Internet Overtakes Newspapers as News Outlet," 23 December 2008.

77. Emily Steel, "Why Web Campaign Spending Trails TV," *Wall Street Jurnal,* 14 December 2008, p. B4.

78. Pamela Johnston Conover and Stanley Feldman, "Candidate Perception in an Ambiguous World: Campaigns, Cues, and Inference Processes," *American Journal of Political Science* 33 (November 1989): 912–940.

79. Kevin Merida, "Racist Incidents Give Some Campaigners Pause," *Washington Post,* 13 May 2008, p. A01.

80. Michael M. Gant and Norman R. Luttbeg, *American Electoral Behavior* (Itasca, Ill.: Peacock, 1991), pp. 63–64. For recent research indicating a growth in issue voting, see Martin Gilens, Jynn Vavreck, and Martin Cohen, "The Mass Media and the Public's Assessments of Presidential Candidates, 1952–2000," *Journal of Politics* 69 (November 2007): 1160–1175.

81. Martin Gilens et al., "The Mass Media and the Public's Assessments of Presidential Candidates, 1952–2000."

82. Craig Goodman and Gregg R. Murray, "Do You See What I See? Perceptions of Party Differences and Voting Behavior," *American Politics Research* 35 (November 2007): 905–931.

83. Conover and Feldman, "Candidate Perception," p. 938.

84. Party identification has been assumed to be relatively resistant to short-term campaign effects, but see Dee Allsop and Herbert F. Weisberg, "Measuring Change in Party Identification in an Election Campaign," *American Journal of Political Science* 32 (November 1988): 996–1017. They conclude that partisanship is more volatile than we have thought.

Chapter 7 / Interest Groups / pages 236–263

1. Elizabeth Williamson and Brody Mullins, "Lobbyists Put Democrats Out Front as Winds Shift," *Wall Street Journal,* 5 November 2008.

2. Matthew Mosk, "Democrats Benefitting from Post-election Lobby Boom," *Washington Post,* 14 November 2008.

3. Jonathan D. Salant, "Obama's Spending Spurs Former U.S. Lawmakers to Join Lobbyists," Bloomberg.com, 9 April 2009; "Robert (Bud) Cramer," http://www.wexlergroup.com/bud-cramer.html.

4. Mosk, "Democrats Benefitting from Post-election Lobby Boom."

5. Alexis de Tocqueville, *Democracy in America, 1835–1839,* repr., ed. Richard D. Heffner (New York: Mentor Books, 1956), p. 79.

6. *The Federalist Papers* (New York: Mentor Books, 1961), p. 79.

7. Ibid., p. 78.

8. See Robert A. Dahl, *A Preface to Democratic Theory* (Chicago: University of Chicago Press, 1956), pp. 4–33.

9. Alan Rosenthal, *The Third House* (Washington, D.C.: Congressional Quarterly Press, 1993), p. 7.

10. This discussion follows from Jeffrey M. Berry, *The Interest Group Society* (New York: Longman, 1997), pp. 6–8.

11. John Mark Hansen, *Gaining Access* (Chicago: University of Chicago Press, 1991), pp. 11–17.

12. David B. Truman, *The Governmental Process* (New York: Knopf, 1951).

13. Herbert Gans, *The Urban Villagers* (New York: Free Press, 1962).

14. Robert H. Salisbury, "An Exchange Theory of Interest Groups," *Midwest Journal of Political Science* 13 (February 1969): 1–32.

15. See Mancur Olson, Jr., *The Logic of Collective Action* (New York: Schocken, 1968).

16. See ibid.

17. See, for example, Edward O. Laumann and David Knoke, *The Organizational State* (Madison: University of Wisconsin Press, 1987), p. 3, cited in Robert H. Salisbury, "The Paradox of Interest Groups in Washington—More Groups, Less Clout," in *The New American Political System,* 2nd ed., ed. Anthony King (Washington, D.C.: American Enterprise Institute, 1990), p. 226.

18. "Health Lobbyist Has Great Sway," Associated Press, 24 May 2009.

19. Federal Election Commission, "Growth in PAC Financial Activity Slows," news release, 24 April 2009, http://fec.gov/press/press2009/20090415 PAC/20090424PAC.shtml.

20. Federal Election Commission, "Table 10: Top 50 PACs by Contributions to Candidates, January 1, 2007–December 31, 2008," http://fec.gov/press/

press2009/20090415PAC/documents/10top50 paccontrib2008.pdf. PAC expenditure data are available online from the Federal Election Commission through its "Summary Report Search" at http://www.fec.gov/finance/disclosure/srssea.shtml.

21. Michael Forsythe and Kristin Jensen, "Democratic Lobbyists Relish Return to Washington's Power Elite," Bloomberg wire service, 10 November 2006.

22. Federal Election Commission, "Table 1: PAC Contribution Summary, 2007–2008," http://www.fec.gov/press/press2009/20090415PAC/documents/1summary2008.pdf.

23. Ibid.

24. Stephen Ansolabehere, John de Figueredo, and James N. Snyder, Jr., "Why Is There So Little Money in U.S. Politics?" *Journal of Economic Perspectives* 17 (Winter 2003): 161–181; Mark Smith, *American Business and Political Power* (Chicago: University of Chicago Press, 2000): 115–141.

25. Marie Hojnacki and David Kimball, "The Contribution and Lobbying Strategies of PAC Sponsors in Committee" (paper presented at the annual meeting of the American Political Science Association, Boston, September 1998); John R. Wright, "Contributions, Lobbying, and Committee Voting in the U.S. House of Representatives," *American Political Science Review* 84 (June 1990): 417–438; Richard L. Hall and Frank W. Wayman, "Buying Time: Money Interests and the Mobilization of Bias in Congressional Committees," *American Political Science Review* 84 (September 1990): 797–820.

26. Kay Lehman Schlozman and John T. Tierney, *Organized Interests and American Democracy* (New York: Harper & Row, 1986), p. 150.

27. Berry, *The Interest Group Society*, p. 166.

28. Frank R. Baumgartner et al., *Lobbying and Policy Change* (Chicago: University of Chicago Press, 2009), pp. 166–189.

29. Eric Pianin, "For Environmentalists, Victories in the Courts," *Washington Post*, 27 January 2003, p. A3.

30. Clay Risen, "Store Lobby," *New Republic*, 25 July 2005, pp. 10–11.

31. Marc K. Landy and Mary Hague, "Private Interests and Superfund," *Public Interest* 108 (Summer 1992): 97–115.

32. Dara Z. Strolovitch, *Affirmative Advocacy* (Chicago: University of Chicago Press, 2007), p. 181.

33. The best available data on this can be found in Kay L. Schlozman, "Who Sings in the Heavenly Chorus? The Shape of the Organized Interest Group System," in *The Oxford Handbook of American Political Parties and Interest Groups*, ed. L. Sandy Maisel and Jeffrey M. Berry (Oxford, UK: Oxford University Press, 2010), pp. 425–450.

34. Kay Lehman Schlozman, Traci Burch, and Samuel Lampert, "Still an Upper-Class Accent?" (paper presented at the annual meeting of the American Political Science Association, Chicago, Ill., September 2004), pp. 16, 25.

35. Jeffrey M. Berry, *The New Liberalism* (Washington, D.C.: The Brookings Institution, 1999), pp. 120–130.

36. Schlozman and Tierney, *Organized Interests*, pp. 58–87.

37. These figures are the authors' calculations, derived from the Center for Responsive Politics at OpenSecrets.org. The number of lobbyists is the aggregate of the categories under "Industry" for pharmaceuticals/health products, hospitals/nursing homes, and health professionals. Figures are current as of 10 November 2009.

38. Baumgartner et al., *Lobbying and Policy Change*, pp. 190–214.

39. Federal Election Commission, "PAC Financial Activity, 2007–2008," news release, 24 April 2009, available at http://fec.gov/press/press2009/20090415PAC/20090424PAC.shtml.

40. Jeff Zeleny and Carl Hulse, "Congress Votes to Tighten Rules on Lobbyist Ties," *New York Times*, 3 August 2007, p. A1.

41. Suzanne Perry, "Nonprofit Lobbyists Protest Restrictions Imposed by Obama Administration," *Chronicle of Philanthropy*, 23 April 2009, p. 35; Dan Eggen, "Lobbying Rules Keep Some Activists Out of Government," *Washington Post*, 22 March 2009, p. A1.

42. *Citizens United* v. *Federal Election Commission*, 558 U.S. ___ (2010).

Chapter 8 / Congress / pages 264–301

1. Mark Mazzetti and William Glaberson, "Obama Issues Directive to Shut Down Guantánamo," *New York Times*, 22 January 2009, http://

www.nytimes.com/2009/01/22/us/politics/22gitmo.html.

2. Nancy Pelosi, "Pelosi Statement on Obama Executive Orders on Closing Guantanamo and Revising Interrogation Policies," press release, 22 January 2009, http://www.speaker.gov/newsroom/pressreleases?id=0972.

3. Associated Press, "House Puts New Restrictions on Gitmo Closing," 18 June 2009; Tim Starks and Joanna Anderson, "Senate Clears Bill That Would Limit Moving Detainees from Guantanamo," *CQ Weekly Online,* 12 October 2009; Anne Kornblut and Dafna Linzer, "White House Regroups on Guantanamo," *Washington Post,* 25 September 2009, http://www.washingtonpost.com/wp-dyn/content/article/2009/09/24/AR2009092404893_pf.html.

4. Keith Perine, "Detainees' Future Tied Up in Policy," *CQ Weekly Online,* 10 August 2009.

5. Mark Mazzetti and Scott Shane, "Where Will Detainees from Guantánamo Go?" *New York Times,* 23 January 2009, http://www.nytimes.com/2009/01/24/us/politics/24intel.html.

6. Clinton Rossiter, *1787: The Grand Convention* (New York: Mentor, 1968), p. 158.

7. James M. Lindsay and Randall B. Ripley, "How Congress Influences Foreign and Defense Policy," in *Congress Resurgent,* ed. Randall B. Ripley and James M. Lindsay (Ann Arbor: University of Michigan Press, 1993), pp. 25–28.

8. Monika McDermott and David Jones, "Do Public Evaluations of Congress Matter? Retrospective Voting in Congressional Elections," *American Politics Research* 31, no. 2 (2003): 155–177.

9. Harold W. Stanley and Richard G. Niemi (eds.), *Vital Statistics on American Politics, 2009–2010* (Washington, D.C.: CQ Press, 2010), p. 46.

10. Bill Mears, "High Court Upholds Most of Texas Redistricting Map," *CNN,* 28 June 2006, http://www.cnn.com/2006/POLITICS/06/28/scotus.texasredistrict.

11. Thomas E. Mann, "Polarizing the House of Representatives: How Much Does Gerrymandering Matter?" in *Red and Blue Nation,* ed. Pietro S. Nivola and David W. Brady (Washington, D.C.: The Brookings Institution and Hoover Institution, 2006), pp. 263–283.

12. Timothy E. Cook, *Making Laws and Making News* (Washington, D.C.: The Brookings Institution, 1989), p. 83.

13. Dennis Conrad, "House Spends Big on Home Mailings," *Boston Globe,* 28 December 2007, p. A2; Michael Glassman, "Franking Privilege: An Analysis of Member Mass Mailings in the House, 1997–2007 (RL34458)," *CRS Report for Congress,* 16 April 2008.

14. Matthew Eric Glassman, Jacob R. Straus, and Colleen J. Shogan, "Social Networking and Constituent Communications: Member Use of Twitter during a Two-Month Period in the 111th Congress," *CRS Report for Congress,* 3 February 2010.

15. Campaign finance data for each election cycle are available from the Federal Election Commission. Cited data were calculated from the FEC's "2009–2010 Financial Activity of All Senate and House Campaigns (January 1, 2009-December 31, 2010)." Available at http://www.fec.gov/press/bkgnd/cf_summary_info/2010can_fullsum/1all2010afinal.pdf.

16. Ibid.

17. Jonathan S. Krasno, *Challengers, Competition, and Reelection* (New Haven, Conn.: Yale University Press, 1994).

18. Paul S. Herrnson, *Congressional Elections,* 5th ed. (Washington, D.C.: Congressional Quarterly Press, 2008), pp. 65–66; Erika Lovley, "Report: 237 Millionaires in Congress," *Politico,* 6 November 2009, http://dyn.politico.com/printstory.cfm?uuid=CA707571-18FE-70B2-A8721899A59ED165.

19. Jennifer E. Manning, "Membership of the 112th Congress: A Profile (R40086)," *CRS Report for Congress,* 1 March 2011. These data do not include territorial delegates or the resident commissioner for Puerto Rico.

20. Hanna Fenichel Ptikin, *The Concept of Representation* (Berkeley: University of California Press, 1967), pp. 60–91; Jane Mansbridge, "Should Blacks Represent Blacks and Women Represent Women? A Contingent 'Yes,'" *Journal of Politics* 61 (1999): 628–657.

21. Carol M. Swain, *Black Faces, Black Interests* (Cambridge, Mass.: Harvard University Press, 1993), p. 197.

22. Mark Hugo Lopez and Paul Taylor, "Dissecting the 2008 Electorate: The Most Diverse in U.S. History," *Pew Hispanic Center Report,* 30 April 2009, p. 2, http://www.pewhispanic.org/files/reports/108.pdf.

23. *Shaw* v. *Reno,* 509 U.S. 630 (1993).

24. *Bush* v. *Vera,* 116 S. Ct. 1941 (1996).

25. *Easley* v. *Cromartie,* 532 U.S. 234 (2001).

26. See David Lublin, *The Paradox of Representation* (Princeton, N.J.: Princeton University Press, 1997); Kenneth W. Shotts, "Does Racial Redistricting Cause Conservative Policy Outcomes?" *Journal of Politics* 65 (2003): 216–226, presents an alternative view.

27. Walter J. Oleszek, *Congressional Procedures and the Policy Process* (Washington, D.C.: Congressional Quarterly Press, 1996), p. 91.

28. See Frank R. Baumgartner et al., *Lobbying and Policy Change* (Chicago: University of Chicago Press, 2009).

29. 111th Congress, H.R. 1966, available at http://thomas.loc.gov.

30. "Megan's Law: Cyber-bullying and the Courts," *Economist,* 11 July 2009.

31. Woodrow Wilson, *Congressional Government* (Boston: Houghton Mifflin, 1885), p. 79.

32. Karen Foerstal, "Gingrich Flexes His Power in Picking Panel Chiefs," *Congressional Quarterly Weekly Report,* 7 January 1995, p. 3326.

33. Joel D. Aberbach, *Keeping a Watchful Eye* (Washington, D.C.: The Brookings Institution, 1990), pp. 162–183.

34. John D. Huber and Charles R. Shipan, *Deliberate Discretion?* (Cambridge: Cambridge University Press, 2002.)

35. Gary W. Cox and Mathew D. McCubbins, *Legislative Leviathan* (Berkeley: University of California Press, 1993); Keith Krehbiel, *Information and Legislative Organization* (Ann Arbor: University of Michigan Press, 1992).

36. Jonathan Franzen, "The Listener," *New Yorker,* 6 October 2003, p. 85.

37. David M. Herszenhorn, "Fuel Bill Shows House Speaker's Muscle," *New York Times,* 2 December 2007, p. 22.

38. Charles O. Jones, *The United States Congress* (Homewood, Ill.: Dorsey Press, 1982), p. 322.

39. Norman Ornstein, "Our Broken Senate," *The American,* May/April 2008, http://www.american.com/archive/2008/march-april-magazine-contents/our-broken-senate; Barbara Sinclair, "The 60 Vote Senate," in *U.S. Senate Exceptionalism,* ed. Bruce Oppenheimer (Columbus: Ohio State University Press, 2002), pp. 241–261.

40. Eric M. Uslaner, "Is the Senate More Civil Than the House?" in *Esteemed Colleagues,* ed. Burdett A. Loomis (Washington, D.C.: The Brookings Institution Press, 2000), pp. 32–55.

41. Cox and McCubbins, *Legislative Leviathan;* D. Roderick Kiewiet and Mathew D. McCubbins, *The Logic of Delegation* (Chicago: University of Chicago Press, 1991); Krehbiel, *Information and Legislative Organization.*

42. Dan Carney, "As Hostilities Rage on the Hill, Partisan-Vote Rate Soars," *Congressional Quarterly Weekly Report,* 27 January 1996, pp. 199–201; Martin P. Wattenberg, *The Decline of American Political Parties, 1994* (Cambridge, Mass.: Harvard University Press, 1996), Chap. 11.

43. See Mark A. Peterson, *Legislating Together* (Cambridge, Mass.: Harvard University Press, 1990).

44. James Sterling Young, *The Washington Community* (New York: Harcourt, Brace, 1964).

45. Barry C. Burden, *The Personal Roots of Representation* (Princeton, N.J.: Princeton University Press, 2007).

46. Richard F. Fenno, Jr., *Home Style* (Boston: Little, Brown, 1978), p. 32.

47. Louis I. Bredvold and Ralph G. Ross (eds.), *The Philosophy of Edmund Burke* (Ann Arbor: University of Michigan Press, 1960), p. 148.

48. For an alternative and more highly differentiated set of representation models, see Jane Mansbridge, "Rethinking Representation," *American Political Science Review* 97 (November 2003): 515–528.

49. Warren E. Miller and Donald E. Stokes, "Constituency Influence in Congress," *American Political Science Review* 57 (March 1963): 45–57. On minority legislators, see James B. Johnson and Philip E. Secret, "Focus and Style: Representational Roles of Congressional Black and Hispanic Caucus Members," *Journal of Black Studies* 26 (January 1996): 245–273.

50. Citizens against Government Waste, *2010 Congressional Pig Book Summary* (Washington, D.C.: CAGW, 2010); available at http://www.cagw.org/reports/pig-book/2010. CAGW also has an online database of over 9,000 earmarks from FY2010 available at http://www.cagw.org/reports/pig-book/2010/pork-database.html.

51. Nancy Cordes, "Earmarks: Who Brought Home the Bacon," *CBS Evening News,* 14 April 2010,

http://www.cbsnews.com/stories/2010/04/14/eveningnews/main6396553.shtml.

52. Cheryl Gay Stolberg, "Ease a Little Guilt, Provide Some Jobs: It's Pork on the Hill," *New York Times,* 20 December 2003, p. A1.

53. Robert Weissberg, "Collective vs. Dyadic Representation in Congress," *American Political Science Review* 72 (June 1978): 535–547.

54. E. Scott Adler, *Why Congressional Reforms Fail* (Chicago: University of Chicago Press, 2002); Eric Schickler, *Disjointed Pluralism* (Princeton, N.J.: Princeton University Press, 2001).

Chapter 9 / The Presidency / pages 302–335

1. Christopher Drew, "Drones Are Weapons of Choice in Fighting Qaeda," *New York Times,* 16 March 2010, http://www.nytimes.com/2009/03/17/business/17uav.html.

2. Ian S. Livingston and Michael O'Hanlon, *Pakistan Index* (Washington, D.C.: Brookings Institution, 24 February 2011).

3. Karen DeYoung and Griff Witte, "U.S., Pakistan Seek to Bridge Divide on North Waziristan," *Washington Post,* 14 April 2010, p. A1. Salman Masood, "Pakistani General Credits U.S. Drone Strikes," *New York Times,* 10 March 2011, p. A12.

4. Peter Finn and Joby Warrick, "Under Panetta, a More Aggressive CIA," *Washington Post,* 21 March 2010; "Remarks by the President on Osama Bin Laden," 1 May 2011, http://www.whitehouse.gov/blog/2011/05/02/osama-bin-laden-dead.

5. Daniel Byman, "Taliban vs. Predator," *Foreign Affairs,* http://www.foreignaffairs.com/articles/64901/daniel-byman/taliban-vs-predator; Jane Mayer, "The Predator War," *New Yorker,* 26 October 2009, pp. 36–45; Mark Hosenball, "U.S. Increases Drone Use in Pakistan," *Newsweek,* 27 October 2009; Finn and Warrick, "Under Panetta."

6. See Louis Fisher, *Presidential War Power* (Lawrence: University Press of Kansas, 1995).

7. Lyn Ragsdale, *Vital Statistics on the Presidency: Washington to Clinton* (Washington, D.C.: Congressional Quarterly Press, 1996), p. 396.

8. Charles Cameron, *Veto Bargaining: Presidents and the Politics of Negative Power* (Cambridge: Cambridge University Press, 2000).

9. Jeffrey Tulis, *The Rhetorical Presidency* (Princeton, N.J.: Princeton University Press, 1987).

10. Cecil V. Crabb, Jr., and Pat M. Holt, *Invitation to Struggle: Congress, the President and Foreign Policy,* 2nd ed. (Washington, D.C.: Congressional Quarterly Press, 1984); Arthur Schlesinger, Jr., *The Imperial Presidency* (Boston: Houghton Mifflin, 1989).

11. "Text of Joint Resolution to Authorize Use of Military Force against Iraq," *Congressional Quarterly Weekly Report,* 12 October 2002, p. 2697.

12. *Hamdan* v. *Rumsfeld,* 548 U.S. 557 (2006).

13. Wilfred E. Binkley, *President and Congress,* 3rd ed. (New York: Vintage, 1962), p. 155.

14. William G. Howell, *Power without Persuasion: The Politics of Direct Presidential Action* (Princeton, N.J.: Princeton University Press, 2003); Kenneth R. Mayer, *With the Stroke of a Pen: Executive Orders and Presidential Power* (Princeton, N.J.: Princeton University Press, 2001).

15. James Risen and Eric Lichtblau, "Bush Lets U.S. Spy on Callers without Courts," *New York Times,* 16 December 2005, p. A1; Lauren Etter, "Is Someone Listening to Your Phone Calls?" *Wall Street Journal,* 7 January 2006, p. A5.

16. James P. Pfiffner, *Power Play* (Washington, D.C.: Brookings Institution, 2008), pp. 190–191.

17. U.S. Census Bureau, *Statistical Abstract of the United States: 2010* (Washington, D.C.: U.S. Government Printing Office, 2009), Table 487: Federal Civilian Employment by Branch and Agency: 1990 to 2008 and Table 460: Federal Budget Outlays by Agency: 1990 to 2009.

18. Richard Tanner Johnson, *Managing the White House* (New York: Harper and Row, 1974); John P. Burke, *The Institutional Presidency* (Baltimore, Md.: Johns Hopkins University Press, 1992).

19. Irving Janus, *Victims of Groupthink: A Psychological Study of Foreign Policy Decisions and Fiascoes* (Boston: Houghton Mifflin, 1972); Andrew Rudalevige, "The Structure of Leadership: Presidents, Hierarchies, and Information Flow," *Presidential Studies Quarterly* 35 (June 2005): 333–360.

20. John Cochran, "GOP Turns to Cheney to Get the Job Done," *Congressional Quarterly Weekly Report,* 31 May 2003, pp. 1306–1308.

21. Howards Kurtz, "Finding Virtue in Vice: Despite Gaffes, Biden Has Blossomed as Obama's Prime Spokesman," *Washington Post,* 10 June 2010, p. C1.

22. Edward Weisband and Thomas M. Franck, *Resignation in Protest* (New York: Penguin, 1975), p. 139, quoted in Thomas E. Cronin, *The State of the Presidency,* 2nd ed. (Boston: Little, Brown, 1980), p. 253.

23. See Richard W. Waterman, "Combining Political Resources: The Internalization of the President's Appointment Power," in *The Presidency Reconsidered,* ed. Richard W. Waterman (Itasca, Ill.: Peacock, 1993), pp. 172–210.

24. Doris Kearns, *Lyndon Johnson and the American Dream* (New York: Signet, 1977), p. 363.

25. See Merrill McLoughlin (ed.), *The Impeachment and Trial of President Clinton: The Official Transcripts, from the House Judiciary Committee Hearings to the Senate Trial* (New York: Random House, 1999); Richard Posner, *An Affair of State* (Cambridge, Mass.: Harvard University Press, 1999); and Jeffrey Toobin, *A Vast Conspiracy* (New York: Touchstone, 1999).

26. James David Barber, *Presidential Character,* 4th ed. (Englewood Cliffs, N.J.: Prentice Hall, 1992); Fred I. Greenstein, *The Presidential Difference: Leadership Style from FDR to Clinton* (Princeton, N.J.: Princeton University Press, 2000); Stanley Renshon, *High Hopes: The Clinton Presidency and the Politics of Ambition* (New York: Routledge, 1998).

27. Donald Kinder, "Presidential Character Revisited," in *Political Cognition,* ed. Richard Lau and David O. Sears (Hillsdale, N.J.: Erlbaum, 1986), pp. 233–255; W. E. Miller and J. M. Shanks, *The New American Voter* (Cambridge, Mass.: Harvard University Press, 1996).

28. Richard E. Neustadt, *Presidential Power,* rev. ed. (New York: Wiley, 1980), p. 10.

29. Ibid., p. 9.

30. George C. Edwards III, *At the Margins* (New Haven, Conn.: Yale University Press, 1989). See also Jon R. Bond and Richard Fleisher, *The President in the Legislative Arena* (Chicago: University of Chicago Press, 1990).

31. See Edwards, *At the Margins,* pp. 101–125.

32. Samuel Kernell, *Going Public: New Strategies of Presidential Leadership,* 3rd ed. (Washington, D.C.: Congressional Quarterly Press, 1997), p. 2.

33. Richard A. Brody, *Assessing the President* (Stanford, Calif.: Stanford University Press, 1991), pp. 27–44; Gary C. Jacobson, "The Bush Presidency and the American Electorate," in *The George W. Bush Presidency,* ed. Fred I. Greenstein (Baltimore, Md.: Johns Hopkins University Press, 2003), pp. 197–227.

34. Paul Brace and Barbara Hinckley, *Follow the Leader* (New York: Basic Books, 1992); Richard Brody, "President Bush and the Public," in *The George W. Bush Presidency,* ed. Greenstein, pp. 228–244; George C. Edwards III and Tami Swenson, "Who Rallies? The Anatomy of a Rally Event," *Journal of Politics* 59 (February 1997): 200–212.

35. Richard C. Eichenberg and Richard J. Stoll, *The Political Fortunes of War: Iraq and the Domestic Standing of President George W. Bush* (London: The Foreign Policy Centre, 2004), p. 8.

36. Jeffrey M. Jones, "Obama Job Approval at 51% After Healthcare Vote," Gallup Poll, 25 March 2010, http://www.gallup.com/poll/126989/Obama-Job-Approval-51-After-Healthcare-Vote.aspx.

37. George C. Edwards III, *The Strategic President* (Princeton, N.J.: Princeton University Press, 2009), p. 188.

38. Sheryl Gay Stolberg, Jeff Zeleny, and Carl Hulse, "The Long Road Back," *New York Times,* 21 March 2010, p. A1.

39. Jeffrey E. Cohen, *Presidential Responsiveness and Public Policy-Making* (Ann Arbor: University of Michigan Press, 1999); Lawrence C. Jacobs and Robert Y. Shapiro, *Politicians Don't Pander* (Chicago: University of Chicago Press, 2000).

40. David McCullough, *Truman* (New York: Simon & Schuster, 1992), p. 914.

41. Bond and Fleisher, *The President in the Legislative Arena;* Mark Peterson, *Legislating Together* (Cambridge, Mass.: Harvard University Press, 1990).

42. Clea Benson, "Presidential Support: The Power of No," *Congressional Quarterly Weekly Report,* 14 January 2008, p. 137.

43. See Sarah H. Binder, "The Dynamics of Legislative Gridlock, 1947–96," *American Political Science Review* 93 (September 1999): 519–534.

44. Sean M. Theriault, *Party Polarization in Congress* (New York: Cambridge University Press,

2008); Nolan McCarty, Keith T. Poole, and Howard Rosenthal, *Polarized America* (Cambridge, Mass.: MIT Press, 2008).

45. "Prepared Text of Carter's Farewell Address," *New York Times,* 15 January 1981, p. B10.

46. Gary C. Jacobson, "George W. Bush, Polarization, and the War in Iraq," in *The George W. Bush Legacy,* ed. Colin Campbell, Bert A. Rockman, and Andrew Rudalevige (Washington, D.C.: CQ Press, 2008), pp. 62–91.

47. *Public Papers of the President, Lyndon B. Johnson, 1965,* vol. 1 (Washington, D.C.: Government Printing Office, 1966), p. 72.

48. Kevin Phillips, *The Politics of Rich and Poor* (New York: Random House, 1990), p. 88.

49. John W. Kingdon, *Agendas, Alternatives, and Public Policies* (Boston: Little, Brown, 1984), p. 25.

50. Richard E. Neustadt, "Presidency and Legislation: The Growth of Central Clearance," *American Political Science Review* 48 (September 1954): 641–671.

51. Seth King, "Reagan, in Bid for Budget Votes, Reported to Yield on Sugar Prices," *New York Times,* 27 June 1981, p. A1.

52. Matt Bai, "Taking the Hill," *New York Times Magazine,* 7 June 2009, p. 35.

53. Jeffrey M. Berry and Kent E. Portney, "Centralizing Regulatory Control and Interest Group Access: The Quayle Council on Competitiveness," in *Interest Group Politics,* 4th ed., ed. Allan J. Cigler and Burdett A. Loomis (Washington, D.C.: Congressional Quarterly Press, 1994), pp. 319–347.

54. The extent to which popularity affects presidential influence in Congress is difficult to determine with any precision. For an overview of this issue, see Jon R. Bond, Richard Fleisher, and Glen S. Katz, "An Overview of the Empirical Findings on Presidential-Congressional Relations," in *Rivals for Power,* ed. James A. Thurber (Washington, D.C.: Congressional Quarterly Press, 1996), pp. 103–139.

55. Sidney M. Milkis and Jesse H. Rhodes, "The President, Party Politics, and Constitutional Development," in *The Oxford Handbook of American Political Parties and Interest Groups,* ed. L. Sandy Maisel and Jeffrey M. Berry (Oxford: Oxford University Press, 2010), pp. 377–402.

56. Richard M. Skinner, "George W. Bush and the Partisan Presidency," *Political Science Quarterly* 123 (Winter 2008–2009): 605–622.

57. For an inside account of the Bush administration's response to September 11, see Bob Woodward, *Bush at War* (New York: Simon & Schuster, 2002). For an account of the decision to go to war with Iraq, see Bob Woodward, *Plan of Attack* (New York: Simon & Schuster, 2004).

58. Alexander George, "The Case for Multiple Advocacy in Foreign Policy," *American Political Science Review* (September 1972): 751–782.

59. John P. Burke and Fred I. Greenstein, *How Presidents Test Reality* (New York: Russell Sage Foundation, 1989); Richard E. Neustadt and Ernest R. May, *Thinking in Time* (New York: Free Press, 1986).

Chapter 10 / The Bureaucracy / pages 336–363

1. Gregory Zuckerman and Kara Scannell, "Madoff Misled SEC in '06, Got Off," *Wall Street Journal,* 18 December 2008; Diana Henriques, "'Lapses Helped Scheme,' Madoff Told Investigators," *New York Times,* 31 October 2009; Liz Moyer, "Why the SEC Missed Madoff," *Forbes,* 17 December 2008; Binyamin Appelbaum and David S. Hilzenrath, "SEC Didn't Act on Madoff Tips," *Washington Post,* 16 December 2008; U.S. Securities and Exchange Commission, Office of Investigations, *Investigation of Failure of the SEC to Uncover Bernard Madoff's Ponzi Scheme, Report No. OIG-509* (Washington, D.C.: U.S. Securities and Exchange Commission, Office of the Inspector General, 2009).

2. James Q. Wilson, *Bureaucracy* (New York: Basic Books, 1989), p. 25.

3. Bruce D. Porter, "Parkinson's Law Revisited: War and the Growth of American Government," *Public Interest* 60 (Summer 1980): 50.

4. See generally Ballard C. Campbell, *The Growth of American Government* (Bloomington: Indiana University Press, 1995).

5. See generally Marc Allen Eisner, *Regulatory Politics in Transition,* 2nd ed. (Baltimore: Johns Hopkins University Press, 2000).

6. See Anne Schneider and Helen Ingram, "Social Construction of Target Populations: Implications

for Politics and Policy," *American Political Science Review* 87 (June 1993): 334–347.

7. Theda Skocpol, *Protecting Soldiers and Mothers: The Political Origins of Social Policy in the United States* (Cambridge, Mass.: Harvard University Press, 1992).

8. Paul C. Light, *The True Size of Government* (Washington, D.C.: The Brookings Institution, 1999).

9. Jessica Holzer and Michael Crittenden, "House to Weigh Dropping Plan for Consumer Financial Watchdog," *Wall Street Journal,* 10 December 2009.

10. U.S. Department of Defense, "Active Duty Military Personnel by Rank/Grade, January 31, 2011," available at http://siadapp.dmdc.osd.mil/personnel/MILITARY/miltop.htm.

11. John T. Tierney, "Government Corporations and Managing the Public's Business," *Political Science Quarterly* 99 (Spring 1984): 73–92.

12. U.S. Office of Personnel Management, *Employment and Trends March 2009,* Table 1: Federal Civilian Personnel Summary, http://www.opm.gov/feddata/html/2009/March/table1.asp.

13. U.S. Office of Personnel Management, *Employment and Trends March 2009,* Chart 4: Distribution of Federal Civilian Employment by Major Geographic Area for March 2009, http://www.opm.gov/feddata/html/2009/March/charts.asp.

14. Lyndsey Layton and Lois Romano, "'Plum Book' Is Obama's Big Help-Wanted Ad," *Washington Post,* 13 November 2008, p. A01. The positions are all listed in what Washingtonians refer to as the "Plum Book" or, more formally, *United States Government Policy and Supporting Positions,* published by the Senate Committee on Homeland Security and Governmental Affairs; available at http://www.gpoaccess.gov/plumbook/2008/2008_plum_book.pdf.

15. Though formally located within the executive branch, the bureaucracy is "caught in the middle" between the Congress and the president. See Barry Weingast, "Caught in the Middle: The President, Congress, and the Political-Bureaucratic System," in *The Executive Branch,* ed. J. Aberbach and M. Peterson (New York: Oxford University Press, 2005), pp. 312–343.

16. Theodore J. Lowi, Jr., *The End of Liberalism,* 2nd ed. (New York: Norton, 1979).

17. Doris A. Graber, *Mass Media and American Politics,* 3rd ed. (Washington, D.C.: Congressional Quarterly Press, 1989), p. 51.

18. Lauren Etter, "Is Someone Listening to Your Phone Calls?" *Wall Street Journal,* 7 January 2006, p. A5; James Risen and Eric Lichtblau, "Bush Lets U.S. Spy on Callers without Courts," *New York Times,* 16 December 2005, p. A1.

19. Tom A. Peter, "Warrantless Wiretaps Expanded," *Christian Science Monitor,* 7 August 2007; Lawrence Wright, "The Spymaster," *New Yorker,* 21 January 2008, pp. 42–59.

20. Jeffrey M. Berry, *Feeding Hungry People* (New Brunswick, N.J.: Rutgers University Press, 1984).

21. Cornelius M. Kerwin, *Rulemaking: How Government Agencies Write Law and Make Policy,* 3rd ed. (Washington, D.C.: Congressional Quarterly Press, 2003).

22. Stuart Shapiro, "The Role of Procedural Controls in OSHA's Ergonomics Rulemaking," *Public Administration Review* 67 (July/August 2007): 688–701.

23. Department of Transportation, "New DOT Consumer Rule Limits Airline Tarmac Delays," press release, http://www.dot.gov/affairs/2009/dot19909.htm; Matthew L. Wald, "Stiff Fines Are Set for Long Wait on Tarmac," *New York Times,* 22 December 2009.

24. Charles E. Lindblom, "The Science of Muddling Through," *Public Administration Review* 19 (Spring 1959): 79–88.

25. See Michael T. Hayes, *Incrementalism and Public Policy* (White Plains, N.Y.: Longman, 1992).

26. Frank R. Baumgartner et al., *Lobbying and Policy Change* (Chicago: University of Chicago Press, 2009); Bryan D. Jones and Frank R. Baumgartner, *The Politics of Attention* (Chicago: University of Chicago Press, 2005).

27. "Bureaucratic culture" is a particularly slippery concept but can be conceived of as the interplay of artifacts, values, and underlying assumptions. See Irene Lurie and Norma Riccucci, "Changing the 'Culture' of Welfare Offices," *Administration and Society* 34 (January 2003): 653–677.

28. Curry L. Hagerty and Jonathan L. Ramseur, "Deepwater Horizon Oil Spill: Selected Issues for Congress (R41262)," *CRS Report for Congress,* 27 May 2010.

29. Justin Pritchard, Tamara Lush, and Holbrook Mohr, "AP IMPACT: BP Spill Response Plans Severely Flawed," Associated Press, http://abcnews.go.com/Business/wireStory?id=10863376; Joel Achenbach and David A. Fahrenthold, "Oil-Leak Gush Hits Record Levels," *Washington Post,* 28 May 2010, p. A1.

30. Scott Wilson and Joel Achenbach, "BP Preliminarily Agrees to $20B Escrow Account to Handle Claims," *Washington Post,* 16 June 2010, http://www.washingtonpost.com/wp-dyn/content/article/2010/06/16/AR2010061602614.html.

31. See generally Terry M. Moe, "The Politics of Bureaucratic Structure," in *Can the Government Govern?* ed. John E. Chubb and Paul E. Peterson (Washington, D.C.: The Brookings Institution, 1989), pp. 267–329.

32. Daniel J. Fiorino, *The New Environmental Regulation* (Cambridge, Mass.: MIT Press, 2006); Del Quentin Wilber and Marc Kaufman, "Judges Toss EPA Rule to Reduce Smog, Soot," *Washington Post,* 12 July 2008, p. A01.

33. Archon Fung, Mary Graham, and David Weil, *Full Disclosure* (New York: Cambridge University Press, 2007).

34. See generally E. S. Savas, *Privatization and Public-Private Partnerships* (New York: Chatham House, 2000).

35. Steven Rathgeb Smith, "Social Services," in *The State of Nonprofit America,* ed. Lester M. Salamon (Washington, D.C.: The Brookings Institution and Aspen Institute, 2002), p. 165.

36. Beryl A. Radin, *Challenging the Performance Movement* (Washington, D.C.: Georgetown University Press, 2006).

37. David G. Frederickson and H. George Frederickson, *Measuring the Performance of the Hollow State* (Washington, D.C.: Georgetown University Press, 2006), pp. 56–57.

38. Vassia Gueorguieva et al., "The Program Assessment Rating Tool and the Government Performance and Results Act," *The American Review of Public Administration* 39 (May 2009): 225–245.

39. See Carolyn J. Heinrich, "Outcomes-Based Performance in the Public Sector," *Public Administration Review* 62 (November–December 2002): 712–725; David Hirschmann, "Thermometers or Sauna? Performance Measurement and Demo-

40. See Amahai Glazer and Lawrence S. Rothenberg, *Why Government Succeeds and Why It Fails* (Cambridge, Mass.: Harvard University Press, 2001).

cratic Assistance in the United States Agency for International Development (USAID)," *Public Administration* 80 (2002): 235–255.

Chapter 11 / The Courts / pages 364–397

1. Philip Elman (interviewed by Norman Silber), "The Solicitor General's Office, Justice Frankfurter, and Civil Rights Litigation, 1946–1960: An Oral History," *Harvard Law Review* 100 (1987): 840.

2. David O'Brien, *Storm Center,* 2nd ed. (New York: Norton, 1990), p. 324.

3. Bernard Schwartz, *The Unpublished Opinions of the Warren Court* (New York: Oxford University Press, 1985), p. 446.

4. Ibid., pp. 445–448.

5. Felix Frankfurter and James M. Landis, *The Business of the Supreme Court* (New York: Macmillan, 1928), pp. 5–14; Julius Goebel, Jr., *The History of the Supreme Court of the United States,* vol. 1, *Antecedents and Beginnings to 1801* (New York: Macmillan, 1971).

6. Maeva Marcus (ed.), *The Documentary History of the Supreme Court of the United States, 1789–1800,* vol. 3, *The Justices on Circuit, 1795–1800* (New York: Columbia University Press, 1990).

7. Robert G. McCloskey, *The United States Supreme Court* (Chicago: University of Chicago Press, 1960), p. 31.

8. *Marbury* v. *Madison,* 1 Cranch 137 at 177, 178 (1803).

9. Interestingly, the term *judicial review* dates only to 1910. It was apparently unknown to Marshall and his contemporaries. Robert Lowry Clinton, *Marbury* v. *Madison and Judicial Review* (Lawrence: University Press of Kansas, 1989), p. 7.

10. Lee Epstein et al., *The Supreme Court Compendium,* 4th ed. (Washington, D.C.: Congressional Quarterly Press, 2007), Table 2-15.

11. *Ware* v. *Hylton,* 3 Dallas 199 (1796).

12. *Martin* v. *Hunter's Lessee,* 1 Wheat. 304 (1816).

13. Epstein et al., *The Supreme Court Compendium,* Table 2-16.

14. Garry Wills, *Explaining America: The Federalist* (Garden City, N.Y.: Doubleday, 1981), pp. 127–136.
15. *State Justice Institute News* 4 (Spring 1993): 1.
16. Charles Alan Wright, *Handbook on the Law of Federal Courts,* 3rd ed. (St. Paul, Minn.: West, 1976), p. 7.
17. James C. Duff, *2010 Annual Report of the Director: Judicial Business of the United States Courts* (Washington, D.C.: U.S. Government Printing Office, 2011), p. 39, Table 11; available at http://www.uscourts.gov/uscourts/Statistics/JudicialBusiness/2010/JudicialBusinespdfversion.pdf.
18. Duff, "Caseload Highlights," in *2010 Annual Report of the Director,* p. 12.
19. Duff, *2010 Annual Report of the Director,* p. 41, Table 13.
20. Duff, *2010 Annual Report of the Director,* p. 16, Table 1.
21. Linda Greenhouse, "Precedent for Lower Courts: Tyrant or Teacher?" *New York Times,* 29 January 1988, p. B7.
22. *Texas* v. *Johnson,* 491 U.S. 397 (1989); *United States* v. *Eichman,* 496 U.S. 310 (1990).
23. *Regents of the University of California* v. *Bakke,* 438 U.S. 265 (1978).
24. *Grutter* v. *Bollinger,* 539 U.S. 244 (2003); *Gratz* v. *Bollinger,* 539 U.S. 306 (2003).
25. *Parents Involved in Community Schools* v. *Seattle School Dist. No. 1,* 551 U.S. 701 (2007).
26. "Reading Petitions Is for Clerks Only at High Court Now," *Wall Street Journal,* 11 October 1990, p. B7; Robert Barnes, "Justices Continue Trend of Hearing Fewer Cases," *Washington Post,* 7 January 2007, p. A4.
27. Jeffrey Rosen, "Supreme Court Inc: How the Nation's Highest Court Has Come to Side with Business," *New York Times Magazine,* 16 March 2008, pp. 38 et seq.
28. H. W. Perry, Jr., *Deciding to Decide: Agenda Setting in the United States Supreme Court* (Cambridge, Mass.: Harvard University Press, 1991); Gregory A. Caldiera and John R. Wright, "The Discuss List: Agenda Building in the Supreme Court," *Law and Society Review* 24, no. 3 (1990): 807.
29. Doris M. Provine, *Case Selection in the United States Supreme Court* (Chicago: University of Chicago Press, 1980), pp. 74–102.
30. Perry, *Deciding to Decide,* p. 286.
31. "Rising Fixed Opinions," *New York Times,* 22 February 1988, p. 14. See also Linda Greenhouse, "At the Bar," *New York Times,* 28 July 1989, p. 21.
32. Jeffrey A. Segal and Harold J. Spaeth, *The Supreme Court and the Attitudinal Model* (Cambridge: Cambridge University Press, 1993).
33. Thomas G. Walker, Lee Epstein, and William J. Dixon, "On the Mysterious Demise of Consensual Norms in the United States Supreme Court," *Journal of Politics* 50 (1988): 361–389.
34. See, for example, Walter F. Murphy, *Elements of Judicial Strategy* (Chicago: University of Chicago Press, 1964); and Bob Woodward and Scott Armstrong, *The Brethren* (New York: Simon & Schuster, 1979).
35. Greenhouse, "At the Bar," p. 21.
36. Justice at Stake, "2009–2010 Contestable Supreme Court Elections," 13 June 2010, http://justiceatstake.org/media/cms/2010_Contestable_Supreme_Court_Elec_56766A73A02C2.pdf.
37. Stephen L. Wasby, *The Supreme Court in the Federal Judicial System,* 3rd ed. (Chicago: Nelson-Hall, 1988), pp. 107–110.
38. Jeffrey Toobin, *The Nine: Inside the Secret World of the Supreme Court* (New York: Doubleday, 2007), p. 269.
39. Federal Judicial Center, "Biographical Directory of Federal Judges," available at http://www.fjc.gov/history/home.nsf/page/judges.html.
40. Ronald Stidham, Robert A. Carp, and Donald R. Songer, "The Voting Behavior of Judges Appointed by President Clinton" (paper presented at the annual meeting of the Southwestern Political Science Association, Houston, Tex., March 1996). See also Susan B. Haire, Martha Anne Humphries, and Donald R. Songer, "The Voting Behavior of Clinton's Courts of Appeals Appointees," *Judicature* 84 (March–April 2001): 274–281.
41. Robert A. Carp, Ronald Stidham, and Kenneth L. Manning, "The Voting Behavior of George W. Bush's Judges: How Sharp a Turn to the Right?" in *Principles and Practice of American Politics: Classic and Contemporary Readings,* 3rd ed., ed. Samuel Kernell and Steven S. Smith (Washington, D.C.: Congressional Quarterly Press, 2006).
42. U.S. Senate, "Supreme Court Nominations, Present–1789," http://www.senate.gov/pagelayout/reference/nominations/Nominations.htm.

43. See Frank J. Colucci, *Justice Kennedy's Jurisprudence* (Lawrence: University Press of Kansas, 2009).

44. "Supreme Court Nominee Sonia Sotomayor's Speech at Berkeley Law in 2001," *Berkeley La Raza Law Journal* (2002), http://www.law.berkeley.edu/4982.htm.

45. *Brown* v. *Board of Education II,* 349 U.S. 294 (1955).

46. Alexander M. Bickel, *The Least Dangerous Branch* (Indianapolis: Bobbs-Merrill, 1962); Robert A. Dahl, "Decision-Making in a Democracy: The Supreme Court as a National Policy-Maker," *Journal of Public Law* 6 (1962): 279.

47. William Mishler and Reginal S. Sheehan, "The Supreme Court as a Countermajoritarian Institution? The Impact of Public Opinion on Supreme Court Decisions," *American Political Science Review* 87 (1993): 87–101.

48. Barry Friedman, *The Will of the People* (New York: Farrar, Straus and Giroux, 2009).

49. *Engel* v. *Vitale,* 367 U.S. 643 (1961).

50. Gallup Poll, "High Court to Start Term with Near Decade-High Approval," 9 September 2009, http://www.gallup.com/poll/122858/High-Court-Start-Term-Near-Decade-High-Approval.aspx?CSTS=alert.

51. Ibid.

52. William J. Brennan, Jr., "State Supreme Court Judge versus United States Supreme Court Justice: A Change in Function and Perspective," *University of Florida Law Review* 19 (1966): 225.

Chapter 12 / Order and Civil Liberties / pages 398–433

1. Jenna Jones, "Pledge of Allegiance Dispute Results in Md. Teacher Having to Apologize," *Washington Post,* 24 February 2010, http://www.washingtonpost.com/wp-dyn/content/article/2010/02/23/AR2010022303889.html.

2. *West Virginia Board of Education* v. *Barnette,* 319 U.S. 642 (1943).

3. *Street* v. *New York,* 394 U.S. 576 (1969).

4. Deborah A. Jeon, Legal Director, ACLU of Maryland to Mrs. Khadija F. Barkley, Acting Principal, *Washington Post,* 5 February 2010, http://media.washingtonpost.com/wp-srv/metro/documents/Pledge02-2310.pdf.

5. Learned Hand, *The Bill of Rights* (Boston: Atheneum, 1958), p. 1.

6. Leonard W. Levy, *The Establishment Clause: Religion and the First Amendment* (New York: Macmillan, 1986); Leo Pfeffer, *Church, State, and Freedom* (Boston: Beacon Press, 1953); Leonard W. Levy, "The Original Meaning of the Establishment Clause of the First Amendment," in *Religion and the State,* ed. James E. Wood, Jr. (Waco, Tex.: Baylor University Press, 1985), pp. 43–83.

7. *Reynolds* v. *United States,* 98 U.S. 145 (1879).

8. *Everson* v. *Board of Education,* 330 U.S. 1 (1947).

9. *Board of Education* v. *Allen,* 392 U.S. 236 (1968).

10. *Lemon* v. *Kurtzman,* 403 U.S. 602 (1971).

11. *Agostini* v. *Felton,* 96 U.S. 552 (1997).

12. *Zelman, Superintendent of Public Instruction of Ohio, et al.* v. *Simmons-Harris et al.,* 536 U.S. 639 (2002).

13. *Engle* v. *Vitale,* 370 U.S. 421 (1962); *Wallace* v. *Jaffree,* 472 U.S. 38 (1985).

14. *Lee* v. *Weisman,* 505 U.S. 577 (1992).

15. *Santa Fe Independent School District* v. *Doe,* 530 U.S. 290 (2000).

16. *Good News Club* v. *Milford Central School,* 533 U.S. 98 (2001).

17. Michael W. McConnell, "The Origins and Historical Understanding of the Free Exercise of Religion," *Harvard Law Review* 103 (1990): 1409.

18. *Sherbert* v. *Verner,* 374 U.S. 398 (1963).

19. *Employment Division* v. *Smith,* 494 U.S. 872 (1990).

20. *Boerne* v. *Flores,* 95 U.S. 2074 (1997).

21. *Gonzales* v. *O Centro Espírita Beneficente União do Vegetal,* 546 U.S. 418 (2006).

22. Laurence Tribe, *Treatise on American Constitutional Law,* 2nd ed. (St. Paul, Minn.: West, 1988), p. 566.

23. Zechariah Chafee, *Free Speech in the United States* (Cambridge, Mass.: Harvard University Press, 1941).

24. Leonard W. Levy, *The Emergence of a Free Press* (New York: Oxford University Press, 1985).

25. *Brandenburg* v. *Ohio,* 395 U.S. 444 (1969).

26. *Schenck* v. *United States,* 249 U.S. 47 (1919).

27. *Gitlow* v. *New York,* 268 U.S. 652 (1925).

28. *Dennis* v. *United States,* 341 U.S. 494 (1951).

29. *Brandenburg* v. *Ohio,* 395 U.S. 444 (1969).

30. Anthony Lewis, *Freedom for the Thought That We Hate: A Biography of the First Amendment* (New York: Basic Books, 2008).

31. *Tinker* v. *Des Moines Independent County School District,* 393 U.S. 503 at 508 (1969).

32. *Morse* v. *Frederick,* 551 U.S. 393 (2007); Charles Lane, "Court Backs School on Speech Curbs," *Washington Post,* 26 June 2007, p. A6.

33. *Miller* v. *California,* 413 U.S. 15 (1973).

34. *ACLU* v. *Reno* (1996 U.S. Dist. LEXIS) (12 June 1996).

35. *Reno* v. *ACLU,* 96 U.S. 511 (1997).

36. *Ashcroft* v. *ACLU,* 524 U.S. 656 (2004); *ACLU* v. *Gonzales,* 22 March 2007, Eastern District of Pennsylvania, Final Order in Civil Action No. 98-5591.

37. *United States* v. *Williams,* 553 U.S. 285 (2008).

38. *United States* v. *Stevens,* 559 U.S. ___ (2010).

39. *New York Times* v. *Sullivan,* 376 U.S. 254 (1964).

40. *Near* v. *Minnesota,* 283 U.S. 697 (1931).

41. For a detailed account of *Near,* see Fred W. Friendly, *Minnesota Rag* (New York: Random House, 1981).

42. *New York Times* v. *United States,* 403 U.S. 713 (1971).

43. *Branzburg* v. *Hayes,* 408 U.S. 665 (1972).

44. *Zurcher* v. *Stanford Daily,* 436 U.S. 547 (1978).

45. *Hazelwood School District* v. *Kuhlmeier,* 484 U.S. 260 (1988).

46. *United States* v. *Cruikshank,* 92 U.S. 542 (1876); *Constitution of the United States of America: Annotated and Interpreted* (Washington, D.C.: U.S. Government Printing Office, 1973), p. 1031.

47. *DeJonge* v. *Oregon,* 299 U.S. 353 (1937).

48. *United States* v. *Miller,* 307 U.S. 174 (1939).

49. *District of Columbia* v. *Heller,* 128 S. Ct. 2783 (2008).

50. *McDonald* v. *Chicago,* 561 U.S. _____ (2010).

51. *Barron* v. *Baltimore,* 32 U.S. (7 Pet.) 243 (1833).

52. *Chicago, Burlington & Quincy R.R.* v. *Chicago,* 166 U.S. 226 (1897).

53. *Gitlow* v. *New York,* 268 U.S. 666 (1925).

54. *Palko* v. *Connecticut,* 302 U.S. 319 (1937).

55. *Duncan* v. *Louisiana,* 391 U.S. 145 (1968).

56. *McNabb* v. *United States,* 318 U.S. 332 (1943).

57. *Baldwin* v. *New York,* 399 U.S. 66 (1970).

58. Anthony Lewis, *Gideon's Trumpet* (New York: Random House, 1964).

59. *Gideon* v. *Wainwright,* 372 U.S. 335 (1963).

60. *Miranda* v. *Arizona,* 384 U.S. 436 (1966).

61. *Dickerson* v. *United States,* 530 U.S. 428 (2000).

62. *Missouri* v. *Seibert,* 542 U.S. 600 (2004).

63. *Berghuis* v. *Thompkins* 560 U.S. ____ (2010).

64. *Wolf* v. *Colorado,* 338 U.S. 25 (1949).

65. *Mapp* v. *Ohio,* 367 U.S. 643 (1961).

66. *United States* v. *Leon,* 468 U.S. 897 (1984).

67. Liane Hansen, "Voices in the News This Week," *NPR Weekend Edition,* 28 October 2001 (NEXIS transcript).

68. *Rasul* v. *Bush,* 542 U.S. 466 (2004).

69. *Hamdi* v. *Rumsfeld,* 542 U.S. 507 (2004); Charles Lane, "Justices Back Detainee Access to U.S. Courts," *Washington Post,* 29 June 2004, p. A1.

70. *Hamdan* v. *Rumsfeld,* 548 U.S. 557 (2006).

71. Michael A. Fletcher, "Bush Signs Terrorism Measure," *Washington Post,* 18 October 2006, p. A4.

72. *Boumediene* v. *Bush,* 553 U.S. 723 (2008).

73. Article I, Sec. 9.

74. Paul Brest, *Processes of Constitutional Decision-Making* (Boston: Little, Brown, 1975), p. 708.

75. *Griswold* v. *Connecticut,* 381 U.S. 479 (1965).

76. *Roe* v. *Wade,* 410 U.S. 113 (1973).

77. See John Hart Ely, "The Wages of Crying Wolf: A Comment on *Roe* v. *Wade,*" *Yale Law Journal* 82 (1973): 920.

78. *Webster* v. *Reproductive Health Services,* 492 U.S. 490 (1989).

79. *Steinberg* v. *Carhart,* 530 U.S. 914 (2000); *Gonzales* v. *Carhart,* 550 U.S. 124 (2007).

80. *Bowers* v. *Hardwick,* 478 U.S. 186 (1986).

81. *Lawrence and Garner* v. *Texas,* 539 U.S. 558 (2003).

82. Ibid.

83. Glenn Kessler, "California Voters Narrowly Approve Same-Sex Marriage Ban," *Washington Post,* 6 November 2008, p. A44.

84. *Perry* v. *Schwarzenegger,* No. 3:09-cv-02292 (U.S. Dist. Ct., N.D. Cal.).

Chapter 13 / Equality and Civil Rights / pages 434–461

1. Nina Bernstein, "100 Years in the Back Door, Out the Front," *New York Times,* 21 May 2006, sec. 4, p. 4, quoted in Aristide Zolberg, *A Nation By Design: Immigration Policy in the Fashioning*

of America (New York: Russell Sage Foundation, 2006).

2. Sam Howe Verhovek, "In Poll, Americans Reject Means but Not Ends of Racial Diversity," *New York Times,* 14 December 1997, sec. 1, p. 1; Jack Citrin, "Affirmative Action in the People's Court," *Public Interest* 122 (1996): 40–41; Charlotte Steeh and Maria Krysan, "Affirmative Action and the Public, 1970–1995," *Public Opinion Quarterly* 60 (1996): 128–158; Gallup Poll, 25–28 October 2000: "Would you vote ... for or against a law which would allow your state to give preferences in job hiring and school admission on the basis of race?" For, 13 percent; against, 85 percent; and no opinion, 2 percent.

3. *The Slaughterhouse Cases,* 83 U.S. 36 (1873).

4. *Civil Rights Cases,* 109 U.S. 3 (1883).

5. Mary Beth Norton et al., *A People and a Nation: A History of the United States,* 3rd ed. (Boston: Houghton Mifflin, 1990), p. 490.

6. *Plessy* v. *Ferguson,* 163 U.S. 537 (1896).

7. *Cummings* v. *County Board of Education,* 175 U.S. 528 (1899).

8. *Brown* v. *Board of Education,* 347 U.S. 483 (1954).

9. Ibid., pp. 483, 495.

10. Ibid., pp. 483, 494.

11. *Brown* v. *Board of Education II,* 349 U.S. 294 (1955).

12. Jack W. Peltason, *Fifty-Eight Lonely Men,* rev. ed. (Urbana: University of Illinois Press, 1971).

13. *Alexander* v. *Holmes County Board of Education,* 396 U.S. 19 (1969).

14. *Milliken* v. *Bradley,* 418 U.S. 717 (1974).

15. Norton et al., *People and a Nation,* p. 943.

16. But see Abigail M. Thernstrom, *Whose Vote Counts? Affirmative Action and Minority Voting Rights* (Cambridge, Mass.: Harvard University Press, 1987).

17. *Richmond* v. *J. A. Croson Co.,* 488 U.S. 469 (1989).

18. *Martin* v. *Wilks,* 490 U.S. 755 (1989); *Wards Cove Packing Co.* v. *Atonio,* 490 U.S. 642 (1989); *Patterson* v. *McLean Credit Union,* 491 U.S. 164 (1989); *Price Waterhouse* v. *Hopkins,* 490 U.S. 228 (1989); *Lorance* v. *AT&T Technologies,* 490 U.S. 900 (1989); *EEOC* v. *Arabian American Oil Co.,* 499 U.S. 244 (1991).

19. *Saint Francis College* v. *Al-Khazraji,* 481 U.S. 604 (1987).

20. Dee Brown, *Bury My Heart at Wounded Knee: An Indian History of the American West* (New York: Holt, Rinehart & Winston, 1971).

21. In 2010 the Shinnecock Indian Nation of Long Island, New York, became the 565th federally recognized Indian tribe. U.S. Department of the Interior, Office of the Assistant Secretary–Indian Affairs, "Skibine Issues a Final Determination to Acknowledge the Shinnecock Indian Nation of Long Island, NY," news release, 15 June 2010, http://www.bia.gov/idc/groups/public/documents/text/idc009847.pdf.

22. Population Division, U.S. Census Bureau, "Summary Table 6: Percent of the Projected Population by Race and Hispanic Origin for the United States: 2010 to 2050 (NP2008-T6)," 14 August 2008, available at http://www.census.gov/population/www/projections/summarytables.html; Jennifer E. Manning, "Membership in the 112th Congress: A Profile (R40086)," *CRS Report for Congress,* 1 March 2011, pp. 6–7. The tally for gender and ethnicity in this publication is updated frequently. These statistics do not include nonvoting delegates from American territories or the resident commissioner of Puerto Rico.

23. Calculated from U.S. Equal Employment Opportunities Commission, "Americans with Disabilities Act of 1990 (ADA) Charges FY 1992–FY 1996," http://www.eeoc.gov/eeoc/statistics/enforcement/ada-charges-a.cfm, and "Americans with Disabilities Act of 1990 (ADA) Charges FY 1997–FY 2009," http://www.eeoc.gov/eeoc/statistics/enforcement/ada-charges.cfm.

24. *Reed* v. *Reed,* 404 U.S. 71 (1971).

25. *Frontiero* v. *Richardson,* 411 U.S. 677 (1973).

26. *Craig* v. *Boren,* 429 U.S. 190 (1976).

27. *J.E.B.* v. *Alabama ex rel. T.B.,* 511 U.S. 127 (1994).

28. *United States* v. *Virginia,* slip op. 94–1941 and 94–2107 (decided 26 June 1996).

29. Melvin I. Urofsky, *A March of Liberty* (New York: Knopf, 1988), p. 902.

30. *Harris* v. *Forklift Systems,* 510 U.S. 17 (1993).

31. *Facts on File* 206B2 (4 June 1965).

32. As quoted in Melvin I. Urofsky, *A Conflict of Rights: The Supreme Court and Affirmative Action* (New York: Scribner's, 1991), p. 29.

33. *Regents of the University of California* v. *Bakke,* 438 U.S. 265 (1978).
34. *Adarand Constructors, Inc.* v. *Peña,* 518 U.S. (1995).
35. *Gratz* v. *Bollinger,* 539 U.S. 244 (2003).
36. *Grutter* v. *Bollinger,* 539 U.S. 306 (2003).
37. *Parents Involved in Community Schools* v. *Seattle School District No. 1,* 551 U.S. 701 (2007).
38. Stephen Earl Bennett et al., *Americans' Opinions about Affirmative Action* (Cincinnati: University of Cincinnati, Institute for Policy Research, 1995), p. 4; Lawrence Bobo, "Race and Beliefs about Affirmative Action," in *Racialized Politics: The Debate about Racism in America,* ed. David O. Sears, Jim Sidanius, and Lawrence Bobo (Chicago: University of Chicago Press, 2000).

Chapter 14 / Policymaking and the Budget / pages 462–492

1. McCain–Obama speeches at Ninety-ninth NAACP Convention, 12 July 2008.
2. Kaiser Family Foundation, "Health Care Costs: A Primer," March 2009, http://www.kff.org/insurance/upload/7670_02.pdf.
3. RAND Corporation, "Consumer Financial Risk," RAND Report on Health Care, 2010, http://www.randcompare.org/current/dimension/consumer_financial_risk.
4. David Himmelstein et al., "Medical Bankruptcy in the United States, 2007: Results of a National Study," *American Journal of Medicine* 122, no. 8 (2009): 741–746.
5. Robin A. Cohen, Michael E. Martinez, and Brian W. Ward, *Health Insurance Coverage: Early Release of Estimates from the National Health Interview Survey* (Atlanta, GA: National Center for Health Statistics, Centers for Disease Control and Prevention, June 2010), available at http://www.cdc.gov/nchs/data/nhis/earlyrelease/insur201006.htm.
6. "Americans at Risk: One in Three Uninsured," *Families USA,* March 2009, http://www.familiesusa.org/resources/publications/reports/americans-at-risk-findings.html.
7. Nancy Lofholm, "Heavy Infant in Grand Junction Denied Health Insurance," *Denver Post,* 10 October 2009, http://www.denverpost.com/ci_13530098; David Hilzenrath, "Acne, Preg-

nancy among Disqualifying Conditions," *Washington Post,* 19 September 2009, p. A03.
8. Huma Khan, "Health Care Bill: What Does It Mean for You?" ABC News, 22 March 2010, http://abcnews.go.com/Politics/HealthCare/health-care-bill-obama-sign-bill-tuesday/story?id=10169801.
9. Associated Press, "Budget Office Estimates Health-Care Law Could Cost More than $1 Trillion," *Washington Post,* 12 May 2010, http://www.washingtonpost.com/wp-dyn/content/article/2010/05/11/AR2010051104714.html.
10. N.C. Aizenman, "Health-Care Overhaul Is Up Against Long Campaign across U.S.," *Washington Post,* 12 May 2010, http://www.washingtonpost.com/wp-dyn/content/article/2010/05/11/AR2010051104719.html.
11. Carol D. Leonnig, "Rep. Murtha's Earmarks Lead to Fewer Jobs Than Promised," *Washington Post,* 31 December 2009.
12. "Espresso Tax Is Defeated," *New York Times,* 18 September 2003, p. A17.
13. Steven Greenhouse, "Mexican Trucks Gain Approval to Haul Cargo throughout U.S.," *New York Times,* 28 November 2002, p. A1.
14. This typology is adapted from Theodore Lowi's classic article "American Business, Public Policy Case Studies, and Political Theory," *World Politics* 16 (July 1964): 677–715.
15. The policymaking process can be depicted in many ways. Another approach, a bit more elaborate than this, is described in James E. Anderson, *Public Policymaking,* 2nd ed. (Boston: Houghton Mifflin, 1994), p. 37.
16. See Christopher J. Bosso, "The Contextual Bases of Problem Definition," in *The Politics of Problem Definition,* ed. David A. Rochefort and Roger W. Cobb (Lawrence: University Press of Kansas, 1994), pp. 182–203.
17. Frank R. Baumgartner and Bryan D. Jones, "Positive and Negative Feedback in Politics," in *Policy Dynamics,* ed. Frank R. Baumgartner and Bryan D. Jones (Chicago: University of Chicago Press, 2002), pp. 3–28.
18. Christopher Trenholm et al., *Impacts of Four Title V, Section 510 Abstinence Education,* report to the U.S. Department of Health and Human Services (Princeton, N.J.: Mathematica Policy Research, 2007).

19. John B. Jemmott III, Loretta S. Jemmott, and Geoffrey T. Fong, "Efficacy of a Theory-Based Abstinence-Only Intervention over 24 Months," *Archives of Pediatric & Adolescent Medicine* 164 (February 2010): 152–159.

20. Mary Dalrymple, "Homeland Security Department Another Victory for Administration," *CQ Weekly,* 16 November 2002, pp. 3002–3007.

21. Walter Pincus, "Intelligence Bill Clears Congress," *Washington Post,* 9 December 2004, p. A04.

22. Senate Select Committee on Intelligence, "Unclassified Executive Summary of the Committee Report on the Attempted Terrorist Attack on Northwest Airlines Flight 253," 18 May 2010, http://intelligence.senate.gov/100518/1225report.pdf; Karen DeYoung and Michael A. Fletcher, "Attempt to Bomb Airliner Could Have Been Prevented, Obama Says," *Washington Post,* 6 January 2010.

23. Derek Willis, "Turf Battles Could Lie Ahead in Fight to Oversee Homeland Department," *CQ Weekly,* 16 November 2002, p. 3006.

24. On the first steps by the Obama administration, see Beryl A. Radin, "The Relationship between OMB and the Agencies in the Obama Administration," *International Journal of Public Administration* 32 (2009): 781–785.

25. Jeffrey M. Berry, *The Interest Group Society,* 3rd ed. (New York: Longman, 1997), p. 187.

26. Michael T. Heaney, "Coalitions and Interest Group Influence over Health Care Policy" (paper presented at the annual meeting of the American Political Science Association, Philadelphia, August 2003), p. 16.

27. Jeffrey M. Berry, "Subgovernments, Issue Networks, and Political Conflict," in *Remaking American Politics,* ed. Richard A. Harris and Sidney M. Milkis (Boulder, Colo.: Westview Press, 1989), pp. 239–260.

28. Paul Peretz, "The Politics of Fiscal and Monetary Policy," in *The Politics of American Economic Policy Making,* 2nd ed., ed. Paul Peretz (Armonk, N.Y.: M. E. Sharp, 1996), pp. 101–113.

29. Jackie Calmes and Michael Cooper, "New Consensus Views Stimulus as Worthy Step," *New York Times,* 21 November 2009, pp. A1, A10; Alec MacGillis, "Economic Stimulus Has Created or Saved Nearly 2 Million Jobs, White House Says," *Washington Post,* 13 January 2010, p. A13.

30. Executive Office of the President, *Budget of the United States Government: Analytic Perspectives, Fiscal Year 2012* (Washington, D.C.: U.S. Government Printing Office, 2011), p. 120, Table 12-1.

31. The Bureau of the Public Debt publishes historical data and a revised total debt figure daily at "The Debt to the Penny, and Who Holds It," http://www.treasurydirect.gov/NP/BPDLogin?application=np.

32. For a concise discussion of the 1990 budget reforms, see James A. Thurber, "Congressional-Presidential Battles to Balance the Budget," in *Rivals for Power: Presidential-Congressional Relations,* ed. James A. Thurber (Washington, D.C.: Congressional Quarterly Press, 1996), pp. 196–202.

33. For a brief account of presidential attempts, from Carter to Clinton, to deal with budget deficits, see Alexis Simendinger et al., "Sky High," *National Journal,* 7 February 2004, pp. 370–373.

34. Ibid., p. 377; Concord Coalition, "Budget Process Reform: An Important Tool for Fiscal Discipline, but Not a Magic Bullet," *Issue Brief,* 5 February 2004.

35. Concord Coalition, "Budget Process Reform," p. 3.

36. J. Taylor Rushing, "Obama Signs Pay-Go Law but Also Raises Federal Debt Ceiling," *The Hill,* 13 February 2010, http://thehill.com/homenews/administration/80981-obama-pay-as-you-go-rules-necessary-and-now-law-along-with-higher-debt-ceiling?tmpl=component&print=1&layout=default&page=.

37. Richard A. Musgrave and Peggy B. Musgrave, *Public Finance in Theory and Practice,* 2nd ed. (New York: McGraw-Hill, 1976), p. 42.

38. Jill Barshay, "'Case of the Missing Revenue' Is Nation's Troubling Mystery," *CQ Weekly,* 17 January 2004, p. 144.

39. Pew Social & Demographic Trends, *A Balance Sheet at 30 Months: How the Great Recession Has Changed Life in America* (Washington, D.C.: Pew Research Center, 30 June 2010), p. i; available at http://pewsocialtrends.org/assets/pdf/759-recession.pdf.

40. Executive Office of the President, "Table 8.7: Outlays for Discretionary Programs: 1962–2009"

and "Table 8.8: Outlays for Discretionary Programs in Constant (FY2000) Dollars: 1962–2009," in *Budget of the United States Government, Fiscal Year 2009, Historical Tables* (Washington, D.C.: Government Printing Office, 2007), pp. 154–155, 160–161.

41. David M. Herszenhorn, "Estimates of Iraq War Cost Were Not Close to Ballpark," *New York Times*, 19 March 2008, p. A9.

42. Executive Office of the President, "Table S-4: Proposed Budget by Category," in *Budget of the United States Government, Fiscal Year 2012, Summary Tables* (Washington, D.C.: Government Printing Office, 2011), p. 176.

43. Times-Mirror Center for the People and the Press, "Voter Anxiety Dividing GOP: Energized Democrats Backing Clinton," press release, 14 November 1995, p. 88.

44. These questions were asked in the 2008 American National Election Survey conducted by Stanford University and the University of Michigan.

45. Fay Lomax Cook et al., *Convergent Perspectives on Social Welfare Policy: The Views from the General Public, Members of Congress, and AFDC Recipients* (Evanston, Ill.: Center for Urban Affairs and Policy Research, Northwestern University, 1988), Table 4-1.

46. Social Security Administration, "2011 Social Security/SSI/Medicare Information Factsheet," 22 December 2010. available at http://www.social security.gov/legislation/2011factsheet.pdf.

47. Social Security Administration, "Nation's First Baby Boomer Receives Her First Social Security Retirement Benefit," news release, 12 February 2008, available at http://www.ssa.gov/press office/pr/babyboomer-firstcheck-pr.pdf.

48. Social Security Administration, *The 2010 Annual Report of the Board of Trustees of the Federal Old-Age and Survivors Insurance and Disability Insurance Trust Funds* (Washington, D.C.: U.S. Government Printing Office, 5 August 2010), p. 2; available at http://www.ssa.gov/OACT/TR/2010/tr10.pdf.

49. U.S. Bureau of the Census, U.S. Department of Commerce, *Statistical Abstract of the United States, 2010* (Washington, D.C.: U.S. Government Printing Office, 2009), Table 7: Resident Population by Sex and Age: 1980 to 2008.

50. Kaiser Family Foundation Fast Facts, "Medicare Benefit Payments, by Type of Service, 2009," 13 May 2009, http://facts.kff.org/chart.aspx?ch=379.

51. Alan Weil, "There's Something about Medicaid," *Health Affairs* 22 (January–February 2003): 13.

52. Centers for Medicare and Medicaid Services, "Brief Summaries of Medicare and Medicaid," 1 November 2010, p. 28; "Table 12.3: Total Outlays for Grants to State and Local Governments by Function, Agency, and Program: 1940–2012," in *Budget of the United States Government, Fiscal Year 2012, Historical Tables* (Washington, D.C.: Government Printing Office, 2011), p. 307.

53. "Critical Care: The Economic Recovery Package and Medicaid," *Families USA*, January 2009, http://www.familiesusa.org/assets/pdfs/critical-care.pdf.

Index